THE KLEIN TRADITION

LINES OF DEVELOPMENT
Evolution of Theory and Practice over the Decades

Series Editors: Norka T. Malberg and Joan Raphael-Leff

Other titles in the series:

The Anna Freud Tradition: Lines of Development—Evolution of Theory and Practice over the Decades
 edited by Norka T. Malberg and Joan Raphael-Leff

Fairbairn and the Object Relations Tradition: Lines of Development—Evolution of Theory and Practice over the Decades
 edited by Graham S. Clarke and David E. Scharff

The Winnicott Tradition: Lines of Development—Evolution of Theory and Practice over the Decades
 edited by Margaret Boyle Spelman and Frances Thomson-Salo

The W. R. Bion Tradition: Lines of Development—Evolution of Theory and Practice over the Decades
 edited by Howard B. Levine and Giuseppe Civitarese

The Klein Tradition: Lines of Development—Evolution of Theory and Practice over the Decades
 edited by Penelope Garvey and Kay Long

THE KLEIN TRADITION
Lines of Development—Evolution of Theory and Practice over the Decades

Edited by
Penelope Garvey
and Kay Long

Routledge
Taylor & Francis Group

LONDON AND NEW YORK

First published 2018
by Routledge
2 Park Square, Milton Park, Abingdon, Oxon OX14 4RN

and by Routledge
711 Third Avenue, New York, NY 10017

Routledge is an imprint of the Taylor & Francis Group, an informa business

British Library Cataloguing-in-Publication Data
A catalogue record for this book is available from the British Library

Library of Congress Cataloging-in-Publication Data
A catalog record has been requested for this book

ISBN-13: 978-1-78220-598-2 (pbk)

Typeset in Palatino LT Std
by Medlar Publishing Solutions Pvt Ltd, India

For ease of reading, "he" is used throughout for general reference to the infant, the patient, or the individual, and "she" for general reference to the analyst, or the student, but at any point the opposite gender can be substituted.

CONTENTS

PART III: WORK WITH CHILDREN

ACKNOWLEDGEMENTS

We would like to express our gratitude to our analysts, our supervisors, our colleagues, our patients and our families who have brought the theory to life.

The figures in Anne Alvarez's "Paranoid/schizoid or paranoid and schizoid positions?" first appeared in her book *The Thinking Heart: Three Levels of Psychotherapy with Disturbed Children*, published by Routledge in 2012. An earlier version of Irma Brenman Pick's essay "Lurching between longing and destruction" was presented at the annual conference of the *Deutsche Physikalische Gesellschaft*, Berlin (March 2015). The chapter "Reparation: waiting for a concept" by Edna O'Shaughnessy was the second in a series of three papers presented during the seminar *Facing the Pain of Crimes and their Reparation* at the 48th International Psychoanalytical Association Congress, Prague, in 2013 and is published on the website of the Melanie Klein Trust. Thanks to New Directions Publishing Corporation for permission to publish sections of the poem *Lament for Ignacio Sánchez Mejías* by Federico García Lorca, translated by Stephen Spender and J. L. Gill, in Shelley Rockwell's paper "A perfect poem of tears: grieving as depicted in Federico García Lorca's *Lament for Ignacio Sánchez Mejías*." The clinical material in Priscilla Roth's "'I used to think you were wonderful': The persecution/idealisation cycle of melancholia" was originally published in *On Freud's Mourning and Melancholia*, edited by Leticia Glocer Fiorini, Thierry Bokanowski, and Sergio Lewkowicz in the Contemporary Turning Points and Critical Issues series, published by the IPA, and is reprinted with kind permission of the International Psychoanalytical Association. Thanks to *Psychoanalytic Quarterly* for permission to publish John Steiner's "Illusion, disillusion, and irony in psychoanalysis", a version of which was published in their volume 85, no. 2, pp. 427–447. Thanks also to *Accounting, Auditing &*

Accountability Journal for permission to publish Richard Taffler and Arman Eshragi's "Hedge funds as phantastic objects: a psychoanalytic perspective on financial innovations", an earlier version of which, "Hedge funds and unconscious phantasy" (2012), was published in volume 25, issue 8, pp. 1244–1265.

Nicola Abel-Hirsch is a training analyst of the British Psychoanalytical Society, and works in private practice. From 2005 to 2012 she taught an annual series of lectures and seminars on Bion in Taiwan, and has given seminars and papers on his work in the UK, America, and Europe. Her forthcoming book, *Bion: 365 Quotes* (2018) will be published by Routledge. She was the 2013–2015 visiting professor at the Centre for Psychoanalytic Studies, University of Essex, and is the editor of Hanna Segal's book *Yesterday, Today and Tomorrow* (2007).

Anne Alvarez, PhD, MACP, is a consultant child and adolescent psychotherapist (and retired co-convener of the autism service, child and family department, at the Tavistock Clinic, London, where she still teaches). She is author of *Live Company: Psychotherapy with Autistic, Borderline, Deprived and Abused Children*; *The Thinking Heart: Three Levels of Psychoanalytic Therapy with Disturbed Children*; and she has edited, with Susan Reid, *Autism and Personality: Findings from the Tavistock Autism Workshop*. A book in her honour, edited by Judith Edwards, entitled *Being Alive: Building on the Work of Anne Alvarez*, was published in 2002. She teaches child analysts at the San Francisco Center for Psychoanalysis, where she was visiting professor in 2005, and candidates at the British Psychoanalytic Society.

Elias Mallet da Rocha Barros is a training analyst and supervisor at the Brazilian Psychoanalytical Society of São Paulo, a fellow of the British Psychoanalytical Society and of the British Institute of Psychoanalysis, past editor for Latin America of the *International Journal of Psychoanalysis*, Latin American chair of the task force for the *International Encyclopedia of Psychoanalysis* (IPA), and received Sigourney Award 1999.

Elizabeth Lima da Rocha Barros is a training analyst and supervisor at the Brazilian Psychoanalytical Society of São Paulo, a fellow of the British Psychoanalytical Society and of the British Institute of Psychoanalysis, child analyst, British Psychoanalytical Society and Tavistock Clinic, DEA in psychopathology Sorbonne University (Paris), and chair for Latin America of the CCM Groups.

David Bell is a training analyst of the British Psychoanalytic Society and a past president. He is a consultant psychiatrist director of the specialist unit for serious/enduring complex disorders at the Tavistock Clinic and an expert in asylum and human rights. His publications include *Paranoia*; *Psychoanalysis and Culture: A Kleinian Perspective*; *Reason and Passion: A Celebration of the Work of Hanna Segal* (Ed.); and *Living on the Border: Psychotic Processes in the Individual, the Couple and the Group* (Ed.).

Rachel B. Blass is a member and training analyst at the Israel Psychoanalytic Society, a member of the British Psychoanalytical Society, and professor of psychoanalysis at Heythrop College, the University of London. She is also a board member and editor of the "Controversies" section of the *International Journal of Psychoanalysis*. She has published a book and over eighty articles which deal mainly with the close study and elucidation of Freud's texts and Kleinian thinking and practice. She has lectured, taught, and offered clinical seminars in many countries and her writings have been translated into fifteen languages.

Michael Brearley is a fellow and ex-president of the British Psychoanalytical Society, and works in private practice in London. He was in an earlier life a professional cricketer. He has written *The Art of Captaincy* (1985), and has recently published a new book, *On Form*, an exploration of being on and off form in many areas of life.

Irma Brenman Pick came to London from South Africa in 1955 and trained first at the Tavistock Clinic as a child psychotherapist, then at the British Institute of Psychoanalysis as an adult and child analyst. She is now a distinguished fellow and training analyst in the British Society, and a past president of the Society. Her published papers include: "On adolescence", "Working through in the counter-transference", and "Concern: Spurious and real", soon to be published in her collected works *Authenticity in the Psychoanalytic Encounter*, edited by M. Fakhry Davids and Naomi Shavit. Together with her late husband Eric Brenman she has taught extensively abroad.

Ronald Britton is a fellow of the Royal College of Psychiatrists and distinguished fellow of the British Psychoanalytical Society. He was given the "International psychoanalytical association award for outstanding scientific contributions" in July 2013 and the "Sigourney award for distinguished contributions to psychoanalysis" in January 2014. His books include: *The Oedipus Complex Today*; *Belief and Imagination*; *Sex, Death, and the Superego*; and *Between Mind and Brain*. Though essentially a clinical practitioner, his writing has emphasised the relationship of analysis to literature, philosophy, and theology.

Roosevelt M. S. Cassorla, MD, PhD, is a titular member and training analyst of the Brazilian Psychoanalytic Society of São Paulo and the Campinas Study Group. He is full professor of psychological medicine and psychiatry at the medical school of the State University of Campinas, and is a member of the editorial board of the *International Journal of Psychoanalysis* and collaborator on the International Psychoanalytic Association's *Encyclopaedic Dictionary of Psychoanalysis*. He has edited five books and is author of a number of book chapters and papers on psychoanalysis and medical psychology. His latest book is *The Psychoanalyst, the Theatre of Dreams and the Clinic of Enactment* (Karnac). He is the 2017 recipient of the Mary S. Sigourney Award for Outstanding Achievement in Psychoanalysis.

Lindsay L. Clarkson, MD, is a training and supervising analyst at the Washington Center for Psychoanalysis and a member of the Center for Advanced Psychoanalytic Studies. She is engaged in private practice of analysis and supervision in Chevy Chase, MD. Her primary interests lie in understanding primitive mental experience to enable better contact with patients, and in a psychoanalytic exploration of our relationship to the natural world and the non-human environment. She co-leads educational efforts in Washington DC supported by the Rita Frankiel Bequest to the Melanie Klein Trust.

Arman Eshraghi is a senior lecturer in finance and director of MSc finance and investment at the University of Edinburgh Business School. He is a fellow of the UK Higher Education Academy, and has held visiting positions at Manchester Business School and University College London. Formerly, Arman was a management consultant in the banking and telecom sectors. His primary research interests lie in the area of behavioural and interdisciplinary finance.

Dr Michael Feldman is a training analyst of the British Society. He trained in psychiatry and psychotherapy at the Maudsley Hospital in London, and is now in full-time analytic practice. He has extensive experience teaching abroad—in Europe and the USA. He is particularly interested in psychoanalytic technique, and the process of psychic change, and has published numerous papers, which have been collected in his book *Doubt, Conviction and the Analytic Process*.

Claudia Frank, Priv.-Doz. Dr med., is a psychoanalyst in private practice in Stuttgart, and a training analyst of the DPV/IPA. Between 1988 and 2001 she was in the department for psychoanalysis, psychotherapy, and psychosomatics of the University in Tübingen, and between 1998 and 2001 was in charge of the chair for psychoanalysis, psychotherapy, and psychosomatics. She is a guest member of the British Psychoanalytical Society. Since 2016, she has been chair of the training committee of the DPV. Publications about technique, theory, and the history of psychoanalysis include *Melanie Klein in Berlin: Her First Psychoanalyses of Children* (Routledge, 2009) as well as papers in applied psychoanalysis. She is co-editor of *Jahrbuch der Psychoanalyse*, and, together with Heinz Weiß, editor of various books on Kleinian psychoanalysis.

Penelope Garvey is a training analyst of the British Psychoanalytical Society. Her first training was as a clinical psychologist and she has worked as a consultant psychotherapist in the NHS.

Currently she is in full-time private practice in Devon. She teaches in the UK and abroad, particularly in Ukraine, and has taught the course "Contributions from Kleinian psychoanalysts" at the Institute of Psychoanalysis in London. She is a co-author of *The New Dictionary of Kleinian Thought* (2011).

Judith Jackson is a child and adult psychoanalyst and a fellow of the Institute of Psychoanalysis. She trained initially as a child psychotherapist at the Tavistock Clinic and worked for many years in child and adolescent mental health services. She teaches at the Tavistock Clinic, the Institute of Psychoanalysis, and was, for many years, visiting lecturer and teacher to Tavistock-linked training schools in Turin and Rome. She has presented child analysis papers at several IPA congresses and has published papers in English and French journals.

Kay Long, PhD. is a psychoanalyst in private practice in New Haven, CT. She is an associate clinical professor in the psychiatry department of the Yale School of Medicine and a training and supervising analyst at the Western New England Institute for Psychoanalysis where she serves as director of the Scholar's Program. Her current teaching and writing interests involve contemporary Kleinian theory and technique. She has served on the editorial board of the International Journal of Psychoanalysis, and is on the editorial board of the Journal of the American Psychoanalytic Association. She co-leads the Melanie Klein Trust-sponsored Rita Frankiel Memorial Fellowship that takes place jointly in New Haven and New York.

Chris Mawson is a training and supervising analyst of the British Psychoanalytical Society and works in private practice as a psychoanalyst. He worked initially with young children and adolescents, first at the Tavistock Clinic and later in the child psychiatry department of the Paddington Green Children's Hospital. His first training was as a clinical psychologist, with a research interest in attention and manic depressive psychosis. He is the editor of *The Complete Works of W. R. Bion* (2014), and *Bion Today* (2010), in the New Library of Psychoanalysis series.

Edna O'Shaughnessy was born in South Africa in 1924. After World War Two she came to England to continue her studies in philosophy at the University of Oxford. Questions that specially engaged her, and on which she wrote, were meaning and its representation, and the freedom—or not—to choose—both topics of continuing interest. Her analytic training began with children at the Tavistock Clinic, followed by training as a psychoanalyst for adults at the British Psychoanalytical Society of which she is a distinguished fellow, a training and supervising analyst, and a child analyst. For a while now she has not seen patients (a huge loss), but she still does some supervisory work with analysts and psychotherapists and in the Tavistock's Fitzjohn's Unit where psychodynamic treatment is offered to adults suffering chronic mental health problems. During more than fifty years of psychoanalytic work Edna O'Shaughnessy has written many papers, now published as her *Collected Papers*.

Kate Paul (Kate Barrows) is a training analyst with the British Psychoanalytical Society and a Tavistock-trained child psychotherapist, and lives and works in private practice in Bristol. Her publications include "Ghosts in the swamp" (*IJPA*, 1999), and *Envy* (Icon Books, 2004). She edited *Autism in Childhood and Autistic Features in Adults* (Karnac, 2008). She has also written several papers about the relationship between literature, music, and psychoanalysis.

Alberto Pieczanski, MD, is a child, adolescent, and adult psychoanalyst. He trained at the Institute of Psychoanalysis-British Psychoanalytical Society. He is a training and supervising psychoanalyst member of the British Psychoanalytic Society, Buenos Aires Psychoanalytic Association (APdeBA), Washington Center for Psychoanalysis, and Washington School of Psychiatry. He is co-editor with Dr Nydia Lisman Pieczanski of *The Pioneers of Psychoanalysis in South America* (Routledge, 2015). He runs clinical workshops in the USA and South America.

Shelley Rockwell, PhD, is a training and supervising analyst with the Contemporary Freudian Society in Washington, DC. She teaches and writes in the area of contemporary Kleinian theory and practice, and co-leads educational efforts in Washington, DC, supported by the Rita Frankiel Bequest to the Melanie Klein Trust. In addition she has a special interest in poetry as it links to psychoanalysis.

Priscilla Roth is a training and supervising psychoanalyst at the British Psychoanalytic Society. She teaches in Britain, Europe, and the United States. She is the author of a large number of papers and the editor of several books, most recently *Imaginary Existences: A Psychoanalytic Exploration of Phantasy; Fiction, Dreams and Daydreams*, by Ignês Sodré; and, with Alessandra Lemma, *Envy and Gratitude Revisited*.

Richard Rusbridger is a training and supervising analyst, and a child analyst, of the British Psychoanalytical Society. He has a background in music and English, and trained as a child psychotherapist at the Tavistock Clinic. He is in full-time private practice in London. He has written papers on theory and on the connection between music and psychoanalysis, and has edited: (with Susan Budd) *Introducing Psychoanalysis: Essential Themes and Topics* (2005); (with Priscilla Roth) *Encounters with Melanie Klein: Selected Papers of Elizabeth Spillius* (2007); and *Inquiries in Psychoanalysis: Collected Papers of Edna O'Shaughnessy* (2015).

Margaret Rustin is a child and adolescent psychotherapist, a child analyst, and an associate of the British Psychoanalytical Society. She was head of child psychotherapy at the Tavistock Clinic from 1985 to 2009 and continues to teach there and in many parts of the world. *Reading Klein*, her latest book, written jointly with Michael Rustin, was published in December 2016.

John Steiner is a training analyst of the British Psychoanalytical Society, and although now retired from clinical practice, he continues to supervise and write. He is the author of *Psychic Retreats*, (1993) and *Seeing and Being Seen*, (2011), and has also edited and written introductions to several books including *The Oedipus Complex Today*, (1989), papers by Hanna Segal, entitled, *Psychoanalysis, Literature and War* (1997), and essays on Herbert Rosenfeld's clinical influence, entitled *Rosenfeld in Retrospect* (2008). Most recently he has edited and written a critical review of Melanie Klein's 1936 lectures, *Lectures on Technique by Melanie Klein* (2017).

Richard Taffler is professor of finance at Warwick Business School. A leading authority on behavioural finance and investment, he has published over a hundred academic and professional papers and books, and is frequently quoted in the media. Among his other research interests Richard is currently developing the new and very practical paradigm of emotional finance. This focuses on the role emotions and unconscious fantasy play in driving investor behaviour and that of the financial markets more generally, including the recent stock market and property bubbles and financial crises, and draws on the insights psychoanalytic theory provides.

Sally Weintrobe, psychoanalyst, is a fellow of The British Psychoanalytical Society. She previously chaired its Scientific Committee, was a member of senior staff at the Tavistock Clinic and honarary senior lecturer at University College London in the department for psychoanalytic studies. She has written on entitlement attitudes, grievance and complaint, prejudice, greed, climate change denial, and our relationship with nature. She edited and contributed to Weintrobe (2012) *Engaging with Climate Change: Psychoanalytic and Interdisciplinary Perspectives* (Routledge and the New Library of Psychoanalysis Beyond the Couch Series). In 2014 this book was short-listed for the International Gradiva Prize for contributions to psychoanalysis.

Prof. Heinz Weiss, MD, is a psychoanalyst (DPV), head of the department of psychosomatic medicine, Robert-Bosch-Krankenhaus (Stuttgart/Germany), managing medical director, Sigmund-Freud-Institut Frankfurt a. M. (Germany), guest member of the British Psychoanalytical Society, and chair of the education section of the *International Journal of Psychoanalysis*.

Gianna Williams is a member of the British Psychoanalytical Society and a former consultant child and adolescent psychotherapist at the Tavistock Clinic. She teaches in both organisations. She has introduced the Tavistock Model Child Psychotherapy Courses in five Italian towns and has developed infant observation for child neuropsychiatry students at the University of Pisa. She consults to "Juntos con los niños", an NGO for street children in Mexico. She has published many articles and chapters and written or co-edited several books including: (1997) *Internal Landscapes and Foreign Bodies: Eating Disorders and Other Pathologies* (1997), and *The Generosity of Acceptance. Vol 1: Feeding Difficulties in Children, Vol 2: Eating Disorders in Adolescence* (2004).

Dr Lynne Zeavin is in full time private practice in New York City. On the teaching faculty of the New York Psychoanalytic Society and Institute, she serves on the editorial boards of *JAPA, The Psychoanalytic Quarterly*, and *Division/Review*. She has published on a variety of topics, including femininity, the nature of the object, and psychoanalysis and the environment. She chairs the Fellowship Program of the American Psychoanalytic Association and she is a co-founder of the Rita Frankiel Memorial Fellowship sponsored by the Melanie Klein Trust and a founder of Second Story, a non-institutional psychoanalytic learning space.

If you have followed "Lines of Development," as we hope you have, you must have noticed that Melanie Klein was present in the Series from the very beginning and all the time. Our eldest is the volume about Anna Freud, the founder's youngest daughter, whose "controversial discussions" with Melanie Klein had huge influence on child analysis and the organisation of training in the British Psychoanalytic Society; the volume on the "Fairbairn Tradition" brings a plethora of reflection about mutual influences and differences between the Scottish psychoanalyst and the then London-based theorist; and what is to be said of our third volume, on Winnicott, Melanie Klein's supervisee, who analysed one of her sons as well as she his second wife; and our fourth, on Bion, an author so deeply immersed in Klein's work that the model is sometimes called "Kleinian-Bionic" (Mitchell & Black, 2016, ch. 4); and the fifth on Jacques Lacan, in press at the moment of writing this preface, like other books compares his work with that of Melanie Klein. And we could not but proceed in the same way: Ferenczi, our next psychoanalytic 'giant', psychoanalysed Klein, encouraged her to become an analyst, inspired her to work with children and may have deeply influenced her concepts of splitting and dissociation (Minuchin, in press). And the same engagement with Klein will no doubt certainly be true for all the books that are still in preparation.

Klein's special position in the "Lines of Development" is due to her special position in the history of psychoanalysis. Indeed, it is only Freud's earliest years of the foundation of the movement before the end of the World War One that Klein was not closely connected to and did not profoundly affect. Her thinking has been part and parcel of psychoanalysis, as it were, "since forever": after the analysis with Ferenczi, she continued with another "secret committee" member, Karl Abraham in Berlin, and finally moved to London in 1926 under the patronage of Ernest Jones, leaving none indifferent. Since then her name is known on all the Meridians of the psychoanalytic globe: in London, in Italy, in Buenos Aires—in psychoanalysis she is "almost everywhere," especially since Otto Kernberg has smuggled her thinking into the US.

The reason for all this seems quite clear. Mrs. Klein pioneered play-analysis, introduced the idea of 'positions', enriched understanding of depressive states, promoted defense mechanisms like splitting and projective identification, and importance of early states like envy and gratitude… Probably more than anything, she is universally considered to be the founder of the so-called object relations theory. All of these, and much more, have attracted so many followers and such opposition that Melanie Klein has grown into one of the strongest sources of gravity psychoanalysis has ever had, so much so that some see her as the very definition of our profession, like Hanna Segal who, as recently as 2006, claimed that true psychoanalysis is epitomised by Freud, Klein and Bion, explicitly dismissing authors of the magnitude of a Winnicott or Kohut.

Numerous books have, naturally, been published over the years about Melanie Klein, her life, clinical work and theoretical contributions. So many that one must wonder what novelty this volume could possibly bring. At this point, dear reader, we must confess. Honestly, we would have published this book even if it brought nothing new, as this series is impossible to imagine without a book on Melanie Klein. However, this collection of essays, we firmly believe, does bring novelty to everyone. Its scope ranges from clinical insights to *King Lear*; it is aimed at students as well as seasoned "Kleinians," and its many rigorously selected contributors deal with central topics in a way that's both intriguing and comprehensive.

As series editors, we can only hope for more books like this one and cannot thank Penelope Garvey and Kay Long enough for all the effort and creativity they have invested in this book! We can also hardly wait for all the new dialogues this book on the "Kleinian Tradition" will definitely provoke in all psychoanalytic corners!

Aleksandar Dimitrijevic
Joan Raphael-Leff
Norka Malberg

References

Anderson, J. W. (2015). Winnicott's constant search for the life that feels real. In M. Boyle Spelman & F. Thomson-Salo (eds.), *The Winnicott Tradition* (pp. 19–38). London: Karnac.

Clarke, G. S., & Scharff, D. E. (Eds.). (2014). *Fairbairn and the object relations tradition*. Karnac Books.

Dimitrijevic, A., Cassullo, G., & Frankel, J. (2018). *Ferenczi's Influence on Contemporary Psychoanalytic Traditions. London: Karnac.*

Hensel, B. F. (2014). On the origin of internal objects in the works of Fairbairn and Klein and the possible therapeutic consequences. In G. S. Clarke & D. E. Scharff (eds.), *Fairbairn and the Object Relations Tradition* (pp. 147–160). London: Karnac.

Levine, H. B., & Civitarese, G. (Eds.). (2015). *The WR Bion Tradition*. Karnac Books.

Lichtenstein, D. & Bailly, L. (eds.) (2017). *The Jacques Lacan Tradition: Lines of Development—Evolution of Theory and Practice*. London: Karnac.

Malberg, N. T., & Raphael-Leff, J. (Eds.). (2012). *The Anna Freud Tradition: Lines of Development-Evolution and Theory and Practice Over the Decades*. Karnac Books.

Minuchin, L. M. (in press). Melanie Klein's development of, and divergence from, Sándor Ferenczi's ideas. In A. Dimitrijevic, G. Cassullo & J. Frankel (eds.), *Ferenczi's Influence on Contemporary Psychoanalytic Traditions*. London: Karnac.

Mitchell, S. A., & Black, M. (2016). *Freud and beyond: A history of modern psychoanalytic thought*. Basic Books.

Segal, H. (2006). Reflections on truth, tradition, and the psychoanalytic tradition of truth. *American Imago*, *63* (3): 283–292.

Spelman, M. B., & Thomson-Salo, F. (Eds.). (2014). *The Winnicott Tradition: Lines of Development—Evolution of Theory and Practice over the Decades*. Karnac Books.

INTRODUCTION

When Norka Malberg and Joan Raphael-Leff, the editors of the Lines of Development series, invited us to edit the volume on Klein, their mandate to us was to collect original papers that would illustrate the development and influence of Kleinian theory over time and across the analytic world. Aware of the many excellent books already written that cover much of this vast and complex territory, we found it a challenge to come up with a concept for a book that would both fulfill our mandate and be an addition to the literature.

We decided that we wanted to demonstrate the far reach of Klein's ideas and the many ways in which they have been developed, including differences of approach within the Kleinian tradition, and so we sought authors across a variety of locations and interests. Most of our authors trained at the Institute of Psychoanalysis in London, others come from Brazil, Germany, Israel, and the United States, and all either trained in the Kleinian tradition or are influenced by Klein's ideas. We wanted also to include some analysts newer to the Kleinian field, as well as those who are well established and recognised for their significant contributions. The majority are involved in work with adults, a number work with children, and several are interested in the application of Klein's ideas to other fields. We would like to thank everyone who agreed to contribute.

The book is organised into four parts. The first part, "Historical frame", contains a chapter written by us to provide an introduction to Klein and her ideas. We give a brief biographical sketch of Klein's life, followed by discussion of her major theoretical and technical contributions, and then trace the development of her key ideas to the present day. While we cover a lot of territory, we make no claim to have done justice to the vast body of Kleinian literature that has been developed by her successors in the past ninety years.

The next two parts, "Theory and practice" and "Work with children", are the core of the book and are comprised of clinical papers containing detailed case illustrations. The final part,

"Applied contributions", consists of papers that apply Kleinian ideas to diverse, non-analytic fields.

What follows is an introduction to the papers, with brief descriptions of each one, which we have organised thematically so readers will have some idea where to turn to pursue their interests.

Introduction to the papers

Many of the clinical papers focus on primitive mental states: how they manifest in treatment, how the analyst understands them, and techniques to reach patients at these deep levels.

Psychotic and borderline states

Tracing the history of a psychoanalytic approach to psychosis from Freud to Klein, **David Bell** argues that these very disturbed, even bizarre, states of mind have a natural connection to ordinary human preoccupations. Through case examples, including Philip Marlowe, the protagonist of the television drama *The Singing Detective*, Bell illustrates the forces within that trap patients in their illnesses and work to prevent good development.

Splitting and idealisation

Making links to Klein's work with Erna, and her description of splitting processes, **Claudia Frank** vividly illustrates the underlying phantasy life in a patient who uses splitting to manage envy, jealousy, and sadistic phantasies of cutting.

Approaching the same topic from a different angle, **Priscilla Roth** describes a patient struggling with envy and jealousy, and focuses on the defence of idealisation. She sets out just how devastating this can be to an individual's capacity to take in and enjoy a good experience. In her case example, she demonstrates the slow but significant progress her patient made as she moved forward into guilt and insight, only to retreat back into splitting and idealisation.

Through Shakespeare's *King Lear*, **Richard Rusbridger** gives us a picture of a personality organised based on splitting and idealisation. He shows us how Lear uses fragmentation to defend against reality, and how shame works to keep him from recognising his damaging effects on his objects and the ensuing guilt, which tragically interferes with his capacity to mourn and repair.

Drawing on Nathaniel Hawthorne's story, "The birthmark", and two case vignettes, **Lynne Zeavin** is also interested in the destructive effects of idealisation of the self and other. She contends that primitive idealisation, especially self-idealisation, protects the patient from recognition of painful psychic realities, in particular broken-down states felt to be irreparable, while in itself inflicting damage.

Richard Taffler and Arman Eshraghi, using Kleinian and Bionian theories, address the question of why hedge funds, in spite of their questionable performance, continue to hold a "magical appeal" for investors. Drawing on insights about the function of unconscious phantasies,

Taffler and Eshraghi show how hedge fund investors search for the excitement of what they, along with David Tuckett, term "phantastic objects", to the point of ignoring their exposure to financial risk and peril.

Sally Weintrobe brings Kleinian ideas to bear on the topic of climate change. She is interested in how to communicate about climate change so as to promote what she terms a "culture of care" in order to counteract the prevailing "culture of uncare", which she argues is based on the defences of splitting and disavowal operating at both an individual and a societal level.

Envy and jealousy

Irma Brenman Pick describes the interweaving of envy and jealousy and argues that these feelings both provoke and are provoked by deprivation and loss. She illustrates how patients become caught up in vicious circles and how shame and guilt can prevent development and, in one patient, lead to physical illness.

Manic mechanisms

Two authors take up the theme of mania as a defence against mourning. **Judith Jackson** writes about the technical challenges in treating a nine-year-old girl who worked hard to convince herself and those around her that she was "normal", but who in fact used manic mechanisms as a fragile defence against persecutory anxieties, crippling phobias, and fragmentation.

Heinz Weiss writes about manic forms of reparation. Through a detailed case report he demonstrates how these primitive attempts at reparation are successful at partially relieving the patient's guilt and anxiety, but leave him in a state of grievance and wrath, forever caught up with damaged internal objects.

Mourning

In a meditation on mourning, **Ron Britton** takes us on a poetic journey through Rilke, Shakespeare, Keats, Wordsworth, Dickens, and Wagner, linking their thoughts to those of Freud, Abraham, Speilrein, Klein, Bion, and Segal. Beginning with the question of what psychoanalysis has to add to our understanding of mourning, he goes on to demonstrate just how much and in what ways it has contributed to our grasp of this fundamental human experience.

Also drawing on poetry, **Shelley Rockwell** takes us through a close reading of Gabriel García Lorca's *Lament for Ignacio Sánchez Mejías*, to vividly trace stages of grief and mourning. She weaves in the ideas of several Kleinian writers, including Segal and Sodré, to add psychological depth to Lorca's poetic description.

Kate Paul is interested in the process by which mourning contributes to psychological development. She argues that Klein's ideas about the working through of loss and the repair of existing internal objects do not fully account for the development that takes place in analysis. Through two clinical cases, she illustrates her view that aspects of early experiences combine with a new experience in the analysis to produce a more robust internal object.

Containment

Nicola Abel Hirsch, in a thorough study of Bion's papers, traces the development of his important concept of container/contained; in addition, she sheds fresh light on the commonalities and differences between Bion's container/contained and Winnicott's holding.

Chris Mawson also carefully traces the evolution Bion's theories, grounding the theories of thinking and container/contained in Klein's theories of projective processes and the depressive and paranoid-schizoid positions. He makes a particular link between Bion's container/contained and an early idea from Freud's pre-psychoanalytic writing in which he describes the infant's communication and need for "extraneous" help.

Gianna Williams is interested in a particular kind of failure of containment: patients who have been projected into in such a way that they internalise a disorganising object. Through clinical examples she illustrates the technical challenges the analyst faces in treating these patients who, in her experience, communicate their longing for an object who can counteract the disorganisation and put order in place.

Reparation

Edna O'Shaughnessy, in a short but powerful paper, traces Freud's ideas about the Oedipus complex, human suffering, and guilt and concludes that Freud's tragic view of man's inescapable suffering left analysts waiting for a concept like Klein's reparation. O'Shaughnessy outlines Klein's theory of reparation and its implications for analysis, indeed for the human struggle to move beyond discontents toward an integration of love and hate that makes the inevitable pain of being human bearable.

Michael Brearley, writing from the point of view of an Independent of the British Psychoanalytic Society, turns to Eric Brenman's ideas about narrow-mindedness and the importance of finding a home for one's feelings to argue for a shift away from guilt and towards generosity as the propeller of development toward a larger sense of self. Generosity, according to Brearley, includes creativity, generativity, taking responsibility for one's attacks on others, and finding room for a wide range of emotions and characteristics.

Technique

Roosevelt Cassorla draws on a wide range of theory to support his unique approach to clinical impasses that are due to chronic mutual enactments. He shows through clinical examples how acute enactments, paradoxically, can provide the stimulus the analyst needs to recognise and address the unseen chronic enactment. His description of the role of dreaming and non-dreaming, including non-dreams for two, is of particular interest.

Using the myth of Narcissus as his starting point, **Michael Feldman**, describes the pressures the analyst must contend with in treating a narcissistic patient. Through a detailed case example, he illustrates a technical approach that emphasises attention to the countertransference pulls on the analyst to behave in ways that conform to the patient's internal object world.

Lindsay Clarkson is also interested in the pressures the patient exerts on the analyst to think and act in order to fit in to the patient's internal world. She explores this through a clinical case of a patient with "as-if" character structure with autistic features.

Alberto Pieczjanski examines both perverse and addictive states of mind and argues that they share a similar defensive organisation and mode of object relating, which rely on pathological projective identification. Through several case examples, he demonstrates his technical approach to treating such patients, and warns of the potential for the analyst to be pulled into a *perversion à deux*.

Writing from the point of view of South American analysts who trained in the Kleinian tradition in London forty years ago, **Elizabeth and Elias Rocha Barros** present an overview, with case examples, of the evolution of their thinking and practice over the past four decades. While remaining true to their Kleinian roots, they have developed technical approaches based on their clinical experiences and interest in different theorists, including Ogden and Ferro.

Reflecting on a particular quality in the analyst's attitude of mind, **John Steiner** discusses two plays, Ibsen's *The Wild Duck* and Sophocles' *Oedipus the King*, to illustrate his thesis that analytic listening is akin to watching a play. In both situations one must adopt a dual identity, first to participate through identification and then to withdraw into the position of an observer. He explores the role of irony in allowing these two attitudes to coexist, so that we can retain a respect for truth alongside an awareness of a need for illusion.

Technique in work with children

Covering a wide range of theory, **Anne Alvarez** argues for a further division within the paranoid-schizoid position to encompass patients who exhibit states of extreme chronic dissociation, emptiness, or perverse attachments to non-human or sado-masochistic objects. She demonstrates through several child cases a technique based on the use of "an intensive, vitalising insistence on meaning", which she believes is more effective than classical analytic technique in helping these very disturbed children.

Margaret Rustin describes the methods that child psychotherapists at the Tavistock Clinic have developed for treating severely disturbed children. Through the detailed case report of an eight-year-old boy who presented for treatment with "no sense of belonging to the human family", Rustin makes a compelling and moving case for the efficacy of a sensitive psychoanalytic approach and underlines the importance of institutional and team support when undertaking this kind of work.

Teaching Klein

Rachel Blass observes that teaching Kleinian theory, with its emphasis on primitive mental functioning, presents unique challenges, particularly when addressing non-analysts and non-Kleinians. She outlines some guidelines for teaching Klein aimed at opening the student to the immediate experience and sympathy necessary for a true understanding of Kleinian theory and practice.

PART I

HISTORICAL FRAME

CHAPTER ONE

Melanie Klein: her main ideas and some theoretical and clinical developments

Penelope Garvey and Kay Long

Introduction

"A woman of character & force some submerged—how shall I say?—not craft, but subtlety: something working underground. A pull, a twist, like an undertow: menacing. A bluff grey-haired lady, with large bright imaginative eyes."

Virginia Woolf on Melanie Klein (1984, p. 208).

While Melanie Klein's theories are controversial in many corners of the psychoanalytic world, their impact and importance are by now undeniable. By any measure she ranks as one of the most influential thinkers in the history of psychoanalysis. From the epicentre of Kleinian theory in London her ideas have spread, taking root in South America, finding adherents throughout Europe, and, after years of antipathy and misunderstanding, are now enjoying a fresh reception in North America. Her seminal concepts have been the source of ongoing theoretical and clinical developments for analytic thinkers throughout the world.

Klein began her psychoanalytic career working with children, and it was through this work that she discovered most of her innovative contributions to psychoanalysis. She began by applying Freud's theories to the mental life of infants and young children, a territory he left largely unexplored. But in the end she extended Freud's theories in directions that led to distinctive psychoanalytic concepts. According to Jean-Michel Petot (1990), she was surprised that her colleagues found her ideas controversial. She believed that any student of Freud who observed young children would come to the same conclusions as she. Of course, that was not true, and famously not true when it came to Freud's daughter, Anna.

Klein's pioneering work mapping the mental terrain of infants and young children led her to enduring theories about the nature of personality development, anxiety, defences, unconscious phantasy, and analytic technique.

Throughout her writings Melanie Klein was careful to connect her ideas to those of her predecessors. She quoted Sigmund Freud extensively in support of her hypotheses; she connected her theories to those of Sándor Ferenczi; she drew on Karl Abraham for her understanding of the importance of object relations, envy, and the oral and anal sadistic impulses; she gave credit to Hermine Hug-Hellmuth for ideas about play; and she linked her theory of the paranoid-schizoid character to a concept of Ronald Fairbairn.

In an interview published on the Melanie Klein Trust website, Hanna Segal, a patient, student, and interpreter of Klein and a major theorist in her own right, tells a story about Klein meeting one of her neighbours. Upon learning that Klein was a psychoanalyst, the neighbour said, "My brother is also an analyst, but he is a Freudian." According to Segal, "Mrs Klein pulled herself up to her full height, which was not considerable, and said, 'My dear, we are *all* Freudian only I am not an Anna Freudian.'"

How did this loyal Freudian develop a branch of psychoanalysis that bears her name, and in the end differ with Freud in some key areas, even as she sought to fit her ideas into his? What are the core ideas that distinguish this psychoanalytic school of thought from others? And how did it all begin?

Biographical sketch

Melanie Klein was born in 1882 in Vienna, the last of four children. Her father broke with his Orthodox Jewish past and dropped his rabbinical studies to become a physician as he neared the age of forty. The anti-Semitism in turn-of-the century Vienna made it difficult for a Jewish physician to thrive, so her mother opened a shop for exotic plants and animals to supplement the family's income, an uncommon practice in that period.

When Klein was four her next oldest sibling, Sidonie, aged eight, became seriously ill and was bedridden. From her sick-bed her sister forged a close bond with little Melanie as she taught her to read and write. Her sister's death a year later was a searing loss that tragically foreshadowed a lifetime of painful losses for Klein. Her father died when she was eighteen, her adored brother Emmanuel, who was sickly his whole life, died of heart failure when she was twenty, her second analyst Abraham died while she was in treatment with him, and perhaps most devastating of all her eldest son, Emmanuel, died in a hiking accident when he was twenty-seven.

At the age of sixteen, Klein passed her medical school entrance examinations and was set to pursue her ambition to become a psychiatrist. However, a year later, she abandoned her plans for medical school when she became engaged to Arthur Klein, a young engineer she had met through her brother. According to Segal, the frequent moves to different factory towns in Arthur's work life would make medical training impossible. After a three-year engagement, during which she suffered the loss of her father and her older brother, she married and soon became pregnant with her first child.

The young family moved several times to various cities in central Europe to accommodate her husband's career as an engineer. Klein became seriously depressed during her second pregnancy, suffering under the weight of an unhappy marriage and life in a series of small, friendless towns. Her mother moved in with them and encouraged Klein to leave her young family and seek treatment for her nervous depression, which in those days involved trips to sanatoriums for rest and carbonic acid baths.

After eleven years of marriage and a series of failed treatment attempts, the family settled in Budapest shortly before the outbreak of the First World War. Pregnant with her third child, she became depressed again. Her mother died three months later and her husband was called into service in the brutal war raging around them. But her life was about to take a turn for the better.

In Budapest, Klein had access to the kind of intellectual and cultural life she had known in Vienna. We do not know who put Freud's popular book *On Dreams* in her hands, but we know from her unfinished autobiography that reading it filled her with excitement about the possibilities inherent in psychoanalysis. According to Segal, "[t]o study psychoanalysis, practice it, contribute to it became the ruling passion of her life" (1979, p. 31). She began psychoanalytic treatment with Sándor Ferenczi, a leading analyst in Budapest and close associate of Freud. This treatment proved to be nothing short of life altering. Under Ferenczi's care Klein's depression lifted and she found an unexpected way to resurrect her career ambitions. In the preface to the first edition of *The Psycho-Analysis of Children* she credited Ferenczi with setting her on the course of her lifework:

> Ferenczi was the first to make me acquainted with psycho-analysis. He also made me under-
> stand its real essence and meaning. His strong and direct feeling for the unconscious and for
> symbolism, and the remarkable rapport he had with the minds of children, have had a lasting
> influence on my understanding of the psychology of the small child. He also drew my atten-
> tion to my capacity for understanding children and my interest in them, and he very much
> encouraged my idea of devoting myself to analysis, particularly child analysis, then still very
> little explored. I had, of course, three children of my own at the time ... I had not found ... that
> education ... could cover the whole understanding of the personality and therefore have the
> influence one might wish it to have. I had always the feeling that behind was something with
> which I could not come to grips. (Klein, 1932a, x–xi)

In 1919, just after the Great War's end, Klein, then age thirty-seven, read her first paper to the Hungarian Psychoanalytic Society, a study of her youngest son, five-year-old Erich, after which she was invited to join the Society as a member. In those days, analysing one's own children was not unusual, nor was writing and presenting a paper as a path to becoming an analyst.

Two years later, fleeing anti-Semitism in Budapest and separated from her husband, Klein moved with Erich to Berlin, while her two older children attended university and boarding school. Klein's five years in Berlin were pivotal for her. During these years her marriage broke up for good; she joined the Berlin Society and under the supervision of Abraham embarked on her first child analysis. She went on to analyse several children, who were to become the basis of her first book, *The Psycho-Analysis of Children*.

While in Berlin she was also analysed by Abraham, and it was here that she first met the members of the British Society who were to become instrumental in her decision to move to London after Abraham's unexpected and tragic death. Encouraged by Ernst Jones, Klein moved to London in 1926 and started her practice, initially by analysing Jones's wife and children. She spent the rest of her life in London developing her ideas—these caused considerable controversy within the British Society.

Work with children

No one before Klein had tried to psychoanalyse children. Although some analysts were treating children, most notably Hug-Hellmuth and Anna Freud, they advocated an educational or psychotherapeutic approach. In the early days of psychoanalysis most believed that children could not engage in analysis as adults do because children do not come to treatment of their own accord; they are still in the midst of the very situations that are causing their illnesses, and they do not have any desire to change or any understanding of an analytic process. Klein disagreed. She believed that a child expressed his inner world in words and actions, including play. And she believed that a child was capable of understanding himself and so could benefit from analytic interpretations.

Klein was not the first to observe that children express their inner world through play. Freud had written about the importance of play for a child in mastering his inner life in his "fort-da" example in *Beyond the Pleasure Principle* (1920g). Klein, however, went beyond Freud's observation that a child uses play to turn a passive experience into an active one when she recognised that a child's play was akin to adult free association.

Klein's first psychoanalytic venture, which she called an "upbringing with analytic features", was with her son Erich, who was inhibited and had difficulties in learning. Following Freud's idea that neurotic conflict is caused by dammed up libido, Klein sought to treat Erich by responding truthfully to his sexual curiosity. In retrospect, Klein (1955) claimed that this work with Erich was when she first began to see the therapeutic potential of play, but it took several years before she developed this observation into a new technique.

Klein began her work with children in Berlin using the same principles and methods analysts used with adults—the couch and free association. However, as she encountered resistances when she tried to help children through these classical methods and as she closely observed the young children she treated, she gradually developed a new method—the play technique.

Klein undertook the treatment of a toddler, Rita, who suffered from severe anxiety attacks, play inhibition, and obsessional rituals. Klein saw Rita in the child's home warily observed by Rita's mother and aunt. At two and a half years, Rita's verbal abilities were limited and so she engaged with Klein largely through play, which Klein was able to interpret to good effect. At this point Klein did not yet privilege play as a means of communication or intervention.

Her experience with Rita showed Klein the difficulties of carrying out a treatment in the child's home and she decided from then on to use her own office. It was when she was analysing seven-year-old Inge that Klein intuitively took a big step forwards in developing play technique. Inge had become averse to school, but was otherwise normal. Klein found the sessions with her dull and monotonous. She noticed that Inge responded to interpretations by telling a new story that was no more revealing than the last. In the midst of another unpromising session, Klein decided to go into her own children's playroom and collect some toys—cars, little figures, bricks, and a train—to bring back to Inge to try to engage her.

Later, Klein wrote:

> The child, who had not taken to drawing or other activities, was interested in the small toys
> and at once began to play. From this play I gathered that two of the toy figures represented
> herself and a little boy, a school-mate about whom I had heard before. It appeared that there
> was something secret about the behavior of these two figures and that other toy people were
> resented as interfering or watching and were put aside. The activities of the two toys led to
> catastrophes, such as their falling down or colliding with cars. This was repeated with signs
> of mounting anxiety. At this point I interpreted, with reference to details of her play, that
> some sexual activity seemed to have occurred between herself and her friend, and that this
> made her very frightened of being found out and therefore distrustful of other people. (1955,
> pp. 125–126)

Klein linked Inge's aversion to school to her fear that her teacher would discover her secret
activities with this little boy and punish her. Klein reported that when she put words to what
Inge had been trying to hide the effect was striking. The little girl's anxiety diminished and she
became freer in her play and speech. As she worked with Klein, Inge's school aversion diminished and her relationship with her mother improved. Most importantly, through this treatment
Klein launched play as an intentional technique.

Although Klein's play technique evolved over time, she adhered to the principle that the
analytic setting and technique should in important respects mirror those of the adult. The setting should be the consulting room, with each session lasting fifty minutes, five days a week.
The room should be adapted for the child's needs, with running water and small toys; while
some toys should be shared, each child should have an individual box containing toys exclusive to him or her, in order to represent continuity with the analyst and the uniqueness of each
relationship.

Play with children became the portal through which Klein was able to discern their drive to
relate to objects in the external world, their need to gain relief from anxieties through externalisation of inner conflict, and their urge to know and to seek new objects to symbolise their inner
world of unconscious phantasy.

Klein wrote:

> In their play, children represent symbolically phantasies, wishes and experiences. Here they
> are employing the same language, the same archaic, phylogenetically acquired mode of expression as we are familiar with from dreams. We can only fully understand it if we approach it by
> the method Freud has evolved for unraveling dreams. (1926, p. 134)

Towards the end of her life Klein made a clear statement about how her discovery of play
technique led to all her subsequent work. In her unfinished autobiography she wrote: "… my
work with both children and adults, and my contributions to psycho-analytic theory as a whole,
derive ultimately from the play technique evolved with young children" (1955, p. 122). However,
Abraham had grasped the magnitude of her discovery early on. In 1924, in response to hearing
Klein's paper on Erna, he declared: "The future of psychoanalysis lies in play technique."

Although Klein's clinical work with children is often criticised for being over-reaching and too penetrating, a close reading of her clinical accounts reveals her extraordinary capacity to sensitively observe and imagine the inner world of a child as well as the interplay of that internal world with the external world. In the following excerpt from her work with Rita we see Klein interpret her young patient's negative transference with striking results.

> Rita suffered from night terrors and animal phobias, was very ambivalent toward her mother, at the same time clinging to her to such an extent that she could hardly be left alone. She had a marked obsessional neurosis and was at times very depressed. Her play was inhibited and her inability to tolerate frustration made her upbringing increasingly difficult.... The first session seemed to confirm my misgivings. When Rita was left alone with me in her nursery, she at once showed signs of what I took to be negative transference: she was anxious and silent and very soon asked to go out into the garden. I agreed and went out with her-I might add under the watchful eyes of her mother and aunt who took this as a sign of failure. They were very surprised to see that Rita was quite friendly to me when we returned to the nursery some ten or fifteen minutes later. The explanation of this change was that while we were outside I was interpreting her negative transference. From the few things she said, and the fact that she was less frightened out in the open, I concluded she was particularly afraid of something I might do to her when she was alone with me in the room. I interpreted this and, referring to her night terrors I linked her suspicion of me as a hostile stranger with her fear that a bad woman would attack her when she was by herself at night. When, a few minutes after this interpretation I suggested we return to the nursery, she readily agreed. (1955, p. 5)

In this next excerpt from Rita's analysis we continue to see Klein's sensitivity to manifestations of an early harsh superego.

> ... before she was two years old, Rita became conspicuous for the remorse she used to feel at every small wrong doing, and for her over sensitiveness to reproach. For instance, she once burst into tears when her father laughingly uttered a threat against a bear in her picture-book. What determined her identification with the bear was her fear of her real father's displeasure. Her inhibition in play originated from her sense of guilt. When she was only two years and three months old she used to play with her doll—a game which gave her little pleasure—and would repeatedly declare that she was not the doll's mother. Analysis showed that she was not permitted to play at being a mother, because, among other things, the doll-child stood for her little brother whom she had wanted to steal from her mother during the latter's pregnancy. The prohibition, however, did not proceed from her real mother, but from an introjected one who treated her with far more severity and cruelty than the real one had ever done. (1932b, p. 6)

Through her work with her young patients, Klein was able to observe and imagine an inner world of such complexity that she was forced to develop many of the Freudian theories that were guiding her. Perhaps her most important departure from Freud was that she noticed that drives and desires are object-seeking, that "relationships to objects are as fundamental as the nature of instincts themselves" (O'Shaughnessy, Chapter Thirteen, this volume). This insight has had far-reaching implications for theory and clinical work.

Her extension of Freud's instinct theory led Klein to a new conception of mental suffering. In Klein's view, the child's suffering was no longer simply due to the inhibition of instincts, but was also due to anxiety and guilt about sadistic attacks on the mother's body, which could be crippling and had to be worked through in order for development to proceed.

Klein's work with children also led her to question the prevailing psychoanalytic view that the superego develops out of the resolution of the Oedipus complex around the age of five. She found in her young patients repeated and dramatic evidence of an early harsh and terrifying self-critical faculty that led her to posit a precursor to Freud's superego. She believed the infant was driven by oedipal jealousy, which has the child's exclusion from the primal scene at the centre. This jealousy leads the child to make phantasised violent attacks on his objects, which results in fear of retaliation. She concluded that the early harsh superego developed out of the introjection of the harsh maternal object retaliating for oedipal attacks. In addition, she observed that the earliest defences are projective rather than repressive, and that children, as well as adults, mediate between the internal and external worlds through splitting, projection, introjection, and symbol formation.

In her 1927 paper "Symposium on child analysis" Klein took up her differences with Anna Freud in a debate that was to stretch throughout their lifetimes and beyond. In this paper, Klein strongly defended her view that transference is as central to the work of child analysis as it is to adult analysis. Klein did not believe, as did Anna Freud, that a young child's relatively "weak" ego required the cultivation of a positive transference through education, reassurance, or instructions. Klein stressed the importance of interpretating the negative transference as a means towards a more trusting, warm relationship. She was convinced of the need to address the patient's "point of maximal anxiety", and she believed that a child could be helped by understanding himself and his unconscious mind.

Anna Freud believed that the superego of young children is strengthened through educational methods. Klein believed the severity of the superego could only be modified through the integration of loving and hating impulses. In her view, analysing the terrifying figures in the child's inner world relieved the child's anxieties and strengthened the ego. It is interesting to note, in this regard, that a rare written endorsement of Klein by Sigmund Freud was in a footnote in which he said he agreed with Klein that the superego does not reflect the real severity of the parents, but is distorted by the child's projections (1930a, p. 132).

Klein found that in the child, as in the adult, the transference was not a one-to-one transfer of attitudes towards real parents, but a projection on to the analyst of internal figures, internalised from external reality but coloured by the child's instincts and anxieties. She wrote: "consistent interpretations, gradual solving of resistances and persistent tracing of the transference to earlier situations—these constitute in children as in adults the correct analytic situation" (Klein, 1926, p. 137). Anna Freud, on the other hand, thought that a child's close attachment to her parents prevented the development of a "new edition", the transference (1927, p. 38).

Klein's theories were rooted in the idea that bodily sensations, the phantasies accompanying them, and phantasies about the mother's body are the foundations of all experience. She was, from the start and throughout her career, interested in the epistomophilic instinct—the drive to learn—and in the inhibitions against it. She came to the conclusion that the central problem inhibiting curiosity and learning is the child's relationship to the mother's body and, in particular, the fear of causing it damage. Klein thought that this fear became extended out into the world through the child's symbolic externalisation of the mother's body into his surroundings. For this reason, Klein thought it important not to shy away from speaking with her young patients directly about their bodily phantasies and experiences.

Many of Klein's interpretations, and those of her early followers, sound bold, even disconcerting, to present-day ears. Indeed, contemporary Kleinians have moved away from interpreting in these bodily terms, preferring, for example, to speak about what is being taken in or pushed out, and how this affects the interactions between the analyst and patient and the anxieties that the patient is trying to manage moment to moment. However, the visceral bodily experience—its immediacy and resonance—adds invaluable weight and depth to the analyst's understanding of the patient's ways of relating to the analyst and beyond.

Controversial discussions 1941–1945

Although tensions had been brewing between Melanie Klein and Anna Freud for many years, they came to a head in 1938 when the Freuds fled the Nazis and moved to London. In 1939, after Freud's death, tensions further increased over the question of who would take over as his successor. Klein and Anna Freud now found themselves members of the same psychoanalytic society, a situation so fraught that it threatened to split the society along lines of loyalty. Added to this a war was raging and many of the protagonists were refugees who had been driven from their homes. A series of scientific meetings, later called the Controversial Discussions, were held in order to debate the ideas, to determine who rightly could claim the mantle of heir to Freud's intellectual legacy, and whose ideas would have the greater influence in the training of analysts within the British Society. The result was a decision to split the British Society into three groups: Kleinian, Freudian, and Independent, a compromise that held for many years. Pearl King and Riccardo Steiner (1991) have comprehensively described these discussions and their implications in their book *The Freud-Klein Controversies 1941–45*.

While issues of power and control of the British Society were at stake, real theoretical differences were heatedly debated. Klein's differences with Anna Freud extended beyond work with children, and by the time of these meetings were focused primarily in the areas of early object relationships, the early Oedipus complex, and the status of unconscious phantasy.

Anna Freud and her followers roundly rejected Klein's theories of infant mental life. They deemed the ideas that the infant had an inner world that contained destructive, even violent phantasies, or was capable of guilt when he recognised that the mother he loved was also the target of these violent phantasies, to be far-fetched and unsupportable. While Klein held fast to a view that object-related phantasy was present from the start of life, Anna Freud believed that the early months were narcissistic in nature, and governed by the desire for instinctual gratification, with object relations developing only gradually. Although Klein was accused of emphasising the death instinct over the force of the life instinct, in fact she attributed as much importance to libidinal impulses as to destructive ones. Klein was also criticised for overrating the unconscious at the expense of attending to conscious experience.

The central paper representing Klein's views during the discussions was Susan Isaac's (1948) "The nature and function of phantasy", in which she made a cogent and compelling case for the claim that the child engages in mental activity long before he is able to express his thoughts in words. However, even among those who could agree to the idea of unconscious phantasies in infants, some continued to be troubled by what they felt was an emphasis on hatred, frustration, and aggression. Many analysts then, as today, find it too difficult to embrace the idea that infants are capable of such dark experience.

The discussions were contentious and hostile, with neither side giving nor gaining ground. Joan Riviere, in her introduction to *New Developments in Psychoanalysis*, a book containing the main Kleinian papers from the discussions, noted that both sides quoted Freud amply but that the Kleinians quoted from his work after 1920—structural theory, internal object, superego, conflicts between love and hate and between the life and death instincts, while Anna Freudians quoted mainly from before 1920.

Many of the issues debated in these discussions remain unsettled. Klein is still criticised for attributing to infants mental states that are too advanced to be credible, such as sadistic and persecutory phantasies in months-old infants, mourning in six-month-olds, and object-related unconscious phantasies from birth onwards. While of course it is not possible to know what goes on the minds of infants, modern infant research and contemporary neuroscience are finding conclusive evidence of complex and nuanced infant mental life. According to Peter Fonagy, Klein's "fictitious developmental ideas" might turn out to have more support in modern infant laboratory studies than her detractors might like to acknowledge (2008, p. 210). Most importantly, one need not subscribe to Klein's exact developmental timetable to find her ideas useful and clinically relevant.

Klein's main theories and their clinical application over time

Unconscious phantasy

As Segal wrote: "Where Freud discovered the child in the adult … Klein discovered the infant in the child, and therefore the depth of the unconscious in the adult" (Segal, N.D.). Klein's observations of infants and children, and her belief in the continuity of mental experience over the lifespan, led her to exptrapolate backwards and posit that unconscious phantasy organised all of mental life "almost from birth" (1936, p. 290). For Klein, unconscious phantasies are not simply one mental activity amongst others, such as dreaming, symbolising, and thinking; phantasies constitute *the* primary mental activity that accompanies all thinking and feeling.

Building on Freud's ideas about primal phantasies and unconscious phantasy as hallucinatory wish fulfillment, Klein concluded that unconscious phantasies are innate, derive from a child's own instinctual and bodily experiences, and are linked to objects from the start. As Isaacs wrote in a much-quoted sentence, for Klein, "[p]hantasy is the mental corollary, the psychic representative of instinct" (1948, p. 81).

According to Klein, the infant is preoccupied with his own bodily experiences, and also with phantasies of the mother's body, and its interior. She thought that primitive phantasies accompany bodily sensations and involve the belief that the sensations are intentionaly caused by objects existing within; good experiences are caused by benevolent objects and bad experiences by malevolent ones. Over time the experience of taking things in and putting them out, actually and in phantasy, leads to phantasies becoming elaborated. Phantasies operate bi-directionally, that is, they structure and colour the infant's perceptions of the external world, and they are in turn affected and built up by external experience. Klein believed, as did Freud, in innate universal phantasies, for example, about the primal scene, birth, and death. Following Abraham's extension of Freud's theory of psychosexual development, Klein pictured infantile phantasies as being influenced by the child's stage of development, with, for example, phantasies of biting and sucking being dominant in the oral stage. Klein wrote:

> The analysis of very young children has taught me that there is no instinctual urge, no anxiety situation, no mental process which does not involve objects, external or internal; in other words, object-relations are at the *centre* of emotional life. Furthermore, love and hatred, phantasies, anxieties, and defences are also operative from the beginning and are indivisibly linked with object-relations. This insight showed me many phenomena in a new light. (Klein, 1952a, p. 53)

As Klein implies in this quote, her observation about the central role of object-related phantasy in mental life opened the door to many of her key ideas. It allowed her to be able to perceive and imagine a complex inner world of anxieties, defences, and object relations, from the earliest and most primitive to the more mature.

A view of unconscious phantasy that includes all of mental activity remains controversial. As was argued against Isaac's classic paper during the Controversial Discussions, some feel that definition is so broad that it lacks conceptual clarity and utility. In addition, many find it difficult to believe that infants are capable of the kind of complex mental activity Klein attributes to them. Isaacs attempted to address this criticism noting the inherent difficulty in using words to describe nonverbal experiences, which can make it seem as if we are attributing thoughts to infants they could not possibly have. To cite one example of Klein's response to this criticism, she wrote: "nor do I believe that the baby would feel that is is full of good milk. It has not any conception of what milk is. It would feel though that something good, satisfactory, something which is equated with the good object, has gone into him" (quoted in Grosskurth, 1986, p. 324).

Unconscious phantasies always involve someone, or a part of someone, doing something to someone else. This one idea, that phantasies of internal objects in interaction underpin all experience, has profound implications for how one listens to and understands patients in the clinical situation.

Life and death instincts

Impressed by man's capacity for destruction, including self-destruction, Freud came to the conclusion that within all of us there is an instinct of destruction—the death instinct. In his 1920 paper "*Beyond the Pleasure Principle*" (1920g) Freud revised his conflict theory so that the central human conflict now became one between the life and death instincts. We have already noted how, throughout her work with children, Klein was struck by the violence of their phantasies, the harsh punishments they meted out and feared receiving, and the great anxiety that this caused them. These observations, together with Abraham's ideas about infantile sadism, had led Klein to argue for the presence of an early harsh superego; she now linked this to Freud's idea of the death instinct, and in 1932 she adopted his theory of the opposition between the life and death intincts.

> Side by side with the polarity of the life-instinct and the death instinct, we may I think, place their interaction as a fundamental factor in the dynamic processes of the mind…. in the early stages of development, the life-instinct has to exert its power to the utmost in order to maintain itself against the death-instinct. (Klein, 1932c, p. 150)

There is no clear "Kleinian" definition of the death instinct and it is not always obvious what exactly Klein intended to convey when she used this term. At times, it seems that she was writing about self-destructive tendencies; at other times she wrote about the anxiety these stirred up—annihilation anxiety. Sometimes she seemed to be referring more generally to destructive tendencies. Freud had written about the death instinct being deflected outwards in the form of aggression and Klein, extending Freud's idea, theorised that at the start of life the death instinct, along with the part of the ego that contains it, is projected out into the mother's breast. This action involves the life instinct—in that it is self-preservative—and involves violent impulses and phantasies of attacking the object. The death instinct that remains within might appear in the form of withdrawal from life or in a state of fragmentation both of which, while preventing and interfering with ego development, may be life-preserving for a fragile ego in extreme circumstances.

While mostly thought of as active, the death instinct can be thought of as passive. In a note (1946, p. 5) Klein referred to Ferenczi's suggestion that every living organism reacts to unpleasant stimuli by fragmentation (death instinct) and that living organisms may fall to pieces in unfavourable conditions. Meira Likierman (2001) outlined some of the continuing debate as to whether fragmented states are due to active splitting processes or passive falling apart in the absence of a holding object.

One way of thinking of these instincts is that the life instinct makes links, reaches out to life, and pushes towards integration, whereas the death instinct rejects and turns away from life and drives towards disintegration. Segal described this beautifully:

> Birth confronts us with the experience of needs. In relation to that experience there can be two reactions, and both, I think, are invariably present in all of us, though in varying proportions. One, to seek satisfaction for the needs: that is life-promoting and leads to object seeking, love and eventually object concern. The other is the drive to annihilate: the need to annihilate the perceiving experiencing self, as well as anything that is perceived. (Segal, 1997, p. 24)

Wilfred Bion, a patient and colleague of Klein, went so far as to say that some individuals have a hatred of life and engage in what he called "attacks on linking" (1959):

> … attacks are directed against the apparatus of perception from the beginning of life. This part of his personality is cut up, spit into minute fragments, and then, using projective identification expelled from the personality. Having thus rid himself of the apparatus of conscious awareness

of internal and external reality, the patient achieves a state which is felt to be neither alive nor dead. (Bion, 1956, p. 345)

Bion made the point that the resulting state is "neither alive nor dead". The death instinct does not just pursue annhiliation; it gains gratification from sucking the life out of developmental possibilities. Michael Feldman has described many of the ways in which this is achieved, such as attacks on meaning, clarity, and creative interchange. His view is that the true aim of the death instinct is not the destruction of the self or object, but rather to maintain them in a near-death state (Feldman, 2000).

It is possible to see in these ideas how it was that Klein thought of envy, the drive to attack objects of desire, as a manifestation of the death instinct (1957). She believed that objects we desire but do not posses provoke a painful kind of desire—envy. The pain of envy can promote a constructive wish to develop and to become like the loved object or, on the other hand, if envy cannot be borne, it may trigger an attempt to steal what is good or to attack and destroy it. In the extreme, envy causes us to experience the good object as bad and leads to confusion and an inability to discriminate good from bad; this reduces the possibility of our taking in and being sustained by good experiences. All experiences then become increasingly persecuting and fragmentation may be employed as a defence.

Klein drew attention to the destructive effects of envy in work with patients:

> The envious patient grudges the analyst the success of his work; and if he feels that the analyst and the help he is giving have become spoilt and devalued by his envious criticism, he cannot introject him sufficiently as a good object. (Klein, 1957, p. 184)

Klein's ideas on envy provoked an outcry against the suggestion that attacks on goodness are inherent in human nature. Klein's successors have built on her ideas about envy and there is agreement that the degree of a patient's envy is of considerable significance, particularly in understanding resistances and the negative therapeutic reaction.

As we have already stated, Klein thought that the life instinct drives the ego to separate the life and death instincts in order to protect the developing ego from overwhelming anxiety, and her view, as quoted above, was that throughout life "the life-instinct has to exert its power to the utmost in order to maintain itself against the death-instinct". For Klein, the life instinct, the projection of loving feelings into the breast and the subsequent pleasurable introjection of a loving object into the self, is crucial for survival, for counteracting anxiety and destructive tendencies, and for providing a central core around which the ego can cohere, a core which then becomes the basis of emotional well-being and development. Conversely, the introjection of the bad hated object, unless mitigated by love, is the basis for emotional disturbance and developmental difficulty.

The issue of whether destructive tendencies, as well as loving ones, are innate or acquired remains controversial.

> I think it is impossible to tell what is innate, what has been acquired through interaction with others, and what is the continuing product of that interaction. What one *can* tell is how deep rooted the patient's negative tendencies are in the present analytic situation. (Spillius, 2007, p. 51)

Environmental factors

Klein's emphasis on the internal world gave rise to the critique that she did not give significance to the role of the child's environment, but this is not true. Although Klein believed in the importance of innate tendencies she placed the infant's relationship to his primary object at the centre of his emotional and cognitive development. Klein's infant is in constant interplay, via projection and introjection, with his mother or caretaker. Klein thought that the introjection of the good object provides the foundation for development, and she held the view that except in cases where there is a greater proportion of death instinct over life instinct, innate destructive forces are mitigated by good experiences and are increased by bad experiences such as neglect and abuse.

> Innate aggressiveness is bound to be increased by unfavourable external circumstances and, conversely, is mitigated by the love and understanding that the young child receives; and these factors continue to operate throughout development. But ... the importance of internal factors is still underrated. Destructive impulses, varying from individual to individual, are an integral part of mental life, even in favourable circumstances, and therefore we have to consider the development of the child and the attitudes of the adults as resulting from the interaction between internal and external influences. (Klein, 1959, p. 249)

As we will describe in later sections, Bion went on to bring detail to the importance of a containing environment in the form of a mother/caretaker/analyst able to take in and transform raw emotion.

The paranoid-schizoid and depressive positions

Perhaps the most outstanding of Klein's achievements is her innovative overarching idea of the two "positions": the "paranoid-schizoid" and the "depressive", each of which describes a constellation of anxieties, the defences against them and the resulting state of the ego and its object relationships—internal and external. These are two distinctive states of mind and each contains its own particular ways of perceiving, experiencing, and being. Klein thought in terms of a developmental progression from one position to the other, but one that involved a certain amount of to-and-fro in the first few years of life, with regression back to the paranoid-schizoid position when under stress.

The idea of a grouping of defences, and of fluidity and movement between one grouping and another, brought an entirely fresh way of thinking about emotional and cognitive development. It set going a great deal of creative interest in the particular defences of each state of mind and provoked exploration of the way in which the defences are organised together, particular focus being given to the point of transition between the two positions.

The paranoid-schizoid position

Klein set out her theory of the paranoid-schizoid position in her 1946 paper, "Notes on some schizoid mechanisms". Here she brought her ideas together with those of Fairbairn (1944) on the splitting of the ego, and set out her vision of the first three months of life. The paranoid-schizoid position describes Klein's understanding of the mental state of the infant. In her view, infants are full of extreme anxieties due to the trauma of birth, the fear of annihilation from the death instinct within, and experiences of hunger and frustration. She thought that the infantile ego needs to protect itself against all of these potentially overwhelming anxieties and, in order to do so, mobilises the omnipotent defences of splitting, fragmentation, projection, denial, and idealisation.

Klein, like Donald Winnicott (1945), pictured the newborn infant as being in a state of un-integration and living in what she called a world of "part objects", in which, for example, the mother is experienced in terms of anatomical parts such as hands or breast. At the same time, these parts are experienced by the infant as concretely providing good or bad experiences and, in phantasy, as malevolent or benevolent: the present feeding good breast relieves hunger and provides warmth and comfort whereas the absent bad breast is felt to be an attacking internal force.

The task of the infantile ego in the paranoid-schizoid position is its own survival and the creation of a sense of safety and order. To achieve this, good experiences are separated and kept safe from bad ones. Klein theorised that the good and bad aspects of the self are, in phantasy, split and projected out into the object (the mother or early caretaker, initially the breast) who, as the recipient of these projections, is then experienced as *being* either good and loving or bad and hating, and as equivalent to the good or bad self. Klein referred to this as "projective identification".

The bad self relates to the bad object or part object (bad breast) and the good self to the good object or part object (good breast). The good object and the good self are at first idealised and, at the same time, the badness of the bad self and object is exaggerated. The good and bad objects are introjected back into the self and there is a wide split between the two. Klein thought that extreme unmanageable anxiety could cause fragmentation and interfere with the achievement of a successful separation of good from bad.

These defensive activities occur in phantasy, but also importantly structure the mind and have real effects. Klein made the point that it is not only the experience that is split-off, but also the experiencing part of the ego, with the result that splitting off and projecting out leave the ego depleted. Conversely, introjecting, or taking in, leads to a sense of containing "internal objects" and, over time, the experience of an increasingly complex internal world. Individuals who omnipotently introject their object's desirable qualities will have a delusional sense of being in possession of those qualities.

This active binary splitting into good and bad is different from the early immature unintegrated state. Klein considered that unintegration lessens over time with maturity, but that the binary split lessens only once the infantile ego has gained sufficient strength from repeated good experiences to bear the experience of knowing about his own bad aspects and those of his object. An infant or individual may achieve the first stage of separating good from bad, but without the introjection of a stable, strong, good object, integration does not occur and he will remain with aspects of his personality cut off from each other, with rigid defences in place, emotionally unstable, and liable to switch between different states of mind—for example, between ideal states and states of persecution. It is important to note here that splitting is not just binary, between good and bad. The ego can be divided along other lines so that, for example, thoughts may be separated from feelings, or bodily activity may be separated from both. Klein described a patient who was crying, but who had no idea why and who did not feel sadness (1946). Splitting also occurs horizontally. Klein had the idea of different levels of consciousness, with different more or less extreme versions of the same object existing at levels that are more or less close to consciousness, with the more integrated objects existing on a plane close to consciousness.

Klein did not explore any further the early unintegrated state that she thought preceded the paranoid-schizoid position. A number of writers, in particular Esther Bick (1968) placed great emphasis on the infantile anxieties of falling apart. A number of psychotherapists and psychoanalysts working with autistic children have described disintegration and dissociation as a response to unmanageable stimuli in an as yet unintegrated child (Alvarez, 2006; Meltzer et al., 1975).

The depressive position

Although the depressive position develomentally follows the paranoid-schizoid position, Klein worked out her ideas about the depressive position first. In her theory, an infant born with a relatively balanced endowment of the life and death instincts and who receives reasonably good responsive care will achieve a separation between good and bad experience and will internalise a good object that will provide a central core of sufficient strength to allow him to move on to the task of integration—the depressive position.

The anxieties and difficulties of integration are considerable; Klein outlined these in the two key papers in which she introduced the depressive position, "A contribution to the psychogenesis of manic-depressive states" (1935) and "Mourning and its relation to manic-depressive states" (1940). Managing the pain of guilt and the losses that arise at this time is enormously important for all future emotional and cognitive development.

Klein thought that the depressive position occurs at about three months of age, at which time the different aspects of self and other are brought together into whole, and therefore more realistic objects. The infant has to gradually acknowledge the bad aspects of his good self and those of his good mother, including, for example, the recognition of the good mother's absences and failures of care. The infant must also recognise his hatred and attacks on his good mother both in reality and in phantasy and the damaging effects of these.

Mourning is central to the depressive position. As the infant faces the reality that the loved and hated mother is one and the same, he has to give up and mourn the sense of being an ideal powerful self in an ideal relationship in which he is the possesor of all that he needs and wants. This is a task that all of us have to achieve not only in infancy, but also throughout our lives. Repeatedly, we have to come to terms with being neither entirely good nor all-powerful. This involves having to bear the anxiety and uncertainty of being alone, of having limited powers, and of experiencing feelings of loss, helplessness, anxiety, jealousy, rage, despair, and guilt. We may long for the earlier, safe, paranoid-schizoid state and will pine for the reassuring presence of a constantly loving object and the comforting sense of our own goodness and power. There is, however, some relief in not being solely responsible for everything that goes wrong.

Klein held that an individual's ability to manage the pain of bereavement later in life involved re-experiencing the infantile depressive position and was dependent on having developed the capacity to mourn when facing depressive anxieties at this early stage.

The capacity to mourn is inextricably linked to the ability to separate oneself from one's object and, as it is the absent object that requires a symbol, mourning is therefore a prerequisite for the development of symbol formation. For example, the early infant will experience a good feed as having a good mother/breast inside. Hunger and the absence of the mother is experienced as a bad object inside. Over time, with sufficient good experience, the frustration of separation is gradually tolerated, omnipotence is given up, projections are taken back into the self, and an increasingly realistic mental representation of the self and the other gradually builds up in the infant's mind. In her paper "Notes on symbol formation", Segal (1957) coined the term "symbolic equation" to describe particular concrete ways of relating that are characteristic of individuals who have failed to achieve this separation and in whom the ego and object remain bound together.

Crucial to mourning and to the work of the depressive position is the growth of a capacity to manage guilt. To recognise that hatred and rage have actually been directed towards a *loved* figure who has provided care, arouses pain, anxiety, concern, and regret about the damage that has been caused. All being well, the awareness of goodness received will inspire gratitude and this, in combination with "depressive guilt", will propel the individual towards trying to repair the damage done. Klein listed some of the difficulties encountered when trying to put things right:

> … there is anxiety how to put the bits together in the right way and at the right time; how to pick out the good bits and do away with the bad ones; how to bring the object to life when it has been put together; and there is the anxiety of being interfered with in this task by bad objects and by one's own hatred, etc. (Klein, 1935, p. 269)

Depressive feelings may threaten to overwhelm the developing individual who may then retreat into a paranoid-schizoid mental state in which he believes himself to be solely good and loving. For example, if the damage is felt to be too great and the task of repair impossible, guilt will be persecutory and the individual may fall back on the defences of splitting and denial in which responsibility and damage are denied. Sometimes the individual may acknowledge the damage, but lacks the capacity to put things right. Like a small child, he may be driven to resort to manic solutions, such as a belief that he is all-powerful and able to repair things by magic. In these situations the need for repair is not denied, but there is a failure to acknowledge either the extent of the damage or the inadequacy of the resources available for repair. Another defence is to try to undo what has been done or to make obsessional attempts to put things right.

Being helpless in the face of suffering and pain is hard to bear and harder still if one feels responsible for causing the suffering. Children with ill parents, for example, may be convinced that it is they who have caused the damage and may be left with little or no sense of having any goodness inside.

Love plays a central and essential part in the negotiation of the depressive position.

> All the enjoyments which the baby lives through in relation to his mother are so many proofs to him that the loved object *inside as well as outside* is not injured, is not turned into a vengeful

person. The increasing of love and trust, and the diminishing of fears through happy experiences, help the baby step by step to overcome his depression and feeling of loss (mourning). They enable him to test his inner reality by means of outer reality …

Unpleasant experiences and the lack of enjoyable ones … increase ambivalence, diminish trust and hope and confirm anxieties about inner annihilation and external persecution. (Klein, 1940, pp. 346–347, italics in original)

Omnipotence decreases as the infant gradually gains a greater confidence both in his objects and in his reparative powers. He feels that all steps in development, all new achievements are giving pleasure to the people around him and that in this way he expresses his love, counterbalances or undoes the harm done by his aggressive impulses, and makes reparation to his injured loved objects. (Klein, 1952b, p. 75)

Oedipus complex and the depressive position

As we described earlier, Klein did not see the superego as the "heir to the Oedipus complex", but rather, in a clear deviation from Freud's theory, she thought of it as an internal force to be reckoned with right from the start of life.

Klein held that the onset of the depressive position occurs at the same time as that of the Oedipus complex (1940), and Ronald Britton (1985, 1989) subsequently set out the similarities and interconnections between the two. He described how the oedipal infant who recognises the parental relationship and who has to overcome his jealousy and give up his sole possession of his mother, is at the same time facing the depressive task of recognising that his own loved good mother is the bad absent one, absent in a relationship with someone else. The infant/patient has to bear the knowledge that his mother/analyst exists as a separate person with relationships from which he is excluded. Britton described patients who retreat back from the knowledge of their exclusion into what he called an "Oedipal illusion" in which they believe themselves to be their analyst's centrally significant other.

Britton (1989) made the point that the link between the parents provides the infant with a container with its own separate point of view from which he can be seen, known, and thought about. In turn, this viewpoint can be internalised to provide a "third position" from which the developing individual can examine himself and his own beliefs, perceive things more as they are, and be able to make realistic judgments. However, some patients can feel provoked by being thought about and experience it as being excluded from a sexual relationship; Britton gives a vivid example of a patient telling him to "stop that fucking thinking" (1989, p. 88).

The interaction between the paranoid-schizoid and depressive positions

Klein's theory posits a to-and-fro between the paranoid-schizoid and depressive positions in which there is a repeated move towards reality followed by a falling back to escape depressive pain. Klein's successors have given a great deal of attention to the movement between the two positions and have come to see the positions less in terms of a linear developmental process and more in terms of two different states of mind in continuous fluctuation, albeit with individuals tending to operate predominantly more in one state of mind than the other.

Bion (1963), using the activities of disintegration and integration as representative of the two positions, came up with the symbol Ps<->D to describe the fluctuations as going either way. Important to his view is that movements in either direction have the possibility of being either positive or negative. His reasoning was that in order to attain new understanding we need first to be able to bear states of disturbance and confusion, including a sensation of disintegration. Following up this idea, Britton (1998) made the point that a non-fluctuating state of D, in which there is no disturbance, is in itself a pathological state of mind; in his words, "yesterday's depressive position becomes tomorrow's defensive organization" (1998, p. 73).

The superego

Klein's theory of the superego changed over time but overall her view was that the early harsh superego is largely composed of the primary introjected bad object, an object that contains the infant's unmodified projected death instinct, and is powerfully bad. The early ideal object is equally harsh in demanding perfection and also plays a part in the superego. Klein's interest was in modifying the harsh superego and some of her papers reveal her uncertainty about whether or not this is possible. In 1958 she resolved the question by making an addition to her theory as follows: she located parts of the earliest extreme good and bad objects in what she refered to as the "deep unconscious", where they remain out of contact with other internal objects or with the processes of introjection and projection; their power and extreme nature is therefore unmodified, with the danger that they may erupt when the individual is under great stress (1958).

In this way of thinking, the superego itself—Edna O'Shaughnessy (1999) would call this a normal superego—also contains the extreme objects. However, it is more modifiable because it exists less deeply and its objects interact via projection and introjection with those in the ego and with objects in the external world. The normal superego, through contact with reality, is realistic in its demands and in the judgements it makes.

There is some debate about whether all internal objects may function as the superego (Riesenberg-Malcolm, 1999) and about the relative functions of the ego and superego. Britton, for example, stated that the ego makes judgements based on experience whereas the superego makes moral judgements based on authority. He argued that problems arise when the superego takes over the functions of the ego and concluded: "we must not simply be judged by our conscience; we must submit our conscience to judgement" (2003, p. 101).

Although for Klein the extreme objects in the deep unconscious were no longer named as superego, she was referring to the same entrenched anti-developmental forces that other analysts from Freud onwards had encountered in their patients. Many of Klein's followers referred to these as a kind of malign superego: "ego splitting superego" (Rosenfeld, 1952), "envious superego" (Klein, 1957), "ego-destructive superego" (Bion, 1959), "abnormal superego" (O'Shaughnessy, 1999). Freud himself referred to the superego as "a kind of gathering place for the death instincts" (1923b, p. 54).

O'Shaughnessy's paper, "Relating to the superego", provides an excellent overview with clinical material illustrating the two kinds of superego. She makes the clear distinction between an abnormal destructive superego and a more helpful normal superego, one which names a crime and is realistic in not demanding perfect behaviour or perfect reparation.

Pathological organisatons of the personality

In 1936 Joan Riviere wrote about patients with a "highly organized system of defence" and following her paper a considerable body of work has grown up on this topic. Herbert Rosenfeld (1964, 1971) and Donald Meltzer (1968) described destructive narcissistic organisations, Segal (1972) and O'Shaughnessy (1981) wrote of defensive organisations, Betty Joseph wrote of patients who are "difficult to reach" (1975), and John Steiner (1982) coined the generally accepted term, "pathological organisation",

Pathological organisations provide the patient with a stable structure that protects him from the anxieties of both positions. For example, a patient emerging from the paranoid-schizoid position and encountering "depressive" feelings of jealousy, may retreat into a pathological organisation, a state of mind, a set of beliefs about himself and a way of experiencing himself in the world, that relieves him of these feelings and provides a sense of security. Pathological organisations may provide more fragmented patients with a means of holding themselves together, a function that Segal made explicit in the title of her 1972 paper, "A delusional system as a defence against the re-emergence of a catastrophic situation". O'Shaughnessy (1981) noted that patients who are defending themselves against fragmentation and confusion may come into analysis when their defensive system is breaking down. Steiner (1987) outlined in detail the interplay between pathological organisations and the two positions.

Herbert Rosenfeld (1971) differentiated destructive narcissism from libidinal narcissism; he thought of the latter as defending both the patient and the analyst. However, currently these organised systems tend to be understood as both defensive and destructive and liable to alternate between the two.

Rosenfeld (1964, 1971) laid out his understanding of borderline and narcissistic personalities in the following way. He saw the patient as being identified with a powerfully good or bad object that dominates his personality and retains control by means of seduction, threats, or cunning, which prevents any contact between the more vulnerable infantile part of the patient and the analyst. The libidinal, or dependent, part of the patient is split-off and kept away from contact with any nurturing figure, leaving the patient trapped in an undeveloped state dominated by a powerful deadly force. This is a variant of the death instinct, which, as we have mentioned, is often thought of as a malign superego.

Rosenfeld described a perverse relationship between parts of the patient, which he thought could be exacerbated by the dependent part colluding in its own imprisonment. A dream from one of Rosenfeld's patients shows how the vulnerable, dependent part of the patient is kept in a dying position.

> A small boy ... was in a comatose condition, dying from some kind of poisoning. He was ...
> in the ... sun which was beginning to shine on him. The patient was standing near to the boy
> in the shade but did nothing to move or protect him. He only felt critical and superior to the

doctor treating the child, since it was he who should have seen the child was moved into the shade. (Rosenfeld, 1971, p. 174)

In this example, Rosenfeld brought his focus to bear on the deadly activity of the patient whilst at the same time recognising the patient's vulnerable undeveloped self. Rosenfeld also pointed out that while deadliness could be noisy, it might be silent, and he warned that some patients could be seduced or lulled into a sleepy idealised state by a split-off psychotic part of themselves.

The many papers on pathological organisations contain very useful, vivid clinical material describing the difficulties encountered by the analyst and illustrate how he can become drawn into the patient's defensive system. A number of writers explore the perverse nature of the patient's relationship both with the analyst and also internally between the parts of himself, noting the excitement and gratification felt by the patient in having the power to destroy his own good efforts and those of his analyst. This excitement in being destructive strengthens the defensive system and makes it hard to penetrate. We will go on to say something more about these ideas in the later section on technique.

Psychic retreats

Steiner (1993) drew attention to a particular type of phantasy content in the material of his patients, often conscious and sometimes represented in dreams, of an idealised, safe, conflict-free *place* into which they retreated in phantasy to avoid difficulties in the external and internal world. Steiner referred to this as a "psychic retreat". Pathological organisations can be thought of as providing a psychic retreat. For example, an Oedipal illusion, itself a version of a pathological organisation, provides a conflict-free zone, an emotional state of mind or a place in a relationship that is free from disturbing feelings such as those of jealousy or envy.

Steiner made clear links between his idea and Henri Rey's (1979) claustro-agoraphobic dilemma: "While trapped in a psychic retreat [the patients] feel claustrophobic, but as soon as they manage to escape they once again panic and return to their previous position" (Steiner, 1993, p. 53). In a later body of work Steiner (2011) went on to write about the difficulties that are experienced by patients when emerging from a psychic retreat, in particular the feeling of shame.

Steiner distinguished the anxieties that must be confronted when emerging from a psychic retreat into those to do with *seeing* and those to do with *being seen*. The anxieties to do with seeing the object more realistically and thus having to contend with painful elements that had previously been hidden have been described and theorised extensively—experiences of envy, jealousy, frustration, rage, guilt, and remorse. Less explored are the experiences a patient confronts when he is exposed to being seen, which can lead to a collapse of narcissistic self-admiration and narcissistic pride and evoke feelings of embarrassment, shame, and humiliation that must be dealt with. In this configuration the analyst will be felt to be a hostile, attacking figure looking down on the patient so that the patient feels inferior. Steiner made the important point that the patient may experience basic aspects of the treatment frame, such as the setting of fees, paying for missed appointments, the use of the couch, and determining holiday dates, as the analyst unfairly exercising power and placing the patient in a position in which he feels inferior and looked down upon.

Projective and introjective identification

In 1952 Klein revised her 1946 paper "Notes on some schizoid mechanisms" and introduced the term "projective identification" to describe the object relations that result from splitting and projection. These activities occur in phantasy but they are also accompanied by behaviours that can effect the recipient. Klein considered that projection and introjection are as basic to us as breathing. Both good and bad experiences and feelings are in a continuous process of being projected out into others and re-introjected back into the self. The taking in of an object and identification with it are known as introjective identification. The result of these activities is that we have within us a complex internal phantasy world of objects that contain a mix of real and imagined aspects of ourselves and others. Central to this way of thinking about emotional development, is that the fate of the ego is bound up with the fate of the object. Furthermore, even though splitting and projection occur in phantasy, these activities have real effects so that, for example, splitting off and projecting out of aggression will cause a weakening of the ego.

An enormous body of literature has grown out of the clinical investigation of projective identification and it has been written about more than any other of Klein's concepts, adding considerably to our understanding of transference and countertransference, and inevitably affecting technique. The term has been expanded and extended in different ways in different schools of thought and in different parts of the world so that it now covers a wide variety of activity. Projective identification should, therefore, be thought of as an umbrella term under which are described a wide range of phenomena that occur in the interchange between patient and analyst and in all relationships.

Projective identification

The concept of projective identification extends Freud's ideas of "deflection" and "projection" to include the projection of part of the ego along with the characteristic or emotion that is being projected. As we have already described, Klein thought that in order to survive, the infant needs to separate and project out the death instinct in the form of a phantasised attack on the mother.

> The vital need to deal with anxiety forces the early ego to develop fundamental mechanisms and defences. The destructive impulse is partly projected outwards (deflection of the death instinct) and, I think, attaches itself to the first external object, the mother's breast. (Klein, 1946, p. 4)
>
> In so far as the mother comes to contain the bad parts of the self she is not felt to be a separate individual but is felt to be *the* bad self. Much of the hatred against parts of the self is now directed towards the mother. This leads to a particular form of identification which establishes the prototype of an aggressive object-relation. I suggest for these processes the term "projective identification". (Klein, 1946, p. 8)

From the much-quoted words above it could appear that projective identification refers only to activities that have to do with an aggressive getting rid of unwanted feelings and aspects of the self, a process that might be better described as "disidentification" (Sodré, 2004). However, as Klein made clear in her paper, the separated good parts of the self are also projected.

> It is, however, not only the bad parts of the self which are expelled and projected but also good parts of the self.... The identification based on this type of projection again vitally influences object-relations. The projection of good feelings and good parts of the self into the mother is essential for the infant's ability to develop good object-relations and to integrate his ego. (Klein, 1946, p. 9)

The activity of projective identification can be thought of as "attributive", in which aspects of the self are attributed to the other, or as "acquisitive", in which the subject gets in to the object and takes over desired qualities (Britton, 1998). Rosenfeld (1971) explored the many aims of projective identification, such as to prevent separation, to inhabit the object, to control the object, to destroy the object, or to place aspects of the self into the object, either to get rid of them or for safe keeping.

Introjective identification

In attributive projective identification, the other is identified as being the self or having aspects of the self; in introjective identification the self is identified as being the other or having aspects of the other. Klein's thoughts about introjection followed those of Ferenczi (1909), Abraham (1924), and Freud, who in 1923 had described the character of the ego as being the precipitate of abandoned object cathexes. For Klein, the infant's introjection of a good object, one that is at first ideal, provides the central core around which his ego coheres. However, just as projection is not solely a destructive activity, introjection is not solely a benign activity, as was very clear to Freud, who famously wrote about the adverse effects of identification with the introjected reproached lost object in his 1917 paper "Mourning and melancholia" (1917e).

Both good and bad objects are introjected. The introjected bad object will, as we have outlined earlier, become the cause of emotional difficulties unless modified by being brought into contact with the introjected good object. Omnipotent narcissistic identification with a powerful object, bad or good, is destructive of development and may, as we have already mentioned, be the pillar of a pathological organisation and a kind of malign superego. Rosenfeld (1971), who had a particular interest in the destructive effects of omnipotent identification, thought that identification occured by projection and by introjection at the same time.

A critical feature in distinguishing pathological identification from normal developmental identification is whether or not the quality of the identification is omnipotent, a point expanded by Ignês Sodrê (2004), who emphasised the significance of whether the identification is concrete or symbolic. In omnipotent introjective identification, we may simply believe ourselves to be the admired person or to possess her desired qualities, whereas in "normal" identification we strive to develop capacities similar to the person whom we admire.

Normal projective identification

Klein thought of projective identification as a fundamental process, but it was Bion who described in greater detail what he thought is transmitted between the patient and the analyst and differentiated between what he called "normal projective identification" and "pathological projective identification". Extrapolating from his work with disturbed patients, Bion built up a theory of development in which the infant is driven to externalise and communicate his raw unmanageable sensations (beta elements) and does so by projection into the mother.

If all goes well, the infant arouses feelings in the mother, which she is able to take in and contain while retaining a balanced state of mind. She then returns them to the infant, modified into a manageable form that conveys a sense that the feelings are understandable and not overwhelmingly destructive of her, the infant, or of their good relationship. The infant introjects the modified feelings along with a sense of a functioning container. Bion called these modified feelings "alpha elements" and considered them to provide the building blocks for thinking and dreaming, in contrast to the unmodified raw sensations, or "beta elements", which are concretely experienced and fit only for evacuation. Bion's theory connects physical experiences, emotions, and thought and adds to the understanding of somatic symptoms and the pressure for action rather than thought.

Pathological projective identification

Drawing on his clinical experience, Bion reasoned that an infant who experiences his mother as refusing to take in his feelings could be driven to project with greater and increasing force. He thought of this as "evacuative" projective identification and came to the conclusion that it can lead the infant to introject a "projection—rejecting object" (1959)—an internal object that is experienced by the infant as attacking him from the inside and stripping him of all sense of meaning. Bion thought that even in cases where the mother provides containment, an excess of envy in the infant can lead him to attack her goodness and thus interfere with his being able to experience the presence of a good object.

Aside from lacking the experience of being contained, some infants may be subject to neglect and abuse. Rosenfeld, particularly towards the end of his life, thought that early traumatic experiences played a large part in his patients' pathology (1987). More recently, Gianna Williams (1997) has written about child patients who had been projected into and used as containers for their caretakers' disturbance. These children as a result had developed what she referred to as "no entry" defences such as, for example, anorexia.

Enactment in the transference/countertransference

Being the recipient of a projective identification may affect how the analyst *feels*, but it can also affect how she *behaves*. That is, the analyst may be pulled or nudged into ways of relating that conform to aspects of the patient's phantasies. This pull to enactment is the subject of many clinical papers; Leon Grinberg (1962) wrote about the analyst being "led" to play a role and Joseph Sandler, a contemporary Freudian, came up with the terms "identity of perception", "actualization" and "role responsiveness" to describe the patient's influence on the analyst's behavior (Sandler, 1976a, 1976b). And, as we will see in the section on technique, Joseph and her followers have explored in great detail particular aspects of this draw towards enactment.

Klein's view of projective identification in countertransference

Klein did not approve of extending the idea of projective identification into the area of the analyst's feelings. In fact, when a supervisee once said to her that her patient had projected her confusion into her, Klein is famously reported to have replied "No dear, you *are* confused" (Segal, 1982). Klein was unhappy about Paula Heimann's (1950) extension of the use of the term "countertransference" to include the use of the analyst's feelings as a means of understanding the patient. Both Klein and Bion continued to follow Freud in using the term "countertransference" to describe the analyst's unconscious pathological feelings towards the patient.

Projective identification in different schools of thought

Although Kleinian analysts in the United Kingdom tend to use the terms "projection" and "projective identification" synonymously, this is not universally the case and across the world definitions differ. Analysts from different schools of thought have explored and written extensively about this subject, particularly in relation to the countertransference, and have made distinctions between one kind of activity and another. For example, Heinrich Racker, who wrote many important papers (1953, 1957, 1958, 1968), made the distiction between concordant countertransference, in which the analyst identifies with the patient, and complementary countertransference, in which the analyst identifies with the patient's internal objects (1968). Grinberg (1979) came up with the term "counteridentification" to describe occasions when the analyst is led to play a part , explaining it as a reaction that would be provoked in any analyst to a particularly intense projective identification from the patient. Madeleine and Willy Barangers' ideas of a "bi-personal field" and "the bastion"—constructed from the projective and introjective activity of both patient and analyst and in which both may become caught up—have influenced clinical thinking in many parts of the analytic world. A more detailed overview of the different ways in which the term has been defined and used can be found in Spillius and O'Shaughnessy's *Projective Identification: The Fate of a Concept* (2012).

Aims, technique, and the analytic attitude

While Kleinian technique has evolved over the years, it still follows a classical Freudian model with close attention to the framework, five-times-weekly meetings, the use of the couch, free association, and interpretation of unconscious meanings with a focus on their manifestation in the transference. In this tradition, the analyst maintains an analytic stance throughout the treatment and across a wide range of patients, even the most regressed or ill. The analyst's role is not to provide reassurance or corrective emotional experiences—in the sense of trying to become the good object or to replace the patient's good objects. The analyst's aim, as described by Eric Brenman (2006), is to help the patient recover his own lost good object, and this is achieved by helping the patient to recognise and work through the reality that the analyst is neither an ideal nor a wholly bad object. Non-interpretive activities are not encouraged, even with regressed patients. The particular focus of interpretations varies, with some analysts giving more emphasis to one aspect of the interaction than to another. This variation can be driven by the patient's vulnerability and also by the analyst's approach. We will touch on some of these differences below.

Transference

Klein viewed transference as ever-present and involving what she termed "the total situation" (Klein, 1952a). Since she understood unconscious phantasy to underlie all thought and feeling, she concluded that everything a patient brings into the analystic situtaion represents aspects of his internal world and has transference meaning. For her, the transference relationship, like all relationships, is mediated by primitive object relations that are projected on to and into the analyst, and the recognition and understanding of these projections form the basis of interpretations that lead to psychic change.

Klein wrote:

> There are in fact very few people in the young infant's life, but he feels them to be a multitude of objects because they appear to him in different aspects. Accordingly, the analyst may at a given moment represent a part of the self, of the superego or any one of a wide range of internalized figures. Similarly it does not carry us far enough if we realize that the analyst stands for the actual father or mother, unless we understand which aspect of the parents has been revived. (Klein, 1952a, p. 436)

Refering to transference as a total situation, Klein wrote:

> For many years—and this is up to a point still true today—transference was understood in terms of direct references to the analyst in the patient's material. My conception of transference as rooted in the earliest stages of development and in deep layers of the unconscious mind is much wider and entails a technique by which from the whole material presented the unconscious elements of the transference are deduced. For instance, reports of patients about their everyday life, relations, and activities not only give an insight into the functioning of the ego, but also reveal—if we explore their unconscious content—the defences against the anxieties stirred up in the transference situation. (Klein, 1952a, p. 437)

Modification of the superego

James Strachey, like Klein, believed it was important to try to modify the anxiety caused by the superego. In 1934 he wrote a landmark paper, "The nature of the therapeutic action of psychoanalysis", in which he spelled out the specific mechanisms by which a focus on the analyst-patient relationship and on the interpretation of transference can lead to therapeutic change through modification of the superego. Strachey described how patients attribute aspects of their "archaic" superegos, archaic because they are derived from infancy and are starkly idealising or punishing to the analyst. Interpretation of these aspects may allow the patient, in small steps, to

begin to see the difference between his "archaic" superego and the analyst's "auxillary" superego. He viewed these incremental insights as the engine of psychic change.

> It even seems likely that the whole possibility of effecting mutative interpretations may depend
> upon this fact that in the analytic situation the giver of the interpretation and the object of the
> id-impulse are one and the same person. (Strachey, 1934, p. 289, n. 18)

In practice, analysts found it very difficult to try to bring about change in the superego. In addition, they were also occupied with the task of identifying and locating all of the split-off parts
of the patient.

Countertransference and containment

Starting with Heimann's 1950 paper on countertransference, analysts began to see that they
could use their countertransference responses to recognise what it was that the patient was
projecting into them. Rosenfeld, who was working with psychotic patients, stressed the importance of the analyst's intuitive understanding, expecially when working with patients who find
it difficult to express themselves in words. He thought of the countertransference as an essential
kind of sensitive "receiving set" (1952).

   In using countertransference as a clinical tool, there is, however, the hazard that Klein was
most concerned about—that the analyst mistakes her own difficulties for a patient's projections.
A great deal has been written about this topic. In an early paper Racker (1953) differentiated
the analyst's specific response to the patient from the intrusion of the analyst's own difficulties.
Roger Money-Kyrle (1956) described in some detail how he understood the analytic process
to work. He thought that the analyst takes in, and becomes introjectively identified with, his
patient before projecting back the now understood part of the patient through an interpretion.
However, he believed that the analyst's understanding of the patient "fails whenever the patient
corresponds too closely with some aspect of himself [the analyst] which he has not yet learned
to understand" (1956, p. 332). When this happens, the analyst is left with a feeling of guilt.
Money-Kyrle gave an example of how his failure to understand led to a situation in which the
patient projected his impotence into his analyst who he then contemptuously attacked. Money-
Kyrle had then to distinguish between his own impotence in failing to understand on the one
hand, and the patient's hated impotence that had been projected into him on the other.

   Irma Brenman Pick (1985) spelt out the way in which patients project into a corresponding
part of the analyst and stir up feelings and dilemmas that already exist there.

> … patients are quite skilled at projecting into particular aspects of the analyst … into the ana-
> lyst's wish to be a mother, the wish to be all-knowing or to deny unpleasant knowledge, into
> his instinctual sadism, or into his defences against it. And above all he or she projects into the
> analyst's guilt, or into the anlyst's internal objects. (1985, p. 161)

In Brenman Pick's view, the analyst's live emotional experience and the way in which the analyst is able to work through her feelings in the session—and this will be under close scrutiny

from the patient—are crucial factors in the effectiveness of an interpretation and in the patient being able to take in the analyst's containing function.

Bion wrote that "[p]rojective identification makes it possible for him [the patient] to investigate his own feelings in a personality powerful enough to contain them" (Bion, 1959, p. 314). But it is not only the analyst's capacity to bear the patient that is important; it is also the patient's perception of the analyst's capacity and state of mind. Bion's theory of container/contained involves the idea that the analyst has to be aware of and contain her own feelings, which includes her feelings about the patient's accurate and inaccurate perceptions about the analyst.

It is important to recognise that working with the negative transference is significantly about the analyst being able to bear being experienced as "bad"—which might be inadequate, overcautious, cruel, or any other characteristic that would limit the analyst's capacity as an analyst. The analyst has to be able to acknowledge the anxieties that the patient may have about the analyst's state. The analyst has to bear and hang on to projected aspects of the patient until such time as the patient is emotionally strong enough to receive them. But containment is not enough on its own. In order to function as fully as he is able, the patient needs to accept back the unwanted parts of himself—good or bad—and face the reality of who he is. And to enable this, the analyst has the emotionally difficult task of making an interpretation (Strachey, 1934). Very often the analyst needs to make the interpretation that causes him the greatest anxiety, the interpretation that he would prefer not to make.

Taking time and working through

The ideas of taking time and working through are well established in the thinking of psychoanalysts and Klein herself was well aware of the need to proceed sensitively and slowly, as the following quotation demonstrates:

> But it is essential not to attempt to hurry these steps in integration. For if the realization of the division in his personality were to come suddenly, the patient would have great difficulties in coping with it. The more strongly had the envious and destructive impulses been split off, the more dangerous the patient feels them to be when he becomes conscious of them. In analysis we should make our way slowly and gradually towards the painful insight into the divisions in the patient's self. This means that the destructive sides are again and again split off and regained, until greater integration comes about. As a result, the feeling of responsibility becomes stronger and guilt and depression are more fully experienced. (Klein, 1957, pp. 224–225)

O'Shaughnessy (1981) went into some detail about the phases of analysis and described how patients who have been traumatised may need to feel that they are in control in order to gain emotional strength. However, she warned that once the patient gains the feeling of being in control a perverse side might emerge to triumph over the analyst. Rosenfeld (1987), also writing about traumatised patients, demonstrated the need for great sensitivity to timing and content of interpretations in work with thin-skinned narcissists; he thought that these patients with early traumatic backgrounds needed to be treated carefully to mitigate the possibility that the analysis would be experienced as a further assault. Steiner's papers on analyst-centred interpretations (1993) and on the shame that can be felt by patients when emerging from a psychic retreat (2011), also suggest technical approaches for dealing with patients who are not able to make use of more straightforward analytic interventions.

The focus on love or hate

Klein and her followers have been criticised for a focus on destructive or negative experiences, which some see as being at the expense of attending to loving or positive ones. In fact, Klein stressed the need to analyse destructive impulses precisely because they interfere with the capacity to love. Spillius (2007) suggested that some of these criticisms may originate from the papers of the 1950s and 1960s, which she described as having a "focus on destructiveness and envy" and as taking "a step backwards from the work of Klein". Spillius noted that there has been a shift over time away from an emphasis on interpretation of the negative transference towards a more balanced and varied approach of attending to both positive and negative aspects of the patient's material.

In a recent paper O'Shaughessy gives a beautiful example of attending to her patient's growing awareness of what has been going on between them, emphasising his positive development:

> During this opening phase Mr. X told no dreams but one day, unusually he brought an image. He described how on the way to his session he had noticed a house and its garden outside. It was a tidy garden that had been swept bare, except, that in a corner, there was a plant with two blue, delicate flowers. What seemed to me foremost and new was that Mr. X had *noticed* the house and how the garden was, and had been able to bring what he had seen to his session and tell it as a communication. It was a significant movement, I thought, from his usual concrete way of "acting in" with me, towards awareness and the gaining of an insight with some small degree (Segal 2008, p. 65) of symbolic representation. I spoke to him about how I thought the house and its garden outside expressed his new awareness of how he and I and his sessions were—we are to be like the two blue flowers in a corner, close and delicate with each other, while the session is swept bare of disturbing things—like his hostiity, or his fear that I get irritated and restive and might not want to be a delicate blue flower with him. (2013, p. 9)

Enactments

While using one's countertransference can be helpful in all treatments, it is particularly important when analysing more disturbed patients whose extensive use of projective identification makes it difficult for the analyst to get her bearings or to understand the patient's communications in a straightforward way.

Analysts working in the Kleinian tradition have shown particular interest in the problem of patients with primitive defences and anxieties that work against contact with the analyst and against understanding. Rosenfeld's technique was to bring the deadly activity to his patient's attention and to try to make links with the part of the patient that wished to live and develop. Joseph brought to light a particular aspect of patients' defensive activity—the way in which some patients relate to their analysts so that they appear to be engaged in real analytic work attuned to underlying unconscious phantasies and their meanings, but in subtle ways they are actually drawing the analyst into a perversion of analysis, a kind of pseudo-analysis. While this may serve to restore their psychic equilibrium, it makes real contact or change impossible. In a large body of work over decades Joseph developed a clinical approach that has attracted a significant following (Hargreaves & Varchevker, 2004). The following is an example of her approach, which involves close attention to what is going on in the room between patient and analyst:

> The patient may tell me that her mother was so fragile that even when she was very young she felt that she had to be very protective towards her mother. It may seem from previous experience that this refers to myself, but I suspect this is not of real use to her, nor convincing to me, unless it is being manifested in some way in the session. But it would alert me to examine for example whether I was talking a bit carefully, was my tone a bit delicate, etc. and if so as a consequence she might have experienced me, whether consciously or not, as pussyfooting round rather than interpreting straight. This can then give me a more global viewpoint—I may come to realise that over a series of sessions the patient and I have been talking to each other "carefully" as if each was more comfortable that way, so that the patient was feeling that interpretations were only "interpretations" and not to be taken too seriously and I was colluding with this. But the statement that the mother was so fragile may of course be stated for some quite other reason, for example—to express understanding she had gained from previous work, to control the analyst and prevent her from being straight and clear. The possibilities are legion and our attempt to understand what is going on in the here and now, means trying to understand not only what is being said, but why it is being said now and in this way, what impact it may be designed to have and what impact it does have. (2013, p. 1)

Dreams

Kleinians, like other analysts, take great interest in their patients' dreams and the clinical literature is full of dream material. Dreams are thought of as an expression of the unconscious world, of the defences against it being made conscious, and also as containing elements of external reality/day residue. Segal (1981) pointed out the need to distinguish between dreams that are symbolic from those that are experienced concretely. She observed that if dreams are the royal road to the unconscious, as Freud believed, it is important not to limit oneself to simply interpreting the content of dreams.

> As I suggested, following only the content of the dream has its limitations. If we analyze not the dream but the dreamer, and take into account the form of the dream, the way it is recounted, and the function it performs in the session, our understanding is very much enriched and we can see how the dream's function throws an important light on the functioning of the ego. (Segal, 1991, p. 73)

For example, in attending to the function of the dream or the telling of it, the analyst might notice how the dream is being used to evoke a particular response in the analyst, such as to excite, confuse, or annoy, and more disturbed patients may use dreams to evacuate painful states of mind. Segal noted that some dreams are predictive in that they become concretely acted out in the session (2007). Jean-Michel Quinodoz (1999) showed how some dreams, while appearing regressive, might in fact communicate a significant point in the patient's growing ability to link parts of himself together.

Meltzer explored and developed Bion's (1962) idea that alpha elements—unconscious mental contents with emotional meaning—provide the basic building blocks for dreaming and thinking. He regarded dreaming as a creative and meaningful activity, shaping inner realities and requiring transformation into symbolic form in order to be thought about and communicated. Dreaming, in terms of the manifest content of the dream, could be regarded as being on a continuum with conscious waking life (Meltzer, 1981, 1983).

Here and now vs. history and the outside world

Most Kleinian analysts attend to the here and now of the patient's expression of internal object relations in interactions with the analyst, but they vary in the extent to which their interpretations focus on the intrapsychic workings of the patient's mind or make connections to the patient's history or to the external world. Klein herself was concerned about too great a focus on the here and now without links being made to the patient's history.

> In recent years the importance of transference to be gathered from the unconscious, as well as from conscious material has been recognized, but the old concept that transference means a repetition from the past seems to have correspondingly diminished. One hears again and again the expression of the "here and now" laying the whole emphasis on what the patient experiences towards the analyst and leaves out the links with the past. (From MK Archive, PP/KLE D17)

Segal described a full transference interpretation as including references to both the past and the present:

> A full tranference interpretation—and though we cannot always make a full interpretation, we aim eventually at completing it—a full interpretation will involve interpreting the patient's feelings, anxieties, and defenses, taking into account the stimulus in the present and the reliving of the past. It will include the role played by his internal objects and the interplay of phantasy and reality. (1981, p. 70)

Interpretations that solely concern the inner workings of the patient's mind or that make links to historical antecedents without any reference to the transference run the risk of being taken up by the patient in an intellectual way and become explanations that have no real power to induce change. However, interpretive work that is focused solely on the immediacy of the clinical moment risks being so narrow that the patient does not acquire the kind of understanding that gives a sense of meaning and continuity over time. Importantly, also, the patient can use a focus on the immediate situation with the analyst as a defensive retreat.

In "Mapping the landscape: Levels of transference interpretation" Priscilla Roth (2001) outlines different levels of transference intrepretations, starting with those that address one of the patient's imagined or actual primary objects, the father in the first case she discusses. The next level of interpretation involves the patient feeling the analyst to be *like* the father—a transference interpretation but not in the here and now. A further level might address the interaction with the analyst at that moment in the session, which is felt to be like the patient's relationship with her father; in the final level of interpretation the analyst takes her own feelings and behaviour into account and considers that she may be involved in an enactment in which she is actually behaving like the father.

Feldman, a close follower of Joseph who works very much in the here and now, makes the point in his paper "The illumination of history" (2007) that a patient's history is embedded in his internal object relations and is expressed in interactions with his analyst. His view is that once these internal object relations have been analysed in the present with the analyst, the patient's anxieties may be reduced to the point that psychic change occurs. The patient may then be able to make a better connection with his past, which would in turn illuminate the present and the future.

Summing up

Attending to the "total situation" Kleinian analysts are attuned to all aspects of a patient's communication, in words and actions, even in the atmosphere of the session and they attend closely to their analysand's responses to their interpretations. Kleinian analysts try to ascertain moment to moment how they are being used by the patient, how they are being experienced, and at what developmental level the patient is operating, in order to try to pitch interpretations to the appropriate level.

Conclusion

In illuminating the inner world of children, Klein also revealed the deepest parts of the unconscious in adults. Her understanding of primitive states of mind and the internal object world of phantasy has influenced clinical work across the world. We have aimed in this chapter to outline Klein's central contributions and to give a sense of the complexity and variety of the ways in which they have been taken up, explored, enlarged, written about, and altered, at times in ways far beyond the original versions.

Klein drew attention to the significance and crippling nature of early anxieties, in particular the individual's anxiety about causing damage to himself and to his objects. She detailed the array of defences that are brought to bear when the persecution of guilt and anxiety becomes too great to manage. Her theory of the two positions and the movement between them provides a model of development, as well as a framework that helps the analyst to appreciate the moment to moment movement in the patient from being open to being closed to thinking about himself.

Klein emphasised the essential part played by projective and introjective processes in development, and the elaboration and exploration of these processes by her successors has become a central focus of clinical work. Close attention is given to the importance of containment and at the same time to the more or less subtle ways in which the analyst may find herself playing a part in the patient's defensive system—often involving the analyst's own defences against facing the difficulties of the encounter—and in this way maintaining the status quo.

For change to occur, the analyst needs not only to contain but ultimately to return to the patient his projected aspects in the belief that this will strengthen him and will increase his capacity to know his inner world and bear the reality of his situation. Importantly, this will increase his ability to make things better and to do things better. All of us depend on the state of our objects. Our mental health is affected by theirs, and being able to repair objects that are damaged, being able to love and to take care of others, and be loved and cared for in return, is the basis of mental well-being.

As analysts, we must recognise that we are not omnipotent, that there are limits to what we know and what we can achieve. Mourning what is not and what we are not is central to the task of psychoanalysis.

Acknowledgement

We would like to thank Richard Rusbridger for his comments on this chapter.

References

Abraham, K. (1924). A short study of the development of the libido, viewed in the light of the mental disorders. In K. Abraham (Ed.), *The Selected Papers of Karl Abraham* (pp. 418–501). London: Hogarth.

Alvarez, A. (2006). Some questions concerning states of fragmentation: unintegration, under-integration, disintegration, and the nature of early integrations. *Journal of Child Psychotherapy, 32*: 158–180.

Bick, E. (1968). The experience of the skin in early object relations. *International Journal of Psychoanalysis, 49*: 484–486.

Bion, W. R. (1956). Development of schizophrenic thought. In: *Second Thoughts* (pp. 36–42). London: Heinemann, 1967.

Bion, W. R. (1959). Attacks on linking. In: *Second Thoughts* (pp. 93–109). London: Heinemann, 1967.

Bion, W. R. (1962). A theory of thinking. In: *Second Thoughts* (pp. 110–119). London: Heinemann, 1967.

Bion, W. R. (1963). *Elements of Psycho-Analysis*. London: Heinemann.

Brenman, E. (2006). *Recovery of the Lost Good Object*. London: Routledge.

Brenman Pick, I. (1985). Working through in the counter-transference. *International Journal of Psycho-analysis, 66*: 157–166.

Britton, R. (1985). The Oedipus situation and the depressive position. In: R. Anderson (Ed.), *Clinical Lectures on Klein and Bion* (pp. 34–45). London: Routledge, 1992.

Britton, R. (1989). The missing link: parental sexuality in the Oedipus complex. In: J. Steiner (Ed.), *The Oedipus Complex Today* (pp. 83–101). London: Karnac.

Britton, R. (1998). Before and after the depressive position. In: *Belief and Imagination* (pp. 69–81). London: Routledge.

Britton, R. (2003). The concept of the ego In: *Sex, Death and the Superego* (pp. 86–102). London: Karnac.

Fairbairn, R. (1944). Endopsychic structure considered in terms of object-relationships. *International Journal of Psychoanalysis, 25*: 70–92.

Feldman, M. (2000). Some views on the manifestation of the death instinct in clinical work. *International Journal of Psycho-Analysis, 81*: 53–65. Later version in: B. Joseph (Ed.), *Doubt Conviction and the Analytic Process: Selected Papers of Michael Feldman* (pp. 96–117). London: Routledge.

Feldman, M. (2007). The illumination of history. *International Journal of Psychoanalysis, 88*: 609–625.

Ferenczi, S. (1909). Introjection and transference. In: E. Jones (Trans.), *First Contributions to Psycho-Analysis* (pp. 35–93). London: Karnac, 1999.

Fonagy, P. (2008). Being envious of envy and gratitude. In: P. Roth & A. Lemma (Eds.), *Envy and Gratitude Revisited* (pp. 201–210). London: International Psychoanalytical Association.

Freud, A. (1927). Four lectures on child analysis: the role of transference in the analysis of children. In: *The Writings of Anna Freud, Volume I 1922–1935*. New York: International Universities Press.

Freud, S. (1917e). Mourning and melancholia. *S. E., 14*: 237–258. London: Hogarth.

Freud, S. (1920g). *Beyond the Pleasure Principle. S. E., 18*: 3–66. London: Hogarth.

Freud, S. (1923b). *The Ego and the Id. S. E., 19*: 3–66. London: Hogarth.

Freud, S. (1930a). *Civilization and its Discontents. S. E., 21*: 59–145. London: Hogarth.

Grinberg, L. (1962). On a specific aspect of countertransference due to the patient's projective identifiation. *International Journal of Psychoanalysis, 43*: 436–440.

Grinberg, L. (1979). Countertransference and projective counteridentification. *Contemporary Psychoanalysis, 15*: 226–247.

Grosskurth, P. (1986). *Melanie Klein: Her World and Her Work*. New York: Alfred A. Knopf.

Heimann, P. (1950). What do we mean by "phantasy"? *International Journal of Psycho-Analysis, 70*: 105–114.

Hargeaves, E., & Varchevker, A. (2004). *In Pursuit of Psychic Change: The Betty Joseph Workshop*. London: Brunner-Routledge

Isaacs, S. (1948). The nature and function of phantasy. *International Journal of Psychoanalysis, 29*: 73–97

Joseph, B. (1975). The patient who is difficult to reach. In: P. Giovacchini (Ed.), *Tactics and Techniques in Psycho-Analytic Therapy, Vol. 2* (pp. 205–216). New York: Jason Aronson.

Joseph, B. (2013). Here and now: My perspective. *International Journal of Psychoanalysis, 94*: 1–5.

King, P., & Steiner, R. (1991). *The Freud-Klein Controversies 1941–45*. London: Routledge

Klein, M. (1926). The psychological principles of early analysis. In: *Love, Guilt and Reparation and Other Works: The Writings of Melanie Klein, Vol. 1* (pp. 128–138). London: Hogarth.

Klein, M. (1927). Symposium on child analysis. In: *Love, Guilt and Reparation and Other Works: The Writings of Melanie Klein, Vol. 1* (pp. 139–169). London: Hogarth.

Klein, M. (1932a). Preface. In : *The Psycho-Analysis of Children: The Writings of Melanie Klein. Vol. 2* (pp. x–xi). London: Hogarth.

Klein, M. (1932b). The psychological foundations of child analysis. In: *The Psycho-Analysis of Children: The Writings of Melanie Klein, Vol. 2* (pp. 3–15). London: Hogarth.

Klein, M. (1932c). The relations between obsessional neurosis and the early stages of the superego. In: *The Psychoanalysis of Children: The Writings of Melanie Klein, Vol. 2* (pp. 149–175). London: Hogarth.

Klein, M. (1935). A contribution to the psychogenesis of manic-depressive states. In: *Love, Guilt and Reparation and Other Works: The Writings of Melanie Klein, Vol. 1* (pp. 236–289). London: Hogarth.

Klein, M. (1936). Weaning. In: *Love, Guilt and Reparation and Other Works: The Writings of Melanie Klein, Vol. 1* (pp. 290–305). London: Hogarth.

Klein, M. (1940). Mourning and its relation to manic-depressive states. In: *Love, Guilt and Reparation and Other Works: The Writings of Melanie Klein, Vol. 1* (pp. 344–369). London: Hogarth.

Klein, M. (1946). Notes on some schizoid mechanisms. In: *Envy and Gratitude and Other Works: The Writings of Melanie Klein, Vol. 3* (pp. 1–24). London: Hogarth.

Klein, M. (1952a). The origins of the transference. *International Journal of Psychoanalysis, 33*: 433–438.

Klein, M. (1952b). Some theoretical conclusions regarding the emotional life of the infant. In: *Envy and Gratitude and Other Works: The Writings of Melanie Klein, Vol. 3* (pp. 61–93). London: Hogarth.

Klein, M. (1955). The psychoanalytic play technique: its history and significance. In: M. Klein, P. Heiman, & R. E. Money-Kyrle (Eds.), *New Directions in Psychoanalysis* (pp. 3–22). London: Karnac.

Klein, M. (1957). Envy and gratitude. In: *Envy and Gratitude and Other Works: The Writings of Melanie Klein, Vol. 3* (pp. 176–235). London: Hogarth.

Klein, M. (1958). On the development of mental functioning. In: *Envy and Gratitude and Other Works: The Writings of Melanie Klein, Vol. 3* (pp. 236–246). London: Hogarth.

Klein, M. (1959). Our adult world and its roots in infancy. In: *Envy and Gratitude and Other Works: The Writings of Melanie Klein, Vol. 3* (pp. 249). London: Hogarth.

Klein, M. Melanie Klein Archive, PP/KLE D17 Wellcome Library.

Likierman, M. (2001). *Melanie Klein: Her Work in Context*. London: Continuum.

Meltzer, D. (1968). Terror persecution and dread. *International Journal of Psychoanalysis, 49*: 396–400.

Meltzer, D. (1981). The Kleinian expansion of Freudian metapsychology. *International Journal of Psychoanalysis, 62*: 177–185.

Meltzer, D. (1983). *Dream Life: A Re-examination of the Psychoanalytic Theory and Technique*. London: Karnac.

Meltzer, D., Bremner, J., Hoxter, S., Weddell, D., & Wittenberg, I. (1975). *Explorations in Autism*. Strath Tay: Clunie Press.

Money-Kyrle, R. (1956). Normal counter-transference and some of its deviations. *International Journal of Psychoanalysis, 37*: 360–366.

O'Shaughnessy, E. (1981). A clinical study of a defensive organisation. *International Journal of Psychoanalysis, 62*: 359–369.

O'Shaughnessy, E. (1999). Relating to the superego. *International Journal of Psychoanalysis, 80*: 861–870.

O'Shaughnessy, E. (2013). Where is here? When is now? *International Journal of Psychoanalysis, 94*: 7–16.

Petot, J.-M. (1990). *Melanie Klein Vols. 1 & II*. Connecticut: IUP.

Quinodoz, M.-M. (1999). Dreams that turn over a page: Integration dreams with paradoxical regressive content. *International Journal of Psychoanalysis, 80*: 225–238.

Racker, H. (1953). A contribution to the problem of counter-transference. *International Journal of Psychoanalysis, 34*: 313–324.

Racker, H. (1957). The meaning and uses of countertransference. *Psychoanalytic Quarterly, 26*: 303–357.

Racker, H. (1958). Counter-resistance nd interpretation. *International Journal of Psychoanalysis, 6*: 215–221.

Racker, H. (1968). *Transference and Countertransference*. London: Hogarth.

Rey, H. (1979). Schizoid phenomena in the borderline. In: J. Le Boit, & A. Capponi (Eds.), *Advances in the Psychotherapy of the Borderline Patient* (pp. 449–484). New York: Jason Aronson.

Riesenberg-Malcolm, R. (1999). The constitution and operation of the superego. In: *On Bearing Unbearable States of Mind* (pp. 53–70). London: Routledge.

Riviere, J. (1936). A contribution to the analysis of the negative therapeutic reaction. *International Journal of Psychoanalysis, 17:* 304–320.

Rosenfeld, H. (1952). Notes on the psycho-analysis of the superego conflict in an acute schizophrenic patient. *International Journal of Psychoanalysis, 33:* 111–131.

Rosenfeld, H. (1964). On the psychopathology of narcissism: A clinical approach. *International Journal of Psychoanalysis, 45:* 332–337.

Rosenfeld, H. (1971). A clinical approach to the psychoanalytic theory of the life and death instincts: an investigation into the aggressive aspects of narcissism. *International Journal of Psychoanalysis, 52:* 169–178.

Rosenfeld, H. (1987). *Impasse and Interpretation.* London: Tavistock.

Roth, P. (2001). Mapping the landscape: Levels of transference interpretation. *International Journal of Psychoanalysis, 82:* 533–545.

Sandler, J. (1976a). Actualization and object relationships. *Journal of the Philadelphia Association of Psychoanalysis, 3:* 59–70.

Sandler, J. (1976b). Countertransference and role responsiveness. *International Review of Psycho-Analysis, 3:* 43–47.

Segal, H. (1957). Notes on symbol formation. *International Journal of Psychoanalysis, 38:* 391–397.

Segal, H. (1972). A delusional system as a defence against the re-emergence of a catastrophic situation. *International Journal of Psychoanalysis, 53:* 393–401.

Segal, H. (1977). Counter-transference. *International Journal of Psychoanalytic Psychotherapy, 6:* 31–37.

Segal, H. (1979). *Klein.* London: Karnac.

Segal, H. (1981). The curative factors in psychoanalysis. In: *The Work of Hanna Segal* (pp. 69–80). Northvale, NJ: Jason Aronson.

Segal, H. (1982). Mrs. Klein as I knew her. Unpublished paper read at the Tavistock Clinic.

Segal, H. (1991). The dream and the ego. In: *Dream, Phantasy and Art: Hanna Segal* (pp. 64–73). London: Routledge.

Segal, H. (1997). On the clinical usefulness of the concept of the death instinct. In: J. Steiner (Ed.). *Psychoanalysis, Literature and War* (pp. 17–26). London: Routledge.

Segal, H. (2007). Interpretation of dreams—100 years on. In: N. Abel-Hirsh (Ed.), *Yesterday, Today and Tomorrow* (pp. 14–24). London: Routledge.

Segal, H. (N.D.). Introduction to the Romanian edition of *The Writings of Melanie Klein in Four Volumes.* Binghamton, NY: Esf.

Sodré, I. (2004). Who's who? Notes on pathological identifications. In: E. Hargreaves, & A. Varchevker (Eds.), *In Pursuit of Psychic Change: The Betty Joseph Workshop* (pp. 53–68). London: Brunner-Routledge.

Spillius, E. (2007). *Encounters with Melanie Klein.* London: Routledge.

Spillius, E., & O'Shaughnessy, E. (2012). *Projective Identification: The Fate of a Concept.* London: Routledge.

Steiner, J. (1982). Perverse relationships between parts of self: A clinical illustration. *International Journal of Psychoanalysis, 63:* 241–252.

Steiner, J. (1987). The interplay between pathological organisations and the paranoid-schizoid and depressive positions. *International Journal of Psychoanalysis, 68:* 69–80.

Steiner, J. (1993). *Psychic Retreats*. London: Routledge.

Steiner, J. (2011). *Seeing and Being Seen: Emerging from a Psychic Retreat*. London: Routledge.

Strachey, J. (1934). The nature of the therapeutic action of psychoanalysis. *International Journal of Psychoanalysis, 15*: 127–159.

Williams, G. (1997). Some reflections on some dynamics of eating disorders: "No Entry" defences and foreign bodies. *International Journal of Psychoanalysis, 78*: 927–941.

Winnicott, D. W. (1945). Primitive emotional development. *International Journal of Psychoanalysis, 26*: 137–142.

Woolf, V. (1984). *The Diary of Virginia Woolf, Vol. 5*. London: Chatto & Windus.

PART II

THEORY AND PRACTICE

"The Devil is in the detail": on the detail of Bion's thought about container/contained

Nicola Abel-Hirsch

The 1950s: beginnings

How did Bion's initial thoughts on container/contained come about? Was there a particular clinical problem or clinical observation that precipitated his thinking? He used the term "contained" for the first time in his 1956 paper, "Development of schizophrenic thought" in which he describes a psychotic patient's projection of "expelled particles of ego" (1956, p. 345) into objects that are then experienced as "containing", even being taken over by, the projection. However, it is in "On arrogance" (1958), a paper given two years later to the Paris IPA Congress, that Bion makes what is a mutative shift in perspective, from focusing solely on the level of disturbance in the patient, to focusing on the analyst's capacity to take in the patient's projections.

In the paper he makes the following observations:

> [I]n so far as I, as analyst, was insisting on verbal communication as a method of making the patient's problems explicit, I was felt to be directly attacking the patient's methods of communication. From this it became clear that … what I could not stand was the patient's methods of communication. In this phase my employment of verbal communication was felt by the patient to be a mutilating attack on his methods of communication. From this point onwards, it was only a matter of time to demonstrate that the patient's link with me was his ability to employ the mechanism of projective identification. That is to say, his relationship with me and his ability to profit by the association lay in the opportunity to split off parts of his psyche and project them into me.
>
> On this depended a variety of procedures which were felt to ensure emotionally rewarding experiences such as, to mention two, the ability to put bad feelings in me and leave them there long enough for them to be modified by their sojourn in my psyche, and the ability to

put good parts of himself into me, thereby feeling that he was dealing with an ideal object as a result. Associated with these experiences was a sense of being in contact with me, which I am inclined to believe is a primitive form of communication that provides a foundation on which, ultimately, verbal communication depends. (Bion, 1958, p. 146)

Bion's recognition that to allow the patient's projection to "sojourn in my psyche" could result in some modification of the patient's "bad feelings" anticipated his imminent thoughts about the container, the contained, and the relation between the two. His conclusion is so familiar to us now that we may be forgiven for not noticing how unfamiliar it may have been then. Certainly the title and the start of the paper do not presage what is to come. Here is the opening statement of the paper:

In this paper I propose to deal with the appearance … of references to curiosity, arrogance and stupidity which are so dispersed and separated from each other that their relatedness may escape detection. (Bion, 1958, p. 144)

Why curiosity, arrogance, and stupidity? All are to do with thinking. At this point Bion was working on his "theory of thinking" and it may well be that he was predisposed to pay attention to these particular factors. Bion does not speak here about what may have been happening at the level of his emotional experience with the patient. What we see is him drawing inferences from his observation of the patient, and in particular his observation of patterns of elements that are not related in a linear way. I wondered at first if this was because the elements observed were fragmented in his psychotic patient's presentation, and he was having to gather them together. I think, however, that one can also see his intention to step back from the linear narrative and observe in a different kind of way.

In his paper "Attacks on linking" (1959) the following year, we find further development of his nascent thoughts about the container and the contained in his now well-known model of mother and infant, derived from his experience with the patient:

The analytic situation built up in my mind a sense of witnessing an extremely early scene. I felt that the patient had experienced in infancy a mother who dutifully responded to the infant's emotional displays. The dutiful response had in it an element of impatient "I don't know what the matter is with the child." My deduction was that in order to understand what the child wanted, the mother should have treated the infant's cry as more than a demand for her presence. From the infant's point of view she should have taken into her, and thus experienced, the fear that the child was dying. It was this fear that the child could not contain. He strove to split it off together with the part of the personality in which it lay and project it into the mother. An understanding mother is able to experience the feeling of dread, that this baby was striving to deal with by projective identification, and yet retain a balanced outlook. This patient had had to deal with a mother who could not tolerate experiencing such feelings and reacted either by denying them ingress, or alternatively becoming a prey to the anxiety which resulted from the introjection of the infant's feelings. The latter reaction must, I think, have been rare: denial was dominant. (Bion, 1959, pp. 312–313)

Bion on the psychoanalyst's countertransference

In the same year we find the following private note, which was later published in *Cogitations* (1992). Bion is contrasting instances when a patient is using projective identification primarily to evacuate, and when, by contrast, the projective identification is more communicative. I quote it in full because it is somewhat unusual to hear about his countertransference experience in detail.

> The grimace of pain or the elbow-rubbing, designed to relieve the psyche of an emotional experience in such a way that the emotional experience can be felt to have been not only excreted but evacuated into a container. In practice, such an omnipotent phantasy can most easily be given the appearance of reality if it expression is not limited to the formation of an ideogram within the psyche, but is expressed through the musculature in an actual grimace of pain or an actual rubbing of the elbow. Muscular action of this kind in the consulting room may sometimes be distinguished from the action designed to change the environment by the peculiarity of the emotional reaction engendered in the beholder. If it is an evacuator muscular expression of an ideogram, the analyst is aware of having feelings aroused in him which have no component appropriate to action to satisfy those feelings—the evacuating patient's aim is to ensure that the unwanted feelings are inescapably contained in their new receptacle. If the act is carried out under the dominance of the reality principle, then the ideogram—whether retained within the psyche or externalised by the musculature—has as its aim a subsequent alteration of the environment. This means that the ideogram expressed by the musculature is felt by the analyst to be by way of a communication and an invitation to do something—not, as is the case in the contrasting state of expression of an evacuator ideogram, to be an intrusion into him to which he feels he is passively to submit. (Bion, 1991, pp. 64–65)

Bion is describing two different kinds of projection (evacuation and communication) and the different effects upon himself. The evacuative projection is experienced as an intrusive takeover to which he is to passively submit; the more communicative projection is felt as an invitation to engage. He is suggesting that, at least sometimes, one can use one's countertransference to distinguish between the two.

Bion's "containing" and Winnicott's "holding": is there a difference?

Following Bion's presentation of his paper "Differentiation of the psychotic from the non-psychotic personalities" (1957) to a scientific meeting of the British Psychoanalytical Society, Winnicott wrote to him about it. This means that, fortuitously, we have a record of the two men's thinking about the same piece of clinical material.

Here is Bion's description of his patient:

> On this morning [the patient] arrived a quarter of an hour late and lay on the couch. He spent some time turning from one side to another, ostensibly making himself comfortable. At length

he said, "I don't suppose I shall do anything today. I ought to have rung up my mother." He paused and then said: "No; I thought it would be like this." A more prolonged pause followed; then, "Nothing but filthy things and smells", he said. "I think I've lost my sight". Some twenty-five minutes of our time had now passed …

The patient jerked convulsively and I saw him cautiously scanning what seemed to be the air around him. I accordingly said that he felt surrounded by bad and smelly bits of himself including his eyes which he felt he had expelled from his anus. He replied: "I can't see." I then told him he felt he had lost his sight and his ability to talk to his mother, or to me, when he had got rid of these abilities so as to avoid pain.

In this last interpretation I was making use of a session, many months earlier, in which the patient complained that analysis was torture, memory torture. I showed him then that when he felt pain, as evidenced in this session by the convulsive jerks, he achieved anaesthesia by getting rid of his memory and anything that could make him realize pain. (Bion, 1957, pp. 270–272)

Bion's emphasis is on the patient's attack on his ability to talk to his mother "so as to avoid pain". He further comments that he, Bion, is in the dark about the patient's actual mother. Here is Winnicott talking about the same material:

It is true that the interpretations you made were very likely right at the moment but if one violates the reported scene by taking it in abstract, always a dangerous thing to do, I would say that if a patient of mine lay on the couch moving to and fro in the way your patient did and then said: "I ought to have telephoned my mother" I would know that he was talking about communication and his incapacity for making communication. Should it interest you to know, I will say what I would have interpreted: I would have said: "A mother properly oriented to her baby would know from your movements what you need. There would be a communication because of this knowledge which belongs to her devotion and she would do something which would show that the communication had taken place. I am not sensitive enough or orientated in that way to be able to act well enough and therefore I in this present analytic situation fall into the category of the mother who failed to make communication possible. In the present relationship therefore there is given a sample of the original failure from the environment which contributed to your difficulty in communication. Of course you could always cry and so draw attention to need. In the same way you could telephone your mother and get a reply but this represents a failure of the more subtle communication which is the only basis for communication that does not violate the fact of the essential isolation of each individual."

Winnicott goes on:

You will see that from my point of view you were talking about the environment although you said you were not going to do so and you were indicating by this clinical material that this man has a relative lack of capacity for communicating because of some experiences in which his mother or whoever was there failed in the original maternal task at the stage when the mother is closely identified with her baby, i.e. at the very beginning.

I know that there is a tremendous amount other than this sort of thing in the psychotic illness and that all the other things that you and others bring in are important, notably the parking out of personal elements in the environment. You happen to give clinical material, however, which screamed out for an interpretation about communication and this is why I want to make this comment." (Winnicott to Bion, 7 October 1955, in Rodman, 1987, pp. 91–92)

Winnicott's emphasis is on a failure "in the original maternal task", whilst Bion's is on the consequences of an innate destructiveness in the patient and the preponderance of this factor in the psychotic part of the personality. I would like to draw attention not to the familiar argument of "nature *vs.* nurture" but to the question of what task the infant/mother couple have in the respective models. In a recent debate between myself and the Winnicottian scholar psychoanalyst Jan Abram on the question of the difference between "holding" and "containing" I was struck by Abram's comment that she does not think of infants as having a fear of dying. I, by contrast, have the notion of an infant's fear of dying in my "analytic blood". The most cited Bionian example of the mother's containment of the infant is of the infant's fear of dying. How come the hypothesised Bionian infant has a fear of dying, and the hypothesised Winnicottian infant does not? It hinges, I think, on whether one is of the view that infants are born with an inherent destructiveness (death instinct). The Kleinian/Bionian model of the infant is that it is born containing a drive that is dangerous to it. This inherent destructiveness has to be projected outwards into the mother for the safety of the infant. One of the key tasks of the infant/mother in this model is to manage the infant's normal inborn destructiveness. Winnicott does not share the view that there is an innate destructive factor that has to be "parked out" and contained by the mother. From this point of view "containing" and "holding" are not being expected to do the same job. Bion is "containing" the patient's attack and breaking of links; Winnicott's focus is on the mother's "holding" the communication of the infant.

The 1960s

Bion was a prominent member of the British Society during the 1950s and 1960s and was president of the British Psychoanalytical Society from 1962–1965.

In 1961 Bion wrote a paper on his conception of man.[1] Here we find his use of the signs ♀♂ to represent container/contained. As well as being a shorthand, these signs designate a phenomenon that is not yet fully (or ever fully) understood. Bion's observations in this period are but the starting point for his own lifelong investigation of the container/contained relation. Although we tend to associate the concept with his earlier work, I will argue later in this paper that his work on container/contained is at its height in his later work.

In 1962 Bion published *Learning from Experience*. The focus of the book is on his newly developing concept of "alpha function". Container/contained (♀♂) is an aspect of alpha function and it is discussed quite late in the book, in the penultimate chapter:

> 5. Melanie Klein has described an aspect of projective identification concerned with the modification of infantile fears; the infant projects a part of its psyche, namely its bad feelings, into a good breast. Thence in due course they are removed and re-introjected. During their sojourn

in the good breast they are felt to have been modified in such a way that the object that is re-introjected has become tolerable to the infant's psyche.

6. From the above theory I shall abstract for use as a model the idea of a container into which an object is projected and the object that can be projected into the container: the latter I shall designate by the term contained. The unsatisfactory nature of both terms points the need for further abstraction.

7. Container and contained are susceptible of conjunction and permeation by emotion. Thus conjoined or permeated or both they change in a manner usually described as growth. When disjoined or denuded of emotion they diminish in vitality, that is, approximate to inanimate objects. Both container and contained are models of abstract representations of psycho-analytic realizations. (Bion, 1962, p. 90)

Klein's work on projective identification was influential on Bion's newly developing thought on container/contained and he refers to this in the first paragraph of the quotation. Although the environment was not the focus of her attention, Klein was aware of its importance. Bion was about to show *how* it was important.

Freud, himself, had been well aware that without the care of the mother, self-regulation through the pleasure principle could not operate; this, however, is different to Bion's model in which the environment not only provides the conditions for an individual's self-regulation, but the regulation of the self is provided by the object. Bion's starting point is different from Freud's in that he begins at the clinical point of a patient's psychotic failure in development. That said, the centrality of the mother in processing the infant's experience is understood to apply to all early development, not only to overwhelming experiences. A question he leaves us with is, I think, whether there can be a spontaneous transformation of infantile experience without the containment provided by an object? André Green (1998), for example, has commented that Bion excludes the spontaneous transformation from beta-elements to alpha-elements without the help of the object.

How do containing spaces come into being?

In the penultimate chapter of *Learning from Experience* Bion continues:

> ♀ develops by accretion to produce a series of sleeves that are conjoined. The result is a reticulum in which the gaps are the sleeves and the threads forming the meshes of the reticulum are emotions. Borrowing from Tarski … his simile of the questionnaire with blanks that have to be filled in, the sleeves can be likened to the blanks in the questionnaire. The structure of the questionnaire has as its counterpart the connecting threads of the reticulum. (Bion, 1962, p. 92)

How do we make "space"? One way, is the provision of the sides or "threads" through one's emotional capacities. Bion also thought that one makes space through an awareness that there is "a something" that is not present. From this point of view we make the space to contain through an experience of absence or loss.

... it is in my experience meaningful to say that "a feeling of depression" is "the place where a breast or other lost object was" and that "space" is "where depression, or some other emotion, used to be". (Bion, 1970, p. 10)

The notion of a space—a container—becoming available through an experience of loss is also intrinsic to Bion's model of the beginning of thinking. An infant can have the rudimentary thought "breast" when able to have a rudimentary experience of the absence of the actual breast.

Is maternal reverie the same as the containing work of the psychoanalyst?

What loss might a mother suffer in order to make space for her baby? It is that of those needs of her own that cannot met. This is somewhat ameliorated for the mother by her identification with the baby, but as therapists and analysts we intend to be available to the patient's projections, without identifying with him in the way a mother does with a baby.

Bion speaks in a condensed way about this when he talks about our having (as analysts) to turn away from our own internal primitive self in order to attend to the patient. He thought that our internal primitive animal part feels lonely as a consequence of this. When an adult turns away from a baby, the baby can be terribly shocked—as if literally dropped and fearing for his life. The turning away is experienced as a total absence. It is this kind of feeling within us that Bion noticed and tried to describe.

> To summarize: Detachment can only be achieved at the cost of painful feelings of loneliness and abandonment experienced (1) by the primitive animal mental inheritance from which detachment is effected and (2) by the aspects of the personality that succeed in detaching themselves from the object of scrutiny which is felt to be indistinguishable from the source of its viability. The apparently abandoned object of scrutiny is the primitive mind and the primitive social capacity of the individual as a political or group animal. The "detached" personality is in a sense new to its job and has to turn to tasks which differ from those to which its components are more usually adapted, namely scrutiny of the environment excluding the self; part of the price paid is in feelings of insecurity. (Bion, 1963, p. 16)

The part of the personality that has prioritised the other above the self is also in a new position. Bion describes this part of the personality as new to its job and turned towards tasks that are different to those it is adapted to. As a result, it also experiences loneliness and separation from what Bion calls the source of its viability.

I think Bion is saying that in order to be available to the patient, we, as analysts, have to learn how to turn away from our own primitive animal self. I am suggesting that this is different from what a mother does naturally in reverie, because we do not simultaneously identify our primitive animal self with the patient, as a mother does with an infant. As a result of this "new job" the primitive animal part of the self feels abandoned, and even the part looking out towards the patient is unsure of its viability.

It is interesting to note that when the young Freud was learning how to use his mind differently, analytically, he reports experiencing a loneliness. Some have questioned whether in his psychoanalytically formative years Freud was as lonely as he claimed. It is sometimes implied that he was exaggerating his loneliness to augment a picture of the heroic nature of the task. It is possible, however, that it was a loneliness caused by his repositioning himself internally, in a way that allowed a new kind of attention to be directed externally. I quote Freud from one of his early letters to Fliess:

> Every now and then ideas dart through my head which promise to realize everything, apparently connecting the normal and the pathological, the sexual and the psychological problem, and then they are gone again and I make no effort to hold onto them because I indeed know that neither their disappearance nor their appearance in consciousness is the real expression of their fate. On such quiet days as yesterday and today, however, everything in me is very quiet, terribly lonely. I cannot talk about it to anyone, nor can I force myself to work, deliberately and voluntarily as other workers can. I must wait until something stirs in me and I become aware of it. And so I often dream whole days away … (Freud to Fliess, 3 December 1897, in Masson, 1985)

Minus container/contained (-♀♂): "without-ness"

In *Learning from Experience* Bion (1962) also introduces his understanding of minus container/ contained. His sign for this is -♀♂. In his description he comments that he has not yet worked out how the different aspects of what he has observed might fit together, but he will let the reader know what he understands thus far:

> … it is necessary to consider—♀ and—♂ and—(♀ ♂) in more detail. There are a number of peculiar features that are difficult to reconcile in a coherent theory. I shall accordingly describe them first without any attempt at explanation.
>
> 8. In the first place its predominant characteristic I can only describe as "without-ness". It is an internal object without an exterior. It is an alimentary canal without a body. (Bion, 1962, p. 97)

What does Bion mean by "without-ness"? Container/contained has the characteristic of "within-ness"—something is put in to something else—something is taken in to something else. "An alimentary canal without a body" by contrast is an attack on the link between taking in food and the growth of the body. Is "without-ness" an object that wishes to put itself in the position of being everything—rather than a link in a chain—an internal object intending to be the whole world?

Bion describes minus container/contained further:

> It is a super-ego that has hardly any of the characteristics of the super-ego as understood in psycho-analysis: it is "super" ego. It is an envious assertion of moral superiority without

any morals. In short it is the resultant of an envious stripping or denudation of all good and is itself destined to continue the process of stripping described in 5, as existing, in its origin, between two personalities. The process of denudation continues till—♂—♀ represent hardly more than an empty superiority-inferiority that in turn degenerates to nullity.

10. In so far as its resemblance to the super-ego is concerned—(♀♂) shows itself as a superior object asserting its superiority by finding fault with everything. The most important characteristic is its hatred of any new development in the personality as if the new development were a rival to be destroyed. (Bion, 1962, p. 97)

This formulation has been clinically very helpful. O'Shaughnessy gives the following example:

The pathological superego also watches the ego from a "higher" place, but it is dissociated from ego functions like attention, enquiry, remembering, understanding. Mrs A's "O God", for example, is not trying to know; it is denuding and condemning me, and with violent projective identifications establishes a transference situation where she and I are relating as abnormal superego to abnormal superego—both extractors of worth and pointers at failure. Nor does Mr B's Sceptic of the Renaissance remember that a living development, a "renaissance" between patient and analyst occurred in the analysis, or enquire how it was that this renaissance came to be destroyed by a rush of erotised fantasies. It is full of hate and prejudice, sceptical of all renaissance; its aim is to destroy links within the self and between the self and its objects. (O'Shaughnessy 1999, p. 868)

Elements of Psycho-Analysis *(1963): "a configuration that keeps on cropping up, both inside and outside the consulting room"*

Bion emphasised that he was not putting forward a new theory but was describing and exploring an observable pattern, a configuration, that keeps on cropping up, both inside and outside the consulting room. At the end of the discussion, Bion reiterated that detecting the underlying pattern was only the beginning of theorising about it and its relationships to other phenomena, and that the status of the ♀♂ configuration, and ideas associated with it, were provisional: a model rather than a theory. (Chris Mawson, personal communication)

In *Elements of Psycho-Analysis*, the book that follows *Learning from Experience*, Bion wants to identify what he calls the elements of psychoanalysis. The first of such elements that Bion identifies (numerically, and perhaps also in certainty and usefulness) is the container/contained. He points out the ubiquity of its occurrence in the way we think and talk:

If a patient says he cannot take something in, or the analyst feels he cannot take something in, he implies a container and something to put in it. ... The patient is "in" analysis, or "in" a family or "in" the consulting room; or he may say he has a pain "in" his leg. (Bion, 1963, pp. 6–7)

An example given in a later work provides some more detail to this picture:

> Thus an extremely greedy patient may want to obtain as much as he can from his analysis while giving as little as possible: we should expect this to show itself by frequent events in which the container was denuding the contained object and vice versa. The patient might show that he made enormous demands on his family but resented doing anything for it. Many patients might show behaviour of this kind on relatively rare occasions but some might show it in many activities and in striking degree as, for example, by habitual incoherence while demanding great precision of interpretation from the analyst. (Bion, 1970, p. 109)

This patient has a characteristic container/contained dynamic (that of a denuding relation between container and contained), and in general it can be clinically very helpful to observe the unique model/s of a container/contained relation operating for any particular patient (or analyst!).

1970: Attention and Interpretation

In 1968 Bion retired from active membership of the British Society and went to live in Los Angeles where he continued to write, practice, teach, and to develop his ideas, until he returned to England in 1979 shortly before his sudden illness and death later that year. The following section is based on the fourth of the quartet of books written in the 1960s, this one, *Attention and Interpretation*, published in 1970.

Familiar as I was already with this book, I was surprised to notice that in it we find Bion's most detailed and wide ranging exploration of his much accepted concept of "container/contained", together with what is arguably his most controversial concept, of the "discipline of memory, desire and understanding".

Clinical example

As I considered how to approach the place of the container/contained concept in this later work I found thoughts of a particular patient pressing on my mind. This patient is someone who could be described as barely *in* analysis and barely *in* herself. On the one hand, my experience of her was like that of a deer glimpsed between the trees, on the other hand, of a frustrating and dismissive figure demanding that I do something to make her life better.

Although intending to be vigilant about assumptions I might be making, I had, on occasion, realised that I was making an assumption so egosyntonic that it had previously passed unnoticed. At such moments of realisation—without saying anything explicitly to the patient—I noticed a change in her own willingness to come forward, in what was otherwise a rather stuck situation. In one instance, I realised that I was assuming that it was only her difficulties that meant she did not enjoy and value symbolisation as I did. In fact, I had chosen a profession that prioritised processes of symbolisation. I enjoyed listening to dreams, found it an achievement when a previously unknown influence on the personality came to be symbolised in dream. The patient didn't necessarily share this! When I realised this about myself and was informed by it in what I said, I noticed that we seemed to gain some separateness, and the patient was able to tell me something she hadn't been able to say before.

This recollection led me on to a thought I'd had reading Bion's previous book *Transformations* (1965). It is a notoriously difficult book, but, without being able to follow the detail, I had thought that Bion was attempting to challenge very basic, taken-for-granted assumptions in his own and in Western thinking, for example, our conception of cause and effect. This process was intended to contribute to his availability to the reality of his patients—through the discipline of memory, desire, and understanding.

Returning to my patient: at the end of a session, the patient—perhaps really for the first time—took *into* herself the problem that had always been externalised. Putting it overly simply, up until this point she had wanted to believe that her problems would be solved by finding a man who would sweep her off her feet. Yesterday she had realised, she told me, that it was she who was not able to allow an internal rush of feelings to happen, for fear that it would make her out of control and vulnerable. Up until this point she had only had glimpses of her feelings (a deer glimpsed between the trees). I had been aware in that particular session, and in the previous one, that I was managing better than before to keep finding my way back, in my own mind, to the reality of her sensitivity and fear, rather than feeling a more familiar frustration at her making her actual life, and our work, an inconsequential poor relative of her wished-for life. I had wondered, previous to this session, whether I was to be a container for her frustration. It was certainly very difficult for her to experience frustration herself. Interpretations of this, however, had not been effective.

I began to wonder whether my frustration might be more a symptom of my not being separate enough from her. Might we consider Bion's injunction to discipline one's memory, desire, and understanding from the point of view of its facilitating an appropriate separateness from the patient? This, of course, is very different to being distant from the patient. Here is a quotation from *Attention and Interpretation*:

> A certain class of patient feels "possessed" by or imprisoned "in" the mind of the analyst
> if he considers the analyst desires something relative to him—his presence, or his cure, or
> his welfare … If the psycho-analyst has not deliberately divested himself of memory and
> desire the patient can "feel" this and is dominated by the "feeling" that he is possessed by and
> contained in the analyst's state of mind, namely, the state represented by the term "desire".
> (Bion, 1970, p. 42)

As mentioned above, when I noticed myself making an assumption, I became more aware of her difference from me, and our contact had deepened. In this more recent example I think my becoming more separate/more in touch with her may have facilitated her own capacity to contain an experience of herself.

My initial hypothesis that the frustration I was feeling may have been my containing the frustration not felt by the patient, was, I think, largely mistaken. This was brought to light as I became more aware of my own assumptions and lack of separateness from the patient. As I changed my position in relation to her, she strikingly became more able to contain her own insight and experience.

Is it possible that Bion's profound work on the "assumptions" he himself held (see particularly *Transformations* and *Attention and Interpretation*) contributed to the wealth of examples of container/contained relations in *Attention and Interpretation*?

I will end with one of his examples, and with a question.

Bion's example of the stammerer

> A man speaking of an emotional experience in which he was closely involved began to stammer badly as the memory became increasingly vivid to him. The aspects of the model (container/contained) that are significant are these: the man was trying to contain his experience in a form of words; he was trying to contain himself, as one sometimes says of someone about to lose control of himself; he was trying to "contain" his emotions within a form of words, as one might speak of a general attempting to "contain" enemy forces within a given zone.
>
> The words that should have represented the meaning the man wanted to express were fragmented by the emotional forces to which he wished to give only verbal expression; the verbal formulation could not "contain" his emotions, which broke through and dispersed it as enemy forces might break through the forces that strove to contain them.
>
> The stammerer, in his attempt to avoid the contingency I have described, resorted to modes of expression so boring that they failed to express the meaning he wished to convey; he was thus no nearer to his goal. His verbal formulation could be described as like to the military forces that are worn by the attrition to which they are subjected by the contained forces. The meaning he was striving to express was denuded of meaning. His attempt to use his tongue for verbal expression failed to "contain" his wish to use his tongue for masturbatory movement in his mouth.
>
> Sometimes the stammerer could be reduced to silence. This situation can be represented by a visual image of a man who talked so much that any meaning he wished to express was drowned by his flood of words. (Bion, 1970, pp. 93–94)

A question

Following on from the example above, Bion discusses the different relations that can occur between container and contained:

> The relationship between these objects, which I shall represent by the male and female signs ♂ and ♀, may be commensal, symbiotic, or parasitic.
>
> By "commensal" I mean a relationship in which two objects share a third to the advantage of all three. By "symbiotic" I understand a relationship in which one depends on another to mutual advantage. By "parasitic" I mean to represent a relationship in which one depends on another to produce a third, which is destructive of all three. (Bion, 1970, p. 95)

What does Bion mean by "a third" and "all three"? Isn't the container/contained a dyadic relationship? Is the "third" the relationship between the two objects? He goes on to give an example of "a third":

[In] a "parasitic" relationship between the contained (or rather, not contained) material and the speech devised to contain it: "container" and "contained" have produced a third "object"—incoherence—which makes expression and the means of expression impossible. (Bion, 1970, p. 96)

Conclusion

The term container/contained is one of the most widely used terms in contemporary psychoanalytic thought. It can acquire a taken-for-granted meaning. I hope to have drawn attention to some of the detail of what Bion says about it, and the fact that throughout his work he "opened up" the meaning of what he had given the name "container/contained".

Note

1. Previously unpublished, "The conception of man" is now published in *The Complete Works of W. R. Bion* (1961).

References

Bion, W. R. (1956). Development of schizophrenic thought. *International Journal of Psychoanalysis, 37*: 344–346.

Bion, W. R. (1957). Differentiation of the psychotic from the non-psychotic personalities. *International Journal of Psychoanalysis, 38*: 266–275.

Bion, W. R. (1958). On arrogance. *International Journal of Psychoanalysis, 39*: 144–146.

Bion, W. R. (1959). Attacks on Linking. *International Journal of Psychoanalysis, 40*: 308–315.

Bion, W. R. (1961). The conception of man. In: C. Mawson, & F. Bion (Eds.), *The Complete Works of W. R. Bion, Vol XV*. London: Karnac, 2014.

Bion, W. R. (1962). *Learning from Experience*. London: Karnac, 1984.

Bion, W. R. (1963). *Elements of Psycho-Analysis*. London: Heinemann.

Bion, W. R. (1965). *Transformations: Change from Learning to Growth*. London: Heinemann.

Bion, W. R. (1970). *Attention and Interpretation*. London: Karnac, 1984.

Bion, W. R. (1992). *Cogitations* (Ed. F. Bion). London: Karnac.

Green, A. (1998). The primordial mind and the work of the negative. *International Journal of Psychoanalysis, 79*: 649–665.

Masson, J. M. (1985). *The Complete Letters of Sigmund Freud to Wilhelm Fliess* 1887–1904. Cambridge, MA: Harvard University Press.

O'Shaughnessy, E. (1999). Relating to the superego. *International Journal of Psychoanalysis, 80*: 861–870.

Rodman, F. R. (Ed.) (1987). *The Spontaneous Gesture: Selected Letters of D. W. Winnicott*. Cambridge, MA: Harvard University Press.

CHAPTER THREE

The development of the psychoanalytic understanding of psychosis

David Bell

"Nothing that is human is foreign to me" (Terence)

Ms T, a woman in her thirties, was prone to sudden outbursts of rage. She formed a precipitately idealised relationship with me (as her psychotherapist) claiming that I was so different from the psychiatrists she had seen who were not "interested in her but only in their theories". In one session I made a mistake as to the age of her son. Suddenly everything changed and she turned on me with scorn and contempt saying I was no different to anyone else; I had never been listening to her at all. The atmosphere was now one of utter hopelessness. Later she recounted that as a child, to escape from a very disturbing situation at home, she "holed up" in some caves nearby, painting over all the cracks in the cave with "magic paint" in order to "stop the monsters getting in".

So in the early phase of her therapy, one might say that she used the magic paint of idealisation to create for herself a kind of personal sacred space, the cave of her childhood, where she could feel safe. My mistake, however, opened a crack and "all the monsters" could now get in (as manifest in her attack on me).

A few weeks later I was informed that when the emergency team visited Mrs K, a known patient with a history of psychotic illness, they had found her in a terrified state. She had sealed all the windows and doors with Sellotape to prevent the evil rays getting into her flat.

These two examples, one from an ordinary neurotic patient and the other from a psychotic person, serve to show how, despite the gross differences in mental state of the two patients, they gave form to very similar psychic situations. That is, the content of their preoccupations was almost identical but the form they took was radically distinct. Both patients worked to create idealised retreats, a kind of personal religion, where they could be protected from destructive forces. In both situations the destructive forces, though taking their origin from internal situations, were felt to exist in the external world—in Ms A's case the fantasied monsters of her childhood now manifest in the psychotherapeutic situation, in Ms X's case the evil rays outside her flat.

Ms D, a psychotic patient on the ward, drank disinfectant in order to clean her insides of intolerable dirty sexual thoughts, calling to mind Lady Macbeth, who in a similar way, treated her own persecuting guilty preoccupation as something quite concrete:

> "Out, damned spot! Out, I say! … all the
> perfumes of Arabia will not sweeten this little
> hand. Oh, Oh, Oh!"

I have introduced this chapter with these three vignettes in order to foreground something that is central to the psychoanalytic understanding of disturbed states of mind. Namely, however bizarre the contents of a psychosis, they have a natural connection to quite ordinary human preoccupations, a connection that, of course, may not be obvious.

A psychoanalytic approach starts from the assumption not of alienation but of communality—certainly Freud would have stood by Terence's famous aphorism "Nothing human is foreign to me".

Before proceeding I will make some further general comments regarding the psychoanalytic attitude.

Psychic continuity

A further important characteristic of the psychoanalytic approach is the assumption of continuity. At a manifest level, of course, a breakdown can seem to evince a marked and even sudden discontinuity with the past. But psychoanalytic exploration will soon reveal a continuity, albeit functioning at a deeper level; that is, a delusion cannot come from "out of the blue",[1] although it may appear that way: it emerges from the personality structure of the person. When an individual's defences break down, what breaks through are disturbing preoccupations that have concerned the individual for much of his life. In fact, the ability to help the patient integrate his pre- and post-breakdown states is an important part of working analytically with such conditions. Recovery is not recovery from the difficulties that brought about the illness. These continue, though at a less manifest level, within the character structure of the individual patient. This commitment, to the restoration of continuity to that which appeared to be discontinuous, emphasises the developmental perspective, central to psychoanalytic explanation.

Personality and illness: a problematic distinction

There is a further conceptual issue here that is of broad relevance, but which is not immediately apparent. In psychiatric diagnosis the distinction between personality disorder and mental illness is helpful for a general appreciation of the patient's difficulties and for the making of rational plans for management. Such distinctions also have important value from an epidemiological perspective, particularly in terms of service planning—the kind of service necessary for mental illness (which generally will be expected to be episodic, although episodes may be very long) will be different from that for personality disorder, where there is a reasonable expectation that the difficulties will be enduring, given they are functions of the whole personality structure.

But when it comes to thinking more directly about the individual, the separation between "personality" and "illness" is highly problematic.[2] What appears as illness will be understood, psychoanalytically, as a personality development under the stress of certain internal and internal conditions.[3,4]

Reasons and causes

When I was a young trainee in psychiatry, we were, in the first seminar, given the "paradigm" (to use Kuhn's term[5]).That is, we were told that the proper interest of the psychiatrist was in *causes* (that is, physical causation of psychiatric illness) and not *reason* or *meanings* of human action; the former were seen as properly scientific and the latter as something one might be interested in when, so to speak, off duty (perhaps when reading novels). However, for a psychoanalyst, reasons/meanings and causes are completely intertwined, inseparable. For example, once we have shown that a man's abdominal pain is based on an identification with his recently deceased father who died of cancer of the stomach, we have at one and the same time given meaning to the symptom *and* explained its causal structure. Similarly, if a person has a breakdown characterised by a dominating preoccupation with themes of guilt, our understanding of the origin of the breakdown will be found by elucidating the (overdetermined) meanings, conscious and unconscious, of this mental content—this provides an account not only of the meaning of what the individual is communicating to us, but of the causal origins of the breakdown.

The subversion of the distinction normal-abnormal

Psychoanalysis does not investigate the human condition from the perspective of "normality", which was for Freud a convenient fiction. The relation of the abnormal to the normal in psychoanalysis is at once more complex and more problematic. Careful study of the abnormal reveals what the normal hides, shows what is immanent in it, for the neurotic (and psychotic) speak loudly about what the rest of us keep secret. It was Freud's appreciation of what was revealed in delusions of observation (an abnormal phenomenon) that led him to appreciate the depth and archaicism of the normal primitive superego. Even within the most ordinary and most disregarded aspects of mental life (such as slips and symptoms), Freud found sublime aspects of the human struggle.

In "Obsessive actions and religious practices", Freud (1907b) showed the clear parallel between the strange private ceremonials and rituals of the obsessional neurotic and those that accompany religious practices. Both centre on the need to keep separate good and bad, the sacred and the profane, and both have intense feelings of guilt and ways of dealing with it as central to their content. The difference is that obsessional rituals are idiosyncratic to the individual, whereas religious ceremonials are collective and stereotyped.

This demonstration of the continuities between the apparently bizarre and abnormal and so-called normality, the insight that the achievements of human culture and the manifestations of human psychological disturbance have more in common than our narcissism would regard as acceptable, is typical of Freud's thought. In *Totem and Taboo* he goes on to say (referring to the difference between the neurotic symptoms and the achievements of culture):

> The divergence resolves itself ultimately into the fact that the neuroses are asocial structures; they endeavour to achieve by private means what is effected in society by collective effort. (1912–13, p. 73)

Freud's attitude to religion is symmetrical to his attitude to neurosis. For both these human creations he showed considerable respect, in particular for their contradictory nature.

Thus, in a certain sense psychoanalysis humanises our attitude to mental illness and serves as a useful break on those culturally endorsed projective systems that seek to view those suffering from mental illness as fundamentally "other", not like us.[6]

Passivity vs. activity

From one extreme psychiatric perspective (and although it is extreme it continues to have an important place in psychiatric education) a patient is a passive object of his experience, he is not involved in constructing his experience. This approach apes general medicine: that is to say, in the same way that the patient with pneumonia is infected with the pneumococcus and is treated with antibiotics that destroy the invading organism, so the schizophrenic patient is viewed as if infected with a kind of "schizococcus" and the treatment is anti-psychotic.[7] This is a profoundly alienating approach, as it regards the language of the patient not as laden with meaning but instead solely as the product of a defective system; it is noise not signal. And there is a further difficulty here—for the patient himself may very well have a vested interest in being thought of in this way; namely, to evade contact with disturbing thoughts and feelings he may act on those around him to consider him as if psychically dead.

Freud on psychosis

Hughlings Jackson, the great neurologist much admired and quoted by Freud, wrote, "'Find out all about dreams and you will have found out all about insanity'" (Freud, 1900a, p 569, n. 2). Freud hoped that by using the same methodology as had been so successful in dreams and symptoms, he might penetrate the depths of psychosis. In fact, the psychosis, as he saw it, was a kind of waking dream. Further, Freud thought that just as the study of the neuroses led us to the understanding of the vicissitudes of the libido, the study of the more disturbed state of the psychotic mind would lead us to the functioning of the ego itself.

Freud's most celebrated account of psychosis is the Schreber case (Freud, 1911c). This work is not only foundational for our understanding of paranoid psychosis but provides the basis for the psychoanalytic approach to psychosis in general. Schreber was a highly intelligent judge who suffered a severe paranoid breakdown. He recorded his experiences in an autobiographical essay entitled, "Memoirs of my nervous illness" (Macalpine & Hunter, 1955), which details the genesis of an intricate delusional system. When this account came into Freud's hands he was clearly fascinated, as it showed that the study of psychosis could indeed provide access to the deeper recesses of the mind.

Schreber believed that the writings in his diary constituted a major contribution to mankind's understanding of himself—this belief being part of his delusional system. That is, he thought he had made profound transcendent discoveries about Mankind, including the nature of our relation to God and the Devil. But in a sense, Schreber was right, for, through the very accurate and detailed recording of his symptoms, their genesis and elaboration, he did indeed make a fundamental contribution to our understanding of our nature, and maybe on a saner lever, he was dimly aware of that too. His diary, then, *did* make a fundamental contribution to human-kind's self-understanding.[8]

Schreber, in the first phase of his illness, believed his body was decomposing and suffered hypochondriacal and paranoid delusions. He recovered sufficiently to live an approximately normal life while, in a manner that is not untypical, maintaining his delusional system rather privately.[9]

Schreber's system centred upon the idea that he was being changed by divine forces into a woman, in order that God would be able to have sexual intercourse with him. The result of this celestial union was to be the bringing into existence of a new race of men who would restore humanity and the world to what Schreber described as a former "state of bliss".[10] Towards the end of the first section of the work, following his description of the main elements of the case, Freud writes:

> The interest felt by the practical psychiatrists in such delusion formations as these, is as a rule exhausted, once he has ascertained the character of the products of the delusion and formed an estimate of the influence on the patient's general behaviour. In his case marvelling at this incredible psychic product is not the beginning of understanding. The psycho-analyst in the light of his knowledge of psychoneuroses approaches the subject with a suspicion that even thought structures so extraordinary as these, so remote from common modes of thinking are nevertheless derived from most general and comprehensible impulses of the human mind, and he the analyst, would be glad to discover the motives of such a transformation as well as the manner in which it is accomplished. With this aim in view, he would wish to go more deeply into the delusion and into the history of its development. (1911c, p. 18)

Schreber's description of his progression from a state of catastrophic anxiety to a delusional system is a familiar one.[11] One might think that living in the grip of such thoughts must be unbearable, but once a full delusional system (whether megalomanic or paranoid) has developed, the patient is often much calmer. He is no longer confused as he "knows" (that is, knows delusionally) what is happening to him.[12] Schreber described the changes taking place inside him as all part of "the order of things", that is, it conformed to a grand, metaphysical, ordered scheme.

It has perhaps now become apparent that for Freud the delusion is *not* the illness, the central catastrophe is the loss and fragmentation of meaningful contact with the world; the delusional system is an attempt at *recovery*, that is, to rebuild a world of meaning, with the limited resources that are available. The delusional system both gives expression to the inner catastrophe and is the attempt to repair it:

> The delusional formation, which we take to be the pathological product, is in reality an attempt at recovery, a process of reconstruction. Such a reconstruction after the catastrophe is successful to a greater or lesser extent, but never wholly so. (Freud, 1911c, p. 70)

This view, which informs the psychoanalytic attitude, has some important implications as regards the therapeutic attitude to patients. From this perspective, patients cannot be "cured" of their delusions; we should not even attempt to argue them out of their delusions, for they provide vital psychic protection.[13]

Returning to Schreber, the initial disintegrating state (accompanied by hypochondriacal delusions) was understood by Schreber to have been inflicted upon him by his physician Flechsig (Schreber called this "Soul Murder"[14]), suggesting a paranoid homosexual transference. As Freud carefully elaborates, as a result of the megalomaniac transformation, a paranoid idea (Flechsig forcing himself upon him) has become part of the grandiose delusion (God seeking to have intercourse with him). As Freud puts it: "a sexual delusion of persecution was later on converted in the patient's mind into a religious delusion of grandeur" (Freud, op. cit., p. 18).

There is an aspect of paranoid thinking that, though implicit in what has been said above, now needs to be made more explicit—that is, the illusory clarity that such systems create. In Schreber's world there was a clear binary division between the good and the bad forces. The good forces that were seeking to protect and promote the Messianic mission were in constant struggle with evil forces seeking to destroy it and bring down the ruin of the world. That is, Schreber has projected on to the external world, and into his grand metaphysical scheme, his own internal struggles—a psychotic version of the only-too-human struggle between love and hate, between the wish to create and the wish to destroy, that is so much part of our nature.[15]

Now, when the patient projects in this way, that is, sees aspects of his own mind in the functioning of the world, he himself, of course, does not know that he is projecting. He sees the world as he believes it to be; for him it is just a fact.

A transient paranoid state

Individuals can develop quite transitory delusional ideas, in order to cope with impending psychic catastrophe, as the following example illustrates.

> Mr D, a forty-two-year-old man in once weekly treatment, started each session as if just continuing the previous session. It soon became apparent that between sessions he carried on imaginary conversations with his therapist. However, he gave the same ontological status to the therapist with whom he continued his conversations as he did to the actual therapist who came and went. The therapist understood this but felt extremely reluctant to talk about it to the patient. Eventually, with some pressure from the supervision seminar, he resolved to raise it with the patient.

Mr D arrived for his next session and, as usual, began to talk as if continuing from where they had left off a week ago. After a while the therapist interrupted and said to the patient that he could see the sessions for him were a kind of seamless event in his mind, his continued talking to the therapist when he wasn't there allowing him to evade any knowledge of the reality of the therapist who came and went. The patient momentarily seemed flustered but then carried on in his normal way. However, after the session he bought a drink from a vending machine in the out-patient department and declared that the drink was poisoned, a sudden delusional idea. One could say that the poison that he had taken in was the insight, experienced as a poisonous assault on the delusional idea of continued contact with his object. He recovered from this momentary breakdown of his defensive structure quite quickly and did not need admission.

Freud's understanding of the mechanism of paranoia, particularly the close relation between paranoia and projection, has stood the test of time. However, we now have a much clearer understanding of the ways in which paranoid thinking derives from primitive mental states and we make important distinctions between different types of paranoia. The theoretical underpinning of these developments is to be found in the work of Klein. But before turning to Klein it is necessary to sketch Freud's theory of identification.

Identification

Given that processes of identification underlie many of the phenomena characteristic of psychosis, it will be clear that the developments in the understanding of this mechanism have been central to the evolution of the psychoanalytic understanding of psychosis. A natural starting point here is provided by Freud's seminal work "Mourning and melancholia" (Freud, 1917e). In this paper Freud showed that the irrationality of the melancholic state is only apparent. When the patient says "I am worthless … I have sinned, etc.", Freud recognised that these accusations are, at a deeper level, directed not against the patient's own self but against another whom he has lost. But because he has managed the loss through taking the lost figure into himself and becoming identified with this figure, the complaints are now levelled against himself, or more properly against his self now identified with the lost object. As Freud poetically put it:

> Thus the shadow of the object fell upon the ego, so that the latter could henceforth be criticized by a special mental faculty like an object, like the forsaken object. (Freud, 1917e, p. 249)

In this way the melancholic sustains the idealisation of his lost object but pays the cost of self-denigration and self-hatred.

Clinical illustration

Tom Freeman (Freeman, 1981), a psychiatrist/psychoanalyst working in Belfast on a psychiatric ward, described a young man who presented himself in an agitated psychotic state and who announced, "I am a traitor. If you look into my eyes I will betray you". Freeman discovered that before the onset of the frank psychosis, there had been a melancholic pre-psychotic phase when the patient had been depressed and introspective, this following a betrayal in love. During this period the patient felt worthless, all recriminations against the girl who had betrayed him being directed not towards her but instead towards himself, that is, himself identified with her (as Freud described); through this process he maintained his idealisation of his lost love.

However, in the psychotic phase there was a further transformation, which broke the continuity with the depressive phase. Now the patient said nothing of his betrayal in love but instead announced, "If I look in your eyes you will be broken-hearted", "I am betraying you", signalling his complete (psychotic) identification with his lost love.

Freud's paper marks a major crossroads in the development of psychoanalytic thinking—the understanding of the processes underlying melancholia opening the door to the recognition that processes of identification are bound up with *all* losses, but particularly the earliest losses (that is, the loss of the parental figures as ideal figures devoted to the self).

The ego develops through internalising these lost figures, an insight subsequently developed by Klein into a picture of a rich inner world with internal figures in complex relations with each other. This work also laid the basis for the understanding that the savage assaults upon the self, so characteristic of melancholia, are but an exaggerated form of the internal self-reproaches that are constitutive of our nature. Later, in 1921, Freud described an internal agency that is the source of these accusations, the superego.

Klein's contribution

It has often been stated that if Freud found the child in the adult, then Klein found the infant in the child. Through her development of the "play technique" Klein found a method of accessing much earlier mental states and so made available to psychoanalysis a model of the mind enriched though this understanding and which, in turn, provided a technique for further exploration of these very early modes of functioning. In "Notes on some schizoid mechanisms" (1946) Klein described the splitting and projective processes that bring about and sustain the states of mind of mind characteristic of psychosis. She also described a psychological mechanism central to the psychopathology of psychotic states—projective identification—whereby parts of the mind are transported, in unconscious phantasy, into external objects that become identified with them.

If we now return to the patient described above who said, "I am betraying you", we can understand that either he has taken his lost lover into himself, a kind of psychic cannibalism, and so has become her (a mechanism Klein described as introjective identification), or he has massively projected his whole self into her (projective identification—see Klein, 1955). The sense of betrayal has taken up residence elsewhere—in those around him whom he believes he is betraying (here too, the mechanism is projective identification).[16]

Clinical illustrations

A psychotic young woman, Ms H, felt she had to protect all the patients on the ward from the evil doctors and nurses, whom she believed were determined to sexually abuse them. In this way, she has located (projected) good aspects of herself in the other patients, who then have to be protected from her own violent and sexual impulses (also projected), now located in the doctors.

As discussed above, the pull towards dividing the world in simple ways between good and bad is a universal human characteristic and, usually, does not result in illness. However, it is also the basis of severe pathology in individuals and in groups who become dominated by this form of thinking. It is helpful here to distinguish paranoid states, which may be transient and which we are all prey to, from paranoid structures that function as institutions, whether in the mind, the individual, or part of larger social formations.

Klein described how in development we move from the paranoid-schizoid mode of functioning to a different way of being in the world, "the depressive position". And for Klein the fixation point for all forms of severe disturbance, including psychosis, is at this point of transformation. Klein's theory, however, is not a stage theory, it describes different psychic structures, different ways of being in the world, and we move back and forth between these modes of functioning throughout life.

The integration brought about by the move towards the depressive position is achieved at considerable cost in terms of psychological pain and suffering—attendant on the awareness of separation and frustration and the pain of guilt. It is the lack of capacity to manage these psychic pains, the inability to contain them in the mind and work through them, that creates the vulnerability to breakdown.

With this understanding in mind, we can go back to the patient who holed up in caves in childhood to protect herself from monsters and recognise that she has projected parts of herself outside the cave, these parts reappearing as the monsters threatening to come in. Thus, at the very point that she created an idealised retreat, she inevitably also brought into being a paranoid universe. The psychotic patient who covered the cracks in her door with Sellotape had similarly projected into the outside word the threatening parts of her mind, but in a much more concrete way.

Following Klein's work we have come to recognise that not only does an individual project aspects of himself in this way but that he can act upon individuals around him in order to bring this projection to life externally. He may disown his own violent impulses and through the process of projective identification experience them as being present in another who is thus imagined as being violent. Then, in a further step, he may act upon this other to make him really feel aggressive and in this way "actualise" the projective process (Sandler, 1976). Betty Joseph (1985) and Michael Feldman (1997) have made extensive studies of these processes as they are lived out in the consulting room between analyst and patient. These processes frequently underlie escalating disturbances on psychiatric wards, as the following example illustrates.

Miss B, a patient in analysis, was internally dominated by a cruel primitive superego, which she felt watched her every move. She experienced any attempt at self-control as in the service of this superego and so could not distinguish between its demands and ordinary ego functions that sought to protect her from danger.[17] This resulted in a wholesale projection of her sane awareness of the danger she was in into her analyst. Left free of any concern for herself, Miss B took increasingly dangerous risks, such as driving whilst under the influence of sedatives with apparent complete equanimity, whilst her analyst became increasingly horrified as the momentum of her self-destructiveness gathered pace. She said that she experienced the ending of sessions "like a guillotine". This was a very apt description as, having projected important ego functions into her analyst, she left the session in a "headless" state. The situation deteriorated to such an extent that it became necessary to admit her to hospital.

On the ward she behaved in a very provocative way to the nurses. She would go off the ward without telling them where she was going, leaving them with an overwhelming anxiety that she was about to carry out a very self-destructive attack. She might say, for example, in an apparently calm way, that she was "going to the shops", as if this was a quite ordinary and banal event, whilst at the same time conveying that she would be near the pharmacy where, by implication, she might buy some paracetamol. At other times she would telephone the ward from outside but not speak when a nurse answered and then hang up. The nurses found this unbearably tantalising. This resulted in an escalation of the need for the staff to control her and so she was restricted from leaving the ward. The situation then further deteriorated and the nurses became worried that she might carry out a serious attack upon herself at any moment. The final result was that she was restricted to a small room where she was continuously observed. She then became acutely anxious and declared in a terrified voice, "I can't stand this place. I'm being imprisoned".

The patient, then, has "actualised" her inner situation. What started out as an inner conflict between aspects of herself, an intra-psychic situation, has now been transported into a conflict between herself and the nursing staff, namely an interpersonal situation. The superego watching her all the time is, of course, inescapable, but temporary relief was achieved through projecting it elsewhere in this way. Now, it is not her own superego but instead it is the nurses on the ward who are felt to be imprisoning her. An inner situation has been transformed into a spatial one.

It is also important to note that the patient's provocative manner did engender a good deal of hostility towards her which was never really owned by the staff. Although the maintenance of the patient under continuous observation served, manifestly, a wish to protect the patient from suicide, at a deeper level it also, I think, satisfied a hatred that had been recruited in the staff and that was associated with some excitement.

A note on adolescence

Mr G, a forty--year-old man, who evinced a profound sense of detachment, revealed after a year of analysis that when he was sixteen he suffered a breakdown—he had become persecuted by very disturbing sexual images that he could not rid himself of and was driven in the end to take several overdoses. However the seriousness of his condition was never picked up and his disturbed state was put down to "exam nerves".

Mr G's story is in fact a very typical one. Many, perhaps a large majority, of those who break down in adult life have suffered an earlier breakdown, often unnoticed, in adolescence. In fact, many serious psychotic conditions make their first appearance in adolescence. It thus becomes clear that from a psychoanalytic perspective adolescent breakdown is a *developmental* disorder.[18]

One of the most fundamental and disturbing aspects of adolescence derives from the psychological significance of the bodily transformations that are its characteristic manifestation. The child is, in a certain sense, free to have fantasies about killing his father, having sex with his mother, and so on, secure in the knowledge that he lacks the bodily capacity to put these fantasies into action. But the changes at puberty bring the realisation that these fantasies can in principle now be actualised and this brings, for all adolescents, a very disturbing situation. But for those who are predisposed to disorder, it can be a catastrophe.

There is a further aspect to this situation that arises from our deeper understanding of the processes of projective and introjective identification. A young girl may, and this is quite ordinary, experience her own sexual feelings as hateful and disgusting and so deal with this by projecting them into her mother, who is now viewed as a disgusting sexual woman. This way of managing maintains a kind of equilibrium that can continue until the girl's body starts to transform and she sees it taking the form of a woman's body. While she knows at a more sane level that this is ordinary development, in a more psychotic register, especially if she is vulnerable, this bodily change is experienced as the sudden eruption within of that which she had projected, like a kind of incubus growing inside her and taking her over.[19] This kind of unconscious phantasy can underlie the disturbed adolescent's attacks upon her body, which seek to remove the terrifying object from inside.

Robin Anderson (personal communication) has put it very well. He made the point that if you don't go mad when you move house, then you really are mad! But he then went on to say that there is something much worse, and that is when you have the builders in and the house starts moving around with you still in it. This is, he explained, the dilemma of the adolescent: it is like having the (anatomical) builders in—you can't go anywhere and everything is moving around inside you.

Further developments

Work with borderline and psychotic patents has led to considerable development in theory and technique. Pre-eminent here are the works of Hanna Segal 1950 (who analysed the first schizophrenic patient without altering the classical setting), Herbert Rosenfeld (who I discuss further below), and Wilfred Bion (whose work with very disturbed states brought a radical transformation of our understanding of psychoanalysis in general, see, for example, Bion, 1956).

I have chosen to focus on Rosenfeld, as his work provides the explanatory framework for the concluding section of this chapter, which makes use of Dennis Potter's television drama *The Singing Detective* to provide an illustration of some of the disturbing processes that exist to some extent in all of us, but which can dominate in some of the very disturbing situations I have been describing.

Rosenfeld (1971) discovered frequent references to gangs, delinquents, or Mafia-like figures in psychotic and perverse patients. He came to understand that what was being communicated was a description of a specific internal situation in which the patient was controlled by a kind of structured internal organisation that had the qualities of a terrifying omnipotent superego, which held the patient in its grip and in thrall to it. These internal figures often spoke to the patient, sometimes as hallucinatory voices, and offered the patient "protection" provided he did not reveal their "secrets". Further, the organisation persuades the patient that madness is sanity and sanity is madness. Rosenfeld also noticed that these figures tended to enter the material as a menacing force just at the moment when the patient was making real progress, was more in touch with himself, and was allowing the analyst more contact with him. In other words, Rosenfeld discovered a new form of negative therapeutic reaction that had a very malignant quality.

Clinical illustration

> Mr M, a schizophrenic patient who I looked after on a psychiatric ward and saw for once-weekly psychotherapy, spent much of his time isolated from other patients, reading comics in bed and giggling to himself. The nurses described him as completely cut-off and noticed that he walked as if floating on air. He came to sessions only because he was, as he put it, "sent". Throughout sessions he would stare blankly at me, responding to my interpretations with a mocking laugh.
>
> However, one day there was a radical transformation. As I walked through the ward, he turned to me and said "Can I see you, Dr Bell?", something he'd never said before. As he sat down in the room I could see he was highly anxious and frightened. He told me that he was in communication with a kind of secret group called "the scientists". The scientists promised him everlasting life and a world where he could be rid forever of all pain and frustration. They (the scientists) also told him that he must avoid, at all costs, contact with, "a dangerous, mad figure" called Dr Bell.
>
> What was central here was that the patient, in telling me about these figures, had moved into a very different state of mind; he was dis-identifying himself from the organisation and seeking my help in obtaining release from them. The patient was thus saner than I had ever known him but now lived in terror of the revenge of the internal organisation (the "scientists"). It was necessary to put him on major tranquillisers, not because he was more ill but because he was saner and therefore at considerable risk.[20]

Rosenfeld gave a considerable emphasis to the unbearable quality of the pain caused by confusion, and this was very evident in my patient. He said to me, with terror, "I no longer know who is mad and who is sane"—this "not knowing" being a manifestation of his sanity, whereas before he delusionally "knew" that he was sane and I was mad.

A literary illustration of "the internal mafia": Dennis Potter's The Singing Detective[21]

Dennis Potter's *The Singing Detective* is regarded by many not just as his masterwork but as one of the pinnacles of British television drama. One of its most remarkable achievements derives from the author's originality in making use of the television medium to provide a complex representation of an inner world and of the movements between inner and outer reality that form the basis of our lived subjective experience. Potter, through his masterly use of his medium, is able to show the interweaving of fantasy, memory, and current reality, and their shifting relationships to each other, as the main character, Philip Marlow, pursues the psychological journey towards integration that forms the central motif of the drama.

The plot centres upon Marlow, a hospital patient suffering the most severe crisis of a disease that has plagued him all his life—psoriasis and psoriatic arthropathy. It is, however, clear that the physical disease is to be regarded as a metaphor for a psychological breakdown—in the text Potter refers to the ward as "a place in the mind".

Because the narrative structure is non-linear and multi-layered, it is difficult to provide a synopsis without doing considerable disservice to the subtlety of the work. In fact, in attempting to provide such a synopsis, one is confronted with the same difficulty one encounters when attempting to summarise an entire psychoanalytic treatment: everything is connected to everything else, the same story is told over and over again, but each time in a different way and in a different context. The drama unfolds over six episodes, and in each episode similar elements appear, although, at first, the relation between them remains vague. But, as the narrative progresses disparate fragments become clearer and the relationship between them more coherent.

Marlow is filled with witty, biting invective that is seductive, but which we soon learn comes from a world of utter cynicism: he believes, *apparently*, in a world where you are either on top or underneath, there are only winners and losers. However, as the narrative progresses, we learn that at the centre of his world there is unbearable psychic pain and guilt, which has formed a central motif in his life. As a young boy Phillip witnessed his mother having intercourse with her lover, who played the piano in the band in which his father sang. Subsequently, the family broke down and he moved with his mother from his beloved countryside (representing something more natural and kind) to the harsh alienating urban world of London. Phillip subsequently confronts his mother with what he witnessed and later we learn of her suicide. Marlow has spent his whole life frozen in three moments now psychically contemporaneous— his observation of his mother's intercourse, his confrontation of her, and her suicide.

During his time on the ward he is helped by what is described as "a clever psychotherapist".

As the drama unfolds we see that Phillip is being pursued and observed by two men in raincoats who, we are informed, work for a security organisation—they seem to represent a kind of internal surveillance system. In the last episode, as fantasy and reality become more distinct from each other and the events of his life cohere, Marlow faces the terrible guilt he has felt for an event from his childhood when he caused damage to a vulnerable classmate. But confrontation with this painful reality, and his capacity to bear it, brings a major transformation in his inner world, which now becomes peopled with friendlier figures. He is then able to turn to his psychotherapist and to his wife for real support. In other words, he accepts ordinary human dependency and relinquishes some measure of cynical scorn for this situation. However, just at that precise moment the men in raincoats appear, they walk out of his fantasy world and on to the ward. Suddenly he is abandoned and left alone with these terrifying figures who loom over him and grab him. He screams out for help.

Now I am quite sure that Potter never read Rosenfeld. In fact, he was not at all interested in psychoanalysis. But these figures in raincoats, who appear just at the point where Marlow makes this fundamental psychic move towards sanity, provide, I believe, a brilliant representation of

Rosenfeld's inner Mafia, who bring the patient back under their control whenever there is a threat to their supremacy.

Conclusion

In this chapter I have traced some of the history of the psychoanalytic approach to psychosis and in the course of this have given considerable space to Freud, as it was this early work that provided both the framework for understanding psychosis and the basis of a psychoanalytic attitude to disturbed states of mind. I have then showed how Klein and her followers have developed this tradition, but, inevitably, a great deal has been left out—I have not had space to describe the major contributions of others such as Segal, Bion, Sohn, Rey , Joseph, and Lucas, whose contributions have been hugely influential.

Times have changed since those early days when it was possible to carry out an analysis or intensive psychotherapy of a psychotic patient, supported by psychiatric colleagues who could provide the structures that make such work possible. This, sadly, is no longer the case.

However, it needs to be said that no analyst who is interested in working with psychotic patients believes that the problems of psychosis are going to be cured by analysis, not least because of the inevitable huge lack of resources. Work with such patients provides a possibility of understanding deeper levels of experience that cannot be as directly observed in less disturbed patients.

The most fundamental challenge in the care of severely ill patients is to ensure that the patient is provided for in a humane world where staff can be helped to see their patients as struggling with human problems, to think of their communications not just as symptoms of their disturbed state, but as real human communications that have a meaning to all of us. The professionals who can make the greatest contributions here are the nurses, doctors, occupational therapists, and creative therapists[22] who are responsible for the care of these patients in both out- and in-patient settings on a daily basis. The recent book by my colleague Marcus Evans, aptly titled *Making Room for Madness* (Evans, 2016) is an excellent example of this work.

The paucity of resources (material and professional) for proper care of these patients has led to a situation where they are increasingly seen as objects to be treated in predetermined ways according to schedules and "care" pathways, leading to the profound alienation of both staff and patients, which I have termed "the industrialisation of human suffering". This degradation of psychiatry does not so much result from the weakening of the place of psychoanalysis within it, but from the broader transformation of the socio-political context that underlies this change (I am referring here mainly to the UK perspective (see Bell, 2013)).

We live in dark times, but through psychoanalytic practice, training, and intellectual engagement we may keep a flame burning and continue to influence coming generations to see that there is a profoundly different way of thinking about mental illness.

Notes

1. This phrase refers to the characteristic quality of certain delusions termed "autochthonous"; that is, it seems to emerge suddenly, out of the blue. The point that is being made is that although this

term is correct phenomenologically, that is, it describes a characteristic feature of psychosis, this refers only to appearance, not to actuality.

2. There is some growing sense that that the simplistic distinction between mental disorder and personality disorder (which underlies the differentiation of axes in DSM-IV) is questionable, see for example (Westen et al., 2006).

3. By this I mean that some individuals may have a kind of psychological "fault-line", which under the pressure of a toxic interaction between the sensitised internal world and particular malign external circumstance is stressed to the point of breakdown. The fault-line, which is often the source of pervasive anxiety, may in other circumstances be managed and so not become manifest.

4. A related issue here is that whereas psychiatrically one may speak of a patient as having more than one illness, from a psychoanalytic perspective the patient has only one illness, which expresses itself in different ways and which is inseparable from his character.

5. Thomas Kuhn (Kuhn, 1962) described the period of ordinary scientific activity as "normal science" (distinct from revolutionary periods). In the periods of normal science each new generation of scientific workers is acculturated into the current paradigm as to what constitutes proper scientific study and what does not. For Kuhn this activity was best understood not in terms of the logic of science but in a more sociological/anthropological manner.

6. Freud elsewhere makes a point that neurotic symptoms can be viewed as a kind of caricature of ordinary cultural phenomena. Hysteria is a caricature of a work of art, obsessional neurosis is a caricature of religion, and paranoia is a caricature of a philosophical system.

7. The same model underlies the viewing of depression as a kind of illness to be treated with anti-depressants. The term "anti-depressant" is a misnomer; what we use are better described as "mood-altering chemicals" that can provide some temporary relief but should not be regarded as capable of providing specific treatment for an illness. For further details, see the work of Joanna Moncrieff, *The Myth of the Chemical Cure* (2008).

8. One is reminded here of Freud's statement that "The patient is always right, but not right in the way he thinks he is right!" (I have not been able to trace the source of this comment).

9. There are many such patients who get by, keeping their delusions and hallucinations secret, although they might reveal them in the privacy of a consulting room.

10. Schreber's delusional system bears a close resemblance to the crazy thinking so well captured in Stanley Kubrick's film, *Dr Strangelove*. The mad general in the film is aiming to bring about an apocalyptic scenario, in order to rid the world of a terrible communist plot that he has endowed with omnipotent power. In this mad paranoid delusion the communist plotters are endeavouring to "sap and impurify all of our precious bodily fluids". Unfortunately, such thinking is not confined to science fiction movies, for many, including those occupying high positions of power in world politics, believe in the coming of an Armageddon (see http://www.huffingtonpost.com/bob-burnett/vote-no-on-armageddon_b_7179908.html) that will bring everlasting peace, presumably conceived as returning to a state of what Schreber termed the lost state of "bliss", or "the order of things". Some think they need to retain access to Tel Aviv, where Armageddon (Har Megiddo) Armageddon is, in order that they can be there when Armageddon arrives in order to witness the coming of the Messiah. Most problematically, those who believe in this delusional system may function in an apparently entirely normal way; they are not, technically speaking, psychotic.

11. Today, as patients are often medicated very early in the evolution of the disorder, the acute early state and its transformation may not be so clearly witnessed.

12. That is, the delusion "cures" the patient of his painful confusion. As will be discussed below, Rosenfeld emphasised the unbearability of confusion.

13. Interestingly, Marx makes a very similar point in relation to religion (which he considered to be a kind of group delusion).

    He writes: "To call on the people to give up their illusions about their condition is to call on them to give up a condition that requires illusions" (Marx, 1843). That is, we cannot ask people to give up an illusion; we can only try to understand the need for it (excellent advice to a psychoanalyst!).

14. This part of the delusional system may have had some relation to the treatment meted out to him as a child by his father, who was a leading figure in a movement that imposed very rigorous discipline on children, including various physical contraptions to prevent masturbation. See *Soul Murder* (Schatzman, 1973).

15. We see a more ordinary version of this projective system in fairy stories: here, for example, the good and malign forces are represented by the fairy godmother and the evil stepmother.

16. There is not space here to go further into the different identificatory processes. Subsequent authors have distinguished between "acquisitive" and "attributive" forms of identification. For a detailed discussion of the history of this concept see Bell, 2001.

17. Bion described this as the "ego destructive superego" (see Bion, 1962); see also O'Shaughnessy (1999).

18. The work of the Laufers on adolescent breakdown is highly relevant here—see Laufer, M. E. and Laufer, M. (1994).

19. In other words the forceful projection is now reversed and she feels as if she is the victim of a forceful re-projection into her.

20. I would like here to express my gratitude to Dr Murray Jackson who I had the great privilege to work with when I was a registrar on the famous Ward 1 at the Maudsley Hospital—perhaps the only ordinary psychiatric ward to provide psychoanalytically informed care of acutely disturbed patients.

21. For a fuller psychoanalytic exploration of *The Singing Detective*, see Bell (1998)

22. Creative therapies such as music therapy and art therapy are much unrepresented in British psychiatry (as opposed, for example, in Scandinavia).

References

Bell, D. (1998). *The Singing Detective*: A place in mind. In: D. Bell (Ed.), *Psychoanalysis and Culture: A Kleinian Perspective*. London: Karnac, 2004.

Bell, D. (2001). Projective identification. In: C. Bronstein (Ed.), *A Contemporary Introduction to the Work of Melanie Klein*. London: Whurr.

Bell, D. (2013). https://chpi.org.uk/wp-content/uploads/2013/12/David-Bell-analysis-Mental-illness-and-its-treatment-today.pdf

Bion, W. R. (1956). Development of schizophrenic thought. *International Journal of Psychoanalysis*, 37: 344–346.

Bion, W. R. (1962). A theory of thinking. In: *Second Thoughts* (pp. 110–119). London: Heinemann.

Evans, M. (2016). *Making Room for Madness*. London: Karnac.

Feldman, M. (1997). Projective identification: The analyst's involvement. *International Journal of Psychoanalysis*, 78: 227–241.

Freeman, T. (1981). On the psychopathology of persecutory delusions. *British Journal of Psychiatry*, 139: 529–532.

Freud, S. (1900a). *The Interpretation of Dreams. S. E., 4–5*. London: Hogarth.

Freud, S. (1907b). Obsessive actions and religious practices. *S. E., 9*: 115–128. London: Hogarth.

Freud, S. (1911c). Psychoanalytic notes on an autobiographical account of a case of paranoia (Dementia paranoides). *S. E., 12*: 3–84. London: Hogarth.

Freud, S. (1912–13). *Totem and Taboo. S. E., 13*: 1–164. London: Hogarth.

Freud, S. (1917e). Mourning and melancholia. *S. E., 14*: 237–258. London: Hogarth.

Joseph, B. (1985). Transference: The total situation. *International Journal of Psychoanalysis*, 66: 447–454.

Klein, M. (1946). Notes on some schizoid mechanisms. *International Journal of Psychoanalysis*, 27: 99–110.

Klein, M. (1955). On identification. In: *Envy and Gratitude and Other Works 1946–1963: The Writings of Melanie Klein. Vol. 3*. London: Hogarth.

Kuhn, P. (1962). *The Structure of Scientific Revolutions*. Chicago, IL: University of Chicago Press.

Laufer, M., & Laufer, M. E. (1994). *Adolescence and Developmental Breakdown*. London: Karnac.

Macalpine, R., & Hunter, R. (1955). *Memoirs of My Nervous Illness: Daniel Paul Schreber*. New York: Random House, 2000.

Marx, K. (1843). Towards a critique of Hegel's philosophy of right. In: D. McLellan (Ed.), *Karl Marx Selected Writings*. Oxford: OUP, 2002.

Moncrieff, J. (2008). *The Myth of the Chemical Cure*. London: Palgrave.

O'Shaughnessy, E. (1999). Relating to the superego. *International Journal of Psychoanalysis*, 80: 861–870.

Potter, D. (1986). *The Singing Detective*. London: Faber.

Rosenfeld, H. (1971). A clinical approach to the psychoanalytic theory of the life and death instincts: An investigation into the aggressive aspects of narcissism. *International Journal of Psychoanalysis*, 52: 169–178.

Sandler, J. (1976). Countertransference and role-responsiveness. *International Journal of Psychoanalysis*, 3: 43–47.

Schatzman, M. (1973). *Soul Murder*. New York: Random House.

Segal, H. (1950). Some aspects of the analysis of a schizophrenic. *International Journal of Psychoanalysis*, 31: 268–278.

Westen, D., Gabbard, G. O., & Blagov, P. (2006). Back to the future: Personality structure as a context for psychopathology. In: R. Krueger, & J. Tackett (Eds.), *Personality and Psychopathology*. New York: Guildford Press.

CHAPTER FOUR

The teaching of Klein: some guidelines for opening students to the heart of Kleinian thinking and practice

Rachel B. Blass

Freud in his *The Question of Lay Analysis* (1926e) addresses the problem of teaching psycho-analysis to non-analysts. Speaking to his imaginary interlocutor of that text, "the Impartial Person", he writes:

> When we give our pupils theoretical instruction in psycho-analysis, we can see how little impression we are making on them to begin with. They take in the theories of analysis as coolly as other abstractions with which they are nourished. A few of them may perhaps wish to be convinced, but there is not a trace of their being so. But we also require that everyone who wants to practise analysis on other people shall first himself submit to an analysis. It is only in the course of this "self-analysis" (as it is misleadingly termed), when they actually experience as affecting their own person—or rather, their own mind—the processes asserted by analysis, that they acquire the convictions by which they are later guided as analysts. How then could I expect to convince you, the Impartial Person, of the correctness of our theories, when I can only put before you an abbreviated and therefore unintelligible account of them, without confirming them from your own experiences? (Freud, 1926e, pp. 198–199)

These reflections on the limitations of theoretical study of psychoanalysis are as relevant today as they were in Freud's time. While the content of psychoanalytic propositions can be abstractly taken in, it is difficult to appreciate their meaning and truth without direct experience. As Freud writes elsewhere, it is not "an intellectual difficulty" per se that makes "psychoanalysis ... hard for the hearer or reader to understand, but an affective one—something that alienates the feelings of those who come into contact with it, so that they become less inclined to believe in it or take an interest in it" (Freud, 1917a, p. 137). And he concludes: "where sympathy is lacking, understanding will not come very easily" (ibid.). Indeed, psychoanalysis puts forth ideas that are intellectually challenging, which require study and clarification, but Freud here emphasises the emotional obstacle that is necessarily involved in meeting the challenge. And yet it is clear that if we wish to make psychoanalysis known and understood to people who have not yet experienced analysis themselves such teaching cannot be avoided. Freud himself did not shrink from the task, and one of the major audiences he held in mind in his lectures and writings was that of non-analysts. The question that Freud faced and is still relevant today is how best to deal with the difficulties, the alienation; how to open students to psychoanalytic ideas that are affectively disturbing (Blass, 2001).

Klein's psychoanalytic ideas are in many ways more disturbing than those of Freud and this is the case not only for non-analysts, but for non-Kleinian analysts as well. Freud maintained that the roles that psychoanalysis ascribes to the unconscious and to hidden sexual phantasies and the blow that this inflicts on our narcissism are mainly responsible for the aversion towards it. But these roles are expanded in the writings of Klein and her followers. The details of phantasy life are elaborated, take central place, and are viewed as more primitive. The focus on such primitive phantasies pose special problems for many non-Kleinians. The infant's murderous wishes towards the maternal object, early phantasies regarding the destructive nature of parental intercourse, and basic fears of punishment and death from the very start of life are regarded as contradicting common knowledge regarding infant development. We all know that preverbal babies are incapable of having such complex ideas. Moreover, the notion of aggression being both deadly and innate, while consistent with Freud's concept of the death instinct, tends to be regarded as ungrounded and pessimistic.

Many also find Klein's consistent focus on phantasy to be disturbing, alienating in its neglect of the important role of reality. I speak here not of those who wrongly think that Klein denies the impact of reality on the person's dynamics and well-being, but those who rightly take note that the Kleinian analytic process is basically concerned with the inner world and its interpretation as it finds expression in the transference; that the understandings that it offers are considerably more removed from the patient's conscious experience of his predicament than other analytic approaches, focusing, for example, on primitive anxieties and split-off parts of the mind, including those experienced as bodily parts and products (e.g., breasts, excrements); and that the ability to live in reality is thought to be attained by facilitating the integration of split-off and projected parts of the self in the inner world, rather than by directly clarifying the unconscious meanings of reality (e.g., interpersonal relations) as described by the patient. Non-Kleinians often find this kind of concern with the inner world to be unreasonable and even if referring to something real in the patient, too far from his actual experience to be helpful and also disrespectful of the patient's wishes to have his reality—the source of his distress as he perceives it—directly addressed.

Finally, from within the analytic world one finds aversion to Kleinian analysis based on a view that it is a rival approach to that of Freud. Loyalty to Freud (often more on an emotional level than in terms of actual practice) then closes off the possibility to learn from Klein.

While some of the difficulties with Klein's ideas may be regarded as intellectual ones (e.g., tied to problems in reconciling her ideas with common contemporary conceptualisations of the mind, of thinking and of the object) their understanding and acceptance require more than clarification. The mind needs to be opened to digesting her ideas.

In what follows I will outline some guidelines on how to teach Klein, with a special focus on how to open the student to Klein's thinking and practice, how to allow for the immediate experience and sympathy that, as Freud explains, is essential for true understanding. Based on my experience over many years of teaching Kleinian psychoanalysis, I've found that these guidelines can be helpful in various contexts (one-off seminars to open-ended courses) and to students with varying degrees of familiarity with Klein and in very different positions (e.g., psychoanalysts, candidates, university students from both within and outside of the mental health fields, psychotherapists with varying backgrounds and experience). Moreover, as guidelines it should be clear that what they offer is one general approach, direction, and stance that can be applied in different ways depending on specific circumstances.

In this paper I speak of *how* to teach, but in doing so through illustration, inevitably, I am also drawn into the very process of teaching. While this makes the paper relevant to students as well as teachers of Kleinian psychoanalysis it should be borne in mind that as an exposition of Kleinian psychoanalysis it is clearly limited. This is unavoidable; given the wealth of Kleinian thinking even an outline of its basic ideas cannot be encompassed in any single paper—what is possible is only illustration of a selected few of them.

Some guidelines

Klein's relationship to Freud

It is important to realise that to teach Klein in effect requires teaching something about the relationship between Freud and Klein. That is, to appreciate Klein's contribution we must consider it in terms of what it *adds* to psychoanalysis, how it goes beyond what was already there. Here there is the danger that in describing Klein's contribution, Freud's will seem constricted. For example, when Klein is described in terms of her being concerned with early object relations, early anxieties, and transference interpretation, what's unique about her thinking gets lost. Freud too, in many places shares these concerns (Blass, 2017). Even the notion of the presence of object relationships from birth, often referred to as a hallmark of Kleinian thinking, is something that can be found in Freud, as has been stressed by Klein and her followers (Heimann, 1952, p. 145; Klein, 1952, p. 52). Discussion of more specific ways in which Klein adds to Freud's thinking on relations, anxieties, and interpretation or differs with it, is necessary.

In this context it is important to emphasise *similarity* as well as difference; how Klein's approach emerges from Freud's and relies on it and how Klein, as she herself put it, is essentially Freudian (Grosskurth, 1990, p. 612). There may be variation among Klein teachers on how to conceptualise this similarity, but it is only when it is clear how Klein is grounded in Freud and adopts his concepts that her unique innovations and their value can be truly appreciated. Moreover, acknowledgement of this grounding helps deal with the more emotional aversion to Klein experienced by some who feel strong allegiance to Freud.

Depending on the context and geographical region in which Klein is taught, comparison with additional analytic approaches may be significant. For example, in the light of current interest in Kleinian psychoanalysis in the USA, it may be important to highlight not only its grounding in Freud, but also its notable differences from American relational psychoanalysis.

A non-apologetic stance

I have noticed that one way in which some teachers of Klein try to make her thinking more accessible is by highlighting how contemporary Kleinian analysts have moved away from some of the more disturbing ideas and practices adhered to by the early generation of Kleinian psychoanalysts. It is emphasised, for example, that Kleinian interpretations tend no longer to be so graphic, referring more to functions than body parts (e.g., Spillius, 1994). Or that contemporary Kleinians are more sensitive than Klein was to the patient's ability to make use of interpretations, better taking into account his immediate experience. Experience-near and analyst-centred interpretations are thought to be more acceptable today than in Klein's time and indicative of the shift that has taken place (Busch, 2015). One may question whether the descriptions of such shifts are accurate (Segal & Meltzer, 1963, p. 511), and if they are, whether they are desirable. But more important for the issue of how to teach Klein, this kind of approach may be used in an essentially apologetic way. That is, it may be used to withdraw from what is disturbing in Klein rather than directly tackle the question of the value of her disturbing positions. In this way Kleinian psychoanalysis can become more acceptable to students, but at the price of possibly losing what distinguishes it from other approaches. A non-apologetic stance, in contrast, is directly concerned with the distinguishing features, even if troubling. In analogy, the non-apologetic stance that I'm proposing would not defend Freud against critiques levelled at his *Totem and Taboo* by stating that the analytic world never shared Freud's belief in the factual accuracy of the "prehistory" it describes. Rather, it would try to understand why Freud maintained this belief and how this impacts the theory he offers us (Blass, 2006).

To take some complex Kleinian examples: to help the student contend with Klein's special concern with the interpretation of the inner world, one may point to texts that show that Klein was well aware of the impact of reality on well-being. But in my view this should be introduced as a preliminary step to considering why, in light of this, she retained such a clear inner world focus in the analytic situation; it should not be used to downplay the fact that she held such a focus. The same effort to understand the essence of Klein's thinking should generally be applied even when dealing with ideas and practices that have undergone significant change since Klein's times. We may, for example, teach that many Kleinians do not interpret in such physical terms as Klein did, but we should not use this as a means to free ourselves of the responsibility to explain why Klein did. Her practice in this regard was not simply an embarrassing error, which we could put aside, and with it the alienation that it arouses in the student. Rather, her practice and the thinking that underlies it is something that may be seen to continue to shape contemporary Kleinian analysis and needs to be contended with.

Worldview vs. models

Psychoanalysis could be taught as a series of models: models of the mind and its structures and functions, models of psychopathology, models of development, models of the process of cure and the mechanisms it involves, etc. This approach could be applied to Kleinian psychoanalysis. One could elaborate the paranoid-schizoid and depressive positions, consider Klein's additions to the model of the superego, to thinking process, to defence mechanisms, to the understanding of early development, to severe pathology. Similarly, Klein's clinical innovations could be taught as a series of findings and recommendations (e.g., regarding where and when to interpret). I have found that this kind of teaching of psychoanalytic thinking and practice furthers knowledge of an abstract kind, of what often seems to be a series of somewhat disjointed and not very well-founded psychological propositions, but does not lead to meaningful understanding or to the development of conviction.

One way to further understanding of a meaningful kind is through presenting the student with the worldview that underlies and guides the various Kleinian models. That is, the models are not merely a set of clinically based insights, but rather share and, in part, emerge from a common perspective on human nature: on what it is to be a person, on what kind of relationships are necessary for well-being, are sought or feared, on life and what advances or threatens it, on love, hate, guilt, knowing, feeling, sexuality, creativity, destruction, loss, and death. Once these are appreciated the clinical insights can be better recognised and their significance understood.

To present the worldview effectively is to allow the student to experience it, to feel it rather than merely learn it as a series of propositions. In other words, I'm suggesting that the student can be opened to Kleinian psychoanalysis, that the sense of alienation that it arouses at times can be overcome, through being experientially touched and moved by its conception of the person. The truth of Klein's thinking can be experientially confirmed not only through direct encounter with it in the clinical setting, but also through the resonance within us of the ideas that lie at its heart. In fact, I would suggest that such resonance is crucial for understanding and conviction even where clinical confirmation is available.

The experiential teaching of the Kleinian worldview is made possible, in part, through close reading of great Kleinian texts, which directly address it and do so very movingly. There are many such texts and there are many aspects of this worldview that are important to cover. I have often found especially useful in this regard the 1936 public lectures of Melanie Klein and Joan Riviere, published jointly in 1937 as *Love, Hate and Reparation*. I bring here a brief example of teaching based on sections from Riviere's lecture "Hate, greed and aggression" (1937). I present the text, discuss it, and then reflect on its role in the teaching process. Riviere writes:

A baby at the breast is actually completely dependent on someone else, but has no fear of this, at least to begin with, because he does not recognize his dependence. In fact a baby does not recognize anyone's existence but his own (his mother's breast is to him merely a part of himself—just a sensation at first), and he expects all his wants to be fulfilled. He (or she) wants the breast for love of it, so to speak, for the pleasure of sucking the milk, and also to still hunger. But what happens if these expectations and wants are not fulfilled? In a certain degree the baby becomes aware of his dependence; he discovers that he cannot supply all his own wants—and he cries and screams. He becomes aggressive. He automatically explodes, as it were, with hate and aggressive craving. If he feels emptiness and loneliness, an automatic reaction sets in, which may soon become uncontrollable and overwhelming, an aggressive rage which brings pain and explosive, burning, suffocating, choking bodily sensations; and these in turn cause further feelings of lack, pain and apprehension. The baby cannot distinguish between "me" and "not-me"; his own sensations are his world, *the* world to him; so when he is cold, hungry or lonely there is no milk, no wellbeing or pleasure in the world—the valuable things in life have vanished. And when he is tortured with desire or anger, with uncontrollable, suffocating screaming, and painful, burning evacuations, the whole of his world is one of suffering; it is scalded, torn and racked too. This situation which we all were in as babies has enormous psychological consequences for our lives … It is our first experience of something like death, a recognition of the non-existence of something, of an overwhelming loss, both in ourselves and in others, as it seems. And this experience brings an *awareness of love* (in the form of need), at the same moment as, and inextricably bound up with, feelings and uncontrollable sensations of *pain and threatened destruction* within and without. The baby's world is out of control; a strike and an earthquake have happened in his world, and this is *because* he loves and desires, and such love may bring pain and devastation. Yet he cannot control or eradicate his desire or his hate, or his efforts to seize and obtain; and the whole crisis destroys his well-being. (pp. 172–173, italics in original)

Riviere's almost poetic description of the infant's earliest experiences opens the student to many essential aspects of Klein's view of human nature and the person's predicament. She speaks of the person's basic relationship to the world. It is felt to be that of a lack of differentiation, but that feeling disappears with the very first moment of desire for the breast. It is then that his fundamentally dependent state becomes known to him. And Riviere speaks of the nature of this primary desire, the desire for the breast. It is not simply presented as a physiological state, the expression of an instinctual biological need. She writes: "He (or she) wants the breast for love it … for the pleasure of sucking the milk, and also to still hunger". Taking in the mother's milk means pleasure and satisfaction, but also love. A little later in the lecture Riviere refers to this love of the breast as an experience of its "goodness" and notes that its tie to pleasure and satisfaction is foundational. She explains:

in babyhood, goodness, pleasure and satisfaction were all one and the same thing, identical— all three experienced in one sensation, a good feeling in body and mind alike, a heavenly content. And they remain thus united in the depths, up to the last breath we draw, in spite of the complications and distinctions that we consciously make between them later.

Striking here is not only the complexity and power of experience that is described, but the concern with "depths". Taking forward Freud's concern with unconscious meanings, the range of meanings of the physical event of nursing at the breast is elaborated. In our depths the experienced feeling of content has moral and epistemological value. It informs us of goodness that indeed we have been given, by our mother and the world. This will have monumental significance for the understanding of the role of guilt and destruction in Klein's thinking. Parts of this role are immediately addressed in the rest of Riviere's portrayal of the infant.

Recognition of dependence on the breast and its absence, Riviere tells us, lead to intense physical reactions, crying, and screaming. These reactions are described as an emotional state of rage, hate, and aggression, which brings about pain, including pain of the most physical kinds, "explosive burning, suffocating, choking bodily sensations". These physical reactions only worsen the emotional state of the infant, intensifying the pain and sense of absence. But what is most important to Kleinian thinking here is that these horrific physical reactions and emotional states are rich with meaning to the infant. Through them, as they are experienced in moments of the absence of the desired breast, the baby learns that there is "no well-being or pleasure in the world", the "world is one of suffering". While this is factually untrue, it is the only conclusion the baby "can draw" given the early state of his mind. In his early state of mind and the hateful reaction that it arouses, the absence is an awareness of death, "of an overwhelming loss, both in ourselves and in others, as it seems".

Riviere adds three crucial points to this dramatic picture. First, the horrific experiences described are the lot of us all. While she first invites us to reflect on the "scalded, torn and racked" world of the infant from the distance of a concerned and empathic observer, she then abruptly informs us that it is ourselves that we have been observing. We all were that infant and have suffered his tortured experience. Second, the upshot of this horror, registered in the minds of us all, is "awareness of love". That is, "at the same moment as, and inextricably bound up with, feelings and uncontrollable sensations of *pain and threatened destruction* within and without" comes the recognition of the goodness of the object. There is a recognition, however primitively felt, that there is pain because there is indeed a beloved object, now absent. "A strike and an earthquake have happened in … [the infant's] world, and this is *because* he loves and desires, and such love may bring pain and devastation." And finally, the interplay of love and hate that is here described and the pain that ensues is inevitable. The infant "cannot control or eradicate his desire or his hate, or his efforts to seize and obtain; and the whole crisis destroys his well-being".

In sum, it may be seen how even a small section of a Kleinian text can open the student to essential aspects of the Kleinian worldview. It poignantly depicts the context and consequences of our foundational experiences and gradually invites readers to find them in themselves. In no way does it downplay the power of the desires, recognitions, and feelings that lie in our depths, as well as the hate and aggression that are dominant there. But they are presented as part of meaningful inner realities, not theoretical postulates. As such they become more accessible to the student, more open to confirmation through considering their resonance with one's own experience. The deadliness of innate aggression with which Klein is concerned can then be more sympathetically considered and the centrality of love to her thinking better appreciated. The student may note that this is not a light-hearted worldview but neither is it a dark or pessimistic one as it is stereotypically thought to be by those unfamiliar with it. It is one that significantly elaborates and enriches Freud's thinking on man's love of others (which finds expression in his models of narcissism, the Oedipus complex, the development of drives, etc.), how this love comes in conflict with a wish to destroy others, the anxiety, pain, and guilt that that conflict arouses, and the manifold ways that man finds to deal with it. And it especially stresses that it is not the events in the infant's life per se that determine his predicament but their *meanings*, what the infant thinks about them; his recognition of the goodness of the breast, not its timely presence per se.

The student may also find that developing a good grasp of the worldview helps make sense of the various models that Klein offers and their inter-relationships. For example, if one can actually feel the inner struggle of the infant it is easier to understand Klein's thinking regarding the positions and the defences and how they are inherently tied to each other. Thus, after examining the worldview students unfamiliar with the basic Kleinian models can benefit from their exposition.

The attempt to apply the worldview to various clinical, theoretical, and daily life situations is an important complement to the reading of the text. Riviere herself offers many examples of such application. For instance, in that same lecture she reflects on the character of "the Don Juan". One may recognise in his behaviour, in his moving on from woman to woman, an apparent greediness coming into play, an insatiable longing. But Riviere goes deeper, inquiring into the meanings of his behaviour in the light of what she has shown us to be man's basic predicament. She describes how because of the greed the Don Juan especially fears his dependence on the loved object and fears attacking it out of frustration. In seeking a way of avoiding terrible destruction important defences are employed:

> All the evil impulses in themselves—the hate, greed and revengeful disappointment—they then expel psychologically into the person or work from whom they had expected so much, and perceive it all there; and then naturally feel it both necessary and justified to turn away and flee from that person or work. (1937, p. 182)

But Riviere then returns to elaborate the worldview and even greater complexity ensues. She explains:

> In fleeing from a good thing which has become more or less bad in our eyes, we are—in our minds—*preserving* a vision of goodness which had almost been lost; for by discovering it elsewhere we seem, as it were, to bring it to life again in another place.
>
> We try to make a fantastic "reparation" by acclaiming the goodness unharmed elsewhere. (1937, pp. 182–183)

In other words, man is powerfully motivated by the desire to save goodness (as experienced at the breast) from his own aggression and will, in fact, destroy the beloved in order to believe that she has survived. "Rejection can even be a method of loving, distorted indeed, but aiming at the preservation of something unconsciously felt to be 'too good for me'" (1937, p. 183).

In other examples that Riviere discusses greed itself emerges as an expression of the effort to prove to oneself and to others that one is indeed loved (e.g., through the accumulation of material goods). And underlying that effort is, once again, the knowledge of one's destructiveness, which renders the person (so he feels) unworthy of love.

Through considering these illustrations and actively reflecting on them the student has the opportunity to become more familiar with the Kleinian perspective. This, too, helps overcome the initial alienation that students may feel.

Making sense of phantasy

In teaching the student about the Kleinian worldview the concept of phantasy inevitably arises. For example, we would naturally refer to Riviere's description of what goes on in the infant's mind as phantasising (about the breast, the mother, the world, absence, destructiveness, etc.). While the concept of phantasy could be regarded as yet another aspect of the Kleinian worldview (e.g., relating to perspectives on the mind, thinking, and the body), the role ascribed to phantasy is so dominant and the alienation it arouses, at times, is so strong that the issue of teaching about phantasy deserves special attention. There are numerous introductory articles on the Kleinian concept of phantasy, but to deal with the alienation and also to bring out Klein's unique contribution there's a question of how to best make use of these texts in the teaching situation.

How to make sense of early phantasy and the notion of preverbal, bodily knowledge

I've found it helpful to directly address the issue of phantasy after the students have already read some Kleinian texts and have become familiar with the *contents* of some Kleinian phantasies. Having done so I can present the students with the problem (which often will have already been raised by them) that Klein's notion of phantasy seems obviously wrong. It ascribes to the infant thought processes that are clearly beyond his capacity. One doesn't need to have examined psychological research to know that the infant can't think the thoughts that having Kleinian phantasies would seem to suggest that he does. This point would be an obstacle even to the student who has begun to warm to the contents of the phantasies that Kleinian psychoanalysis offers. She may sense their truth, and yet feel that their early origin is surely mistaken.

To address this issue and to explain phantasy I always have found it useful to first turn to Isaacs' classic text, "The nature and function of phantasy" (1948). And again, I offer here a brief illustration.

In introducing the text I mention the fact that it is one of the papers of the Controversial Discussions, highlighting that the Kleinian understanding of phantasy has distinguished it from the start from other analytic approaches and that the objections that it has aroused have always been openly addressed. This suggests that the Kleinian response, its justification of its notion of phantasy, is not a simple one that can be readily digested; the difficulties with it are not simply intellectual ones.

Through the study of Isaacs' text the student can come to see how the response has to do with the non-propositional, nonverbal nature of Kleinian phantasy. Isaacs gets to the relevant points seven pages into her paper. She first outlines the basic Freudian grounds of the concept, explaining that unconscious phantasy is what Freud referred to as the mental expression of instinct (Isaacs, 1948, p. 81). She then tries to elaborate what this means exactly, and it is apparent that this isn't an easy task. She states that "[a] phantasy represents the particular content of the urges or feelings (for example, wishes, fears, anxieties, triumphs, love or sorrow) dominating the mind at the moment." But what this "representation" means is hard to explain. Isaacs suggests that turning to examine some specific phantasies may help, but that too is problematic:

> In attempting to give such examples of specific phantasies we are naturally obliged to put them into words; we cannot describe or discuss them without doing so. This is clearly not their original character and inevitably introduces a foreign element, one belonging to later phases of development, and to the preconscious mind. (p. 82)

She later asserts that phantasies originally "spring from bodily impulses and are interwoven with bodily sensations and affects" and goes on to explain that in the bodily experience there is a kind of inherent knowledge that differs from conscious knowledge associated with mature understanding and words. Isaacs' text is very direct and explanatory. She writes:

> It has sometimes been suggested that unconscious phantasies such as that of 'tearing to bits' would not arise in the child's mind before he had gained the conscious knowledge that tearing a person to bits would mean killing them. Such a view does not meet the case. It overlooks the fact that such knowledge is *inherent* in bodily impulses as a vehicle of instinct, in the excitation of the organ, i.e. in this case, the mouth. The phantasy that his passionate impulses will destroy the breast does not require the infant to have actually seen objects eaten up and destroyed, and then to have come to the conclusion that he could do it too. This aim, this relation to the object, is inherent in the character and direction of the impulse itself, and in its related affects. (pp. 86–87, italics in original)

The illustrations that she goes on to offer help grasp this complex idea. Here's one such instance:

> In the phantasy: "I want to drown and burn mother with my urine", we have an expression of the infant's fury and aggression, the wish to attack and annihilate mother by means of his urine, partly because of her frustrating him. He wishes to flood her with urine in burning anger. The "burning" is an expression both of his own bodily sensations and of the intensity of his rage. The "drowning", too, expresses the *feeling* of his intense hate and of his omnipotence, when he floods his mother's lap. The infant feels: "I *must* annihilate my bad mother." He overcomes his feeling of helplessness by the omnipotent phantasy: "I can and *will* destroy her"—by whatever means he possesses; and when urinary sadism is at its height, what he feels he can do is to flood and burn her with his urine. Doubtless the "flooding" and "burning" also refer to the way in which he feels *he* is overcome, flooded, by his helpless rage, and burnt up by it. The whole world is full of his anger, and he will himself be destroyed by it if he cannot vent it on his mother, discharging it on her with his urine. (p. 87, italics in original)

Isaacs then explains that when one meets in the external world events that correspond to the bodily experience the knowledge contained in the experience can be expressed verbally.

> The rush of water from the tap, the roaring fire, the flooding river or stormy sea, when these are seen or known as external realities, link up in his mind with his early bodily experiences, instinctual aims and phantasies. And when he is given names for these things, he can *then* sometimes put these phantasies into words. (p. 87, italics in original)

I have found that it's important to help the student grasp these new ideas; how the enraged frustrated baby feels that he is burning with anger and this experience contains in it knowledge of destruction, both of the self and the object, but not knowing the meaning of "burning" and "destruction" or the causal relationship between the two he obviously can't think about destruction through burning in the regular sense of thinking. Another, nonverbal, non-propositional sense of thinking or knowing here comes into play. It is only when the baby encounters fire that he can then say that he was burning with anger and speak of the destruction felt, but he knew it beforehand. In fact, I suggest to the students that what we feel about fire in our first encounter with it is because we knew about it beforehand. Similarly, our first reaction to ocean waves may be tied to our personal early experienced knowledge of being emotionally overwhelmed. Once again, such examples from daily life, from personal experience, are helpful—here to grasping notions of knowledge that at first seem alien.

It's important to note that the preverbal knowledge of phantasies that Isaacs presents is also about goodness, not only destruction. Isaacs writes:

> Phantasies of fæces and urine as beneficent are certainly strengthened by the fact that mother is pleased when he gives them at the proper time and place; but his observation of his mother's pleasure is not the primary origin of his feeling of them as good. The source of this lies in his *wish* to give them as good—e.g. to feed his mother as she has fed him, to please her and do what she wants; and in his feeling of the goodness of his organs and of his body as a whole, when he is loving her and feeling her good to him. His urine and fæces are then instruments of his potency in love, just as his voice and smile can also be. (p. 86, italics in original)

Exploring rich sections such as these allows the student to reflect on additional aspects of phantasy, for example, different meanings of Klein's notion of goodness and the role of reality in phantasy. And indeed, having opened the student to the very meaning of phantasy and the nonverbal knowledge that it contains, other central aspects of phantasy can and should be addressed.

Phantasy as the material of the mind

When coming to understand the concept of phantasy, students tend to equate it with representation. This may in part be due to the influence of Otto Kernberg's thinking and of cognitive theories; however, it's interesting to note that this tendency was recognised and considered to be problematic already at the time of the introduction of Klein's ideas. Isaacs writes:

> The problem of how best to describe the process of introjection related to the phantasy of incorporation is often dealt with by saying that what *is* introjected is an image or "imago". This is surely quite correct; but it is too formal and meagre a statement of a complex phenomenon to do justice to the facts. (Isaacs, 1948, p. 92, italics in original)

Bringing out similarities and differences between representation and phantasy sharpens awareness to the Kleinian contribution (see Blass, 2015). Of special importance is the fact that while representation may be conceived as something that takes place in the mind, from a Kleinian perspective phantasy is not *in* the mind, but rather the material (so to speak) that the mind is made of. What this means is that changes in our phantasies have a direct and concrete impact on our states of mind. Elsewhere I have explained that this position is based on two foundational ideas:

> first, that both I and my objects are me. For example, in my relationship with a maternal object in my inner world, both myself and the maternal object are parts of myself and are composed

of various parts of myself. The second idea is that my objects *are* my mind. Thus if in my phantasy I have attacked the maternal object, not only is part of myself under attack, put also part
of my mind may be damaged. (Blass, 2017, italics in original)

Isaacs presents a very potent illustration of this state of affairs (in a different version of her
phantasy paper). She refers to a child who phantasises cutting up his mother:

> *When the child feels he has dismembered his mother, his mental life is split and disintegrated*—he
> shows the most acute anxiety, he is confused and behaves chaotically, he cannot see or hear or
> control what he does and says, and so on. It is not that, *first*, his mental life becomes disinte-
> grated and he *then* interprets this as having dismembered his mother; it is *because he wants to
> dismember his mother*, intends to, tries to and in imagination does so, that he feels his own ego
> to be split and disintegrated, and shows in his behaviour that "mental disintegration" which
> we can describe and label and talk about.
>
>   We, for our purpose of comparing one mind with another and making generalizations,
> can see what happens to the child, the way he behaves, and can describe it as "mental dis-
> integration." But the child experiences it as "my-mother-inside-me-is-in bits." (Isaacs, 1943,
> pp. 275–276, italics in original)

It is very important to bring this distinction to the student's attention as it is a major distinguishing feature of Kleinian psychoanalysis, one that effects theory and practice alike. Conceiving
of phantasies not merely as content of the mind, but its material, means that changes in phantasy have real effects on the capacity to think. From this follows the central role of thinking in
Kleinian psychoanalysis and the analyst's attunement to it in the analytic setting (a fact that provides the grounds for teaching Bion's main ideas on "thinking" as a development that's integral
to the Kleinian framework). It effects other aspects of the individual's reality as well. Speaking
of the phantasy of incorporation Isaacs writes:

> It is not an actual bodily eating up and swallowing, yet it leads to actual alterations in the ego.
> These "mere" beliefs about internal objects, such as, e.g. "I have got a good breast inside me",
> or, it may be: "I have got a bitten-up, torturing bad breast inside me—I must kill it and get
> rid of it", and the like, lead to real effects: deep emotions, actual behaviour towards external
> people, profound changes in the ego, character and personality, symptoms, inhibitions and
> capacities. (p. 92)

Isaacs highlights how this way of thinking about phantasy relies on Freud's thinking, but in so
doing she also makes the difference ever more clear. What are fears, wishes, and feelings of loss
in Freud become relational events of the mind that shape its functioning. The "dread of being
killed by the mother" of which Freud speaks is, Isaacs explains, "obviously a way of describing
the child's phantasy of a murderous mother" (p. 84). And the child's sense of having lost the
mother of which he speaks "means his phantasy is that his mother has been destroyed (by his
own hate or greed) and altogether lost" (p. 83). The child's mind is formed by these phantasied
mothers and they determine his way of being and thinking as well as how he experiences being

and thinking. That is, for example, a phantasy of splitting the object may lead to a disintegrated way of thinking and will also be present in the act of thinking in that way. Similarly a phantasy of projection of parts of oneself into the other may lead to a sense of emptiness or stupidity (depending on how in phantasy the original location of the object is conceived of), but also one of the meanings of the feeling of emptiness will be that objects have been projected, that the person feels emptied out of his objects. Here it becomes apparent that Klein's contribution to Freud is not merely the addition of themes and dynamics, but in a more foundational way changes the way we think of the person.

The ongoing presence of phantasy in life and pathology

Another crucial aspect of phantasy, important to the understanding of the Kleinian perspective and to making it accessible to the student, has to do with the ongoing role of phantasy in our life. As the mind is made of phantasy, we always perceive reality through it. As Isaacs explains:

> In their developed forms, phantasy thinking and reality thinking are distinct mental processes, different modes of obtaining satisfaction. The fact that they have a distinct character when fully developed, however, does not necessarily imply that reality thinking *operates* quite independently of unconscious phantasy. It is not merely that they "blend and interweave"; their relationship is something less adventitious than this. On our view, *reality-thinking cannot operate without concurrent and supporting unconscious phantasies*. E.g. we continue to "take things in" with our ears, to "devour" with our eyes, to "read, mark, learn and inwardly digest", throughout life. (1948, p. 94, italics in original)

The fact that the metaphors that are integral to our everyday language are in tune with this idea of phantasy makes the idea more convincing to the student; she can feel their relevance in her own life. It also facilitates comprehension of some aspects of phantasy that are not always easy to grasp; how phantasies are not actually representations or imaginary ideas as opposed to realistic ones. They are rather the very prism through which reality is seen.

In light of this understanding of phantasy the Kleinian conception of pathology can be better understood. It can be seen how it's not a matter of the presence or absence of phantasies or of phantasies of certain kinds, but rather the omnipotent imposition of phantasy in disregard for reality, imposition which usually involves projective identification. It is the projection of good or bad parts of oneself in a way that doesn't fit with the actual nature of things that is problematic.

In turn, reflection on this notion of pathology opens the student to additional important aspects of the Kleinian worldview, and a more integrated picture emerges. What becomes apparent is that like other traditional analytic theories the notion of health or normality is very much tied up with that of being able to see reality clearly (Klein, 1950, p. 46), but Kleinian analysis emphasises that reality is not simply the objective facts of the matter. Rather it is rich in meaning and relational and moral significance. To recognise reality as it is, is to experience it deeply and this means to be able to involve our phantasies in our encounter with it; to emotionally encounter it (ibid.). It is for aspects of the phantasy of the good breast to come alive when faced with good and of the bad breast when faced with bad. Here, too, examples from daily life are helpful. For instance, it may be pointed out how in enjoying a good meal phantasies of the good breast may enrich the meal, bringing out for us in an experiential way the significance of the meal, its goodness, the sense of gratitude that that arouses in us. The phantasy will deepen the pleasure and satisfaction. Of course, the situation would be very different if the good breast shaped our experience of a terrible meal. We would then have imposition and distortion.

Reflection on the relationships between pathology and the imposition of phantasy on reality sheds light not only on how reality is conceived in the Kleinian worldview, but also how this worldview conceives of the nature of man's relationship to it. For example, it reveals how the person's openness to reality and his desire to know it is posited from the start and is seen as a manifestation of loving phantasies and the life instincts. In contrast, distortion of reality through imposing phantasies on it may be regarded as a hateful relationship to reality, involving destructive phantasies and the death instincts, the imposition itself entailing not only a wish not to know it but also the denial of the very otherness of reality, of its independence of the mind of the person who omnipotently projects on to it. In other words, what becomes apparent is that love and hate are directed not only towards objects in reality, but rather reality itself is an object that arouses love and hate and that health is founded on love of reality, of respect of its otherness (Blass, 2016; Segal 1962).

Considering things in this way the student gains a deeper understanding of the place of narcissism in the Kleinian worldview. She not only learns that Klein posits object relations from the start and does not have a concept of primary narcissism, or that these ideas are based on her clinical work. Rather, coming in touch with Klein's broader perspective on the person, the student can see how integral to the heart of her thinking is the notion that the healthy person would not want to impose himself on reality and narcissistically take it over and hence destroy it, he would love its otherness and independence even though this may be a source of pain.

My point here is that elaborating this broader perspective through the readings of Kleinian texts helps the student contain, make sense of, and confirm through her own experience many different Kleinian propositions, even in the absence of the direct clinical experience, which as Freud claimed, is normally needed for conviction.

The Kleinian stance and the analytic process

Another central aspect of the Kleinian worldview that deserves special attention has to do with how the analytic process should take place and the role of the analyst within it. Here too, there is the possibility of teaching Klein in terms of basic principles, for example, that Kleinian analysis is focused on the interpretation of transference "in the here and now", that one seeks to interpret the most dominant anxiety, that it's important to take note of the projective identification, that one should be attentive to countertransference (although it's usually emphasised that Klein herself objected to this). The process too can be summarised in terms of moves towards the depressive position and integrating split-off parts of the self. But for such principles to be meaningful they have to be considered as integral to the Kleinian perspective on the person and on phantasy. One has to consider *how* in light of this perspective interpretation within the here and now of the transference furthers change and how it changes the phantasies or the tendency to omnipotently impose on reality. Without such meaningful integration not only may the principles seem arbitrary but also both rigid and unreasonable. Why stick to transference interpretation when there are apparently other things going on, for example, life problems that the patient is talking about and seeking help with? How can the analyst make interpretations that are outside of the patient's immediate experience (seemingly therefore emerging from the adoption of an authoritarian stance)?

There are many Kleinian texts that are helpful to teaching in this regard. These include papers that directly attempt to clarify the heart of the analytic process and the analyst's role, such as Strachey's (1934) "The nature of the therapeutic action of psycho-analysis", Klein's paper "On the criteria for the termination of a psycho-analysis" (1950), Segal's "The curative factors in psycho-analysis" (1962), her "Postscript on technique"(1964), or her "Uses and abuses of countertransference" (1997) or some of Betty Joseph's papers on the Kleinian uses of transference (e.g., 1985, 1987) or on her view of psychic change (1992). Equally important are papers that offer clinical illustrations that powerfully illustrate how Kleinian analysis conceives of the analytic process or the change that takes place through it. One illustration of an analytic process, which I find particularly helpful, actually takes place outside of an analytic situation proper. This is the case of Mrs A in Klein's "Mourning and its relation to manic depressive states" (1940). Closely reading parts of this case brings out different basic aspects of the process of analytic change, for example, how insight has the power to change our phantasies and the very nature of our inner objects. Again, I offer a short illustration.

I briefly summarise for the students parts of the background of the case and the events leading up to the central transformative moment, which centre on the death of her son. I refer to Mrs A's difficulty in dealing with the death and how she, in part, denied this reality by maintaining the idea in her inner world that "my mother's son died, and not my own". Having ambivalent feelings towards both her brother and her mother allowed for feelings of triumph in relation to them to arise and take the place of sorrow Mrs A would have felt (and in a sense was feeling) over the death of her own son. These underlying thoughts, which emerged through analysis of Mrs A's dreams, are presented by Klein as important expressions of Mrs A's manic defences.

For some students this view of the dynamics is first felt to be proof of Melanie's Klein's negative view of the person and the morbid focus of her approach. Rather than recognise Mrs A's pain and sorrow in the face of her terrible loss she's concerned with the hate that emerges from old family rivalries. But the disdain that students feel here precisely helps bring out the power of Klein's thinking and of the analytic process. It provides the opportunity to help the student see how this understanding of Mrs A reflects Klein's willingness to face head-on the depths of the mind, including the dark sides of the mind that come to the fore at moments of pain. It also demonstrates how this willingness enriches our appreciation of the person's great forces of love and her poignant struggles to give them expression. It may be seen that Klein understands how Mrs A's denial is also "denial of the psychical reality that she and her internal mother were one and suffered together" (p. 357).

I then address Klein's description of the process of change that Mrs A underwent. It entails recognition of her rivalry with her mother and brother and murderous feelings towards them. In her mind, Mrs A, Klein explains, "made reparation to her parents for having, in phantasy, killed their children, and by this she also averted their wrath" (p. 358). This psychic process, in turn, opens her to other experiences, good ones, of her maternal object, formerly felt to be punishing and retaliating, which then allows her to weaken the hold of the manic defences. We focus on the following section in which Klein emphasises the positive cycle that ensues (pp. 142–143):

> It seems that the processes of projecting and ejecting which are closely connected with giving vent to feelings, are held up in certain stages of grief by an extensive manic control, and can again operate more freely when that control relaxes. Through tears, which in the unconscious mind are equated to excrement, the mourner not only expresses his feelings and thus eases tension, but also expels his "bad" feelings and his "bad" objects, and this adds to the relief obtained through crying. This greater freedom in the inner world implies that the internalized objects, being less controlled by the ego, are also allowed more freedom: that these objects themselves are allowed, in particular, greater freedom of feeling. In the mourner's situation, the feelings of his internalized objects are also sorrowful. In his mind, they share his grief, in the same way as actual kind parents would.... This experience of mutual sorrow and sympathy in internal relationships, however, is again bound up with external ones. As I have already stated, Mrs. A.'s greater trust in actual people and things and help received from the external world contributed to a relaxing of the manic control over her inner world. Thus introjection (as well as projection) could operate still more freely, more goodness and love could be taken in from without, and goodness and love increasingly experienced within. Mrs. A., who at an earlier stage of her mourning had to some extent felt that her loss was inflicted on her by revengeful parents, could now in phantasy experience the sympathy of these parents (dead long since), their desire to support and to help her. She felt that they also suffered a severe loss and shared her grief, as they would have done had they lived. In her internal world harshness and suspicion had diminished, and sorrow had increased. The tears which she shed were also to some extent the tears which her internal parents shed, and she also wanted to comfort them as they—in her phantasy—comforted her.

This paragraph offers a succinct description—both exceptionally clear and moving—of one way in which understanding can bring about dramatic inner change. It allows for recognition of goodness, which in turn contributes to release of manic control, which allows for a fuller, truer, and hence less paranoid, experience of the object. While there is a great emphasis here on love and its transformative power, it is important for the student to distinguish the Kleinian approach from other approaches that instead encourage the patient to give expression to unconscious loving forces or even offer the patient parental love and support in an effort to bring about change. It may be seen that the kind of change that Klein regarded as analytic was change through understanding, through an encounter with truth, through a struggle with the inner realities that blind us to it. It is only when love is made available in this way that a meaningful psychoanalytic process—not one of suggestion and seduction—has taken place. The students' experience of the power of these insights into human nature is usually enhanced when at the end of the study of the case of Mrs A I mention that it is now known that she is Melanie Klein herself.

Through texts like these, which bring out the depth of the Kleinian process, the initial aversion to the Kleinian perspective that students feel often undergoes dramatic change. Through them the students have the opportunity to some extent to "actually experience as affecting their own person—or rather, their own mind—the processes asserted by analysis" as Freud had put it (Freud, 1926e). They let one feel how opening to the inner world of phantasy that Klein sets before us one encounters destructive forces, but of a very human kind, not blind aggression, and how the person's struggles with these forces are meaningful ones, understandable, and painful. In the understanding and compassion that students come to feel towards Mrs A they also tend to experience some sense of the transformative value of such understanding, its reparative potential, and, more generally, the richness and value of the person as seen in light of Klein's thinking. And they then wish to come to know it more.

Conclusion

Teaching psychoanalysis is a difficult task and I have argued that this is especially so when it comes to the teaching of Kleinian psychoanalysis. To meet the task the teacher must find ways of countering feelings of aversion and alienation that students often first feel towards Kleinian ideas and in this chapter I have suggested a few ways of doing so. They all involve boldly bringing out what is unique to Kleinian psychoanalysis and reflecting on the view of the person and of life that it relies on. It is important that these reflections come alive for the student, for true learning and conviction is gained through immediate experience. Close study of important Kleinian texts allows this experience.

References

Blass, R. B. (2001). On the teaching of the Oedipus complex: On making Freud meaningful to university students by unveiling his essential ideas on the human condition. *International Journal of Psychoanalysis, 82*: 1105–1121.

Blass, R. B. (2006). The role of authority in grounding and concealing truth, "Truth and Tradition in Psychoanalysis". *American Imago, 63*: 331–353.

Blass, R. B. (2015). Conceptualizing splitting: On the different meanings of splitting and their implications for the understanding of the person and the analytic process. *International Journal of Psychoanalysis, 96*: 123–139.

Blass, R. B. (2016). The quest for truth as the foundation of psychoanalytic practice: A traditional, Freudian-Kleinian perspective. *Psychoanalytic Quarterly, 85*: 305–337.

Blass, R. B. (2017). Bion as a Kleinian: An elaboration of the phantasy of the mind in "Attacks on linking". In: C. Bronstein, & E. O'Shaughnessy (Eds.), *Attacks on Linking Revisited: Psychoanalytic Ideas and Application Series*. London: Karnac.

Busch, F. (2015). Our vital profession. *International Journal of Psychoanalysis, 96*: 553–568.

Freud, S. (1917a). A difficulty in the path of psycho-analysis. *S. E., 17*: 135–144. London: Hogarth.

Freud, S. (1926e). *The Question of Lay Analysis. S. E., 20*: 177–258. London: Hogarth.

Grosskurth, P. (1990). Review of *Between Freud and Klein: The Psychoanalytic Quest for Knowledge and Truth*, Adam Limentani. London: Free Association Books, 1989. *Psychoanalytic Review, 77*: 612–614.

Heimann, P. (1952). Certain functions of introjection and projection in early infancy. In: M. Klein, P. Heimann, S. Isaacs, & J. Riviere (Eds.), *Developments in Psychoanalysis* (pp. 122–168). London: Hogarth.

Isaacs, S. (1943). The nature and function of phantasy. In: P. King, & R. Steiner (Eds.), *The Freud-Klein Controversies 1941–1945* (pp. 264–321). London: Routledge, 1991.

Isaacs, S. (1948). The nature and function of phantasy. *International Journal of Psychoanalysis, 29*: 73–97.

Joseph, B. (1985). Transference: the total situation. *International Journal of Psychoanalysis, 66*: 447–454.

Joseph, B. (1987). Projective identification: Some clinical aspects. In: *Psychic Equilibrium and Psychic Change: Selected Papers of Betty Joseph* (pp. 168–180). London: Routledge.

Joseph, B. (1992). Psychic change: Some perspectives. *International Journal of Psychoanalysis, 73*: 237–243.

Klein, M. (1940). Mourning and its relation to manic depressive states. In: *Love, Guilt and Reparation and Other Works, 1921–1945* (pp. 344–369). London: Karnac, 1975.

Klein, M. (1950). On the criteria for the termination of a psycho-analysis. *In: Envy and Gratitude and Other Works, 1946–1963* (pp. 43–44). London: Karnac, 1975.

Klein, M. (1952). The origins of transference. In: *Envy and Gratitude and Other Works, 1946–1963* (pp. 48–56). London: Karnac, 1975.

Riviere, J. (1937). Hate, greed and aggression. In: A. Hughes (Ed.), *The Inner World and Joan Riviere* (pp. 168–205). London: Karnac.

Segal, H. (1962). The curative factors in psycho-analysis. *International Journal of Psychoanalysis, 43*: 212–217.

Segal, H. (1964). Postscript on technique. In: *Introduction to the Work of Melanie Klein* (pp. 117–123). London: Hogarth.

Segal, H. (1997). The uses and abuses of counter-transference. In: *Psychoanalysis, Literature and War* (pp. 90–96). London: Routledge.

Segal, H., & Meltzer, D. (1963). Narrative of a child analysis. *International Journal of Psychoanalysis, 44*: 507–513.

Spillius, E. B. (1994). Developments in Kleinian thought: Overview and personal view. *Psychoanalytic Inquiry, 14*: 324–364.

Strachey, J. (1934). The nature of the therapeutic action of psycho-analysis. *International Journal of Psychoanalysis, 15*: 127–159.

CHAPTER FIVE

The sense of self: generosity or narrow-mindedness?

Michael Brearley

Introduction

As a young Army doctor during the Second World War, Eric Brenman, an independent-minded Kleinian analyst, who died in 2012, was sent up-country in Ghana, then the Gold Coast, to treat a man in a wild state, accused of a serious crime. The chief of the man's tribe observed: "That poor fellow has no home for his feelings." Eric was struck by this phrase and remembered it in his subsequent thinking as a psychoanalyst. In one of his papers (1985) he describes some of the ways in which we find ourselves in, or resort to, homeless states, rather than find ways of coming to terms with our hatred, guilt, and anxiety, often originally towards our parents (and later our analyst). In my paper I will make use both of Brenman's notion of narrow-mindedness, and of the central importance of finding a home for ones feelings, in determining what kind of a self, or selves, we develop.

The self

We have quite opposite views of the self and its significance in our lives. On the one hand, there is the need for a strong self, and for a sense of it; on the other hand, there is a meaning of "self" according to which the small, petty (from the French "*petit*") self dominates and limits us. Religions invoke the need for control of and lessening of self and selfishness. Buddhism invites us to give up our desires; yet we are to desire this desire-less state. Perhaps we need to think of two versions of the self, even two selves; to recognise a narcissistic self, narrow, two-dimensional; and also a broader, more generous self, a bigger self, one that is three-dimensional, a true subject of thoughts and feelings, a self that knows it does not know itself fully. One self desires in a possessive and narcissistic way, or it undoes wanting in a deadly way; the other, though not without passion, is capable of desiring more dispassionately, more reflectively and compassionately, with less need to control.

There are differing degrees of integration between these selves. At times, and with some people, the split is absolute enough to warrant the description "two selves", with experiences, thoughts, and feelings appearing, in different veins, under the aegis and according to the agenda of one or other self; in other people the two are more interwoven, and it feels more accurate to think of aspects or sides of the self rather than separate selves. Certainly, some babies are born more generous than others, more accommodating towards their mother's and the world's failings towards them. Such accommodation may be a sort of insensitivity—they feel less hurt, whether by nature or by denial—but it may also be that these infants are more capable of tolerating pain, discomfort, or frustration. And, of course, the more generous and solid the mother and others are towards the child, the more chance the child has of developing a sound and generous self.

A central aim of analysis is the growth and integration of the self. It is a human tendency to restrict ourselves, to shut out parts of ourselves. D. H. Lawrence coruscatingly attacks Benjamin Franklin for envisaging the self too narrowly, too tamely. He writes: "The *wholeness* of a man is his soul. Not merely that nice little comfortable bit which Benjamin marks out ... The soul of man is a dark vast forest, with wild life in it. Think of Benjamin fencing it off!" (Lawrence, 1923, pp. 16–17).

This enlargement of the self often frightens us. This fear must be the origin of the contemptuous term for a psychoanalyst, namely, "shrink". In fact, psychoanalysts aim to do just the opposite: we aim to enlarge.

The generous self and the narrow-minded self

I want to emphasise the element of generosity in the depressive position. This way of speaking offers a somewhat different emphasis from, but a similar meaning and reference to, Melanie Klein's distinction between paranoid-schizoid thinking and depressive position thinking.

Klein emphasises that: "The fact that at the beginning of post-natal life an unconscious knowledge of the breast exists and that feelings towards the breast are experienced can only be conceived of as a phylogenetic inheritance ... We have good reasons to assume that the infant's impulses bound up with the sensations of the mouth direct him towards the mother's breast, for the object of his first instinctual desires is the nipple and their aim is to suck the nipple" (1952, p. 117, n. 1). We are object-seeking from the beginning, no doubt often voraciously so.

Klein wrote directly about generosity only rarely. Here is an example: "Enjoyment is always bound up with gratitude; if this gratitude is deeply felt it includes the wish to return goodness received and is thus the basis of generosity. There is always a close connection between being able to accept and to give, and both are part of the relation to the good object" (1963, p. 310). For Klein, generosity is present in the earliest self in its response to the bounteous good breast. Such idealised generosity needs modification, of course, both in terms of realism about the self and the object (neither is so all-giving), and in terms of recognising that (apparent) generosity may be self-serving, or admiration-seeking, or based more on guilt and duty than on love.

My emphasis on generosity chimes with Donald Winnicott's highlighting of "concern for the other" (1963, p. 73) in preferring this term to Klein's "depressive position". The latter term may sometimes be used to imply that concern grows primarily out of a sense of guilt for attacks on loved figures, so that it can be thought of as a wish to make good for these, rather than as (also) something more expressive of love and the wish to give than only a matter of reparation. I think Klein sometimes represents love as if it were essentially reparative, and for an idealised object.

Especially in her later papers, however, Klein does emphasise both the actual giving of the parent-figures, and the loving impulses of the infant and child. In "Envy and gratitude" (1957), for example, she writes: "The more often gratification at the breast is experienced and fully accepted, the more often enjoyment and gratitude, and accordingly the wish to return pleasure, are felt. This recurrent experience makes possible gratitude on the deepest level and plays an important role in the capacity to make reparation, and in all sublimations (1957, p. 189)." She goes on: "Gratitude is closely bound up with generosity. Inner wealth derives from having assimilated the good object so that the individual becomes able to share its gifts with others. This makes it possible to introject a more friendly outer world, and a feeling of enrichment ensues. Even the fact that generosity is often insufficiently appreciated does not necessarily undermine the ability to give." And the fact that "[w]e frequently encounter expressions of gratitude which turn out to be prompted mainly by feelings of guilt, and much less by the capacity for love", and that "the distinction between such guilty feelings and gratitude on the deepest level is important"—these facts do not impugn but enhance the recognition that gratitude, generosity, and love are central features of the depressive position.

Indeed, they must be present in the paranoid-schizoid position too, though in that case they are more split-off from the hostility, and there is less capacity for reparation and integration. What the depressive position (or "the capacity for concern"), ushers in is the gradual bringing together of the objects of love and hate, and the wish to protect the object from one's attacks without splitting them off from each other so absolutely. It includes not only a less persecutory guilt, but also, as Winnicott suggests, concern. A more mature love accommodates ambivalence, giving a home to both love and hate, and includes a wish to repair and make amends for the damage done to the object. The generosity of the depressive position embraces not only the loving impulses but also a greater degree of integration in which love predominates over hatred. There is also the thread of love woven into the wish to make reparation.

Brenman's opening remark in his paper "Cruelty and narrow-mindedness" (1985, p. 273), — "In normal development, love modifies cruelty; in order to perpetuate cruelty, steps have to be taken to prevent human love from operating"—seems right to me, reflecting the presence of both tendencies and the tussle between them.

Generosity, then, includes taking responsibility for one's attacks on the other, attacks in which the object is denuded of good qualities. The generous self regards others as unique centres of experience rather than as merely means to our own ends, or as merged with ourselves. It values freedom and responsibility, since, given the right support at the right time, we all have some capacity to rise above our more or less unfortunate contexts and backgrounds, above our narcissistic tendencies, to go beyond our gut reactions or our merely following rules compliantly. The generous self is open to challenges (up to a point); it knows that it doesn't have the last word on its own history and current state, and that it doesn't know the limits of its possibilities. Novelist and essayist Marilynne Robinson writes of a vision of the soul, which is "wholly realist in acknowledging the great truth of the centrality of human consciousness, wholly open in that it anticipates and welcomes disruption of present values in the course of finding truer ones" (2012, p. xiv). I would say that we are never "wholly" realist or "wholly" open; but we may be more or less so, and the vision is there as an ideal. The generous self is also generous *to* the self; it does not readily resort to despair or to *mea culpa* states of mind; or, finding itself in such places, it is better able to recover rather than become trapped there.

Generosity includes in its penumbra of meanings or associations the notion of creativity—another element that Klein recognises. The passage from the paper "On loneliness" I quoted earlier continues: "Furthermore, the feeling of generosity underlies creativeness, and this applies to the infant's most primitive constructive activities as well as to the creativeness of the adult" (1963, p. 310). It also implies what I would like to call generativity, for it tends to call forth more generous responses from others.

The contrasting state—the narcissistic self—is indeed a narrowing of what we are capable of. We limit ourselves in self-protective, self-indulging ways. We inhabit a different frame of mind, a different kind of mentation. One patient described such a state as "being in a tunnel".

In my analysis, I remember being disconcerted by my analyst's way of picking up this kind of limitation in me. When I would come to a pause in what I had to say about whatever we were discussing, he might ask: "Do you have anything else to say about that?" Feeling harried, I would reply, touchily, perhaps, or defiantly, "No, I don't think so". There would be a short pause. "You surprise me," he would respond, tersely. Once I had got over my outrage and offence, I could see that there was in fact something encouraging in this apparently sardonic comment. He thought I had more in me than I knew; he was not only, or not primarily, pointing up my limitation. Rather he was giving me credit for being capable of more awareness than I was showing, or knowing, at that moment. I was bigger than I thought.

We may well switch from one state to another, sometimes in alarmingly sudden ways, so that we quickly become cut off, or cut ourselves off, temporarily or more permanently, from our larger selves. Our trains of thought and feeling are (in the image of a patient I refer to later) on different rails or tracks, and we can't easily jump back to the mainline.

Psychoanalysis is in part the recognition, restoration, and enlargement of the loving, generous self. This process embraces the slow growth of recognition of the attacks on that self (and on others) from within us. Such repair and development were recognised by Homer in his memorable allusion to sin and reparation: "Destructiveness, sure-footed and strong, races around the world doing harm, followed haltingly by Prayer, which is lame, wrinkled, and has difficulty seeing, but goes to great lengths trying to put things right" (*Iliad*, Book 9, lines 502ff, my translation). The enlarged self not only sees the faults and limitations of the self, it also takes steps to address them.

Example from Ian McEwan

Here is an example, from Ian McEwan's novel *Solar* (2010, pp. 117–118), of the power of the narcissistic self to influence and take over from a saner self. The main character, an overweight, alcoholic, physicist, Michael Beard, arrives back at Heathrow from a trip to Berlin. During the flight he has drunk champagne, a large gin and tonic, and three glasses of Burgundy, and has eaten everything business class had to offer for lunch, including three bread rolls—all this barely two hours after a meaty Germanic breakfast. The delayed flight has made him an hour and a half late for the talk ("for an unnaturally large fee") he is about to give on climate change at an energy conference at the Savoy (where he looks forward to another lunch).

Further delayed in immigration,

> he crossed the departure hall, fully aware that he was not quite taking a direct line to the stairs that led down to his train, nor was he quite aiming for the down-at-heel airport shop that sold newspapers, luggage straps and related clutter. Was he going to be weak and go in there as he always did? He thought not. But his route was bending that way. He was a public intellectual of a sort, he needed to be informed, and it was natural that he should buy a newspaper, however pressed for time. At moments of important decision-making the mind could be considered as a parliament, a debating chamber. Different factions contended, short—and long-term interests were entrenched in mutual loathing. Not only were motions tabled and opposed, certain proposals were aired in order to mask others. Sessions could be devious as well as stormy. (p. 161)

Beard buys four newspapers ("as if excess in one endeavour might immunise him in another" (p. 162)); but at the last minute "as he handed them across for their bar codes to be scanned, he saw at the edge of vision, in the array beneath the till, the gleam of the thing he wanted, the thing he did not want to want, a dozen of them in a line, and without deciding to he was taking one—so light!—and adding it to his pile" (p. 162).

"It"—the "thing he did not want to want"—was a bag of salt and vinegar crisps. "What defeated him," McEwan writes, "was always the present, the moment of vivid confrontation with the affirming tidbit, the extra course, the meal he did not really need, when the short-term faction (in his interior parliament) carried the day" (pp. 162–163). (I am reminded of our societal short-term blindness towards climate change.)

The image of a person noticing that his footsteps are not taking a direct line to where, in his better self, he wants to go (the direct route to the appointment for which he is late) but nor are they quite aiming for the site of the alluring crisps (alluring, that is, to his unworthy self), seems to me a perceptive illustration of how the mind can be divided into two parts that pull this way and that, with anxieties, values, and motivations on each side that would be foreign to the self that directs and inhabits the other scenario. The two pulls lead him at first on a compromise course. Michael Beard's compulsive greed seems to function like an arm of a destabilising and corrupting secret organisation within the overall self.

Narcissism—that partly secret organisation—overtakes us all to some degree, often in the form of narrow-mindedness, a mind narrowed so as to concern itself only with the self-centred self, and its short-term desires. As Shakespeare wrote: "Th'expense of spirit in a waste of shame/Is lust in action" (1985, p. 143). We revert to our own forms of it under pressure of anxiety. We may retreat into depersonalisation, undoing the self, perhaps trying to revitalise ourselves by ultimately unsatisfying sexual excitation; we may become false, over-compliant selves; or we may be overtaken by grievance and a feeling of being the victim, victim of, it may be, self-righteousness and cruelty; or we may fall into psychosis. In group contexts we revert to a touchy tribalism, a state in which, as the outcome of hatred and projection, we identify "we"—*our* group—narrowly; competition and opposition become more significant in our attitudes to others than the possibilities of reconciliation, co-operation, and learning from differences.

Mental space and giving house-room to one's narcissism

When the generous self prevails, it accommodates, has some affectionate relation to, and stands up to the narcissistic self, rather as generous parents look after their children and help them grow up. The good enough parent not only accommodates the tantrums, the regressions, the taking for granted of the "His Majesty the King" child; she not only helps the child move beyond this natural narcissism, she also loves the child-self, with its spontaneity, passion, living in the moment, and capacity for love. The child's hurt and vulnerability to loss, to separation, to jealousy and other painful feelings, all which may give rise to hatred and cruelty, these too need to be understood with empathy and love. Brenman spoke of how much patients come to appreciate an analyst who appreciates what it is like to be in their situation and under their pressures. He conveyed, by his stance as well as by his words, a sense that he knew that "there but for the grace of God go I".

This idea of accommodation—giving a home to (remember Brenman's story of the man in the Gold Coast)—resonates with the notion of mental space. Our patients sometimes show us moments of movement out of constrained states. One, who was exceptionally prone to blame the environment, or fate, or his partner, for his self-centred anger and despair, had a rare moment of insight in which, briefly, something of a broader self appeared, when he said: "I realise that I go berserk if someone goes missing and I have no means of forcing them to be there." Until then he had in effect simply gone berserk, a state of mind that he represented to himself and to me as an inevitable, natural, and wholly normal reaction. Instead of going out of his mind ("berserk"), he had the capacity to have the thought, to recognise this tendency in himself. This was a shift in the self, however temporary, in that he not only now had the chance to act differently, he was already in a different, more enlightened, state.

I am inclined to use the word "luminous" to describe such enlarging states, as contrasted with the darkness, impoverishment, enclosure of the state of mind when the narcissistic self is prevalent. A man who is obsessed with sex writes: "Seeing every woman as a potential sexual adventure leaves me feeling vacuous and shallow and ultimately lonely."

I hope to describe how analysis aims to facilitate the development of this luminous, bigger self, and how a narcissistic narrower self objects to and resists this process. I want to underline the role of generosity in this process of growth—both in the analyst's attitude and in the patient's.

Clinical examples: the spoiling self

First, a borderline patient: Ms B was a lawyer, whom I heard about in supervision. Her split-off, narcissistic, and paranoid self would tyrannically attack the analyst and overwhelm her generous self. This cruel and narrow-minded self devalued her analyst, turning him into a dangerous figure in her mind. Whenever she began to work well with him and make progress, coming to trust him more, a negative therapeutic reaction occurred, taking the form of a gang-like menace that blackmailed her into the conviction that her analyst was dangerous and untrustworthy. Ms B was herself often in a terrified state in the analysis, and felt she had to defend herself. Hostile and terrified, she would crouch in a corner of the consulting room, hiding as far from the analyst as she could. She also feared that he would violently retaliate against her. For many months she secretly took a knife into the consulting room, to protect herself against him.

One such takeover of her more loving side by this spoiling reaction occurred when she was required to write to officials to justify her continuing need for the health authority care package that included financial support for her analysis. In two letters she wrote movingly and insightfully about the vital importance to her of her analysis. She then wrote a third letter warning the authorities to ignore the first two letters.

On another occasion she dreamed of all sorts of ordinary and real exchanges. Suddenly a spider sits on the analyst's face and she wakes up. The spider was I think a part of herself (or a split-off self), which, in reaction to the ordinary, real exchanges, with its clever and legalistic web, squashes the analyst. This spider-self won't let him have any satisfaction, both as a result of envious possessiveness, and as a result of her fear that he (perhaps as constituting a combined object with the spider) attacks her with his intrusive, spider-like interpretations. There are clear oedipal elements in this central scenario—the narcissistic self, jealous and envious of the couple that consists of her more generous self and her good parent, sadistically and excitedly attacks this fruitful relationship. Thus, one target of the attack is her saner self, which is damaged and put out of action by such destructive assaults.

Ms B also expressed some understanding of the overall situation with her analyst. She spoke of having two very unmatched legs to stand on—her two selves, I think. It was not that she had no leg to stand on; rather she had two different legs.

Over some weeks she agonised over which of two flats to choose—one having no windows and being disturbed by the noises of a neighbouring family, the other having a balcony and windows, but liable to street noise and exposure. This gave an accurate picture of her transference predicament: the first flat representing her withdrawal inwards, where she is not exposed, but is liable to be troubled by her gang (the neighbouring family); the second flat expressed her capacity for insight (the windows), a possibility of looking inside and outwards (the balcony), but a move that risked her being seen (exposure) and noise (conflict and difficulty). She dreamed:

there are several tracks with different trains on. Someone leaps from one to another, and is then in a particular world, absolute and complete. She is afraid of falling between the tracks.

This dream shows understanding of the different worlds/tracks (trains of thought and feeling)—selves—that she is liable to; of her jumping from one track or frame of mind to another; and of her fear of losing the security of either track. If she acknowledges the different tracks will she fall between the different worlds? And if she joins the analyst in a therapeutic alliance she opens herself to the perverse and cruel attacks from the self that is identified with an internal gang.

In his paper Brenman describes the narrowing of perception and judgement in the narcissistic self. He says (1985, p. 274) of one patient that she was "acutely switched on to my faults, showing the acumen of a specialist." This patient's narrow self was like a consultant skilled in sniffing out a disease, like the doctors of earlier times with a "nose" for cancers. It specialised in this process, with all the acumen, sharpness of an expert. She was also in this incarnation (or transubstantiation) a brilliantly destructive superego, a fundamentalist who could spot a sin in any activity, and strip down her object, as she did herself, wiping out any good qualities. Humanity and mercy were non-existent for this patient of Brenman's. The situation was similar in Ms B.

Gradually, as a result of the analyst's patience in tolerating Ms B's hatred and her stripping him of all good qualities, and his steadiness in interpreting her terror of internal and external destructive figures, Ms B's suspicion became less violent, her anger more direct and focussed, and her capacity for love and gratitude—from her broader self—more solidly grounded. For the first time she wanted to give her analyst a Christmas card. She meant to bring it to the last session before the break, but "forgot" (a small enactment, I presume, by the narrow self). She sent it by mail after Christmas, and very moving it was, with a warm message of gratitude to her analyst for saving her life. The card portrayed the restoration of a beautiful monastery damaged in fighting by a powerful guerrilla force. This was, the caption said, a progress report: a great deal of work was still to be done. But one could see from the series of photographs, some of which were close-up, others more panoptic, how much richness there was in the original building (she too had a rich potential), and how much work had already been done. The analyst was touched by this card.

On her return, however, the sessions were filled with her fury at his absence over the break. As one might have predicted, she had lost access to the feelings expressed in the card; but neither the analyst nor I expected the degree of scotomisation of the card itself and of the concern and love that went into her giving it—she apparently had no knowledge of the card, she denied sending it, "it had nothing to do with her". Gradually, however, the card could be acknowledged, as for example in a dream in which:

> there was a monastery at the back of the building where she lived. She had not noticed this building before, though it was large, like the Tate Modern. When she tried to get into it there were all sorts of obstacles. The path was dangerous and steep. The doors were barred. She eventually was let in, but only into an annexe to the monastery. She could not get served food there.

This newly discovered ("modern") monastery held all sorts of riches, it seemed, but there were many obstacles to her being able to enter it and get nourished there. It was, however, real. She now knew of its existence. She was not all bad, and nor was the analyst. Even the anger at his absence during the break was straightforward and explicit, unlike the more generalised terror and fury that had so often prevailed.

Ms B's predicament was that her narcissistic self repeatedly overwhelmed the fuller, more generous self. When under the control of that cruel self, hope was not permitted, all shoots of growth overthrown by the self that preferred grievance. Thus the home was ravaged, and disparagement and disappointment, often verging on despair, prevailed. The fear and hopelessness were also violently projected into the analyst, giving him a sense of how much of Ms B's life was overwhelmed by such feelings of despair and worthlessness.

Shakespeare again, in the same poem quoted above, refers to the lust that is: "Enjoyed no sooner but despisèd straight,/Past reason hunted; and, no sooner had/Past reason hated as a swallowed bait." And he ends: "All this the world well knows, yet none knows well/To shun the heaven that leads men to this hell" (1985, p. 143).

All this material, as in the sonnet, makes one wonder about a pure destructive narcissism, fuelled no doubt by defensive elements: the patient, like the man liable to this "expense of spirit in a waste of shame", is not only defensive (defending, as I suggested above, against awareness of dependency), and envious and jealous of the oedipal couple consisting of the generous self and the analyst, but is also perverse. There was, I think, an erotised sadistic gratification through power and destructiveness.

Another patient, Mrs C, would attack her husband when he did something helpful or needed. One day he worked hard to eradicate weeds in the garden. The patient was clearly delighted. But at once she turned on him: why was it easier for him to do this than for her? And why had he not done it before? The transference implications of these complaints were apparent: this patient devastated her home, whether the literal home (she would create chaos and undo tidying); or the potential analytic home worked on by both her and her therapist; she would thereby attack any potential home in her own mind. Mrs C could not bear the fact that the help she had received had not come sooner, nor that, as it seemed to her, it was less of a struggle for her analyst than for herself to eradicate weeds. Her narrowed perception quickly made these the salient facts of the situation, much more so than the plain fact of the help that had been given. For several reasons, the narcissistic self cannot maintain its (generous) gratitude to the helpful other; it prefers grievance and the role of hard-done-by victim.

Of both these patients, Ms B and Mrs C, we could say that they had little sense of a home in themselves, or rather that they repeatedly trashed or destroyed it and their awareness of it. Ms B became, during her analysis, able to know (for more of the time, and in more detail) that she had a rich resource in herself and in the analyst (there was a newly revealed and beautiful monastery that was being restored by the work of the analyst and herself). She also knew how hard it was to enter it, let alone to get to the food on offer in it, or to own it. And as we have seen, she could lose all knowledge of it in her subservience to the malign gang within. Mrs C, whose problems were perhaps less extreme, could see at times how much she damaged her actual and her inner home, and the home, and help, offered her by her husband and her analyst. Both patients also made their analysts feel for long periods of time that there was no home for them or their interpretations.

Analysis offers an opportunity for finding a home for the projection and eventual ownership of the narcissistic self, and for the stirrings of a generous self, and thus finding and growing a bigger self that can function in a more generous way, both socially and privately.

The good object recovered

As Brenman stresses, we all need help with the vicissitudes of life. We all need actual good figures; but we also need an internalised good object, not as a possession but as a separate person, whose separateness can be mourned, allowed, and even generously celebrated; an object reliable enough in our minds not to be too radically attacked and thus lost. Without such figures we cannot in analysis or in life hear uncomfortable truthfulness about ourselves as inspired by generosity and love, and then make good use of it, but will instead see such recognition of ourselves as a superego attack from a narrow-minded and superior other. Without such secure enough internal figures to identify with, we cannot be loving and generous ourselves.

I was struck by one of Brenman's comments in the seminars that are reported in his book (2006, p. 122). There is a discussion of a patient who has to deal with primitive feelings of exclusion and jealousy relating to his analyst's weekends. Brenman mentions how, for the child to come to terms with his mother's other life and other relationships, especially with father, it is necessary to give him good experiences of his own, for instance, by arranging for a friend to come over to play with him. I think this simple reminder acts as a corrective to a trend in psychoanalytic thinking, namely the innuendo or implication that the patient/child has simply and austerely to learn to deal with and mourn disappointment and loss, especially in relation to the analyst, that this reconciliation is the main task of growing up. Such lessons do indeed need to be learned; but Brenman with his humanity and common sense reminds us that we can't mourn alone, that we need a parent/analyst who understands how difficult that is (and can face his or her own separation anxieties). He also reminds us that the analyst needs to bear in mind that jealousy is lessened if deprivation for the patient is not too great; if the patient has good things of his own apart from the necessary access to an appropriately loving mother, father, or analyst (he needs friends of his own, and for such friendships to be encouraged and fostered). We may need to interpret that our patient has the idea that we expect him to sit around mourning our absence all the time; if he feels we understand his need for a life of his own, he may take a further step and come to believe that we do want him to have a good time and good relationships outside analysis. We should not, in short, speak (possessively and narcissistically) as if the patient's attachment to us is the only one that counts.

Having said this, there is no escape from discomfort and pain, and bearing discomfort is a difficult sine qua non for both parties to the analytic process. Giving up exclusive possession and control of the other, originally the mother, allowing her to be separate, is, when done willingly, a generous act, for it entails the experiencing and tolerating of jealousy and loss, as well as giving permission, even welcoming, her having good experiences away from ourselves. Real generosity involves emotional cost. The patient (partly prompted by his bigger and more generous self) voluntarily puts himself on to the couch, where he has to come to terms with the peculiarly destabilising realisation of how much he is not in control of, or even at times conversant with, his own thoughts, motives, and characteristics. He has to encounter primitive aspects of himself in relation to an analyst distorted by his own projections. For his part, the analyst has to face the uncertainties inherent in patients' projections. He has to open himself to doubt, and question his own assumptions and presumptions. He has to risk making interpretations without being sure which of the patient's selves will react, or how the conflict between the two selves will turn out. He has to stand aside from his responses to the patient in order to challenge them. He, too, has to realise that he himself is not all sweet reason, that he, like the patient, is sometimes thrown and even perhaps disabled by what the patient sets going in him, and that he has his own limitations. Or, alternatively, he may have to reflect on the blandness of his experience: Why am I not more disrupted? Is that a defensive arrangement I have put in place, perhaps encouraged to do so by the patient?

For us all the growth into a larger self, and the strengthening of the larger self, involve both the recognition of the good we have, which entails gratitude for the help given, and also a capacity to mourn and let go what we have not had, and the bad things that we have done, or that have happened to us, including in the analysis. We also have to mourn what we have not been able to allow, and the cruelty or envy that we have inflicted on the other. Forgiveness, understanding, and remorse are needed, alongside gratitude. Then gradually the larger self can give a home to the narcissistic self, rather than being relegated and usurped by it.

References

Brenman, E. (1985). Cruelty and narrow-mindedness. *International Journal of Psychoanalysis, 66*: 273–281.

Brenman, E. (2006). *Recovery of the Lost Good Object*. London: Routledge.

Klein, M. (1952). On observing the behaviour of young infants. In: *Envy and Gratitude and Other Works* (pp. 94–121). London. Hogarth, 1975.

Klein, M. (1957). Envy and gratitude. In: *Envy and Gratitude and Other Works* (pp. 176–236). London: Hogarth, 1975.

Klein, M. (1963). On the sense of loneliness. In: *Envy and Gratitude and Other Works* (pp. 300–313). London: Hogarth, 1975.

Lawrence, D. H. (1923). *Studies in Classic American Literature*. London: Penguin, 1971.

McEwan, I. (2010). *Solar*. London: Jonathan Cape.

Robinson, M. (2012). *When I Was a Child I Read Books*. London: Virago.

Shakespeare, W. (1985). Sonnet 129. In: S. Wells (Ed.), *Shakespeare's Sonnets and A Lover's Complaint* (p. 143). Oxford: OUP.

Winnicott, D. W. (1963). The development of the capacity for concern. In: *The Maturational Processes and the Facilitating Environment*. London: Hogarth, 1982.

CHAPTER SIX

Lurching between longing and destruction

Irma Brenman Pick

I wrote this paper for a conference, in which the unlikely title was: "Desiring admiring envying (object relations) between longing and destruction". I scratched my head over the complexity of the chosen topic! I struggled. I even consulted the *Oxford English Dictionary* (1977) in my attempt to clarify the terms.

So what do they say about desire? Desire, is defined as that "emotion which is directed to the attainment or possession of some object from which pleasure or satisfaction is expected: longing, craving; a wish ..."

Interestingly, desire is presented in an ambiguous way—it is not clear whether it is a longing for what is provided by the object in a relationship, out of which may come development and growth; what we may think of as a loving intercourse. Or whether desire is, as they seem to suggest, for possession of the object. Desire appears to move from desire for something from the object, which would imply a relationship with the object, to possession/being. Freud (1941f) wrote of having and being in children—saying that "having is the later of the two" (p. 299). He gives the example of the infant's first experience of the breast: "the breast is a part of me, I am the breast", and only later can they feel, "I have it—that is I am not it" (p. 299). And these states of mind are present not only in children; like the response you frequently hear from an adult to a small baby: you are so sweet I could eat you all up!

Considered developmentally, Freud, early on, gave an account of His Majesty the Baby (1914c), with his wish to have it all and be it all. The hungry baby, we presume, understandably, would wish to possess the breast so that he would not have to feel his own hunger/need. When the breast is unavailable, not yet able to long for it, he wishes instead to possess it, so that he does not have to feel the pain of wanting that which is not available to him.

He may suck his own thumb, wishing to believe that there is no difference between his thumb and that which the breast provides; he may even, in the process, hallucinate the breast at that moment. When his thumb and his hallucinations fail to assuage his hunger, however, he has a problem. The question then is: How does the baby manage the deprivation of that which he desires, and in fact needs, for survival? And how does he manage to bear that his thumb and his phantasies have failed him? It is the breast, after all, which "has it". How does the baby manage this experience—that the breast is able to provide something which he cannot?

Does he admire the wonder of this capacity of the breast to understand and provide what he needs? Does he feel grateful that it is there, despite the agony of having to wait? And if so, does this capacity to feed, despite being "deprived" presuppose some rudimentary awareness of the wondrous capacity of the mother, in the first instance, to understand and provide for his need? Perhaps this is linked at the most primitive level to a loving response, an answer to the life instinct—a kind of "thank goodness you're here" which allows for a genuine admiration for the breast and the flow of milk that comes with it.

Or does his anger at having experienced frustration get in the way?

In this instance, the baby may shout or scream, attacking what is not there, and, by turn, feel attacked by the absent breast. Perhaps the baby, when the mother finally returns, turns his head away and will not or cannot feed. I think here of the paper by Edna O'Shaughnessy (1964) in which she illustrates Bion's (1962) idea of the way in which, rather than being longed for, the absent good object is experienced as a bad object present, an object to be turned away from and attacked.

And is this response of turning away always to be understood as simply an angry reaction? Or might it be a persecuted reaction—the fear of retribution from the attacked breast? Or could it be a self-protective reaction—not linking up with someone who will desert you? Deprivation can stimulate not only an angry response, but a deadly envious resentment that the mother/breast has the capacity to provide that which is not part of his own equipment.

So, to return to the *Oxford English Dictionary* (1977); they speak of envy, in fact, in two different ways: to feel envy at the superior advantages of another; or (in what they term a more neutral sense) to wish oneself on a level with another. I would call this conscious envy, in which the admiration for the other remains more or less intact and alive, and the envy of the advantages of the other is acknowledged, as the *OED* suggests, in a more "neutral" way, one which may even stimulate positive efforts to develop.

Later there is a third definition of envy: to regard with discontent another's possession of some superior advantage; and further yet—to feel a grudge against, to begrudge, to have malevolent feelings.

And it is these malevolent feelings (of which the origin is often unconscious), which point in the direction of destruction, and which may eliminate awareness of the admiration of the other, because the goodness has already been destroyed. The envy then is often more unconscious. Melanie Klein famously wrote of this spoiling of the goodness in her book on envy and gratitude, published posthumously, in 1962.

Here she described the way in which the more grudging, malevolent feelings, the discontent for not being in possession of the good thing, may lead to destruction, even eradication of the good, such that it is not even seen. Hanna Segal, in 1993, writing on the usefulness of the concept of the death instinct, says: "I contend that the death instinct from the beginning is directed at both the perceived object and the perceiving self, resulting in such phenomena as pathological projective identification, as described by Bion. The defences against the death instinct create vicious circles leading to severe pathology" (p. 60).

In this paper I will address these vicious circles or "interwoven snakes", an image that I am taking from one of the cases I will present; I will argue that envy is interwoven with deprivation and loss (not only as cause but also as consequence) and, further, interweaves with jealousy, and guilt, and creates or perpetuates, infinite vicious circles. I will illustrate my theme with clinical examples.

First, a deprived, suicidal adolescent girl who reported looking exclusively at a black spot on the wall, seeing only what was black and faulty, defects or deficits, and in that way, protected herself from feelings of both loss and envy. The envious attack, whilst in her case fueled by deprivation, is inevitably as a consequence, impoverishing and depriving to the subject. The destructive attack may not only be on the object, but also on the loving or libidinal part of the self. We may say, in such a scenario, that that part of the self which desires the object is despised and attacked for its very desiring. If both object and libidinal self are attacked, however, the subject is deprived of good experience, and in this impoverished state, has more cause to feel envious. Segal (1993) described this, as I said, as the basis of the death instinct; the attack both on the breast and on the wanting mouth or lips, in which one does not know which is primary—the murderous or the suicidal emotions.

In stressing the spoiling quality of envy, Klein differentiated it from jealousy. In the Oxford dictionary, jealousy is defined as: troubled by the belief, suspicion, or fear that the good that one desires to gain has been, or may be, diverted to another. In biblical terms: "for I am a jealous God", a God who will tolerate no unfaithfulness in the beloved object.

Jealousy then, implies an omnipotent (God-like) self that insists on being in possession of the object, tolerating no unfaithfulness. Yet jealousy does at least acknowledge the value of the object. Klein (1962) suggested that envy comes before jealousy, although she also posited a very early Oedipus complex. (I (2008) stressed the interweaving of envy and jealousy in an earlier paper I wrote on envy, in which I cited Shakespeare's *Othello*.)

We quite frequently see the interweaving of envy and jealousy in operation in our clinical work.

For example, the adolescent girl, who I mentioned earlier, focusing on a black spot, frequently cut herself; she had grown up in dreadful circumstances, with a rejecting mother and an alcoholic father. She was very bright and longed to be accepted into a good school; she had every possibility of achieving this. She was helped by an able therapist. Yet she continued to cut herself. She took a "token" overdose after a holiday break during which she had been offered care by both a psychiatrist and a family therapist in the unit; this family therapist had helped her access a library where she could have a place to work.

Following the overdose she claimed that she couldn't concentrate. She saw only a black spot on the wall, and was so taken up with that she lost her focus on her work.

There is much to suggest she cut herself to avoid the pain of the deprivation she had suffered, and that she may have "overdosed" her wishes for revenge against depriving objects. She also set up rivalry between her therapists—it was the "other" therapist who provided the good (library) space. But, I suggest, finding the black spot, the fault or the blemish on the wall (it is not pure white/good), provided her with justification for wreaking vengeance. And focusing on the black spot protected her from the sadness of loss, or any danger of longing for the therapist to be present, or any of the pains associated with being alive, and blurred her knowing about any gratitude for what had been offered to her.

So the therapist's holiday became, instead of an absence, a malign action against her, the patient. The vicious cycle then begins; the therapist's "malign action" justifies the patient's attack on the work they had done together. She was, further, unable to concentrate on her work, for she feared that if she did, others would treat her as she had treated them. Thus, she feared that the examiners would focus only on the "black spot" in her work, and in her. No matter what constructive efforts she made, all that would be seen would be her failings—that which was not there. She would be the black spot that had to be got rid of. But of course, her desperate assaults, on herself and on the work, ensured failure. We could say that she also sought punishment by failure, so as not to feel responsible for the way in which she caused her analyst to fail. The black spot took her then into a despairing black hole into which any good from the object, or herself, had been and was now, made to vanish.

Melanie Klein (1962) said that greed, envy, and persecutory anxiety (connected with persecutory guilt) compound a vicious circle. She also referred to deprivation exacerbating envy. I suggest that not only do these factors intertwine with each other, but also may intertwine with a particular form of sexuality. I think that this young girl's focus on the black spot became the basis of a sado-masochistic relationship in which she excited herself, both as victim and as perpetrator. And this excitement in turn helps defend against painful, even tragic, feelings of gratitude, dependency, and loss.

I want, as the title of my paper suggests, to show ways in which this interweaving is manifest. An analyst happened to wear a silver brooch featuring interwoven snakes; her patient, as we will see, referred to this brooch, which, I believe, illustrates features of interwoven states of mind.

When Mrs B came for treatment she was divorced; she has an adolescent daughter. She sought help for depression and severe hypochondriacal anxieties. Mrs B grew up on a collective farm in the then Soviet Union; from the first weeks she was kept in a crèche during the week. Her mother herself had experienced deprivation, growing up in great poverty.

In a session, which I shall present in some detail, we see, I believe, the interweaving of envy and jealousy, as well as an intertwining of her envious self, projected into her mother, who may, in fact, herself, actually have been envious; her child had a better life than she. And, of course, projections from the child into the mother may well interweave with the mother's own difficulties. Currently, as we shall see, Mrs. B is shocked at the idea that she now may be envious of her own daughter.

We see an interweaving of the past (she frequently says "I feel like a child") and the present. The envy she experiences may reflect not only the early envy of the breast, as described by Melanie Klein, but also current envy of her analyst, not only for her analytic gifts, but because the patient believes that she, the analyst, almost certainly had, and has, a better life than that of the patient.

The sessions

Patient:

"I feel really bad today. I am hurt and angry that you will not be here on Friday [deprivation: the Friday session has been cancelled by the analyst]. Maybe you celebrate your birthday.

I know these feelings are completely childish, but I don't know where you will be, who will
be with you [jealousy]. It is a feeling which in the beginning of the analysis would have led to
another illness, today it is only the muscles that are like stone."

Note the acknowledgement of change, presumably thanks to the analysis. She conveys that
in the beginning this would have led to another illness, now only the muscles are like stone.
We may note, too, the interweaving of the psyche with the soma, and also how quickly her
acknowledgment of change disappears and she complains, as though the gratitude one might
have anticipated "turns to stone".

She continues:

"At home I am totally angry, but when I am here I can't be angry any more. I want to be
right near to you [desire] and at the same time I feel I will never come again [I'll get rid of
you/destruction], I want the good connection to you. I am so happy about that, but at the
same time I feel ashamed about my wishes to want to know what you will do at the weekend.
I really feel very ill, like at the beginning."

Consciously she refers here to the beginning of the analysis, but is there also a reference to the
beginning of life—her birthday? In addition, we see signs of a negative therapeutic reaction—
the moment she feels better she goes back to the beginning, to where she was before the
treatment.

She says:

"I am ashamed because of the envy and aggression I have when I think of you and your family
together, and I am not with you; I know it sounds crazy but it is like that. You will despise me;
I am sure you jeer at me."

She feels not only left out, jealous of her analyst's time with her family, but also ashamed of
these feelings. Although she has spoken of envy, here she seems to be stressing a more healthy
jealousy, in which she feels left out of her analyst's relationship with her family. Yet she fears
that her analyst will despise her and jeer at her for having these "baby" feelings. Is this a realistic
fear of the analyst's contempt, or does this come from a part of herself that despises herself for
being a baby who wants a mother?

All this interweaves, too, with the social system in which she grew up, which apparently disregarded the infant's need for a mother and puts babies in a crèche. And the patient, I imagine,
experiences the analytic relationship as one in which the analyst thinks that it is in order to send
her patient/baby away for a long weekend. But she herself, perhaps partly in identification/
interwoven with the system, despises her own wishes and needs to be mothered.

The analyst says: "There seems to be no room for feelings of anger and envy."

Mrs B adds:

"And hatred. I hate this dependency. I feel imprisoned, powerless. You are free. This morning I thought of not coming, but then I would still have to pay for the session. It feels like a
punishment … these feelings I have of not being invited, not being part of your surroundings,

feel unbearable; they take me back to the beginning of analysis [and we note that she believes that it is the analyst's birthday, perhaps the beginning of life, for both analyst and patient)."

When the analyst then speaks of Mrs B's deep hurt at not being able to participate, Mrs B responds:

"Yes that's it! I hate to imagine who is with you. I told you how I hate your brooch of the snakes which are interwoven. I imagine your husband gave it to you. Thank God you don't wear it today. The envy, the fury of not being invited. It can happen that you kill the relationship."

The analyst suggests that these feelings now seem dangerous, and that the patient wants to know if she, the analyst can survive them, or whether she gets into an angry state like the mother.

Mrs B continues:

"My mother was hard; she put a veil over it—as if everything was okay with us. It had to be so. At home there was always envy, rivalry and envy. My father got rice soup in the morning when we went back to the crèche. I hated him. I didn't want him to come back. For us my mother only gave some bread. For all these years I never said aloud that I wanted rice soup. My mother used to provoke envy in us, then she hit us for it. Yes—she herself provoked the envy, and then she condemned us for it [the mother's projected envy perhaps mixed with her own]"

The analyst says: "Like I provoke envy now by cancelling the Friday session."

The patient goes on to speak of her rivalry with her sister, and her aggression towards her and then shocks herself by confusing her sister with her daughter. "My sister was ten years old when I left her alone with her school problems—I deserted her really." She declares herself guilty for having deserted her sister, yet this is intertwined with her reproach toward the analyst for abandoning her at the weekend—projecting her guilt into the analyst. She then says that though she, the patient, had earlier threatened to cancel two sessions the following week, now she wishes to attend. But she fears that her analyst would have rejoiced had she failed to attend.

So we see that there is a moment when she feels guilt and perhaps even sadness at having deserted her sister; a moment when she realises that in her rivalry she also deserts the part of herself that needs to be looked after. Perhaps this is what enables her to reclaim the sessions she threatened to cancel. But all this quickly intertwines with her reproach against her analyst for leaving her; as I said, projecting the guilt into the analyst. In these circumstances she then fears that her analyst wants to be rid of her; "You won't want me back, indeed you want to triumph over me." So depressive guilt interlocks with persecutory fears.

* * *

Finally, I will bring some more detailed material from a patient in her mid-thirties. She is an intelligent, perceptive person, born in South America, and living now in London. She holds a position in the administration of a prestigious university. She came into analysis because she was unable to maintain a relationship. She had often engaged with men who had treated her badly. She very much wanted, one might say longed for, a marriage and children, yet whenever she came close to fulfillment of these wishes she broke off the relationship.

She had a difficult relationship with her mother, who was very young when she was born, and whom she believed had deprived her, favouring her younger brother. She was closer to her father. She felt there was something really bad inside herself, which she pictured as a snake. She also, currently, has a difficult relationship with her (female) analyst, complaining bitterly that her analyst failed to help her too.

After some years of analysis, she is now in a relationship with a caring partner, and has, with trepidation, just given up her rented apartment, to move into a new apartment with him. She is in reach of that which she has longed for. Her parents, who she had always complained were so unhelpful to her, came down from Scotland, where they now live, to assist the young couple with the move.

She starts the session, unusually, saying: "These days I feel that I need you very much. But it is very hard to tell you this." She goes on to speak of some uncertainty in relation to her work; there are to be new placements. She says that her hands shook with anxiety when she asked a senior colleague for help. The more difficult thing to talk about is that she took her mother to the train (mother is now returning to Scotland to rejoin father, who had already returned, and to the home where the brother and family live too). She, the patient, was depressed all weekend. "I'm sure I am ill. It's a repetition of what happened with B [an earlier relationship where her partner B, who had been unfaithful, had then developed a rare illness, and she had left him]. Only, now I'm the one who is ill. I will let Simon [her partner] be free, as I should. Then I will have to go through the process of finding another house."

In these opening remarks, it seems to me, we see the intertwining of many factors. She begins, unusually for her, acknowledging her need for her analyst, and implies that she has been longing for her analyst: "These days [the weekend without analysis]—I feel I need you very much." And she says how hard it is to ask for help—her hands shook with anxiety as she did so. But the more difficult thing, she says, is loss; "I took my mother to the train." But then the loss, almost instantly, becomes depression, with a conviction that now an illness is located inside her body. The "snake" resides physically within her. We may note that she neither directly expresses feelings of loss at the departure of her mother, nor open gratitude to her mother for helping her. Instead she is focused on a black spot, the "conviction" that she has a black spot, an illness. Now she has the illness, like her former partner, and has to protect her partner from her. Might it be that as she spoke the words "I need you", a toxic envious spit froze her tongue, and, in her mind, returned as a malignancy in her body (as in the previous patient of whom I wrote)—the psyche interwoven with the soma.

Her physical and emotional move, her new arrangements, are then threatened with breakdown—a new physical illness enters the scene. One might consider whether a negative therapeutic reaction threatens. Indeed, there has, in psychoanalysis, been much debate about whether the negative therapeutic relationship is a consequence of guilt or of envy. I recall a European Psychoanalytical Federation conference in London, in 1973, where Joseph Sandler argued that the negative reaction was based on guilt, whereas Elizabeth Spillius argued that the cause was envy.

I suggest that the material of this patient of whom I have just written might persuade us that these two factors are interwoven, and are further mingled with fears of loss too. If she acknowledges her love and need for her partner/analyst, she is threatened at every level. There is uncertainty about the future (the new placements); where might she be placed? There is loss: she has to say goodbye to her old apartment and to the former position she held at work, as well as to the position she held psychically where she could experience herself as the victim of bad treatment, and hold herself together, focused on a grievance—another version of a black spot. And if she perseveres, she fears that she (her illness) will be damaging to Simon and to her analyst.

To add to all of this, she has had to say goodbye to her mother, who is returning to Scotland and is not, even now, hers exclusively. This must arouse both loss and jealousy (mother rejoining father and brother). And of course, if she continues to improve, some day she will have to say goodbye to her analyst, hopefully, without recourse to malignant denial and grievance.

Now she is faced with her growing love and need for her mother/analyst and the associated threat of having to mourn loss. Intertwining with love and need is not only destructive defensiveness, but also hope—she can have a life of her own, she can move in with her boyfriend, etc. And then there is the poisonous guilt. The patient feels persecuted by guilt that she abandoned her earlier partner who had a terminal illness. I think she also believes that she abandoned her mother in some way, in her claim that she, mother, was a malignant person. And in the background is the malignant, poisonous, envious, snake part of her, threatening to spoil it all.

Of course we cannot interpret everything at once. A choice about what might be the most urgent anxiety has to be made. In an earlier paper, "Concern: spurious or real" (1995), I argued that the patient needs to be held with two hands; one firmly to hold the destructiveness of the patient, the other to hold the vulnerability. I would say here how important it is to be aware that, whatever we interpret, we also need to keep in mind that there are other factors. Bion (1967) said when we know something we also know that there other things we don't know, and when we make a choice we also give something else up.

I think we see in this session the malignant part of the patient that wishes to threaten (now ostensibly with a physical illness) all that has been achieved. But there is another part terrified by (intertwining) persecutory and depressive guilt, and loss, and still another part, smaller and less robust, cathecting with a love object. There is a way in which the envious, destructive part of her is partly owned (felt to be caused by her, represented as a snake within her), and simultaneously disowned—an illness that is "visited upon her". And in the face of this illness there is an intertwining of the psyche with the body, which might ultimately kill her. Would she die rather than be grateful for the help she has been given by the mother/analyst, or is she desperate for her analyst to help her and, indeed, doubts her capacity to manage without her?

As the session continues she laments that she was so tired and depressed all weekend; she doesn't want to lose Simon. She recalls a friend having expressed great joy when she and her partner had moved into a home together; so she allows a glimpse also of her own wish to enjoy and celebrate this great step; but she cannot hold on to this. Instead she says: "I feel like I have a lot of pain inside me. I don't want to lose Simon, get sick and die, and I feel like all three will happen." She goes on to say that mother was so pleased that she, the patient, has found Simon and continues: "I feel that I want to attack her joy. I hate the sense she has that she made her contribution to make all this happen."

It seems that the patient is willing to destroy her own happiness in order to attack her mother and eliminate any awareness of what mother and analyst have given her. And now, in the session, she sets about attacking any joy the analyst might have had in her achievement. She goes so far as to accuse the analyst of not giving her anything. Is this an envious attack or is it unbearable for her to move on when she feels so guilty and so ashamed?

She now reports a dream:

> I went to ask someone if I could go to human resources. The person I asked, said, "There will now be only one place there, not two." That made an impression; not two places, only one. There will be only one person left in the house, Simon.

She becomes rather histrionic, lamenting that she is terminally ill. There can be only one person—the other has to be eliminated, will die. She cannot consider that two people, she and her analyst, worked together to bring about this improvement; instead the analyst will take all the credit and leave her to die. But we might also think that she would die of envy, or die rather than acknowledge the help the mother/analyst has provided. She has a further thought that she says is weird. She read an article about a patient who had seen her father's penis when she was a child; this person was subsequently unable to have a sexual relationship, or achieve orgasm. She explained that she thought of this because she recalled seeing her father coming out of the bathroom naked; she saw that "it" was very big.

> "How will I go home [to the new apartment]? It's too good to be true. I shouldn't be enjoying this. It's all too much for me. I will get cancer and die. The new house is very lovely. I feel I shouldn't be there, it's too nice for me ... I want to vomit."

We might think that the patient is walking a tight rope between a negative therapeutic reaction and a successful outcome. We see her lurching between longing to be able to enjoy her new life, and wishing to destroy the improvements she has achieved. Envy then is not only a cause of deprivation, but also a consequence. And we see the intertwining of many factors; her fear of dependency and her loving heart, and of loss, and also her fear of envy of her mother's and her analyst's capacity to help. Her nasty attack on her mother—"I want to attack her joy"—is followed by feelings of unworthiness and guilt—"I shouldn't be there"—in this better place—"It's too nice for me."

I think there is also an ongoing anxiety about the analyst appropriating the good work. As if in the face of the patient's improvement, the analyst will become intensely excited and "big", like father's naked penis, which would expose the analyst in what the patient sees as her self-congratulatory narcissism. Partly she fears that this may be a true picture of the analyst. But I believe that she also fears that it may not be true. For if it is not true she would be faced with having to take responsibility for her own narcissistic assault on a caring analyst.

The following weekend she leaves a message for the analyst saying that she is in a panic; she requests a session. By the time the analyst returns home and responds to the call she has recovered. What emerges in the session following is that, in part, she was in real panic; in part, though, she was wanting to manipulate her analyst into "getting it wrong". That is, either failing to respond to her genuine *cri de coeur*, or succumbing to the patient's manipulations—a genuine needy part of her quite entangled with something more poisonous. The analyst is placed in a very difficult position. And so we see also how she drives the analyst one way or the other, into an enactment—an entwining with the other, with the object, in which the other becomes either too solicitous or too neglectful.

There is the threat of a tragic ending; she has so longed for this good outcome, and now on the brink of achievement it may all be destroyed, or she may destroy it all! Or not? By continuing to make the analyst uncertain and anxious she ensures not ending, as she also projects into the analyst doubts about her own capacities. A joyous analyst would more easily feel able to separate without guilt. There is only room for one and that is the patient! But behaving in this omnipotent way promotes her own guilty feelings that she does not deserve a good place.

Conclusion

I have tried to illustrate the intertwining of many different factors. And there is, of course, a huge literature on the ways in which one might say patients intertwine with others, not least their analysts, and how the other may then be nudged into enactments of one sort or another. Of course, to a greater or lesser extent these are the problems of life, and I suppose the particular forms these intertwinings take go to make us the people we are! The question that remains, in each case, is whether that analyst can help that patient to make the huge move from entrapment in these vicious circles, this lurching between longing and destruction, towards a more hopeful outcome.

References

Bion, W. R. (1962). *Learning from Experience*. London: Heinemann.

Bion, W. R. (1967). Notes on memory and desire In: E. Bott Spillius (Ed.), *Melanie Klein Today, Vol. 2: Mainly Practice*. London: Routledge, 1988.

Brenman Pick, I. (1995). Concern: spurious or real? *International Journal of Psychoanalysis, 76*: 257–270.

Brenman Pick, I. (2008). Reflections on "Envy and gratitude". In: P. Roth, & A. Lemma (Eds.), *Envy and Gratitude Revisited*. London: Karnac.

Freud, S. (1914c). On narcissism. *S. E., 14*: 67–102. London: Hogarth.

Freud, S. (1941f). Findings, ideas, problems. *S. E., 23*: 299–300. London: Hogarth.

Klein, M. (1962). *Envy and Gratitude*. London: Tavistock.

O'Shaughnessy, E. (1964). The absent object. *Journal of Child Psychotherapy, 1*: 34–43.

Oxford Dictionaries (1977). *Shorter Oxford English Dictionary*. Oxford: OUP.

Segal, H. (1993). The clinical usefulness of the concept of death instinct. *International Journal of Psychoanalysis, 74*: 55–61.

CHAPTER SEVEN

"The mountains of primal grief"

Ronald Britton

Mourning is older than psychoanalysis; it is older than poetry; it may be older than mankind, for we are not the only species to manifest the process. Biological reasoning would therefore suggest that it must be advantageous. The poets, dramatists, and novelists who have best described its manifestations and the feelings also seem to say so, and to say it very well. So what does psychoanalysis if anything have to add? I think its contribution is threefold: it provides some understanding of the unconscious mental processes involved in mourning; it makes clear why it is necessary for psychological development; and it throws light on failed mourning and its pathological consequences. It may by extrapolation suggest that collective mourning is necessary for the health of societies.

The practice of analysis provides many opportunities to see evidence of the value of mourning in increasing adaptation to reality and the enrichment of mental life. It also enables us to see the adverse consequences of the failure to mourn: sometimes in the form of depression; sometimes in the form of manic activity; sometimes in the loss of a capacity to form deep, intimate relationships. Analysis also provides us with examples where, like Miss Haversham in Dickens' *Great Expectations*, grief can become pathologically arrested in an attempt to freeze time; so that present loss cannot be transformed into a past event; so clinging to the pain of loss, prevents the recently departed from becoming the long gone.

Probably the worst consequence of a failure to complete mourning is repetition: the model of the loss being endlessly reiterated. How often we see in our practices the re-enactment of old events in new forms, in which the individual subjects himself, or someone else, to some untransformed experience of former times.

Freud suggested that mourning is a form of psychic work analogous to the concept of working through in analysis. In normal mourning the process of overcoming the loss of the object absorbs all the energies of the ego. He suggested that the representation internally of the attachment to the lost person is made up of single innumerable impressions; and all of them have to be reactivated to be relinquished. As Freud put it, the laments always sound the same, but have different unconscious sources. If the object does not have this great significance, reinforced by a thousand links, its loss will not be of a kind to cause either mourning or melancholia.

As Rilke wrote:

> Joy *knows*, and Longing has accepted,—
> Only Lament still learns; upon her beads,
> Night after night, she counts the ancient curse. (1987, "Sonnets to Orpheus", I: 8)

Repetition and reiteration seems to be at the heart of mourning as we hear when King Lear, realising his daughter Cordelia is dead, cries:

> Howl, howl, howl, howl!
> … She's gone forever!
> … Thou'lt come no more,
> Never, never, never, never, never. (Shakespeare, 1969, *King Lear*, 5.3)

That unusual reiteration with a fifth "never" going beyond what might seem to be the end of the line captures the strength of the urge to repeat and prolong through protracted grief. Such prolongation and reiteration is facilitated by a sense of injustice; as analysts we can testify that for some people old grievances sustain a sense of immortality. There are, however, many others who would like, through denial, to dismiss death: to consign personal loss to the dustbin of significance.

The argument between those who would quickly turn to new life after a death and those who would have us wear the winter foliage of lamentation longer, is most tellingly represented by Shakespeare between Claudius and Hamlet. Claudius reproaches his nephew, now his stepson, Hamlet, for continuing to mourn his dead father,

> To persever
> In obstinate condolement is a course
> Of impious stubbornness. 'Tis unmanly grief.
> It shows a will most incorrect to heaven. (1969, *Hamlet*, 1.2)

Hamlet's scathing response is couched as a reproach to his mother on her rapid remarriage; it makes clear that he regards, for a time at least, that the continuing relationship to the dead is a necessary part of the human condition: "[A] beast that wants discourse of reason/Would have mourned longer", he says and continues with irony, when she claims not to have forgotten her dead husband: "O Heavens! die two months ago, and not forgotten yet? Then there's hope a great man's memory may outlive his life half a year".

I have taken my title, " the mountains of primal grief" from the climax of Rilke's *Duino Elegies* where "*Die Klagen*", the "Laments", take the young man to the foot of the mountains of primal grief where is located the fountainhead of joy. And then "Alone, he climbs up the mountains of primal grief". Rilke implies that making that journey is the means of resolution and renewal.

In his own retrospective account of the composition of the *Elegies* that took him ten difficult years, Rilke wrote:

> Two inmost experiences were decisive for their production: the resolve that grew up more and more in my spirit to hold life open toward death, and, on the other side the spiritual need to situate the transformations of love in this wider whole differently than was possible in the narrower orbit of life (which simply shut out death as the other). (Rilke, 1969, p. 330)

In the *Elegies* he proposes the idea that it is our function to transform the visible external world into the invisible internal world. This he sees as creative and reparative, and crucial to this process is the recognition of death. He had already proposed we should give psychic life to things by naming them, so that they had a life beyond their own material, transient, existence. He now makes it clear that experiences and feelings are among the things that need a name. Grief, he decides, is an experience of great value:

> … How we squander our hours of pain.
> How we gaze beyond them into the bitter duration
> To see if they have an end. Though they are really
> Our winter-enduring foliage, our dark evergreen,
> One season in our inner year—not only a season
> In time- but a place and settlement, foundation and soil and home. (Ibid., p. 205)

This was written in 1922 and the use of winter as symbolic of mourning echoes other poets, notably Shakespeare, who introduces, in Sonnet 97, winter as a metaphor for absence, and therefore implicit is the promise of spring's return. But, running through the sonnet is the threat of death and permanent absence that might make winter out of summer.

> How like a winter has my absence beene,
> From thee, the pleasure of the fleeting yeare?
> What freezings have I felt, what darke daies seene?
> What old December's barenesse everywhere?
> And yet this time removed was sommers time … (2014, p. 114)

The metaphor of winter for mourning is also central in an essay called "On transience" (1916a) that Freud wrote in 1915, as a contribution to a commemorative volume produced by the Berlin Goethe Society. What adds interest to this is that it has been suggested by some scholars that Rilke was the anonymous poet referred to and that the taciturn friend was Freud's analytic colleague Lou Andreas Salome, who was also Rilke's former mistress. I will quote a few sentences from this essay. He wrote it during the First World War, like a postscript to "Mourning and melancholia" (1917e)—the paper that moved the centre of gravity of psychoanalysis from sexuality and hysteria to object loss and depression. It introduced the concepts of introjection and identification into the psychoanalytic landscape and changed it forever.

In his short essay "On transience" Freud wrote:

> Not long ago I went on a summer walk through a smiling countryside in the company of a taciturn friend and of a young but already famous poet. The poet admired the beauty of the scene around us but felt no joy in it. He was disturbed by the thought that all this beauty was fated to extinction, that it would vanish when winter came, like all human beauty … I could not see my way to dispute the transience of all things … But I did dispute the pessimistic poet's view that the transience of what is beautiful involves any loss in its worth. … As regards the beauty of nature, each time it is destroyed by winter it comes again next year, so that in relation to the length of our lives it can be regarded as eternal … What spoilt their enjoyment … must have been a revolt in their minds against mourning … I believe that those who think thus, and seem ready to make a permanent renunciation because what was precious has proved not to be lasting, are simply in a state of mourning for what is lost. Mourning as we know, however painful it may be, comes to a spontaneous end. When it has renounced everything that has been lost, then it has consumed itself, and our libido is once more free …"
> (1916a, pp. 303–307)

Whilst working on "Mourning and melancholia" Freud also wrote, in the early part of 1915, "Thoughts for the times on war and death" (1915b). This was prompted by the war and by the new work on depression; it is clear that it turned his mind to themes of loss, guilt, and aggression. In "Thoughts for the times on war and death" he deals with our denial of our own death; our destructive instinct and our ambivalence towards our love objects. On the latter he wrote:

> [Our] loved ones are on the one hand an inner possession, components of our own ego; but on the other hand they are partly strangers, even enemies. With the exception of only a very few situations, there adheres to the tenderest and most intimate of our love-relations a small portion of hostility which can excite an unconscious death wish … (p. 298)

He concludes:

> … our unconscious is just as inaccessible to the idea of our own death, just as murderously inclined towards strangers, just as divided (that is ambivalent) towards those we love, as was primeval man. But how far we have moved from this primal state in our conventional and cultural attitude towards death.
>
> It is easy to see how war impinges on this dichotomy. It strips us of the later accretions of civilisation and lays bare the primal man in each of us. It compels us once more to be heroes who cannot believe in their own death; it stamps strangers as enemies whose death is to be brought about or desired; it tells us to disregard the death of those we love. *But war cannot be abolished* … (p. 299, my italics).

As I see it, the implication in these essays is that although we might struggle to contain the instincts that find satisfaction in war, we cannot abolish them anymore than we can abolish death. He also suggests that we can recover from wars, and from the deaths of loved ones, and that the world will not end with our own death.

If, however, we cling to our dead loved one, he writes: "Our hopes, our desires and our pleasures lie in the grave with him, we will not be consoled, we will not fill the lost one's place. We behave as if we were a kind of Asra, who die when those they love die" (1915b, p. 290). On the other hand, we need to recognise that the world does not end when *we* die. Freud quotes the motto of the Hanseatic League: "'*Navigare necesse est, vivere non necesse*' ('It is necessary to sail the seas, it is not necessary to live')" (p. 291).

The opposite of believing in re-finding and renewing love is vividly expressed by Shakespeare through the mouth of Venus. When she discovers her adored Adonis to be dead she declares that love is dead and wishes suffering on all future lovers:

> For he being dead, with him is beauty slain,
> And, beauty dead, black chaos comes again.

Shakespeare shows us in the poem that this determined ablation of beauty by Venus, as a reaction to the death of Adonis, is based on what we now would call the narcissistic nature of her love for him. He writes:

> She lifts the coffer-lids that close his eyes,
> Where, lo, two lamps burnt out in darkness lies;
> Two glasses, where herself herself beheld
> A thousand times, and now no more reflect.

Venus, suffering the loss of her lover, takes revenge on love and those who love with a curse:

> Since thou art dead, lo, here I prophesy
> Sorrow on love hereafter shall attend …
> Since in his prime death doth my love destroy,
> They that love best, their loves shall not enjoy. (2004, p. 415)

If we personify beauty; if we equate it with *one* living thing; if we believe it is irretrievably incarnate in mortal flesh, then mourning as a process of release is blocked and the only recourse is some form of posthumous idolatry. Such a belief, Shakespeare implies, is a consequence of being madly in love. And he appears to share with Freud the view that "being madly in love" is a kind of temporary insanity that any of us might experience.

> Lovers and madmen have such seething brains,
> Such shaping fantasies, that apprehend
> More than cool reason ever comprehends.

> The lunatic, the lover, and the poet
> Are of imagination all compact. (1969, *A Midsummer Night's Dream*, 5.1)

In his paper "On narcissism" Freud wrote that when "the satisfaction of love is impossible, and the re-enrichment of the ego can be supplied only by a withdrawal of libido from its objects, the return of the object libido to the ego and its transformation into narcissism represents, as it were, a happy [primal] love once more; and, on the other hand", he writes, "it is also true that a real happy love corresponds to the primal condition in which object libido and ego libido cannot be distinguished" (1914c, pp. 99–100). Suddenly in this last sentence we are presented by Freud with the notion that the fully fledged libidinal narcissist is in love with himself in just such a way as someone else might be "in love" with another person. But is it really another person, if "happy love corresponds to the primal condition in which object libido and ego libido cannot be distinguished"? In this passage Freud implies that this "primal"—"happy love"—is essentially narcissistic object love, whether pursued with another person in the external world or as a love affair with the self in the internal world. This narcissistic way of loving, it seems, proves to be one obstacle to the process of mourning and its resolution.

So how do we rescue ourselves from such a mental state as that attributed to Venus by Shakespeare? The analytic answer is, once again, through mourning, this time not for the lost object but for the ideal object. The ideal object is a personification of beauty, or goodness. However, the existence of an ideal object in the material world depends on there being a physical object identical with its precursor in the mind. In the psychoanalytic terms that Wilfred Bion (1962) used, it depends on the realisation in the physical world of the preconception of a good object being absolute. Alas, in our imperfect world this cannot be the case. As we gain experience we discover that the ideal can only retain its perfection by remaining immaterial: thus it lacks one most important quality we would wish it to have, that of being real and substantive.

The alternative is made clear by Keats in his "Ode on a Grecian urn": he suggests that the static state of the potential lovers, frozen forever in a preliminary position, represent a perfection that any progress would impair.

> Heard melodies are sweet, but those unheard
> Are sweeter …
> Bold Lover, never, never canst thou kiss,
> Though winning near the goal—yet, do not grieve;
> She cannot fade, though thou hast not thy bliss,
> For ever wilt thou love, and she be fair! (1956, p. 209)

Here the price of perfect love is non-consummation; this is an attitude met with in a number of analyses where the illusion of existing in the anteroom of life is unconsciously believed to make time stand still.

Since realisations can only be possessed in their imperfect forms, unrealised perfection has to be mourned in order for the real and imperfect to be loved in our real world of space and time. Idolatry, on the other hand, requires time to stand still and for things to remain unchanged, and fundamentalism seeks truth, beauty, and goodness only in words.

If Venus's words can be said of beauty—"For he being dead, with him is beauty slain,/And, beauty dead, black chaos comes again"—so they can be said of goodness and of truth. When such a belief is embraced I think there is great danger. When we convince ourselves that truth and goodness have been personified, realised in a person once and for all, we will be disposed to fight ruthlessly to maintain his representations, whether in material form or in his words, as idolatry or as fundamentalism, thing worship or word worship. These tendencies obviously exist in religions, but if we look at other spheres of life we find them everywhere—in politics, letters, even in the sciences, and certainly in psychoanalysis itself.

The discovery of an unconscious world of sexual phantasy was at the centre of the first phase of psychoanalysis; the second phase was narcissism; discovering the vital importance of mourning and its relationship to depression was its third phase. In "Mourning and melancholia" (1917e), written in 1915, Freud built his theory on the work of Karl Abraham with psychotic depressive patients and his own earlier speculations.

Mourning was to become, and to remain, central to psychoanalysis, but interest in it arose from the analysis of those depressive states that arose for no manifest reason and were not linked consciously to object loss. It began with Karl Abraham, the first true psychoanalyst in Germany, who wrote his paper on depressive states in 1911. Abraham was probably second only to Freud as the major early influence in psychoanalysis. He developed his analytic practice and training organisation in Berlin. He was born in Bremen in 1877 of an old Jewish family that had long been resident in the Hanseatic towns of North Germany. He studied medicine in Wurzburg, and worked in psychiatry in Berlin and then the famous Burgholzi psychiatric hospital in Zurich. Being Jewish he could not become a chief physician or professor in Switzerland and so he returned to Germany.

Abraham suggested, in 1911, that depression stood in the same relation to normal mourning for a loss as did morbid anxiety to ordinary fear. "Anxiety and depression are related to each other in the same way as are fear and grief", he wrote. "We fear a coming evil; we grieve over one that has occurred" (p. 137). The cause of the apprehension in neurotic anxiety states is unconscious and so is the cause of grief in the depressions. He made other very significant findings in his analyses of these cases, notably that an unconscious attitude of hate was paralysing the depressive's capacity to love. Ambivalence was, he thought, the hallmark of both the depressive and the obsessional. In a later paper Abraham suggested that in melancholia regression to the earliest stage of development occurred and that unconsciously the patient's wish was to incorporate his sexual object, to devour it. What are repressed, he asserted, are cannibalistic wishes, and the reaction to these unconscious wishes is to refuse to take food. This in turn leads to a fear of dying of starvation. "[In depression] the edict has gone forth that the mouth zone shall never experience that satisfaction it longs for; and the result is a fear of dying of starvation" (1916, p. 278).

Psychoanalytic ideas like this provoked opposition and excited ridicule from the moment they were first put forward. When I read in December last year of a case of cannibalism in Rotenberg, Germany, I could not resist paraphrasing Wordsworth to say "Abraham! Thou should'st be living at this hour". Armin Meiwes admitted that he had advertised for a victim on the internet and had killed, him chopped him up, and eaten him, thus fulfilling a fantasy he had had since childhood. Meiwes own comments perfectly illustrate Abraham's ideas about incorporation.

"With every bite," Meiwes said, "my memory of him grew stronger". Since eating Brandes (the victim) he felt much better and more stable. "Brandes spoke good English," he said, "and since eating him my English has greatly improved."

This case apparently illustrates an old dictum of Freud that the neuroses are the negative of the perversions; one might put it the other way round, that the perversions are the negative of the neuroses. But I think a more modern psychoanalytic view would be that both the neurotic inhibition and the perverse practice are the consequence of a miscarriage of a normal process. As we find in anorexia on the one hand and bulimia on the other.

Whilst illustrating Abraham's thesis this case raises even more questions. How and why is this unreconstructed primitive phantasy actually enacted in such a literal way? What has this outrageous event to do with normal mourning, you might ask? Meiwes himself gives us a clue; he felt lonely and neglected as a child after his father abandoned the family and fantasised having a blond younger brother whom he could keep forever by consuming him. Later he had fantasies of eating his schoolmates. For me there is an even more intriguing question raised by this case. What were the motives of the man who sought out Meiwes in order to be consumed? I will try to address both those questions.

One could say that in both depression and the perversion the normal process of mourning has gone wrong and that it has gone very wrong in the early stages of development. Abraham suggested that there was in his depressive cases a "primal depression" of early childhood reactivated in life by adult circumstance. He was reinforced in this view by the analyses of children that Melanie Klein was undertaking in Berlin. He wrote to Freud in 1923: "I have something pleasant to report … In my work on Melancholia … I have assumed the presence of an early depression in infancy as a prototype for later melancholia. In the last few months Mrs. Klein has skilfully conducted the analysis of a three year old with good therapeutic results. This child presented a true picture of the basic depression that I postulated in close combination with oral erotism" (Freud & Abraham, 1965, p. 399).

Just as Freud had hypothesised on childhood neurosis from the analyses of adults, Melanie Klein hypothesised on the nature of infantile phantasy from the analysis of young children. This led her to a concept of an infantile depressive position, which she believed underlay the tendency to depression later in life; she then linked the depressive position to mourning. At first she used it as an explanation of depression; later she realised that it was ubiquitous; psychopathology therefore was a consequence of some break-down in negotiating what is a normal developmental step. The depressive position is, in fact, the prototype for mourning and has to be renegotiated in life with each loss and each new development. Why with each new development? In Klein's theory the infantile depressive position is a consequence of the development of the child's mind. What, prior to the depressive position, was timeless, total, unintegrated, ideally good or irredeemably bad, loved or hated, became one source of experience, good and bad, loved and hated. The hatred that initially belonged to a bad object was now seen to be directed towards the same loved object, and thus fear of damaging that relationship led to what later would be called guilt.

At the heart of Melanie Klein's thinking was the notion of internalisation; of the building of an internal world of object relationships through the process of introjection. The idea of a good internal object, that can be relocated in the outside world, underlies her thinking on the depressive position and on mourning. The investment of a figure in the external world with the significance of the good internal object means that loss of the external figure provokes fear of losing the internal object. In other words, losing a loved person can provoke the fear of losing love and of living in a loveless world incapable of love oneself. Similarly, projecting the internal bad objects into external figures can initiate the belief that badness can be eliminated by annihilating them. Living in a world free of ambivalence but occupied by unambiguously good and unambiguously bad figures Klein described as the paranoid position and saw it as a defensive organisation against the depressive position. We are all familiar with these positions as we move through them in our lives, at times feeling the discomfort of the depressive position with its mixed feelings as we exchange the pure culture of affection for ambivalence; at other times we indulge in the paranoid position, loving our friends and hating our enemies.

There are many aspects to the depressive position and a great deal has been elaborated on it in the last half century of psychoanalysis. One particular line of thought I would like to speak about, as it relates to the question of mourning and the consequences of a failure to mourn. It was described by Hanna Segal in two important papers on symbolism (1957, 1978). In essence what she suggested is that there is a difference between a symbol and what she termed a symbolic equation, and that the difference came about through mourning. Where the original object is lost and mourned the symbol is a creation of the ego to replace it. A symbol is more than an emblem, it partakes in the qualities of the original but it is *not* a new version of the original. What Segal showed is that symbolic equations are used *as if they were* replacements so that they might appear to gain supernatural power. The symbolic equivalent is at the heart of the case of cannibalism that I referred to: a man's actual flesh symbolically representing the flesh of the lost object that has to be literally consumed and incorporated. The contrast with that symbolic equivalent could be, for example, taking the bread and wine in the Christian Church's Eucharist, *symbolising* the body and blood of Christ. The argument about the literalness of that transaction—between those who see it as symbolic and those who see it as the real presence, a symbolic equation—has been felt deeply enough in Christianity to condemn some to death and others to war.

Recent developments

If I can summarise what I have been saying, it is that for our species mourning began when life began. It is a process of relinquishment and renewal that can be impeded by both internal and external factors. It takes time and is an active process; the length is likely to be commensurate with the scale and significance of the loss. Three parallel processes seem to be involved. First, withdrawal of the emotional investment in the object bit by bit; each bit accompanied by pain. Second, re-introjection of the primal loved object as an internal presence newly shaped by the character of the departed person; third, the symbolic representation of the lost object and its use in the commemoration of the departed. All these processes require relinquishment and all of them therefore will be opposed internally. Mourning, therefore, is not only painful, it is a struggle against the desire for the reinstatement of the pre-existing state, which can only be achieved through illusion.

The true symbol, as Segal said, is part of a triangle composed of the original object, its symbol, and the self. The tolerance of triangularity is an accomplishment in development that is part and parcel of working through the depressive position and involves the early Oedipus situation, that first version of triangularity. As I wrote some years ago (1989, 1998), we work through the depressive position by working through the Oedipus situation and we work through the Oedipus situation by working through the depressive position. It entails relinquishing the phantasy of total possession of the object of desire; it involves observing the relationship of two others from the point of view of the self and thus creating triangular space. In triangular space the relationship between the lost object and its symbolic representative can be observed because when we have triangular space we can observe the relationship of others in which we are not included. That position, when tolerated, creates a third position in which we can witness the relationship of others, and in our inner world it enables us to observe ourselves whilst being ourselves in interaction with others. It integrates subjectivity with objectivity. The collapse of that inner triangle into a dyadic relationship in which the world is only composed of one self and one other can lead to a regression to the most primitive of object relationships in which we desire to have the object totally inside us or to be totally inside the object.

This urge to enter helps us to understand the peculiar self-sacrifice of the volunteer victim of cannibalism that I referred to earlier. Just as Abraham described an incorporative wish, there is also its counterpart, a wish to be incorporated, to be lost in a merger with the love object.

Sabina Speilrein, in 1912, described a kind of love that meant self-destruction. She thought this was universal, whereas I think it is characteristic of a particular kind of hysteria from which she herself suffered. For Spielrein, *love* meant *identification*. For the development of her ideas on love and death, she turned to Wagner. She quoted from "Tristan and Isolde" and "The Ring Cycle" where, when Siegfried is killed, Brunhilde on her horse rides into the flames of his funeral pyre.

If we look at the Nordic mythology that informed Wagner's operas it throws some light on the link between sex and death. If a hero died in battle he went straight to Valhalla. Women also had a place in Valhalla, if they suffered a sacrificial death. They could be strangled and stabbed and burned after a hero's death in the name of the god. Should they be burned on the hero's pyre, their reward would be a marriage in the afterlife that they could not have in this one. Hilda Ellis Davidson (1964) quotes a mythic example of a slave-girl on the Volga who was stabbed and strangled so that she could be burned with her master. She consented to this sometime before the funeral ceremony, and was treated with great honour—as though, in fact, she were a true wife—until the day of the burning. If we equate these myths with the phantasies of hysteria, we could say that living means facing separation, whilst death provides union. If mutual death is the destiny of the primal couple, then unity by death becomes the erotic fulfilment of the excited imagination.

Suicide bombing is a short step away from this; the phantasy of union with God by self-sacrificial suicide. Osama bin Laden's fatwa urging his young men to take a certain step to paradise by suicidal attack has an uncomfortable resemblance to Nordic mythology; in that "Those who died in the god's service, undergoing a violent death … had entry into his realm". As Nordic mythology, infatuation with Wagner, and a bad reading of Nietszche all contributed to Hitler's idealism, this link is not a comforting one. The denial of real death, separation, and loss, and its replacement with the manic phantasy of eternal life, redemption, and union, under-lies all these idealistic ideas.

Such denial is the antithesis of mourning: as we mourn we become more ourselves, as we become more aware of who and what we have lost. Successful mourning means an enhancement of the internal world and an enrichment of the self. I will give the last word on this to Rilke:

> Whoever does not, sometime or other, give his full consent ... to the dreadfulness of life, can never take possession of the unutterable abundance and power of our existence: can only walk on its edge, and one day, when the judgement is given, will have been neither alive nor dead. (1987, p. 317)

References

Abraham, K. (1911). Notes on the psycho-analytical investigation and treatment of manic-depressive insanity. In: D. Bryan, & A. Strachey (Eds.), *Selected Papers of Karl Abraham*. London: Hogarth, 1973.

Abraham, K. (1916). The first pregenital stage of the libido. In: D. Bryan, & A. Strachey (Eds.), *Selected Papers of Karl Abraham* (pp. 248–279). London: Hogarth, 1973.

Bion, W. R. (1962). The psycho-analytic study of thinking. *International Journal of Psychoanalysis, 43*: 306–310

Britton, R. (1989). The missing link: Parental sexuality in the Oedipus complex. In: J. Steiner (Ed.), *The Oedipus Complex Today*. London: Karnac.

Britton, R. (1998). *Belief and Imagination*. London: Routledge.

Davidson, H. E. (1964). *Gods and Myths of Northern Europe*. London: Penguin.

Freud, S., & Abraham, K. (1965). *A Psycho-Analytic Dialogue* (Eds., H. C. Abraham, & E. L. Freud). London: Hogarth.

Freud, S. (1914c). On narcissism. *S. E., 14*: 99–100. London: Hogarth.

Freud, S. (1915b). Thoughts for the times on war and death. *S. E., 14*: 273–302. London: Hogarth.

Freud, S. (1916a). On transience. *S. E., 14*: 303–307. London: Hogarth.

Freud, S. (1917e). Mourning and melancholia. *S. E., 14*: 237–258. London: Hogarth.

Keats, J. (1956). Ode on a Grecian urn. In: H. W. Garrod (Ed.), *The Poetical Works of John Keats* (p. 209). Oxford: OUP.

Rilke, R. M. (1969). *Letters of Rainer Maria Rilke* (Trans. & Eds., B. Greene & H. Norton). New York: W. W. Norton.

Rilke, R. M. (1987). *The Selected Poetry of Rainer Maria Rilke* (Trans. & Ed., S. Mitchell). New York: Random House.

Segal, H. (1957). Notes on symbol formation, *International Journal of Psychoanalysis, 38*: 391–397.

Segal, H. (1978). On symbolism. *International Journal of Psychoanalysis, 59*: 315–319.

Shakespeare, W. (1969). *Complete Pelican Shakespeare* (Ed., A. Harbage). London: Penguin.

Shakespeare, W. (2004). Venus and Adonis. In: *The Illustrated Library of Shakespeare, Vol 3*. Glasgow: William Mackenzie.

Shakespeare, W. (2014). *Love Sonnets of Shakespeare*. Philadelphia, PA: Perseus.

Spielrein, H. (1912). Destruction as a cause of coming into being. *Journal of Analytical Psychology, 39*: 155–186.

CHAPTER EIGHT

Dreams, symbolisation, enactment

Roosevelt M. S. Cassorla

Contemporary psychoanalysis gives considerable importance to intersubjectivity, defined as involvement between patient and analyst in analysis. This involvement, accompanied by emotional turbulence, is strengthened by these subjects' encounters even though their relationship is regulated by the rules of the setting. The analyst allows herself to be led by what is happening and, at the same time, observes in detail the facts that occur. That is, the analyst makes objective what she experiences subjectively.

Countertransference, as a valuable instrument for understanding what is taking place in the analytic field (Heimann, 1950; Racker, 1948, 1953), constitutes a common ground for many different theoretical conceptions in contemporary psychoanalysis (Gabbard, 1995), and the concept of enactment is a part of this scenario. Detailed studies on the Kleinian concept of projective identification, by several different psychoanalytic groups (Spillius & O'Shaughnessy, 2012), have increased our interest in intersubjectivity. Money-Kyrle (1956) describes normal countertransference, which he sees as the appropriate oscillation in the analyst between projective and introjective identification. Money-Kyrle also described what came to be known as normal, or realistic projective identification (Bion, 1962; Rosenfeld, 1965), that is, identification that serves as a means of communication and recognition of the other.

Grinberg (1957, 1962) broadened the idea of projective identification by introducing the notion of projective counter-identification. Besides being a fantasy of the patient, projective identification can bring about something real in the analyst that is independent of the analyst's own conflicts. Bion (1962), without being acquainted with Grinberg's work, described the beta screen, which consists of elements that are expelled by projective identification. This projection arouses emotions in the analyst and results in the reaction that the patient unconsciously desires. In various papers, Joseph (Feldman & Spillius, 1989) describes in detail how the patient can recruit the analyst to play certain roles in order to maintain the status quo.

Joseph also describes the function of the analyst, based on what Klein (1952) called total situations. Joseph wrote that

> Total situations [...] include everything that the patient brings into the relationship. What he brings in can best be gauged by focusing our attention on what is going on within the relationship, how [the patient] is using the analyst, alongside of and beyond what he is saying. Much of our understanding of the transference comes through our understanding of how our patients act on us to feel things for many varied reasons; how they try to draw us into their defensive systems; how they unconsciously act out with us in the transference, trying to get us to act out with them; how they convey aspects of their inner world built up from infancy—elaborated in childhood and adulthood, experiences often beyond the use of words, which we can often only capture through the feelings aroused in us, through our countertransference, used in the broad sense of the word. (Joseph, 1985, p. 447)

It is evident that analysts can only understand "how patients act on [... or] capture the feelings ..." if they can symbolise these aspects.

The facts described take place in the analytic field (Baranger, M. & Baranger, W, 1961–62), which consists of the space/time where patient and analyst work. Everything that happens in one member of the analytic dyad has repercussions in the other. The field comprises the whole of spatial and temporal structures, including the unconscious fantasy of the dyad, something that is created between the two and is radically different from what each one, taken separately, is.

The Barangers describe the term *bastion* as indicating obstacles in the face of progress in the analytic process. The presence of bastions suggests paralysis in the field, which may include the feeling that nothing is happening or that strictly stereotypical speech is being produced. The bastion is a field precipitate that can only take place between this analyst and this analysand, and shows aspects of the interaction between them. From outside, the bastion may appear to be static, while the analytic process may apparently follow its course or the bastion invade the entire field, which then becomes pathological. These ideas contain the seeds of recent work on intersubjectivity (Brown, 2011; Ferro, 1992, 1996, 2009; Ogden, 1994, 1999, 2005) and the importance of the real person of the analyst. A break in the bastions bring about the destruction of the status quo and the split-off parts can return to the emotional world.

Enactment

As of the 1990s the term enactment, first used by American analysts, was accepted by a number of psychoanalytic groups. Enactment refers to behaviours that take place in the analytic field as the result of mutual emotional induction. The phenomena had been recognised years earlier but this nomenclature drew attention to them.

Controversies over the new term were amply discussed in a symposium edited by Ellman and Moskovitz (1998). The word enactment is drawn from the field of law, related to figures such as decrees or laws (McLaughlin, 1991). Thus, enactment indicates induced emotional facts that involve both members of the analytic dyad, similar to court orders that are carried out under obligation. So, due to the legal connotation, when we refer to enactment as a concept related to the verb to enact, it goes beyond acting, playing, or representing.

I have considered two categories of enactment, the chronic and the acute (Cassorla, 2001, 2005, 2012). Chronic enactment is expressed through behaviour that involves both members of a dyad, whereby an obstructive collusion is formed with neither patient nor analyst being aware of what is happening. The analytic process becomes paralysed in certain areas. Chronic enactment is similar to the ideas of bastions and mutual recruiting.

Chronic enactment is perceived after it has been undone. That is, knowledge of it occurs *a posteriori* (*Nachträglichkeit, après coup*, deferred action) (Freud, 1918b). Chronic enactment can be undone abruptly, thus threatening to destroy the analytic field and, in this case, a traumatic situation comes on, known as acute enactment. These aspects will be taken up in detail farther below.

Many analysts have described situations that are similar to what we call enactments without their being clearly named as such. Freud, for example, describes them in the case of Dora (Freud, 1905e) and in the dream of the injection of Irma (Freud, 1900a). Breuer and Anna O. constituted the first collusion described in psychoanalysis. Today the term tends to be used by analysts of various backgrounds, including Feldman (1997), Britton (1999), Hinshelwood (1999), Steiner (2006), Mann and Cunningham (2009), and Bohleber et al. (2013).

One proposal of a definition leads us to see chronic enactments as intersubjective phenomena where, on the basis of mutual emotional induction, the analytic field is taken up by conduct and behaviour that involves both members of the analytic dyad, without their being aware of what is happening. Such conduct and behaviour refer back to situations where verbal symbolisation was weakened. When words exist they serve as instruments for discharging or forms for expressing affects that involve the listener emotionally. Words function as acts in the sense of "saying is doing" (Austin, 1990). They include ways of remembering through feelings, which Klein (1957) called memory in feelings.

Enactment can also be understood on the basis of Bion's theory of thinking (1962). We have access to our patients' capacity to think through its manifestations in the analytic field. Fantasies, objects, object relations, and functions of the mind emerge as affects, acts, scenes, narratives, and behaviour. These data allow the analyst to come into contact with both the patient's inner world and his thinking apparatus.

The functioning of this apparatus can be seen as a continuum that reveals the capacity to transform raw emotional experiences (beta elements) into symbolic representations that allow dreaming and thinking (alpha elements) to appear. This capacity results from what we call the alpha function, which is a product of the intersubjective relationship between baby and mother. Through her reverie the mother gives meaning to the beta elements projected by the baby. The baby's capacity to symbolise results from the introjection of the maternal functions.

When the alpha function is operating adequately, the individual is able to think, that is, to give psychic quality to non-mental facts (beta elements), which are then transformed into alpha elements. Their connection constitutes a "contact barrier" that separates and, at the same time, communicates both consciousness and the unconscious. The alpha elements become evident through predominantly visual images, which have also been called affective pictograms (Barros, 2000). The connections among these pictograms make up highly visual scenes and scripts, called "dreams" (both when the individual is awake and when sleeping). These dreams are experienced and recounted in the analytic field. When faced with them, the analyst deduces that he is in contact with functioning of the non-psychotic part of the personality (Bion, 1957), able to form symbols.

Dreams, as compromise formations, both reveal and conceal aspects of the patient's inner world and psychic functioning. Transferentially, the analyst is included in the patient's dreams. The ways by which this inclusion is carried out show how reality is processed and the difficulties of the relationships between the inner and outer worlds.

Therefore, in areas of non-psychotic (symbolic) functioning, the patient places his dream in the analytic field and stimulates the analytic capacity of the analyst. The analyst, in turn, uses his intuition to detect aspects of the patient's dream that, although still part of the symbolic chain of thought, have been deformed or blocked by the defences. The analyst then re-dreams the dream on other bases, allowing new symbolic connections and broadening meanings. The patient, in turn, re-dreams the analyst's dream and so forth. Analyst and patient are thus involved in dreams-for-two, phenomena that include facts beyond the individual dreams of each one.

When the patient's alpha function is attacked, or is not available in a suitable form, he cannot think. Non-symbolised sensorial and emotional stimuli are experienced as nameless terror and are expelled through projective identification. This expulsion may include split parts of the thinking apparatus (mental functions) and constitute bizarre objects. Here we are in an area of functioning of the psychotic part of the personality, where it is impossible to dream.

The product of these projective identifications is expressed in the analytic field through discharges in the form of acts, physical symptoms, hallucinations, beliefs, fanaticism, delusions, and other transformations into hallucinosis (Bion, 1965), in other words, into non-dreams (Cassorla, 2005, 2008). The prefix non-indicates that, potentially, these non-dreams can be dreamed if they find an alpha function. When the analyst fulfills this function he dreams the patient's non-dreams, giving them meaning and including them in the symbolic network of thought.

At times, pictograms may appear in non-dreams but the pictograms are not connected to one another. When there are outlines of scenes or scripts, they appear paralysed. The material has no meaning and there is space neither for connections nor for emotional resonance.

In Meltzer's words (1983):

> What seems to happen is that the analyst listens to the patient and watches the image that appears in his imagination. It might cogently be asserted that he allows the patient to evoke the dream in himself. Of course that is his dream and will be formed by the vicissitudes of his own personality. [...] From this point of view one might imagine that every attempt to formulate an interpretation of a patient's dream could imply the tacit preamble, "While listening to your dream I had the dream which in my emotional life would mean the following, which I impart to you in the hope that it will throw some light on the meaning that your dream has for you." (p. 90)

Meltzer stresses that the dream dreamed by the analyst, even if it is an attempt to dream that of the patient, is a dream of the analyst. This makes it evident that factors proper to the real person of the analyst come on-stage. They will be all the more necessary for patients who are less able to dream.

When the analyst listens to the dream of a patient and then has a dream of his own, he is mostly in contact with non-psychotic functioning. But in a psychotic area (with symbolic deficit) the analyst also listens but, especially, suffers in himself the action of the patient's projective identification, his non-dream, which, as we saw, tries to induce the analyst into avoiding psychic change. At the beginning, the analyst should let himself be recruited by experiencing the aspects that the patient is trying to eliminate. But simultaneously, or soon after, he should disengage himself from this identification by dreaming, thinking about and interpreting what is happening. That is, the analyst dreams the patient's non-dream. The analyst's interpretation becomes part of the patient's symbolic network.

But the analyst may sometimes let himself be engulfed by the patient's massive projective identification and thus lose his analytic capacity. He becomes unable to let the patient's non-dream be transformed into a dream. In these situations, analyst and patient run the risk of remaining indiscriminate, or symbiotic, in an area of mutual sluggish psychic functioning. In this case we are in the presence of a non-dream-for-two, which I consider to be the raw material of chronic enactment (Cassorla, 2008, 2013a).

Projective identifications hook on to aspects that belong to the analyst, but other identifying facets besides those described above (Franco Filho, 2000; Sandler, 1993) may also participate in enactment as forms of contact with primitive areas of the mind.

The developments described here were influenced by discussions on reverie (Barros, E. M. R., & Barros, E. L. R., 2014; Bion, 1962; Ogden, 1999), a mental daydreaming state needed for the analyst to intuit unconscious aspects in the patient. Reverie is activated when memory and desire are set aside (Bion, 1967, 1970). Through reverie the analyst comes into contact with projective identifications and suppressions as well as empty spaces and inscriptions that are parts of primitive aspects of the patient's mind (Green, 1998).

In fact, the two extremes mentioned (dreams and non-dreams) are hypothetical abstractions (Cassorla, 2013b). In practice we find intermediate and mixed situations because psychotic functioning oscillates and coexists with non-psychotic functioning, such as PS< >D (Bion, 1963). For example, there may exist non-dreams that seek to become dreams, quasi-dreams, dreams with meanings that are difficult to expand, dreams being transformed into non-dreams, interrupted dreams (Ogden, 2005), and states of confusion that blend non-dreams with dreams. In this continuum, many different levels of symbolisation can be seen, such as raw elements, precarious symbols with little capacity for connecting, symbolic equations (Segal, 1957), obstructed or sophisticated symbolic networks, etc.

Behaviours that show up as acts resembling theatrical mimicry or a silent movie (Sapisochin, 2013) are a part of this continuum. In this case there is externalisation in the analytic field of early mental inscriptions that were not symbolised verbally because they occurred when the symbolic mind had not yet been constituted. They are related to what Freud (1914g) called Agieren and fall into the category of chronic enactments (Cassorla, 2013b, 2014).

The clinic: dreaming acts of the analytic dyad

The analyst welcomes his male patient, who comes in and walks over to the couch. The analyst suddenly realises that he has forgotten to replace the paper napkin on the head rest where the patient is about to lie down. He steps in front of him and takes away the used napkin while the patient watches on, still standing. The analyst takes a clean folded napkin from a package and has trouble opening up the napkin. The more he tries the harder this simple task becomes. The analyst thinks to himself, "This is hard." Later he was not sure whether he just thought this, or if he said it out loud to the patient.

All this movement was barely noted by the analyst, although he felt embarrassed for a minute or two. Only after the session did he become aware of what had happened. For the time being, these movements were non-dreams.

The session begins and the patient lies in silence, not knowing what to say. He is tense and reticent, and says that yesterday he was disappointed with the analyst and felt him distant.

The analyst immediately remembers the session of the day before. The patient had described a panic attack, a relapse, after many months. The session had been very difficult. The patient was sad and disappointed and no idea came to the analyst's mind. The analyst was also sad and disappointed. Both felt helpless.

But the analyst remembers that, at the end of the session the day before, he had managed to articulate an interpretation showing how creative situations of the patient had put into action an envious internal object, filicide, which had attacked the patient from inside. The patient associated and seemed to think, and both left the session feeling satisfied.

And now, this session. Yesterday the analyst had been distant and the patient felt that it was his fault and he is certain that he disappointed his analyst, etc. The analyst tacitly agrees with the patient as the patient describes in detail what he (the analyst) himself had felt yesterday. He also notices that nothing is said of the interpretations made at the end of that previous session.

In silence the analyst remembers the interpretations and begins to suspect that they were theoretical. They were based on ideas about early states of mind and about panic. Suddenly he imagines the possibility that the patient may have let himself "fit into" the analyst's theory in order not to disappoint the analyst even further. Or might he, the analyst, be attacking his own ideas? The evolution of the process will show him that the first hypothesis was correct.

Only after the patient had left, as the analyst was once again placing a clean napkin on the head rest for the next patient (an easy operation this time), did the analyst remember his difficulty during the session that had just ended. His phrase, "This is hard", was clearly referring to the blockage towards the closed minds of the analytic dyad. His inability to open the napkin symbolised, in act, his closed mind. The near-panic at not being able to open the napkin showed his incapacity to think. The non-dreams were now being dreamed. The analyst is grateful to the patient when, in the following session, the patient brings in a theoretical paper about panic and says, "This is what I have", praising the author of the paper. The analyst clearly sees how the patient encourages competition.

Now the analyst is certain that one of the constituting factors of previous collusions between the members of the dyad was a personal dispute (over theories), which sometimes alternated with mutual idealisation. This previous unconscious collusion can be classified as a chronic enactment, and it was undone by the episode of the napkin on the couch. This episode is classified as an acute enactment. *Après coup*, the analyst perceives the dispute and that he is dreaming the non-dream. This dream of the analyst continues after the session is over and becomes clear later when it was seen that the non-dreamed aspects covered up early situations of helplessness and terror.

The clinic: dreaming primitive aspects

The analyst woke up feeling "uncomfortable" that day but he could not pin down what he himself meant by "uncomfortable". Words like boredom and fatigue were not really exact but were sufficient for him to be concerned with the vitality of the analytic function he would need during the day.

Now the analyst is about to see his first patients and realises that the "uncomfortable" feeling is gone. He works well. At mid-morning, during his coffee break, he remembers patient S. She is to be his last patient this morning and he notes that he is worried.

As he sips his coffee he thinks about his work with S. At the beginning she had complained a great deal of physical symptoms such as indescribable uneasiness and dread of deadly diseases. The analyst was impressed at the patient's quick response to his attempts to name this dread and his dreaming of non-dreams. Although the work was difficult, it was also enjoyable.

But something has happened in recent weeks and it seems that all the work done up till now has fallen apart. S has begun to complain again and suffers in a different way. The analyst has felt lost and powerless. His interventions, which for a time had been useful, are no longer taking effect. Little by little he has noticed that he feels sleepy, as if he is being lulled by the repetitious prattling of S. It has been hard to stay awake and he feels that his analytic powers are "dwindling". He finds it hard to discern his own feelings (and only later was he to realise that he had almost disconnected himself from S).

The strange taste of the coffee he is drinking leads him to put more sugar in it. He notes that he is intrigued by a change in his feelings. Until just a few sessions back he was struggling to stay awake, but now he feels afraid. The patient, S, has been crying. It is frightened crying. The naming of the affect leads the analyst to perceive that both he and S have been terrified. He now knows why his drowsiness has been transformed into a warning.

The analyst has perceived outlines of dreams that ended up not developing. They were confusing agglomerations, somewhat frightening, on topics related to death and suicide. Suddenly the analyst understood: the perception of finiteness, of nothing after death, was unbearable. With this realisation he threw out the rest of his bitter coffee and began thinking about his own children.

The analyst had been shocked at the unthinkable realisation of his own death, both physical and, especially, psychic death, in short, non-existence. But this only became clear later on.

Let us stop here for a moment. We can say that the analytic process, which had once been productive, had now declined. Neither of the members of the dyad was able to dream. The analyst had been through two phases in recent weeks. In the first he had experienced symptoms such as drowsiness, almost giving up on the patient. Now he was living with fear, or dread, and being very much on the alert. He realised the presence of beta elements in search of dreamers. He was aware of his difficulties but was unable to transform them into thought. But this morning he was better able to observe himself and he managed to clumsily name something like discouragement, terror, or death.

As we saw above, the analyst had been comfortable with the first patients that day, but now, after his coffee break, he is distressed. His outlines of thought are unable to overcome his concern and he knows that this can warp his perception of the analytic field. He sternly and actively forces his "non-desire and non-memory" to activate his intuition. But it will not be easy.

If, when he opened the door for S, the analyst had paid attention he would have noticed his heartbeat go up. But then it went down again when he saw her, alive. Fantasies about death and suicide become obvious when he looks at the patient's face, resembling that of a prisoner in a concentration camp waiting for death and unable to commit suicide for lack of strength.

S comes in and drags herself to the couch. The analyst moves from a state of preoccupation to one of discouragement and fear of becoming desperate. He sees himself wondering about the competence of the psychiatric treatment that S is undergoing at the same time that she is in analysis. Later he will realise that he projected his own helplessness, guilt, and despair on the psychiatrist.

As S drags herself to the couch the analyst moves to his own chair and feels that his analytic capacity is also simply dragging along. The rest of the session might have continued like others before it, but, in fact, something very different happened during this session. Before S gets to the couch the analyst surprises himself by asking her not to lie down, but to sit in one of the upholstered chairs.

S stops, looks at the analyst, and hesitates. Then she painfully turns and sits in the chair. The analyst sits facing her and both know that something different is happening, but they do not know what.

This episode shows an action by the analyst, certainly not conscious and possibly consisting of acting out.

Now back to our considerations. We can remember the state of the analyst when he woke up in the morning. It would not be inappropriate to suppose that, during the night, he had tried to dream non-dreams prompted by his work with S. The uneasiness he felt in the morning indicated that he had not been successful in his attempt to dream. The attempt continued during the morning and the difficulties became evident while he was on his coffee break.

When he opened the door for S to come in, the analyst became more aware of how difficult it was to dream. S, in turn, shows her non-dreamed suffering. The invitation by the analyst for her to sit facing him could give the impression of discharged helplessness, an attempt to change the script by changing the setting a bit. The analyst may have been trying to get closer to S in a non-analytic way, through a more informal conversation. Would he be able to tell her, face-to-face, that he could not analyse her any longer? Or was he seeking sensory contact? These hypotheses passed through the analyst's mind later when he was reviewing the session. Let us now look at the sequence that takes place in the session.

The analyst looks at S seated before him. He can hardly see her face because of the angle she is sitting at and she seems to be hiding from him. He can see that her hands and feet are tense. Later the analyst was able to describe this impression as that of a person who is trying to hide and yet communicate a conflict between existence and non-existence.

Without knowing why, the analyst looks directly into the patient's partially hidden face but says nothing. Powerless, he has no idea of what to say but is a bit fearful about the possible consequences of his invitation for her to sit down.

At this moment the analyst notices that S is crying. Little by little her face becomes more visible and the tears that roll down her cheeks move the analyst. His fear disappears and is replaced by an immense sadness. The tears seems to "bathe the soul" of both members of the dyad. Then S searches for words amidst sobs. Looking directly into the analyst's eyes she says: "This is the first time anyone has ever looked at me. It's the first time anyone has ever actually looked at me!" Then, furtively looking at the analyst, but sometimes looking away, she slowly tells how her mother never gave her any consideration or attention, nor listened to her. But, especially, her mother never looked at her. It is clear that she wanted to be looked at in order to feel alive, rather than have to face the "non-look" that almost annihilated her.

This moment broke the possible dead-end story. Now the analyst realised that S also did not feel "looked at" by him. S had been re-living situations of emptiness, of non-existence, for lack of contact with living beings. This lack of contact, brought to the analytic field as a raw element, required the analyst's alpha function (the look) beyond what was available. It had become a non-dream-for-two, in fact a "void for two", haunted by the static noise of the symptoms and mental destruction.

The analyst, later reviewing the beginning of the analytic process, which had seemed productive, concluded that he had indeed dreamed non-dreams, but in areas on this side of the void. They may have been false dreams that S took as true dreams, in her anxiety to fill in this void or to please her analyst, so that he would look at her. The action of the analyst, permitting a look, indicated an interruption of the chronic enactment through its expression as acute enactment.

The analyst does not know exactly why he invited S to sit in the chair, but we can suppose that, during the night and early morning, his mind sought to dream, hesitatingly, almost giving up (when the idea of his own death took hold of him). He insisted and eventually invited her to sit facing him, which seemed like a non-dream discharge. But it was more than this. It may have been an expression of an earlier implicit alpha function.

Now the analyst has contact with the influence of facts from his own life, his real person, on what happened. His thoughts, blocked until that moment, move about easily through a complex symbolic network and make him remember and work through personal experiences more thoroughly. Terrible losses and deaths, for generations, non-looks, searches for meaning, for being, the impotence of medicine, of politics, the encounter with psychoanalysis, the difficulty in learning to accept losses, reality, without ceasing to feel indignant. He also perceives specific factors that might have limited his work with S, and then later facilitated it.

Acute enactment and attenuated trauma

Chronic enactment can be understood as regression to a symbiotic dual relationship whose function is to avoid contact with triangular reality. It can be seen through distinct scenes and scripts that fail to stimulate images in the analyst's mind or, when they exist, they are volatile. The analyst is swallowed up by the situation and fails to perceive what is happening. This fact of being swallowed up makes the analyst seem stupid (Bion, 1958; Cassorla, 2013c). He usually has the impression that some progress is being made but, in fact, what we have are false dreams that conceal collusions of mutual idealisation and violence.

Situations of this type show how initial traumas can induce the patient to "fuse" with the analyst, who thus becomes immobilised. This is similar to what happens when a drowning person grabs on to another, trying to save them, and uses the rescuer as a "protective shield" (Freud, 1920g). The dual relationship covers up potentially traumatic situations in the patient by calling up early bonding situations. A paralysed analyst should neither abandon the patient nor be intrusive, since going in either direction can be traumatic. But neither is the analyst able to think, and this situation keeps him from making contact with triangular reality

As was seen above, at certain moments there may be abrupt discharges, technically referred to as acute enactments. The analyst feels uncomfortable, imagines that he has lost his analytic function and attributes the fact to personal defects. But when he sees the facts that are taking place, he is surprised. He realises that before the discharge he was involved in a chronic enactment. Thanks to acute enactment the collusion is undone as soon as the analyst realises what has been happening. There is another surprise when one realises that the analytic process has become more productive.

The study of these situations shows that, during chronic enactment, in areas parallel to the obstruction, the analyst works with the patient to the extent that the analyst's implicit alpha function gradually restores the patient's traumatised symbolic network (Cassorla, 2008, 2013a). When there has been sufficient recovery the trauma can be re-lived in a controlled way because symbolisation is now taking place. The defensive dual relationship is undone and triangular reality comes to the fore. In short, acute enactment is nothing more than the trauma being re-lived in an attenuated way. At the same time, this re-living shows that there is contact with reality, the dual relationship is undone and the patient is able to think. These two situations take place at the same time. Thus, acute enactment involves more than simple discharges. Non-dreams being dreamed and, sometimes, dreams reverting to non-dreams, are also a part of the process. The dyad lives *in statu nascendi* as the intersubjective relationship develops the symbolic formation.

As was seen above, after the acute enactments are understood the analytic process develops, but chronic enactment can return. In fact, this happens frequently during analytic processes, often in ways that are not clear to the analyst. These facts are part of the process of working through traumas. Only when there has been sufficient working through can the triangular relationship be sustained.

To summarise, the natural development of the analytic process with traumatised and borderline patients includes several different configurations, namely: 1. Dual relations that protect against the trauma (chronic enactments); 2. Implicit alpha function which rebuilds the symbolic network; 3. Acute enactment, which indicates the undoing of dual collusion; and, 4. Resumption of the capacity for dreams-for-two. The relationship between enactments and pathological organisations (Steiner, 1993) was described in earlier papers (Cassorla, 2008, 2012, 2014). Chronic enactments can arise as collusions of mutual idealisation alternating with sadomasochistic collusions. The former, collusions of mutual idealisation, are organisations of the "thin skin" type (Rosenfeld, 1987), whereas the latter collusions are of the "thick skin" type.

There is always some personal factor of the analyst involved in enactment and this makes him more vulnerable to induction by the patient. The patient, in turn, is induced by the analyst and does not usually know who started the enactment. It is to be hoped that it was not the analyst. These facts distinguish enactment from projective counter-identification even though they may overlap. Some authors, including Gabbard (1995), give greater importance to the role of the analyst, using the term countertransferential enactment.

The difference between enactment and acting out is that in the latter the analyst is not included and can only observe the patient's discharges. In enactment the analyst is led by the relationship instead of merely observing it (Bateman, 1998).

We can classify enactments as normal, or pathological. When the analyst detects the communicational aspects of normal and pathological projective identification (but does not let himself be recruited by such identifications), he momentarily identifies with his patient. These are normal enactments because they are undone through the analyst's interpretations at the same moment they occur. This happens all the time in the symbolic area. It is here that mutative interpretations (Strachey, 1934) are indicated and possible. The difficulty of making a mutative interpretation (Caper, 1995), when the analyst imagines that his interpretation is going to traumatically undo the dual relationship, can be understood as normal enactment that has become pathological through factors of the analyst. But we cannot rule out the possibility that the analyst is sensing a true traumatic factor, that is, that he is in contact with a non-symbolic area where, at least for the moment, there is no indication of a breach in the continuity of the dual relationship. Rather, the dyad should work to redo or to broaden the capacity for symbolisation. Therefore, a mutative interpretation will be useful (and non-traumatic) only after sufficient symbolic fabric has been created to sustain the triangularity.

In summary, pathological enactments, or simply, enactments, resulting from factors of the patient interacting with aspects of the analyst, are considered chronic when they are prolonged without being identified or when they evolve into impasses. On the other hand, enactments are considered acute when they mobilise the analytic dyad, and they last for short periods if they are understood. In the literature the term enactment usually refers to acute enactment.

To conclude

It is certain that, due to personal difficulties of their own, analysts can be blind to material provided by their patients and they can thus be responsible for possible enactments. In this paper, however, we have discussed situations where enactment enabled very close contact with areas that are deficient in their symbolisation. The analyst's understanding made it possible to expand the patient's symbolic network beyond what had occurred before it was obstructed.

It is not clear exactly how the alpha function operates. In this text we associate it with the deep unconscious communication going on between the members of the analytic dyad, and raise the hypothesis that chronic enactment may have this function, beyond its obstructive aspects. As we saw, it seems here that the analyst's unconscious dream, his implicit alpha function, was caught up by the patient, a possibility that deserves further investigation. Stern et al. (1998) present hypotheses on implicit intersubjective movements that coexist with the explicit knowledge of the transferential relationship. These movements evolve into what Stern et al. call moments of meeting, which occur when each participant (especially the analyst) "has actively contributed something unique and authentic of his or herself as an individual" (p. 912), beyond their routine therapeutic roles. These moments of meeting alter the intersubjective context and enable rearrangements in the defensive processes.

These ideas are similar to what we suppose happens when acute enactment makes a break in a chronic non-dream-for-two. Enactments therefore correspond to obstructive processes in which both members of the dyad are involved and the processes result in damages and impasses in the analytic process. But they can become very useful when they are undone and understood, and even more so if their presence has allowed the introduction of implicit alpha function. The gains and losses result from factors involved in each enactment and from the possibility of a second glance (Baranger et al., 1983) or listening to listening (Faimberg, 1996).

References

Austin, J. L. (1990). *How to Do Things with Words*. Oxford: OUP.

Baranger, M., & Baranger, W. (1961–1962). The analytic situation as a dynamic field. *International Journal of Psychoanalysis, 89*: 795–826.

Baranger, M., Baranger, W., & Mom, J. (1983). Process and non-process in analytic work. *International Journal of Psychoanalysis, 64*: 1–15.

Barros, E. M. R. (2000). Affect and pictographic image: The constitution of meaning in mental life. *International Journal of Psychoanalysis, 81*: 1087–1099.

Barros, E. M. R., & Barros, E. L. R. (2014). The function of evocation in the working-through of the countertransference: projective identification, reverie and the expressive function of the mind. In: H. B. Levine, & G. Civitarese (Eds.), *The W. R. Bion Tradition: Lines of Development—Evolution of Theory and Practice over the Decades*. London: Karnac.

Bateman, A. W. (1998). Thick and thin-skinned organisations and enactment in borderline and narcissistic disorders. *International Journal of Psychoanalysis, 79*: 13–25.

Bion, W. R. (1957). Differentiation of the psychotic from the non-psychotic personalities. In: *Second Thoughts: Selected Papers on Psycho-Analysis* (pp. 43–64). London: Heinemann, 1967.

Bion, W. R. (1958). On arrogance: In: *Second Thoughts: Selected Papers on Psycho-Analysis* (pp. 86–92). London: Heinemann, 1967.

Bion, W. R. (1962). *Learning From Experience*. London: Heinemann.

Bion, W. R. (1963). *Elements of Psychoanalysis*. London: Heinemann.

Bion, W. R. (1965). *Transformations*. London: Heinemann.

Bion, W. R. (1967). Notes on memory and desire. In: E. B. Spillius (Ed.), *Melanie Klein Today: Mainly Practice* (pp. 17–21). London: Routledge, 1988.

Bion, W. R. (1970). *Attention and Interpretation*. London: Tavistock.

Bohleber, W., Fonagy, P., Jiménez, J. P., Scarfone, D., Varvin, S., & Zysman, S. (2013). Towards a better use of psychoanalytic concepts: a model illustrated using the concept of enactment. *International Journal of Psychoanalysis, 94*: 501–530.

Britton, R. (1999). Getting in on the act: the hysterical solution. *International Journal of Psychoanalysis, 80*: 1–14.

Brown, L. J. (2011). *Intersubjective Processes and the Unconscious: An Integration of Freudian, Kleinian and Bionian Perspectives*. New York: Routledge.

Caper, R. (1995). On the difficulty of making a mutative interpretation. *International Journal of Psychoanalysis, 76*: 91–101.

Cassorla, R. M. S. (2001). Acute enactment as resource in disclosing a collusion between the analytical dyad. *International Journal of Psychoanalysis, 82*: 1155–1170.

Cassorla, R. M. S. (2005). From bastion to enactment: The "non-dream" in the theatre of analysis. *International Journal of Psychoanalysis, 86*: 699–719.

Cassorla, R. M. S. (2008). The analyst's implicit alpha-function, trauma and enactment in the analysis of borderline patients. *International Journal of Psychoanalysis, 89*: 161–180.

Cassorla, R. M. S. (2012). What happens before and after acute enactment? An exercise in clinical validation and broadening of hypothesis. *International Journal of Psychoanalysis, 93*: 53–89.

Cassorla, R. M. S. (2013a). Reflections on non-dream-for-two, enactment and the analyst's implicit alpha-function. In: H. B. Levine, & L. J. Brown (Eds.), *Growth and Turbulence in the Container/ Contained: Bion's Continuing Legacy* (pp. 151–176). London: Routledge.

Cassorla, R. M. S. (2013b). In search of symbolization: The analyst's task of dreaming. In: H. Levine, G. Reed, & D. Scarfone (Eds.), *Unrepresented States and the Construction of Meaning. Clinical and Theoretical Contributions* (pp. 202–219). London: Karnac.

Cassorla, R. M. S. (2013c). When the analyst becomes stupid: An attempt to understand enactment using Bion's theory of thinking. *Psychoanalytic Quarterly, 82*: 323–360.

Cassorla, R. M. S. (2014). Commentary to case Ellen: the silent movies. *International Journal of Psychoanalysis, 95*: 93–102.

Ellman, S. J., & Moskovitz, M. (Eds.) (1998). *Enactment: Toward a New Approach to the Therapeutic Relationship*. Northvale, NJ: Jason Aronson.

Faimberg, H. (1996). Listening to listening. *International Journal of Psychoanalysis, 77*: 667–677.

Feldman, M. (1997). Projective identification: the analyst's involvement. *International Journal of Psychoanalysis, 78*: 227.

Feldman, M., & Spillius, E. B. (Eds.) (1989). *Psychic Equilibrium and Psychic Change: Selected Papers of Betty Joseph*. London: Routledge.

Ferro, A. (1992). *The Bi-Personal Field: Experiences in Child Analysis*. London: Routledge, 1999.

Ferro, A. (1996). *In the Analyst's Consulting Room*. Hove: Brunner-Routledge, 2002.

Ferro, A. (2009). Transformations in dreaming and characters in the psychoanalytical field. *International Journal of Psychoanalysis, 90*: 209–230.

Franco Filho, O. M. (2000). Quando o analista é alvo da magia de seu paciente: considerações sobre a comunicação inconsciente de estado mental do paciente ao analista. *Revista Brasileira de Psicanálise, 34*: 687–709.

Freud, S. (1900a). *The Interpretation of Dreams. S. E., 4*: 1–627. London: Hogarth.

Freud, S. (1905e). Fragment of an analysis of a case of hysteria. *S. E., 7*: 1–22. London: Hogarth.

Freud, S. (1914g). Remembering, repeating and working-through. *S. E., 12*: 146–156. London: Hogarth.

Freud, S. (1918b). From the history of an infantile neurosis. *S. E., 17*: 1–124. London: Hogarth.

Freud, S. (1920g). *Beyond the Pleasure Principle. S. E., 18*: 1–64. London: Hogarth.

Gabbard, G. O. (1995). Countertransference: the emerging common ground. *International Journal of Psychoanalysis, 76*: 475–485.

Green, A. (1998). The primordial mind and the work of the negative. *International Journal of Psychoanalysis, 79*: 649–656.

Grinberg, L. (1957). Perturbaciones en la interpretación por la contraidentificación proyectiva. *Revista de Psicoanálisis, 14*: 23–32.

Grinberg, L. (1962). On a specific aspect of countertransference due to patient's projective identification. *International Journal of Psychoanalysis, 43*: 436–444.

Heimann, P. (1950). On countertransference. *International Journal of Psychoanalysis, 31*: 81–84.

Hinshelwood, R. D. (1999). Countertransference. *International Journal of Psychoanalysis, 80*: 797.

Joseph, B. (1985). Transference: the total situation. *International Journal of Psychoanalysis, 66*: 447–454.

Klein, M. (1952). The origins of transference. In: *Envy and Gratitude and Other Works, 1946–1963* (pp. 48–56). London: Hogarth.

Klein, M. (1957). Envy and gratitude. In: *Envy and Gratitude and Other Works, 1946–1963* (pp. 175–235). London: Hogarth.

Mann, D., & Cunningham, V. (2009). *Past in the Present: Therapy Enactments and the Return of Trauma.* Hove: Taylor & Francis.

McLaughlin, J. T. (1991). Clinical and theoretical aspects of enactment. *Journal of the American Psychoanalytical Association, 39*: 595–614.

Meltzer, D. (1983). *Dream-life: Re-Examination of the Psycho-Analytical Theory and Technique.* Reading: Clunie.

Money-Kyrle, R. E. (1956). Normal counter-transference and some of its deviations. *International Journal of Psychoanalysis, 37*: 360–366.

Ogden, T. (1994). The analytical third: working with intersubjective clinical facts. *International Journal of Psychoanalysis, 75*: 3–19.

Ogden, T. (1999). *Reverie and Interpretation: Sensing Something Human.* London: Karnac.

Ogden, T. (2005). *This Art of Psychoanalysis: Dreaming Undreamt Dreams and Interrupted Cries.* Hove: Routledge.

Racker, H. (1948). La neurosis de contratransferencia. In: *Estudios sobre Técnica Analítica* (pp. 187–221). Buenos Aires: Paidós, 1977.

Racker, H. (1953). A contribution to the problem of counter-transference. *International Journal Psychoanalysis, 34*: 313–324.

Rosenfeld, H. (1965). *Psychotic States: A Psychoanalytical Approach.* New York: International University Press.

Rosenfeld, H. (1987). *Impasse and Interpretation.* New York: Tavistock.

Sandler, J. (1993). On communication from patient to analyst: not everything is projective identification. *International Journal of Psychoanalysis, 74*: 1097–1107.

Sapisochin, S. (2013). Second thoughts on Agieren: Listening the enacted. *International Journal Psychoanalysis, 94*: 967–991.

Segal, H. (1957). Notes on symbol formation. *International Journal of Psychoanalysis, 38*: 391–397.

Spillius, E. B., & O'Shaughnessy, E. (Eds.) (2012). *Projective Identification: The Fate of a Concept.* New York: Routledge.

Steiner, J. (1993). *Psychic Retreats: Pathological Organizations in Psychotic, Neurotic and Borderline Patients.* London: Routledge.

Steiner, J. (2006). Interpretative enactments and the analytic setting. *International Journal of Psychoanalysis, 87*: 315–320.

Stern, D. N., Sander, L. W., Nahum, J. P., Harrison, A. M., Lyons-Ruth, K., Morgan, A. C., Bruschweiler-Stern, N., & Tronick, E. Z. (1998). Non-interpretative mechanisms in psychoanalytic therapy: the "something more" than interpretation. *International Journal of Psychoanalysis, 79*: 903–921.

Strachey, J. (1934). The nature of the therapeutic action of psycho-analysis. *International Journal of Psychoanalysis, 50*: 275–292.

CHAPTER NINE

Autistic features encountered in the world of "as-if"*

Lindsay L. Clarkson

Introduction

Analysis is an ongoing endeavour for each analyst to deepen her capacity to take in all aspects of her patient's experience. We utilise, as best we can, our emotional, intellectual, and creative capabilities as a person to come into contact with aspects of ourselves and our patients that are disturbing, disheartening, and downright terrifying. We encounter forces in ourselves and pressures from our patients that work against full exploration, and we are aware that there are forces that encourage us in our dangerous and rewarding endeavours. Feldman has described the pressures on the analyst to make herself comfortable colluding with certain aspects of the patient's archaic internal object relations, and the strain the analyst is under to see things just one way (Feldman, 1997). Counterbalancing such pressures, we are strengthened in our work when we sense a growing sense of emotional reality developing in our patient's understanding and our own. Bion describes that a sense of reality is vital for life, in the way that air and food are essential (Bion, 1962). With patients who present with little contact with internal or external reality and challenge us to enter an "as-if" world we must do without the relief of emotional reality for long periods of time. In this paper I will address the autistic phenomena encountered in the defensive organisation of "as-if", to illuminate both the pressures on the analyst from within and without to remove herself from the encounter, and the understanding that may help the analyst stay in contact with her patient.

*Acknowledgments: During my last conversation with Betty Joseph, we discussed this paper. I am grateful to her for her comments, as well as her role in my development as an analyst and a person. I will miss our shared love of psycho-analysis and gardens. I would like to thank Drs Shelley Rockwell, Kay Long, and John Kress for their thoughtful, close reading and encouragement as this paper developed.

In the "as-if" world, opposites smoothly coexist without contradiction, but this shapeless quality is paired with a constriction that pinches awareness of internal and external reality. Joseph recognised that in certain patients beyond the dominant archaic object relationship evident in the transference, there can be an obscured dependent and ill person. This is the aspect of the patient that needs attention, and that might be able to be enlisted in more normal growth (Joseph, 1989). The analyst can find the wherewithal to sustain her work through the preservation of an awareness that she must stay open and receptive to a small part of her patient, alive and observing who might be capable of contact.

Harold Searles has the capacity to turn an observation on its head. Searles describes his work with a patient who could not allow his analyst to have emotional meaning to him. After Searles ventured an observation, his patient replied with some contempt: "You are of no more significance to me than that fly-speck over on the wall there." Over time, Searles came to appreciate that to prevent certain collapse, the patient could only tolerate a speck of awareness of the analyst's separate and meaningful being. Unbattered by his patient's forceful contempt, Searles recognised that it was the immensity of his value to the patient that could not be acknowledged to exist outside of the patient's command. Searles saw not just the way the awareness was diminished and put into a little bit out there, but also that there was some preservation of a tiny portion of this knowledge that could be communicated to his analyst if the analyst could receive it in this form (Searles, 1979, p. 163).

"What is wrong with this person?"

There are many aspects of Helene Deutsch's 1942 article, oddly entitled "Some forms of emotional disturbance and their relationship to schizophrenia", that sound old-fashioned to our ears, but the problems she described are still alive and confounding. In Deutsch's original paper she depicts patients whose "emotional relationship to the outside world and to his own ego appears impoverished or absent", but the situation is "not perceived by the patient himself". She comments on the pressure an analyst experiences in trying to understand an "as-if" mode of relating, which

> forces on the observer the inescapable impression that the individual's whole relationship to life has something about it that is lacking in genuineness, and yet outwardly runs along "as if" it were complete ... something intangible and indefinable obtrudes between the person and his fellows and invariably gives rise to the question, "what is wrong?" (Deutsch, 1942, p. 302)

There is a disturbing disjunction between what seems on the surface to be an emotional sensitivity, but on closer observation is revealed to lack emotional reality. The person responds to others as though attuned, but there is no depth or inside process. Everything happens at the level of surface imitation or mimicry of responsiveness. As an analyst, one knows something is off. One can perceive that what is being reproduced is a facsimile of a containing relationship; the form lacks live resilience and responsiveness to actual emotional experience. This false structure has a tendency to spring a leak, which reveals the looseness and jumble inside that is always threatening to pour out. The goal of the "as-if" patient is to keep things intact and seamless without reference to internal or external reality. The analyst is to function as an inanimate matrix that is under the control of the patient, supporting the false structure. In response the analyst may feel useless, unnecessary, and alien. The containing aspects of the analyst's understanding are perceived as threats to a defensive organisation that is designed to forestall the threat of dissolution caused by awareness of separation.

Mr R had been talking in a seamless way (in his own mind, free-associating as he would imagine I would expect; to my mind, using words about emotional situations in others without any live emotional resonance to his own experience or real empathy with the people he was describing) when I made a comment. The patient paused, and after a few moments, went on. This time he incorporated what I had said as though he had already included the knowledge in his previous remarks. When I took up the way my comment was smoothed in to his narrative, he said he knew what I was talking about. He went on to say: "It is as though you are walking along smoothly, and suddenly there is a slight twist in your ankle. You can continue on after a small wince and a pause, but not quite so smoothly. It takes a moment to regain your smooth pace." I did get through a bit; there was a wince, and Mr R conveyed the effort he had to exert to not be rattled. It was my impression that he used the pause not to think about what I had said, but to bind his ankle, and resume my/his gait as best he could. The perturbation disappeared into his pace.

Strains on the analyst

The analyst in close contact with a patient who treats reality as fantasy, feels in a sensory deprivation chamber, as there is no ordinary sensory or human feedback that one has any trust in. This situation may induce some disorganisation and panic in the analyst, or sudden need for sharp closure. The floating quality of the "as-if" organisation in which nothing is ever settled, may move the analyst to impose her own views of reality on the patient out of a desperate need to get someone's feet on the ground. What is lost in such a refusal by the analyst to bear with the disintegrative tendencies and mechanistic recoveries in her patient is the communicative aspect of the forces from the patient. Since words are not used in their ordinary emotional or symbolic sense, the analyst is often perplexed or irritated. She may speak to her patient as though the words were being used symbolically to communicate feeling, when the words are being used to create a seamlessness to prevent awareness of a gap. I will highlight the autistic anxieties and defences that play a role in creating an "as-if" quality of relating and that I think disturb and trouble the analyst.

As I read through the literature about the "as if" phenomenon, it was apparent to me that I was not alone in my difficulty in finding a place of reverie within myself that felt meaningful and receptive. The following two examples give the flavour.

Riesenberg-Malcolm comments:

> On occasion the patient reports intense suffering or pain or difficulties, but the analyst's feelings usually do not correspond to those reports, as they do with other patients. There is often an atmosphere of morality, and the analyst has vague feelings of guilt, sometimes mingled with irritation or despondency. (1990, p. 386)

... often gives the analyst a curious feeling of hovering between thinking the patient's action is voluntary or conscious or an unconscious bizarre behavior and between the feeling that the patient is re-enacting something or that he is plainly lying. (1990, p. 388)

Harold Searles notes:

... much "as-if" behaviour, which strikes us as repellently contemptibly "phony" relates to an early life impoverishment ... viewing these patients in such a light yields a sense of compassion which one badly needs in one's work with these exasperating persons. (Searles, 1979, p. 141)

Such thoughts and feelings are distressing for the analyst to be aware of in herself. If we go toward the irritability and propensity to distance ourselves, it may be feasible to understand the quality of the object relationship that is being activated and that seems at the moment intolerable. The analyst is provoked in part because she feels such futility in trying to get through; her efforts are continually and subtly dismantled. In addition, the patient communicates a deep disturbance, a sense that the most basic trust and dependence on another being is awry and that he has turned his intelligence to a delusional self-sufficiency, which the analyst is required to join. The analyst may in turn be disturbed by such profound disorientation. There are uncomfortable pressures on the analyst to conform to a non-human status or to accept a position, without inquiry, as a figment of the patient's imagination. The idea of a patient's mimicry of the external form of the analyst, in person and in mind, does not do justice to the analyst's perception of an annihilating attack on her self and on meaningful links to the rest of the world. The patient treats the analyst as a non-human entity entirely under the patient's control, with no reality except what the patient confers. The purpose from the patient's point of view is not to find reality but to go by the book of how someone behaves, and the analyst is influenced to conform to this plan. The recovery of the analyst to round herself to empathy with the patient is essential to finding a way to talk to the patient and to creating some disruption of a profound stasis.

What lies beneath

Keeping in mind the potential for a reachable speck of awareness in the patient, it is the realm of autistic experience that has seemed most helpful in explicating the qualities of the world the analyst must enter to find her patient. If the analyst can take a perspective that the best the patient can do is utilise the analyst as an inanimate object, an assembly line, a movie camera recording, then the analyst already has some purchase. If the analyst can further understand the threat of catastrophic dissolution that lurks if there is anything other than a seamless contiguity, she has a position from which to work. The mechanisms that seem most operative here are evidence of pathological interference with normal projection and introjection. These patients are sticking to the outside, moulding themselves to another, mimicking. There is no interior space for words, thoughts, feelings to enter into or be contained within. Such patients look to intense perceptual and body sensations controlled by themselves to hold themselves together. Without rigid obsessional methods there is a terrifying feeling of dissolution, incoordination, evaporation.

Most of our theories of psychic change depend upon the ability of the analysand and analyst to find a way to develop a relationship that has the quality of the container and contained. The analyst's capacity for reverie allows her to take in disturbing and unmodulated terrors, desires, phantasies from her patient and understand them emotionally in such a way that they are moderated and put into a form that can be taken in by the patient in a more tolerable conformation. The patient's ego is strengthened incrementally not only by the tolerance of his own urges and fears, but by an introjection of some of the mother/analyst's capacity to cope. If we can comprehend the situation, the patient has the experience of being safely held in his analyst's mind. The language we use, of being held, implies a body experience of being gathered up in the arms of one's mother, with the sensations from all modalities: intimate looks, familiar smells, rhythms of the maternal body, sounds of her voice, accustomed touches, experience of her affective tone, etc. Daniel Stern's work extends the observation that babies from earliest infancy are able to weave the various sensory modalities together in the context of affective exchange, between mother and infant. The baby experiences intensities, shapes, temporal patterns, hedonic tones and is constantly moving toward integration of experience. Stern describes a baby's ability to take in early rhythmicity and patterns in a multi-sensory way, that become the underpinning of a time and spatial sense in relationship to the human and nonhuman world. It is when there is some stability of being held that an interior space may be perceived in the maternal object and in the infant's own developing self (Stern, 1985).

In an "as-if" experience, the attention of the other creates an awareness of separateness and difference from the object that feels catastrophic. Much of what we see as action in relation to the analyst reflects a defensive structuring to take apart this awareness. Such patients often use their considerable intelligence in highly detailed obsessional organisations that mimic the artless flow of spontaneous emotional interactions, in lieu of the dangers of true creativity or freedom to be alive that would expose the faulty nature of the earliest object relationship.

Mr N recounted that his mother, who from his point of view had always been remote and inaccessible, now had become demented. He arranged to have a photograph made in which he placed his mother's arm around his shoulders to form the image of a mother who loved and was attentive to her son. Mr N was ostensibly pleased with the photograph, as though it were the real thing. In some ways it was better than the real thing, as he was in complete control of the image, and was not at all in contact with any real sense of wishing for a dependable mother, nor of the loss involved in her diminished mind and impending death. Time was collapsed; the Alzheimer's deterioration was "exactly the same" as the mother's original vagueness. An arm around the shoulders in a set-up performance was "equivalent" to love or reverie. As his analyst I was placed in the position of onlooker at the posed dyad to confirm the pose, not to reflect upon it. My day in day out experience with Mr N was "arm around the shoulder for show"; it did not appear to matter whether or not anything I said had any bearing on internal or external reality. It was more important to go through the motions of analysis. Mr N treated me, when I functioned as an analyst, as an intruder who interfered with the tableau of an idealised open access mother that he was orchestrating.

Ordinarily in development of a responsive baby with an available mother the strengthening of the body ego and the sensory floor of our early experience becomes implicit. We then go on to privilege what we consider our more "human" capabilities, our use of language and symbolic thought. However, when the earliest emotional relationship is faulty and does not provide an underlying structure of safety, the infant is left in a desperate state. A defect at such a basic level deprives the infant of an underpinning of sturdiness. The infant has to turn to emergency measures to create a modicum of safety. In such a transference situation the analyst may be utilised, taken into the structure of her patient's experience by being stripped of her human integration, and employed as a surface to lean against, or a rhythm to which the patient can synchronise. The patient turns away from what the analyst offers, preferring his own creation as ghostly as it is, to awareness of the disaster of a separate object. It is a relief to the patient to reduce the analyst to appointment times handwritten on a page.

At a moment when Mr N felt slightly more integrated, he described the analysis as "a figment of his imagination". I felt this was when he was most truthful, or at least there was some truth to this observation. If the analyst is seen as a figment of the patient's imagination, then the patient is not forced to face the hard edge of the analyst's separateness. "Imagination" is used by the patient, but, in fact, is too differentiated a word for the function he means, as it implies there is an integrated internal self operating. However, like Searles' speck, there is a possibility of a small aspect of the patient that is an alert hidden watcher.

Working with Mr N, I could better understand what I had previously considered odd enactments by Helena Deutsch in her original paper. Deutsch had reported giving her patient a ticket to her lecture, and giving another patient's artwork to an expert to assess. I thought Deutsch must feel compelled to assert that she is a psychoanalyst and will give a lecture ensuring her patient's attendance so that her patient would be convinced of this reality. In my view, Deutsch must have believed there needed to be an objective expert, definitively judging the lack of creativity and real interiority in her patient's work, as the floating lack of reality in which mimicry was treated as identical to live and painful creation was intolerable. Faced with such a lack of ordinary perspective, the analyst may feel a desperate need to assert some authority or meaning. However, the sense of being intolerably unmoored helps us understand our patient's situation.

Thoughts on development

Esther Bick has drawn our attention to early states of being that she feels precede the processes that Bion describes in his model of container-contained. From close observation of infants, Bick delineates two basic states, a way of being that coheres, or an uncoordinated, dissolving, process of annihilation (Bick, 1968, 1986). In ordinary situations, because of the fragility of its ego, a baby too hungry, or cold after a bath, before being cuddled in a towel, would fall into such a state of dissolution. The mother steps in, and from the baby's point of view, gathers the baby up. The skin to skin contact creates a boundary of self that is secure and relieving. Without the intervention of the mother's cohering self, the infant feels loose and in mortal danger of evaporating. Bick describes how "in its most primitive form the parts of the personality have no binding force from amongst themselves"; thus the baby depends on the mother in the earliest post-partum days to perform a function for her baby by responding, holding the baby in her mind, and body. She does this in the most basic sensory ways, rocking, soothing, singing, keeping the baby together, or gathering the baby when it falls into states of dissolution. Bick thought the baby felt this passively, done from the outside. Although Bick's description of a pathological development is compelling, I find myself in disagreement with Bick's idea that this level of passivity is ever a normal state. Under ordinary circumstances there seems much evidence for a powerful, cohering push by the baby from very early life to seek engagement with another, with the expectation of an actively receptive other to be found (O'Shaughnessy, 2006; Stern, 1985).

From Bick's understanding, the baby gradually develops a capacity to introject through reciprocal interaction with the mother, as the baby must be able to sense an internal space in the mother. Bick felt that the infant with a nipple in the mouth closed a hole in the boundary that the mouth represents, and if this relationship worked harmoniously the baby could develop a sense of interior space. If there is no internal object that inspires and safeguards a coherent self, then the infant will be unable to project into an external object. Bick initially focused on the sensory experience produced in the skin by tactile pressure, but later developments have emphasised aspects of rhythm, patterning that is visual or auditory, familiar scents, accustomed moods, that also serve the function of creating a bounded sensory floor.

If all does not go well, either from the infant's side—of extremes of sensitivity, defects, or marked unevenness in sensory processing, or other neurological dysfunctions—or from the mother's side—of vacancy, inability to relate, depression, psychosis—the baby will not find a mother who can help with the binding needed for a beginning sense of coherence. A mother may not be able to tolerate the awareness of otherness or separateness of the baby, and so treat the infant as part of herself. If the skin in relation to the mother's containing function fails to operate as a boundary, the infant is left in a state of unintegration, dissolution, with catastrophic anxieties. Bick describes:

> The need for a containing object would seem, in the infantile unintegrated state, to produce a frantic search for an object—a light, a voice, a smell, or other sensual object—which can hold the attention and thereby be experienced, momentarily at least, as holding the parts of the personality together. The optimal object is the nipple in the mouth, together with the holding, talking, and familiar smelling mother. (Bick, 1968, p. 484)

Most relevant for the "as-if" defensive measures are the "second skin formations" described by Bick. In response to primitive terrors that emerge as a consequence of defects in the early skin relatedness, children develop in an omnipotent way to deny the reality of the problem. A false independence may be instituted; there is often a hypertrophy of muscular or verbal capacities (chatterboxes), which may mirror the business of mental functions that desperately try to hold the personality together. This protective strategy has terrible consequences; there is no space between the mother and infant for a relationship to develop. A certain kind of existence can be ensured but there is no room for growth.

A number of years ago I was wearing new shoes that were slightly pinching my feet. Before I went out to find Ms. G in the waiting room, I had the fleeting sensation of wanting to take off my shoes and stretch my toes. I suspect I was anticipating the constraint of the upcoming hour. When Ms. G came in, she first smiled widely as she did each time she entered. She then sat on the couch, and began to remove her shoes, which she had never done in the course of many years of treatment. She caught herself, to say, "What am I doing, I meant to straighten the napkin for my head [as she invariably did each day]. I have confused my head with my feet." I was momentarily disoriented. My first inclination was to recoil from her impulse to remove her shoes as uncanny, detailed, and unsettling. Slowly I relaxed, regained my wits, and became interested to experience a world in which minds are read. I thought I had understood that my patient was acutely aware of me. Ms G characteristically took things in with a quick peripheral glance that appraised me and my office each time she entered. Suddenly the rapidity of the operations involving seamless perception and a move to alleviate discomfort was apparent to me at a whole new level. Now, how can we understand how such a transmission occurs? I suspect that my patient is a bit like an "idiot savant" in her ability to read me, that she is able to scan and process unconsciously my facial expression, my walk, my body movement. Although there is an appearance that she was in my head, I think she was reading me from the surface, leaning into me, to mimic me, which made it feel uncanny. Just as a person who can calculate the day of the week for any date in any year couldn't tell you how the process works, I think her scan of me, which occurred each day during the smile, was a robotic function gathering mechanical feedback in minute detail. I have the impression that she experienced something not the same in me this day, and this glitch produced an unbearable separateness and lack of identity that created an ominous threat. Ms G unconsciously moved quickly to create an experience without a wrinkle between us; we indivisible had reason to take off our shoes. The disturbance between us had disappeared. In this session I did experience some dislocation and irritation that I thought reflected a glimmer of Ms G's response to my lack of uniformity.

The underpinnings of a sensory nature underlie our basic sense of consciousness, orientation, and security in the world. For most of us this awareness lies in the background, unless a disruption suddenly puts uneasiness or precariousness in the foreground. The sensation of the tremor during an earthquake or a disorientation that can occur when a swimmer is tumbled by a breaking wave are examples of such physical dislocations. These are transitory; is it imaginable that one would have to endure this sensation permanently? I suspect that it is this kind of disruption in the analyst's sense of self that causes some of the countertransference disturbance in "as-if" relatedness.

Tustin has explored the defensive nature of the use of autistic objects and shapes. These are called into play when the child has experienced a separation before there is a sense of a sustaining, cohering force from within. Tustin describes bodily separation from the mother at this stage of emergent self (before continuity and integrity have been established in a body way supported by the mother) as having been experienced concretely as a disaster. The nature of the terrors, of dissolution, or of falling into limitless space, spurs the infant to turn to a pathological self-sufficiency. The child tries to create a surround out of sensations that the child can provide and control himself. The autistic child utilises powerful perceptions and bodily sensations as a means to hold himself together. Instead of projection into an object, he utilises mimicry and sticking to an object, which denies the two-person problem. If the defences fail, vertigo, fears of falling into a void, or leaking away emerge.

The nature of the sensations employed to prevent dissolution is two-fold: autistic objects and autistic shapes. Autistic objects are inanimate, tactile, hard, impervious, unvarying impressions on the skin, gripped against one's hand. In later life, manifestations may be quiet or unspoken preoccupations with lines, appointment times, visual grids, deep obsessionality, necessity for sameness and predictability into which an analyst may be incorporated. The analyst may be relegated to a matrix viewed by the patient as his own construction. The other sensations, autistic shapes, are more liquid and flowing, slippery and malleable, moulding to a surface. In conformity to such sensations the analyst may be treated with subtle pressures, of a kid-glove softness, that may disguise the omnipotent control exerted. It is only gradually that she may realise she has been reduced to static, under the patient's control. The sensation has become a substitute for containment, and prevents real containment or contact with a separate object from occurring (Tustin, 1992).

Bick, and later Meltzer, who elaborates the concept slightly differently, have described "adhesive identification". This is a primitive form of object relation at the skin level, where a sense of cohesiveness is derived from contiguous contact with the other. They emphasise the difficulty of growth in the absence of a sense of interior space. Meltzer describes coming to discover the two-dimensional world inhabited by autistic children, in which there were no spaces, nothing changed. He movingly described children who could lean up against something, mimic something from the outside, but couldn't hold things in their pockets. Meltzer depicted a drawing of a house, in which one stepped in the front door only to exit the back door; there was no interior. The analyst of the "as-if" patient is made to feel two-dimensional in a disturbing and flattening way (Bick, 1968; Meltzer, 1975; Meltzer et al., 1975).

Trying to understand what we observe

Daniel Stern reports that he was called in to observe the interaction between a mother on the psychiatric ward and her ten-month-old daughter, as there was a disagreement among the staff about the mother's potential danger to the child. Some on the staff thought the mother should have more time with her daughter; others felt that there was something terribly wrong going on and that the baby was in danger when in her mother's company. Stern describes that his team was interviewing the mother when her baby was brought to her:

> The mother gently took her sleeping baby and began to lay her on the bed so that she would stay asleep. The mother did this with enormous concentration that left us closed out. After she had ever-so slowly eased the baby's head onto the bed, she took one of the baby's arms which was awkwardly positioned, and with her two hands carefully guided it to a feather-like landing on the bed, as though the arm were made of eggshells and the bed made of marble. She poured herself into this activity with complete and total participation of her body and preoccupation of her mind. Once this was done she turned to us and picked up the interrupted topic of conversation in a normal manner. (Stern, 1985, p. 205)

In a structured observation to measure attunement, the mother was found to be vigilant about the baby, but absolutely not attuned to her baby.

> Gradually she revealed to us that she was almost exclusively attentive to the external environment and not to her daughter. She concerned herself with the hard edges of the desk, the sharp things on the floor, and the sounds from outside. If the horn that she had just heard beeping,

beeped a second time, she would alter what she was doing with the baby at that moment. If it did not beep again, she would continue doing what she was doing and await some other external signs, all of which were non-specific to her and open to her interpretation. Because of her preoccupation with trying to both read and control the external world impinging on the baby, she remained unavailable to enter into the baby's experiences and share them.... The baby had presumably become accustomed to the shifting of the mother's interactional tack. She seemed to have adapted passively, falling in with the mother's new direction of activity when it shifted. (Stern, 1985, p. 206)

The mother's exquisite care looks like attunement (unless one can bear to look closely), hence the disagreement of the staff. A catastrophe is already in evidence in the material. Stern imagines that the child at some later date would probably perceive that there are interactions between others that she herself knew nothing about. A patient later in life might describe a sense of being from another planet. The language is reminiscent of Tustin's: the eggshell quality of the arm, the hard surface of the marble bed, the beeps, the edges of the desk, the mother pouring herself into her daughter without boundary. What is poignant is the infant's necessary compliance to a completely incomprehensible world, such that there is apparently a mother infant dyad interacting, but in fact there is no containing relationship that responds to the infant's internal or external experience. It is essential to the infant's survival to go along. Physical annihilation is the alternative to psychic annihilation.

If we think of the countertransference in an "as-if" world, it is along these lines. We are being asked to comply with an "as-if" relatedness, although neither party has a belief in the reality of containment. Given the complexity of the infant's primary relationship, one can see how important and valuable the relative simplicity of interacting with the inanimate, apparently self-generated world might be for the baby. As no true inner self could be built up under such circumstances, the child will develop an encapsulated, in this case, compliant, "second skin" to prevent a total breakdown.

However, inside, the patient feels an alien being who has no belief in human containment as a solace. Temple Grandin's "squeeze box" is a good example of a mechanical solution devised by an autistic person to the problem of debilitating, catastrophic anxiety. She imagined and constructed a machine that she controls to provide a variable deep pressure on her whole body. This pressure offers her a sensation of profound relaxation (Grandin, 1984). For Temple Grandin, the "squeeze box" at her disposal is much more relieving than the demands of the complex and confounding interactions with humans. However, it is difficult for the analyst to perform the function of a squeeze box without recoiling. And if the patient is using words, and psychological words, we are often tempted to take up the words, ignoring the way the words are being used, that is, not symbolically, but more concretely as a squeeze. It is a difficult task for the analyst to hold both in mind, the tolerance of the felt necessity of the mechanical aspects of being, and an openness, without pressure, to the emergence of more differentiated insight, or a tiny speck of awareness from within the patient. It is hard for the analyst to live with the experience of one's life being squeezed out of one's perceived being. If the analyst stresses more integrated aspects prematurely, then the patient goes right along "as-if".

In a session

In the final section, I will report on a Monday session occurring four years into an analysis that commenced following the breakdown of a relationship. The session is used to illustrate the surface level of the patient's psychic organisation. Of particular interest is the nature of the watching eye alluded to in the material, that is not, for the most part, human. In fact, a live and aware being is suspect. As in Stern's description, the analytic dyad is already a problem, as there is a lack of a sufficiently robust good internal object to build upon. Instead, an inanimate construction is substituted for an animate world.

Mr N is attractively dressed, and presents in a completely different entire ensemble one day to the next. The dress and demeanor that accompanies his outfit is carefully thought out to create the situation he is entering. He "knows where he is" if he has (in phantasy) orchestrated the scenario in which he is now located.

> Mr N begins: "I took a half a klonopin, then woke at five am. I went to sleep quickly, and I feel alone and unprotected on lying down so I want to rush by this. I wake up gingerly. Am I in one piece? Then I put myself back together to approach the day. I put on a mantle of proficiency.
>
> I had been on line last night with three different women. One sounded nice; she worked in the helping profession. Another called. I do not answer, I do not call back. They are left waiting, wondering why I do not call.
>
> I went to visit my family this past weekend. When I arrived at the local airport, I felt like weeping. I feel I would want to kiss the ground."
>
> [He goes on to describe waiting for his family. When they arrive, they rush in and stop to greet another man while my patient watches. As yet unmet, he tells me about his outfit, a suede jacket, blue jeans, boots and that he is standing next to his suitcase. Finally his family notices him and come running over to welcome him.]

Where are we? As his analyst, I am listening to his talk, which seems to have coherence, and at some level does. He recognises how klonopin obviates the need to face a transition to sleep or dream. There seem to be emotions; "feeling like weeping", "wanting to kiss the ground", "waking gingerly" suggesting he might fall apart if not careful, but there is no emotional grounding. Rather the words are like articles of clothing put together for effect. There are references to the three-day break we have just had, and the three analysts he has encountered, who wait for him to call; it is not he who waits. "A mantle of analytic proficiency" is a good description of the quality of the patient's "free associations". There is more solidity in the suede jacket (soft and moulding) or the suitcase (more angular and edged) than there is in the emotional display of the family towards him, or in himself towards the situation he is in. His family greets with identical enthusiasm the person who is not him. Mr N has rushed in on me with about the same level of recognition. It takes work to approach this material with a real appreciation of Mr N's need to seem to belong while recognising that he has no belief that the object has any capacity to relate to him as an individual. Instead of collapsing, leaking away, he is in a jacket or in a suitcase or a mantle of proficiency. Mr N limits his awareness not just in relation to others, but within himself. I comment that he wanted me to be sure to see him in one piece. That it was important that we rush past any uneasiness about the transition from his morning alone to being with me. I think he saw me as an object who has no capacity to tolerate or hold his worries of collapse.

> Mr N answers: "Well, I am fine, once I get in motion." [I think he is now in the motion he is talking about, chattering along. My words have oriented him. He now has been "greeted" and knows what to do.]

Mr N goes on to talk about his ease and relief once he is in the security line at the airport. He gives himself over to the situation. Gracefully, and effortlessly, he follows the rules, unlike his ex-girlfriend who was anxious and awkward. He does give the impression he is relishing his superior handling of the process as he is telling me about his proficiency. The effect on me is to feel I have been subsumed in the security process, which, of course, is in place to prevent catastrophe. On the other hand, the security process often seems quite futile; no one has any belief in its real effectiveness.

Mr N speaks from on high, and likes the experience of the camera recording him. He makes it clear that the camera's eye is linked in his mind with the pilot, whom he trusts and admires. The watching eyes link the inspector and the pilot and produce an unblinking constant watching focused on his grace and subtlety. The camera admires how quickly and effortlessly he seems to manage. There is a watcher of minute and intimate details in a completely impersonal way, having nothing to do with himself or his internal world. Mr N is no longer frightened of dissolving in transit, he leans into the process of the transition, relaxing in the squeeze box he has created. I am the condescended-to girlfriend struggling with the indignity of exposure and the awkwardness of being human, or the pilot at the helm. Neither is invested with real weight.

I comment that I think it is relieving to be watched at every step, and there is no sense of being unmoored. I think he feels I am watching as he speaks to me, and he feels I admire and am relieved by how smoothly he talks to me.

> Mr N then responds: "I am also aware that inside I am loose, and not held together." [I feel for a moment that he could bear to talk about an awareness *inside* without collapsing. I observe: when I spoke about the importance of his smoothness, he felt I understood he was uneasy inside.]
>
> Mr N pauses slightly and then goes on to discuss a family whose child he teaches. The family is going through a difficult time as the father is ill, and the mother said hopelessly, in the course of a meeting about the child, that she had never worked and wouldn't even know how to write a cheque or do the basics about taking care of the family. Mr N felt immediately that he would have to take over all of the functions the husband had fulfilled, for the rest of his life.

I say that I think he feels he would be endlessly tied to this woman without any sense that anything could change or develop, and that he feels with me that this is what he could hope for from our work, a way of thinking that he experiences briefly with me, but doesn't hold away from me. There seems no real reason that I am working with him; I simply have agreed to take on these functions for the rest of his life.

> Mr N responds: "Well, all my life I have been afraid of being like that. Not being able to function at all. [For a moment he is serious, and then moves to cut me out.] In contrast, yesterday I was at such a high speed, very busy indeed. I did three hours of gardening, power-washing the back deck. I was not alone, because the workmen were out in the yard. It's funny, I don't like gardening or housework; I wouldn't have been out there, but for the company. I had thought yesterday of getting back together with my girlfriend. No questions asked. Nothing would be different except that then I would have someone in the house. It makes me think of my mother. I have no sense that she was *doing* anything in the house. My mother is so perfunctory; she treats me as though she cared for me, and I go along."

Here Mr N has become manic, busy in the external world, busy in the internal world. In response to my comment that drew attention to his location with me, he briefly recognises there is a human me, not just a fly on the wall or a security camera, but a real person with some capacity for emotional containment. This awareness threatens and disturbs him and has to be dismantled. Mr N describes the altered analyst, a woman of no capacity, whom he now is fated to care for. The situation is hopeless, so without choice or the possibility of development, but he has moved into high speed. The analysis now is a site of power-washing and rapid gardening. There is no sense that there is a home in himself that has to be put right. He is doing it because the other workers are there and will see his fast work. He will be like them and seem to have a purpose. He is reinstalling the archaic object, a perfunctory mother that will create an impression of a mother at home. His interest in the home is for show, unrelated to any real concern, and the mother is not actually thought to be capable of doing anything inside.

I say that I thought he was rushing to fill in when he is talking to me this way. We are both very busy, all is supposed to look right but I did not think he felt there was anyone home to cope with his worries, that he is not held together inside.

Mr N. pauses, then responds with a description of the clothes he set out the night before, and that it looked to him as though he were getting dressed up for me. This morning he ran upstairs to add one more detail.

He has entered his clothes as a second skin. I respond, "You felt you had to present yourself, put together, graceful, so I would see you turned out, and would think I was doing good work." I thought he didn't have much belief in this, as he did not feel I could manage if he showed me anything awkward or worried.

> Mr N, in a slower voice, goes on to say: "When I would go to the store with my mother, she didn't notice me. I felt I disappeared, and she could easily wander off without me [which is what I feel he has just done to me]. At eight years old I had a fantasy that a movie camera would watch my every move, followed me wherever I went. I liked to be watched. My mother would say go outside and play. I don't think she was thinking it would be fun for me to be

outside. I would go out as I was told, and feel aimless. I was not sure what to do. [This description, as empty and at a loss as it is, has a more genuine feel to it than the whole rest of the hour.] I think she was tired of me asking questions or following her about. I found a crack in the sidewalk and watched the ants. I crouched down, and I would follow their business and lose all sense of time. [Mr N was being drawn into the ants' movement. He was pulled out of his head into tiny little bits of aliveness going in and out of a crack endlessly, without interruption or development.]"

I comment that he feels this camera watching is more reliable than me as a person who can be distracted or develop a crack. He watches me, and tries to fit in; that helps when he would otherwise feel frantic.

Mr N responds in an unusual way, recognising the end of the hour.

This is a complicated communication, as he has jumped ahead to end the hour, but I thought, because of my comment, he was tolerating a slight awareness that there was a separation about to occur, and that time was passing, not static. I think when I was able to accept the way he saw me as a mechanical eye, that something more alive from within him could emerge. His despair about making human contact with an object who is human and receptive to his emotional experience became briefly available to him (not just to me). He was for a moment aware of a sense of desperation and a feeling that he was doing something to me that might make me weary of him. The aliveness often slips back into the cracks. I often have to face a feeling of discouragement when what seemed for a moment a gathering slips away like sand through my fingers.

Final thoughts

Despite the unreality of much of the emotional experience of the session, there are small moments of genuine contact that have gradually emerged in the analytic work. In this paper I have tried to explore the quality of relatedness within the "as-if" world, not with judgment but with an appreciation of the necessity for this way of being. The patient who presents as a facsimile of a person, where the second skin is the only area of interface with the analyst, is very difficult to engage in a way that allows the analyst any confidence in the reality of her emotional perception. Repeatedly, the analyst's attempts at thoughtful communication have been parsed and dismantled, and are so altered that the meaning has gone out. If the analyst can comprehend that the mechanical aspects of control, smooth operation, and the need to look artless, but to act without emotional aliveness, are felt to be essential for survival, it can lead to greater empathy for the patient's dilemma. The analyst can then withstand the despair engendered as the momentary gathering of emotional meaning abruptly disperses, to stay receptive to whatever glimmer of communication is occurring.

It is never certain; as analysts we are always trying to discern how our responses have evolved: out of understanding, or out of intimidation and compliance, to forces from within or without. For growth to happen, the analyst must introduce perturbation to the "as-if" system, otherwise we are enacting the seamless phantasy that is imprisoning the patient. In a paper on the defensive uses of compliance Feldman describes the subtle but forceful and intimidating pressures on the analyst to conform with the patient's phantasy that there should be no separateness or difference between the patient and object. He describes such a person:

> She has a capacity unconsciously to tune in to the other person's needs in a way which can be extremely rewarding, since she becomes exactly what the other person requires of her, and this reinforces her sense of triumph over and superiority to the person to whom she is so sensitively compliant.
>
> However, what does become apparent is that this compliance by the patient, or by her object, has a quasi-mechanical quality, as if one object is fitting in with another in a plastic fashion: it is not mediated by thought or understanding. (Feldman, 1999, p. 29)

I have been emphasising the more mechanical aspects of relatedness in the patients I have discussed, who initially do not seem to evidence awareness of internal needs in themselves or in another. Because we as analysts are sensitive to feelings, we may be aware that the patient is responding to a fleeting awareness of an internal state, but I do not think the patient is aware of the feeling that leads to forceful defensive maneuvers. We may be tempted to fill in the emotional blank in our patient prematurely with our own awareness, out of uneasiness with the dislocation we experience in the weightlessness due to lack of emotional gravity. It is the reflexive, automatic, alien quality of the reaction that I think we fight against. It is not just the ways we don't understand, but the ways we are familiar with such experiences that may impel us to move away from re-experiencing such terrors that impede our reception of our patients (Ogden, 2014). If the analyst can face her own discomfort and simply describe the skin level or gridlike frame the patient inhabits, she may be able to find some moments of real communication conveyed by the patient who perceives himself to be a being without a home in the human universe. If there is not too much pressure on the patient to be other than he is, the patient may be able to experience some gathering sensation from the analyst, and a beginning awareness of sensation originating inside himself. In the course of an hour with one young patient there was a movement from a contemptuous, hateful comment about "the rocks" on my shelves to a gradual acknowledgement that they were "fossils", with a history and a life, and the potential for seeds, long dormant, to grow.

References

Bick, E. (1968). The experience of the skin in early object relations. *International Journal of Psychoanalysis,* *49*: 484–486.

Bick, E. (1986). Further considerations on the function of the skin in early object relations: findings from infant observation integrated into child and adult analysis. *British Journal of Psychotherapy,* *2*: 292–299.

Bion, W. R. (1962). *Learning from Experience*. London: Heinemann.

Deutsch, H. (1942). Some forms of emotional disturbance and their relationship to schizophrenia. *The Psychoanalytic Quarterly, 11*: 301–321.

Feldman, M. (1997). Projective identification: the analyst's involvement. *International Journal of Psychoanalysis, 78*: 227–241.

Feldman, M. (1999). The defensive uses of compliance. *Psychoanalytic Inquiry, 19*: 22–39.

Grandin, T. (1984). My experiences as an autistic child and review of selected literature. *Journal of Orthomolecular Psychiatry, 13*: 144–174.

Joseph, B. (1989). The patient who is difficult to reach. In: M. M. Feldman, & E. B. Spillius (Eds.), *Psychic Equilibrium and Psychic Change* (pp. 75–87). London: Tavistock.

Meltzer, D. (1975). Adhesive identification. *Contemporary Psychoanalysis, 11*: 289–310.

Meltzer, D., Bremner, J., Hoxter, S., Weddell, D., & Wittenberg, I. (1975). *Explorations in Autism*. London: Karnac.

Ogden, T. (2014). Fear of breakdown and the unlived life. *International Journal of Psychoanalysis, 95*: 205–223.

O'Shaughnessy, E. (2006). A conversation about early unintegration, disintegration and integration, *Journal of Child Psychotherapy, 32*: 153–157.

Reisenberg-Malcolm, (1990). As-if: the phenomenon of not learning. *International Journal of Psychoanalysis, 71*: 385–392.

Searles, H. (1979). *Countertransference*. Madison, CT: International University Press.

Stern, D. (1985). *The Interpersonal World of the Infant*. New York: Basic.

Tustin, F. (1992). *Autistic States in Children* (revised edition). London: Routledge.

CHAPTER TEN

Responding to narcissism

Michael Feldman

Hera, the sister and wife of the great god Zeus, found it difficult to endure her husband's constant infidelities. She became aware that whenever Zeus turned his attention to yet another young and beautiful creature, one of her own nymphs, Echo, would distract Hera's attention with her chattering and singing. When she discovered this, she deprived Echo of the gift of speech, condemning her to repeat only the last syllable of words spoken in her presence. Shortly afterwards Echo fell in love with a young Thespian named Narcissus. As she was unable to declare her love, she was spurned by him and went to hide her grief in solitary caverns. She died of a broken heart, her bones turned into stone, and all that was left of her was the echo of her voice.

Narcissus in turn was punished for having spurned Echo, by making him fall in love with his own image. The soothsayer Tiresias had predicted that Narcissus would live only until the moment he saw himself. One day, when he was leaning over the limpid waters of a fountain, Narcissus caught sight of his own reflection in the water. He conceived so strong a passion for this phantom that nothing would tear him away from it, and he died there of languor. He was changed into the flower that bears his name and which grows at the edge of springs.

The question I wish to raise is this. If we can imagine ourselves coming upon the scene in which a handsome youth is gazing adoringly at his reflected image, impervious to everything around him, how do we respond? Do we stand back, and take a scientific interest in the scene, wondering about the psychological mechanisms that operate with such profound effects? Do we try to intervene, ruffling the water, pointing out it is just an illusion? Or interpose ourselves, shake him, or try and turn his head so he should see us and take note of his surroundings? Do we try and talk to him in a sensible and reasonable way, warning him that he is locked into something deadly? Or do we become so intrigued, so fascinated, so drawn into the scene that we begin to lose ourselves in the tragic beauty of it? Or, perhaps, we come to believe, after a while, that Narcissus is indeed aware of our presence, finely attuned to our interest and responses, involving and controlling us in a subtly cruel fashion? I hope to explore some of these possibilities in relation to the clinical material I am going to present.

In his paper "On narcissism", Freud (1914c) wrote as follows:

> Women, especially if they grow up with good looks, develop a certain self-contentment which compensates them for the social restrictions that are imposed upon them in their choice of object. Strictly speaking, it is only themselves that such women love with an intensity comparable to that of the man's love for them. Nor does their need lie in the direction of loving, but of being loved; and the man who fulfils this condition is the one who finds favour with them … Such women have the greatest fascination for men, not only for aesthetic reasons, since as a rule they are the most beautiful, but because of a combination of interesting psychological factors. For it seems very evident that another person's narcissism has a great attraction for those who have renounced part of their own narcissism and are in search of object-love. (pp. 88–89)

He speaks of the charm exercised by the person's self-contentment and inaccessibility, and goes on to suggest: "It is as if we envied them for maintaining a blissful state of mind—an unassailable libidinal position which we ourselves have since abandoned" (p. 89).

I am going to describe some of the issues that arose in working with an attractive, intelligent, narcisstic young woman—the pull into becoming fascinated and absorbed by the way she spoke and functioned, the responses she elicited from her analyst, and the problem in finding ways of engaging her analytic work that might lead to psychic change.

The patient had a particular way of speaking, using a quiet, modulated voice. She would hesitate, apparently struggling to find just the right word or phrase, describing events and interactions in the greatest detail. It was important to her to get the nuance right, to include as many perspectives as she could, all the while assuming my intense interest and concentration. Or she would explain her thoughts and interpretations in complicated and subtle ways, not so much that I might understand or be able to help her in any way, but so that I might observe in admiration and fascination. It often felt as if one was watching, gripped, a sensitive musician preparing herself for a wonderful, artistic performance, or a gymnast preparing herself for a feat of grace and skill. I sometimes became uncomfortably aware that I was responding to her by speaking at great length myself, often quite repetitively, trying to explain and describe in detail my view of what was going on.

I trust I did not exactly mirror her—I hardly ever felt there was anything to admire in what I said or did with her, but on these occasions I talked as if I was addressing someone who might be interested and might be able to listen and think about what I was saying. I now recognise the way I addressed her arose out of a quiet hopelessness in me, my despair about the patient being able to understand and respond to my interpretations as symbolic and meaningful communications.

In response to what I said to her, the patient would often pause, give a token "nod" in the direction of what I had spoken about, perhaps repeat or confirm some small point, and then proceed with a further complicated and beautiful elaboration of her own experiences and thoughts.

It was as if I had been driven, a little desperately, to find an interesting and persuasive interpretation to engage the patient's attention, to draw her away from the fascinated contemplation of her own beautiful reflection in the pond.

At times, it felt that I too was becoming lost in fascinated contemplation of the complexity of her mind, and her language. It was difficult to find a way of addressing the peculiar lack of real engagement, the sense I had that the patient often did not, perhaps could not, link up with the meaning of what I was saying. And behind this were doubts about the possibility of anything really changing—perhaps we were indeed engaged in a fascinated, but sterile and deadly contemplation of a phantom, with which one couldn't really make contact.

To the extent to which the analyst is in contact with the more deadly, psychotic aspect of the patient's narcissistic disorder, this inevitably has a disturbing effect upon him. Instead of an apparently beautiful and innocent scene, one is confronted with something that is profoundly anti-understanding, and anti-development. It is always difficult for the analyst to recognise and to find words to capture these underlying forces, and the primitive phantasies they embody, because of the disturbance that is evoked in him. As I will illustrate, this situation may drive the analyst into speaking to the patient in ways that represent his attempts to make sense of the situation for himself, to deal with the experience of turmoil, uncertainty, and confusion that is evoked in him, which make it very hard to find ways of thinking and speaking about the situation. Thus what he interprets to the patient may take little account of what is happening between them in the room, and the extent to which the patient is unable to think or to understand what is going on in his own mind and what the analyst is saying to him.

I will say very little about the patient's background. Several members of her family are quite disturbed: her parents have been separated for many years, and her mother lives abroad. The patient has little contact with her, and when they do communicate, she finds her mother largely self-preoccupied and unavailable, while going through the motions of being concerned. The patient was much entangled with her younger sister, for example, both sharing and competing over their pathological relationship to food. When her sister moved abroad, they would have two-hour conversations on the telephone, each narrating the most minute details of their lives, thoughts, and feelings, giving the other her turn, and then proceeding. She feels distressed, hurt, and angry that her sister has now apparently disentangled herself. She is married, and refuses to get drawn into the kind of intimacy they previously shared.

In the course of the analysis the patient, who is intelligent and attractive, has been able to resume studying, and has indeed been very successful, often gaining the highest honours. Friends, tutors, professors are filled with excitement and admiration for her, and often behave in extraordinary ways with her. She has moved from an interest in the arts, increasingly towards psychology, and she is currently involved in a postgraduate clinical psychology course, where she conveys that she is unquestionably the most sensitive and talented student.

Clinical material

In the first session I want to describe, the patient spoke about a phone call with her mother. She explained that they had not spoken for two and a half months. When her mother phoned on Sunday, she couldn't speak for long, so Miss A phoned her back the following night. She then gave me a detailed report of their conversation, indicating how her mother spoke as if she were interested in hearing about Miss A's work, and as if she were expressing concern about Miss A finding it so exhausting. What her mother said made Miss A feel tearful, and she said to her mother, "Gosh, I'm going to get upset, I'm going to cry", and she told me she had cried silently for a bit. Her mother said, "Am I asking too many questions, or saying too much?" Miss A responded, "No, no, it's nice that you're interested."

Miss A went on to say to me, "… I don't know, it's so sad, it's so sad. I couldn't just think Oh, how lovely. Part of me did think that, but it also felt as if she was just saying the right thing; saying what she had learnt to say. Anyway I had to finish writing up my report, so we couldn't talk for long then either because my mother had to go, she had some other telephone call she had to make, some important telephone call."

Miss A went on, without a pause, "And then last night I had this dream, of being in a changing room place at the swimming pool. There was this woman there, just walking across the room, naked, and I was looking at her. I was particularly looking at her breasts, absorbed with how perfect and wonderful they were. They were perfectly young and shaped and full. I was looking at her hungrily, in some sort of emotional way. She caught me looking and she looked away, but she knew that what she had was very special and beautiful. I felt so ashamed, so absolutely devastated, that I *so* wanted to look, and yet I knew somehow that I wasn't allowed to look.

"But it felt so innocent to me, all I wanted to do was to be allowed to be somehow part of this beauty and look at her. The woman *knew* she had something beautiful and there was a way in which she was swanning herself, parading it in a slightly teasing manner. [Silence.] That was all. Also, in the dream I was feeling just so … awful and dirty and impure and ugly in comparison … [long silence]"

> I simply commented on the way she had emphasised the purity and innocence of her interest and longing, and yet she felt so uncomfortable when the woman, who knew that what she had was very beautiful, noticed her looking.

The patient responded very quickly, saying "I think that's a story that I tell myself a lot. I was talking to my mum about my sister last night. I see myself as having this innocent pure desire to be friends with my sister. It's a desire to meld or join in some complete way. When that is met with a look which is forbidding, that somehow casts my impulse into a different light, then I feel terribly ashamed and … it feels like there is something initially sort of sexualised about this wanting, not so much sexualised as being erotic or wanting some very delicious and luxurious joining, and then I feel like I'm told no, you can't. Then I feel terrible."

> At the start of the session the patient went into great detail about the difficulty in communication between herself and her mother. Their attempts to speak to one another on the telephone are repeatedly disrupted by each being busy with other affairs.
>
> The patient portrayed herself as longing for any gesture that created the illusion of intimacy. Both she and her mother felt obliged to say the "right things", but she recognised the empty quality of their interaction and became, briefly, sad and hopeless. I think she might also have become uncertain how her "story" was being received by her analyst—whether I was

gripped and absorbed in her narrative and her images, or whether I was looking and listening from a different perspective.

I think it was when she began to doubt the version of an idealised relationship with her sister, her mother, and her analyst, and indeed became painfully aware of the emptiness of her mother's expressions of affection and concern, that the patient quickly went on to describe a dream, where she was absorbed in the contemplation of the beauty of a woman's breasts. She referred to herself looking "hungrily", wanting to be part of this beauty.

In the Narcissus myth, Echo's punishment renders her unable to express her love for Narcissus, and he spurns her, condemning her to a tragic lonely demise. Narcissus in turn is condemned to fall in love with his own image—leading eventually to his own death as well. In the session I have been describing, the failure of proper contact between the patient and her mother, and her doubts about the contact with her analyst in the early part of the session, result in her evoking a dream. In the dream she too "falls in love", becoming lost in admiration of a young woman's body, wanting to merge with her. While it is ostensibly another woman's body she is absorbed with, I think it is in fact an idealised version of herself, a beautiful young woman with perfect breasts (and a beautiful mind) that she identifies herself with. Her description of the woman "swanning herself", teasingly aware of the admiring gaze of the other, vividly and accurately captures elements of the atmosphere the patient creates, or seeks to create, in the consulting room. It is as if the analyst, too, should become lost in the fascinated contemplation of her body and her mind, and not have to recognise, or think about, the difficult, even tragic, elements of her situation, and the problems in communication that exist in the analysis as well as outside.

In the course of the session I did indeed find myself being drawn into paying close attention to what was in front of me—not just her vivid, familiar, and painful description of the interaction with her mother, but I was very interested in the shifts in her narrative, and the complex pattern of identifications that I struggled to give meaning to. I found it difficult to have any confidence in my *understanding* of what was going on, either between the patient and her mother, or between the patient and myself. Indeed it took some work to move into the mode where I could even *attempt* to understand what was going on, as if this required me to free myself from an underlying pressure. It felt as if there was a powerful requirement to listen carefully, to become involved, and to *react* to what I was being presented with. It became evident that the patient did not primarily *require* understanding from me, and could probably not make use of what I could offer her.

I think one can see the extent to which what appears to be a narcissistic structure contains a powerful dynamic. There is an underlying desperation that *requires* the object to be drawn into a mutual idealisation—in Miss A's case, between her and her sister, or her mother, and now with her analyst. When the object escapes from this pressure, and looks at her from a different perspective, and thus "casts her impulse in a different light", the narcissistic defence collapses, and she feels terrible—terribly ashamed.

As quoted earlier, Freud referred to the great attraction of another person's narcissism, and the charm exercised by the person's self-contentment and inaccessibility. "It is as if we envied them for maintaining a blissful state of mind …" If we are indeed charmed, I think we become seduced into a kind of *folie à deux*—sharing an idealisation of the narcissistic figure that persists until we—or someone else—ruffles the water. On the other hand, if we consider Freud's reference to our envy of the other person's blissful state of mind, in so far as we are excluded from this, such envy entails hatred and the wish to disrupt the other person's admiring contemplation of her own image.

I thought my patient was aware that she stirred up complex reactions in the other—excitement, admiration, frustration, and resentment, and she feared that this would elicit a response—an observation, a comment, or an action that would disrupt the benign, idealised version of herself suddenly exposing her to feeling awful—dirty, impure, and ugly.

Thus, on the one hand, I felt like a fascinated, helpless spectator, impressed and gripped by her narrative, and, she assumed, admiring the beauty of her dream narrative. On the other hand, I had some awareness of an impulse to challenge, to disrupt, to try to engage with the patient—to be allowed to make a meaningful contribution. I think I responded to this dilemma by trying, in an inappropriate fashion, to make "sense" of what she had described. In my first intervention I had simply observed how she had emphasised the innocence of her interest, and yet she had felt so uncomfortable when the woman in her dream had noticed her looking. This comment did not address the difficult and frustrating quality of the interaction in the session, and the underlying despair. I think her response confirmed that she could not make any use of what I had said.

What I can now more easily recognise is how much the situation between us in the session recapitulated her dream. I thought the analyst had become the spectator mesmerised not only by the beauty of the patient's body and mind, but drawn to watching a very particular scene. In it, although the patient is herself apparently admiring another young woman's beauty, it seemed clear that she was, in fact, absorbed in the fascinated admiration of herself, and her own ideas, and I was required to join her in this.

My intervention was followed immediately by the patient saying "that's a story that I tell myself a lot"—she did not engage directly with the analyst and what he had said, but with her own "story", which was already present in her mind, and had come up in her dream. Thus the patient could acknowledge that I had spoken, and she repeated one or two words that I had used, but she did not, apparently, engage with the content or the meaning of what I had said. Instead, she continued in her absorption with her own thoughts, experiences, images, and words. The analyst is once again put in the position of having to observe her and witness her admiring preoccupation while also having to manage the impulse to challenge and to confront her.

I think in the patient's mind, and to some degree in reality, the analyst has two alternative sets of responses. Ostensibly, he is invited to join her in fascinated contemplation of her physical beauty, the beauty of her thinking, and the vivid and erotic dream she brought. I think she believes that although the analyst tries to maintain a professional neutrality, he must be excited by her and what she offers him—he too must become filled with needs and desires for the beautiful breasts, and what they offer, although he may also be anxious about *her* penetrating, "forbidding" look.

At the same time, behind this erotised phantasy there is a much more disturbing view of the analyst's responses, namely the presence of the analyst's "forbidding look". I think this probably refers to her belief that he is aware of the patient's hostility and her perversity, and his "look" expresses his own feelings of frustration, disapproval, and resentment.

Returning to the session, the patient went on to say, "I know about the kind of excitement that was in my dream. I remember telling my father and his wife about the baby I'm observing, describing the breastfeeding, and then describing the way the mother couldn't let the baby touch her. My father was obviously really excited by the whole thing. It disturbed me as I thought it was because *I* was talking about it. On Monday, as I was watching the baby playing with a plastic toy, and … I can't remember if I told you this yesterday … and also [she mumbled] I presented my observation to the course seminar yesterday. [Then she suddenly began to speak in a bright, animated and coherent way.] She was playing with this toy, and she is amazing, she can be on her own for quite a while with this toy … I am sure I have told you this already … and she was munching it and she became completely victorious in her enjoyment and began shouting. It was a shout that was loud and exuberant. She filled the air with her shouts of joy. I was surprised how loud she was. When I was with my sister at Christmas I felt I couldn't show her that I wanted to be with her, that I like to be with her, that I need her. It all has to be secret and hidden away. And there is something of that in the dream, as if I am not allowed to show how beautiful I find the woman's breasts."

> The patient begins by saying she knows about excitement, and she gives a vivid sense of the way her objects become excited—her father, the baby, and, she assumes, her peers and her analyst are impressed and excited by her observations and lively descriptions, which she is clearly proud of. She portrays the baby's mother as an anxious inhibited woman who has difficulty with being touched, even by her own baby. She conveys that her responses, her understanding, and her responses are better and more admirable than the responses of her object. However, always accompanying this narcissistic view is the sad and painful view of her mother and her sister in particular, not wanting to be touched physically or emotionally, so she has to restrict herself, unlike the exuberant baby. This was reflected in her hesitancy and mumbling when referring to the way her presentation had been received. While she can allow herself a degree of exuberance, pleasure, and excitement in her narrative, I think she is always uneasy about my reactions. On the one hand, she assumed I would admire her vivid and lively descriptions, perhaps even become excited, like her father, about this talented patient. On the other hand, I thought she was also fearful that her talent and sensitivity would evoke an envious, negative, hostile reaction—I would become this critical "forbidding" figure, who would wish to put her down.
>
> I said it was difficult for her to be open and direct with me, and to take pleasure in her achievements. She couldn't speak directly about the success of her work because she was worried about what she stirred up in me, whether she evoked pleasure and excitement, or something more hostile, resentful, and forbidding. It was difficult for her to experience, and to know in any direct way, what was going on in herself. This meant that she had to focus her attention anxiously on the other person's reactions to her.

The patient said, "I feel like the implication of what you're saying is that I'm just sort of forgetting or scooting over the fact that I know that often, what is going on in me is something much more greedy and aggressive and devouring."

I thought the patient found it difficult to listen, to understand or make any use of what I had actually said. The way she spoke confirmed her difficulty in knowing what went on internally: she thus discussed "the implication" of what I was saying, and speculating in a rather disconnected way. Although she spoke in an apparently "knowing" way, she introduced descriptive words—"greedy", "aggressive", "devouring"—that she had previously used, but which seemed to have little immediate reference.

I commented on her need quickly to try to work out what I was thinking, how I might be seeing her, to show that she herself was able to know and understand things. I thought she needed to protect herself from having to recognise or take seriously any interpretation that might disturb her, and make her feel worried about herself.

After a silence, she said, "I do—I think there is this innocent impulse to want to eat, I suppose [laugh]. In some ways I feel the problem is that I missed the boat, it should have happened a hell of a long time ago and it never happened—now it's too late, and as it gets later and later, I get more and more frustrated. It doesn't go away."

Although the patient seemed to respond to what I had said, in fact I thought there was only a very tenuous connection with the content of the interpretation. It is difficult to know to what extent she couldn't make sense of what I had said, and to what extent she was disturbed by the content of the interpretation. Instead, she seemed once again irresistibly drawn to focusing on words, phrases, and ideas that were already in her mind, and which were familiar. One could, however, understand her as conveying an awareness that while she might have an "innocent" wish to make use of what I offered her, something was wrong with her capacity to take in anything. She believed this went back a long way, and when she could allow herself to recognise that she had "missed the boat", as she put it, he briefly felt rather sad and desperate about whether anything could now change.

I suspect I found this disconnected, but rather despairing, communication difficult to deal with in the session, and I responded by making a long, explanatory, and reconstructive interpretation. It was as if I also had to invoke familiar elements from her history that I knew were important to her, to try to engage her attention. I referred to what she had always conveyed about the quality of her contact with her mother, and how she felt deprived of the innocent pleasure of being the infant at the mother's breast. Something went wrong then, and now she has to be alert to what the other person has in mind, how they will construe her look or her actions. She herself has some inkling that her desires are not entirely innocent and straightforward, but if I try to talk about them in a way she doesn't already know, and hasn't anticipated, she becomes hurt and defensive and easily feels misunderstood.

The patient responded in a bright, vigorous fashion, and at this point any pain or despair seemed to have vanished. She said, "There is a way that even those other things I think, you know, I mean, it seems to me it's a bit like a child stroking a cat and they go 'nice pussy cat, nice pussy cat', and they like the softness of the fur, the warm fire, and the sound of purring and everything, and then they yank its tail [laughs]. And you can understand why it yanks the tail. It's partly an aggressive thing, but it's also bound up with the niceness of this cat, and wanting um .... It's funny, because I don't like cats at all—that kind of devouring thing, there is also something innocent about it, something understandable about it, and I feel it was kind of never allowed, and the voracious appetite was never allowed."

> Although the patient spoke in a peculiar, disconnected way, she gives a vivid description of the way she lulls her object, saying "nice pussy cat" or "nice analyst, I agree with you", which conceals the teasing cruelty and sudden violence towards the object. She briefly indicates it is the good qualities of the object that provoke her attack—presumably because of her envy of the capacity of the cat, or the analyst, to have some feeling of satisfaction and contentment. She herself is never free of the experience of deprivation. I think she felt her object could tolerate neither her appetite, her desires, nor her aggression, and she was left to try to cope with powerful primitive violence and greed.

The patient continued: "Yesterday in the session you interpreted the way I might not be able to take things in within the cycle of things but became voraciously hungry and needy later. I think that happened but I managed to remember what you had said and actually it was okay, the evening was okay, but I felt very tired. Yesterday I ate more carefully, and felt okay in the evening, and woke up having slept very well last night, partly because I had eaten properly. I woke up feeling very refreshed, and I did some good reading this morning, and I did things I felt good about. I noticed that because of the relief about getting out of this destructive zone, things were better this morning, and then I want to ride this wave pretty quickly, and scoot away from the recognition of the other things.

> It was quite unusual for the patient to describe feeling better, eating in a more careful way, sleeping better, and able to work. She referred to what I had said in the previous session, and implied that that had contributed to the improvement. She then spoke in a more obscure way about wanting to "ride this wave" and scoot away from the recognition of other things.
>
> What came to my mind was the way she had mumbled something about the presentation of her observations in her course earlier in the session, but she had made no further reference to it. As I knew how important the responses of others to what she presents has always been, I commented that she had told me about her father's reaction to her description of the breastfeeding, how interested and excited he became. This raises the question of who the woman is with the perfect breasts that are so admired in the changing room. I thought part of the "wave" she spoke about arose when she felt that she made such good observations and presented them in a way that she knows will make people look at her with admiration and excitement, wishing they could do it like her, and have what she has got. I thought she was worried about how to speak about it here, and how I would react.

The patient responded quickly, in a lively way: "You're absolutely right [she laughed], and the presentation went very, very well in fact. I had introduced it by saying I thought I had rushed it and that I was in such a state and hadn't done it properly, but the tutor said that she thought it was excellent and everyone really enjoyed it. She said I should use it as one of the papers for my qualification. After the seminar, walking down the stairs she came alongside me and she said, 'Antonia, you observe *so* beautifully, you really just have a natural gift for it.' And this had to be kept secret, had to take place on the stairs, where she could be more openly enthusiastic than in the seminar with the others present. Perhaps that was why I liked the fact that Gaby, the baby, could shout so victoriously about what she was doing. That there was room for her to do that, and her mother was encouraging, enjoying her achievements. I have always felt aware of the person I was going to trample upon."

> One of the things that interests me is the way such a narcissistic patient leads one to behave. I think I felt intrigued, frustrated, and provoked by the patient's way of speaking. There was something subtly controlling and intimidating about the way she listened for, anticipated, and pre-empted whatever I might think or say. Whether she is stressing her identification with an idealised version of the baby she observed, or the remarkable, sensitive observer, I think she consciously or unconsciously believes she knows what responses she elicits, whether it is fascination, excitement, fear, or paralysis, and I suspect she exerts some powerful control over what can or cannot be said to her.
>
> I had had little doubt about her identity as the beautiful woman in the changing room, or the beautiful observer or psychoanalyst in the consulting room, but I did not initially interpret this directly to the patient. I am not entirely sure why, but I suspect it is because, paradoxically, I suspect she anticipated that I would make such interpretations. It then felt as if I would either be fitting in, confirming what she already knew, or provoked into saying something to disrupt her complacency.
>
> When, in response to her mumbled reference to the presentation of her observations, about which I had already heard a great deal, I did speak about her identification with the beautiful woman, she became excited, acknowledging more openly her triumph and excitement, and her fears about her effects on others. It is not only that they are filled with envy, but also, in her triumph, she feels she "tramples" on the object, her sister, her mother, or her analyst. Thus, in the session she has to watch me extremely carefully—she is anxious in case I get excited like her father, feel trampled on like the other members of the seminar, or get provoked into "trampling" on her. She thus has to resort to constant efforts to propitiate me.

Next session

After a long silence the patient began: "I just don't know what to talk about, but it also feels there's so much to I need talk about. Like the way I didn't drink any tea or coffee yesterday. When I do drink tea or coffee it is very effective in helping not to look at these things. I slept well and didn't eat too much, and that sustains me. At lunchtime yesterday I made this salad, no it wasn't lunchtime, it was for supper. I was watching the news, and I caught myself eating the salad like a dog devouring its food. I was just stuffing it into my mouth. Then I thought about it, and I thought that's somehow what I want, just to have a very full mouth … That is what was left out of the dream yesterday …

"[Silence—five minutes] It's actually terrifying to me to feel better, not to feel that my body is wound up with some physical process … It feels like a kind of freefall, a feeling of indeterminateness … nothing to hold on to. And I realise how attached I am to things that make me feel ill. Things like drinking tea or coffee always make me feel ill, but to have illness almost feels like, sort of health."

After a long silence she said, "I feel very uncomfortable now, sort of awkward, like I haven't really got anything to bring."

> After more silence I said that she had actually brought quite a lot, indeed she indicated how she stuffs her mouth and her mind with the salad of news and talking that fills her up, so she doesn't feel vulnerable. She did worry, however, that I might feel left out and dissatisfied.

After another silence, she said, "I feel worried about being just sort of panicked and vulnerable. Right now I feel I don't want to be looked at; I don't want to be seen. I ate too much yesterday, and this has to be hidden. I have to get through somehow, without being seen as fat.

> I said I thought she did feel she had filled herself up with the news in the session yesterday, in a way that disturbed her, and that left no room for anything else. It didn't satisfy her and she depended on some response from me to reassure her. I thought it was all right if she felt I was involved and gripped by what she was describing and explaining, because one way she protected herself from this "freefall" was to talk, explain, and describe, saying, "It's like this" and "I thought about that", assuming that I am absorbed by her, and responding to her in ways she can anticipate and knows about. However, there was always a danger that I might look with my own eyes or think with my own mind, forming my own judgements about her mind or body, which would threaten and disturb her.

After a while the patient responded, "I think that's right. In the way I dress, I think I control things, by dressing in clothes that are sort of hiding, or sort of straight up and down. I don't like to have my arms bare, and I don't like wearing jeans with just a T-shirt. I don't like to be seen in places which it seems perfectly normal for other people to display."

> I said I thought she recognised the extent to which she felt she had to cover herself up; it was very threatening to be seen or known about directly. If she could talk in familiar ways, as if we were understanding each other, this seemed to offer her some protection.

After another long delay, she responded, "I think all of that's excruciating to me, and I can't bear it. I see myself so reflected in other people, I so depend on other people to reflect back and I try and control what they see. But when that goes out of my control, I worry, 'What are they thinking?' I feel anxious and slightly paranoid … And then I often resort to trying to challenge people to make compliments and jokes so I see their reactions in a form I recognise.

"[Long silence] Now I feel, this is a problem for me, I'm trying to read your thoughts, and I feel you think I'm missing the point. In fact I'm just doing the same thing over and over again and I'm not able to let you have your own thoughts about me and make your interpretations without taking it over somehow.

"[Silence—ten minutes] I'm so attached to this image of myself as … it's what I present. It is probably the way I make people see me, sort of hoodwinking them and myself that I am somebody who is capable of doing all these different things. And so perfectionist."

> I said it was important to see herself as the beautiful woman with perfect breasts that everyone gazes at with such admiration and desire, like the responses she elicited when she presented her work to the seminar. Although she suspects there is something like hoodwinking going on, it is nevertheless desperately important for her to find a way of speaking that also drew me into this kind of admiration, and prevented me from thinking, or doing anything that threatened her. When she didn't feel confident about controlling what I saw and thought, and knowing what was in my mind, she becomes worried, what she describes as anxious and slightly paranoid about what I might recognise was going on in her, which was excruciating.

The patient was silent for about ten minutes, and then said, "I feel pretty sort of exhausted, and hopeless trying to think about it because if feels like its so much its own kind of machine, and involved with all this kind of circular business that I do."

> In this session one gets a clearer sense of the patient being caught up in desperate activities, stuffing her mouth with a salad of food, drinks, and my words from the previous session ("the news"). The broken-up, confused world that lies behind her narcissism becomes more apparent. She seems to have some inkling of her perverse addiction to illness, and things that make her feel ill. However, without them she has nothing to hold on to, she refers to "freefall", with nothing to hold on to, and she is filled with anxiety.
>
> She also conveys that part of the disturbance arises when she feels she doesn't know and cannot control what goes on in my mind. She becomes panicked, vulnerable, and what she describes as "paranoid", and I thought one could see how she tried desperately to do what she called "hoodwink" me, creating the illusion of understanding and agreement in response to my interpretation, but actually missing the point, getting into her own familiar clothes, which conceal her disturbance. When this didn't work very well, I think she became more aware of a mechanical, circular quality to her way of functioning, and at the end of the session gave a brief glimpse of an exhausted hopelessness.

Discussion

The patient I have been describing seemed at times to show the self-contentment and inaccessibility that Freud suggested was present in certain narcissistic women. He thought that they had a great fascination for men, partly because we envy them for maintaining blissful state of mind—"an unassailable libidinal position which we ourselves have since abandoned." Such a figure is vividly present in the patient's dream of the beautiful woman in the changing room, with perfect breasts, knowing that "what she had was special and beautiful". However, the description of her "parading them in a slightly teasing manner", aware of the patient looking at her breasts hungrily, implies an interesting and complex object relationship.

It became clear that the patient not only filled her mouth with something very desirable, but she had to some degree incorporated the desirable qualities, thus becoming partially identified with the beautiful object with special qualities. If she could believe her object—whether her analyst, her father, mother, sister, or teachers and fellow students gazed at her with excited admiration—she could keep at bay the awareness of anything bad, disturbed, or disturbing within her.

Her narcissistic organisation thus depended on her capacity almost to convince herself of her own beauty, talent, and goodness, but also on her capacity to draw her object into sharing this perspective. At the same time, the object had to carry the experience of desire, guilt, and shame that the patient could partially and temporarily disavow.

If there was any sense that the object escaped this mesmerising hold, and viewed and thought about her in a different way, this was very threatening. The narcissistic structure collapsed, leaving her, for the time being, coping with feelings of badness and inadequacy that she strove so hard to cover up.

Reference

Freud, S. (1914c). On narcissism: an introduction. *S. E., 14*: 73–102. London: Hogarth.

CHAPTER ELEVEN

Getting to know splitting as an organising unconscious phantasy, then and today

Claudia Frank

Introduction

A fifty-one-year-old patient replies to my thoughts in her third assessment session: "Now there once again is this kind of line cutting off my foot." She sits opposite me, her right leg folded over the left one and while she talks, she points out to me with her hand this horizontal line that appears as if it is cutting off her right foot. After a short moment she adds in a slightly contemptuous tone that we are dealing with a phantasy here, of course. I have the impression that she has to reassure the two of us with this afterthought. As I would learn later, some years previously an analyst had refused to treat her, as he considered her condition to be too close to being psychotic. In her first two assessment sessions Mrs A had been preoccupied with the question of how best to travel to the sessions should she decide to start an analysis with me. Which would be the most sensible way, which the fastest? Should she take the bus or would it be better to come by tube, or perhaps to use her car? And then there was all the time that she would waste on her journey … I had interpreted in several ways that there was a wish to come and to take the time but alongside it another tendency aimed at preventing her from really getting something here. Following this, she had opened the third session with the remark that perhaps she had inflated the problem of the journey. Later in this session she mentioned the line in the room, as I described earlier: she had made a cut—instead of approaching my thoughts and taking them up.

Mrs A had been suffering for more than thirty years from very tormenting, shame-inducing obsessive thoughts. Over the years she had received several treatments for this and some provided her with temporary relief, but none of them had led to a real and sustainable improvement in her condition. After a renewed increase of her obsessive thoughts, which had brought her to the verge of a nervous breakdown, she decided, as a last attempt, to get help. She found her obsessive thoughts aggressive and gruesome—on the one hand, (dividing) lines, knives, and similar objects constituted a threat against her own bodily integrity, on the other hand, knives were stabbing into the pregnant bellies of others. She found these horrible images inexplicable, since she experienced herself as completely inhibited in aggression and as peace-loving and harmony-seeking. Her problem, as she saw it, was always being "too good" a girl. Yet, as you may imagine, I had already got to know her stabbing side. At the end of the second assessment session, as soon as I had offered her an analysis four times a week with me, she wondered whether she should not rather consult a colleague in a different location, whether she should think of other alternatives. After a while she was able to add, however, that while her husband would think about decisions, then make them and stick to them, she would immediately question a decision as soon as she had made it.

The patient, referring to the line, had spoken about it as a "phantasy" in the sense of "only a phantasy", and so had tried to downplay and deny the dynamic hinted at in the room, which in the course of the analysis would unfold its full force. Thus, she indirectly let me know how, on one level, she was quite aware of the possibly terrible consequences such phantasies can yield in internal and external reality. In the room it seemed they could be so gruesome that under no circumstances should she get in touch with them; they should, as it were, remain separate ("cut-off") and split-off. And yet, her preoccupation with the journey could also be understood as a question to me, whether I would find a way of being with her that would allow her to get in touch and live with herself. Thus, on one level it seemed clear that the way in which I handled "the phantasy" would be crucial—whether I would and could stand up to it (or also had to downplay it) in order that we might examine and get to know its meaning on different levels in the context of the transference-countertransference relationship. The line cutting off the right foot is a conscious phantasy, which contains at the same time central unconscious facets; these are acted out and as such are not known and not wanted to be known. Of course this raises many questions, for example, the phantasy provides a key for the task but what we do not know is what the balance between truth seeking and truth avoidance will be both in the patient and in the analyst.

These questions that came to my mind hint at a fundamental continuum of "in a certain way conscious—in another way unconscious", and in my opinion Melanie Klein proceeded from such an assumption quite naturally—in fact, I believe that she took it as a matter of course and saw no reason or need to work it out explicitly. Underpinning all these questions and thoughts is an understanding of phantasy as mental expression of the activity of both the life and the death instinct from the outset (e.g., Klein, 1952, p. 58). But what does this mean in particular? In 1946 Klein formulated the relevant connections in the following way:

> The more sadism prevails in the process of incorporating the object, and the more the object is felt to be in pieces, the more the ego is in danger of being split in relation to the internalized object's fragments. The processes I have described are, of course, bound up with the infant's phantasy-life; and the anxieties which stimulate the mechanism of splitting are also of a phantastic nature. It is in phantasy that the infant splits the object and the self, but the effect of this phantasy is a very real one, because it leads to feelings and relations (and later on, thought-processes) being in fact cut off from one another. (1946, p. 6)

How did Klein come to this view? I think, she was grounded in the theory and technique of her time, particularly, of course, in those of Freud. Looking at Klein's early lectures and papers, I note that she mentions amongst other things those phantasies that determine the symptoms, actions etc. (see her early publications, "little notes", and others, listed in Frank, 1999, p. 64, 2009, p. 68). In 1921, when she began her analytic practice, she started from the assumption that oedipal impulses and phantasies determine the child's activities, possibly inhibit them, lead to symptoms, etc.—and accordingly she was interested in them and interpreted them. Based on my research of the estate documents of the Melanie Klein Trust in the archives at the Wellcome Institute for the History of Medicine in London, I believe, however, that she was rather intuitively driven by a feeling of not having properly understood something, which made her want to/ need to get things straight about what she had experienced with her little patients. In my opinion, she was from the beginning convinced of having discovered something "new" with her patients, only in so far as each case is individual and unique and revealing hitherto unknown phantasies and connections. Long-term and high frequency analyses with severely disturbed children led her in the following years to engage in intense interactions with her little patients. In attempting to figure out what lay underneath what she was observing, Klein came up with a description of fundamental phantasies linked to mental functioning. I would like to illustrate this with the example of what I believe to be her first description of the splitting of the self.

Let us briefly bring to mind the actual state of theory at that time: Freud had, at the inception of his work, talked about a "splitting" of consciousness—conscious/unconscious—but by and large he then dropped the term. It was not until 1927 that he wrote about a splitting of the ego; sporadic approaches in this direction are to be found a few years before, when Freud conceptualised the ego as the centre of the psychic apparatus. Concerning its relation to reality, he formulated, for example, that "[…] it will be possible for the ego to avoid a rupture in any direction by deforming itself, by submitting to encroachments on its own unity and even perhaps by effecting a cleavage or division of itself" (Freud 1924b, p. 152). As far as I know, Klein does not quote this paper and it remains open as to whether she read it, and if so, how. (In my opinion it was probably not decisive for her own discovery, since her starting point was not a theoretical concern with the instances of the psychic apparatus and reality.)

Klein's discovery of splitting as it emerges in the clinical situation—without her fully realising the discovery as such

A manuscript (captioned "Erna = work, 2nd part"), which Klein had probably written in the spring of 1926, begins with the following assertion: "The material in the drawings clearly indicates the *fragmentation* [*Zerlegung*—dissection] of the personality into two parts" (italics added). In this simple sentence Klein summarises a psychic reality, which had revealed itself to her during her more than two and a half years of analytic work with Erna, the six-year-old girl who had been suffering from a severe obsessional-compulsive disorder. In everyday language she clearly and simply denominates a revolutionary insight into the complex conditions of the self: we are not dealing with a coherent, integrated ego, but with a split personality. As will be typical for the seeds of all her conceptual developments, it is not theoretical concerns and theories that constitute the starting point, but her clinical observations and experiences. It appears to me that her concerns were not primarily about "new theories" and this could explain why she left the manuscript to rest and neither pursued nor published it. My hypothesis is that, at that point in time, she had not yet quite realised just how fundamental were the insights that she had gained from the—often very challenging—process of Erna's high-frequency analysis.

But, first of all, let us listen to the relevant paragraphs of this amazing manuscript:

> The material in the drawings clearly indicates the fragmentation [*Zerlegung*] of the personality into two parts. The opposition between the beautiful princess and the peasant girl or between the witch and the good princess etc. signifies the opposition between good and evil that she feels within her own personality, which is also repeatedly represented in games and phantasies by the alternating angel and devil figures. In the drawings, the evil principle, as for example represented by the witch, regularly and indeed increasingly clearly comes to take on particular characteristics of the good princess, who conversely takes on the other's traits, so that, as it finally turns out in individual drawings, the two opposing figures come to resemble each other. I refer in particular to the representation in which at the sound of a thunderbolt the ugly figure repeatedly turns into the beautiful one and the beautiful figure into the ugly one. In this way, the unsuccessful endeavour somehow to fuse together the two parts of her personality is expressed again. This *splitting* actually arose from the necessity to ward off this evil principle in herself. She is trying somehow to alienate herself from this part of the personality by this *splitting* and manages to do this by projecting it outwards. The witch, the peasant girl [...] emerge in this part of the analysis, [...] as the evil part of her own personality that she rejects. The mechanism of this projection is thus that she has to project the part of her personality that she cannot tolerate outwards on to someone else. By doing this, however, the other person becomes an entirely evil and sadistic figure about whom Erna feels guilty because of her projection. In her phantasy, Erna herself then becomes the victim of the external sadistic person ... (in Frank, 2009, p. 178, italics added)

In my view Klein describes here, in a tremendously lucid way, the cause (the evil felt to be unbearable within oneself) and the effects of splitting (one feels oneself to be the victim of the projected evil). Now, what are the concrete clinical situations with Erna, on which these propositions are based?

Let me first of all remind you of the starting point: Erna's analysis begins in the year 1924. At the age of six, Erna's behaviour at home was "unbearable". She displayed "marked asocial tendencies in all her relations", "suffered from great sleeplessness, excessive obsessional onanism, complete inhibition in learning, moods of deep depression, obsessive brooding, and a number of other serious symptoms" (1927, p. 160). Erna had been able to let Klein know that "there is something about life I don't like" (1932, p. 35). As Klein observed in her session notes, Erna displayed an "especially strong sadism" (in Franck, p. 193), and she was aggressive and contemptuous in her first few sessions. Amongst other things Erna cuts as much paper as she can get into pieces, since she wants to force Melanie Klein to keep giving her "lots of new paper to cut up while taking special pleasure in using up [...] as much as possible to destroy" (in Frank, 2009, p. 196). Klein puts a boundary on this and interprets her "will for power and destruction". Eventually Erna brings her own paper to the sessions and cuts up on her own. Shortly after this, Klein notes Erna's first drawings.

In her notes taken after the sessions Klein only comments on the first picture (Image 1). Here Erna dominates the scene as "the laughing house (because the mother is in heaven) that is covered over in black" (p. 376). In heaven mother finds herself surrounded by two angels. Klein writes: "beginning to understand anal material!" Erna knows, as she says, that she wants to soil herself ("would like to smear herself with small and large") (p. 375). Viewed with Erna's second drawing of the same day [Image 2], these pictures—originating in the seventh session of her analysis—allow us a first glimpse into Erna's complex inner world. The bad girl, having pulled down mother's trousers and smashed her benches and chairs, is now being banished into hell (in Frank, 2009, p. 377). Instead of angels, we are now dealing with various devils. (I will come back to these drawings later.)

The first play-phantasies had been about angels and devils: for example, children who initially had been courteous towards their teachers, but then assaulted, killed, and roasted them.

Image 1

Image 2

The "children are devils" and enjoy themselves. Eventually they are in heaven, "the former devils are angels" (2009, p. 190) and, according to Erna, do not know about ever having been devils, "it wasn't them at all". Right from the start of Erna's analysis Klein had been confronted with the "cliffs and splits" in Erna's personality, as the first drawings impressively bear witness. How one might understand and conceptualise this in detail was part of Klein's analytic research over the following years and it led her, amongst other things, to denominate splitting and to describe the partitioning of the personality into two parts.

The clinical material on which the manuscript is based

We are in the fortunate position that some of the drawings, to which Klein refers in the above manuscript, are preserved. Let us take, for example, the statement at the beginning that in the drawings "the evil principle, as for example represented by the witch, regularly and indeed increasingly clearly comes to take on particular characteristics of the good princess, who conversely takes on the other's traits, so that, as it finally turns out in individual drawings, the two opposing figures come to resemble each other." Pictures such as the second drawing dated 14 November 1925 would have provided a foundation for this. Here, Erna had been drawing two figures (Image 3) and explained that X (the figure drawn in black) was a beautiful girl under the spell of a witch ("black hair poo"). The figure drawn in red would be the witch, who had been put under a spell too and therefore had to do evil; the witch would be crying "bloody tears". And Klein adds in brackets: "recognizes red body etc. bloodily cut to pieces, by her" (in 2009, p. 212).

What went on before this? Klein notes, about the first drawing in the above session, that Erna takes on the role of a strict teacher, dictating the letter B, which her analyst is supposed to copy badly. She "[a]ssociates: B: lower part of bottom & stomach; red line (she made) cut up, bloody." Klein explains in brackets the reversal: now Erna is the strict mother who "punishes me [her] for cutting up" and "taking out [the] stomach". Eventually she notes that Erna becomes listless at playing school and draw instead. Concerning the third B, Klein adds: "+ ... whole person that she constructs from B" (p. 211).

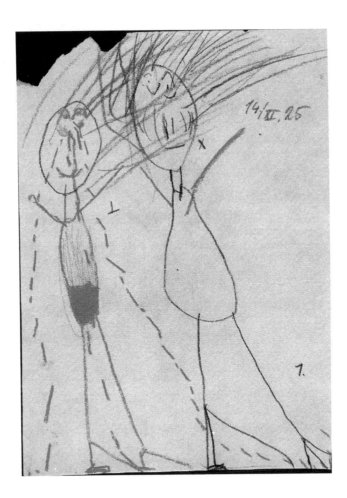

Image 3

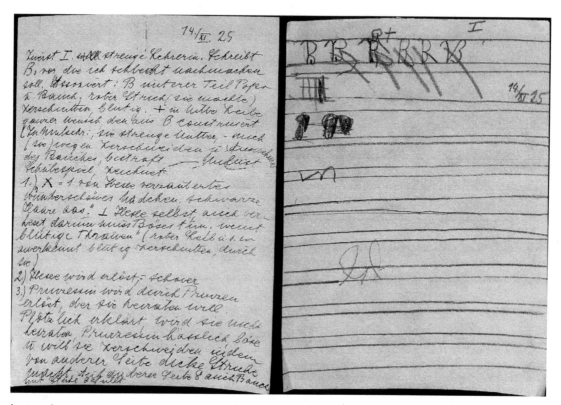

Image 4

Let us try to understand the events by looking at the picture (Image 4): Erna obviously tries very hard to get the first B right, which has an excessively large upper belly—the further evolution of this B allows a reading of this large upper belly as breast. Erna plays school and takes up the role of the strict teacher, as she says. It seems to me that she is identified with aspects of a "teacher"/analyst who gives her interpretations, breastfeeds her with them, and so facilitates (emotional) learning and growth. This fruitful relation can be found eloquently expressed in the oversized lower belly of the second B, a pregnant belly. The third B symbolises the fruit emerging from it: a new little human being. Erna can feel the difference between herself and her analyst. This is difficult for her to bear and so she seeks to reverse the roles. With the instruction that Klein should make it badly, she ensures, that the "bad" is now located in her object (has to remain projected into it), and which she can now "legitimately" attack: Erna cuts and destroys with the red lines the fruitful intercourse, she declares the belly as bum, and we can therefore interpret the small black areas in the third row as faeces. Erna knows that she can go no further with this and turns towards drawing something.

Let us have another look at the drawing (Image 3) that emerges now. We can assume that Erna thinks about what has happened with the help of her drawing. She wants to be a "beautiful girl", expressing her admiration and appreciation for her analyst with a "beautiful" B;

but the experience of the fruitful process transforms her, puts her "under a spell"—instead of Bs/hair/thoughts being beautiful and fruitful they are emptied and Bs/"poohs"/faeces come out of herself/her head. A tempestuous internal movement—a "storm of feelings" (of envy, jealousy etc.)—turns her into another person. The one who transforms/puts on a spell is called "witch"—the figure in the picture has similarities with the beautiful girl, but is phantasised with a more potent body. And Erna is more specific about this witch: she herself is under a spell and so can't help but do evil. In a certain way, Erna seems to depict the principle of talion: what she had done first to the Bs/the belly of the mother, she now has to suffer from the witch. I am impressed by the way in which the bewitched girl and the witch increasingly look the same. Although still depicted as two figures—that is, split and projected—, one might well think that for a moment she gets close to an insight that both (figures) represent aspects of her own self.

We also have the drawings of 5 November 1925, to which the following sentence refers: "I refer in particular to the representation in which at the sound of a thunderbolt the ugly figure repeatedly turns into the beautiful one and the beautiful figure into the ugly one." With regards to the first drawing (Image 5), Klein notes that Erna draws a queen and explains that she has short hair, a moment later that she has none, and finally that it is only a wig. Subsequently she draws the flowers with particular care. But then she paints them over with red—alleging that it would be nicer this way. This is followed by lines crossing the face, a mutilation. Let us look at this strikingly rich and colourful picture. We see a queen with dense blond hair, adorned on the right side with a red bow. We learn how Erna attacks her—by robbing her of her splendid coiffure. Then, with the carefully drawn beautiful flowers, attempts at reparation seem to get the upper hand, but those cannot survive and have to be painted over—and consequently further damage is done. Let us now look at the three following drawings in this session. In the second (Image 6) we see a face in red surrounded by yellow hair that reaches down to the floor and on the right again the outlines of a red bow—altogether more scribbled than worked out. Klein's notes say Erna "[b]egins to draw more beautiful princess. Does not succeed, gives up" (in Frank, 2009, p. 210)

She has another go at it (Image 7). In the third drawing we see, as in the second picture, a splendid yellow coiffure reaching down to the floor. A very broad crinoline fills the space in the middle of the picture and underneath are red stick-like legs and black high-heel shoes (?). Erna comments: "Meant to be a beautiful princess—but finds this not worked, legs thin" (pp. 210–211) And here we have the last drawing of this session (Image 8): a huge head with an oversized mouth, raised hair, a relatively thick neck, and, in comparison to this, a small and shapeless body. Black lines fill the neck and the body. Below, one can read the two thin black strokes as legs and the firmer little rectangle as "pipes", as we know them from the first year. In the former drawing we have seen it in red with the queen. From the notes we learn that Erna had associated that after a thunderbolt the princess lost all her hair, turned ugly, and her bottom was full of poo. What followed was an inhibition in her play, depression, remorse, and then the school lessons.

You will remember that the 'thunderbolt' also figured in Klein's impressive fragment where she describes splitting: "I refer in particular to the representation in which at the sound of a

Image 5   Image 6

thunderbolt the ugly figure repeatedly turns into the beautiful one and the beautiful figure into the ugly one. In this way, the unsuccessful endeavour somehow to fuse together the two parts of her personality is expressed again." Thus, after Erna has destroyed the attempts at reparation, she cannot compete with the mother/queen/analyst in a "healthy" way and the "dissection" into different parts of the personality, and splitting gains the upper hand.

I think we can comprehend how Erna as the princess triumphs over the queen with an excessively splendid coiffure but is not really happy with the result—perhaps because any relation to reality is lacking (no body, no legs). Therefore she aborts the effort, but then has another go at it. This time, with the whole figure in view, she tries to force the triumph over the big crinoline, but then she realises that her whole endeavour is based on week/thin feet. And in the next picture, what remains after the "thunderbolt" is a baby crying, feeling ugly with all her shit. In the first drawing the eyes were black, here it is faeces that are black. Might one assume that eventually the principle of talion gained the upper hand and made her feel just as ugly and bald as she believed her attacks had made the queen?

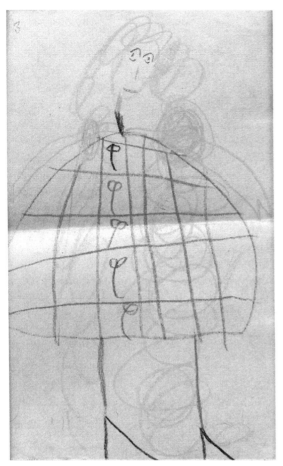

Image 7   Image 8

Erna's first drawings of the 16 January 1924 as conscious phantasies, slowly revealing their unconscious roots in the course of the analysis

We have already had a first look at Erna's drawings of 16 January 1924 and I now want to come back to them to consider what has unfolded and differentiated in the meantime. Those first drawings are about heaven and hell, contrasting worlds or spaces, which Erna tries to demarcate with several lines. In the first drawing (Image 1) we have an above and a below. Above, in the sky, far away, hardly differentiated and rather pale, we can see mother with two angels. Below, dominating the picture, the little girl is a squatter in the house/mother's body, laughing in view of her triumph and demonstrating her anal might. In the second drawing (Image 2) this order has started to skid. Although Erna still tries to maintain a separation of the two worlds, the separation has veered already into a slanted position. Moreover, the angels in the sky have vanished and instead we can see devils in both worlds: mother is provided with a devil giving her consolation—what kind of solace is he going to give? And what kind of tears are being shed by the crying devil next to the girl on the right? They are devils, so presumably they are therefore devilish tears and devilish solace, which cannot really pacify. Thus it is the laughing and, presumably, in view of his tricks, the triumphant, devil next to the girl on the left, who dominates the dynamics in the scene. Although mother, given her size, is now the commanding figure, she also seems at the same time helpless and damaged. This comes as no surprise, since Erna had obviously wanted to attack her and deprive her of her peace (bench and chairs can be understood as places to settle down, come to rest). Then there also is "St. Peter['s] clouds" and the comment that "the mother also [is] a Chinese man". It seems that the sky is populated by rather strange, dubious, and partly bizarre objects.

In a certain way, the first drawing might remind us of Freud's initial use of the term split-ting in terms of conscious and unconscious experience. Whereas Freud's later structural theory (where he does not speak of splitting any longer) with the id below, is possibly even more fit-ting. But, as the second drawing shows, the dynamic is much more complex and confusing and not instantly comprehensible with the help of these models.

If we look again, almost two years later, at the drawings (Images 3 and 4), which had helped Klein to describe the partition into two parts of the personality, it seems as if the whole world could be contained within a B: the breast and belly, so to speak a "heaven" composed of flesh and blood, but also buttocks having correspondingly hellish attacking weapons at their dis-posal. Erna can make use of and learn from such an object and, as becomes apparent in her effort for B, a part of her personality really loves and admires this splendid and creative analyst. However for another part of her B is the trigger for attacks, and this part of her personality is under the spell of the witch. Instead of angels and devils, we are now dealing with beautiful and ugly girls—and we are close to the picture of a child that recognises beautiful/good and ugly thoughts and impulses within herself.

I cannot describe in detail the course of the analysis but, again and again, contemptuous con-stellations dominated the situation and it appears that these prompted Klein to seek advice from Abraham. To illustrate, I will give you a brief excerpt from Klein's session notes of 22 September 1924 (see Frank, 2009, p. 420). In this session, Erna initially is the strict teacher, and the children "must behave as quietly as mice". Then she suddenly demands that Klein should play mother and child with her. Erna is the child whom Klein discovers has soiled herself. To this, Erna reacts scornfully, asserting that before she had only pretended to be friendly. Klein is supposed to force-feed her with semolina, which she then vomits out. Klein notes that also at home Erna is again more aggressive and difficult, but "also depressive—over-tender". Erna complains that Klein does not help her: "I don't know what it should mean that I am so sad". And then Klein makes the following entry: "sometimes she loves, she bad—Abraham suggests." I understand this comment as Klein having consulted with Abraham about this difficult treatment and his having suggested that Erna sometimes loves to be bad. Presumably both of them had been preparing their papers for the first German conference of psychoanalysis in October 1924 in Würzburg, where Klein for the first time presented her work with Erna in detail.

From the material I have just quoted, I would like to pick up one moment that appears to be repeated, and that is how Erna scornfully tries to dismiss her own state of mind. It therefore makes sense that Klein, in the manuscript of her Würzburg lecture (1924/5, p. 16B; PP/KLE/C40 III, unpublished text, Klein Archives), reached the conclusion that Erna negates the relation to reality. Although after some time Erna had acknowledged that her sadistic phantasies were definitely directed towards the mother, it had not been possible to link her phantasies with reality. I think that here we can recognise the trace of a parallel configuration to the splitting of the ego, which Freud described in 1927: different parts of the ego vary in their relation towards reality—and "the sealing off reality", as Klein denominates one kind of dealing with it, characterises one of the parts. One can assume that Klein's own analysis helped her to live and work through difficult enactments and interactions that were often hard to bear, in particular in the sessions from November till December 1925. This led to her eventual description of splitting.

Excursion to a phantasy of S. Freud

Whereas in my view Klein understands psychic reality as equivalent to phantasy, Freud's grappling with the term phantasy extends from understanding it on the one side as solely being tied to the pleasure principle (e.g., 1911b) to, on the other side, as a notion of (phylogenetically transmitted) primal phantasies (e.g., 1915). I believe this is closely connected to his attempts to gain clarity about the fundamental principles of mental functioning. He talks (1911b) about a "governing purpose", the pleasure-unpleasure principle (in short, the pleasure principle) as the only tendency that primary processes follow. Only later—prompted by the lack of the expected satisfaction—does the "new principle" take over, the reality principle:

> It was only the non-occurrence of the expected satisfaction, the disappointment experienced, that led to the abandonment of this attempt at satisfaction by means of hallucination. Instead of it, the psychical apparatus had to decide to form a conception of the real circumstances in the external world and to endeavour to make a real alteration in them. A new principle of mental functioning … (p. 219)

Naturally, it does not escape Freud's attention that this construction would not be compatible with real life:

> It will rightly be objected that an organisation which was a slave to the pleasure principle and neglected the reality of the external world could not maintain itself alive for the shortest time, so that it could not have come into existence at all. The employment of a fiction like this is, however, justified when one considers that the infant—provided one includes with it the care it receives from its mother—does *almost* realise a psychical system of this kind. (ibid., p. 220, n. 4, italics added)

In this footnote Freud thus adds something crucial, although, with regard to his theoretical construction, he keeps treating it as *quantité négligeable*: in the context of a good enough object relationship the predominance of the pleasure principle appears possible, although he needs to restrict it to "nearly possible". (Later on, Klein defined more clearly the mechanism applied by the pleasure principle: projective identification.)

In this footnote Freud summarises his vision as follows: "A neat example of a psychical system shut off from the stimuli of the external world, and able to satisfy even its nutritional requirements autistically (to use Bleuler's term (1912)), is afforded by a bird's egg with its food supply enclosed in its shell; for it, the care provided by its mother is limited to the provision of warmth." It appears to me that through the characterisation "autistic" something enters the picture through the back door, which doesn't quite fit into the idea of life being "exclusively" determined by the pleasure principle. His picture of "normal" development includes a component that fundamentally negates the reality of another—while at the same time assuming optimal (or at least very good) relatedness between mother and child.

What I would like to emphasise in my considerations is the fact that Freud, in his attempt to rescue the sole dominance of the pleasure principle, despite the obvious contradictions, cannot but embed it within a relationship to an object. Here an intense exchange takes place, which however gets completely negated by the infant's psychic apparatus. The fact that he draws on Bleuler's expression "autistic" demonstrates in my view his intuitive knowledge that one component in this happening is far from harmless and does not sit easily with the concept of the sole pleasure-unpleasure principle. As I see it, Freud indirectly concedes two things with this footnote: one point—in my view quite openly stated—indicates that something like a reality principle must exist in some rudimentary form right from the beginning; the other one—this time more intuitively—points at the fact that, besides the pleasure principle, there must be another one at work.

I would suggest that with his "phantasy" of the bird's egg he captured the relationship a baby has from the beginning with the object more precisely than he did with his theoretical formulations of the pleasure-unpleasure principle.

Unconscious phantasy today—back to Mrs A's analysis

We left my patient at the end of her third preliminary meeting, when she spoke of the line cutting off her right foot. The fact that I did not turn away, but could see and talk about something in her that cruelly wanted to prevent her from taking the step into analysis, enabled her to decide for it. This was immediately followed by compulsive thoughts of having her tongue cut off, and then by a memory of her aunt (with whom she had a good connection) who had fallen ill with cancer of the tongue.

For a long time in her analysis she would not/could not consciously know about her "real" aggressive actions. She experienced utter shame and outrage, to "have to" come to her analysis, and I turned into the one who was demanding slavish obedience. She was convinced of belonging to the group of beings considered unworthy of life, who in Nazi times would have ended up straight "in the rubbish".

When, after many years of analysis, she was able to dream and experience herself as someone who could have impulses, such as throwing a baby out of the window, or destroying a fruitful and satisfying interaction with a ricocheting bullet, or attacking with a knife in a dream (and not an isolated knife out of the blue at that) she experienced great relief. Naturally it was also painful for her to realise that in truth she was not solely peace-loving. However, this was outweighed by what she gained through knowing herself, and knowing in an emotionally significant way about all the impulses that she had and owning and confronting them. And she conveyed how, in this way, her life had become much happier and more contented and how much more able she felt to face life and be curious about it.

I would like to briefly illustrate with some condensed clinical material from her seventh year in analysis, how this was manifested. Triggered by a particular situation, she spoke one Monday session about how long she had held on to her particular omnipotent illusions. She moved on to speak of her discovery of a new (female) patient of mine who she knew by sight from a different context. She had heard about the patient's great commitment as a teacher and felt envious of her "rich life". This reminded her of her sister's popularity, in particular with her parents, and her sister's ability to share her enjoyment with others. I picked up on her knowing about her desire to outdo everybody else, to have a very special position, but to then find herself isolated; she now seemed able to also experience the pain of her envious feelings towards my new patient. I said that at the same time she seemed to convey that there was also a sense of having things in common with others, which she could be glad about and which grounded her. The patient reacted with relief, and agreed. After a moment's silence she mentioned that, "funnily", she had become tearful, although she wasn't crying. After this, various images occurred to her of reconciliation between arch-enemies (de Gaulle and Adenauer). She went on to wonder whether, if one looks out for more realistic ways of managing, it might be possible to take back omnipotent phantasies. But, she said, this is where she would often get cold feet, although some things would work out, "it's that simple—or not". I interpreted that she knew that for one part of her it was far from simple, but another part sensed this to be a rewarding and realistic path to take.

She began the Tuesday session with the comment that yesterday's session had been good, had touched her, she had felt understood. Yet once again she felt distanced from it! She went on to tell me how once again she had demanded that X give her special treatment. I described how hurt she felt when a good session came to an end, how she then felt provoked in her "tried and tested" ways to enforce a special position. The patient described an image that emerged in her mind: a knife over a belly. And she remembered how, some years ago, she had taken part in a weekend seminar on antenatal psychology. I interpreted her phantasy of a fetus to whom just about everything is boundlessly available, and how this evokes great envy. At this point the patient was able to speak to me, in a quite different tone of voice, and to tell me that she saw me as someone who sometimes (much more so in the past) appears to her to be a "different type of human being", who can master everything in a superior way, and who doesn't have to "struggle to make ends meet". It became evident how the "knife on the belly" had come to represent an emotionally significant image of her way of psychic functioning, namely her splitting.

You will remember that earlier on we dealt with Erna's cutting up of the "B"s (belly, breast). We now have Mrs A's image of a knife on a belly. Both managed, in the course of the intensive process of a high-frequency analysis, to better face their impulses and to struggle with them. The areas that initially were split-off and kept well apart could, despite all the ups and downs, be successfully brought closer together and be partially integrated. What was important in this process was to take up the images (line; devil) in the here and now. Notwithstanding the obvious differences, in the case of Erna as well as of Mrs A the decisive factor appears to be that it was possible to get in touch in different ways with the unconscious aspects of their conscious phantasies about their psychic functioning.

Acknowledgement

All images within this chapter copyright (c) the Melanie Klein Trust, London. Reproduced with kind permission.

References

Frank, C. (1999). *Melanie Kleins erste Kinderanalysen—die Entdeckung des Kindes als Objekt sui generis von Heilen und Forschen*. Stuttgart: frommann-holzboog.

Frank, C. (2009). *Melanie Klein in Berlin: Her First Psychoanalyses of Children*. London: Routledge.

Freud, S. (1911b). Formulations on the two principles of mental functioning. *S. E.*, *12*: 213–226. London: Hogarth.

Freud, S. (1915). *A Phylogenetic Fantasy: Overview of the Transference Neuroses* (Ed. I. Grubrich-Simitis, Trans. A. Hoffer, & P. Hoffer.) Cambridge, MA: Harvard University Press, 1987.

Freud, S. (1924b). Neurosis and psychosis. *S. E.*, *19*: 147–154. London: Hogarth.

Klein, M. (1927). Symposium on child-analysis. In: *The Collected Works of Melanie Klein Vol I* (pp. 139–169). London: Hogarth, 1975.

Klein, M. (1932). *The Collected Works of Melanie Klein Vol. II: The Psycho-Analysis of Children*. London: Hogarth, 1975.

Klein, M. (1946). Notes on some schizoid mechanisms. In: *The Collected Works of Melanie Klein Vol III* (pp. 1–24). London, Hogarth, 1975.

Klein, M. (1952). The mutual influences in the development of ego and id. In: *The Collected Works of Melanie Klein Vol III* (pp. 57–60). London: Hogarth, 1975.

CHAPTER TWELVE

The projective process and the two positions today

Chris Mawson

"My present work, which I hope to publish, convinces me of the central importance of the Kleinian theories of projective identification and the interplay between the paranoid-schizoid and depressive positions. Without the aid of these two sets of theories I doubt the possibility of any advance in the study of group phenomena."

W. R. Bion (1961b, p. 8)

In this chapter I describe how two interrelated ideas from Melanie Klein's pioneering work in child analysis have been developed to become a core part of the contemporary Kleinian development of Freud's work. I begin with Klein's description of something she referred to initially simply as a projective process, followed by her description of two configurations occurring in the mental life of all human infants, continuing to operate throughout life; this is intended as preparation to show how the ideas were expanded by Wilfred Bion to form clinical tools for use in adult and child analysis, and for the study of group and institutional processes.

Anxiety and the projective process

For Melanie Klein, anxiety, and how it was managed by the early ego, was at the core of psychoanalysis. In this she was following Freud, who early on in his "A project for a scientific psychology", had described pain as "the most imperative of all processes", observing, "the nervous system has the most decided inclination to a *flight from pain*" (1950a, p. 307, original italics).

In his earliest explorations, Freud began from the fact that the experience of pain mobilises the body/mind system as a whole, and—alone amongst psychophysical processes—the transmission of pain meets no effective obstacles, being discharged along every pathway available to it, hence his remark about its imperative nature. Originally the boundary between conscious and unconscious, thought Freud, was fully permeable to pain, and with it the whole integrity of the mental apparatus became threatened unless an intervention could be made from outside that limited the irruption and somehow bound the escalating anxiety psychically. At first, the infant is helpless to effect this vital function of "binding" for themselves, and today we would call this "containing", for which they first have to experience the mother's capacity to contain the feelings aroused inside her as a result of taking in and suffering what the infant cannot. I see an early foreshadowing of such a process in Freud's pre-psychoanalytic writing in the "Project":

> It takes place by *extraneous help*, when the attention of an experienced person is drawn to the child's state by discharge along the path of internal change. In this way this path of discharge acquires a secondary function of the highest importance, that of *communication*, and the initial helplessness of human beings is the *primal source* of all *moral motives*. [By this Freud means social and group mentality.]
>
> When the helpful person has performed the work of the specific action in the external world for the helpless one, the latter is in a position, by means of reflex contrivances, immediately to carry out in the interior of his body the activity necessary for removing the endogenous stimulus. The total event then constitutes an *experience of satisfaction*, which has the most radical results on the development of the individual's functions. (1950a, p. 318, original italics)

This connection to Freud, and the nature of the intervention required in the situation of urgency, is something to which I will return later, when in the final section I relate Freud's concept of the requisite or specific action to interpretation and Bion's version of Klein's two positions.

In her work with children and adults, Melanie Klein identified a particular form of projection, a response to the fear of being overwhelmed by persecutory experience, which, before naming it as projective identification in her 1946 paper, "Notes on some schizoid mechanisms", she called simply a "projective process" (1946, p. 102).

Even before the mother can be conceived of as a whole person, wrote Klein, there arises an early form of projection and introjection in which the first object of satisfaction, hostility, and protection—the breast—is attacked in phantasy by the infant in distress, in experiences that suggest that the psychic reality is one in which the infant (a) has pushed, with violence, parts of himself, together with associated bodily products, right into the body of the mother, and (b) has sucked and scooped out of the mother its beneficial contents. The former is an early form of what Freud called "deflection", that is to say, projection. The latter is the prototype of introjection.

Klein wrote that the mother is, as a consequence of these operations, felt to *contain* the unwanted parts of the self, and is also felt to have been depleted of good parts of herself. Thus Klein spoke of these processes as leading to a particular kind of identification, because the mother containing these projections is felt concretely to *become* those split-off parts of the infant, and the identity, the *being*, that is, of the infant is also affected by the associated introjection of the altered mother. According to this model, primitive hatred and consequent rejection of parts of the self are directed by the infant against the mother and take residence inside her, a set of events that affect the actual relationship between mother and infant and, although they take place in phantasy, the effects and consequences are real. She theorised that the structure of the infant's self, or ego, was altered too. In the original 1946 paper in which Klein described this theory she mentioned this kind of identification as a prototype of an object relation, and, in passing, she used the term "projective identification". She wrote: "I have referred to the weakening and impoverishment of the ego resulting from excessive splitting and projective identification" (p. 104). In the 1952 version of the paper she introduced some footnotes to show how the idea already had been used clinically, and also a paragraph making the new term for the concept more definite.

> Much of the hatred against parts of the self is now directed towards the mother. This leads
> to a particular form of identification which establishes the prototype of an aggressive object-
> relation. I suggest for these processes the term "projective identification". (Klein, 1952, p. 8)

Klein wrote, importantly, that good parts of the self also are separated off and projected in this way—into an object. This too affects seriously the normal development of object relations, permanently if the processes are carried out with excessive violence and excessive splintering of parts of the self. She wrote:

> Excrements then have the significance of gifts; and parts of the ego which, together with excrements, are expelled and projected into the other person represent the good, i.e. the loving parts of the self. The identification based on this type of projection again vitally influences object relations. The projection of good feelings and good parts of the self into the mother is essential for the infant's ability to develop good object relations and to integrate his ego. However, if this projective process is carried out excessively, good parts of the personality are felt to be lost to the self, and the mother becomes the ego ideal; this process, too, results in weakening and impoverishing the ego. Very soon such processes extend to other people, and the result may be an extreme dependence on these external representatives of the good parts of the self. Another consequence is a fear that the capacity to love has been lost because the loved object is felt to be loved predominantly as a representative of the self.
>
> The processes of splitting off parts of the self and projecting them into objects are thus of vital importance for normal development as well as for abnormal object relations.
>
> The effect of introjection on object relations is equally important. The introjection of the good object, first of all mother's breast is a precondition for normal development. I have already described how the internal good breast comes to form a focal point in the ego and makes for cohesiveness of the ego. (Klein, 1946, p. 103)

Wilfred Bion's extension of Klein's concept of the projective process

Klein had stated that in the projective process the mother was felt to *contain* the disowned part of the infant, and therefore she felt that the appropriate terminology was to describe the projections as being made *into* the mother. Bion's first use of the term "container" in relation to Klein's concept of projective identification was in his 1958 paper, "On hallucination". Concerning the patient's fear of his impulses harming or killing his analyst, Bion wrote:

I was able to show him that he was splitting off painful feelings, mostly envy and revenge, of which he hoped to rid himself by forcing them into me. There the session ended. Melanie Klein has described how this mechanism produces problems for the patient by engendering fear of the analyst who now is a container of a bad part of himself. (Bion, 1958, p. 68)

In 1961, in a paper called "The conception of man" (1961a), Bion stated his intention to make an expanded use of Melanie Klein's concept of projective identification, which, following Freud, he believed constituted an essential normal factor, both in the inception of communication and in mental development in the infant, which occurs successfully only with the irreplaceable help through the repeated understanding and timely intervention of his mother. This is the nub of what today we refer to as container-contained, or—as shorthand—containment. Its earliest form is in the anxiety situations occurring daily in the mother-infant relationship, and the analytic situation itself both arouses its basic features and constitutes a later model of it. The phenomena of transference and associated countertransference depend upon this fact. It enables the theory of projective identification, and those derived from it, to

> explain more than what their propounder intended.... I shall use the theory of projective identification as a model for early development of the processes that have later come to be known as thinking. The model supposes the existence of a couple; I use it to represent an internal apparatus in the individual. What originally represented a relationship between mother and infant, or breast and mouth, now represents these objects internalized. The representation of these internalized objects is used as a model for the mental mechanisms involved in thinking. The signs ♀ and ♂ can be used to represent the internal apparatus by the sign ♀♂. (Bion, 1961a, p. 16)

This is an early formulation of what has become known as Bion's container-contained (♀♂) model of mental development. For Bion, container-contained extends Klein's concept of projective identification by taking it as being effected into a containing object, and expands upon it (see later). Its origins are in his clinical observations of patients in psychotic states, made in the late 1950s, which supported Klein's contention that the projective process, the identificatory process that she had observed, was a phantasy with actual consequences, and one which operated on the idea of getting *into* the object and altering it, and not merely projecting on to its surface and thereby altering attributions. In a footnote to her 1946 paper Klein had written:

> The description of such primitive processes suffers from a great handicap, for these phantasies arise at a time when the infant has not yet begun to think in words. In this paper, for instance, I am using the expression "to project into another person" because this seems to me the only way of conveying the unconscious process I am trying to describe. (Klein, 1946, p. 102)

Two years earlier, in "Attacks on linking" (1959), in a section called "Denial of normal degrees of projective identification", Bion had made a crucial clinical observation about the impact on a patient of his analyst's failure adequately to take in the patient's urgent communications. That observation enabled Bion to consider the consequences in analysis, and earlier, in infancy, of the denial by the primary object of normal and necessary degrees of projective identification. This was in fact the beginning of Bion's use of what we now know as his container-contained model. His statement of it at that stage is worth reproducing here because of its importance in showing the clinical foundation for his later work:

> When the patient strove to rid himself of fears of death which were felt to be too powerful for his personality to contain, he split off his fears and put them into me, the idea apparently being that if they were allowed to repose there long enough they would undergo modification by my psyche and could then be safely reintrojected.
>
> On the occasion I have in mind the patient had felt … that I evacuated them so quickly that the feelings were not modified, but had become more painful. Associations from a period in the analysis earlier than that from which these illustrations have been drawn showed an increasing intensity of emotions in the patient. This originated in what he felt was my refusal to accept parts of his personality. Consequently he strove to force them into me with increased desperation and violence. His behaviour, isolated from the context of the analysis, might have appeared to be an expression of primary aggression: the more violent his phantasies of projective identification, the more frightened he became of me. There were sessions in which such behaviour expressed unprovoked aggression, but I quote this series because it shows the patient in a different light—his violence a reaction to what he felt was my hostile defensiveness. The analytic situation built up in my mind a sense of witnessing an extremely early scene. I felt that the patient had experienced in infancy a mother who dutifully responded to the infant's emotional displays.
>
> The dutiful response had in it an element of impatient, "I don't know what's the matter with the child." My deduction was that, in order to understand what the child wanted, the mother should have treated the infant's cry as more than a demand for her presence. From the infant's point of view she should have taken into her, and thus experienced, the fear that the child was dying. It was this fear that the child could not contain. He strove to split it off together with the part of the personality in which it lay and project it into the mother.
>
> An understanding mother is able to experience the feeling of dread, that this baby was striving to deal with by projective identification, and yet retain a balanced outlook. This patient had had to deal with a mother who could not tolerate experiencing such feelings and reacted either by denying them ingress, or alternatively by becoming a prey to the anxiety which resulted from introjection of the infant's feelings. (Bion, 1959, p. 312)

In *Learning from Experience* (1962), Bion extended this model further, by incorporating another idea of Klein's, based on her two basic configurations of anxieties and object relations, the paranoid-schizoid and depressive positions of early infancy. It is to this that I will return after outlining this second of Klein's major contributions.

The two positions: configurations of mental suffering and defences against them

As well as developing a theory of projective processes, Klein had also described what she called two "positions"—emotional constellations of phantasies, anxieties, and defences against them—each detectable in periods of the early mental life of infants, and present in all of us, in constant oscillation throughout life. She favoured this formulation over that of stages of development. In 1935 Klein wrote:

> In my former work I have described the psychotic anxieties and mechanisms of the child in terms of phases of development. The genetic connection between them, it is true, is given full justice by this description, and so is the fluctuation which goes on between them under the pressure of anxiety until more stability is reached; but since in normal development the psychotic anxieties and mechanisms never solely predominate (a fact which, of course, I have emphasized) the term psychotic phases is not really satisfactory. *I am now using the term "position" in relation to the child's early developmental psychotic anxieties and defences.* It seems to me easier to associate with this term, than with the words "mechanisms" or "phases", the differences between the developmental psychotic anxieties of the child and the psychoses of the adult: e.g. the quick change-over that occurs from a persecution-anxiety or depressed feeling to a normal attitude—a change-over that is so characteristic for the child. (Klein, 1935, n. 14, p. 159, italics added)

Klein had described an early persecutory phase in the mental life of infants, sometimes called a paranoid position. Klein agreed with Fairbairn's use of the term schizoid position, which she felt was appropriate if it included both persecutory anxiety and schizoid (splitting) processes.

The leading anxiety, she wrote, was a fear of imminent destruction of the self. The principal defence against the dread of annihilation and fragmentation was held to be psychic splitting, an earlier defence than repression.

Klein (1935) wrote:

> In paranoia the characteristic defences are chiefly aimed at annihilating the "persecutors", while anxiety on the ego's account occupies a prominent place in the picture. As the ego becomes more fully organized, the internalized imagos will approximate more closely to reality and the ego will identify itself more fully with "good" objects. The dread of persecution, which was at first felt on the ego's account, now relates to the good object as well and from now on preservation of the good object is regarded as synonymous with the survival of the ego.
>
> *Hand in hand with this development goes a change of the highest importance, namely, from a partial object-relation to the relation to a complete object. Through this step the ego arrives at a new position, which forms the foundation of that situation called the loss of the loved object. Not until the object is loved as a whole can its loss be felt as a whole.*
>
> With this change in the relation to the object, new anxiety-contents make their appearance and a change takes place in the mechanisms of defence. (Klein, 1935, p. 147, italics added)

The leading anxiety in the depressive position centres on the lost good object, whose welfare is felt to be essential to the integrity of the self. The fear is that the infant's own uncontrollable destructive impulses and phantasies have damaged or destroyed the loved and needed mother.

In 1946 Klein developed further her ideas about the infantile depressive position. The urge towards reparation of damage done in psychic reality, about which she had written earlier (Klein, 1929), she now harnessed with the identification made by the infant with its good object to provide the ego with a creative urge as well as constituting a defence. She wrote in a section called "The depressive position in relation to the schizoid position":

> With the introjection of the complete object in about the second quarter of the first year marked steps in integration are made. This implies important changes in the relation to objects. The loved and hated aspects of the mother are no longer felt to be so widely separated, and the result is an increased fear of loss, a strong feeling of guilt and states akin to mourning, because the aggressive impulses are felt to be directed against the loved object. The depressive position has come to the fore. The very experience of depressive feelings in turn has the effect of further integrating the ego, because it makes for an increased understanding of psychic reality and better perception of the external world, as well as for a greater synthesis between inner and external situations.
>
> The drive for reparation, which comes to the fore at this stage, can be regarded as a consequence of a greater insight into psychic reality and of growing synthesis, for it shows a more realistic response to the feelings of grief, guilt and fear of loss resulting from the aggression against the loved object. Since the drive to repair or protect the injured object paves the way for more satisfactory object relations and sublimations, it in turn increases synthesis and contributes to the integration of the ego. (Klein, 1946, p. 105)

The taking care and the protection of the mental growth made possible by the organisation of pain and defence against it in the depressive position was thought by Klein and her colleagues to promote symbol formation, thinking and to be the source and foundation of all creative sublimations. Both positions, the paranoid-schizoid and the depressive, entail inevitable suffering, with the concomitant tendency in both towards fragmentation and the associated confusional pain.

I will return now to Wilfred Bion's extension of Melanie Klein's concept of projective identification, and those stemming from it, which, as you will recall, he had said "explain more than what their propounder intended".

Projective identification as the container-contained relation

The container-contained relationship was, for Bion, how projective identification operated. It required the existence of at least two minds. Bion's idea of an interaction within a containing mind of parts of the infant in distress, under urgently felt pressure amounting to life and death anxiety, extends out into an elaborated model of the various different possible consequences of transactions between an impacted living mental container—in the infantile setting it is the mother, in an analysis it is the person of the analyst—and an equally living, and turbulent, "contained", that is to say, whatever is projected into the caregiver as a receptacle. The turbulence produced when a mother willingly suffers (allows) her child to enter her heart and mind with its cries and communications, and its unspoken mental actions and ingress into her feelings, can, according to Bion, result in three classes of mental events: the transaction between container and contained can: (a) produce conditions conducive to growth of both, which he termed a "symbiotic" ♀♂ relationship; (b) the members of the pair can be apart but still have the potential to affect one another, which he called "commensal" (the literal meaning being at the same table, side by side); and (c) the containing structure can constrict the potentially contained elements, damaging or destroying it, or the expansive force of the contained elements can threaten to burst the capacity of the containing object; both these eventualities are in their own way harmful to the distinctive qualities of both ♀ and ♂; this relation is termed "parasitic".

Between 1958 and 1970 Bion produced landmark contributions to develop this model, which later became a theory of mind and a theory of thinking. According to this, once the mother has established with her infant the secure anticipation deriving from the emotional experience of repeated cycles of projective identification, met by mother's provision of a containing mind capable of meeting an emotional storm in a state of relative receptive calm, in which dread and terror can be reduced to anxiety and pain. Thinking and symbolisation can then take place, and the possibility arises for the infant to take into himself the fundamentals of this process and to build it into a functioning version of his own, in his developing psyche, as a new function. Bion called it "dreamwork-alpha", or "alpha-function". Its origin is a function in the mind of the mother, and its momentous significance in the life of the human infant is well summed-up by Freud's description, which I described earlier, of something that is, in my view, the same process:

> When the helpful person has performed the work of the specific action in the external world for the helpless one, the latter is in a position, by means of reflex contrivances, immediately to carry out in the interior of his body the activity necessary for removing the endogenous stimulus. The total event then constitutes an *experience of satisfaction*, which has the most radical results on the development of the individual's functions. (1950a, p. 318, original italics)

I think Freud in his earliest writings felt this to be the most important thing that a mother does for her infant. In his "A project for a scientific psychology" (1950a), Freud used an energic model to explore the origins of mental activity in the earliest mother-infant situation. At first, the infant's primary need is to turn to the mother not only for satisfaction of instinctual needs, but also for help with alleviating the worst of the pain and frustration involved in attempting to do so. Under propitious conditions this evokes an orienting response in the mother (Di Ceglie, 2013), which corresponds to Freud's description of the need for the attention of an experienced person to be drawn to the child's state by what he called, "discharge along the path of internal change". This amounts to a mental movement enabling the mother to align herself optimally with the powerful projective identifications of her infant in order not only to weather the storm of them, but to take them into herself and to discern their meaning for her child and herself.

On Bion's expansion of Freud's early theory, this makes possible the establishment within the psyche of the infant of the prototype of a means for modifying the impact of reality, both psychical and material, rather than evading it. It eventually becomes a capacity for thinking emotional thoughts, and for making emotional and cognitive links. The essential factor in the mother is the capacity to orient herself along these lines, and to intuit the requisite or specific action needed to meet the child's anxiety.

The mother's capacity for reverie and the two positions

In taking up this fundamental situation, over seventy years after Freud's earliest descriptions, Bion (1962) wrote of the mother's radical openness to the infant's earliest communications and evacuations of mental pain in the following terms:

> … when the mother loves the infant what does she do it with? Leaving aside the physical channels of communication my impression is that her love is expressed by reverie.
>
> … If the feeding mother cannot allow reverie or if the reverie is allowed but is not associated with love for the child or its father, this fact will be communicated to the infant even though incomprehensible to the infant. Psychic quality will be imparted to the channels of communication, the links with the child. What happens will depend on the nature of these maternal psychic qualities and their impact on the psychic qualities of the infant, for the impact of the one upon the other is an emotional experience subject, from the point of view of the development of the couple and the individuals composing it, to transformation by alpha-function. The term reverie may be applied to almost any content. I wish to reserve it only for such content as is suffused with love or hate. *Using it in this restricted sense reverie is that state of mind which is open to the reception of any "objects" from the loved object and is therefore capable of reception of the infant's projective identifications whether they are felt by the infant to be good or bad.* In short, reverie is a factor of the mother's alpha-function. (Bion, 1962, p. 36, italics added)

So, reverie is the term Bion used for the capacity of the mother to be receptive to her infant's evacuations of mental pain in order for some modification of the rawness of them to take place—first of all in her mind, and later as something that could be "taken back", as it were, by the infant, where it could lead to the development of a corresponding human capacity within the developing child. Alpha-function is Bion's term for the process he was exploring for that capacity in the nursing pair in which linking of emotional thoughts became possible by the building of a container with the resilience to withstand the tensions and pressures arising from housing the mental conflict and emotional turbulence inevitable in human object relations.

This returns us to Klein's two positions, as the conflict and turbulence are forms of mental pain existing at different levels of coherence and meaning, which is what Klein's theory enabled us to explore in the clinical situation.

The persecutory and depressive feelings experienced concretely by the infant and, to quite an extent, by the mother, Bion (1963, p. 31) describes in terms of feelings of being "filled with painful lumps of faeces, guilt, fears of impending death, chunks of greed, meanness and urine".

The terrible sense of the non-existence of a fellow human being—in Freud's term (1950a, p. 331), the *Nebenmensch*, the infant's "first satisfying object and further his first hostile object, as well as his sole helping power", or the breast that initially is the earliest form of one—is alleviated by being met with a *real* match for the innate preconception, the pre-existing model of the experience. Repeated, timely experiences of satisfaction in which not only the hunger, for example, is met properly, but also the associated *terror*, lead to transformations in which the mother performing the "specific action" (Freud) for the infant enables, within the infant, the absent object (breast) to be perceived as a functioning breast, which at first, associated with idealised omnipotent phantasies, is felt, paraphrasing Bion (1963, p. 31), to convert concrete equations of phantasies of persecuting urine and faeces and burning urine into an experience of soothing milk; turn paralysis and fear of extinction into vitality, and faith in what Winnicott called "going on being" (1960, p. 587).

This description reads as an elaboration of what Freud meant when he wrote, "The total event then constitutes an *experience of satisfaction*, which has the most radical results on the development of the individual's functions" (1950a, p. 318).

In order to function with reverie, as described by Bion, in order to perform the specific action (Freud) to meet the urgent psychological situation of anxiety, the mother needs to be able to manage, without breaking under the strain, the primitive feelings in relation to her infant that pull her towards excessive paranoid-schizoid and depressive anxieties and defences against them. But this is not the only significance of the two positions in this context. I will conclude this chapter by outlining another sense in which an understanding of Klein's two positions relates to Bion's version of projective identification in the transition from the containment of primitive anxiety, in both mother and infant, towards the growth of a capacity for thinking.

The two positions as mental coherence/incoherence and the development of thinking

As well as referring to the mental strains undergone by the mother in being a container for her infant's projected distress, Bion built on his colleague Hanna Segal's (1957) finding that the growth of the capacity to form symbols and to make use of them was an achievement made possible by the depressive position. How is this brought about?

In order to explore the connection between containment and the growth of thinking, Bion (1962) coined the new term Ps $\rightleftharpoons$ D. This did not signify Klein's original description of her two positions of infant mental life, but was used to highlight the degree and type of *coherence* found in each position. It was thus an *analogy* of Klein's system, an extension of it in a particular direction, just as he had done with her concept of identification and projection. Bion drew on an idea in the work of a mathematician, Henri Poincaré. He did so because he wanted a way of describing how learning from experience, and thinking based upon it, requires that experiences are derived from previously existing, and more basic forms, or models, and that in this process, however it operated, the relative *coherence* of experience was a central feature. Using an idea of Poincaré's, called the "selected fact", Bion related his analogue of Klein's positions, Ps $\rightleftharpoons$ D, to the container-contained ($\female\male$) concept and to the identification of the relevant central elements around which there could be a development of meaning. Bion believed that forms present in our emotional experiences, to the extent that they can be contained symbiotically (see earlier description), specific recognisable, flexible, and transferrable models can be intuited, abstracted, and used to build an apparatus to think thoughts, which can under favourable circumstances evolve and be promoted to different levels and for different uses. This relates to Bion's Grid, a discussion of which is beyond my purposes in this chapter.

Here is how Poincaré (1914), as quoted by Bion, described his idea of the selected fact idea in his own field, concerning mathematical objects:

> If a new result is to have any value, it must unite elements long since known, but till then scattered and seemingly foreign to each other, and suddenly introduce order where the appearance of disorder reigned. Then it enables us to see at a glance each of these elements in the place it occupies in the whole. Not only is the new fact valuable on its own account, but it alone gives a value to the old facts it unites. Our mind is frail as our senses are; it would lose itself in the complexity of the world if that complexity were not harmonious; like the short-sighted, it would only see the details, and would be obliged to forget each of these details before examining the next, because it would be incapable of taking in the whole. The only facts worthy of our attention are those which introduce order into this complexity and so make it accessible to us. (Bion, 1962, p. 72)

Bion made use of this idea to advance his understanding of the capacity for thought, stimulated by Segal's work on symbol formation. She, in turn, felt inspired by his work on normal and pathological forms of projective identification and his work on the container-contained relationship. To conclude, I show how this latter aspect, in particular, of Bion's expansion of Klein's ideas on the projective process and the two positions, found its way into Bion's conception of a psychoanalytical attitude. In two passages he condensed his clinical findings into the following recommendations to psychoanalytic practitioners:

First, in *Elements of Psycho-Analysis* (1963, p. 102):

> The patient may be describing a dream, followed by a memory of an incident that occurred on the previous day, followed by an account of some difficulty in his parents' family. The recital may take three or four minutes or longer. The coherence that these facts have in the patient's mind is not relevant to the analyst's problem. His problem—I describe it in stages—is to ignore that coherence so that he is confronted by the incoherence and experiences incomprehension of what is presented to him. His own analysis should have made it possible for him to tolerate this emotional experience though it involves feelings of doubt and perhaps even persecution. This state must endure, possibly for a short period but probably longer, until a new coherence emerges; at this point he has reached → D, the stage analogous to nomination, or "binding" as I have described it. From this point his own processes can be represented by ♀♂—the development of meaning.

And second, towards the end of *Attention and Interpretation* (1970, p. 124), Bion described what he called, "perhaps the most important mechanism employed by the practising psychoanalyst". He added that it derived from Melanie Klein's description of the positions:

> In every session the psychoanalyst should be able, if he has followed what I have said in this book, particularly with regard to memory and desire, to be aware of the aspects of the material that, however familiar they may seem to be, relate to what is unknown both to him and to the analysand. Any attempt to cling to what he knows must be resisted for the sake of achieving

a state of mind analogous to the paranoid-schizoid position. For this state I have coined the term "patience" to distinguish it from "paranoid-schizoid position", which should be left to describe the pathological state for which Melanie Klein used it. I mean the term to retain its association with suffering and tolerance of frustration.

"Patience" should be retained without "irritable reaching after fact and reason" until a pattern "evolves". This state is the analogue to what Melanie Klein has called the depressive position. For this state I use the term "security". This I mean to leave with its association of safety and diminished anxiety. I consider that no analyst is entitled to believe that he has done the work required to give an interpretation unless he has passed through both phases— "patience" and "security".

The passage from the one to the other may be very short, as in the terminal stages of analysis, or it may be long. Few, if any, psychoanalysts should believe that they are likely to escape the feelings of persecution and depression commonly associated with the pathological states known as the paranoid-schizoid and depressive positions. In short, a sense of achievement of a correct interpretation will be commonly found to be followed almost immediately by a sense of depression.

I consider the experience of oscillation between "patience" and "security" to be an indication that valuable work is being achieved.

I think it is now possible to appreciate that it is particularly in this area of a conception of a psychoanalytical attitude that Klein's concepts of projective identification and the two positions have found their most lasting and contemporary clinical significance, largely through the contributions built by Bion on the pioneering work of Freud and Klein.

References

Bion, W. R. (1958). On hallucination. *International Journal of Psychoanalysis, 39*: 341–349.

Bion, W. R. (1959). Attacks on linking. *International Journal of Psychoanalysis, 40*: 308–315.

Bion, W. R. (1961a). The conception of man. In: C. Mawson (Ed.), *The Complete Works of W. R. Bion. Volume XV* (pp. 11–29). London: Karnac, 2014.

Bion, W. R. (1961b). *Experiences in Groups and Other Papers*. London: Tavistock.

Bion, W. R. (1962). *Learning from Experience*. London: Karnac, 1984.

Bion, W. R. (1963). *Elements of Psycho-Analysis*. London: Karnac, 1984.

Bion, W. R. (1970). *Attention and Interpretation: A Scientific Approach to Insight in Psychoanalysis and Groups*. London: Karnac, 1984.

Di Ceglie, G. R. (2013). Orientation, containment and the emergence of symbolic thinking. *International Journal of Psychoanalysis, 94*: 1077–1091.

Freud, S. (1950a). Project for a scientific psychology. *S. E., 1*: 295–346. London: Hogarth.

Klein, M. (1929). Infantile anxiety-situations reflected in a work of art and in the creative impulse'. *International Journal of Psychoanalysis, 10*: 436–443.

Klein, M. (1935). A contribution to the psychogenesis of manic-depressive states. *International Journal of Psychoanalysis, 16*: 145–174.

Klein, M. (1946). Notes on some schizoid mechanisms. *International Journal of Psychoanalysis, 27*: 99–110.

Klein, M. (1952). Notes on some schizoid mechanisms. In: M. Klein, P. Heimann, R. Money-Kyrle, & J. Riviere, (Eds.), *Developments in Psycho-Analysis*. London: Hogarth.

Poincaré, H. (1914). *Science and Method* (Trans., F. Maitland). New York: Dover, 1946.

Segal, H. (1957). Notes on symbol formation. *International Journal of Psychoanalysis, 38*: 391–397.

Winnicott, D. W. (1960). The theory of the parent-infant relationship. *International Journal of Psychoanalysis, 41*: 585–595.

CHAPTER THIRTEEN

Reparation: waiting for a concept

Edna O'Shaughnessy

Sophocles' tragedy of *Oedipus* is known well to psychoanalysts. Sophocles' world is a world of destiny. Oedipus is fated to murder his father and marry his mother, crimes that will bring disaster upon himself, his family, and his city. No matter how Oedipus tries—and he does try, for example, he leaves Corinth where he grew up to save, as he thinks, his King and Queen—he cannot escape his destiny. That is his tragedy. Sophocles located this world of tragic humankind in external reality in ancient Greece under the realm of the Gods. Centuries later, as Jonathan Lear (1998, p. 18) describes, "Freud put Sophocles' world inside us".

In one of his late, marvellously innovative papers, written after long years of psychoanalytic inquiry into the human psyche, Freud describes in *Civilization and its Discontents* (1930a), what it is to make a journey from a "state of nature", as he calls it, to becoming a civilised human being. Civilisation, he tells us, demands the renunciation and repression of many sexual and aggressive instincts—which makes us unhappy. Also, our ego suffers under a cruel superego for our oedipal crimes, a superego that is vigilant and all-seeing, that knows our actions and our impulses and phantasies. Freud writes: "The super-ego torments the sinful ego ... and is on the watch for getting it punished by the external world" (ibid., p. 125). "Life, as we find it," he concludes "is too hard for us; it brings us too many pains, disappointments and impossible tasks" (ibid., p. 75).

Freud then discusses a wide range of ways in which we try to make life more bearable. "There are perhaps three such measures: powerful deflections, which cause us to make light of our misery; substitutive satisfactions, which diminish it; and intoxicating substances, which make us insensitive to it. Something of the kind is indispensable" (ibid., p. 75). He thinks "Voltaire has deflections in mind when he ends *Candide* with the advice to cultivate one's garden". Freud thinks scientific activity is a deflection too, and that art offers only substitutive satisfactions, though these are "psychically effective, thanks to the role which phantasy has assumed in mental life. The intoxicating substances influence our body and alter its chemistry" (ibid., p. 75). Freud goes on to describe the inner measures suffering humanity also takes, such as remaining aloof from others, turning away from the external world, or becoming manic, which, in his view, is like intoxication. And if reality is altogether intolerable we resort to illusions, or even a delusional remoulding of reality.

Even those sublimations of the instincts that bring us solace—he cites "an artist's joy in creating ... or a scientist's in solving problems or discovering truths ... [and how] such satisfactions seem 'finer and higher'", yet even so, Freud contends *their intensity is mild as compared with that derived from the sating of crude and primary instinctual impulses*" (ibid., pp. 79–80, italics added). Alas, Freud concludes, these can neither restore our lost happiness nor lighten our guilt. They are "palliative measures" only.

Here is the kernel of Freud's thinking. Happiness depends on the satisfaction of our instincts. Civilisation means we lose some of this happiness, and, furthermore, that we will suffer under a cruel burden of guilt for our Oedipus complex and the murder of the father. However, he recognises that our situation is conflicted. He writes:

> ... if the human sense of guilt goes back to the killing of the primal father, that was after all a case of "remorse" ... this remorse was the result of the primordial ambivalence of feeling towards the father. His sons hated him but they loved him too ... Now I think we can at last grasp two things perfectly clearly: the part played by love in the origin of conscience and the fatal inevitability of the sense of guilt. (Ibid., p. 132)

Our civilisation is an expression of Eros, and with all its discontents of instinctual renunciation and the severity of the judgments of the superego, in Freud's view, civilisation is to be preferred to remaining in a state of nature. Near the end of *Civilisation and its Discontents*, on a magisterial note, he says "I bow to their reproach [meaning the reproach of his fellow-men] that I can offer them no consolation" (ibid., p. 145). Thus, we are no longer—as the ancient Greeks saw us—tragic humankind with a destiny given to us by the gods, but we are guilty humankind because now our crimes come from within ourselves. Freud's investigations have changed Sophocles' play.

This is where Freud took us and left us. Intriguingly, though, in a short paper on "Humour" (1927d), he had glimpsed a superego very different from the cruel watcher of the ego he describes in *Civilization and its Discontents*. He saw a superego that can offer consolation by means of humour and, in this way, comfort the troubled ego.

I think psychoanalysis was waiting, was ready for some such concept as Klein's "reparation".

As Freud was reflecting on these discontents of humankind, Melanie Klein was analysing small children. Her analyses confirmed Freud's findings of an Oedipus complex and an inner world of crime and guilt in small children and extended them to pre-oedipal times, including what had not been there before—the early relations to the mother, and daughters as much as sons. Klein also made some new observations. She noted that the psychic state of her young patients was closely bound up with the state of their objects and she began to conceive of instincts as "object-seeking".

This was a change in psychoanalytic theory away from an instinct theory in which the object has only a secondary role as the means of gratifying the instinct, to a theory in which the relations to objects are as fundamental as the nature of the instincts themselves. Such a change in theory was being made at that time in the UK not only by Klein but by others too, for example, Fairbairn, Winnicott, and Balint.

Indeed, this was a time of big changes in general psychoanalytic theory. In Freud's work there had always been two currents. One was an instinct psychology, such as we saw in *Civilization and Its Discontents*, where, for example, he sees happiness as due to the satisfying of instincts. The other current is an object relations psychology, in which he sees the state of the individual as dependant on identifications and relations to objects, as in "Mourning and melancholia" (1917e). In Freud's writings, sometimes one perspective predominates, sometimes the other.

And at this very time, Freud himself in his late years made a change in general psychoanalytic theory with a new classification of the instincts into life and death instincts. This innovation placed the sexual instincts in the category of Eros, as one of the instincts of love and life, and put aggression under Thanatos as an instinct of hate and death. Here is Freud's formulation in *Civilization and its Discontents*: "besides the instinct to preserve living substance and to join it into ever larger units, there must exist another, contrary instinct seeking to dissolve those units" (p. 118). Implicit in his formulation are also notions of connection and contact, and their preservation or their destruction. In her work, Melanie Klein used Freud's new theory of the instincts. In the course of many years she formulated a theory different from Freud's theory of psycho-sexual progression, a new, original theory of the human psychic journey. She conceived of a human journey from the state of nature to civilisation as happening in two psychic constellations of relations to objects and anxieties. We are born into a paranoid-schizoid position from which we develop towards a depressive position. In Klein's new account, love and hate, the preservation and destruction of parts and wholes of self and objects, their splitting, and their later integration, all become central ideas.

Klein has recorded how, when in distress with anxiety, guilt, and sometimes feelings of remorse, her young patients (Greta, Erna, Rita) would try to repair the damage they felt they had done to their objects and themselves. It was this that led her to notions of "making good" and "repair", the forerunners of the concept of reparation. From these early findings in children, and later also in adults, Klein's ideas slowly developed. She differentiated the wish to repair from reaction formation and sublimation, and in 1935 (Klein, 1935) reparation became a key concept in her theory of a depressive position.

What is reparation?

Reparation is an impulse of Eros. In Freud's words cited above, Eros is "the instinct to preserve living substance and to join it into ever larger units". In the depressive position the ego attempts to do just this with its objects and itself—to preserve or restore life and to integrate the different aspects of self and object.

As the ego becomes more integrated, what happens to the discontents of civilisation that Freud described—the renunciations of instinctual gratification and the inevitability of guilt?

Instinctual renunciation could become a loss to be mourned and endured, less from fear, more from empathy with others. And if things go well, a humanist conscience will develop.

The chief difference in understanding between Freud and Klein concerns the "discontents" of civilisation: Freud sees these as due to the restriction of instincts, while Klein sees the unhappiness as coming more fundamentally from the ego's identifications with its objects—if these are felt to have been humiliated, damaged, even murdered, the ego feels guilt and pain and in identification is mortified, broken, deadened.

If guilt and pain for hatred of primary objects can be faced and to an extent worked through and some reparation made, the depression of containing damaged objects changes to a sense of there being alive objects within. The ego feels better able to enjoy life, mourn its losses, recover from its lapses and failures, and, importantly, unconscious phantasies of making reparation can also come to inform sexual life.

Freud was a realist. You will recall his pessimism at the end of *Civilization and its Discontents*: "The fateful question for the human species seems to me to be whether and to what extent their cultural development will succeed in mastering the disturbance of their cultural life by the human instinct of aggression and self-destruction" (ibid., p. 145). Melanie Klein too was a realist. In "Envy and gratitude" she describes this instinct of aggression and self-destruction, the death instinct in its form of envy, and shows that it can "disturb or annihilate all attempts at reparation and creativeness" (1957, p. 231).

And reparation itself is difficult. Klein charted the struggle it is to make true reparation—even as we try, there may come a recrudescence of hate and grievance. There is the task of taking responsibility for our crimes, naming them, and facing external and internal reality. If this can be done it lessens anxiety and brings relief by replacing what Bion (1962, p. 62) calls "nameless dread"' by named deeds. This brings consolation that our guilt is limited, and not, as we unconsciously feared, immeasurable.

Even so, it involves recognising the painful truths that there are no new beginnings—what's done cannot be undone, and facing also that while some destruction can be repaired, guilt continues for things we feel to be irreparable, unforgivable. Under the burden of our guilt, we may yearn for absolution, redemption, forgiveness from an all-merciful being. Reparation differs from religious conceptions of God's mercy or absolution given to sinners. Reparation occurs in a human context, limited and conflicted, closer in some ways to the South African idea of truth and reconciliation.

Klein distinguished between true and manic reparation. Manic reparation is an omnipotent manic defence, often needed in early struggles in the depressive position when emotional pain and guilt are still too persecutory. Manic reparation, while reparative, is too weighted with triumph over the object, which is seen with contempt and so fails to relieve guilt or to repair the object. In the psychic endeavour to make reparation, the state of the internal and external objects on whom the patient depends—Are they alive or injured? Are they *forgiving*?—becomes of vital importance.

Reparation is psychic work, a part of the journey of integration in the depressive position. It is limited, uncertain, often conflicted—impelled by love, obstructed by anxiety and hatred. It is a crucial developmental step humankind tries to take, each along an individual path and to an extent that is possible—which is very various.

We could see all this as the continuation of Freud's "journey of civilisation". Klein saw how we can struggle on beyond discontents and a punishing superego—in her terms "the paranoid-schizoid position", and because of our love and identification with our objects, with a new integration of love and hate, try to make reparation to them as part of, in Klein's terms, "the depressive position".

References

Bion, W. R. (1962). *Learning from Experience*. London: Karnac, 1984.

Freud, S. (1917e). Mourning and melancholia. *S. E., 14*: 237–258. London: Hogarth.

Freud, S. (1927d). Humour. *S. E., 21*: 159–166. London: Hogarth.

Freud, S. (1930a). *Civilization and its Discontents. S. E., 21*: 59–148. London: Hogarth.

Klein, M. (1935). A contribution to the psychogenesis of manic-depressive states. In: *The Writings of Melanie Klein* (Vol. I). London: Hogarth.

Klein, M. (1957). Envy and gratitude. In: *The Writings of Melanie Klein* (Vol. III). London: Hogarth.

Lear, J. (1998). On killing Freud (again). In: *Open Minded*. Cambridge, MA: Harvard University Press.

CHAPTER FOURTEEN

Mourning and the development of internal objects

Kate Paul

We know that internal objects can develop in the process of mourning. People can mature in response to loss, but how does it happen? The study of mourning has been central to the development of psychoanalysis. "Mourning and melancholia" (1917e) is one of Freud's most moving and creative papers. The same could be said for Klein's "Mourning and its relation to manic-depressive states" (1940). Freud (1917e) touches the reader in his discovery of the internalisation of the lost object, evocatively casting its shadow upon the ego, and this paper becomes a cornerstone for subsequent discoveries in several areas, including internalisation, projective identification, and that "critical agency", the superego, and, last but not least, melancholia. He vividly describes the difficulties of letting go of the lost object and emphasises the looking back, the going over in detail before the object can be relinquished and the world embraced anew.

> Each single one of the memories and expectations in which the libido is bound to the object is brought up and hypercathected, and detachment of the libido is accomplished in respect of it. Why this compromise by which the command of reality is carried out piecemeal should be so extraordinarily painful is not at all easy to explain in terms of economics. It is remarkable that this painful unpleasure is taken as a matter of course by us. (p. 245)

Freud emphasises a stark contrast between a capacity for relinquishment in normal mourning and the relentless and punitive hold of melancholia, which cannot let go of the object. His account of melancholia is fuller than that of mourning, and his conjecture about the eventual recovery from a loss only takes us part of the way. It is put in terms of how "the ego is persuaded by the sum of the narcissistic satisfactions it derives from being alive to sever its attachment to the object that has been abolished" (p. 255). This is a surprising conclusion, as we would like to think that the outcome of mourning consists in more than narcissistic satisfaction. Interestingly, Freud's response to that most painful of losses, the loss of a child, was deeper and went further than his theory. In a letter to Binswanger (1929), who had just lost a son, he writes of the death of his own daughter Sophie in 1920:

> [W]e know that ... the acute mourning resulting from such a loss will subside [but that] ... we shall remain inconsolable and will never find a substitute. No matter what may fill the gap ... it nevertheless remains something else. And actually this is how it should be. It is the only way of perpetuating that love which we do not want to relinquish. (p. 386)

Here, love, not narcissism, is the key. In *The Ego and the Id* (1923b) Freud takes his theory further and describes the installation of objects within the ego as integral to its development. This is in contrast to the pathological melancholic identification, riven with ambivalence, that can impede emotional growth.

By the time Klein writes her paper, the complex and emotional internal world of relations to and between internal objects has become the focus.

> The poignancy of the actual loss of a loved person is, in my view, greatly increased by the mourner's unconscious phantasies of having lost his *internal* "good" objects as well. He then feels that his internal "bad" objects predominate and his inner world is in danger of disruption ... he not only takes into himself (reincorporates) the person whom he has lost, but also reinstates his internalised good objects (ultimately his loved parents), who become part of his inner world from the earliest stages of his development onwards. (Klein, 1940, p. 353, original italics)

This is a huge advance, and greatly extends and deepens the exploration that Freud had begun. Klein's work on the depressive position underlies this development and is taken further by it. She describes the need to face one's aggression towards the lost or disappointing object and the guilt and despair that can ensue. She suggests that in normal mourning there is a phase of mania that protects the mourner from awareness of destructive feelings, followed by a period of despair and depression leading eventually to acceptance of loss. Her distinction between mania as part of the mourning process and the working through that she views as integral to development, is a particularly useful one, since mania can be mistaken for recovery. She suggests that the necessity of this painful emotional work may "go some way towards answering Freud's question" (p. 354) about the painful unpleasure and why we take it as a matter of course.

It is striking that these two papers arose in part from their authors' experiences of mourning. Freud's older half-brother, Emmanuel, died in 1914 at exactly the age that Freud's father had been when he died. The war itself then led to a depression from which he found it hard to emerge. He writes to Abraham in 1915: "I still think it is a long polar night, and that one must wait for the sun to rise again" (Freud & Abraham, 1965, p. 209). Two of his sons were at the front, though they were later to return unharmed. So there were losses enough to be mourned as well as the disillusionment and anxiety of war. Klein writes about her own response to the tragic early death of her son. That both these papers emerged from times of loss in their authors' lives adds poignancy and conviction to their content. Both papers introduce new and very important ideas. This in itself illustrates the point that I want to add: the development of a new relation to the lost object is an integral part of mourning. People do not only reinstate the lost object or their loved internal objects as if these were static and unchanging; their relationship to their objects also develops and the objects themselves undergo change.

Klein writes vividly of this. She describes how "a renewal of life inside sets in, with a deepening in internal relationships ... At this stage in mourning, suffering can become productive ... [the mourner] becomes more capable of appreciating people and things, more tolerant in their relation to others—they become wiser" (1940, p. 360).

However, though it is in itself a major development, I do not think that her description of working through the loss and reparation of familiar internal objects sufficiently accounts for this capacity for development through mourning. I would like to give more thought to the idea of renewal and to suggest that in the process of mourning the mourner continues to get to know the lost object, to think about the lost object differently. It is not only a matter of reinstating the lost objects within the ego but of seeing them in different lights. Hence the internal objects change as do aspects of the self. Perhaps another aspect of the "painful unpleasure" that we take for granted is that we know that our internal objects will not just remain the same, we do actually have to say goodbye to them in their immediacy, since however much we may value them and retain them internally, our relationship to them will change and cannot be frozen in time.

In following this line of thought I will turn to Bion's ideas (1962) about the importance of K, the capacity to learn from experience, as a life force. Bion would see the capacity to seek truthful understanding as central to emotional development. If we think of this in the context of mourning, one might say that learning from experience is central to the capacity to mourn. The mourner comes to know himself and his object anew, as well as reinstating familiar object relationships. In this way, the process of life also affects the quality of mourning. To give a simple example from everyday life: a young man whose father died during his turbulent adolescence had retained a picture of his father as strict and forbidding in relation to his adolescent rebellion: it was not until he had teenage children of his own that he was able to recognise that an important element of his father's strictness was born of love and concern rather than of rigidity. He had maintained an adolescent stance in some regards until this point, and then learning from his own and his children's experiences helped him to see his father differently and to be grateful for the fact that he had cared about his welfare. Mourning is a lifelong process.

This process clearly goes hand in hand with development. The paradox entailed in Klein's view of mourning is that just when the individual most urgently needs his internal objects to help him deal with an external loss, these internal objects too are felt to be destroyed and therefore unavailable for containment or support. "His internal 'bad' objects predominate and his internal world is in danger of disruption" (Klein, 1940, p. 353). Loss can be overwhelming at this stage. Klein acknowledges the importance of the presence of the external object, the mother in infancy or, for the mourner, "people he loves and who share his grief" (p. 362). She writes of the need to internalise goodness and love, and to find mutual sorrow and sympathy. I am interested in how this internalisation takes place and how it leads to development. The capacity to mourn is intimately linked to the internal and external containment that is available to help the individual to be able to bear loss. The quality of one's internal objects is crucial to being able to bear the pains of loss, as is the quality of the external support that is available. This is recognised in societies where support for the mourners is enshrined in social traditions. The wake, the visiting of the mourners, music, dancing, and other rituals all provide vital support and containment for the bereaved. It has to be said that our modern society is often woefully lacking in such customs. Though the support of family and friends remains paramount, it is subject to the vagaries of what each family can manage at the time, and the greater the need for support within disturbed families, the less likely it is to be available.

So far, I have been talking about successful mourning, but of course in many instances there is a failure to manage the mourning process. In fact, this is often what brings patients to analysis, even where it may not be the stated reason for seeking help. The individual may have difficulty in mourning, for instance, the loss of a close family member or the end of a close relationship, a professional disappointment, or the disillusionment entailed in ageing. There may also be difficulties in mourning within the family, which are passed down from generation to generation (Barrows, 1999). Coming to terms with loss may only occur through containment of the distress that has been avoided through lack of mourning. Indeed, the failure to mourn may underlie the most severe forms of disturbance, where the avoidance of depressive pain has led to breakdown of the personality. Rosenfeld (1965) pointed out the depressive pain that may be avoided through psychosis, and Tustin, to her astonishment, stumbled across the sorrow expressed by an autistic child whose first word was "Gone!", soon to be followed by "Broken!" (1986, p. 76). He then had to mourn the loss of the object that he had felt to be part of himself and which he experienced as irreparable.

Bion (1963), Segal and others have emphasised the importance of the internalisation of the container and its containing functions. "An identification with a good container capable of performing the alpha function is the basis of a healthy mental apparatus" (Segal, 1991, p. 51). In this chapter I will be illustrating developments in internal objects that are affected by the internalisation of aspects of the container. I shall describe work with two patients whose internal objects seem to have developed during the process of mourning.

Mr A

Mr A, a teacher, was a likeable and highly articulate middle-aged man who never felt himself to be fully himself. He was kind, thoughtful, and caring but could be shocked by sudden eruptions of anger that made him want to throw away everything he had—his family life, his profession. He would return to picturing himself in the gutter, with nothing. His father died when he was a toddler. His mother had suffered a series of losses and seems not to have recovered and to have remained very isolated, depending on her son for support and an idealised relationship. She became physically disabled in later life. She died in her eighties when Mr A had been in analysis for three years. It was not easy for Mr A to mourn her loss.

When he started analysis with me it seemed that his main aim was to please and to co-operate. Early in his analysis he seemed convinced that he was there to look after me, reassure me of my usefulness to him. He would greet me with a kindly, avuncular smile, leaning over towards me and slightly inclining his head in a caring fashion, so that I sometimes felt that I was his pupil rather than he my patient. On several occasions he thought that he had the keys to the front door and tried to open it, forgetting to press the bell and wait for me to operate the intercom. He would chat affably to all in my neighbourhood. He is a good talker, yet despite the richness of his vocabulary there was a poverty of emotional experience and an underlying emptiness. Sydney Klein (1980) described patients who use words as an autistic barrier to protect themselves and their objects from underlying feelings of emptiness and non-existence. I felt at once walled out and soothed. He could not feel things much and neither did he have the capacity to project strong feelings into me. On one occasion he had a small cyst removed and said he had a feeling of loss, of missing the cyst, which had become part of him. It became clear that he experienced me, like the cyst, as a part of him which he did not want to lose. He also had to be the cook, the provider, and came to analysis partly in order to learn from me the recipe for understanding himself, hence bypassing his feelings of dependence. I wondered whether, when he was "looking after" me, he was also projecting into me feelings about being looked after in a way that actually offers little containment or room to be oneself, to develop as an individual.

Things gradually changed and his omnipotence and feeling of being my helper diminished. After a few years in analysis he started to bring many dreams, which shocked him as they were graphic and transparent. One such dream was as follows:

> He was in a theatre with the A couple. [They have in reality been very supportive to him and his wife through difficult times, they are kind and loving. His family went round to theirs recently and enjoyed themselves. But in the dream] they were watching a play in which the women were naked and splaying their legs apart, showing their genitals very explicitly. The men looked as though they had huge erections but in fact the penises were false as were the erections.

This reminded him of an article in the paper about people looking as though they were naked on stage, but actually having false pubic hair, breasts, penises, etc. He brought this dream near the end of the session. I pointed out that something fake had replaced a feeling of a genuinely loving couple. In the same way, he can feel what I say to be genuine, and then suddenly become alarmed that it may be fake. This seemed to represent both his view of the analyst as part of a genuine couple now seen as fake, and the way in which he becomes part of the couple, with a fake penis pretending to have intercourse with a gaping vagina. This horrific picture of the parental intercourse and the way in which he can become part of it, with a feeling that the show must go on, seemed an all too apt illustration of the falseness and bravado of many of his communications, his anxiety being hidden behind the pretence. He may also have felt that he was exciting me by giving me what he thought I wanted, until his dream revealed the falseness of this. However, his omnipotence and over-involvement with me as someone whom he felt to be in need of him did diminish over this period in the analysis.

A few weeks later, he came back after a difficult holiday with the following dream:

> he had been grossly obese and had now become thinner. He had folds of flesh hanging down, and sagging breasts, but with penises instead of nipples.

In the session it was possible for him to see how this dream, connected to his feelings of having felt at sea in the holidays, seemed to represent his sagging omnipotence; his feeling that he has the penis breasts is laid bare and he feels grotesque and empty. The next night he had another dream:

> his mother was able to walk again and had shapely feet in good shoes. He was looking for a better flat for her.

He said somewhat guiltily that in reality the flat she had lived in had been run down and in need of repair (his mother having died the previous year). I interpreted that he had been keeping me in a run-down state, needing to be kept going by him, and that now he felt that he wanted to find me a better place inside him. He protested that he does not see me as being in need of his support or run down, and I replied that it may be that he consciously feels that he appreciates me and his analysis, but perhaps he also feels me to be in need of his support, excessively dependent upon his co-operation in the analysis to make it work. I added that this has fostered the omnipotence of the obese him with penis-nipples and when this is exposed and seen for what it is he seems to find a stronger version of me/his mother, with healthy feet on the ground in good shoes, a good connection to reality. He said that it did feel a relief to see it so clearly.

It could be argued that the dream of the mother with healthy feet illustrates just what Melanie Klein described, the recovery of the internal good mother of the first year of his life. This entails mourning both the disabled and depressed mother whose feet were distorted and who had to lean on him and the analyst who was experienced as too much in need of his co-operation. It also means facing the aggression entailed in keeping the analyst/mother in a run-down state. However, I am suggesting that in addition to the recovery of the original stronger object, a new experience with his analyst led to a change in his internal mother. He needed to experience me as having my feet on the ground with a healthy perspective on his emotional reality, and this may have combined with an early lost experience of his young mother as healthier and happier, to produce a strengthened version of his older mother in his dream. It seems likely that this stronger version of his mother is not just based upon past experience, a replica of the past, but is added to by his relationship to his analyst in which he works through some of the distortions that also occurred in relation to his mother and takes in some strength and straightforwardness. I am suggesting that he takes back his projected feelings but also takes in something new that helps his internal objects to develop. He internalises a capacity to contain the anxieties, which he had previously been unable to face. So one could say that the development in the dream, of his mother as an old person with good feet, included both a revival of qualities, which she may have possessed in his first year of life, and new strength and capacity for containment taken in from his older analyst.

Occasionally some material relating to a hidden, more childlike, part of himself came to light with startling clarity. A couple of months after the session above, he described looking at the *Guardian* online: there was a bat, which had fallen through layers of shale thousands of years ago. It looked as though it was still asleep, as if put to bed by its mother. Now it had been discovered and was on view. He felt very affected by this. The creature formed a link in the history of evolution. He had thoughts about his transience. Then he thought of another article about looking at the world from space. He felt a strong wish to use the time in his life, to know what *he* wants or thinks, to have his own perspective on it.

I talked of a part of himself that may have been as if asleep for a long time, buried beneath layers of things inside him. It is a part of him that can feel looked after and wants to wake up to his own feelings and be able to have his own thoughts. (I might have added, had I thought of it at the time, that the view from space may feel like his father looking down on him from far away with a different perspective. He is likely to have been told as a child that his father was up in heaven with the stars.)

He replied that he loves it when things come to light quietly and simply (I think that he meant in contrast to a familiar fanfare of articulateness and co-operativeness). A little later in the session he talked of a space he had found under the bathroom floor while he was repairing the plumbing, that there were layers of newspapers from bygone years, the debris of generations under the bathroom floor and he had been clearing it out. He thought of his father and his enjoyment of his workshop.

It seems to me that he was talking about a part of himself that had got buried under the debris of generations of loss and unresolved mourning. This is a sleeping child who has been put to bed by his mother—a child who is looked after and protected. He rediscovers this child, at the same time invoking a father to give him sufficient distance from his mother to have an independent perspective or to support or repair her. He also feels that he discovers a space inside the object where the importance of the influence of the generations can be acknowledged rather than buried (Barrows, 1999). Do we think of this simply in terms of the recovery of lost objects or parts of the self, or do we think of it as deriving from a new experience in the analysis? It seems to me that as well as the important rediscovery of the buried part of the self, there is a new perspective, a new experience of acknowledgment of loss, which adds something to the original objects and their rediscovery. I think that this newness is integral to the process of mourning.

Something much more genuine gradually came in to the atmosphere between us. In a later session he said that he now realised that I had been concerned all along about his grandiosity and the damage it did to him, though he could not realise it at the time. He mourned earlier dreams of being sole cultivator of an apple orchard, another place in which he tills the land and is self-sufficient, unimpinged upon by feelings of envy, rivalry, or loss. He became able to be more critical of me and to genuinely question the meaning to him of his analysis, rather than attempting to shore up an idealised symbiotic union that protected us both from damage and loss.

During this period I think that he took in strengths that enabled some of his internal objects to develop—as well as, undoubtedly, some weaknesses in his analyst that will have limited the scope of these developments.

I shall now go on to give a brief example of a similar kind of dream and development in the analysis of a rather different kind of patient.

Mr B

Mr B, a writer, came to analysis suffering from high anxiety and writer's block. His mother left the family when he was four or five for a new man and for dreams of an exciting new career. Neither the new relationship nor her career worked out and by the end of her life she had become reclusive and tormented. She died when Mr B had been in analysis for a few years and his mourning was complex, involving his anger and disappointment with his mother as well as his sorrow about her unhappy last years and his guilt at being able to make more of his own life than she did of hers. However, doubt and indecision affected all areas of his life so that he could feel quite paralysed. In his analysis he gradually became much more aware of the attacking nature of his doubt, as well as his identification with an aspect of his mother who was felt to envy and devalue his—and her own—achievements and engagement with life, and whom he felt his anger had damaged.

There was a session in which I was able to show Mr B how something inside him was enviously attacking, relentlessly scuppering and undermining any chances of contentment or stability in his life and in his analysis. He literally could not settle in the room, lying on the couch but constantly moving, moving his head from side to side, interrupting his own sentences, so that everything was broken up, nothing stayed with, nothing followed through or properly concluded. In the next session, he started off by talking a bit about the difficulty of negotiating with someone difficult at work. Gradually I related this to having to negotiate with a difficult part of himself. He then brought a dream:

> his mother was showing him a photograph, which she had kept of him age two or three walking along a little wall. It was a nice picture and she was kind. She was making sure that he would keep his balance. He was very interested in the wall and she supported his interest.

He added by way of association that the wall had things growing in it and interesting stones, and it was between two different gardens, one cared for and the other neglected. He added later

> that he was lonely at the beginning of the dream, missing his girlfriend Anne but then someone said that they knew where she was.

He said that there was in reality only one photo of him and his mother looking alright together and it was a bit like the one in his dream, except that in the actual photo he is in his mother's arms. I said that he wanted to feel that I can support his interest in the wall that he walks along, between two very different states of mind, cared for and neglected, optimistic and negative, and to feel that I care about whether he keeps his balance. (He could in fact feel frightened at feeling so unhinged.)

He responded with agreement and told me two more dreams: one was about

> being in a lift that was going down too fast but then it slowed down and they got out okay. Then there was another dream about being in an aeroplane that was out of control but then managed also to land okay and safely.

He seemed to feel less out of control and less identified with an out-of-control object. The lift and the aeroplane can slow down and he can get out, in contrast to the times when his identification with a disturbed, out-of-control object has felt unassailable.

Towards the end of the session he talked about how he can feel lonely on Friday (the last session of the week). He said there is a lonely building at work with no one to talk to and he finds it hard to bear. This is in contrast to another building where there is someone he can share things with (this seemed reminiscent of his missing Anne at the beginning of his dream). I suggested that these places were also places where he feels I leave him: he can feel left in a lonely place by me, but wants to be able to hold on to me in his mind as someone to share things with, to be able to be in the better place.

As with Mr A, a more benign version of the mother comes into Mr B's dream. He seems to have gone back to the good picture of himself and his mother and adapted it to his present enquiring state of mind, where he is extremely interested in what supports him and the border that he finds himself on between contrasting states of mind: bleak versus someone to share things with, neglected *vs.* cared for, out-of-control *vs.* able to manage, loving *vs.* hating, and other contrasting states as well, too many to name here. As with Mr A, the rediscovery of a good aspect of the object combines with a new experience to create a changed version of his internal object. As he learns more about himself and accepts more about his object, his internal world develops. It was important for him at times that I did not repudiate observations that he made about me—my moments of impatience, for instance, when he was going over old ground yet again. He also, I think, noticed that I supported his capacity for real interest and recognised it as a life force in a very chaotic world. This, too, is present in his dream and his more evolved picture of his mother. His interest in the stones and the things that are growing in the wall may represent his curiosity both about elements from the past, the stones, and present developments, plants that are growing. At this stage in his analysis, the writer's block diminished and he was able to move forward in his career.

Conclusion

Both patients eventually began to be able to mourn their mothers and to see them differently. For both, it was important to gradually feel aware of the difficulty in perceiving their objects as separate and feel that it is acceptable to do so. This also entailed relinquishing their hold on their objects. Mr B's hold was an all-pervasive doubt, and Mr A's a conviction that he kept his object going. They both became aware of omnipotent feelings of being the cause of all the damage, and this awareness enabled them to recognise their objects more fully as separate, with both damage and strengths that were not caused by them. There was great sadness as well as anger and disappointment about something broken, aspects of a mother that could not be repaired. But there was also a revival and development of some strengths in their objects. In taking in and containing these situations in the analysis, the analyst inevitably returns them with some added quality, as it were, for instance, straightforwardness or a sense of balance, which were previously in short supply.

Through the analytic work it seems possible to gain a stronger internal object, which may well have been present to some extent early on. I am suggesting that qualities in the internal object can develop, can be enhanced or strengthened. We might, of course, say that the patients' dreams, arising in the analysis, simply represent the good object that has been attacked by the subject and is now repaired. We may also wonder about wish fulfilment or a defensive aspect of idealisation. But this may not be the whole story: an aspect of the past, an early experience, may combine with a new experience in the analysis to produce a more robust internal object.

Alongside these changes in the internal objects the older versions remain and in times of difficulty the individual will return to them, so that versions of the internal object are many-layered. Mr A will always have a tendency to return to the idea that he is someone's "prop and stay", and Mr B will tend to return to a sado-masochistic state of doubt and negativity. However, containment of these states may make it possible to recover the developments that have taken place in their internal objects, such as the mother with healthy feet or the mother who supports her son's lively curiosity and who can help him to keep his balance between contrasting states of mind. These developments comprise aspects of the analyst and her function as well as of the original objects. They could be seen as arising from the relationship between the internal objects of analyst and analysand.

I have discussed two men whose dreams about their mothers showed developments. However, I am not suggesting that it is only the internal mother who develops: clearly there are many internal objects and part objects that can evolve as the personality changes. These changes take place partly through containment of the patient's anxieties and gradually returning the patient's projections, but an important aspect of change also consists in the patient's internalisation of qualities of the container that allow the internal objects to develop. (Denis Flynn (2004) has written of the "vital response" of the mother as part of her containing function, matched by vitality in the infant.) This seems to me another aspect of Bion's idea of containment and transformation, since it represents the particular qualities and characteristics of the container and their impact on the patient's internal objects as well as the insights which arise from containment and thought. The internalisation of these qualities contributes to changes in the internal world of the patient and to his capacity for containment, leading to the enrichment and deepening of the personality. Nothing in life stands still.

Though I have written this paper about adult work, it seems important to mention work with children, since I think that the type of developments that I have described are an integral part of childhood. The child's internal objects are established early on, but they develop in relation to many figures in his life—relatives, teachers, other influential figures. In some cases psychoanalytic work is needed to set these processes in motion. In work with adults the kind of changes I have described arise through arduous and painstaking psychoanalytic work. While the same type of commitment is needed in work with children, the personality of the child tends to be considerably more flexible than that of the adult. The amount of change, the development of the internal objects, can be surprising and can have enormous implications for the future of the child, although it should also be said that this is not always the case. A brief example would be a child whom I discussed at greater length in a recent paper on mourning and perversity in *The Turn of the Screw* (Barrows, 2013)—a child who was fostered at six months, thought to have suffered malnourishment and abuse. He was physically and emotionally unmanageable at home and at school and lived in a violent and a dangerous inner world, which coloured all his relationships. In his psychotherapy his internal objects and his capacities developed a great deal. In particular, he was able to develop a sense of perspective, which is in itself a very significant aspect of containment. His drawings were initially absolutely chaotic and violent, lacking in perspective or form. In his psychotherapy he developed a real talent for drawing and communicated his feelings through this. As he gained a capacity for a perspective on his feelings he started to use perspective in his drawings. The sense of perspective helped him to tolerate strong ambivalence, saying "I like coming here but you are so annoying" or "I love my dad but he is so annoying!" He relished being able to say and feel these things without it leading to a disastrous fight and it paved the way for other important developments. He internalised a sense of perspective, which enabled him to live with his feelings rather than being governed by them. His internal objects acquired depth, as did his relationship to me as his therapist and to his adoptive parents from whom he began to be able to take in good qualities. A colleague working with his adoptive parents also helped them to contribute to these changes. With good support and understanding for himself and his family, the child is sometimes developmentally more open than is the adult to internalising aspects of his analyst and of other central figures in his life and to his internal objects developing as a result of this.

One could see the dreams of my adult patients as harking back to a stage in childhood when things have gone wrong with the natural processes of development and internalisation. Containment in the analysis leads not only to insights but also to introjection of qualities of the container and developments in the patients' internal objects. However, alongside the strengthened versions earlier ones remain and there is damage to be mourned. The analyst is used to provide insight and functions that may go some way towards enabling the patient to face and repair the damage, and to accept what cannot be fully repaired, freeing him and his internal objects to develop anew.

References

Barrows, K. (1999). Ghosts in the swamp. *International Journal of Psychoanalysis, 80*: 549–562.

Barrows, K. (2013). No place to mourn: Loss and perversion in *The Turn of The Screw. BPA Annual Bulletin*, 2014.

Bion, W. R. (1962). *Learning from Experience*. London: Heinemann.

Bion, W. R. (1963). *Elements of Psychoanalysis*. London: Heinemann.

Flynn, D. (2004). *Severe Emotional Disturbance in Children and Adolescents*. Hove: Brunner-Routledge.

Freud, S. (1917e). Mourning and melancholia. *S. E.*, 14: 237–258. London: Hogarth.

Freud, S. (1923b). *The Ego and the Id. S. E., 19*: 3–68. London: Hogarth.

Freud, S. (1929). Letter to Ludwig Binswanger, 11 April 1929. In: T. & J. Stern (Trans), E. L. Freud (Ed.), *Letters of Sigmund Freud 1873–1939* (p. 386). New York: Dover.

Freud, S., & Abraham, K. (1965). *A Psycho-Analytic Dialogue: The Letters of Sigmund Freud and Karl Abraham 1907–1926* (Trans., B. Marsh et al.) London: Hogarth.

Klein, H. S. (1980). Autistic phenomena in neurotic patients. *International Journal of Psychoanalysis, 61*: 395–402.

Klein, M. (1940). Mourning and its relation to manic-depressive states. In: *The Writings of Melanie Klein Vol 1* (pp. 344–369). London: Hogarth, 1975.

Rosenfeld, H. (1965). *Psychotic States*. London: Hogarth.

Segal, H. (1991). *Dream, Phantasy and Art*. London: Routledge.

Tustin, F. (1986). *Autistic Barriers in Neurotic Patients*. London: Karnac.

CHAPTER FIFTEEN

Some thoughts on addiction and perversion in psychoanalysis: theory and technique

Alberto Pieczanski

Introduction

Addiction and perversion share a number of structural features and frequently co-exist, confronting the analyst with similar technical problems. The clinical material and discussion in this paper are an attempt to demonstrate some of the technical difficulties and similarities I encountered in the analyses of patients with these characteristics.

The processes described in this paper can be found, although less prominently, in every analysis.

Inspired by H. Etchegoyen's (1991) ideas, and by the technical difficulties reported by most analysts working with these pathologies, I focused my attention on the detailed analysis of the transference-countertransference field from an object-relations perspective. It is my contention that object-relations theory and technique, specifically the close monitoring and interpretation of the transference and the use of countertransference as an extension of our exploratory tools, are essential to visualise the perverse and addictive modalities of relating that shape the relationship between analyst and patient.

In this paper I propose to focus on addictive and perverse states of mind, and suggest that they may not really constitute separate entities.

The approach of studying the transference/countertransference has led to the identification of what can be termed a perverse modality of object relation, with an identifiable and distinct emotional picture. Following the psychoanalytic tradition that generated concepts such as transference neurosis and transference psychosis, the idea of a transference perversion and transference addiction is being incorporated into our clinical conceptual armory and enhances our ability to work in this field.

Having sensed the existence of the configurations in my work does not mean that I can propose a definition of perverse and addictive transference in ways other than sharing what has happened when trying to work with these patients. A premature definition could create a false sense of knowing what I do not actually know to my satisfaction. However, some of the identifiable features will, in my view, confirm their existence and allow further investigation.

Projective identification seems to be the predominant organiser of the defensive structures that I have been able to identify. The clinical material I present will make clear that I am referring here to pathological projective identification as described by Rosenfeld in "On the psychopathology of narcissism: a clinical approach" (1964) and particularly in "Contribution to the psychopathology of psychotic states: the importance of projective identification in the ego structure and the object relations of the psychotic patient" (1971). Rosenfeld states that an important motive for projective identification is to control the mind of the object; this ultimately leads to a kind of mental parasitism.

Being the recipient of projections can adversely affect the analyst's capacity and lead to a loss of his painfully acquired skills, and to acting out. The survival and progress of the analysis depends on the analyst's capacity to preserve and keep his separate thinking mind, while holding on to his capacity to put himself in the patient's shoes; empathic but separate. The analyst's part in this process was described by Grinberg (1979) as projective counteridentification, a component of countertransference that can develop when projective identification is predominantly used for evacuative, controlling, and destructive purposes.

Another feature that seems to consistently appear in these relational modes is the patient's hatred and attack on the different components of the analytic situation, for example, on the setting, interpretation, and the emotional and thinking capacity of the analyst.

Theoretical background, nosology, and technique

My clinical work has frequently led me to think of addictions and perversions as psychological organisations that belong to the same register of human experience. This intuitive approach has been reinforced by the confirmation of frequent coexistence of perverse phantasies, acting out, and addictive symptoms.

This paper's theoretical background is primarily (although not exclusively) informed by a combination of Freudian, Kleinian, and post-Kleinian models, particularly as developed by Bion, Etchegoyen, Rosenfeld, Segal, and Joseph who, in "Addiction to near-death" (1982), describes the addictive qualities of perverse configurations. More recently, Feldman has described similar analytic configurations in "Some views on the manifestation of the death instinct in clinical work" (2000).

I will make some direct references to specific contributions, but I will not explore those ideas in depth.

I will use a nosological approach based on psychodynamic understanding, and not on external symptom manifestations. My understanding will be based mainly on the exploration of the specific transference-countertransference processes that constitute what Etchegoyen (1991) has named "transference perversion", which in my experience shows up in addictions as well as perversions.

The analysis of perversion and addiction confronts the clinician with patients who seem to be ill-equipped to exist in the real experience of life. Unlike those affected by other pathologies, they seem to completely obliterate some links with reality, particularly in regard to frustration and boundaries. This they do in a manner that is experientially more radical and unreachable than that of other patients, including those affected by some types of psychosis. Freud (1925h, 1927e) anticipated this when, as a result of his ideas about the death instinct, he introduced the notion that the dynamic understanding of perversion may require factoring in aggression as well as libido, and he also indicated that fetishists have a peculiar contact with reality. Psychoanalysts from different schools have used disavowal (Strachey's translation of *Verleugnung* in the *Standard Edition*) to designate the dissociation of the ego that leads to the obliteration of reality that we find in perversion and addiction.

Perversions and addictions show an important degree of destructive acting out. They employ a language of action that partly originates in phantasies of damage to primary objects and their external representatives, and partly are a defence to neutralise psychic pain, defuse unconscious guilt, and preserve psychic balance. In this system, "doing" is not an attempt to implement thinking and understanding, instead, it replaces thinking, particularly the linking with the consequences of hostile desires.

This dynamic alters the sequence in which thinking leads to action, replacing it with acting out. I assume it is self-evident that this psychological blueprint will result in serious difficulties to working in analysis.

As stated above, pathological projective identification is the main component of these patients' defensive organisations. It is their most effective tool with which to implement their need to unburden their internal world from guilt and persecution and to control psychic pain. The prevalence of projective identification defines a style of communication that shapes the transference-countertransference experience.

Rosenfeld presents a patient's dream that very concisely addresses the unconscious phantasies associated with excessive and pathological projective identification and the implications for analytic technique. In the dream, the patient

> … saw a famous surgeon operating on a patient who observed with great admiration the skill displayed by the surgeon, who seemed intensely concentrated in his work. Suddenly the surgeon lost his balance and fell right inside the patient, with whom he got so entangled that he could scarcely manage to free himself. He nearly choked, and only by administering an oxygen apparatus could he manage to revive himself. (1949, p. 49)

This dream shows how the object relation is conceived as a concrete intrusion into the other person's body and how both participants in the process can be affected. The surgeon/analyst has to save himself from the depletion of analytic "oxygen". He has to "cure" himself from the effects of the intrusive projective identification. Furthermore, the dream suggests identification with the patient, in so far as in the dream it is the analyst/surgeon who is the one that is performing the "operation" (a body/mind penetration).

Glover, a contemporary of Klein, defined perversions as the negative of psychosis, a counterpoint to Freud's idea that they were the negative of neurosis. I understand Freud to mean that perverse patients do what neurotics imagine or repress and Glover to mean that perversions are a defensive formation that protects or prevents psychosis. Although most Kleinian contributions have shifted the understanding of perversion towards psychosis, using a paradigm of a continuum neurosis/psychosis, my work leads me to think that perversion/addiction, as perceived from within the daily clinical experience, constitutes a different conceptual entity with specific clinical features.

Moving it closer to psychosis opened up the field, but it did not explain the specific features that show that we are not dealing with a clinical psychosis. It is not my experience that the analysis of perversions and addictions uncovers a latent psychosis.

The concept of perverse transference has opened up the study of aspects of this pathology based on inferences that can be drawn in the process of overcoming technical challenges that these patients present to the analyst.

Regarding addictions, Freud's contribution can only be inferred from his papers on other subjects and from a reference to them he made in a letter to Fliess. He first mentions addictions in the context of the possibility of using hypnosis (1890a), adding the warning that hypnosis itself can be addictive. Then he writes to Fliess (1897) that masturbation is the "primary addiction", all the others being a substitution for masturbation. He then links addiction to the actual neurosis (neurasthenia), which in contrast with psychoneurosis, according to Freud, could not be treated with psychoanalysis. So, it looks as if Freud gave up on addictions.

In all cases in which I dealt with addictions, I repeatedly found the development of a transference very similar to the perverse transference. Etchegoyen named it "addictive transference" (it is included in his book on technique as a sub-item in the chapter on perverse transference, with some differences mainly related, in my view, to the clinical consequences of substance use). The fundamentals of the addict's personality are very similar to those found in perversions, resulting in an object relations mode that resembles addiction to substances. This includes an addiction to analysis, which can become a source of impasse.

Clinical material

The material that follows intends to highlight the common features of patients with a perverse or addictive transference. These notes intend to convey the prevailing emotional mood that develops following persistent attacks on the good objects, good experiences, and love, and the difficult countertransference experience that can easily lead to a loss of the analytic instrument.

The prevalence of malignant projective identification and the non-symbolic use of words compound the technical problems the analyst has to deal with. I do not expand here on the non-symbolic use of language, ("symbolic equation") introduced by Segal in her 1957 paper "Notes on symbol formation", but I hope, its meaning will become clear in the clinical presentation.

Ms A was a young woman addicted to alcohol, some illegal substances, and psychiatric medication that was prescribed unbeknownst to me while she was in analysis. In her analysis, we established that her addictive behaviour originated in a set of unconscious phantasies of parental failure.

The unconscious phantasies that fueled the addiction fed two parallel processes. First, she tried to kill the awareness of her damaged internal world and the potential emotional debacle that could follow and second, addictions were part of an attempt to poison the internal objects (parents and siblings) trapped inside. The analysis showed that, in her mind, fighting me was a way of keeping me trapped inside her, a bonding through hate; making me "go where she wanted me to go" (like a baby inside her) and stopping me from doing what I wanted to do. This dynamic used to increase her persecutory anxiety because it led to phantasies of retaliation. While in this mode, any interpretation, no matter how carefully or caringly constructed, ended up sounding resentful and sadistic to her (and at times even to me). The attack on our good analytic intercourse and her good analysis was also being performed by the medication, which turned the analysis poisonous by virtue of her deception.

It is difficult to present clinical verbatim vignettes because the aspects of the process I am trying to describe are mainly experiential and can be strongly felt in the interaction but not necessarily expressed by either of us in words.

This short example is a rather routine and pervasive one.

Words in brackets are countertransference thoughts and feelings. Square brackets are further elaborations that developed while writing this paper. This is an opening of a session that felt very familiar.

Ms A: I feel great today.

A: (already this opening triggers some anxiety in me I don't trust. She does not celebrate progress, she enjoys mindlessness. Short silence. Perhaps she is checking my mindset depending on what I say and how I say it. I don't want to engage in a fight. I say nothing.) [We can see that the hopelessness has already installed itself in my mind. I could not emotionally stay with no memory and no desire as Bion recommends and I risk losing my balance.]

Ms A: I had dinner with J not very exciting, but I like his attention. I drank a little bit too much. We went to bed. Not much of a lover; such a small penis.

A: (I can't really pay too much attention to the content. I connect mainly with the futility and the denigration of the object. It sounds: business as usual.) [I can see I am becoming the rancorous small penis.]

A: It is business as usual, not much hope; nothing to celebrate, and yet, you feel great. [Trying to open up the field, inviting reflection.]

Ms A: Well yeah. (Silence) (Abruptly) Are you bored? Is that all you have to say?

A: [Such a small penis!!! Here there is a perverse distortion: I think that at this point I am in a parental transference. I am trying to help her to be in touch with her internal truth. She erotises, and then denigrates, turning the breast into a small penis.]

A: (It feels that at this point I refuse to engage in a sense of satisfaction about the lack of hope in love, and she tries to provoke me again.) You dislike feeling that I refuse to join in the excitement of witnessing how love fails again.

Ms A: Okay, okay!! I know what you think. I am not going to come here and cry. I have a meeting after this.... (Silence) Do you really believe in this shit?

A: [This is possibly a split second of insight (Okay, okay) that she rapidly obliterates through trivialisation: the only thing that mattered is that her make-up could be ruined. It becomes another insightful moment perversely lost. She was right; my interventions, if successful, could help her lose her make-up, and connect her with painful reality; she also knows that it is my belief in analysis that had kept her going, and she envies my fidelity.]

The obliteration in her mind of my dangerous thoughts always had an initial soothing effect that eventually became persecutory anxiety due to her belief in the inevitability of my retaliation, an inextricable part of her inner world. Another example of this is her repeated exciting daydream that I, in a state of total impotence and rage, watch her using drugs or drinking too much and am powerless to stop her. This manic triumph has frequently turned into a state of persecution and fear; in my view, evidence of the often described combination of sadistic and masochistic perverse unconscious phantasies.

At other times, particularly those when she perceived me as still alive, she could be overcome by hate. This was part of a transference in which I was the envied "sane" sibling. "Sane", in this case, meant the loved and thoughtful sibling.

Ms A's mood shifts were abrupt and catastrophic, due to the lack of "as if" psychological quality that allows playing and thinking with ideas. When the perverse transference dominated, one could clearly see the progressive loss of thinking ability. Her words, at such times, lost their ability to communicate and generate understanding. She was aware of this, and her picture of herself in that predicament could be so painful that at times it forced her to abruptly interrupt the session and leave the office.

Ms A also perceived my psychological qualities and skills, my ability to interpret, for example, as something she could take from me. She tried to copy my interventions with family and friends, becoming their analyst, an object to admire and envy. She felt she was entitled to this since she was the paying customer. When doing it, she was acting out a stealing phantasy that I could not control.

A key emotional aspect of the transference was her clear awareness of the destructiveness of her behaviour, the ludicrousness of most of her excitement, and the masochistic nature of her predicament, particularly if, to any degree, an attack on the analysis was successful. It is an intrinsic feature of the perverse transference that it exposes the analyst to witnessing how a patient consciously attacks the lifeline inside and outside the analysis with no manifest sense of loss. These attacks seem to increase as the analyst is increasingly perceived as good, analytically and as a human being, because eventually the conclusion is inevitable: only a good person, somebody that really believes "in this shit", would stay the course.

It was hard, although not impossible, to rescue her loving and reparatory qualities. In the sessions I described, these could easily be ignored. My disposition to hold on to her good and loving self was constantly tested. In this analysis, for extended periods I was the keeper of the goodness. While she provoked me to ignore the good objects—hers and mine—her survival depended on me never doing so. I was unconsciously expected to be the ultimate loving mother who would love the baby whatever the circumstances.

Mr B was a moderate alcoholic with obsessive sadomasochistic and paedophiliac phantasies. In his daydreams boys and adolescents obeyed him blindly, and that caused him a lot of satisfaction and sometimes also sexual excitement. As the transference-countertransference unfolded it became increasingly clear that in our relationship I was supposed to be the "thinker" while Mr B was the "doer", the child totally dominated by my thoughts; a "perfect team" that no one could stop. Mr B's thinking mind was the disowned and projected part. This phantasy defined the emotional flavour of the sessions. He became intensely hopeless about the analysis as he recognised that I refused to dominate, make decisions for him, or force him to follow my orders, equated in his mind with my thoughts. In his view, this would be the only way to show that I really cared. His "solution" to this problem was to use the analytic hour to "convert" me to his view. Furthermore he was puzzled by my reluctance to enter into an agreement that would give me all the power I could wish over him, as was the case for him with the children in his fantasies.

Mr B did not have manifest guilt. However, I understand many of the masochist components of his obsessing as resulting from unconscious guilt. During sessions in which I think he was not quite sober, although relatively in control, he imagined he was becoming my servant. In those fantasies I was strict and cold. He told me that the fantasy had a soothing effect. I understood it to be a projective identification of his abusive sadistic component, making me the child abuser, a cold and neglectful parent.

The pair—abuser/abused—showed up in another aspect of the transference. He would project his neglected and devalued self on to the analysis itself. He then thought we were having what he called a "disposable session", one in which I was considered to be so stupid and irrelevant that he would rather dispose of it in his mind, as if it never existed, rather than get angry about it. The fact that I could become such a pathetic creature was exciting enough to make him feel that he did not mind paying for it. I think that it was not too much to pay for unloading his mind of such a painful image of himself.

As in Ms A's case, when the perverse transference dominated, Mr B's use of words showed a progressive deterioration as tools for understanding and communication. With Mr B, rather than experiencing the deterioration as a loss, as was the case when Ms A stormed out of a session, he thought that words should be weapons.

The impoverishment of the symbolic function also generated disruptive countertransference responses. His concrete use of words led him to use language to elicit emotions to distort, nullify, and control my capacity to understand. The assault on my mind increased his persecutory anxiety and fear of retaliation, and generated a frustration in me that was hard to hide.

As with Ms A, the ongoing acting out in the transference plus the threat of the addiction were used to inhibit the analytic process. As with Ms A, I was supposed to collude with his defences rather than interpret, lest his mental state deteriorate.

Language and words were the main tools Mr B used to create the transference perversion. He enjoyed these mind games and excitedly used to talk about himself as being "very good with words", particularly when his language made others feel confused and humiliated. A frequent comment of his was that he could use words as sharp knives that could hurt and cause pain, adding: "I think words are useless unless they can be knives".

As I increased my clinical and technical understanding of these interactions I learned to recognise pockets of perverse phantasies in almost every analysis and found it very useful to keep in mind what I learned in these more extreme cases.

I find that the perverse transference can generate a blurring of internal boundaries in the countertransference. We can fall prey to the fear of using language as the patient does, to hurt and humiliate. The fear that we might camouflage attacks as interpretations can impair our capacity to think and interpret and this was particularly so when in moments of intense paranoid anxiety Ms A became very suspicious. She thought that I was a dirty old man using analysis and the analytic inquiry as some kind of mental masturbation in which I took advantage of her dependence to influence her. This anxiety was compounded by her feeling that I was running out of patience with her lack of progress. There was a further perverse twist. She accused me of doing exactly what I was supposed to do: influence her with the analysis. In this way she was corrupting the concept of the good analysis by claiming it to be bad if it actually brought about change.

We can here observe two different situations. First there is a countertransference anxiety about indulging in a destructive behavior similar to the patient's, and second, there is a fear of doing something that is in fact what we are supposed to do. These processes do not necessarily take place in an openly confrontational way and their subtlety and intricacy can make them hard to detect until it is too late.

The constant intertwining of perverse and addictive phantasies plus their mutual strengthening seems to be the main source of the atmosphere of clinical impasse that analysts report when presenting these patients.

A further complication that arises in the treatment is connected with envy, which is Klein's (1957) major contribution to the understanding of anti-life psychological processes. In the pathologies I am describing I find that envy expresses itself frequently as intolerance of the asymmetry of the analytic situation. Most attacks on the process tend to eliminate the patient/ analyst asymmetry, rendering the analyst's mind as useless as the patient feels his own mind to be at that moment.

Mr C, an intelligent man with serious addictive problems (alcohol and marijuana) and frequent sociopathic behaviour, characteristically followed a moment of analytic progress with a variety of irritating "smart" criticisms of me and the analysis. This attitude, when not interpreted (and many times even if interpreted), obliterated any good feeling or acknowledgement of progress. The arrogant attack on my working mind was at times intense enough to render me analytically useless. When I could not contain the envious attack, I could not think or, at other times, I could only formulate a partially "digested" interpretation in a tone of voice that gave away my irritation and frustration.

When the analyst is caught in this "mental indigestion", the patient experiences it as parental failure, and it can act as a confirmation, in his mind, of the damage done to the parent in the transference. The clinical situation is now one that confirms the patient's fears of being at the mercy of a damaged, uncontaining, and uncontained parent. As in the dream reported by Rosenfeld, the analyst is "losing his balance and falling right inside the patient".

Ms H, another patient, expressed her attacks on the good analytic couple by a relapse into drinking and promiscuous sexual activities, the symptoms that brought her to me in the first place. As in my previous examples, the acting out increased her unconscious guilt. On those occasions, she tried to find relief by trying to make me feel guilty (a projection of her own intolerable guilt) about "all those wasted years of analysis".

In one session, with no manifest anxiety, Ms H described in detail a sadistic sexual encounter that reminded her of the anal rape she had recently seen in Bertolucci's 1972 movie "Last tango in Paris".

This sexually exciting experience was followed by alcoholic bingeing. We had previously identified this combination of sex and drunkenness as evidence of analytic failure, and, in her mind, a source of intense frustration for me. She then added, in an anxious tone of voice, that she knew that I hated what she was telling me, but said also that she knew it would be hypocritical were she to hide this material from me. In other words, she was portraying herself as truthful even if it meant disappointing or hurting me. I think that she was actually confessing to being insincere, since, as in Ms A's daydreaming, it was very exciting for Ms H to expose me as a failure.

The analysis showed how this was an attack on what she felt was my "smug" sense of being a good analyst and a good person. Her masochistic behaviour (rendering the session useless) was a small price to pay if she could prove that I was a complete failure.

In the context of this session, the movie was a paradigm of an envious attack by the old man, representing her perverse self, on the beautiful adolescent, possibly representing our creative, lively parts. She was degrading goodness by killing our link with life and love, after which she tried to fend off the unbearable idea that irreparable damage has been done. Ms H oscillated between a manic denial of the damage done by her omnipotent attacks (for such was her perception of her aggression) and a resentful envy, mostly unconscious, of what she felt as my youthful lively side.

Even though the predominance of excessive projective identification is an obstacle to communication and understanding, I believe that intermingled with the perverse and addictive phantasies there is a genuine search and desire for love and hope—that this time the outcome will be different, preventing murderousness from taking over. It is part of the tragedy in these patients' lives that the combination of their sadism and defensive system can so consistently make good objects look ineffective and stupid.

To a great extent, the capacity to preserve the life in the loving objects is an uphill battle that requires an analyst with a strong belief in the process and the goodness of our technique. This is possible if our training and supervision, in so far as they help to preserve the analyst's binocular vision (Bion 1962b), enable us to sustain the analytic stance in the face of the interactions that I have described. Our stance is particularly critical when patients get caught-up in vicious cycles of increasingly destructive acting out, which trigger, in both the patient and the analyst, conscious and unconscious feelings of guilt and persecution that then restart the cycle with new acting out, a source of constant frustration for the analyst.

The preservation of the analytic setting, important as it is in every analysis, is here critical to preserve the process in the mind of the patient and the mind of the analyst. Any violation of analytic technique has an intensely damaging effect on us, due to the conscious or unconscious awareness of the damage done to our "baby"—psychoanalysis—and our failure to protect our patient from his own murderousness.

When the analyst loses the necessary internal stance, the balance between in-touchness and separateness is altered, and this results in the danger of colluding in a perverse transference that manifests itself as a divorce from technique and erasure of the clinical asymmetry that allows us to work. This collapse of the analytic process leaves therapist and patient confined in a dyadic delusional system in which the oedipal third, the Other—in this case the observing, trained analyst in internal dialogue with his analytic parents and siblings and the healthier part of the patient—is kept out of the process. I think of this clinical situation as a psychic retreat (Steiner, 1993) fueled by an unconscious claustrophilic phantasy.

In supervisions of analyses in which the therapeutic couple has become entangled in situations like these, I have regularly found that the analyst has ignored or changed, through a variety of rationalisations, some of the fundamentals of analytic technique with the excuse that "in this case", it will facilitate the process. The perverse collusion that develops, a *perversion à deux*, is unconsciously designed to protect each member of the dyad from the persecutory anxiety triggered by the attack on the constructive analytic process (like two children acting out while parents are not watching).

Mr L, a child abuser, used to bitterly complain that he was the victim of the culture's ignorance of how much children love and enjoy sex. Furthermore, he thought that if only I agreed with that, it would be possible for him to trust me. By that, he meant that we "should not be interfered with by the outside world". He expected me to become part of a closed, insulated system, where I could be seduced to reject my analytic understanding and technique. My professional identity was pictured in his mind as an intrusion that prevented him from being able to trust me and open himself up to me. It was an idealised and exciting attempt to enslave my mind to his perverse point of view, an attack on what he thought was my love for my work and my thoughts. The reward for betraying my analytic family was the unique special place he would let me occupy in his life.

A key aspect of this phantasy was that it would bring me "closer" to him. I understood and interpreted that he was trying to proselytise and seduce me into becoming a replica of him, a lonely and guilty outcast, whose only option would be to find refuge and comfort in my relationship with him after giving up my world. The alternative—to let me analyse him—he felt would expose him to an unbearable internal struggle, given the irreparable damage he believed he had done to his internal and external objects.

Summary

The analysis of patients with perverse and addictive symptoms shows that they have similarly perverse and addictive internal configurations, relational experiences, and defensive organisations.

Analytic psychopathology frequently describes patients in terms of their relationship to neurosis and psychosis. I think that the pathologies explored here belong to a register that does not fit the polarity psychosis<>neurosis and should be seen as a separate entity. Their connection with reality is seriously disturbed in a manner that differs from other clinical entities. The use of projective identification is also quite distinctive.

The specific qualities I described can be best identified when the analytic focus is on the transference and countertransference. If in the transference repetition a perverse modality takes over, the interaction with perverse and addictive personalities can seriously affect our analytic capacity. If this countertransference disturbance is not properly worked through it leads to a perversion of the analytic process that I have come to call a *perversion à deux*, in which the therapeutic asymmetry is eliminated.

The use of a consistent technique focused on a detailed analysis of the transference-countertransference field is indispensable to stay close to the main source of disturbance of the analytic process. In parallel, this approach seems to be, in my opinion, the one that most clearly allows visualising the perverse and addictive pathological organisation as well as helping the clinician to preserve the analytic function, his sanity and professional integrity. As Betty Joseph says in her bold style in "A clinical contribution to the analysis of a perversion" (1971, p. 441): "my impression is that, while one may deduce a great deal from these patients' symptoms, activities, and history, this is therapeutically comparatively useless unless one can analyse the manifestations of the perversion in the transference."

References

Bion, W. R. (1962b). *Learning from Experience*. London: Heinemann.

Etchegoyen, H. (1991). *The Fundamentals of Psychoanalytic Technique*. London: Karnac.

Feldman, M. (2000). Some views on the manifestation of the death instinct in clinical work. *International Journal of Psychoanalysis, 81*: 53–65.

Freud, S. (1890a). Psychical (or mental) treatment. *S. E., 7*: 281–302. London: Hogarth.

Freud, S. (1897). Letter to Wilhelm Fleiss, 22 December 1987. In: J. M. Masson (Trans. & Ed.), *The Complete Letters of Sigmund Freud to Wilhelm Fleiss 1887–1904* (p. 287). Cambridge, MA: Harvard University Press.

Freud, S. (1925h). Negation. *S. E., 19*: 235–242. London: Hogarth.

Freud, S. (1927e). Fetishism. *S. E., 21*: 149–158. London: Hogarth.

Grinberg, L. (1979). Countertransference and projective counteridentification. In: L. Epstein, & A. H. Feiner (Eds.), *Countertransference* (pp. 169–191). New York: Jason Aronson.

Joseph, B. (1971). A clinical contribution to the analysis of a perversion. *International Journal of Psychoanalysis, 52*: 441–449.

Joseph, B. (1982). Addiction to near-death. *International Journal of Psychoanalysis, 63*: 449–456.

Klein, M. (1957). Envy and gratitude. In: *The Writings of Melanie Klein* (Vol. 3). London: Hogarth.

Rosenfeld, H. (1949). Remarks on the relationship of male homosexuality to paranoia, paranoid anxiety and narcissism. In: *Psychotic States* (pp. 34–51). London: Hogarth.

Rosenfeld, H. (1964). On the psychopathology of narcissism: a clinical approach. *International Journal of Psychoanalysis, 45*: 332–337.

Rosenfeld, H. (1971). Contribution to the psychopathology of psychotic states: the importance of projective identification in the ego structure and the object relations of the patient. In: P. Doucet, & C. Laurin (Eds.), *Problems of Psychosis* (pp. 115–128). Amsterdam: Excerpta Medica.

Segal, H. (1957). Notes on symbol formation. *International Journal of Psychoanalysis, 38*: 391–397.

Steiner, J. (1993). *Psychic Retreats*. London: Routledge.

CHAPTER SIXTEEN

Evolutions in Kleinian-inspired clinical practice

Elizabeth L. da Rocha Barros and Elias M. da Rocha Barros

Our aim in this article is to examine the evolution of our clinical approach over the past forty years of work. We have, as a starting point, the mode in which we thought and worked clinically right after completing our training in the London Kleinian Group. Our finishing point is the current moment; that is, how we think clinically today, and for such we will each of us present a patient of ours today. We moved to London in January 1977 and there we stayed until May 1986. During this period we did our training in the Kleinian Group of the British Psychoanalytic Society. On our return to Brazil we had been accepted as full members, being today fellows, of this society.

If there are differences in our present ways of thinking and working, this does not mean that they derive from paradigmatic ruptures, since many of them may be thought of in terms of an evolutionary process. Even so, some important issues are posited on the nature of these differences.

For instance, on thinking of our work today, here are a few of the questions we meet with: Could we still be considered Kleinian analysts since we have incorporated influences from many other orientations outside the English group? In what has our way of working changed as a function of increments resulting from our appropriation of the core concepts of the Kleinian approach? We don't intend to fully answer these questions and will leave it to the reader to reflect on them based on our contemporary clinical work soon to be exposed below. Finally: What would the theoretical influences that articulate our present clinical work be?

This article is divided into two parts: first, the commented presentation of two clinical materials, and second, a commentary about some of the clinical-theoretical topics that seem to us to permeate the main changes in our clinical approach.

We would like to reflect on these questions based on the clinical vignettes. The clinical vignettes are instances that capture the core of, and changes in, our theoretical-practical trajectory along these forty years, and act as a springboard to the following more general, theoretic appraisal of the Kleinian system.

Commented clinical vignettes

Clinical vignette—Elias M. da Rocha Barros

We start off in illustrating some aspects of our clinical work today, with the material of a patient attended by the second author—Elias M. da Rocha Barros. It is presented in the first person.

Julia was fifty-eight years old when she came to me on the recommendation of her psychiatrist, who had been treating her for several years with antidepressants and sleeping pills. J did not understand why she had been referred to analysis. She had several reasons for feeling this way and listed them: she was fine and only had problems getting to sleep; she did not believe that a fifty-eight-year-old person could change and, in fact, believed that no one could change; she lived alone, was a widow without children and did not want to be disturbed by an examination of her past. She did not want to speak of, and be led to think about it, the story of her life. She was born in Brazil but came from a rich European family. Her mother had died when she was six years old. After her mother's death her father returned to Europe with his children and later got married to another Brazilian, a fact that led him to move once again to Brazil. Nine years ago, by chance, J discovered that she suffered from a very serious cancer with a ninety-five per cent death rate, but had survived it thanks to the expertise of a surgeon. The surgery caused her to have diabetes and had led her to monthly consultations with an endocrinologist over the past nine years. She told me she had not been shaken at all either with the discovery of the illness or with the surgery. This was all my patient had to tell me about her life.

J was very agreeable to be with, seemed to have an active social life, travelled a lot, and described in a very interesting fashion her trips, her interest in cooking, and her work as a designer, which brought her great social recognition. During the sessions I felt it must be very pleasant to have her as a friend but to be with her analytically was quite distressing as most of the time I did not know what to say to her and most of the time I felt incompetent. J was in touch with the feelings and perceptions of people she described, but when I tried to use these descriptions to point out something about her mental functioning, she denied my observations and retreated into herself. At such times she insisted that she did not know what she was doing here. J was bilingual. During the sessions she sometimes described an emotional state with words from the other language, "more precise", as she put it.

J sometimes told me jokes in this other language. These jokes had usually to do with linguistic misunderstandings between a couple. Initially I tried to suggest that these stories could be seen also as an expressive metaphor of what happened between us, suggesting that as an analytic couple we remained together and even appreciated each other but that I had the impression that there seemed to be a misunderstanding between us, to more accurately describe which there was a lack of words, and the amusing and always pleasant atmosphere existing between us served to avoid the unease that otherwise would establish itself here. She denied this and in time I left off making these connections and only listened, searching to observe the emotional atmosphere created between us. Once, after one of these jokes, I told her it seemed to me she said these funny things but there was a sadness lurking in her talk. For the first time she agreed with me saying, "Maybe!"

This situation suggested the existence of impairment in her capacity of symbolisation, but of what nature? She was capable of symbolic representation of some emotional experiences and some of her dreams drew on quite a large number of symbols, but she was not able to recognise the full meaning of the emotional experience that appeared to be conveyed by the symbolic forms[1] used in her dreams. She seemed to have lost her ability to understand the connotative[2] (subjective) aspect of the symbolic representations and only grasp its denotative[3] (objective) side. The analogies involved in denotation became indications of concrete equality, as in symbolic equations. Thus she was not sensitive to expressive[4] aspects of the symbols conveying potential meanings for the emotional experience represented. It seems to me this limitation already occurred during the process of symbol creation and affected mainly her capacity for symbolic expressiveness. I don't think that this impairment in the process of symbolisation can be explained only by impairments in the process of projective identification, though this may well play a part. Along these lines I also suggest that we cannot reduce the matter simply to a theory of splitting off parts of the self and I cannot just say that she was evacuating unpleasant experiences of her past.

At this point I wish to suggest that there is a discontinuity in her mind, a kind of fracture that interferes in her capacity to apprehend or construct symbols for certain kinds of experiences. This suggestion results from a recent deepening in our research on the processes of symbolisation and its profound intricacy (Rocha Barros, E. L., & Rocha Barros, E. M., 2011, 2016).

In one session she brought a dream that differed from the usual. The dream was about a stone. The stone initially was just strange, as it seemed to want to communicate something, but it was a stone and said nothing. So as she was on the beach she decided to put it against her ear, as we do with shells and then it produced a sound.

By way of associations, she tells me that a few times on her trips she saw spectacular aurora borealis. She says she recalls this because some people in the group heard sounds that accompanied the auroras, others did not. At this moment her eyes filled with tears. I notice the fact and ask her what she could say about these tears. She answers that she does not understand them and that they tell her nothing and she further comments that she was neither sad nor moved right then although she had been, during her trips, when the lights started dancing in the skies. Apparently out of nowhere, she says she remembered a time when she was preparing a typical pasta of her country, lots of work, together with her father, and at that time her eyes had also filled up with tears. Her father noticed and likewise asked her why she had tears and she answered in the same way as here. Next, in a whisper, she comments that she found out from friends that I like to cook. I feel touched by all she has just told me and afraid of saying anything that might seem like a simplistic and mechanical comment or a simple analogy. I say nothing and become quite exasperated for not finding the words to say something in this moment that seemed special; I feel blocked and scared of spoiling everything. After battling with my own self, I tell her, hesitantly, that for the first time she says we might have something in common, our fondness for cooking, but I noticed that this had to be said in a very low voice, in a whisper, in such a way that we hear and don't hear what she is saying. I risk telling her that the stone between us started to want to talk and produced a faint sound not yet articulated in words that not everyone could hear. I add that this atmosphere of quasi dialogue seems to have something to do with the relationship between her and her father in the past and perhaps reflects still in the present moment, a wish to speak about things they and we could never talk about. I believe that my countertransference and reverie were at that instant being used as support for the expressive working out of symbolic expression that for her had been blocked. I would say, using a term of Ferro's (1999) that there was starting to exist between us the delineation of an "affective hologram".

She doesn't deny this and says jocularly that it seems a miracle, like the aurora borealis. I add that just as in her experience of the sight of the aurora, some lights accompanied by sounds not yet articulated with words indicate perhaps a wish to talk with me about flashes of emotions that are appearing for the first time and can be seen by both of us, and that this might be the aurora of something.

In the next two sessions, she brings me an excruciating problem: she does not know whether or not to stop working and if so, she would consequently close her design studio. She wants no more commitments, is tired, wants to travel more; however, she likes what she does. What calls my attention is the growing tension that comes along with this doubt, which at the end of the second session becomes almost unbearable to me. She insists that there are good arguments in favour of her stopping work and equally fine reasons not to close the studio. What to do? I think that I could say to her that the dilemma she presents to me also refers to whether or not to continue working on the building of a dialogue between us, but I decide not to say this as it seemed too simple and mechanical to make this transposition.

I feel sometimes, before interpreting something more specific, that it is helpful to describe the atmosphere of the session when I am reasonably sure of being able to capture it. And so I tell her that our last two sessions were progressively dominated by a feeling of not knowing what to do, what decision to make, or what to say regarding this. I said I thought the atmosphere was likely becoming unbearable to her and she might feel the same was true for me. The feeling between us was one of being tortured by the need to do something, but at the same time feeling that something was keeping us from proceeding. She surprises me, saying, "So then let's tell a joke!" I'm baffled, I did not expect this reaction in face of the growing sense of torment between us and the lack of a way out in our conversation. I get irritated and once more feel very incompetent. I torment myself searching what to say to her.

That night I dream that I had a very good conversation with a son of mine, which relieves me a lot, but in the dream the son did not look like any of my children and the conversation was about a trip and the possible obstacles and setbacks that we might face. Something tells me that the dream referred to a certain perception of my relation with my patient. There was the wish for a dialogue between me, in the role of father, and her as my daughter, but something kept us from going on this trip.

Three days later she begins the session commenting that she had received an enigmatic phone call from her sister-in-law and she was left not knowing what was expected of her in the family, and then she says, "You know, when my mother died and my father took us to Europe I had to change languages from one day to the next. I stopped speaking Portuguese even with my brother. I only went back to speaking Portuguese some years later when I returned to Brazil. In Europe we lived in a *palais* which today is a historical site. It was pretty but gloomy and enormous and only we and our employees lived there. Then my father took us to the house of some friends and told us he needed to travel and we only met again some months later. I didn't know these friends, who were very kind to us, very warm, the house was pretty, comfortable, and unlike the *palais*, full of life. We moved once again to another city. Apparently I didn't take much notice of the moving, I even liked it." She becomes silent. I notice the reference to the loneliness in the residence, its gloomy atmosphere, and the lack of communication between her and her father.

I decide not to say anything. The atmosphere gets heavy! After a few minutes she says: "When I saw my father again eight months later, I felt a mixture of happiness, hate, and a wish to ignore him. He was very warm and had tears in his eyes, smiling a lot, accompanied by a woman I did not know and who seemed to be his girlfriend. That day my father cooked for all of us, but no one spoke about his trip, where he had been, what he had gone to do, who the woman was, etc. I realise that up to today I still don't know where he went, nor the reason for his trip."

I am moved by what she says and risk commenting that perhaps both of us have this experience when we meet, of liking to see one another, a pleasure in there being an affection between us, but at the same time we end up without knowing what to say to each other, nor what to expect of the other and under such conditions we can even talk of things we have in common but at the same time there are many things we do not know about each other. This kind of atmosphere seems to be very difficult for her to face since something disastrous or painful might ruin the good mood of our meeting.

The happenings along these last two weeks lead me to think that she was enacting in the sessions an experience that was not formulated on the discursive level, that is, put into words, which delineated itself under the form of the feeling that she liked her father and felt he liked her very much but, after the death of her mother, this father was at a loss and did not know what to do with his children, especially her. It seems to me there is also an enormous anxiety regarding her sense of impotence in face of the anguish and suffering of her father with the loss of her mother. She never knew what was expected of her.

I believe these feelings to be at the roots of a form of relating in the present. This emotional nucleus manifests itself in a hardship in deepening a dialogue that could take two people to getting to know each other more intimately. Getting to know is painful because it involves examining one's own painful feelings and those of others.

Clinical vignette—Elizabeth L. da Rocha Barros

Let us now turn to the clinical vignette of the first author—Elizabeth L. da Rocha Barros—to further our reflection on the evolution of Kleinian practice in our work. This, also, is a first-person presentation.

The patient is a twenty-eight-year-old man who began analysis with me some years ago. The material presented was produced eighteen months after he started therapy. We worked initially with three, and after a year, went on to four sessions a week. Daniel comes from an intellectual family. He sought analysis of his own volition although at first he had thought he would have only one or two sessions a week. He said he felt confused professionally, a bit lost and paralysed. He became over-anxious, which led him to eating compulsively and consequently he also had an obesity problem. He felt highly devitalised and was very afraid of coming to suffer depression. In the family there are various cases of depression and his mother, though a very sensitive and proper person, had gone through several depressive periods in her life. His parents had been separated for ten years and both had remarried. His father is a successful businessman and both parents have been in analysis for various years. I will not expand on his story for I wish only to discuss some issues linked with clinical practice.

The material I will relate happened ten days prior to a two-week vacation break of mine.

During a Monday session Daniel seems tense and restless. He starts giving a long account of all the preparations for a party there will be at his house that day for his girlfriend's birthday. This is a relationship of two years, and about a month ago they started living together. He speaks factually and in a monotone. He describes in detail the organising of the celebration, the preparations, the food that will be served, the list of guests, and so on. As he relates the various measures he has taken he appears to me irritated. He tells me he did not want to fight with Solange (his girlfriend) but when he called her before the session, he found out she was at the supermarket getting Nutella for that night, as she feared that the buffet catering service they had contracted would not have it in its provisions. He got very angry over this and at the same time he was upset and did not want to ruin the night, although he was afraid this might happen.

What might have been my possibilities for interpretation? I could say that what is not unconsciously tolerated is my "party-vacation", which he seems to need to deny; that is, deny his need (of his infantile I/self) of the analyst and as such prove that he is capable of taking care of everything alone. In this interpretation the patient is projecting his infantile self into the analyst who is kept excluded from his talk. The long speech would consist of an enacting in the transference through which Daniel is actively excluding the analyst from an active role. Or I could, as well, understand his irritation with his girlfriend as the enacting of his anger at my independence relative to him evidenced by my autonomy in exercising my right to a vacation when I wished. These would be direct interpretations of his unconscious phantasies shaping his experience in the here and now of the session.

These, however, seemed to me very distant from the general mood of the session, though they were congruent and consubstantiated (Bolognini, 2008) with the feelings expressed towards his girlfriend and, so to speak, not "wrong". I decided on waiting and, rather than interpret the more prominent anxiety (loss of control over the object) and his defence (of a maniac character, denying the need through the imposition on me of an exclusion), I sought first to *elucidate* better the feelings involved. I believe I was searching the part of his self most accessible for listening to what I was saying to him and which would best reflect the atmosphere of the session in order next to suggest a meaning to what was happening. These two interpretive options are not contradictory and differ above all in the way of arriving at each one of them. This second approach is the result of many considerations. I would not feel comfortable going directly to the interpretation of the unconscious phantasy without first clarifying the feelings underlying his enactment in the session.

In the session, I showed him initially that he had experienced the buying of the Nutella as a doubt about his capacity to handle everything and prepare alone the party for S.

Daniel is very surprised and seems quite relieved with my observation. The atmosphere changes totally and he seems to me more reflective.

I add that it appears to me that to feel he is competent and powerful he must be especially self-sufficient and take care of everything without the least help, and I suggest that this interfered with and hindered the chance of his forming a partnership with me in analysis and with S in his life, as a form of shared work. The session was ending and I added no more.

The point I wish to highlight is the need I feel today not only of knowing which part of the patient I am talking to, but of making a hypothesis about how the different parts interact with one another. As Daniel is a young man who is continually defending himself from his more infantile aspects and his needs, I opted to first clarify the feelings involved and describe the impasse he put himself in. From my present experience I considered that to interpret the infantile aspects in the classic fashion mentioned above might have led Daniel to closing himself in even further, aggravating his maniac defences in a way as to deny any sort of dependence. As I did it, I sought to interest him in the paradox of his functioning; that is, how he cannot receive help without feeling at risk of losing his competence. In this case, Daniel confuses dependence with a lack of autonomy and competence. My interpretation addressed an adult aspect of his that could listen to me so as to invite him to observe, with me, the functioning of his infantile self.

In the next session the patient comes in saying that the party had been great and gives a long description of it. This session precedes my vacation. Then he tells me he had a dream, a dream that to him seemed strange, without rhyme or reason, and says: "I wasn't able to understand the *why* of a dream so strange, so incomprehensible!"

> It was a sort of oriental palace, something very open with grass lawns. This palace was made of various tents. I was with my grandfather and others of the family. We were sitting in a circle, it may seem strange but it was as though we were watching the grass growing. A short, reddish, kind of English-looking man appears and tries talking with us. That ruined the atmosphere. Then this man goes to the next tent. I see in another tent a very tall man criticising my partner, Socrates. I push him into the pool. I say to him: "I want to see you have the courage to get out of there!" The man stays in the water and never comes out.

In his associations the palace has him recall a caravanserai, which he explains to me is a place that serves as a shelter for the nomads in the desert. It is a protected place where there is food and room for sleeping. He had visited a similar place during his last vacation. The entrance was very beautiful, all carved in stone. Stones reminded him of Kyoto, due to the beauty and peace of its gardens. He also says that he was upset because his father had not called his girlfriend the day before, when he himself always called on his stepmother's birthday.

Let me deepen my understanding of this dream to then comment on my way of working.

Some of the observations I made about the difficulty in my speaking about his infantile self in the previous session, here did not seem to me inadequate. Daniel told his dream in perplexity; however, the general mood of the session was of greater emotional accessibility to understand his dream.

The countertransference experience I had was curious, for while Daniel spoke of something completely incomprehensible (paralysing), my experience happened in the opposite direction, in my seeming to understand his dream.

I interpret how he felt the analysis as being this shelter—the caravanserai—and that he was very angry with this Englishman who, I suggested, was a representation of my husband (he knew he had lived for many years in England) who interrupted this intimate and atemporal process of contemplating his interior, and distanced me from him. I understand there is an unconscious phantasy that I would not go on vacation were it not for this man. He interrupts me and tells me that he remembered that during a period when his father was sick in hospital he had, at his father's request, filmed the lot where he intended to build his house. The lot had been cleared, some trees taken out, and grass planted. When he took the film for his father to see, it was out of focus and tremulous. His father then asked that he film it again, telling him: "You must stay still with the camera, as though watching the grass grow." On bringing me this association he becomes very surprised and moved.

Upon hearing this account, I recalled that on this same visit to his father at the hospital, his father had said, "Daniel you are my *sol* (sun in Portuguese)." This comment had left him very happy, flattered, and likely triumphant in relation to his siblings. The reverberations of the words "sol", "Socrates", and "Solange" articulate with one another, making me understand that this issue is again present in this session.

In this dream we are faced with experiences and affects that are completed in a single image, as we will see next.

The most available affects are his anger towards the analyst due to the forced interruption by the untimely vacation break, the issue of possessiveness of the analyst/mother whose inner-session-caravanserai is experienced as a shelter. The disappointment in not feeling he is the sol/sun of his father (or mine in the context of the session) at that moment of forgetting his wife's birthday is linked with his anger at the Englishman who interrupts our intimacy, distancing me from him. I could also think that the tall man (his father is a very tall man) who criticises his partner represents his father who hurt and humiliated him when he made a criticism of the work he had done some days before. In this dream D expresses all his hatred of the paternal figure, which in the transference would be my husband indicated by the Englishman (as mentioned, D knew my husband and I had lived in England for ten years) in the dream, something which is present but still very unconscious. In the context, my vacation is experienced as "being forgotten by me" on his no longer occupying a privileged position (that of being my "sun"/"sol", not forgetting *Socrates*, *Solange*) with the analyst.

The interpretation of the expression of hatred in this dream is especially difficult and important. I was careful in interpreting his anger, as it seemed important that he had made this feeling more available for himself to reflect on. An interpretation of this feeling just as an attack could be experienced as an onslaught against his person. Here I took into consideration that my patient is a highly vulnerable person who feels inhibited and paralysed.

Reflections on the evolution of our clinical approach

From these vignettes we now move on to the broader reflections that complement and expand upon what they touched on.

We look on the Kleinian system as a live ensemble that is constantly being reinterpreted by the multiple readings of its founding authors, by the accrual of observations, and by the cultural context that took it on, both in its place of origin and in other parts of the world not directly associated with the core English Kleinians. Within this context we proceed with our views on the evolution of our practice.

Canestri (1995) pinpointed well a basic development on suggesting that what best characterises present psychoanalysis is a form of interpreting that incorporates the process of listening and the subsequent process happening in our own selves.

We believe that the changes in our clinical approach observed today follow on from a special form of listening that incorporates something more than what Paula Heimann (1950) considered countertransference to be, and from a deeper, more reflective attention to the processes of transformation happening in the mind of the analyst as a result of the elements in it evoked up to the point when these can acquire the form of an interpretation. Moreover, our experience has led to a great concern over the question of the formal aspects of the language in which the interpretations are being conveyed so as to emotionally touch the patient.

Among these preliminary considerations we must also mention that little by little we began to observe that something more than insight must happen to produce changes in the mental functioning of the patient. This "something more" became increasingly prominent and led us to reflect on the role we are playing in the process of psychic change. We add further our concern over the way by which unconscious phantasies transform themselves into forms of thought and are construed through complex symbolic processes.

In this context, what was to become essential to our present clinical practice are the notions of intersubjectivity, the analytic third or thirdness, reverie, issues in the constituting of subjectivity, and also a deeper understanding of the processes of symbolisation and meaning-making.

The progressive complementation (and/or advancement) of the concept of countertransference into that of reverie has its origins in the works of W. Bion and is one of the outcomes of exploring the phenomenology of projective identification. This notion has, since 1986, been significantly broadened in the United States by Thomas Ogden and in Europe by Antonino Ferro (1995).

We think that in our clinical work today are present some developments derived from our works (Rocha Barros, E. L., & Rocha Barros, E. M., 2000, 2011, 2016) on the building of symbols and the constituting of meaning/meaning-making, besides the contributions of some analysts outside the Kleinian circle such as Thomas Ogden, A. Ferro, A. Green, and likely many other analysts we are unable to identify. Ogden (1992) contributed immensely with his works on the function of reverie and his emphasis on the importance of intersubjectivity also central to Ferro. The concept of the analytic third, as an instance created from the interaction of the pair/couple, was fundamental to the development of a perspective of observation of our reverie. We need say also that the works of André Green (1987) on *la tierceté* (thirdness) reinforced this stance.

If it may be problematic (but not incompatible) to suggest that these developments are part of Kleinian thought, it must be said that they did influence a great number of Kleinian analysts outside of England.

Among the contributions of Kleinian contemporaries we underscore the work of Ron Britton (1998) on triangular space and the Oedipus complex and of John Steiner (1987) on psychic retreats.

Some developments of Kleinian thought, produced in the heart of the English group in the years subsequent to our training period, will likewise influence its clinical practice towards what could be called "modern Kleinian clinical practice". Before we talk of the influences outside the English Kleinian group, we will try to summarise the contributions of the authors of this London group, which are at the core of our clinical approach.

From the beginning, Rosenfeld, Segal, Betty Joseph, and Bion gradually furthered the understanding of the nature of the internal object through their clinical observations and began to characterise it as something that takes on its significance and function in the multiple relations that it establishes with the self. Within this we can understand the impact of broadening the concept of part objects introduced by Bion (1962) in 1962, when he characterises it less as analogous to an anatomical structure and more closely related to its mental function. Spillius (1983), the author who so far has carried out the most profound and significant studies of the development of Kleinian thought in England, underscores the shift in emphasis from a structure-based concept to one based on functions exercised within the mind. Complex defensive organisations are built to maintain the more needy aspects of the self, isolated from the objects that fulfill a nourishing function promoting emotional development. Several clinical studies are presented, showing that in the good parts of the self are also lodged bad aspects, just as in the bad aspects there are good aspects too. In this way the analysts of this group, especially John Steiner, with the description and investigations of the virtual collusions between different aspects of the self, go significantly deeper into the nature of the interaction operating in the transference and the nature of the defences in action therein.

We can, for instance, note the profound influence of this synthesis of ideas on examining the concepts of pathological organisations and psychic retreats, as well as Britton's papers on oedipal situations and Feldman's on projective identification. In 1964 Rosenfeld (1964) suggests that narcissistic object relations are defences against any recognition of separateness between self and object. Recognition of the separateness would lead to feelings of dependence on the object and to anxieties; on acknowledging that the object has something good and nourishing on which one depends, envy is aroused, producing hostile feelings. Here we have one of Rosenfeld's most original discoveries, that is, that narcissism is a defence against envy. The most immediate implication of this discovery is that envy rarely can be seen directly in the patient's material. The focus of observation and interpretation then becomes the narcissistic type of object relations and the different mental organisations that can be built to avoid contact with feelings of hostility, humiliation, and shame, and that frequently imply splitting of the ego in order to eliminate the part of the personality that can have feelings; in other words, the capacity of feeling, in itself, is projected out. As an outcome of these ideas, the interpretation of envy and destructiveness changes focus. Analysts prefer to keep from interpreting directly the attacks on the analyst, paying greater attention to the effects of the destructiveness on the mental life of the patient and its consequences.

Britton, deeply influenced by Rosenfeld, concentrates on investigating the difficulties resulting from the non-perception of the self as separate from the object and on the problems created by this impediment on working through the oedipal conflict. In order for the oedipal situation to be worked through and the resulting sense of subjectivity to be developed, it is necessary, on the one hand, that the child feel separated from his object, and on the other, that he be able to differentiate the parents from each other and develop a specific relationship with each of them.

John Steiner adopts the same focus in this conceptual development. Based on his clinical observations, he goes further into the problems of creating psychic retreats as a way of not facing the psychic reality of separateness, and consequently of one's feelings of hatred (and thus its effects on the unconscious phantasy regarding the integrity of an object) and of hurt towards the parents by whom one feels betrayed. Within this, Steiner develops complementarily to Britton, on some of the consequences of the feelings of resentment and remorse, and so of the need for experiencing and verbalising indignation, and of the conditions under which reparation may occur. He shows the importance of the frustration of childhood wishes (of becoming part of the parental couple) and consequently the disappointment that causes indignation towards the parents as part of the developmental process and the depressive working through of the oedipal situation. We might say that here he discusses the positive role of facing the hatred the child feels for his parents in the process of development, which favours the depressive solution of the oedipal conflict. The investigation of the oedipal situation by these authors leads them to stress the role of mourning as a factor that either facilitates or, in the impossibility of mourning, makes the oedipal working-through process more difficult. This concept (mourning) ultimately becomes a key concept in their respective works, and very central to promote contact with the psychic reality and to integrate the ego. The processes of working through mourning now take up major space in the study of psychic development and in the symbolisation processes. Mourning is no longer simply a stage to be reached, but becomes the very process by which development is achieved and through which the mind develops.

As the emphasis of observation of what happens in the transference changes from the individual to the analytic dyad and to the acting out invited by the patient and sometimes complemented by the analyst's responses, we suggest that a new kind of clinical thinking is being created and, correspondingly, a new metapsychological approach. Green (2002) refers to this change of emphasis as producing a kind of "third topic" whose poles are the self and the object. He attributes this new concept to

> a pressure aroused from the experience that led psychoanalysts to need a theoretical frame that is more deeply rooted in clinical work. In other words, we would not have in consequence the clinical practice on the one hand and the theory on the other, but a theory that would be only—which is not the case in Freud—*a theory of clinical thinking*. (Green, 2002)

Bion has been an enormous influence on analysts in general, in addition to the great impact his work has had on analysts of Kleinian inspiration, above all on those living outside of England. His oeuvre is immense. We will mention here only three of his concepts of importance: his notion of "container/contained", his hypothesis of the existence of an "alpha function" that would enable a mental representation of emotional experiences initially not representable, and his concept of "transformations".

Besides the contributions from the core group, we find that other aspects related to the bases of our practice also merit being reflected on. In both clinical cases presented, the interpretations are more descriptive than conclusive, aim to clarify in the sense of understanding more than of concluding and are conveyed in a colloquial language. Both analysts in these two cases leave more room for the patient to reach his own conclusions, and their interpretations are, to use a language much in vogue today, less "saturated". The idea of saturation deserves reflecting on, it being that Kleinian analysts are often criticised for offering saturated interpretations to their patients. Here saturation is understood by the critics of the Kleinian clinical approach as a procedure similar to decoding the unconscious phantasies underlying the clinical material. Besides being considered decodings, the Kleinian interpretations would be formulated, still according to these critics, independently of an evaluation of the patient's capacity for understanding them and for living them as a meaning-making emotional experience. In sum, these interpretations would leave no space for the patient to contribute with his own outlook and experience of the issue in focus. It is important to note here that Hanna Segal in many of her clinical papers after 1962 was very critical of this kind of interpretation, which, according to her, downgraded the importance of transference and acted against the aliveness of the emotional experience taking place in the here and now of the session.

Ferro (1999), in answer to Elizabeth Spillius' question about what he considered to be a saturated interpretation, says: "I consider interpretations like cargo which has to be found a place on board a ship, but instead of a ship, there's a boat. We first must expand the boat (develop the [patient's] alpha function of the apparatus for thinking thoughts) before the weighty contents can be taken on board" (Spillius, 1999, p. xvi).

Ferro's reflection is still important even if we believe that in our initial stages as analysts we (and our supervisors, such as Hanna Segal, Betty Joseph, H. Rosenfeld, E. Spillius) did not adopt this kind of approach to the patient. Surely Rosenfeld and John Steiner warned us constantly to guard against this danger, using a vocabulary different from Nino Ferro's. They insisted on the importance, before formulating an interpretation, of our searching to adjust the communication with the patient to the level (cognitive and emotional) within which his mental functioning happened. Betty Joseph also highlighted the need to identify from which position (paranoid-schizoid or depressive) the patient was bringing his material, so as to build an emotionally meaningful interpretation that would touch the patient, this being the only way to produce psychic change.

The reflection, as we said, is valid even if the criticism may not be precise in relation to contemporary Kleinians and the work of the London group after the 1980s. Ferro's formulation points to the fact that the success of analysis depends basically on the growth of the psychic apparatus, which is evaluated by the qualitative deepening of mental contents and the greater containment capacity of the thinking apparatus. Containment here means the transformative capacity, above all, of the symbolic forms available for thinking about emotional experiences. There follows from this reflection, focused on the patient, that it also holds true in relation to the analyst.

As we see it, guarding against saturation means the analyst being attentive to any tendency towards associative and anti-intuitive rigidity. While a non-saturated mind is open to reverie, the analyst needs equally to know that the mental work necessary to go from reverie to interpretation is extremely complex, as we next suggest.

Bion (1952, 1958, 1962a, 1962b), rather than using the term countertransference, prefers to underline the impact of projective identifications on the analyst and the use of reverie to deal with them. In this context, intersubjective exchanges become the central focus of the study of the analytic relation. Based on the mechanism of projective identification, Bion proposed the existence of a continual flux of unconscious phantasies taking place as much in waking life as in dreams. In the session, this flux implies a continual invitation for the analyst to abandon her analytical attitude and enact aspects of the patient's internal world. Bion's ideas, according to Ferro (2007), introduce not only the notion that projective identification can have a communicative function but also, and above all, that that which is projected into the mind of the analyst can and must be transformed.

From what has been said, evocation takes shape in a process that generates an affect or a representation that will have to be worked through in the analyst's reverie. At the moment of the initial impact the evocation produces a deconstruction in the mind of the analyst, a disorganisation followed by a new articulation, which allows for the manifestation of unconscious links between affects that interfere in the meaning-making of an emotional experience. These links are not available to the conscience and as such are not felt as a lived experience.

Before building her interpretation, it is necessary for the analyst to go through a complex psychic working through, in part conscious, in part not. It is not enough for her to be aware of what feelings are projected into her mind by the patient; she also needs to trace back in what way the experience of these feelings have affected her. This second stage is essential to make efficient use of reverie and to characterise it conceptually as such. The identification of this experience, in self-analysis, allows the analyst to apprehend the aspect of the patient that is dynamically unavailable. This process bears a certain similarity to what happens in dream production. We think the expression "to dream the patient's dream" (Cassorla, 2013) is born out of this situation. In this context the word dream does not hold a total identity with the phenomenon that takes place while we are sleeping but rather more directly with the dreamwork similar to that which takes place during sleep. The central characteristic of this "dreaming the patient's dream" is that it happens in an oneiroid state during which the mind is unfocused and follows the same principle of the evenly suspended attention proposed by Freud as one of the basic analytic rules for listening to the patient. To dream together—patient and analyst—happens upon the transformation of an emotional experience into an expressive phenomenon that makes itself present in the mind of the analyst in the form of an affect. Why does this transmission generate a visual form? We must recall that an imagistic form is highly prone to simultaneously hold within it complex syntheses of experiences and a condensation of links. An example of this is the sketch (think of satirical political sketches) that very often is more forceful in conveying an idea than a hundred written pages. This symbolic visual form within the process of building an interpretive comment for the patient, must be recaptured in the form of verbal symbols. In this process of symbolic transformation it is necessary that the affect that was transmitted in an encoded way by the projection keep its expressive qualities, which then acquire the semantic character of a metaphor.

Within this context the interpretation is only a proposal of a meaning, never exhaustive and necessarily ever open to new expansions. The processes described above constitute what Ferro (1999, p. 118) calls the unsaturated relational model, today incorporated in our practice.

Not only do we have here an expansion of the concept of position, but also a different standing before what we would call the transference matrix. We mean, by this, our not being primarily concerned with relating the patient's affects and emotional experience to projections with the figures of his internal world or of his life story present in the here and now of the session, but in allowing also to take into account the broader context in which the transference seems to be expanding. We are interested not only in communicating to the patient what the analyst may be representing in the transference at that moment, but also, and most importantly, in showing to the patient his particular ways of thinking and apprehending the internal and external world, especially within the workings of his unconscious phantasies that will shape his affects.

We can say that in our present way of working, the language used in formulating interpretations is built from the metaphors provided by the descriptions of the many emotional situations lived by the patient. This consists in learning the language of each patient from these implicit or explicit metaphors dealing with his emotional experience. We believe this point to be crucial in discussing the changes in our way of formulating interpretations when we compare our early work and that of today. In adopting a language as close as possible to the patient's way of referring to his experience, we are concomitantly suggesting to the patient how we arrived at the interpretation without having to prolong ourselves in a complex and detailed explanation of an intellectual character, very proper to rationalisations.

Psychic causality is complex and we seek, in our listening, to hear expressions or references to the multiple layers of sense and meaning present in the mental life of the patient. In our listening today we continue to attribute meaning to the content of unconscious feelings and actual conscious ideas present in the patient's mind and we try to interpret them together with the notion that they are the expression of his affective unconscious architecture. On interpreting, we think we have to make a bridge between the conscious content, including its conscious meanings, and the unconscious communication, in order to mobilise the more available aspects of the patient's self, capable of listening.

We suggest that on formulating an interpretation based on the working through of the countertransference grasped by our reverie, we operate, among other processes, what linguists call the transmutation of the symbolic bases. We believe that this concept is very useful for understanding the function of symbolisation in psychoanalysis.

On interpreting, we place these evoked experiences on another symbolic basis; that is, we transmute from a specific symbolic basis, in this case the language evocative of the visual symbols of the dream or the metaphors or even the expressive experiences of countertransference, into verbal language descriptive of meanings (another symbolic basis), thus broadening the capacity to think about the experience, on giving meaning to the feelings involved. The changing (mutation) of one symbolic basis into another widens the power (of the possibility of a resonance of states of mind) of a communication. This broadening is due to a progression in the communicative capacity ensuing from the new symbolic basis. In this context, the interpretation is neither a causal explanation nor a mere description, but becomes the tool for expanding the links between significant emotional experiences and promoting new links between affects or affective networks.

In this way the inner evoked image is analogous (contains in itself a metaphoric virtuality), but not identical, to the feelings of the patient. The interpretation, in its turn, indicates connections between affects and affective networks that did not exist in the conscious mind. This activation (in philosophical terms, presentification) of the patient's affective networks makes visible something that was not present in the initial talk or behaviour of the patient and can give us access to his unconscious phantasies and beliefs, which constitute kernels of meaning that organise his feelings and behaviour.

We find also that today we relate to the concept of positions and the notion of a bi-personal field present in the session in a way different from that emphasised in the 1980s. We might add as well that today we take into greater account what Ogden (1986) calls the "state of being" and how this interconnects with the matrix of transference. We utilise the concept of "positions" not only as a special defensive organisation in response to a specific type of anxiety (paranoid or depressive), but also as a mode of generating and organising an emotional experience and as a mental optic (Ogden, 1992). We can likewise say that this approach denotes a different emphasis in the concepts of defences that have become, for us, "modes of thinking", that is, modes of organising the emotional experience.

So numerous are the influences of new clinical concepts or perspectives that it is difficult to summarise them in this space.

Our reflections on symbolism (Rocha Barros, E. M., & Rocha Barros, E. L., 2011, 2016) based on studies of E. Cassirer, Susan Langer, and Alain Gibeault and grounded on the seminal work of Hanna Segal, as well as various articles by Ricardo Steiner on the same theme, produced some alterations in our theoretic and clinical focus. In addition to the existing theories, the idea that is not only *what* the symbol represents but also *how* it does so, became central for us. Likewise, the observation that the capacity to build symbols can be attacked during the moment of being created came to be an object of our scrutiny. On acknowledging not only the representative aspect of the symbol but also its expressive aspect derived from the form chosen to give representation to the feeling or current emotional experience, these become the object of our attention in the speech, as well as in the metaphors, used by the patient and in his dreams. We began by pointing out that the very process of building symbols, in its diverse components and vicissitudes, is of central importance to contemporary psychoanalysis, since symbols are essential for thinking and storing emotional experiences in our memory, and for communicating our affects to others and explaining them to our own selves. Further, in relation to building symbols, today we consider that internal attacks are not directed only at the internal objects but also include attacks on the structure or forms of the mental representations before, and while, they are constituted in symbols. It is by these means that destructive impulses invade the processes of symbolic construction. Symbols can lose their plasticity and thus silence the emotions, and therefore cut off the patient from their meanings.

In a previous work (2000) we said: "When we think of the suppression of contents from the conscience, we are before a psychoanalysis that has for central notion, repression. On speaking of the suppression of mental functions, we are addressing something more than repression." In this latter case we are suggesting that the patient did not have the conditions of experiencing certain affects or of formulating a more explicit and precise thought because the mental function necessary to do so was not available. In such a case, we are not dealing with something suppressed from conscience, which could, through an interpretation, be liberated. It becomes in this instance a matter of restoring the capacity to think, to represent and build symbols, so that this something never thought or felt comes into being.

We believe that part of our emotional life does not yet acquire full mental representation because the psychic apparatus itself is lacking in mental functions that could produce them.

As such, part of our lives translates itself into automatic actions or somatic states experienced as concrete facts without meaning, existing therefore outside symbolic processes. In the process of building interpretations we are before a new task. Our listening presupposes an availability to undergo the emotional experiences of the patient that could not be lived nor represented by him. We are not dealing, of course, with an intellectual availability, or a function that can be carried out intellectually. It is these new concepts that have changed the way of psychoanalytical listening.

The complexity of clinical work today is greater than in the past, for we must expand our listening, identify the timing so as to make contact with our analysands, and have ever present the phantasies, viewed as expressions of a way of unconscious thinking enacted in the transference relation. Nevertheless, we must bear in mind that this expanded form of listening does not imply its trivialisation. Psychoanalysis today has become even more intricate and sophisticated in its means of understanding the human psyche. The analyst herself is an important work tool and, as such, her training must be even more rigorous and careful, for beyond understanding the communications of our analysands, we must be an instrument of quality in resonating their reverberations.

Notes

1. Langer (1930, p. 87; Innis, 2009, p. 15) says that the form of a thing is "the way its parts are put together." Cassirer says "by symbolic form is meant here all the energy of the spirit in whose structure a spiritual content with meaning is linked to a concrete sensible sign. In this sense, language, the mythical-religious world and art show themselves as so many other specific symbolic forms. Because in all of them is manifest the fundamental phenomenon that our conscience is not satisfied in just receiving the external impression, but interlinks and penetrates all the impression with an act of free expression" (Cassirer, 1956, p. 163).
2. Connotation: a meaning, ideas, or associations, brought to mind or suggested by a word or thing apart from this word or thing.
3. Denotation: a direct specific meaning as distinct from an implied or associated idea.
4. The most basic and primitive type of symbolic meaning is *expressive* meaning, the product of what Cassirer calls the expressive function (*Ausdrucksfunktion*) of thought, which is concerned with the experience of events in the world around us as charged with affective and emotional significance, as desirable or hateful, comforting or threatening (*Oxford Dictionary of Philosophy*).

References

Bion, W. R. (1952). Group dynamics: a review. *International Journal of Psychoanalysis, 33*: 235–247.
Bion, W. R. (1958). On hallucination. *International Journal of Psychoanalysis, 39*: 341–349.
Bion, W. R. (1962). *Learning from Experience*. London: Heinemann.
Bion, W. R. (1962a). A Theory of thinking. *International Journal of Psychoanalysis, 43*: 306–310.
Bion, W. R. (1962b). *Learning from Experience*. London: Heinemann.
Bolognini, S. (2008). *O Abraço de Peleu: Sobrevivência., Continência e Com-Vencimento na Experiência Analítica com Patologias Graves*. Conferência na SBP de São Paulo.

Britton, R. (1998). *Belief and Imagination*. Hove: Routledge.

Canestri, J. (1994). Transformations., *Int. J. Psych.*, 75: 1079–1092. (Publicado também no Livro Anual de Psicanálise, 1996; São Paulo: Editora Escuta.

Cassirer, E. (1956). *Esencia y Concepto del Símbolo*. México: Fondo de Cultura Econômica.

Cassorla, R. (2013). In Search of symbolization: the analyst's task of dreaming. In: H. Levine, G. S. Reid, & D. Scarfone (Eds.), *Unrepresented States and the Construction of Meaning*. London: Karnac.

Ferro, A. (1995). *A Técnica da Psicanálise Infantil*. Rio de Janeiro: Imago.

Ferro, A. (1999). *The Bi-Personal Field*. London & New York: Routledge.

Ferro, A. (2007). Il paziente miglior colega: transformazione in sogno et transformacione narrative. *Rivista di Psichanalisi*, 53 (4): 1083–1090.

Green, A. (1987). La capacité de rêverie et le mythe étiologique. *Révue Française de Psychanalyse, 51*: 1299–1315.

Green, A. (2002). *La Pensée Clinique*. Paris: Éditions Odile Jacob.

Heimann, P. (1950). On countertransference. *International Journal of Psychoanalysis*, 31: 81–94.

Innis, R. E. (2009). *Susanne Langer in Focus*. Bloomington, IN: Indiana University Press.

Langer, S. K. K. (1930). *The Practice of Philosophy*. New York: H. H. Holt.

Meltzer, D. (1978). *The Kleinian Development Part III: The Clinical Significance of the Work of Bion*. Perthshire: Clunie Press.

Ogden, T. (1986). *The Matrix of the Mind: Objects Relations and Psychoanalytic Dialogue*. London: Karnac.

Ogden, T. (1992). The analytic third: Working with intersubjective clinical facts. *International Journal of Psychoanalysis*, 73: 613–626.

Rocha Barros, E. R. (2000). Affect and pictographic image: The constitution of meaning in mental life. *International Journal of Psychoanalysis, 81*: 1087–1099.

Rocha Barros, E. L., & Rocha Barros, E. M. (2011a). Reflections on the clinical implications of symbolism. *International Journal of Psychoanalysis*, 92: 879–903.

Rocha Barros, E. L., & Rocha Barros, E. M. (2011b). The conundrum of time in psychoanalysis. In: S. Lewkowicz, & T. Bokanowski (Eds.), *On Freud's "Constructions in Analysis"*. London: Karnac.

Rocha Barros, E. M., & Rocha Barros, E. L. (2016). The function of evocation in the working through of the countertransference: projective identification, reverie, and the expressive function of the mind: Reflections inspired by Bion's Work. In: G. Civitarese, & H. B. Levine (Eds.), *The W. R. Bion Tradition*. London: Karnac.

Rosenfeld, H. (1964). On the psychopathology of narcissism: a clinical approach. In: *Psychotic States*. London: Hogarth.

Spillius, E. (1983). Developments from the work of Melanie Klein. *International Journal of Psychoanalysis*, 68: 69–80.

Spillius, E. (1999). Introduction. In: A. Ferro (Ed.), *The Bi-personal Field*. London: Routledge.

Steiner, J. (1987). The interplay between pathological organizations and the paranoid-schizoid and depressive positions. *International Journal of Psychoanalysis*, 64: 321–332.

CHAPTER SEVENTEEN

"I used to think you were wonderful": the persecution/ idealisation cycle of melancholia

Priscilla Roth

In this paper I discuss how a patient strove to protect herself from the pain of object loss by rearranging her perception of reality—and often my own—in order to maintain her internal attachment to a pathological object relationship. This relationship was characterised by the idealisation of the object, believed to be almost available but cruelly withheld, and, simultaneously, rage at this object for its refusal to be what she needed it to be. By contrast, I was required, over and over again, painfully to experience the loss that the patient herself largely managed to avoid.

I describe some of the shifts that occurred in the sessions, reflecting the patient's slowly increasing capacity to face pain and the awareness of loss.

Idealisation and persecution

Idealisation is described by Melanie Klein in two different ways. When she writes that "[t]he whole of [the infant's] instinctual desires and his unconscious phantasies imbue the breast with qualities going far beyond the actual nourishment it affords" (Klein, 1957, p.180) and repeatedly stresses that the mother's introjected loved and loving good breast, forms "the core of the [infant's] ego" (ibid.), Klein is suggesting that the original good object must be experienced as ideal—nothing less than this would adequately convey "the whole of (the infant's) instinctual desires". In this view, the infant projects "his entire loving capacity.... on to the object, and this [projected-into object] is then introjected together with the object's actual goodness to become his very core" (Likierman, 2001, p. 95).

At other moments, though, idealisation is viewed differently, for Klein also frequently maintained that much of what the infant experiences as positive is in fact the result of a defensive exaggeration of the object's goodness: "Idealization is bound up with the splitting of the object, for the good aspects of the breast are exaggerated as a safeguard against the fear of the persecuting breast"; that is, a defence against persecutory anxieties stemming from the infant's projection of hateful impulses and hate-filled parts of the self into the (bad) breast/mother (Klein, 1946, p. 7).

These two views are not, I think, contradictory: it was Klein's view that at the beginning of life splitting must be sufficiently impermeable to ensure the normal necessary separation of good from bad. In this view, idealisation was not simply a psychopathological mechanism, but an essential intermediate "process in the young child's mind, since he cannot yet cope with his fears of persecution". Not until a second stage, that is, "... not until early anxieties have been sufficiently relieved owing to experiences which increase love and trust, is it possible to estab-lish the all-important process of bringing together the various aspects of objects (Klein, 1940, n., p. 315). Thus, "... the neonate can cope with life only by actively separating out the forces of destruction from those energies considered constructive.... the forces tending toward life, object love and integration of the ego must be united into a coherent whole before the unity of the real object in its good and bad aspects can be faced" (Petot, 1991, p. 211).

It is thus only in a second phase—as ego capacities develop and depressive possibilities thereby arise—that splitting must become more porous—allowing confrontations—temporary at first—between love and hate. But it is worth noting that in her last paper, Klein returned to the problem of idealisation, remarking that, "In my experience, the need for idealization is never fully given up, even though in normal development the facing of internal and external reality tends to diminish it" (Klein, 1963, p. 305).

Since the most pernicious factor in developmental disturbances is the blurring of primary splitting between good and bad—that is, envy—it follows that a defence against envy would have to include undiminished impermeable idealisation.

Envy is born of the gap between the expectation accompanying the fantasy of an inexhaust-ible breast, and reality, which inevitably brings deprivation. This "inexhaustible" breast is conceived as giving perfect satisfaction to a perfect self. Essential to this phantasy is no differ-entiation whatsoever between perfect self/perfect breast: a unified and undifferentiated couple. When it exists—however briefly—it is subjectively the totality of experience. The ideal-ness of the ideal breast is not only that it nourishes and loves: the ideal breast creates an ideal self—an entirely loving self from whom all feelings of badness—of hatred, rage, persecution—have been expunged

The bad, that is, persecuting, breast is not the self. Because it contains, by projection, the split-off destructive impulses and parts of the self, it is conceived as cruelly and malevolently withholding satisfaction, thereby projecting bad feelings—hatred and envy—into the self. For the small infant, this too, when it exists, is the whole world, now intolerable, and these experi-ences have to be got rid of and are re-projected into the bad breast, which becomes both more terrifying and more vengefully re-projecting badness—anxiety/hatred/terror/rage—back into the self.

What I intend to show in the material that follows are, first, the contours and the strength of my patient's dependence on the melancholic solution to manage overwhelming anxieties pre-sented by the intrusion of reality into her omnipotent phantasies. Her "solution" involved the maintenance of a powerful split in her object, allowing the possibility of a perfect ideal object with whom she is inseparably bound in pure love; irrevocably kept distinct from a terrifying hateful persecuting object. This, of course, is a configuration we all know well. What I will then explore is the movement/transformation of this impermeable split into another, no less destructive, form when the analysis, and ordinary life, confront the patient with the beginnings of an awareness of reality.

While idealisation is used by K to protect her from powerful experiences of envy of her good object, in fact it imprisons her in a world of dissatisfaction, disappointment, and self-hatred, and indeed, proliferating experiences of envy and jealousy of other people who come to stand for the idealised primal object.

Clinical material

In her early thirties, when her analysis began, K had had several boyfriends but none of the relationships had lasted. She was puzzled about this; afraid she would never get married and have children, never be "normal".

She is a lawyer in an established firm: beautiful, from a wealthy family, her parents divorced when she was at university. She reports that she had constant temper tantrums as a child and was felt to be impossible to control. She has one sister who is three years younger.

For the first year K expressed only positive feelings about the analysis, often remarking on how much "progress" she was making. She had had a previous unsuccessful analysis, and she saw this new analysis as full of promise. From the beginning, her material was strikingly narcissistic—a running commentary on her "feelings", in a vacuum, with almost no content. After the first year, there was a change, as she became angry about breaks or occasional alterations to the structure of the analysis; the rare changed session-time infuriated her, as did any variation in what she saw as usual analytic practice: "No one else's analyst takes off the week *before* Easter; everyone else's analyst takes the week *after* Easter."

Looking back now, what becomes clear was a hopeful beginning, where it was possible that I would fit perfectly into her expectations and hopes of me. And then: disappointment.

During the first two years, K went on occasional dates and had some sexual relationships; none of these had any importance to her. In the third year, she had a date with a young man, B, which became a "wonderful" weekend spent together. She was delighted with him and soon reported that she was in love. However, within weeks, these feelings of attraction transformed into complaints, demands, and assertions of entitlement. By the third week after the exciting "wonderful" weekend, the patient was irritated with B for not being sufficiently "committed": she nagged him with increasing bitterness about smoking, untidiness, not having a driving license, not answering her text messages quickly enough, not "going around the car and opening the car door" for her like her friend's boyfriend did, and not taking her on romantic holidays. He was her possession, expected to provide her with all the accoutrements of a "relationship". From this point on, I never heard about the pleasures of getting to know B, delight in his company, or anything specific to him that might interest or please her. He was consistently described in terms of what her idea of "a boyfriend" or "a relationship" should be. When he occasionally rebelled and became angry, she would arrive at her session in despair about having gone too far, wanting help to control her behaviour. This never lasted long; within minutes she would find reasons to justify her attack on him and to find further fault with him.

It was not difficult to recognise this as a repetition of the analytic relationship, and, of course, as repetitions of a fundamental primitive relationship.

Two sessions

One day I spoke to K about a fee raise. The following day she responded:

> "I really don't want to come to analysis any more. Don't want four times a week. I'd rather sleep. I want to come once a week. I want to be able to come if I feel bad … but not all the time. I used to feel bad, needed to come more. Now I don't. I came to analysis because I wanted to have a relationship—well, now I've got one, I just want to live my life. Not have to analyse myself all the time. Like normal people."

The proposed fee-raise had insulted her and hurt her feelings. The very fact of the fee—and the raising of it—stood for everything that keeps her out and differentiates her role from mine, her position from mine. She experiences this as an expulsion. Threatened with the loss to her sense of herself and to the reality she has created, she instead incorporated a particular picture of me into herself and, as it were, became this view of me: she identified with a cold and unavailable version of me and became herself cold and unavailable, someone with no needs and who herself contains everything desirable. At the same time she projected all her sense of inadequacy and worthlessness into me. Once in the grip of this two-way projective identification, why would she want to come to useless me for analysis? The threat of object-loss is avoided by an identification with the loved and hated object: the patient pulling her analyst into an enactment of her primary libidinal relationship. In this situation: I raise her fee/she feels contemptible, becomes cold and smug/I am contemptible. The relationship—subject to object, child to parent—remains the same; one person is a useless supplicant, the other a cold and impenetrable figure. Relations between the two are exploitative and ruthless one way or the other, but the basic relationship stays the same.

Melancholia is a narcissistic condition; at base, the hatred of the object in melancholia is because of its separateness from the self, but this situation is complicated by other feelings. The wished-for perfect object is inseparable from the perfect self and the perfect self is entirely loving and therefore lovable. Made of love. The horrible thing I do by raising K's fee is make her feel hate-full and therefore hateful (to me) and therefore the object of willful persecution from me.

That night the patient had a dream that she brought to the next day's session:

> I was coming here, to my session. Maybe it was summer, because it was warm and sunny. All around the building was water, there was a big lake and a beautiful garden—a beautiful landscape. To get to the door I had to climb on to a ladder, and there was a pulley system which pulled me in, over the lake, as if over a moat. At the door, three girls came out—they'd been in the consulting-room with you. They said "She's marking one of your essays—she's got some of your work on her table." I realised that they were just supervisees, and they thought I was just a supervisee; they didn't realise I'm in analysis. When I went in you said "S", very warmly and friendly and nice, and you showed me pictures of plans for the gardens. As if we were friends.

This dream—a response to the proposed fee raise—is the other side of the melancholia. In the dream, K recovers the ideal place from which she is now *not* excluded. If the fee-raise was felt to put her down, in *this* place I reach out and "pully" her up, like a small infant, and bring her to me. And I have her on my table—in my mind—all the time. Not coming (and of course having to go) every day—but in my mind all the time. A never-ending session in which I show her beautiful gardens and we are friends forever. This is the idealised relationship, felt to be lost the previous day and magically restored in her dream. In this place she is entirely loved and loveable and loving, as am I. We are "friends".

The dream reality is so clearly about "up" and "down". The fee-raise threw her down; the dream image is concretely about being pulled back up. "Up" is not only being together, parallel, with me, but is "upper" than the "just supervisees", who are looked down on. When she is up with me, I am warm and she is warm—the hatred of the previous day is completely non-existent—as if it never was. When she is up with me she can feel love-full. Not hate-full.

A few months later, after a summer break, K announced that things had been terrible the whole time "we were away". She was horrible to B, critical and nasty, feeling that he wasn't good enough.

Yesterday, she said, they nearly got to the end. Saturday her sister gave birth. "We went to see them in the hospital yesterday. B and I were both born in that same hospital. On the way in, I said to B, "Isn't it amazing that we were born here too?" He said, "Yeah"; he was not very interested. I just went nuts! And then, there they were: my sister and brother-in-law, there with their baby. My younger sister now has two children!! And I was furious! I hated B, I told him he isn't what I want, he isn't good enough."

I said I thought the experience of visiting the new baby was both upsetting to her in itself, but also powerfully representative of a frequent experience she has: I said there is always a picture in the back of her mind of where she'd really like to be and can't be. It is where she is *not*. Mother and father and baby together—with her having to look on, completely left out—is the awful apotheosis of it. After a moment, I said I thought that in the background is the picture she'd had of me on holiday, when things had been, as she said, "terrible" for her: me "not interested" in her and not remembering that she was born here too—that she has a place here in my mind too. When she feels so forgotten, so jealous, then B—who can't or won't make everything perfectly better—seems to her not good enough, however he behaves.

I felt sympathetic and tender towards her.

K immediately said she didn't understand. The baby visit only happened yesterday, and she was horrible all through the holiday.

I explained again that this was only the culmination … that the whole holiday, "when we were away", felt like having to watch a happy family—from which she was excluded—in her mind. I mentioned also her parents and baby sister—that watching this new baby brought back these memories and ever-threatening feelings.

(I felt uncomfortable explaining this again; I thought that her not understanding was disingenuous: I felt thrown.)

She responded: "But how can I have felt that about two parents who were always fighting with each other?"

(I again felt she was being disingenuous—a kind of perverse mock stupidity.)

After a few minutes she said, quietly, "I *was* jealous of L (her friend) this weekend. I was mad with jealousy." L's new boyfriend had "whisked L away to Prague on a holiday to a glamorous hotel. He planned it all!" S had said to B, "You never do this!" She was overcome with jealousy—thought she wouldn't be able to bear it, wouldn't be able to live. There was a long pause. Then she said that during the holiday she didn't love B at all. Didn't even respect him. She had to go through the motions. (This was said with sadness.) She paused. And then: "So what does what you've been saying have to do with *that*??? I mean, why didn't I feel any respect for him?"

This is a complicated message, and I want to look at it carefully:

On the one hand, I believe that for a moment there actually had been a shift in K's thinking: she had taken in what I'd said about jealousy and could tell me that she is able to be aware of jealousy and how powerful it is—so powerful that, drowning in her jealous and, I think, envious feelings, she was unable to love B during the holiday. For a moment she is sad about this. But as soon as she experiences a wish that I help her to understand it, two things happen: she immediately feels envious of the privileged position this wish of hers gives *me*—as if I am now the lucky one, like L, who is being "whisked off"—and up—now by her—to a glamorous, enviable place—"So what does what you've been saying have to do with *that*?"; and I am suddenly dropped again and have no link to her and am in a contemptible position.

At the same time, I am being told about someone—her—who doesn't respect someone—B, me—and has to "go through the motions". If this second scenario is what is going on here, now—if she is contemptuous of my concern for her and condescendingly placating a me who has been trying to get through to her—what does it suggest about the first scenario?

It is my belief that both are true. I think that K is actually able to remember and communicate to me something about her own jealousy and envy. And then the envy—provoked from this movement towards a me experienced as helpful and at the same time not-her—attacks and corrupts a meaningful communication. "So what does what you've been saying have to do with that?" is an envious attack on her sudden picture of me who has been "whisked off" to an enviable place in her mind. But the attack is more sinister and destructive than that: it is also a corruption of her own sense of the ordinary helpfulness of her analyst; from one second to the next, she is "going through the motions".

Being on the receiving end of this is a temporarily difficult experience: feeling dropped, confused, wrong-footed.

But for K, something much more substantial has taken place: a moment's communication, a moment's sadness about herself and what she can do, what she is like. And then the recognition and understanding is not only destroyed, it is corrupted. K's nature, and the nature of her psychopathology, forces her into a hate-full state of mind, produced by envy of the even momentarily satisfying object; directed at her good, and therefore hated object.

Being full of hatred is a horrible state of mind.

As a defence against this awareness of a self full of hatred, and therefore hateful, and therefore hated, K needs to create or cling to those few moments when she somehow, as if magically, felt completely loving. She knows this perfect place exists because she once had it: that first "wonderful" weekend with B before it all went wrong, the idyllic landscape dream. These remain perfect and always possible and attainable in her mind. This perfect state is all that saves her from an impossible state of mind.

K can only be alright if she is together, absolutely, with her object: the object as a "we" with her. In this sense "We were born here too" doesn't only mean "We were both born in this hospital—the hospital where my sister's baby was just born." It means "You and I were born at exactly the same moment, came into existence as a 'we'. There was no you before me." B's uninterested "Yeah", dropped her from a "we" to a hateful "me". Similarly, I must only begin my existence as she opened her eyes to me. My crime is that being myself—remaining her analyst—I don't protect her from an increasing awareness that I am not born here in this room as she notices me.

I think it is likely that "normal" for K means everyone else in the world, imagined as existing in perpetual unity with an object. I also think that, paradoxically, K's envy for everyone else is envy that they can be an "I" without desperation or devastating envy, and without possession of an object.

Appreciating the goodness of the object makes her instantly vulnerable to terrible persecution. The split idealised object/bad object having to be so rigidly maintained means that the bad object—who contains her bad, murderous, hateful projections, and her bad, murderous hateful self—will, by its very imagined nature, attack her with all the rage and envy she has projected into it. Furthermore, if I *am* felt to have been able—even for a moment—to withstand and contain her projections, she is besieged by envy of my ability for some actual goodness, momentarily recognised by her. This is the problem: the object has to be perfect—and then can never be real or actualised—because its actual good qualities are always under terrible immediate attack.

Sometime later, two weeks before a three-week break:

The patient has four sessions a week—Monday through Thursday. She had, unusually, cancelled two Monday mornings in a row.

When she returned on Tuesday, she reported that she'd had a miserable weekend, and that she now felt depressed, mean and ungenerous. She reported a dream. In this dream,

she and B take her sister's two small children into their bed. They were all in bed together; it was very very nice.

She added that on her way to analysis she always sees women in big cars, with children. Why can't she be happy like them? They always look so happy. She is fed up with B, wondering if she'd be happier on her own.

I thought—and said to her—that the dream was like her dream about coming to the consulting room in the idyllic landscape. Here it is about grownups and children all in her bed, all very happy. Like the idyllic landscape dream, this is a dream about something she feels she should have, did once have, and, compared with which everything else is tormentingly disappointing. This in bed with children dream is also a dream solution to the hospital experience where she had visited her sister and brother-in-law after the birth of their second child. In this new dream, not only does she, together with B, replace the sister and brother-in-law, standing for the parents with their new baby, her sister, but she and B are also the children she has taken into her bed. All jealousy, all envy, all sense of being left and alone is obviated by this dream.

But it is also worth noting that the phrase "in bed together" suggests "in collusion with", corruption. In this sense, I think this is not simply a day-dreamy dream of a wished-for event sometime in the future. As itself, it is an envious takeover of everything in the primal scene: stealing and thus attacking every position, every identity, every experience.

I suspect that K knows that something is corrupt about the omnipotent dream/phantasy; and perhaps that she continues to maintain a corrupt position in her analysis in collusion with an analyst who either is blind to her corruption or in collusion with it for her own reasons.

One of these reasons is felt to be my own narcissism—a view of her object who, in possession of good things, doesn't give them to her, (is not ever-bountiful, ever-generous) but who, instead keeps them for herself. The women with the big cars, the mother with the full breast—kept for her own smug self-satisfied self.

When she returned the following week, she was very angry:

"What you said Thursday really irritated me. I slept badly again. You said I was feeling fragmented because I missed the sessions last Monday and this. A stupid thing to say."

(This was not what I had said, and I thought she knew this. I felt in a familiar uncomfortable spot.)

I said: "It sounds like this has become something I have said in your mind, though it's not what I said."

She said, "I know … you said it's because you are taking the holiday as well. That makes me even more irritated. You're saying that I sleep badly, that I feel bad, because of something you do. *You always take things up in terms of here.* Maybe you think it's your job. It's just stupid. And the answer is obviously to stop coming; if analysis is my problem, why bother coming? I can solve my problems by not coming."

What "irritates" K is my insistence that there is an "I"—separate from her—who *matters* to her. To have to be aware of my—felt to be—incorrigibly narcissistic insistence on my importance to her is intolerable. We are not a "we"—I am a "me" and I am insisting that something I do matters to her. She can only deal with this by annihilating me: not coming.

"You should think about the impact on me when you say these things. I leave on Thursday, you tell me it's my fault for missing last Monday and this Monday. Your job is to make me feel better. *And if what you say is true,* how come I slept fine on Thursday and Friday, then terribly on Saturday, Sunday, and Monday? How does that make sense? I don't find what you say interesting … I'm not interested in analysis."

Here she is absolutely clear: my job is to make her feel better. To take away all her bad feelings, including her resentment and hatred of me. But a moment later there is a very slight movement … "and if what you say is true"—the possibility of being able for a second to consider. And then, "How does that make sense. I'm not interested in analysis". The door between us, open for a second, is snapped shut.

I think this is a powerful and immediate projection of an experience of K's when the implacably maintained delusion of unity between self and object is pulled from her: when she is suddenly dropped; repeating what I picture as an infantile experience: that the nipple—believed to be her possession—is suddenly pulled from her mouth.

Aware of the brief opening, I reminded her of previous weeks, when I thought she had been interested, and I said something had happened to her interest.

There was a pause and then she said, "I haven't felt that in a long time." She paused again. "I used to think you were wonderful. You understood me *perfectly* … all I ever wanted." And then: "How do you explain *that*!?"

Again, just for a moment, K was thoughtful: remembering, considering, describing. And talking to me from a place where we were at the same time separate from each other and able to helpfully communicate something.

But the last statement—"How do you explain *that*?", taunting and triumphant—shuts the door in my face.

After a few minutes I tried to talk to her about some of this.

I said my impression is that at these moments I'm kept on a very thin ledge, that I can't make any contact with her—can't get in, can't feel any real understanding between us ... that she swats me away so that I can't touch her. We're allowed only the thinnest moment of contact, and then her mind closes suddenly, as if she doesn't want understanding either way between us—for me to understand her, or for her to understand me.

She was silent and then said, "That's like my father. What he does. There is no contact, he doesn't allow it. This is just what it feels like to be with him. He talks only in clichés. And my mother ... only neediness." She paused. "My father is moving house—after thirty years—the house I grew up in has been torn to the ground—they're building a new house on the property. The house is gone. It's very odd. He says it is a difficult time for him, but he only talks in clichés. 'It's a very emotional time for me.' Meaningless".

She was again silent for a minute. In fact, she said, she's in quite a good mood today. Not here—she's been in a bad mood since she got here—but she woke up in a good mood even though she didn't get much sleep. On the weekend they moved B's stuff into her flat—the vans came and delivered everything. On Saturday they put his stuff away. It was fun. There is still lots of crap around ... boxes and things. But they did a lot. On Sunday they went to a wedding—then came back last night. ... She's excited about the coming holiday, but not about the flights: there will be a long flight, then two internal short flights ... she is afraid of the short flights.

I said I thought that what I had said had made sense to her, and that as well as talking about her trip, she was describing a change that seems to have taken place now, in which her mind can actually move and travel. I thought this was very different from where she had been earlier in the session: that her thoughts seemed now to be able to move out of the flatness and thinness, the batting back. She now had thoughts about her father and mother, about moving house, and putting stuff away, about travelling, and how it will all be. ... Her mind and thoughts seemed freer, with more possibilities. I thought she had been able to make room for me in her mind, as she is able to make room for B in her flat.

She paused and then said, "I am meeting the woman from human resources today at work. She is a psychotherapist. She is apparently very odd. E says this woman will offer me supervision. That'll be weird." She spoke again about the trips and that she wished she could stay in one place.

I said I thought that she was finding it "very odd" that something had happened inside her, that she felt freer and less constricted, without her being in charge of it, being able to predict it or explain it. I thought she didn't know how to think about that and found it "weird", but I thought that she felt it had something to do with my human resources.

The session ended.

The following day she announced that she was furious at B. She had come home from work and found that he hadn't moved any of the boxes she'd asked him to get rid of.

"He doesn't do anything for *us*," she shouted. "He will do all sorts of things for himself, he tidies up *his* room, but he left boxes all around the house ... he never thinks about *us*. Either he should earn the money, and drive me around in his car, or else he has to help me clean up the flat. He has to do one or other. He has to be a partner."

What has happened? For some minutes in the previous day's session—longer than usual—K had been able to be more available, more open, her mind moving and connecting and flexible; freer to follow her thoughts and wanting to communicate them. This is, for these minutes, an emergence from a narcissistic state into a real relationship with another person and it is an accomplishment. But as she experiences ordinary helpful contact with another person, she is aware that it is "weird" and "odd". Me being me—with my ordinary *human resources*—talking to her, telling her something that interests her, is disturbing and dangerous because almost immediately it provokes envy.

And then the session ended. I ended the session; I am suddenly up, she is down. I am "supervising" her.

At that point she needs to revert to her narcissistic defences as powerfully as ever, and this includes the projection of narcissism into me: "He (she) doesn't do anything for *us*". He (she) will do all sort of things for himself—tidying up his/*her* room. ..." These are hate-full feelings, by which I mean both full of hatred and also felt to be hateful—bad. Not "normal". When I don't protect her from them, when I just take care of *me*, I am not tidying up her mental room—her mind. I am leaving her with the horrible mess while I drive around in my big car.

It is at the moment of separateness that the good object becomes cruel: keeping her resources for herself, looking down on the patient who suddenly doesn't have any. For as soon as we are not as-one, every good interpretation is a bad interpretation: I have become superior and narcissistic. And the ordinary goodness of the object creates unmanageable envy. No longer an absolute split, this state is much worse than persecution by the persecuting object: this state provokes constant attacking, constant undermining.

For K, there *are* moments of "wonderful": a first weekend and maybe two short weeks with B, when she could actually love him. An idyllic landscape dream of being in my mind and heart forever. An imagined scene in which she is the parents and she is the children and—since she has created this and occupies every position in it—there is only love: no hatred, no jealousy, no envy. And, of course, the first weeks of her analysis when she thought I was wonderful—I understood her "perfectly". What characterises these idyllic events is the absence of bad feelings: jealousy, envy, persecution, and hatred. And within them K is able to be entirely loving and entirely good; joined with her object in perfect goodness forever.

What I have been hoping to illustrate in this paper is that period in an analysis when an initial rigorous and implacable splitting begins to soften; when it is possible for the patient to have momentary experiences of the goodness of a separate whole object.

It is at that moment that envy becomes most poisonous and dangerous, because as it destroys the goodness of the object, it prevents an introjection of, and partial identification with, the object in its goodness, and this impedes emotional growth and flexibility. But this level of destructive envy is also dangerous and destructive to the self by adding to a proliferation of bad feelings, which then have to be projected and become the imagined or real provocateurs of persecution from the object.

This period in an analysis—when powerful envy has been released—is always very difficult, requiring both strength and sensitivity in the analyst.

References

Klein, M. (1940). Mourning and its relation to manic-depressive states. In: *Contributions to Psycho-analysis: 1921–1945*. London: Hogarth, 1965.

Klein, M. (1946). Notes on some schizoid mechanisms. In: *Envy and Gratitude and Other Works 1946–1963* (pp. 1–24). London: Hogarth, 1975.

Klein, M. (1957). Envy and gratitude. In: *Envy and Gratitude and Other Works: 1946–1963* (pp. 176–235). London: Hogarth, 1975.

Klein, M. (1963). On the sense of loneliness. In: *Envy and Gratitude and Other Works: 1946–1963*. London: Hogarth.

Likierman, M. (2001). *Melanie Klein: Her Work in Context*. London: Continuum.

Petot, J. -M. (1991). *Melanie Klein: Volume II, The Ego and the Object*. Madison, CT: International Universities Press.

CHAPTER EIGHTEEN

Illusion, disillusion, and irony in psychoanalysis

John Steiner

In this paper I am going to draw a parallel between an analyst listening to a patient and a member of the audience watching a play. I will propose that in both situations it is important to be able to adopt a dual identity, first in order to participate in the action through identification and then to withdraw from the identification to adopt the position of an observer.

I will discuss two plays, Henrik Ibsen's *The Wild Duck* (1884) and Sophocles' *Oedipus the King* (5th century BC, a) to suggest that both in the theatre and in analysis it is necessary to adopt an ironic attitude if we want to sustain this dual identity. When we identify with our patients and engage with them as participants we take a subjective view and empathise with their plight. We recognise that reality may be so difficult to bear that illusions are often necessary and useful. Then when we withdraw to adopt the position of an observer we take an objective view and recognise the value of truth and the importance of facing reality. I will argue that it is through irony that these two attitudes can coexist so that we can retain a respect for truth alongside a sympathetic awareness of a need for illusion.

Dual identities: participant and observer

As we listen to our patients we need to be able to engage in their conflicts and also to retain a sceptical, questioning attitude in which our primary aim is to observe the patient in order to understand how his mind works. Normally, we alternate between these two states, emotionally engaged as participants on the one hand and becoming separate to be able to observe, on the other, and to achieve this dual role requires a capacity to identify, and to disidentify, in a flexible and reversible manner. Keeping a proper balance is not always easy, and the analyst may behave inappropriately if he allows himself to get trapped in identifications with his patients or their objects. He may then become over-involved in their drama and fail to see what is happening. Equally, however, he will fail to understand his patient if he behaves only as a detached observer without feeling himself into the patient's experiences.

The parallels between the role of the analyst when listening to his patient and that of the spectator of a classical drama are deepened if we refer to the classical theory of catharsis put forward by Aristotle, who highlights two emotions, namely terror and pity, which are evoked in the audience of a tragedy. As we watch the drama unfold, the response of terror involves a fear of something happening to ourselves, while pity, by contrast, is based on feelings for the person whom we are observing (Turri, 2015). When we feel terror, we have identified with the hero of the drama and are feeling what we imagine he is feeling, while when we feel pity, we have withdrawn from this identification and are observing the suffering as it is happening, not to us, but to someone we have come to care about.

To understand a play and the effect it has on us requires that we engage in both roles, and I believe that this dual identity as participant and observer is achieved through a capacity for irony. The two states are irreconcilable: we cannot be both involved and detached at the same time, but when we are involved there is a lingering awareness of a capacity to observe, and this makes us question our sympathetic identification. Equally, when we are observers we know that we have been, and again will become involved, and we are less certain of our capacity to be objective. Because neither position is stable, this awareness leads to self-doubt, which is essential to irony and can serve as a reminder of our human frailties. Without irony, the situation can become so real that there is no gap between the drama and the audience, or so unreal that the drama seems to have nothing to do with us. The parallel with the psychoanalytic situation raises the possibility that we can learn something about the analytic attitude from a consideration of the impact of a theatrical performance on the audience.

The nature of irony

Irony is an elusive concept, divided into three main categories by Fowler, in his *Dictionary of Modern English Usage* (1926).

In its everyday usage verbal irony involves a figure of speech in which the intended meaning is the opposite of that expressed by the words used. For example, "What a lovely day", when it is raining.

Socratic irony involves a dissimulation or pretence such as that used by Socrates when he claimed ignorance to confute his adversaries. The *Oxford English Dictionary* adds that Socrates "was famous for proclaiming that he knew nothing, and that the only wisdom he had was the wisdom to realize how ignorant he was."

Dramatic irony, of which Sophocles' *Oedipus the King* is commonly given as the classical example, involves the situation in which the audience observes the tragedy from a position of knowledge that is not available to the protagonists in the drama. For example, Fowler states:

> [Ironic] drama had the peculiarity of providing the double audience—one party in the secret & the other not.... All the spectators, that is, were in the secret beforehand of what would happen. But the characters, Pentheus & Oedipus & the rest, were in the dark, ... the dramatist working his effect by irony. (pp. 295–296)

Irony as an attitude to life

Later I will utilise the ideas of Schafer (1970) and others (Lear 2003, 2014; Stein 1985; Walsh 2011) to think of irony as a self-questioning attitude to life. Lear (2003) has explored this through the work of Kierkegaard to make a comparison between a self we claim to be—the pretender to the self—and the ideal self that we aspire to become. Kierkegaard feels that if he claims to be a Christian he becomes aware of a gap between what he is and what a Christian should be and that the gap can only be bridged through irony. He could claim to be a Christian only if he realised that he was far from the Christian he should be. The example is easily applied to any claim concerning our identity, as an artist say, or even as a human being, so that I can claim to be a writer and a psychoanalyst as I give this paper only with a sense of irony. Being aware of the gap and the recognition of the hypocrisy of a literal version of the claim, is the essence of the ironic attitude. Again it involves a double approach: a subjective one in which we engage in the pretence that we are psychoanalysts; and an objective one in which we observe ourselves and recognise how far we fall short of the ideal of what a psychoanalyst should be.

I will suggest that this double attitude, one engaged and participating and one detached and observing, reflects an internal situation in which we know what is happening from our observations of ourselves and others, and at the same time split off that knowledge as we engage in actions. An ironic stance straddles the two attitudes, recognising that a denial of reality is necessary for a full-blooded engagement in life, while a recognition of reality is required in order to draw lessons from what has happened and learn from experience. Oedipus would never have searched for the truth of his origins if he had known what he was doing and he would have learned nothing from the tragedy if he had not been able to observe and face the truth when it was revealed. I have discerned a similar issue in the idea of the myth of the hero who needs to embrace omnipotence in order to embark on his adventures but then has to relinquish it to return to the ordinary world and learn from his experience (Steiner, 2015).

Dramatic irony and illusion

In the absence of irony, a world based on illusion comes to have a concrete existence that we take for granted because we do not realise that we have split off and ignored our capacity to observe. The impact of reality, when it finally gets through to us, can then be devastating, exposing as it does the extent to which we have been in a state of denial. A capacity for irony would make such revelations less catastrophic because we would be more aware of both views and would anticipate the impact of truth when it came. Irony can also make us more sympathetic and less righteous when we observe those trapped in illusions because we know that we ourselves are subject to our own denials of reality.

I will explore this theme in Sophocles' *Oedipus the King* (Sophocles, 5th century BC, a), and in Ibsen's *The Wild Duck* (Ibsen, 1884), where in both plays we can see the devastating impact of reality on lives that have been based on evasion of truth. These evasions have allowed an assumption of superiority and complacency to develop, which does not appear to be a problem until it collapses into catastrophe as the truth becomes known. This is a common, if not universal, theme in tragedy, and it is also a recurring, if not universal, experience in analysis. To varying degrees, we all have a Garden of Eden fantasy of an idealised time when we were sole possessors of the breast and from which we were cruelly expelled, and this may support a belief that the idealisation can be recovered and does not have to be relinquished (Steiner, 2013, 2015). Our awareness of pretence, falsehood, and self-deception varies from the gross lying of the impostor to a dim awareness that all of us have something to hide because none of us can live up to the standards of the ideal (Deutsch, 1955; Greenacre, 1958; Steiner, 2011).

Both these plays deal with the growing impact of reality on the lives of protagonists who have been living under the spell of an illusion, and it is the sudden dramatic impact of reality as it shatters illusions that gives rise to the plays' tragic element. Examining this theme can remind us that illusions serve important functions, and that there are dangers if reality is forced on to an individual who is not equipped to deal with it. In both plays, we have a protagonist who is determined to expose the truth, and in both, the truth proves to be unbearable, and the consequences tragic, once it is revealed.

Henrik Ibsen's The Wild Duck

The brutality of truth

The drama in *The Wild Duck* (Ibsen, 1884) centres on a confrontation between truth and illusion that follows the reunion of two childhood friends, Hialmar Ekdal and Gregers Werle. They knew each other when their fathers were business partners prior to the disaster that struck Hialmar's father, Old Ekdal. He was convicted of a fraudulent forestry deal, imprisoned, and stripped of his army rank, while Gregers's father, Hakon Werle, was acquitted and went on to become a prosperous merchant.

The humiliated, lowly status of the Ekdal family compared to that of the Werles is evident when the play opens with a sumptuous dinner given by Hakon Werle for his son, who has accepted his father's invitation to return after some seventeen years of resentful absence following the death of his mother. In defiance of his father, Gregers invites his friend Hialmar to this dinner, in the course of which Hialmar gives an account of his recovery after his family's disgrace. Thanks to Gregers's father, Hakon, Hialmar has been able to establish a photographic studio and to meet the woman to whom he is now happily married. He adds that his wife, Gina, was once in service with the Werles, and Gregers is shocked when he realises that she was the person who not only kept house for them during the last year of his mother's illness, but also the one with whom he suspected his father had a relationship.

Hialmar's presence is an embarrassment to the gathering, and the awkwardness is even more painful when the shabby, doddering Old Ekdal walks through the company and is looked down on by everyone—even by his own son, who averts his gaze.

Hialmar leaves early, and Gregers then confronts his father and attacks him for allowing old Ekdal to take the blame for the crime that both partners were guilty of. This, Werle denies, and Gregers goes on to accuse him of helping the Ekdals with money to cover up his guilt. Moreover, he also accuses him of covering up his relationship with Gina by marrying her off to Hialmar. Hakon asks if it was Hialmar who has accused him of this, and Gregers tells him that it was his mother who told him about his liaison with Gina. Exasperated, Hakon responds by saying that Gregers sees everything through his mother's eyes and has ignored her clouded vision. Despite the long-standing animosity between father and son, Hakon is seeking a reconciliation with Gregers and has invited him to return home to join the business as a partner, so that Hakon himself can retire to the country and marry his present housekeeper.

Gregers sees this as an attempt to get him to collude with yet another cover-up by condoning his father's behaviour and concealing the family's ugly secrets, including rumours about his mistreatment of Gregers's mother. As the two argue, Gregers's idealisation of his mother and his hatred of his father clearly emerge, and their row ends with Gregers refusing to support his father and leaving, insisting that they will never meet again. When his father asks him what he will do if he will not join the business, Gregers proclaims that he has now found his mission in life. It is clear that this mission is to expose the lies of Hialmar's marriage, and we realise this has more to do with exposing his father than with helping his friend.

The remainder of the play takes place in Hialmar's studio, where we see the various illusions and self-deceptions that the Ekdal family live by. Despite these, and perhaps because of them, Hialmar and Gina manage to live a contented life and, albeit with hardships and tensions, they care for each other, so that Hialmar can say, "Our roof may be poor and humble, Gina; but it is home. And with all my heart I say: here dwells my happiness" (Ibsen, 1884, p. 35.) They gain great comfort from their love for their daughter, Hedvig, now age fourteen, who is described as their greatest joy, but also as their deepest sorrow because she is going blind.

Hialmar, his father, and Gina each cope with their humiliation through enacting a pretence. Old Ekdal escapes to the attic in which his family have created a make-believe forest where rabbits and hens are kept, and where he can put on his uniform and pretend he is still an officer shooting bears. Hialmar, instead of working in his studio, dreams of his great invention, which will restore the family name and allow him to rehabilitate his father. Gina supports these illusions, keeps the business going, economises to make ends meet, and pretends that it is Hialmar who is the breadwinner. Hedvig adores her father but, like her mother, she treats him as a difficult child, and she overlooks the growing evidence of his selfishness and neglect.

Also in the attic, in a special basket, sits the wild duck, shot and wounded by Hakon and given to Hedvig, after being rescued from the "depths of the sea" by Hakon's dog. The wounded wild duck has many resonances—most obviously standing for Hedvig as a symbol of objects damaged by Hakon and given to Hialmar to look after.

Gregers becomes the Ekdals' lodger, and his passion for truth grows as he sees the make-believe world they inhabit. He invites his old friend Hialmar for a long walk, in the course of which he reveals Gina's secret liaison with his father and the dubious motives for his support of the family. He has embarked on his mission to rescue Hialmar from a life based on illusion to one founded on truth.

Gregers has always been an idealist, and he expects Hialmar to have identical views, which would lead him to embrace the truth, accept what has happened, and rebuild his marriage on a new, sound footing. However, Gregers in his narcissism has completely misread Hialmar who, far from embracing the truth, reacts with horror and indignation when he discovers Gina's past and the support that Gregers' father Hakon Werle has secretly provided. He declares his intention to leave Gina and Hedvig and to reject everything that he has received from Hakon Werle.

In his outrage he even tells his daughter that he would like to strangle the wild duck and that the only thing that prevents him from doing so is that he knows how much it would upset her.

A further blow to Hialmar's pride takes the form of a letter from Hakon Werle that contains a deed of gift, which Hialmar tears up in a rage when he learns that it provides a pension for Old Ekdal passing to Hedwig after his death. However, the final blow comes when he begins to recognise that Hedwig may not be his daughter. It becomes clear that Hakon is himself going blind, and this creates the conviction in Hialmar that Hedwig's blindness is hereditary, and that Gina was already pregnant when she married him. Gina confesses her affair and admits that she cannot be sure who Hedwig's father is. Hialmar's cruelty becomes most poignant when he rejects Hedwig and calls her an interloper.

Gradually, however, Hialmar allows himself to lean on Gina once more, and as he begins to feel less righteous and more needy he glues together the fragments of the torn letter so that the legacy need not be given up. When he hears that Hedwig intends to sacrifice her precious wild duck to demonstrate her love for him, his rejection of her also softens—but it is too late, because the drama comes to its tragically fatal conclusion when Hedwig, instead of shooting the wild duck, shoots herself. She has come to believe that it is she who is the burden on her family, having been damaged by Hakon Werle and shunned by Hialmar.

A voice of reason appears in the form of Dr Relling, who explains that, in his view it is Gregers whose mind is diseased, saying, "But one disease he has certainly got in his system.... He is suffering from an acute attack of integrity" (Ibsen, 1884, pp. 71–72). Dr Relling has been trying to support Hialmar without disturbing his illusions because he argues that: "Rob the average man of his life-illusions and you take away his happiness at the same stroke" (p. 100). Gregers has failed to recognise that Hialmar is an average man, and he has no understanding of his feelings. Moreover, Gregers's motivation for revealing what he did had less to do with Hialmar's happiness than with the wish to expose the alleged wrongdoing of his father. Gregers's hatred arises in part from his idealisation of his mother and his denial of her paranoia and alcoholism, which led to her husband's alienation and hastened her death. This means that the truth Gregers wants to impose does not take into account the wider picture and is equally based on illusion.

Kindness and truth: the role of irony

In *The Wild Duck*, Ibsen forcefully reminds us that truth can be cruel and that we can become blind to the tragic consequences of its impact. The tragedy raises the importance of feelings such as pity and kindness, as these are evoked in the audience who are made aware of Gregers's inability to feel them.

The need for kindness is a theme pursued by E. M. Forster, an admirer of Ibsen (Forster, 1936) who argued that kindness is as important as truth—not only to mitigate the harshness of truth, but also to make it more true. In *A Passage to India* (1924), his heroine, like Gregers, felt only "cold justice and honesty" and "no passion of love for those whom she had wronged" (p. 217). Forster asserted that: "Truth is not truth in that exacting land unless there go with it kindness and more kindness and kindness again" (p. 217).

Forster's point is not simply that truth without kindness can be cruel, but that truth without kindness is not fully true. Nevertheless, we also know that truth is essential for our mental health and that pursuing truth is one of the basic goals of psychoanalysis. We find ourselves in agreement with Freud when he asserts that "we must not forget that the analytic relationship is based on a love of truth—that is, on a recognition of reality—and that it precludes any kind of sham or deceit" (1937c, p. 248).

Moreover, in *The Wild Duck*, Gregers's view of the benefits of truthfulness is close to that held by psychoanalysts in their model of healthy development. We argue that facing the reality of loss allows us to mourn our lost objects, to recognise our guilt, and to repair the damage we have done. What we sometimes forget is that, in order for guilt to be accepted and to motivate us toward reparation, it has to be bearable—and this is often the critical factor, as it proves to be for Hialmar. As we relinquish and mourn our illusions, we must also relinquish and mourn our omnipotence; paradoxically, this means that facing reality includes an acceptance of our limitations, including the limits to the reality we can accept.

Freud recognised that a love of truth is not the same as an idealisation of truth. He was very aware that we all need defences and that neurotic compromises are part of ordinary existence. In his words:

> It is not his [the analyst's] business to restrict himself in every situation in life to being a fanatic in favour of health … We must allow that in some cases that flight [into illness] is fully justified, and a physician who has recognized how the situation lies will silently and solicitously withdraw. (1916–17, p. 382)

Freud was a great admirer of Ibsen, and in relating one of his own dreams, he described a sentence "written in a positively *norekdal* style" (1900a, p. 296). Freud's self-analysis revealed that "*norekdal*" was a condensation of Nora and Ekdal—the first, a character in *A Doll's House* (Ibsen, 1879) and the second, in *The Wild Duck* (Ibsen, 1884). In discussing this dream, Anthi (1990) suggests that, at the time, Freud was beginning to become aware that his studies in hysteria were exposing him to criticism from his colleagues, and that, in identification with Old Ekdal, he feared humiliation and disgrace. Anthi also suggests that Freud's partnership with Fliess was coming to an end, and that the imprisonment of Old Ekdal reminded him of his guilt about their dangerous collaboration in the case of Emma Eckstein (Masson, 1984). I suspect, however, that Freud was also becoming aware that, in his treatment of hysterical patients, he had been exerting pressure on them to accept the truth, and that the portrayal of Gregers in *The Wild Duck* may have alerted him to the harm that can be done by over-zealous idealists.

Freud could recognise both the value of truth and the dangers of an insensitive imposition of it on others, and this capacity is essential to irony. By contrast, Gregers's concrete solution to the problem shows that he is completely without a capacity for irony, and he cannot extricate himself from identification with Hialmar; hence, he cannot observe what he has done or feel pity for those whom he has exposed. He cannot feel tolerance or kindness towards them and is intent only on taking action that is unrestrained by thought or self-doubt.

Oedipus the King

Collusions to avoid reality

In *Oedipus the King* (Sophocles, 5th century BC, a), we have a similar, though even more dramatic, example of a determination to expose the truth that results in tragedy. This time it is Oedipus who pursues the truth without realising where it will lead, and we identify with him as he gradually discovers what a disaster this exposure will be. If we emerge from our identification, however, and temporarily become sufficiently detached, we can also observe how the collusions and evasions among the drama's participants led to a denial of the truth for so many years. Having triumphed over the sphinx, Oedipus, his family, and indeed the whole city of Thebes, lived under an illusion that all would be well as long as they did not pursue the truth, until a plague disturbed the status quo.

Like the original Greek audience, we are familiar with the story, but we do not always recognise that each of the main characters had his or her own reasons for evading reality, and how this led them to collude in establishing and sustaining their ignorance of the facts. At the beginning of the play, Oedipus is confronted with the crisis of the plague, which leads him to embark on a quest to determine its cause. Seventeen years previously, he had entered Thebes as a homeless fugitive from the court of Corinth, to be welcomed in triumph because he had solved the riddle of the sphinx. He was made King of Thebes in place of Laius, who had been killed a few days earlier, and accepted Jocasta, the former queen, as his wife. However, in order to enjoy his good fortune he had to evade a number of facts that, had he pursued them, would have led him to discover the truth and to avoid the false premises on which his good fortune was based.

Moreover, the other characters in the drama—Jocasta and Creon in particular, but also the elders of the city—found it expedient to turn a blind eye in order to ignore events that would have enabled the truth to emerge (Steiner, 1985; Zachrisson, 2013).[1] It was this unconscious collusion that established Oedipus as an upright king and a respected father in what turned out to be an illusion of normality. Furthermore, it was an illusion that has enabled the family and the city to survive until it is shattered as the facts emerge in the course of the play.

When the tragedy's disillusion arrives, we in the audience are moved to terror and pity as we witness the unfolding events. In identification with Oedipus, we share in his determination to discover the truth, and we are terrified as each new discovery implicates him more certainly as the source of the corruption. However, we are also able to disidentify with the hero and observe the total situation, and this allows us to acknowledge the facts that Oedipus has been evading, as well as the complex involvements of all the characters in the cover-up. As we withdraw from the identification and stop to observe and think, we are bound to ask: "If these things can be brought to light now, why were they not discovered seventeen years ago when Oedipus first entered Thebes?"

The attitude of Oedipus

We can begin by imagining the thoughts going through the mind of Oedipus when he first entered Thebes to be acclaimed as a hero. He has left Corinth determined to avoid the prophecy at the centre of the play, and he has just killed an older man with a retinue outside the city. He has married the widow of the king, a woman old enough to be his mother, and he did this within a very short time of being told by the oracle that he was destined to kill his father and marry his mother.

We know the fateful history, but we watch attentively as it becomes clear that Oedipus has failed to make the crucial connections. The city must have been buzzing with news of the recent murder of King Laius, but Oedipus had not asked where the king had been killed, by whom he was attended, or what he looked like. Instead of pursuing the obvious inquiries, Oedipus has erected a plausible facade to cover up the truth, which he persuaded himself and others to accept. He felt safe in Thebes because he convinced himself that the one thing he feared was a return to Corinth, where he might kill King Polybus and marry Merope, the couple he believed to be his parents. He overlooked the fact that he had gone to Delphi expressly to ask about his parentage because doubts had been cast on it, and the oracle had failed to provide the answer. He accepted his new situation without qualm because, as Green (1987) suggested, the desire to enjoy Laius's throne and Jocasta's bed made him a poor logician.

The testimony of Teiresias

One of the remarkable moments of the play occurs quite near the beginning when Oedipus swears to find and banish the killer of Laius, and the ancient soothsayer Teiresias is sent for. At first he refuses to identify the guilty man, but when Oedipus becomes childishly abusive, Teiresias gets angry and tells him in plain terms, first that the killer Oedipus is seeking is himself, and then that it is he who is "the cursed polluter of this land … living in sinful union with the one you love" (Watling, 1947, p. 36).

Creon, the elders, and Oedipus all hear this, and all go on to act as if they have not heard it. The remarkable thing is that we in the audience also hear it and, while knowing it to be true and witnessing the wholesale denial, we identify with Oedipus and join in the collusion, apprehensively waiting for the denouement as the play gradually and with many diversions leads inexorably toward the truth.

Jocasta's attitude

Jocasta must have been told of the death of her husband, and she knew of the prediction that led Laius to fear that his son would murder him. Despite this she agreed to the marriage and repeatedly expressed her contempt of prophecy. In the play, she reassures Oedipus by insisting that guilt is inappropriate because all lives are ruled by chance. Marriage to the youthful Oedipus offered her the opportunity to remain Queen of Thebes and once again to bear children. It is not difficult to suppose that these advantages led her to turn a blind eye to the truth and to collude in the cover-up.

As psychoanalysts, we recognise that the oedipal illusion is universal and includes a fantasy of mutual love between mother and child, irrespective of differences in age. Jocasta's fate, however, reminds us of the tragic consequences if these illusions remain untouched by reality.

Creon's attitude

Jocasta's brother, Creon, was responsible for ruling the city after Laius was killed. He explains that he had no ambition to rule and was content to retain an influence in the background. He shows no surprise when told of Teiresias' accusations, despite their terrible import, saying only

"If he did so, you know best" (Watling, 1947, p. 40). Earlier, when Oedipus asks what stopped them from tracking down the King's killer there and then, Creon replies, "The Sphinx with her riddles forced us to turn our attention from insoluble mysteries to more immediate matters" (Watling, 1947, p. 29).

Oedipus asks why Teiresias was not summoned to identify the murderer at that time, only to be told that he *had* been summoned but had remained silent. When Oedipus asks why he has now spoken after staying silent for so long, Creon answers simply, "I do not presume to say more than I know" (Watling, 1947, p. 41). It makes sense for Creon to deny his complicity; Oedipus cannot be saved, but Creon can—and in fact he comes out of the drama unscathed.

The attitude of the elders

Finally, the chorus of elders, on stage throughout the unfolding of the drama, are shown to be concerned with their own interests as they begin to suspect that all is not well with Oedipus. When Oedipus proclaims that he will find the guilty party, they deny having had anything to do with it and indicate they prefer divine knowledge to that arrived at by investigating reality.

Even though the elders heard Teiresias make clear that it is Oedipus who is the killer of Laius and the polluter of the land, they avoid all reference to these accusations. Instead, they speak of an unknown robber with blood-stained hands who has committed the most unspeakable of unspeakable crimes, and refer to him roaming the countryside at large. Eventually, they admit that Teiresias' testimony is disturbing, but they affirm their compliance and decline to take sides. They are terrified of the chaos that they think will arise if their king is dethroned, and they are also playing it safe while there is a chance that he might survive.

The cover-up

A cover-up requires conspirators who agree either overtly or tacitly to collaborate. If Creon had called for a proper inquiry, the witness would have been interrogated and the truth would have come out. If Jocasta had not ignored the oracle that she so hated, she might not have turned a blind eye to her young husband's resemblance to Laius, to the fact that his age was precisely that of her son had he lived, or to the scars on his feet that must have puzzled her. If the elders, too, had been more vigilant and not so concerned about backing the winning party, they might have demanded an inquiry, or at least asked about their new king's background.

The cover-up could only take place because it suited several parties at the same time, and thus enabled the participants to be of mutual service to each other. We in the audience also collude in the cover-up because we empathically identify with everyone's need to do so.

Oedipus' remarkable pursuit of truth, and the horrible denouement

If we recognise the only-too-human evasions of truth that led to the massive cover-up in *Oedipus the King*, then the determination and courage shown by Oedipus as he faces reality is even more remarkable. We see him vacillating and struggling with his ambivalence, but this only makes his final achievement more impressive.

The climax of the play occurs when the shepherd who took Oedipus away as a baby makes the whole truth clear, and Oedipus accepts it with great courage and without prevarication or excuse. He admits everything, saying simply, "Alas, all out! All is known! No more concealment! Oh light! May I never look on you again, revealed as I am, sinful in my begetting, sinful in marriage, sinful in the shedding of blood" (Watling, 1947, p. 56).

At this point, the truth, although awful, seems to be accepted by Oedipus, but the next event in the tragedy—the final blow of Jocasta's death—seems to make the situation unbearable. A messenger announces the suicide of the queen and describes what happens next: when Oedipus sees her suspended body, he cuts her down and then puts out his own eyes with her brooches. We are moved with horror and pity as we recognise that his guilt has led to this tragic self-mutilation, which seems to indicate that looking at the truth became impossible when it included responsibility for Jocasta's death. Her death was unexpected and doubly shocking. The murder of his father and his marriage to his mother were part of the prophecy, but nowhere was Oedipus warned that his crime would devastate and destroy his mother as well.

Moreover, the hero is now alone, with neither parent able to serve as a good object to make tragedy and guilt more bearable. After his determined pursuit of the truth and his courageous acceptance of responsibility, his self-blinding initiates a move away from truth, which deepens in *Oedipus at Colonus* (Sophocles, 5th century BC, b), where Oedipus adopts a God-like status and emphatically denies his guilt (Steiner, 1990, 1993).

Sophocles highlights the conflict between the wish to face the truth and the wish to evade it, surely one of the deepest of human conflicts, and one that every patient who embarks on an analysis has to wrestle with. We can identify with the hero who espouses such devotion to truth, but I believe that looking again at *Oedipus the King* and *The Wild Duck* can lead us to temper our love for truth with a recognition of its cruelty and an acceptance of the need for evasions that can make life bearable. This means that the acceptance of reality is more complex than a simple facing of facts, and that different visions of reality are required to enrich our understanding and to make it more true. To support the patient as he embarks on developments in accord with reality requires the analyst to appreciate how complex, multi-layered, and rich our relationship with reality is. The analyst needs to accept that reality can be cruel, that evasions and illusions are universal, and that understanding them is often possible only in a wider context, where the total situation can be taken into account.

The ironic attitude

I have used *The Wild Duck* and *Oedipus the King* to argue that the discovery and acceptance of reality is complex, and that the history, circumstances, and personalities of the participants must be taken into account to gain a broader and truer view of the total situation. Some of this complexity is brought out by Roy Schafer (1970), who suggested that the observer can adopt one or more of a variety of attitudes towards, or visions of, reality, summarised under the headings of comic, romantic, tragic, and ironic. Of these I believe that the ironic vision is the most significant for the present theme.

I have argued that in *The Wild Duck* and in *Oedipus the King*, it is the catastrophic disillusionment that gives the tragedy its bite, as we witness how the people who have come to matter to us are crushed by the impact of reality, and we are moved to feel both terror and pity, which fills us with dread but which also enriches our understanding. We can see that a gap has emerged between the experiences of the protagonist in the throes of relinquishment of his illusion and those of the audience aware of the reality he has so energetically been avoiding. Moreover, this gap exists in all of us as we alternate between participation and observation in the dramas of others, but also in our own dramas, which we both live through and reflect on. The *ironic* vision involves an awareness of this gap and a willingness to tolerate both points of view. We realise that all along we have known something of the truth; we feel pity for the blindness of the protagonists, as well as for our own blindness, and we shudder as collusions and seductions are exposed.

Because these attitudes are contradictory, they cannot be resolved, and the conflict has to be recognised as inevitable and permanent. It is part of the human condition that we wish both to deny and to accept reality. I think it is a sense of irony that allows us to live with this contradiction and also with other contradictions, such as that between subjective and objective, symbolic and concrete, actual and ideal.

Irony and humour

The relationship between irony and humour is complex and always somewhat uncertain and ambiguous. Because it aims at partial detachment, irony may be used defensively to lessen the impact of tragedy. Fowler (1926) speaks of the delight of irony in a "secret intimacy" (p. 296) with those in the know, and it is these delights that may lead to feelings of superiority if we disengage from the tragedy and look down on those suffering it. This relief may contribute to the humorous element in irony, which causes us to smile as we see the discrepancy between the tragic struggles of the protagonists on stage and our own apparently superior knowledge.

In tragedy, however, humour is supressed and replaced by sympathy and pity: we do not laugh at the suffering of the Ekdal family or of the torments of Oedipus. It seems to me that the humour is proportional to the degree of detachment. At one extreme, we enter the drama through a concrete identification with the hero, trapped in his experience, which is factual and humourless. As we detach ourselves we pass through a phase when we are less identified and feel pity as well as terror. Humour becomes possible but we recognise the need to be sensitive to the feelings of the participants. With further detachment, ironic humour with its tinge of pain predominates and we can enjoy a bitter-sweet pleasure at our amusement tempered by self-reflection. When detachment is more nearly total the humour becomes more mocking, sarcastic, and cruel and involves a splitting off, projection, and disowning of our vulnerability into those we are observing.

The potential cruelty of irony is illustrated in a story told by Freud (1905c), of a brother and sister who put on a play for their family of uncles and aunts. The boy of ten plays a fisherman who leaves his poor and honest wife to make his fortune. He returns a rich man and tells his wife of his adventures in foreign lands. His sister of twelve, playing the wife, interrupts him, proudly saying, "I too have not been idle", and she opens the door of her hut to reveal twelve large dolls lying asleep on the floor. The grown-up audience who have been listening with close attention until then bursts into laughter, to the bewilderment and chagrin of the children. This is an example of dramatic irony, in which the adults believe that they know where babies come from while the children apparently do not. Like Oedipus, the children have to face the humiliation of not having realised what later becomes obvious to them in a most painful way. To retain a sense of irony and avoid mocking the children the audience too must realise the insensitivity of their laughter and remember their own painful acquisition of the facts of life.

Irony is always somewhat risky, tipping over into a humourless concreteness on the one hand or into sarcasm, mockery, and superiority on the other, the outcome depending on the balance of involvement and detachment. It is the intermediate positions that are truly ironic, where we are able to feel pity and also able to smile because while we are observing we are simultaneously laughing at ourselves through identification with the protagonists of the tragedy.

Even though irony can be cruel, its great value lies in the way it can mitigate the cruelty of the superego that demands a literal interpretation of the truth. The ironic view allows us to appreciate the importance of both sides in the conflict between reality and illusion. It encompasses the comic and the tragic, the subjective and the objective, the concrete and the symbolic. If we are able to experience each of these states in turn, we can become aware of the conflict and contradictions in our complex relationship with reality. We can also recognise how easily the ironic view can collapse into a concrete certainty with the potential for insensitivity and cruelty.

Irony in analysis

Having looked at the complexity of our responses to the characters portrayed in *The Wild Duck* and in *Oedipus the King*, we can see a similar complexity as we listen to and try to understand our patients. I have stressed the fact that the ironic stance is also relevant to an intra-psychic conflict within ourselves. We can become keenly involved in our beliefs and actions if we are also able to stand back from them to observe what we have done and what the consequences of our actions have been.

This sequence of action, followed by observation and reflection, repeats over and over as the analytic session proceeds, and we can observe the patient's responses to our interpretations and use them in part to understand the patient better, and in part to detect flaws within ourselves and to correct errors in our constructions.

If we admit a need for illusion, we are accepting our frailty as well as that of the patient, and we manage this through the use of irony. We both believe our patients and remain sceptical, and similarly we have a belief in our work and remain sceptical of it. We know that both the patient and the analyst defensively distort reality to make life bearable. But we also know that there is a truth, which we strive to be aware of and respect.

In her unpublished lectures on technique, Klein suggests that a good analytic attitude involves a "rather curious state of mind, eager and at the same time patient, *detached from its subject and at the same time fully absorbed in it*" (1936, p. 30, my italics). She says this requires a "balance between different and partly conflicting tendencies and psychological drives, and … a good co-operation between several different parts of our mind".

These characteristics seem to me to be part of an ironic stance that, when it is functioning well, can allow an eager involvement with our patients, while a capacity to laugh at ourselves protects us from dangerous over-involvement with passionate beliefs.

Note

1. In an earlier paper (Steiner, 1985), I use the term "to turn a blind eye" to denote a situation in which we have access to reality but choose to ignore it because it proves convenient to do so. This mechanism involves a degree of ambiguity as to how conscious or unconscious the knowledge is; most often, we are vaguely aware that we are choosing not to look at the facts, but without being conscious of what it is we are evading. These views of Sophocles' play are based on the work of Philip Vellacott, an idiosyncratic classicist who is known for his translations of Aeschylus and Euripides but whose views on Oedipus (Vellacott, 1971) have not been generally accepted.

References

Anthi, P. R. (1990). Freud's dream in norekdal style. *Scandinavian Psychoanalytic Review, 13*: 138–160.

Deutsch, H. (1955). The impostor: contribution to ego psychology of a type of psychopath. *Psychoanalytic Quarterly, 24*: 483–505.

Forster, E. M. (1924). *A Passage to India*. London: Edward Arnold.

Forster, E. M. (1936). Ibsen the romantic. In: D. B. Christiani (Trans.), *The Wild Duck* (pp. 143–146). New York: Norton, 1968.

Fowler, H. W. (1926). *A Dictionary of Modern English Usage*. Oxford, UK: Clarendon, 1937.

Freud, S. (1900a). *The Interpretation of Dreams. S. E., 4–5*. London: Hogarth.

Freud, S. (1905c). *Jokes and their Relation to the Unconscious. S. E., 8*: 3–249. London: Hogarth.

Freud, S. (1916–17). *Introductory Lectures on Psycho-Analysis. S. E., 16*. London: Hogarth.

Freud, S. (1937c). Analysis terminable and interminable. *S. E., 23*: 211–253. London: Hogarth.

Green, A. (1987). Oedipus, Freud, and us. In: M. Charney, J. Reppen, & J. A. Flieger (Eds.), *Psychoanalytic Approaches to Literature and Film* (pp. 215–237). London: Associated Press.

Greenacre, P. (1958). The impostor. *Psychoanalytic Quarterly, 27*: 359–382.

Ibsen, H. (1879). *A Doll's House*. Clayton, DE: Prestwick House, 2005.

Ibsen, H. (1884). *The Wild Duck* (Trans., D. B. Christiani). New York: Norton, 1968.

Klein, M. (1936). *Lectures on Technique by Melanie Klein* (Ed., J. Steiner). London: Routledge, 2017.

Lear, J. (2003). *Therapeutic Action: An Earnest Plea for Irony*. London: Karnac.

Lear, J. (2014). *A Case for Irony*. Cambridge, MA: Harvard University Press.

Masson, J. M. (1984). *The Assault on Truth*. New York: Straus & Giroux.

Schafer, R. (1970). The psychoanalytic vision of reality. *International Journal of Psychoanalysis, 51*: 279–297.

Sophocles (5th century BC, a). *Oedipus the King*. In: R. C. Jebb (Trans.), *The Complete Works of Sophocles*. New York: Bantam, 1982.

Sophocles (5th century BC, b). *Oedipus at Colonus*. In: R. C. Jebb (Trans.), *The Complete Works of Sophocles*. New York: Bantam Books, 1982.

Stein, M. (1985). Irony in psychoanalysis. *Journal of the American Psychoanalytic Association, 33*: 35–57.

Steiner, J. (1985). Turning a blind eye: The cover up for Oedipus. *International Review of Psychoanalysis, 12*: 161–172.

Steiner, J. (1990). The retreat from truth to omnipotence in *Oedipus at Colonus*. *International Review of Psychoanalysis, 17*: 227–237.

Steiner, J. (1993). *Psychic Retreats: Pathological Organisations of the Personality in Psychotic, Neurotic, and Borderline Patients*. London: Routledge.

Steiner, J. (2011). The impostor revisited. *Psychoanalytic Quarterly, 80*: 1061–1071.

Steiner, J. (2013). The ideal and the real in Klein and Milton: some observations on reading *Paradise Lost. Psychoanalytic Quarterly, 82*: 897–923.

Steiner, J. (2015). The use and abuse of omnipotence in the journey of the hero. *Psychoanalytic Quarterly, 84*: 695–718.

Turri, M. G. (2015). Transference and katharsis, Freud to Aristotle. *International Journal of Psychoanalysis, 96*: 369–387.

Vellacott, P. (1971). *Sophocles and Oedipus: A Study of Oedipus Tyrannus with a New Translation*. Ann Arbor, MI: University of Michigan Press.

Walsh, J. (2011). Unconscious dissemblance: the place of irony in psychoanalytic thought. *PIVOT, 1*: 143–158.

Watling, E. F. (1947). *The Theban Plays*. Harmondsworth, UK: Penguin.

Zachrisson, A. (2013). Oedipus the king: quest for self-knowledge—denial of reality: Sophocles' vision of man and psychoanalytic concept formation. *International Journal of Psychoanalysis, 94*: 313–331.

CHAPTER NINETEEN

Primitive reparation and the repetition compulsion in the analysis of a borderline patient*,**

Heinz Weiss

Mature and primitive forms of reparation

It is generally assumed that attempts at reparation occur when the damage that was done to the object in reality or in phantasy can no longer be denied and feelings of guilt occur to prevent the loss of the loved object and to protect it from further injury or hurt. This development is made possible at the transition to the depressive position when persecutory anxiety lessens and splits can be overcome, and the individual makes the discovery that his feelings of love and hatred are directed towards the same object (Klein, 1935, 1940, 1946). This experience may in turn be accompanied by intense feelings of conflict, which may lead to renewed splitting and escape into a psychic retreat. If all goes well, the processes of integration of the self are strengthened and the development of an internal space in which loss and mourning can be dealt with is promoted.

In this way reparation is seen as an elementary psychic process, which counters destruction and disintegration. In their work, Melanie Klein and Hanna Segal (1978, 1991) have shown that processes of reparation in the depressive position are closely linked to processes of symbol formation. These processes enable the small child to acknowledge separation and to symbolically restore the damaged and, to a certain extent, lost object.

But what happens in patients who are only partly or momentarily capable of such integration? Are there any observable moves towards the depressive position? What do such primitive attempts at reparation look like and what effects do they have on the analytic treatment process?

---

*Translated by Ursula Haug, London, and Kristin White, Berlin.
**Parts of the clinical material have been used in a previous publication (Weiss, 2012) and in a communication by the Melanie Klein Trust, London (www.melanie-klein-trust.org.uk).

Henri Rey (1986) was one of the first authors to describe the precursors of the processes of reparation in schizoid and borderline patients. He regarded reparation as a universal occurrence, akin to such biological processes as maintenance and renewal of the organism. Referring back to Freud (1911c), he pointed out that even schizophrenic patients endeavour to repair their fragmented internal world. In this way, delusional ideas can be regarded as desperate attempts to protect the self from complete disintegration and fragmentation. However, the price to be paid for this restitution by omnipotent and psychotic means is the loss of contact with reality.

In patients with pathological personality organisations the conditions are somewhat different. Here too we find different forms of primitive reparation, but without overt breakdown in external reality.

For example, compulsive rituals can be understood as an attempt to magically repair an object, which has been damaged by sadistic attacks and has possibly become vengeful. In contrast, other efforts of compulsive neurotics predominantly serve the prevention of further damage and the control of the object, rather than any real acknowledgement of separation and guilt.

Grievance and resentment is another significant clinical constellation. The patient ceaselessly demands reparation from his objects, but keeps the wounds open and ultimately does not allow for reparation to take place (see Feldman, 1997). Grievance can therefore be described as a condition in which the need for reparation is projected and recurs as an unrealisable demand for reparation.

Manic forms of reparation are predominantly seen in narcissistic patients. They show traits of omnipotent denial, which is supposed to get rid of guilt and in this way actually renews the hurt and damage done to the object. The godlike grandiosity of Oedipus (Steiner, 1990) or the grandiosity of King Lear (Rusbridger, 2011) are examples of this.

Lastly, if we regard the self-mutilation of some borderline patients as a concrete attempt at reparation, it becomes clear how measures aimed at sanctioning and control possibly rob them of the only means they possess to repair their damaged internal objects.

In comparing these primitive precursors with more mature forms of reparation they seem to promote continual damage to the object, thus leading to a vicious circle. Certain manifestations of the repetition compulsion can thus be seen as desperate, failed attempts at reparation. These patients resemble the figures of Greek mythology (Sisyphus, Prometheus, Tantalus), whose rebellion against the gods (the primitive superego) leads to endless torment and punishment.

Attempts at reparation and the evolution of the superego

This section of the paper introduces the role of the superego into the processes of reparation and their success or failure. In the following discussion, I would like to look at those processes that make reparation possible in some cases and block it permanently in others. I will take Melanie Klein's thesis as a starting point, that it is the evolution of the superego that makes reparation possible, whilst under the domination of an archaic superego the damage is repeated endlessly.

Klein published her thoughts on this in her late paper "On the development of mental functioning" (1958). She argues that the early archaic superego originates from split-off, destructive parts of the self. In its early stages one could conceptualise it as a kind of "bad bank", in which primitive destructive impulses as well as persecutory projections are stored in order to protect the ego from fragmentation. However, in the course of development, elements of the life instinct and loving experiences are continuously introduced into this rudimentary superego structure, thus gradually changing its character and allowing for a beneficial development of its relationship with the ego.

Klein describes it thus:

> As the process of integration ... goes on, the death instinct is bound, up to a point, by the super-ego. In the process of binding, the death instinct influences the aspects of the good objects contained in the super-ego, with the result that the action of the super-ego ranges from restraint of hate and destructive impulses, protection of the good object and self-criticism, to threats, inhibitory complaints and persecution. (1958, p. 240)

If the positive qualities predominate, the sadistic traits of the superego recede into the background. While the primitive superego poses a constant threat to the ego, the developing superego can increasingly assume a containment function for the ego. In my view, Klein has clearly described this intra-psychic containment function of the superego in relation to the ego when she writes: "The super-ego—being bound up with the good object and even striving for its preservation—comes close to the actual good mother, who feeds the child and takes care of it" (p. 240).

One of its functions is to continue with the imposition of prohibitions and prescriptions, which, however, are no longer directed in a sadistic way against the ego. To some extent, when development goes well, Klein continues, "the super-ego is largely felt as helpful and does not operate as too harsh a conscience." One of its functions now is "to protect the good object as well as safeguard him against persecutory anxieties" (p. 240).

What Klein describes here is the evolution of a superego from a "bad bank" to a "container" and eventually to an agency that enables the ego to make reparation. Hand in hand with this goes the development of the ego functions as well as an increasing tolerance of the superego by the ego with whom it "shares the different aspects of the same good object" (p. 240).

Klein summarises:

> With the strengthening of the ego and its growing capacity for integration and synthesis, the phase of the depressive position is reached. At this stage the injured object is no longer predominantly felt as a persecutor, but as a loved object, towards whom a feeling of guilt and the urge to make reparation are experienced. (pp. 241–242)

What is significant about Klein's approach is the idea of an evolution of superego structures in close connection with the development or the blocking of ego functions. This means that the primitive superego structures have a lifelong existence alongside the mature superego and there is an ongoing exchange between them, just as there is between ego and superego. Depending on how this exchange works out, different configurations will develop, which will either promote processes of reparation or maintain a status quo where internal objects are constantly damaged and correspondingly have a detrimental influence on the ego functions (Malcolm-Riesenberg, 1988; O'Shaughnessy, 1999).

Processes that facilitate reparation and processes that systematically prevent reparation

I would like to go on to examine those processes that prevent genuine reparation using clinical material.

According to my assumptions, primitive attempts at reparation are mainly distinguishable from mature reparation by (1) being relatively concrete, (2) serving primarily to control anxiety, (3) not having a real capacity to acknowledge separation, all of which lead (4) to a pseudo-acceptance of reality.

Nevertheless these primitive attempts at reparation can be successful to a degree as long as they relieve anxiety and unbearable feelings of guilt. However, they deplete themselves in their attempt to avoid the experience of loss and to uphold the control over the object. I would like to show how these circumstances can lead to a situation in which the individual is forever caught up with his damaged internal objects.

Pathological organisations

Clinically such configurations manifest as persistent reproaches, tortuous self-accusations, rancour, grievances, chronic contrition, or as a longing for utopian states (Weiss, 2011). Characteristically, the suffering is kept going over long periods of time and each move towards change is often accompanied by a worsening of the clinical condition. As long as the patient clings on to misrepresentations of his internal and external reality, stability is achieved at the cost of contact and development.

In theory, such states of psychic equilibrium have been described as "pathological organisations of the personality" (Steiner, 1993). Even earlier, Klein (1935) had considered the possibility of a "manic" and "obsessional position" at the transition between the paranoid-schizoid and depressive positions. These "positions" could consequently be characterised by disturbed and distorted processes of reparation under the dominance of a powerful, cruel superego. John Steiner (1992) expanded these conceptions and coined the term "borderline position". The borderline position is an example of a pathological psychic equilibrium. Among other things it is characterised by a resistance to change, as well as an addiction-like adherence to states of psychic retreat.

I will now go on to describe a clinical example of a psychic retreat, which was mainly based on grievance and wrath repeatedly leading to impasses and dead ends in the analysis. I would like to show how the underlying organisation was based on a near delusional misrepresentation of reality, which drove the patient to suicidal crises whenever he moved closer towards reparation, which made me doubt whether the treatment could be of any benefit to him. This evoked feelings of irritation and resignation in me, so that my capacity for reparation, too, was undermined and I found it difficult to maintain an attitude of unbiased understanding.

Clinical example: wrath, grievance, and the impossibility of reparation

Mr B is a thirty-year-old student, who grew up in a family that had moved to Germany from a completely different cultural background. Because of his foreign origins he was often picked on and teased as a child. This, together with his parents' pressure to conform and their traditional style of child education, which included beatings, led to the repeated experience of humiliation and shame. He tried to overcome this by doing well at school and subsequently by acquiring detailed knowledge of the financial markets. Through clever transactions he accrued a fortune of several million dollars by the age of twenty one. After feeling wrongly criticised by a superior he resigned from his job in an insurance company and decided to study economics, with the aim of becoming a fund manager in an international stock exchange. In order to devote all his time to his studies, he entrusted the administration of his fortune to his father. However, when his father did not act fast enough during a crisis in the financial markets, most of the fortune was lost in a short time.

Mr B's ensuing depression and feelings of disgruntlement made it difficult for him to study. He narrowly failed his exams several times, moved to another university, and eventually gave up after the death of an idealised professor and after a previously passed exam was not recognised. Since then he had withdrawn from the world and was full of resentment and contempt. He blamed his father's "stupidity" for his failure and refused to try a new start in life. Instead he expected to be reimbursed for his unjust losses.

Thus he lived at home and tyrannised his parents, whom he accused of living in derelict squalor because they had not followed his "instructions". Related to this, I later learned, were accusations against the father that he had had an affair when the patient was around fourteen years old and disappointment with his mother for having stayed with her husband. He had only once been able to voice his feelings towards a young woman and he could not cope with her rejection. In the same year he witnessed the terror attack on the World Trade Center in New York. In my view the collapse of the Twin Towers seemed to represent the collapse of his omnipotent self as well as the murderous rage against his parents. So he spent most of his time in financial analyses in front of his computer, occasionally self-harmed, and let his parents feel his resentment. After several suicide threats he started psychoanalytic treatment, which he experienced as a humiliating confirmation of his condition as well as a futile effort to give him back his pride, success, and financial independence.

Course of treatment

During one of our first sessions Mr B mentioned that he was not sure whether he might not put a knife through his heart immediately afterwards. I was shocked and alarmed but also angered by his attack and interpreted that he was putting a knife to my chest and giving me the responsibility if things did not go the way he wanted. He made me to understand that the treatment could not change much in any case and he returned to his enraged accusations. At the end of another session, he said he could not imagine that any human being had ever been as unjustly humiliated as he had.

In the subsequent sessions, his attitude towards me varied between admiration, contempt, or subjugation in relation to me as a cruel figure who demanded "absolute obedience". I will go on to show that all three constellations contained aspects of a cruel, persecutory superego.

In the subsequent long period of his analysis Mr B was almost exclusively preoccupied with the past, whereas my attempts to look at his current state were rejected. For instance, he described in minute detail the ups and downs of the share prices in 2001, the failures of his father, the unjustified criticism by a former course leader, and the failure to be credited for an exam passed at a previous university. When he filled the sessions with such monotonous accusations he seemed difficult to reach. I often felt tired, hopeless, or annoyed, while my futile efforts to establish emotional contact were ignored with charitable negligence. For Mr B it was clear that this treatment came "too late" and that his misery was *not* my fault.

Many months passed in this tug of war. While I was trying to bring him into the "here and now", he kept ignoring my interpretations and drew me back into the "there and then" (O'Shaughnessy, 2013). I could sense a powerful grievance and rage. The only solution, the only form of "reparation" he could imagine, he said, was a return to the state prior to the loss of his fortune and the failure of his studies. As he well knew that I would not be able to bring about this state, my interpretations were experienced as irrelevant or as taunts, which left me feeling rejected and angry. In particular, when he presented his father as simple, lazy, and useless, I was more than once provoked into getting carried away pointing out that he was unbearably arrogant. Such "rebuke", as he called it, hurt him, but he did not let on.

The retreat to an inaccessible island

Nevertheless his condition stabilised after about two years and he tried to rebuild his fortune by skilful financial investments. He continued to refuse to seek regular employment and experienced it as a "punishment of fate to have such incompetent parents as his". On the surface of it I was excluded from this accusation, but I experienced myself as unable and unsuccessful in relation to the patient. Repeatedly, Mr B let me know that he experienced relationships with people as disappointing and it seemed clear to me that the relationship with me could only be another disappointment.

At a time when the conflicts with his parents were coming to a head, he contemptuously said that he wanted "no more to do with this world".

Then he created the picture of a desolate island, on to which he had retreated and from which he kept people off with a large "No trespassers" sign. From this island, he was going to follow the worldwide stock exchanges in the hope of reconstructing his former wealth through clever investments and thus be able to live a life of independence and abundance. While no one was allowed to come close to the island, I was permitted to land from time to time in a small boat to bring him provisions. But even I was not permitted access to the "darker areas" inside the island.

To me this picture seemed as much imaginative as provocative. While I was trying to interpret his self-righteous wrath, he made me feel that indeed I did not have access to these "darker areas" in his internal world. A kind of helplessness spread in me and one day I even caught myself carefully checking the share prices in the mad hope that if they rose, my patient would get better.

It seemed that I had lost confidence in my work and instead had become identified with my patient's omnipotent belief system. I thought the "provisions" I was allowed to deliver to the island were upholding the status quo without finding real access to his internal world.

Emerging from the retreat and moving back into it

There were times, however, when a better contact developed. When he once again began a session by saying "In the year 2000 …", and I expected him to continue with his usual complaints about his father's failure, he continued by saying: "In 2000 I would not have understood your interpretations". To my surprise, he added, if he understood me correctly, his greatest problem was his attitude of all or nothing and thus he was his worst enemy. And after a short pause he let me know that he was invited to visit friends in Switzerland who organised white-water rafting tours for tourists with expert guides from New Zealand.

I had the impression that telling me about this invitation expressed an appetite for life, and I said that he was considering trusting my guidance in moving off his desolate island into rough waters. He responded that someone who has never had the experience of failure like me would probably never understand him, and immediately I had the impression that I was being given another lesson on failure and misunderstanding.

For Mr B, of course, it was difficult to feel understood by me. From his point of view I was in an ideal situation, equipped with all the attributes he longed for; money, prestige, academic achievement, and a family. This made him envious and, although he acknowledged my "analyses" as "correct", he was insistent that I could never empathise with him.

Mr B "understood" my interpretations on an intellectual level but could not really take them in and make use of them. His problem was that he lacked a capacity for reparation. Instead of acknowledging the damage he inflicted on others, he was preoccupied with the injustice done to him. He projected his wish for reparation and demanded reparation for what he felt was rightfully his and was unjustly kept from him; in particular, money, success, and respect. For this reason, reparation meant concrete restitution rather than making amends.

Thus Mr B experienced life and his analysis as a constant humiliation. He despised dependency and sought to recreate an illusory state in which everything belonged to him and he was not dependent on anyone. He tolerated treatment on his solitary island as long as this provided food for his illusions and his campaign of revenge. However, he seemed to reject analysis whenever it was likely to get him in touch with the reality of mourning and loss.

Wrath—the impossibility of reparation

In this hopeless situation, time passed by without any prospect of change. It became increasingly clear that Mr B was dominated by a cruel superego, which forced him into a stance of either moral superiority or absolute obedience. He claimed the higher moral values for himself and thus justified his withdrawal from other people, though he regretted not having been able to have a relationship with a woman.

Feelings of humiliation could quickly flip into states of rage and indignation, where he looked down on other people. He complained endlessly about the "stupidity" of his parents and their numerous shortfalls. He could spend whole sessions in disdain of his mother, who had used a fork in a Teflon frying pan despite his "warnings", and his father, who had no table manners, drove like an idiot, did not use his hearing aids, and generally did not follow his advice and "instructions". And this was why he had stopped talking to him. Talking like this, his voice grew louder and louder. He escalated into an excited rage, described his parents as "hopeless cases", and asked himself how much longer he would be "patient with them".

In turn, *I* increasingly experienced him as a hopeless case and sometimes lost patience with him. He indulgently ignored my attempts to interpret his accusations as directed towards me. If he experienced my comments as criticism he either submitted obediently or stopped talking to me and at times this led to loud confrontations in which I found myself carried away into reproaching him.

In the case of the scratched Teflon pan, he had accused his mother of "poisoning" the food, while I accused him of not wanting to see that he was poisoning other people's food with his angry accusations.

There followed a long silence until he got back into his reproachful and hurt manner of talking about his mother's misdemeanours. I interpreted that he had experienced my comment as a sharp fork, which had scratched his thin internal protective layer and thus poisoned his food.

Although he seemed to experience this interpretation as far-fetched, he listened carefully. In a more lively and engaged way he protested against my view of his moral superiority by saying that he had a right to think like this. But then his protest flipped into indignation and he declared: "Because of my failures and unjust humiliations, I have developed a strict moral code. And if you think that I have an attitude of moral superiority or you think that an attitude of 'laissez faire' towards my parents would be a better solution, I am definitely of a different opinion."

This indignation could rapidly change into anger and then his contempt and hatred assumed self-destructive proportions. In angry indignation reparation can only be thought of as mercy and this is exactly why it makes the idea of reconciliation nearly impossible. In this state of mind the patient seemed to prefer "to reign in Hell than serve in Heaven" (Milton, *Paradise Lost*, Book 1, 263).

Thus the therapy had to be conducted in this "hell". And why should I be spared from going through this hell with him? In the transference I was identified either with the contemptible parents or with a vengeful superego, and he imagined that *I* felt in possession of higher moral standards in my omnipotent belief that I could change him. Evidently I had to admit my own failure to understand him, before I could take in some of his desperate isolation. After his self-righteous moral declaration, he felt alone and let me know after a long weekend that he felt worse without the sessions. On this occasion a more desperate sadness and clinginess became apparent, which had previously been absent.

On the threshold to the depressive position—despair and retreat

Nevertheless, the conflict with the parents escalated when they accepted an invitation to a wedding abroad. He had declined to accompany them and despised them for accepting the relatives' offer to pay for their travel costs. With "absolute obedience" he drove the parents to the airport, but did not speak a word or even look at them. At home he unplugged the phone so that they could not contact him. He wanted them to remain in doubt about his well-being, while suicidal fantasies and projections of guilt dominated his ideation.

This situation was mirrored in the treatment by his "advice to anyone" *not* to contact him. He said that he was on "the path to self destruction" once again, that "the coldness inside" himself was coming to a head and that he could do to himself what others had done to him previously.

I interpreted that here too he had unplugged, sent me warning signals and let me know that nobody could prevent him doing harm to himself. He reacted with angry bouts of rage, saying that he was pleased that his parents were away. He claimed to be the only person who could help him by rebuilding his fortune. Otherwise life was meaningless for him.

I suggested that he regarded my endeavours as pretty useless, felt terribly lonely, and doubted that anyone could understand his despair. As I said this, I had little hope of being able to reach him and was close to giving up.

It was at moments like this that Mr B occasionally got into a state of deep sadness. Then his superiority and rage collapsed and he became completely desperate and helpless. I feared that he would harm himself at the point of relinquishing his destructive system. I said to him that he attempted to hold himself together by sustaining his grievance, so as not to be overwhelmed by sadness, dependency, and guilt. He replied that he agreed with my "analysis, but *just could not forgive*".

Much to my surprise, he told me in the last session before the Christmas break that he had replied to Christmas cards for the first time in years and was planning to visit friends. After he had said his goodbyes and wished me a good Christmas, he turned round and said with tears in his eyes: "And thank you very much for being always here for me in the past year!"

Such moments could be very moving and gave a glimpse of a capacity for gratitude, which had been hidden for a long time. Mr B worried that he might not be able to finance the four-times-weekly sessions once the health insurance stopped paying, although I had indicated that I was prepared to make financial accommodations for him. He wanted to know whether he was allowed to return to the analysis at a later date and whether I was prepared to have him back and he announced that if he were to make money on the stock exchange, he would invest it in his analysis. His mother had said to him he should not worry so much about his future and he had begun to talk more with his father.

These movements made me feel hopeful, but could easily be obscured when humiliation and shame dominated. At such times, his accusations and wrath grew to monstrous proportions and he retreated into his rageful defensive system in which he "ordered about" his parents like unruly children and wished them dead. At such times, he spoke of his three "basic premises" for any kind of possible change. First, he had to get back his lost fortune, second, others were the guilty ones and they had to change first, and third, the clock had to be turned back and the bad experiences of his childhood had to be undone.

Conclusion

Mr B's three anti-therapeutic "basic premises" illustrate the foundation of his defensive system and his almost psychotic misrepresentation of reality. Because of his professional failure and the demeaning experiences of his childhood, he felt humiliated and demanded that others take responsibility for this. The persistence of his grievance and the omnipotence of his wrath made, for a long time, any attempt at reparation nearly impossible. His way of dealing with his-primitive superego was to identify with its ideal, omnipotent aspects as well as its cruel and persecutory ones. In this way he felt superior to his parents and entitled to look down on them and to humiliate them. In this context Money-Kyrle (1962, p. 384) wrote of an envious usurping of the superego by the ego.

In the analysis both aspects of his superego were projected into me so that I was either an ideal object who constantly evoked his envy, or a cruel object who demanded "absolute obedience", put him down, and relentlessly rebuked him with "sharp criticism".

For a long time there seemed to be no way out of this situation and I had to resist my own sense of failure and disappointment. During this period I would put the blame on him and demand that *he* change. I was identified with my patient as I dealt with my sense of failure by projecting it into him. In so doing we got into a situation where each demanded that the other change. It was a dead end, in which grievance and feelings of revenge thrived and the possibility of reparation was made very difficult.

In her 1958 paper, Melanie Klein points out that ego and superego can only change *collectively*. (This is somewhat different from Ron Britton (2003) in his essay "Emancipation from the superego".) This means that changes in the ego functions can take place when the superego relinquishes some of its cruelty and omnipotence. Only then do guilt feelings become more bearable and a process of reparation can begin. Again I would like to quote Klein:

> At this stage the injured object is no longer predominantly felt as a persecutor, but as a loved object towards whom a feeling of guilt and the urge to make reparation are experienced. (Klein, 1958, pp. 241–242)

In other words, it is the transformation of the superego from a pathological organisation into a helpful entity that limits the ego but also encourages it to come to terms with its worst anxieties by maintaining the good object. In Mr B's case such endeavours of reparation became observable when his mood became more mournful and he felt helpless.

However, such movements could trigger a degree of despair, and during those times I feared he could harm or kill himself. It was as if he could only survive by holding on to his grievance and wrath. I think at those moments Mr B approached the threshold of the depressive position, but then retreated into his defensive system when the emerging anxieties and feelings of guilt became unbearable.

I think of grievance as a state in which the wounds are kept open and the wish for reparation is projected into an object whose every attempt at reparation will be denied (Weiss, 2008). On the other hand, in his wrathful righteous indignation Mr B seemed identified with a morally superior position. At times he felt like a god and that the world was not good enough to deserve his love. In such a position, reparation is only possible in the form of mercy.

Both states of mind, grievance and wrath, render the processing of guilt very difficult. Instead of enabling reparation, they trigger feelings of humiliation and contrition or nourish feelings of revenge, thus perpetuating the damage to the internal objects. Mr B was well able to see this vicious cycle and even agreed with my "analyses", but he just could not forgive.

I believe, though, that genuine understanding is bound up with the possibility of reparation. While humiliation and shame require immediate relief (Steiner, 2006), reparation requires time,

time to acknowledge transience and loss. And it is exactly this experience that Mr B tried to avoid by withdrawing to a timeless state of mind. The only possibility of reparation, as he put it in his third "premise", was the reversal of time, a return to paradise.

When the path to reparation fails, the compulsion to repeat takes over, maybe not just in the individual mind, but also in certain social and historical developments. In this way, Mr B's third premise appears like a backward-looking historic utopia (Weiss, 2011).

I would like to conclude with a thought by Money-Kyrle (1956) in his early paper on countertransference, where he says that by projecting his internal objects into the analyst the patient comes to stand for the analyst's own damaged internal objects. In his view, true understanding goes along with the *analyst's* capacity for reparation. In Mr B's analysis I had reached a point more than once where I had lost all hope for development and change. Then I projected my helplessness back into my patient and held him responsible for my failing.

Only in those moments when I had to acknowledge my limits to tolerate and understand, did it become possible for Mr B to admit to himself how lonely and desperate he actually felt. It seemed as though both analyst and patient had to experience the collapse of their omnipotence in order to recognise the limits of what is achievable and devise realistic goals (Steiner, 2011).

In the case of Mr B that meant, as he once put it, that the "breaking waves" against his lonely island were getting softer and he could ask me whether he might be able to return. I think that this question contained an expression of his uncertainty as to whether I would be able to forgive him. In his paper on reparation Rey (1986) suggests that the development of a capacity to forgive is in turn linked to the possibility of being able to imagine *being forgiven*. In this sense, I think, the analysis of Mr B could not solve his problems, but might at least have helped him to live with them.

References

Britton, R. (2003). Emancipation from the superego. In: *Sex, Death, and the Superego* (pp. 103–116). London: Karnac.

Feldman, M. (1997). Groll: die zugrundeliegende ödipale Konfiguration. In: R. Britton, M. Feldman, & J. Steiner (Eds.), *Groll und Rache in der ödipalen Situation. Perspektiven der Kleinianischen Psychoanalyse* (pp. 733–758). Tübingen: edition diskord. (Grievance: The underlying oedipal configuration. *International Journal of Psychoanalysis, 89*: 733–758.)

Freud, S. (1911c). Psychoanalytic notes on an autobiographical account of a case of paranoia (dementia paranoides). *S. E., 12*: 3–82. London: Hogarth.

Klein, M. (1935). A contribution to the psychogenesis of manic-depressive states. In: *The Writings of Melanie Klein* (Vol. 1, pp. 262–289). London: Hogarth, 1975.

Klein, M. (1940). Mourning and its relations to manic-depressive states. In: *The Writings of Melanie Klein* (Vol. 1, pp. 344–369). London: Hogarth, 1975.

Klein, M. (1946). Notes on some schizoid mechanisms. *International Journal of Psychoanalysis, 27*: 99–110.

Klein, M. (1958). On the development of mental functioning. In: *The Writings of Melanie Klein* (Vol. 2, pp. 236–263). London: Hogarth, 1975.

Malcolm-Riesenberg, R. (1988). The constitution and operation of the superego. *Psychoanalytic Psychotherapy, 3*: 149–159.

Milton, J. (1668). *Paradise Lost. A Poem in Ten Books*. London: 1668.

Money-Kyrle, R. (1956). Normal countertransference and some of its deviations. In: D. Meltzer, & E. O'Shaughnessy (Eds.), *Collected Papers* (pp. 330–342). Strathtay, Perthshire: Clunie, 1978.

Money-Kyrle, R. (1962). Megalomania. In: D. Meltzer, & E. O'Shaughnessy (Eds.), *Collected Papers* (pp. 376–388). Strathtay, Perthshire: Clunie, 1978.

O'Shaughnessy, E. (1999). Relating to the superego. *International Journal of Psychoanalysis, 80*: 886–870.

O'Shaughnessy, E. (2013). Where is here, when is now? *International Journal of Psychoanalysis, 94*: 7–16.

Rey, H. (1986). Reparation. *Journal of the Melanie Klein Society, 4*: 5–35.

Rusbridger, R. (2011). Narcissism and grandiosity in *King Lear*. Unpublished lecture, Robert-Bosch-Krankenhaus, Stuttgart, 22 October 2011.

Segal, H. (1978). *Delusion and Artistic Creativity and other Psychoanalytic Essays*. London: Free Association.

Segal, H. (1991). *Dream, Phantasy and Art*. London: Routledge.

Steiner, J. (1990). The retreat from truth to omnipotence in Sophocles' *Oedipus at Colonus*. *International Review of Psychoanalysis, 17*: 227–237.

Steiner, J. (1992). The equilibrium between the paranoid-schizoid and depressive positions. *New Library of Psychoanalysis, 14*: 46–58.

Steiner, J. (1993). *Psychic Retreats: Pathological Organisations in Psychotic, Neurotic and Borderline Patients*. London: Routledge.

Steiner, J. (2006). Seeing and being seen: Narcissistic pride and narcissistic humiliation. *International Journal of Psychoanalysis, 87*: 939–951.

Steiner, J. (2011). The numbing feeling of reality. Unveröffentlichter Vortrag, gehalten am 25.06.2011 am Robert-Bosch-Krankenhaus, Stuttgart.

Weiss, H. (2008). Groll, Scham und Zorn. Überlegungen zur Differenzierung narzisstischer Zustände. *Psyche—Z Psychoanal, 62*: 866–886.

Weiss, H. (2011). Utopien und Dystopien als Orte des seelischen Rückzugs. In: M. Teising, G. Schneider, C. E. Walker (Eds.), *Leben und Vergänglichkeit in Zeiten der Beschleunigung*. Frankfurt a. M.: Geber und Reusch.

Weiss, H. (2012). Wiedergutmachung beim Borderline-Patienten. *Jahrbuch der Psychoanalyse, 65*: 59–80.

CHAPTER TWENTY

The perfect is the enemy of the good: on idealisation and self-idealisation

Lynne Zeavin

In Nathaniel Hawthorne's story "The birthmark" (1844), the author tells the tale of a young couple recently wed. The groom is a man of science whose devotion to his work has only recently been paired with his love for a beautiful woman. He wins her hand in marriage only to discover some trouble quite soon thereafter. One day, contemplating her perfection, he is unsettled to find a tiny birthmark on her face, which, until that moment, he had overlooked. All at once, he is overcome by its presence and he asks her if she has ever considered having it removed. Embarrassed by the question, she tries to deflect it by calling on previous experience of this birthmark as "charming". In response, the husband replies, "On another face [it might be a charm] … but never on yours. You came so nearly perfect from the hand of Nature that this slightest possible defect, which we hesitate whether to term a defect or a beauty, shocks me, as being the visible mark of earthly imperfection" (p. 148). His shock is a poignant depiction of the failure of idealisation; the birthmark signals a kind of intrusion into his vision of perfect and pristine beauty. Even this minute blemish is enough to wreak havoc with his need for absolute perfection. The husband cannot live with even the slightest threat to his vision of the ideal.

The seemingly unobtrusive birthmark illustrates what Klein knew well—that the ideal is necessary, vital even, for protecting against the encroachment of terrible paranoid anxiety, anxiety that in certain cases requires an intricate, if delicate, set-up based on idealisation of self and object. This situation requires that all awareness of the less than ideal be vigorously split off.

As readers, we are meant to know that the birthmark is inconsequential, that for everyone else in the wife's young life, if it has registered at all, it has only been seen as an endearing feature. But for the husband it is the unbearable testimony of the "hand of Nature" itself. Imagining the wife's perfection has given rise to the idea that the wife is "beyond nature's grasp" and as such unmarked by any prior relation. She is absolutely his. Being beyond earthly limit situates each of them outside the realities of time and mortality, and of separation and loss.

For the husband, a scientist, that she is in fact thus marked becomes a most personal challenge. He sets about finding a cure for the birthmark—which for him is conceived of as an act, not of modification, but of restoration, as benign as restoring a flawed painting to its original form. At the outset we can see that the husband's effort will never be really reparative. He is so furiously and manically driven, so imbued with the need to restore his own idealisations (of his wife and, reflectively, of himself) that we anticipate a terrible end. One has the sense of his frailty, that he would dissolve, his ego in bits, if not held together by the fantasy of absolute dominion over a perfect object.

Driven in this way, the man of science sets out to eliminate the birthmark.

After some exhortation from her husband, the wife agrees with his proposal to find a tonic that will cure her. Over the course of their discussions she too becomes horrified by the once inconsequential birthmark. Once only the repository for her husband's disturbance, the birthmark now functions to join the two of them in a shared quest to establish perfection. After several unsuccessful attempts, the husband administers his final cure, entering a state of ecstasy as he watches the birthmark fade. His exclamations over his wife's perfection are simultaneously exclamations of his own—a divine grandeur envelopes them both. But quickly, fatefully, he is made to comprehend his error. Holding up a mirror to her face so that she can view his handiwork, the wife realises the terrible conclusion of his/their efforts. She knows that she is dying. "At last the crimson tint of the birthmark—that sole token of human imperfection—faded from her cheek, the parting breath of the now perfect woman passed into the atmosphere, and her soul, lingering a moment near her husband, took its heavenward flight" (p. 162).

Hawthorne's tale is at once a critical commentary on American Enlightenment ideals in the nineteenth century—the quest of science to triumph over nature—and an apocryphal tale of a woman's ultimate renunciation of herself as she attempts to become the object that her object requires at any cost to herself. At the same time, it is the tragic story of a deeply narcissistic man who requires a sense of perfect mastery of himself and his object as a way of managing a terrible internal state that any site of imperfection seems to evoke. His need to be in total possession of his object leads him to make an unspeakable mistake, a mistake that unmasks his own marked destructiveness.

"The birthmark" takes us into a psychic world where brittle primitive idealisations protect against the awareness of a broken-down object, a disintegrated object for whom more ordinary care is insufficient, an object beyond repair. Idealisation is the solution to what is felt to otherwise be encroaching, leeching, impossible damage. The degree of damage felt to be in one's object (and therefore in oneself) is evidenced by the all-out perfection required to eradicate it.

Such an object relation aims at the perfect fit of an idealised union. This impregnable union will ward off all flaw. But, as "The birthmark" illustrates, the union, far from being actually stable, depends upon keeping reality at bay. Reality itself (both internal and external) is the source of danger and persecution. The result is an untenable split: idealisation here, reality there. Idealisation remakes our objects in innumerable ways—loving not hating, smooth instead of flawed, robust rather than in need of repair. As long as idealisation holds, the split-off dimension stays where it needs to be. But when the split weakens and the relation cannot be maintained, the overwhelmed and persecuted ego essentially comes undone.

"The birthmark" describes the frantic and driven effort of manic reparation. Tiny though it is, the birthmark bears witness to a threatening and hateful presence. For our scientist in the story, it is a reminder that he is not in sole possession of his object, that there has been "the hand of nature" before him. The unendurable hand of nature references all that preceded him—beginning with the parents' relation that conceived her. Perfection via idealisation is his only solution to a kind of madness. But the solution itself is madness. The need to idealise his object and possess the object entirely and forever obliterates time and history—it obliterates reality.

Melanie Klein wrote about the relation between idealisation and persecutory anxieties in 1946:

> One characteristic feature of the earliest relation to the good object—internal and external—is the tendency to idealize it. In states of frustration or increased anxiety, the infant is driven to take flight to his internal idealized object as a means of escaping from persecutors. From this mechanism various serious disturbances may result: when persecutory fear is too strong, the flight to the idealized object becomes excessive, and this severely hampers ego-development and disturbs object relations. As a result the ego may be felt to be entirely subservient to and dependent on the internal object—only a shell for it. With an unassimilated idealized object there goes a feeling that the ego has no life and no value of its own. I would suggest that the condition of flight to the unassimilated idealized object necessitates further splitting processes within the ego. For parts of the ego attempt to unite with the ideal object, while other parts strive to deal with the internal persecutors. (1946, p. 103)

Idealisation for Klein represents a necessary but transient state in normal development: idealisation is the "safeguard against a retaliating or dead mother and against all bad objects" (1940, p. 157). In the states of mind that I am considering here, idealisation has persisted and constitutes a central aspect of psychic reality; I think of it as constituting a preserve in the mind, where time is stopped, and development cannot proceed. Self-idealisation occupies an important place in this preserve. When the object is idealised as a means of diminishing the sense of threat, there is a corresponding idealisation of the self. Some patients for whom this is true speak of feeling not quite grown up, which makes sense because growing up depends on the capacity to face realities that require that idealisations be gradually given up. To my reading, in many reports of idealisation, self-idealisation is often in the background while we concentrate on the idealisation of the object. I want to explore the ways that self-idealisation enters the scene and the ways the two necessitate each other.

Here I mean to follow Klein, who did write about the very important place of self-idealisation. I hope to offer some elaboration of these ideas with clinical material.

Self-idealisation is a part of the early need for idealisation, and just like idealisation, protects the ego from the sense of internal persecutors. Klein described how in identifying with an ideal object, in an act of introjective identification, one might have the sense of being in possession of everything good. But this sudden being-in-possession of everything good is quite different from the development over time of a stable good object inside. Being in possession of everything good generates a sense of triumph and as such bears witness to the fantastic idealisation and manic defence that allows for it.

In the following clinical material, I want to highlight the uses of self-idealisation, which, along with idealisation of the object and the implicit manic defences involved, are dominant organisers of psychic life. In the first example, the patient is moving toward the depressive position; in the second case, the patient is locked down by omnipotent mechanisms and paranoid/schizoid functioning.

Ms A

Ms A is a woman in her mid-thirties who, after having twin daughters, came to analysis to address a debilitating inhibition in her work as a creative writer. She was obsequious in her attention to the analyst, offering thanks at the end of the session, or having an impossible time even imagining asking for a change in the schedule, or a delay in paying her bill—anything at all that would ask something of the analyst or risk inconveniencing me. At the same time it seemed that Ms A was conscious of being likeable—wanting and needing to be likeable (the referring person had described her in utterly glowing terms). In time, this was something she came to speak about. This moment in her life was confusing to her. She had always felt herself to be happy, always enthusiastic and engaged in her world, and now she felt anxieties that she thought were new (though, of course, as we talked we could see these anxieties early on but fended off).

Her sense of being at the centre of other peoples' attention had started in childhood—and she knew this from having watched movies of herself as a little girl where she would push her way into the centre of the frame. She said that if she didn't have this central place things would go dark and she wouldn't feel very sure of her existence, but early on in treatment she laughed this off—a silly fact of her childhood that was meant more to illustrate how central she was than to illuminate her fears of being left out or discarded, frightened of the implications of being outside and alone. In fact, Ms A's initial efforts at polite gesturing with me could feel like a clamouring for attention, which oddly I didn't mind—I felt pulled into a sense of it being agreeable to find her charming, engaging, very worthwhile. There was some pressure to notice and affirm what a special person Ms A was. Gradually I came to feel that this kind of response was compulsory, that she needed it as a way to manage both her own and my state of mind—our moods, my whole manner of responding to and treating her. That is, if I didn't feel her to be so special and central, her anxieties began to emerge.

O'Shaughnessy (1992) describes the establishment of an enclave in analysis as a situation in which the patient engages the analyst in an overly close bond that can stave off and screen out the patient's world of painfully envious internal objects while keeping a curious hold over the analyst's mind and creativity, denuding the analyst and her interpretive efforts. For the purposes of this paper, I want to emphasise the ways in which the object relationship that O'Shaughnessy describes as "over-close (but not close in a truer sense) and too well-attuned", is part of a psychic structure founded on early idealisations. The role of envy and jealousy, which are prominent forces in Ms A's psychic structure (and perhaps are forces at work whenever idealisation remains compulsory) are beyond the scope of this paper, where I want to develop the role of early self-idealisation as a defence against envy and difference and the unbearable experience of internal reality.

As work with Ms A proceeded it became clear that the enclave she created in the room was meant to keep a version of myself and of her out of sight and out of awareness. Very subtly she would evade my interpretations, mostly by emphasising her own great interest in what I had to say. Initially I mistook her self-reflective-sounding responses for real insight. What I eventually could see was that it was a way of putting herself at the centre of our frame—very visible, very much appreciated, but that little of what we talked about actually sunk in, as though the real aim was to be in the centre, the pleasurable object of my attention. One of the things under discussion was her need to feel me absolutely attentive and responsive to her—her response to this was often an amplification of yes, and how, and why. But the deeper anxiety, regarding a me who could either wish to disappear or be done with her, could not come into focus for a long time. What I want to emphasise is that it was stated and I would feel myself in this position, but there was an overwhelming force at work precluding us from actually getting in touch with the aspects of me in the treatment that correspond with this very troubling internal object.

Ms A's object is felt to be damaging, damaging by virtue of absence—absence in a literal and emotional sense (her mother seems to have been gone quite a lot throughout her childhood, including on birthdays and holidays), and absent particularly when a younger sister was born with a deformity that required multiple surgeries and intensive care from birth until about three years of age, and then absent again in adolescence when the parents' divorce meant that the mother herself was often out and preoccupied with her own recently rediscovered sexuality and love of dancing. Absence is important, for as Klein (1940) describes, the external real object puts a check on the internal world, and vice versa. Furthermore, the absence of the mother was not merely absence of something good but the presence of a tormenting and unpredictable object.

Ms A would claim to have a close relation to her mother while frantically working in the analysis and outside of it to be always the admired focus and centre of attention. Only when she was successful feeling admired and adored—which she seemed often to be—would she seem to "know where she was", that is, feel that she was filled up and pleased and free of anxiety. In other words, without the sense of being the centre of attention in the real external world she succumbed to a feeling of darkness inside, sometimes described as emptiness, sometimes described as an acute, nearly unbearable, feeling of anxiety. She once said that the first thing she had to do when arriving anywhere was to contact her mother. Only when her mother knew her whereabouts, could she then begin to relax and feel that she herself knew where she was. She described how as a child and adolescent the worst thing was to arrive home and be alone. She said, "It was so dark inside, I would just go next door where there was light." It has taken some years of analysis for Ms A to recognise the darkness as a state of mind, related to her early experiences of self and object. Light was associated with people who were happy to see her. But the people haven't consolidated as reliable figures inside. I have the sense that what makes this impossible is how painful it is to contend with the reality internally of being sent away, of being less than central (which seems to mean actually dropped and forgotten, actually in darkness) with an object who had other interests, other pulls—which were intolerable to consider.

What has gradually emerged are my patient's anxieties about my states of mind, particularly any sense that I am somewhere else in my attention, or wishing to be elsewhere. She worries that my efforts at caring for her are only partial and only because I have to. We have had moments in sessions where she feels she isn't succeeding in eliciting my admiration (or her own) and she feels dropped, suddenly, her eyes feel blurry, things "go dark". This was a theme of the analysis for some time, accompanied by a series of dreams in which I transformed in her presence from someone light and recognisable to a dark house or room where someone was hiding or was menacingly in shadow. In one dream she was playing a kind of "dress-up", taking quite a lot of time putting clothing and jewelry and make up on a woman she "didn't quite recognise". At the time, I interpreted that she goes to great lengths to dress me up and make me appear pleasing to her, to have me be exactly to her liking—and the other way round—but how just underneath there is a sense of being very worried by who I actually am were she not busy making all this effort (effort that sounded as though it was manically excited and driven in her dream), how in effect menacing and critical and unknowable I might be.

Ms A was disturbed by these dreams, disturbed by the suggestion and then feeling that she didn't really know me. The reality of not really knowing me made it possible that I could be anything, not simply someone of her own contriving. At this time she discussed being upset with one of her daughters and feeling that she "could not read her". This ushered in various thoughts about her relationship with her mother and with me, the sense of a mother who could actively disappear, both externally and internally, and who required her to be "a big girl", and to set aside all feelings save for the ones where she was knowing and strong. Once when she was about five years old her mother left her and her sister in the car to wait while she went to a dental appointment. My patient remembers being terrified, but her mother upbraided her for her unnecessary concern. She then stoically managed her fear, but felt very keenly the sense that she was deserted. Her ability to arrive at the stoical position did elicit praise, and the sense inside of being very good indeed. But the catch was—and is—that the only way to keep hold of her mother is to be without any disruptive feeling, to be captivating (articulate, poised, strong)—lest she feel utterly let go of and belittled, and dropped into darkness, eliminated, perhaps as a result of her failure to be the perfect object her mother required (hearkening back to the situation of "The birthmark").

In her paper "The absent object" O'Shaughnessy (1964) illuminates this clinical situation from a slightly different, though complementary, vantage point:

> For the wanted breast is in fact not a bad breast present, but a good breast absent when needed. The infant has in the course of time to come to know this fact, which is a fact of both inner reality—his need, and outer reality—the missing good breast. That is, the infant has to advance from experiencing the needed absent breast in the phantasy of a bad breast present, to being able to think of the real missing good breast. This crucial advance in his development is hard, since the bad breast, which in phantasy is present, is felt au fond to be starving him to death, and it is only by tolerating the pain and terrors of his frustration enough that he can put himself in the position of being able to think about them, to think, eventually, that what he needs is the missing good breast. Such knowledge, in thought, of the good breast will also help him to endure his state of need. Since tolerance of frustration is essential for thought to develop, the infant who predominantly avoids facing his frustrations and in phantasy simply gets rid of them, is employing methods actively antagonistic to thinking, so that the development of his mental powers will be, at the least, inhibited, and may be disturbed. Thus we may say that the absent object gives the child his first opportunity to know reality through thought, and also gives him the incentive, viz., to make frustration more tolerable. (p. 35)

It seems to me that part of what Ms A contends with is her lifelong difficulty coming to terms with her mother's real absences, and the enormity of her own fury and despondency in the face of this. Her internal predicament could not easily be assuaged by the external one—except through her efforts to be the centre of attention whenever possible. As a strategy early on, Ms A put herself in the centre of the frame, her way of describing her clamouring need to be always at the centre of the action, a desperate effort to feel the presence of an external object relating to an ideal her. In fact to feel something like an ordinary good object inside, the object that O'Shaughnessy describes as a result of contending with the object's absence and one's own fury and despondency, is still a long way off.

The good object inside can only be felt through a cycle of idealising/self-idealising that unfortunately vitiates the object's real usefulness. Ms A can express fury—but it is always rationalised as the other's failure to properly attend to her. She can now say that she knows her need for attention places an unfair burden on others, which she voices some regret about.

Ms A brought a dream that she said was the most terrifying of dreams, leaving her feeling nauseous and upset for the whole day until she could recount it. In the dream she is asleep and her father comes to waken her. Her father says to her, "Wake up, something terrible has happened—your mother has been killed in an accident. Oh my poor baby, you have lost your mother." As she told the dream she was crying. I thought it was significant that she was sleeping in her dream. It seemed to me that the part of her mind given over to self-idealisation was asleep to her despair and despondency, at least partly over her own murderousness and her early terror of being without her object. She feels her object eluding her grip, disappearing—which for her is akin to dying, but she also has her father being tender and concerned. What O'Shaughnessy makes clear is that the object being able to be felt alive inside, even while absent, has a great deal to do with one's own ability to tolerate without too much rage the object's independent life. Ms A's self-idealisation precludes her being able to tolerate for very long any awareness of her own destructiveness or greed, which then requires further self-idealisation and splitting. My patient's terror is grounded in a sense that the absence is forever, that she has killed off her object and that she can only refind the other in a oneness that follows from her own sense that that of them is absolutely all there is. If she isn't, compellingly, the centre of attention or takes her eye for a second off that aim, she feels she risks losing her object and her place in her object's mind.

Inasmuch as Ms A's world is dominated by underlying persecutory fears, she begins to show some capacity to accept understanding that goes beyond mere affirmation. Ms A is at times grappling with anxieties related to the onset of the depressive position and her pining for her objects is real and unmistakable—the father who can hold her, the analyst who can talk to her and help put real fears and unease into words. This vicious cycle is beginning to change with analysis—as her capacity to "pine" expands, the necessity for self-idealisation very gradually diminishes.

Idealisations recast what is a frightening world both internally and externally. What has been unloving and bad in oneself and one's object is written off, projected, denied, and remade by what Klein calls (1940) "violent or secretive or cunning methods"—only to return in dream images or persecutory anxiety and guilt that infiltrate one's sense of goodness and stability. Sodré (2015) refers to this as "the consequence of excessive splitting and projection of everything that is painful and disturbing is the simultaneous eruption of a hell which is then felt to be all around the self as a constant threat, always potentially returning and invading the mind" (p. 87).

Ms A's initial presenting symptom included the idea that she would be punished for having children, for thriving. Such success would then place her as a rival to a mother from whom she required a feeling of absolute primacy and importance in order to feel loved. If she succeeded, she would lose her mother; if she maintained her mother, she could not succeed. Appeasing an object is different from making reparation for the damage that has been felt to be done. Appeasing the object draws on a sense of one's own omnipotent capacities borne of self-idealisation—the ability to make everything whole and good again just by a particular sort of relating or fitting in. Self-idealisation always has a hand in appeasement, and appeasement itself can only generate a false sense of something reparative.

With Ms A, there is coming to be some sense of movement: as the need for idealisation lessens, loosens, there are moments of felt anguish, genuine self-reflection and insight, moments when she can receive interpretations without calling attention to the ability to respond. These oscillate with moments where her self-reflectiveness returns to being a way of fitting in with me, taking hold of me, and a source once again of self-idealisation and reprieve. Sorting this out and moving through it constitutes much of our work, but as we go on there is a growing sense of Ms A's capacity to show real interest and concern for her objects and to believe more realistically in the capacity of her objects to care for her.

Mr B

Mr B is a man in his early forties, who married and had a child in the course of his first five years of analysis. Though very successful in his career, and presenting as easy-going and confident, he came to analysis with what he described as a fear of breaking down and being revealed as "small, crumbling" by colleagues in his profession. As the eldest boy in a family of boys, he was his mother's favourite, but he particularly emphasises how his special love and care of his brothers led them both to always "look up at me". His sense of himself as concerned about his brothers, taking care of them, tending to them, harmonises with his experience of himself as an especially loving son and brother. He repeatedly notes, though, that, in spite of this love, his mother could be particularly harsh with him, because her expectations were so high. Proud of his multiple degrees from prestigious universities and the only child in his family to have thus succeeded, he laughingly refers to himself as needing to be the "smartest person in the room".

Mr B has a friendly manner and is very quick with words, adept at argument. He seemed to take easily to the work of analysis. What appeared initially as curiosity and a capacity for insight soon transformed into a pressure for me to see everything coming from him in much the same way: to admire/to affirm/to reassure him of its—and his—goodness. Anything that strayed from this would be felt as a lack of pleasure taken in him, or even a sign of taking offence at him. Complicating matters, of course, is the fact that I can indeed feel irritated and manipulated by his transparently extravagant humility and his overblown expressions. He doesn't so much take in an interpretation as seem to memorise it, often repeating it, and over the course of several repetitions the interpretation comes to be as lifeless and removed as can be, a ditty or refrain that he plays back to himself, but which has lost all its original heart and meaning. His idealisation of my interpretations strips them of their "imperfections" and also, similar to the activity of the scientist in "The birthmark", of their life. The interpretations themselves become rote explanations for what is going on, assuagements, rather than something that might need to be looked into or faced.

In our work, Mr B has the rather unusual habit of referring to me (frequently, compulsively) by my name. What has become clear is that there is an idealised "Dr Z" in his mind that obtains at the same time that he navigates and manages a real analyst in the room. In another time and in another space (one of his own making) I can be the Dr Z he admires and learns from, but in the room with me a much more fraught, indeed persecutory, experience has taken hold.

Mr B's need to control me, to dominate me in the sessions, keeps a me that has a mind of my own (a mind marked by the "hand of nature") at bay. But equally, and I think more importantly, it works to keep split off a damaged and frightening figure—while at the same time maintaining that he has only good feelings about me. Those good feelings form something like a preserve, untouched, unmarred by actual interaction.

Klein (1940) wrote:

> The young child, who cannot sufficiently trust his reparative and constructive feelings, resorts to manic omnipotence. For this reason in an early stage of development the ego has not adequate means at its disposal to deal with guilt and anxiety. When the defences of a manic nature fail, the ego is driven to combat the fears of deterioration and disintegration by attempted reparations carried out in obsessional ways. Obsessional mechanisms are a defence against paranoid anxieties as well as a means of modifying them. (p. 153)

The object must be managed in this way. As the management has over time broken down, the hell that Sodré describes—the threat of an all-encompassing persecutory guilt over the object's presence as a deteriorated figure—has made its presence amply felt, both within sessions and outside of them.

When Mr B was first in treatment everything was on a grand scale. He extolled his giving to charities, his concern over children dying in the world, wars, refugees, disasters. He wanted to be the person who could lift up the other, and be so large that he and he alone would be able to repair the damage. In smaller, more local, ways this would obtain, with me, where he seemed at great pains to lift me up (I hope you had a nice weekend)—or reassure me of my usefulness and a kind of fixed, brittle way of thanking me after each and every session. His need for a manic reparation required a sense of himself as being ingratiatingly kind, what he calls "humble", as a means of evading the sense of being damaging to his internal and external objects.

Mr B has one very unique relationship in his life. Besides his brothers, whom he refers to as "my guys", and his wife and new baby daughter, Mr B has a deeply private and compelling relation with what he calls his "to-do" list, a large document on his computer comprised of everything he must do—it is his ideal life in some sense, characterised by the novel he will write, the good work he will do, his plans to run for public office, etc., all the trips he will go on, because as he tells me, it would be terrible to die without doing it all. In addition he writes down everything he loves: his favorite people, films, works of art and literature—as though without writing them down he will lose them or lose track of them. Recorded, written down in an indestructible file, they are there for him and they are him. Not written down he worries that he will forget—that they won't be there inside, no reminders, only a kind of barren world.

Once they are in the to-do list they become the self-affirmation he needs to turn to for respite from the world of objects that inhabits and torments him.

The to-do list appears in sessions often as a form of reassurance, a virtual version of auto-eroticism in its way—that is, he turns back toward himself in frank self-idealisation, achieving distance between himself and me, where so often he feels hounded by my knowledge of him, by what he feels I might actually see and know in him. In other words, his efforts to turn our relation into an ideal one (the Dr Z relation), with him the ideally building-up son, I the ideally built-up other, are infiltrated and weakened by the inevitable disharmonies he encounters when I offer a view different from his own or different from that which he is comfortable hearing. Mostly this will happen if I ever attribute motivation to him; that is, if I locate in him destructive feelings such as contempt or a wish to control me, he reacts as though aghast, how could I possibly suggest this … at these moments he recruits others (brothers, friends) who think just the opposite, who have reassured him that in fact he is kind, not too aggressive, etc. At these moments I become the aggressive one, he can feel me as cruel, and I can feel myself turning cruel, or dismissive, in the countertransference. The world between us is simultaneously awash in persecutory anxiety—I can feel his dread of my intentions toward him—and yet at the same time there is his powerful retreat into the self-idealising world whose intention it is to quell such anxieties, to fill his mind with reassurances: he will say, "I worry about being destructive to K, but then I tell myself, 'C'mon buddy, there is nothing wrong with being angry once in a while'; I mean I know that I can be angry, but can't everyone? C'mon Dr Z, isn't it true that it's a good thing that I can admit my feelings—it doesn't mean these things have actual consequence." And then a little while later he will be describing with great relish his to-do list and the relieving feeling that nothing will ever be left undone.

Mr. B's to-do list gives me the sense of an alternate world where everything is possible, there is no limit, there is no loss. He can have everything. By putting it on paper it is as if it is already in his possession, where it remains forever. There is also the sense that in controlling things in this way he has control of his mind, but without it he can in fact become lost, his mind fails him. (He worries he won't remember his interests, his experiences—so they are catalogued, they are static). But as Sodré (2015) points out, "the narcissistic withdrawal from the object doesn't really mean that the attachment to the object is diminished or extinguished; on the contrary, there is in fact a tremendously possessive, intense relationship with the object taking place unconsciously in the internal world" (p. 166).

In the fourth year of treatment Mr B brought a dream.

He is with his wife, they are going out into the ocean (an idealised place for Mr. B). But suddenly it becomes clear that there is going to be a tsunami. He tells his wife to go back, to go back into the sea, when in the dream he knows better that she should come in. [He feels a nudge of guilt about this as he tells me about the dream but quickly reassures himself that this particular element doesn't mean anything.]

The very next scene in the dream is his wife coming back on to shore, carrying him in her arms. He can see himself, but he is not himself, but a him who, as he describes it, is quite damaged, in great need of help, and may be dying.

The dream conveys so well, I think, the split that Mr B is dealing with, a split that his self-idealisation helps to maintain. The serene and beautiful ocean is threatened by a terrible storm—the analysis that threatens him with a feeling of great danger both from without and from within. The life-threatening storm comes when idealisation falters. He tries and fails in this instance to control his object—to send her out into the threatening sea rather than to have her be "in" where she can threaten him. His destructiveness, which he makes light of and attempts to hide, is warded off, along with the potential damage to the object. The dream exemplifies what Klein describes in the following:

> The desire to control the object, the sadistic gratification of overcoming and humiliating it, of getting the better of it, the triumph over it—may enter so strongly into the act of reparation that the benign circle started at the beginning of this act becomes broken. The objects that were to be restored again become persecutors and paranoid fears are revived. (1940, p. 132)

This also happens in analysis in the day-by-day efforts to build me up that often feel like thinly disguised efforts to control my thinking and my mind, a way to manage me, to keep me away or to get away himself. The reparative effort is so infiltrated by triumph that of course it collapses. When I do get in, when I do make contact, which increasingly can happen for a brief moment, he misses sessions, or demeans the understanding that has felt to be very real that day or that moment before. This is obviously very complex, more complex than idealisation alone can account for, but the world he slips into, the to-do list world, bears similarities to the states of mind described by Sodré as pathological daydreaming: "Pathological daydreaming takes over the mind, replaces life with a made-up thing, and has a purely defensive, anti-life, but anti-internal reality function" (p. 72). The self-idealising world, restrictive as it is, means that nothing can be relinquished, nothing can be mourned, and reparation is constantly failing, infused as it is with triumph and contempt. Another way of considering the self-idealisation is as the remnant of a failure of a capacity to bear guilt. As Sodré (p. 24) also suggests, guilt becomes unbearable when reparation is felt to be impossible. And as such we can well imagine the retreat to an illusory internal world where the realities of loss and guilt are permanently held in abeyance.

To sum up then, idealisation and self-idealisation are crucial aspects of early normal development, preserving and strengthening the ego and helping to build up the presence of a whole good object inside. But self-idealisations can persist, leading to a turning away from reality, particularly an inner reality that cannot be faced. The presence of idealisation (just the other side of persecutory fantasies) interferes with the building up of a good object inside, as what is required instead is the presence of an ideal figure regarding one's goodness or being an ideal figure oneself. Such an organisation leads to what Sodré calls "replacing life with a made up thing" (p. 72). When very fixed, as with my second patient, it can lead to a retreat from life, to be anti-life, which is, of course, ironic given the great investment in being everything. But we see how the everything comes crashing down, like the terrible tsunami wave of my patient's dream, like our scientist's effort in "The birthmark", causing damage to oneself and one's object.

References

Hawthorne, N. (1844). The birthmark. Kindle Editions, 1987.

Klein, M. (1940). Mourning and its relation to manic-depressive states. In: *The Writings of Melanie Klein, Vol. I* (pp. 344–369). London: Hogarth.

Klein, M. (1946). Notes on some schizoid mechanisms. In: *The Writings of Melanie Klein, Vol. III* (pp. 1–24). London: Hogarth.

O'Shaughnessy, E. (1964). The absent object. *Journal of Child Psychotherapy, 1*: 34–43.

O'Shaughnessy, E. (1992). Enclaves and excursions. *International Journal of Psychoanalysis, 73*: 603–614.

Sodré, I. (2015). *Imaginary Existences: A Psychoanalytic Exploration of Phantasy, Fiction, Dreams, and Daydreams*. Hove: Routledge.

PART III

WORK WITH CHILDREN

CHAPTER TWENTY-ONE

Paranoid/schizoid position or paranoid and schizoid positions?*

Anne Alvarez

Introduction

It is well known that Melanie Klein made a vital distinction between the anxieties, defence mechanisms, and processes characteristic of the depressive position, and those characteristic of the paranoid-schizoid position. Her original distinction, in 1935, was between the depressive position and the "earlier paranoic position", but in the 1952 revision of her 1946 paper, "Notes on some schizoid mechanisms", impressed by the contributions of Fairbairn and Winnicott on the nature of unintegrated states, Klein extended the term paranoid to the paranoid-schizoid position (Fairbairn, 1952; Klein, 1935, 1946; Winnicott, 1945). She saw that schizoid withdrawal from feeling, with states of fragmentation and unintegration, were characteristic of these more disturbed states of mind in adults, but also, in slightly different ways in very young babies (Klein, 1946; Likierman, 2001).

I have used the following figures to illustrate the quantitative element implied in Klein's concepts. I apologise for their simplistic and two-dimensional quality. Figure 1 shows the depressive position, where love is stronger than hate, and goodness stronger than badness. In Figure 2, where the sense of badness outweighs the sense of goodness, I have termed the lower section the paranoid position, not the paranoid-schizoid position. In Figure 3, where the sense of goodness and badness are both weak, I have termed the lower section the schizoid position.

---

*An earlier version of this chapter was first read to, and then published in the proceedings of, the German Psychoanalytic Society's Annual Conference in Berlin, May 2012 (Reiser-Mumme, U., Tippelskirch-Eissing, D. von, Teising, M., & Walker, C. (Eds.) (2012), *Spaltung: Entwicklung und Stillstand*. Berlin: DPV. An even earlier, and very condensed, form of some of these ideas was published in the concluding chapter of *The Thinking Heart* (Alvarez, 2012a).

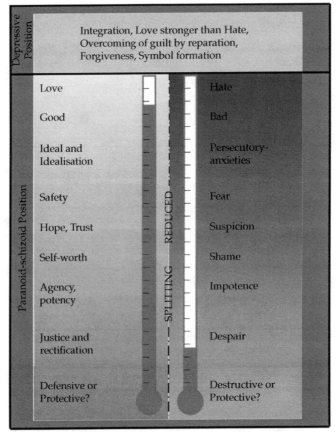

**Moments when the Sense of Goodness
is Stronger than Badness**

Figure 1. Integrated depressive states.

This is very over-simplified, because the kind of children I am thinking of as being in these affectless states include autistic children and neglected children, both of whom are different from schizoid or dissociated children. Yet I think that some subtypes of all these conditions do have something in common in terms of their deficit. In my view, although Bion's theory of "attacks on linking" has been taken to imply that all fragmentations are the result of disintegrating processes acting upon prior integrations, I think there is no need to see them as such (Alvarez, 2012b; Bion, 1959).

The concept of deficit (Stolorow & Lachmann, 1980) and Bick's somewhat similar concept of helpless unintegration (1968) have led to controversy for good reasons. They have seemed to challenge Freud's great insight into the dynamic nature of thought processes—their inherent meaningfulness and purposiveness. This is an old issue. Fairbairn pointed out that, although Freud's concept of repression was the foundation-stone upon which the whole explanatory

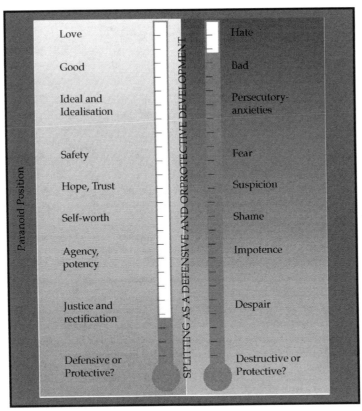

**Moments when the Sense of Goodness
is Too Weak to Overcome Badness**

Figure 2. Paranoid and/or persecuted states.

system represented by psychoanalytic theory had been built, this had nevertheless not been an unmixed gain, because it left no room for the idea of ego weakness (which, he pointed out Charcot had ascribed to the hysterics he and later Freud were treating) (Fairbairn, 1954, p. 14). In child work, we might add, the dynamic model that implies that every state of mind, however pathological, arises from meaningful motivation leaves no room for ego *immaturity* and therefore for the idea of something like helplessness (in relation to the advancement of certain more advanced states of mind).

I am suggesting that certain pathological, empty, affectless states do differ from even the most persecuted of states of mind. So I have divided the more persecuted or paranoid states from those characterised either by deficit, or by dissociation so chronic that it amounts to a deficit. Of course, schizoid and paranoid elements may coalesce in the same patient, but the diagnostic manuals for adult psychiatric patients themselves distinguish between paranoid types of schizophrenia characterised by disorganisation of speech, behaviour, and affect, and those more purely paranoid types, which are more organised (APA, 1994, p. 149).

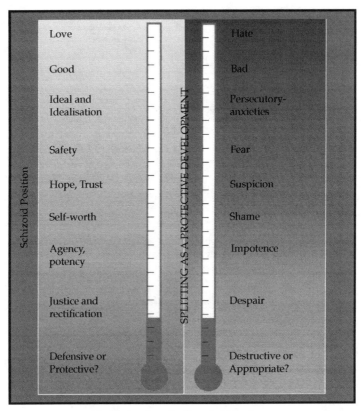

**Moments when the Sense of Goodness
and Badness are Both Extremely Weak**

Figure 3. Empty and/or dissociated states.

*But to stay for a while with the usual Kleinian term, that is,
the paranoid-schizoid position*

I have been suggesting for some years (1992, 1997, 2012b) that we need much more study of the tiny steps toward recovery *within* the paranoid-schizoid position, long before certain patients are anywhere near the depressive position. Most of these steps I first described involved tiny increments in the positive side of the split, for example, increases in trust, or hope, or love. But first, as a general concept, I suggested that we needed a concept of "overcoming" of persecuted states, rather than only a concept of defences against them. I borrowed the term "overcoming" from Klein's great meta-concept regarding the depressive position, where she insisted that reparation was not a defence *against* guilt—nor was it a reaction formation—it involved an *overcoming* of guilt that involved growth and creativity, not dead-end static defences (Alvarez, 1992; Klein, 1937). I suggested that we also needed a similar concept of overcoming for the paranoid-schizoid position. That is, how do we help a terrified child to overcome fear as opposed to deny or omnipotently control it? I thought we needed terms such as potency to stand alongside omnipotence; a sense of agency and pride to stand alongside defensive narcissism; relief, joy, and hope to stand alongside manic denial; order, structure, and predictability, and, for that matter, a sense of safety, to stand beside obsessional defences (Alvarez, 1992).

André Green suggested that, following Freud's great broadening of psychoanalytic theory beyond the sexual instincts to the idea of the conflict between the life or love instincts and the death instincts, we have neglected to pursue the study of the nature of these life instincts (Freud, 1920; Green, 1995, p. 877). Klein herself did insist on the importance of the gradual strengthening of the good object and of the individual libidinal (life instinct) impulses: this, she said, enabled the integration of the persecutory impulses and thus the move from the paranoid-schizoid position to the depressive (Klein, 1952). I am attempting to identify some of the elements in this strengthening, including elements in the development of the self as well as in the nature of the internal object (Alvarez, 1992).

Subsequently I suggested that a sense of rectification at the paranoid-schizoid position (not reparation as at the depressive position) may offer healing phantasies of a sense of justice, and even, of revenge (Alvarez, 1997, 2012b). I also suggested that certain psychopathic children, while in no way moving directly towards depressive position concern and empathy, seem sometimes in treatment to begin to be less grandiose and thus more concerned for their own well- being—thus a bit sobered down (Alvarez, 1995, 2012b). This is certainly paranoid-schizoid position level functioning—there is no remorse for damage done—but the child may be less grandiose, and thus a little saner, less dangerous to himself and others out of fear for himself, (such as expulsion from school or home). But it may nevertheless be a development. I have also suggested that certain states of despair, which probably belong in the paranoid-schizoid domain, have been seriously under investigated—they are very different from the depression of the depressive position, and yet also different from states of persecution (Alvarez, 2010b).

In "Notes on some schizoid mechanisms" Klein (1946) described in great detail the way a patient of hers could cut himself off from feelings and from her at the point when anxiety was being evoked: the defensive elements in his withdrawal are clear, and her subsequent interpretations served to bring him back in touch with feeling. Nevertheless, her description of the level of unreachability of her patient at such moments is very powerful. We might, with our modern understanding of post-traumatic stress disorder, describe such moments as moments of dissociation. And, with some of our most terrified child patients, interpretation of anxiety may serve only to escalate it.

John Steiner has added to the literature on the P-S position by distinguishing what he calls "psychic retreats" from more persecuted states. I have added that it would also be essential to disentangle elements of the near atrophy found in something like a psychic desert from those involved in the "psychic retreat" (Alvarez, 2010a; Steiner, 1993b) A psychic desert in infancy may gather defensive or addictive motives during the development to adulthood, and these motives would certainly need analytic attention. However, so also would the accompanying or underlying deficit where the object, rather than being avoided, is hardly found, due to its remoteness or weakness. In such states of mind, the patient is not hiding, he is lost. A retreat offers, at the very least, a place to go; a desert offers nothing.

In this chapter, I am interested in a more general issue, a quite fundamental development: that from affectless schizoid or autistic states to more alive states, regardless of whether the affect then experienced is positive or negative. Many patients make contact with a good object and it settles them. The same sometimes holds true for the integrating capacity of bad objects: I have occasionally seen autistic and psychotic patients move from a state of fragmentation to hallucinating, say, a terrifying object—where such a progression may be a development, because some part of the world is finally *not* inhabited by the bad object (Alvarez, 1992). (And see Rodriguez, 1955, on a similar case.) Badness is focused, contoured, and finally locatable within a confined space.

I would also want to add in to the group of affectless children those with marked psychopathic features (Alvarez, 1995, 2012b). One group of researchers has suggested that preschool disruptive behaviour needs careful study, and fine distinctions need to be made between more normal types of reactive aggression and those that seem more deliberate and calculating. Two important emerging markers are callous and unemotional states. Careful psychoanalytic clinicians make such distinctions all the time, and it is heartening to see these new researchers insisting that current psychiatric classifications for children are too crude and therefore still inadequate to the task of good assessment of the needs and suffering of the child and the risks he presents (Wakschlag et al., 2010). De Jong also pointed out that the then current classification system, DSM-IV, inadequately captured the range and type of psychopathology seen in the "in care" population of children (De Jong, 2010). And Van der Kolk, an expert in child abuse, has suggested that DSM-V should have included a new diagnostic entity, which he termed "Developmental trauma disorder," (Van der Kolk, 2009). And see Reid's proposal that a group of children with an "Autistic post-traumatic developmental disorder" may make up an important sub-group of children with autism (Reid, 1999).

To return to the addictive aggressive children: psychoanalysts, too, have had to learn to know when symptoms have deep symbolic meaningfulness, and when, as in the case of some psychotic preoccupations, some addictive behaviours, and some autistic repetitive behaviours, they do not (Alvarez, 1992; Joseph, 1982; Segal, 1957; Tustin, 1980). Such processes have become habitual, and are more like a "bad habit" and the patient becomes what Reid has termed "stuck"; and this may require different analytic techniques. Cognitive behavioural treatment is documented as having helped numerous patients with obsessive-compulsive disorder, depression, and anxiety, and it is my guess that this happens where the symptom has outworn its motivational usefulness. Where it has not, I believe they need psychoanalytic psychotherapy.

Concerning the deprived and neglected children: many of the children in these affectless states have gone beyond states of despair, to giving up or to dissociation. A more severe possible outcome is the blunting of mind and feeling, and the stunting of brain growth with its attendant emotional and cognitive delay, which can result from severe emotional neglect in infancy (Music, 2009; Perry, 2002). Perry has described a condition arising from emotional neglect leading to lack of dendritic and synaptic growth in the brain. It is possible to imagine that a baby or child with weak brain growth would be less likely to summon necessary defences against stress. The type and the sophistication of the "defences" available to the infant seem to depend on his age and stage of emotional and cognitive development (Papousek, H., & Papousek, M., 1975). Such children or babies seem to lack integrating processes, not, I suggest, to be attacking them. It is important to note also that the brain researchers see dissociation as an automatic, protective, and initially much-needed mechanism, which can become unproductively habitual. I think we clinicians sometimes need to be reminded of this element of need in order to ensure that we move very carefully in helping patients to give up their defences. We can sometimes tend to see the underlying feelings of, for example, fear or despair, as truer than the rightful need for safety or love expressed in the defences.

We may also need to leave room for the possibility that chronic dissociation in infancy and childhood produces such an extreme level of cognitive delay that, in other words, chronic disintegration may lead to unintegration. Chronicity and severity are major factors in all pathology: children and adolescents with these histories of neglect fail to pay attention, not necessarily because they are defending themselves against thinking, nor because they are suspicious of and hate teachers; they simply expect nothing of interest to emerge from an encounter with another person. They have internal objects that are unvalued, not devalued. Something similar may be seen in a type of autism where the autism has turned the child away, in earliest infancy, from the world of other human beings to his own repetitive preoccupations with inanimate objects.

A further attempt to calibrate developments within the P-S position: a differentiation between the paranoid and schizoid positions

I wish to draw attention to states of mind that are no longer so evidently defensive but which, sometimes due to the regular and repeated nature of trauma, have become chronic and habitual. Children in such states may have shut down so early that certain life-giving and interpersonal connections in the mind-brain are barely functioning. So I want to distinguish chronic general dissociation from temporary defensive dissociated states. We are, therefore, in the realm of deficit—deficit not only in the self, but also in the internal object. That is, it is not a question of whether other people are loved or hated, it is whether they are felt to be interesting, whether, that is, they *matter*. Certain blunted empty children—different from the chronically dissociated children—are blunted emotionally but also cognitively; their minds seem empty of affect and of curiosity, and they pose similar problems in terms of our technical problems in finding ways of reaching them and finding something alive in them to which to relate. With the dissociated children, connections have been made, but cut: in the case of the blunted children, certain connections were never made in the first place. In some cases—those with autism—the child's autism has led to a situation of emotional neglect, because the child has not shown the usual object-seeking tendencies, and parents unknowingly have begun to give up trying to get their attention (Acquarone, 2007).

Five clinical vignettes; two persecuted and three dead and affectless

A paranoid state where necessary projective identification of badness played a part in recovery

A disabled and deformed girl, Jill, condemned to live life in a wheelchair, became desperate and suicidal when she moved from her primary school to a large secondary school. After a few months in therapy, she began to make her therapist sit in a chair with Sellotape wrapped around her legs. She told the therapist that she (the therapist) would never get out, she would have to stay there forever. The game was pretend (the therapist was not really trapped) but the tone was deadly—acidly—serious. Clearly this figure represented Jill, but from the clinical point of view it was important for the therapist to imagine—and to describe—this extremely disturbing experience as belonging to herself and not to return the projection in the early stages. The patient not only wanted, she needed to *try on* the identity of being the healthy one, while seeing someone else experience despair and bitterness on her behalf. She felt it ought to be somebody else's turn. The sense of urgent and rightful need is very different from a wish—even a passionate wish—that things be otherwise, and the therapist's words, countertransference responses and dramatisations can reflect that. The game began sadistically, but as the weeks progressed, it became more symbolically dramatised, and eventually—at moments—humorous. Returning the projection prematurely would only have increased the child's already unendurable frustration and despair and prevented the slow exploration of painful truths. She knew perfectly well how disabled she was and how deep was her despair. But somewhere she had a preconception of herself as a healthy able being, and here she found an opportunity for that to be realised, if only in fantasy. I am stressing here that the usefulness of such containment by the therapist need not only be seen as a step along the way to subsequent re-introjection of the sense of disablement, but rather also as a necessary step in the growth of hope and agency (and the desire for a decent, partially able life) in the self that has been left behind while carrying out the needed projection. Kundera described the way in which justice and even revenge phantasies could lead to the "rectification" of a lifelong feeling of bitterness (Kundera, 1982). The therapist's containment of projective identification seemed to enable Jill to recover from her despair and to begin to see herself as more able. Careful monitoring should warn us of the danger of going on too long and too passively with such receptivity, and of therefore denying reality, or worse, feeding narcissism or sado-masochism.

A second example of a child needing help in processing severe feelings of persecution

Here the therapeutic process did not involve containment of projective identification—rather, the therapist provided, by sharing the experience of choking with his little patient, a kind of self-resonance. This helped a five-year-old child, David, to process some very dangerous respiratory failures in his infancy. He got his therapist to cough and choke with him in unison, in exact replays, until, over time, the gagging sounds became part of their playful joint repertoire. I have suggested that patients deep in the paranoid–schizoid position may need much help in getting "alpha function" around various elements within each side of the split, either the good or the bad, long before they are ready to integrate the two. In David's case it was a so far unthinkably terrifying experience, and alpha function, the function of the mind that makes thoughts thinkable (Bion, 1962) assisted him, not through containment in and by someone else, but through joint sharing of the terrible experience in all its detail (Alvarez, 2010a).

Moving from a dead to a more alive state

An autistic patient of mine, Robbie, told me one day, at a period when he was becoming more reachable, that, long ago, his uncle had helped him out of a deep freeze, where he had been stuck and "left to be dead forever and ever with no eyes, no ears, no mouth, and no penis". He demonstrated what it had been like to struggle out of the ice, with his legs moving terribly slowly at first. It seemed to me a vivid illustration of the difficulties of overcoming not only the autism, but its chronicity and is a reminder of the *practice* it takes, once the patient is more alive, to stay alive. Robbie gradually became much better at catching himself drifting off or, for that matter, sinking.

A second illustration of the patient coming alive

Many years later, when Robbie was in his twenties, he was much more independent, less engaged in his ritualistic talk and altogether saner. His conversation now made sense, but it was terribly compliant and dull. He would, for example, begin the session by telling me that he had helped his father sweep the leaves in the garden yesterday. In the transference, he was telling me what he thought I wanted to hear, and although I had interpreted this many times, it had not had much effect. He tended to hear it as a confirmation. However, I had recently begun to notice that I greeted him at the start of the session in a very different manner from the way I greeted another, much more severely autistic child whom I saw at the clinic. Samuel was a very embittered frustrated child, but nevertheless full of a powerful compressed vitality. I began to notice that when I greeted Samuel, my eyes were probably alight with some kind of energised anticipation, but when I greeted Robbie, although I was relieved at his sanity, my eyes were probably dull. I had been worrying about this a lot, wondering what I could do about my countertransference. One day Robbie came in, glanced at the brass doorknob that we passed on the way to the consulting room, and said, longingly, "I want to be that doorknob". My heart sank, as this remark of his was so similar to an autistic repetition of his from a decade ago, when he used to "want to be the weathervane". I had never really understood at the time, what I believe I understand now, which was that he wanted to be *someone* or *something* that people watched, followed, and admired—as Marlon Brando said to his brother in the film "On the waterfront", "I could have been a contender, Charlie …" Robbie had wanted to be a contender: but, in those early years of child analysis, I had taken it, in too part-object a way as an identification with a penis or breast, but also as something an oedipal child had to learn to relinquish. I did not, in those years, understand that, in his pre-oedipal self, he had a rightful need to be admired, as all babies do (Trevarthen, 2001). Some types of admiration tend to feed narcissism, but the kind of admiration and confirmation of achievement that conveys awe and pleasure in the existence of the life force and its strength and development can encourage pride, rather than shame, and this may lead to a sense of potency rather than despair or narcissistic omnipotence.

In any case, as I followed him down the hall with my heart sinking, I realised that what he had said had been said in a quite emotional way—nothing autistic about it. So when we got down to the consulting room, I asked him why he wanted to be that doorknob (it was brass). He answered slowly, "Because it's so shiny." I found myself thinking about research I had been reading cited by Allan Schore (1994, p. 74) about how the pupils of people's eyes enlarge when they look lovingly at a baby, and that this allows more light to get in and hit the retina. Thus, when our students of infant observation say that someone's eyes lit up, they are describing a physiological fact. I found myself thinking of the need and right every baby has to bring a light to the mother's or father's eyes, and so what I said to Robbie (he was only coming up to London on a monthly basis now) was this: "I know what I should have said, at the door, Robbie, I should have said,

'How lovely to see you, I haven't seen you for a whole month!'" As I said, this, my own feelings toward him changed: I felt quite moved, and, as I spoke he became enlivened too: his eyes lit up, and colour came into his cheeks. I learned subsequently to be extremely vigilant about my own countertransference and about the quality of the eye contact I was maintaining with him, and I believe it helped him to find ways other than the old autistic perverse excitements to feel alive.

A third patient preoccupied with aliveness, in this case, in the object

Another autistic boy, eight-year-old Jesse, had been making somewhat better contact with me in recent months. He was also somewhat better able to play out stories with longer dramatic sequences, and even, occasionally, to share them and let me know what was happening in the narratives. Recently he had been placing a large cushion on a wooden armchair, pretending that it was an enemy alien, and then bashing it. But on this occasion, he explained that it was a zapper, not a bad zapper, but a good one. When it zapped you, it made you move. He then spoke for the zapper. He told me to move, and then to jump, and then to fall. I did the first two, and then pretended to fall, and he seemed to love this and be very enlivened by his idea.

These three clinical examples illustrate a particular form of aliveness where coming to life seems to involve an interpersonal relationship and the life is facilitated by someone else. In the first instance with Robbie, his "uncle" coaxed him out of the deepfreeze; in the second, my emotional welcome finally brought colour into his cheeks and a light to his eye. With Jesse, for that moment at least, it was the other way around: the zapper was him bringing me to life. I think he was experiencing potency and agency, not omnipotent control. Gradually, in normal infant development, such object relations get internalised, so the relationship to a psychic-life-giving and psychic-life-receiving object is intrapersonal, not only interpersonal. And the communication is reciprocal: the baby changes the way the parent unfolds, and the parent changes the way the baby unfolds. However, as we know from countless infant observations, newborn babies vary enormously in the amount of life force, even psychic life force with which they enter the world. Some have a stronger sense already that the world out there is fascinating and draws them to it like, as Donald Meltzer said, a magnet (Meltzer et al., 1975).

A few comments on some brain research

Biven pointed out that there are two major ways of feeling good; one is evoked by the opioids which give feelings of pleasure and happiness, and the other is evoked by the dopamine system which evokes curiosity and anticipatory excitement. Note that she was stressing the differences between them (Biven, personal communication, 2011; Panksepp & Biven, 2012). It is energising and stimulating. She suggested that Panksepp's ideas on something he calls the "seeking system" in the brain, are of great interest for this question of emotional deadness/aliveness. He distinguishes this system from attachment, sex, and hunger, although he points out they can and do combine. His descriptions correspond somewhat to Bion's concept of "K". Here are some speculations. I think that the sense of wonder plays a part here. Stern suggested in his last book that it was not only the content of mental/emotional life that matters, it was also the quality of the forms of expression and of experience that required greater study, for example, the vitality contours, that is, the quasi-musical shaping (e.g., explosive, flat, elated, over the top, or more regulated) of emotional experience, expression, and communication. He thought that the neuroscience underpinning this may lie in the arousal system, which is providing the force behind and under all mental/emotional activity—"a force that throws the motivations (sex, hunger, attachment, etc.) into action, that triggers the emotions, sharpens the attention, starts up cognitions, and initiates movement" (Stern, 2010). Solms has suggested that the seeking system seems related to Freud's life instinct, or the life force, even the drives (Solms, 2000).

Gerhardt tells us that when the mother smiles, the baby's nervous system is pleasantly aroused and his own heart rate goes up.

> These processes trigger off a biochemical response.... "Endogenous" or homemade opioids like beta-endorphin are known to help neurons to grow, by regulating glucose and insulin (Schore, 1994.) As natural opioids, they also make you feel good. At the same time, another neurotransmitter called dopamine is released from the brainstem, and again makes its way up to the prefrontal cortex. This too enhances the uptake of glucose there, helping new tissue to grow in the prefrontal brain. (Gerhardt, 2004, pp. 41–42)

Panksepp himself writes of Leonard, a grown man whose dopamine circuits were destroyed in childhood; only with the introduction of L-dopa by Oliver Sacks, could he partake again of worldly delights. Panksepp says that now we know that ascending dopamine circuit tracts lie at the heart of powerful, affectively valenced neural systems that allow people and animals to operate smoothly and efficiently in all of their day-to-day pursuits. Panksepp suggests that "'intense interest,' 'engaged curiosity,' and 'eager anticipation' are the types of feelings that reflect arousal of this system in humans" (Panksepp, 1998, p. 149).

Technical implications

It is important to say that when a patient, however weak and lost, is in a state of mind where there is some ego function and capacity to think, interpretations drawing attention to the fact that he cannot imagine that his utterances could be interesting to anyone may offer a chink of light. Or we may suggest that he cannot imagine that his therapist could possibly say anything interesting, or that their encounter could ever produce anything of import. This is addressing deficit in the self, object, and relations between them via classical technique. However, in more far-gone states, something else may be required. Panksepp goes on to say that, "without the synaptic 'energy' of dopamine, these potentials remain frozen, as it were, in an endless winter of discontent. Dopamine synapses resemble gatekeepers rather than couriers that convey detailed messages. When they are not active at their posts, many potentials of the brain cannot be readily manifested in thought or actions. Without dopamine, only the strongest emotional messages instigate behaviour" (1998, p. 144). I myself have previously suggested that there are certain states of mind, and perhaps states of brain, where what is required is a more intensive, vitalising insistence on meaning, because it creates what some developmentalists call a "heightened affective moment" (Beebe & Lachman, 1994). The pulse and pitch of our voices changes at such moments of urgency where we "reclaim" our patients into the world of meaning (Alvarez, 1992,

2010a, 2012b). Panksepp says that some research has found that the insistent rhythms of music can increase the synthesis of dopamine in animals (Panksepp, 1998, p. 131). Something like this happened between me and Robbie when I felt and then showed great urgency about his nearness to psychic death, and I felt that the urgency in my voice finally reached him.

I want to turn now to the issue of curiosity. We can be curious about what lies over spatial horizons, beyond the next mountain or country, but we can also have intense curiosity about the future, that is, temporal as opposed to spatial curiosity. Sometimes we fear the future, sometimes we dread it, sometimes we experience eager anticipation and confident expectation. Here I want to say something about Bion's concept of "K", the desire to get to know someone or something (Bion, 1962.) He thought it was a third emotional link, which needed to be added to the emotional links arising from love and hate. Fisher pointed out that the word curiosity is inadequate to describe Bion's insistence on it as an emotional link between self and object. Fisher suggested that expressions such as "feeling interested" or "intrigued" are a bit closer. He adds that adjectives such as "attentive, inquiring, or questioning" seem even closer to what Bion is talking about (Fisher, 2011). Certainly K is not about the desire to *have* knowledge, it is about the desire to get to *know*. There is no endpoint, there is mystery, maybe some excitement, as with the Romantics, but, somewhere, also awe about that which is unknown. It is interesting that the German word for curiosity has much more emotion in it: *"neugier"* means a "craving for the new". And in Italian, according to an Italian friend, it sometimes means a type of intrusive curiosity. Fisher discusses the danger when love and hate overwhelm and stifle K, and I have had at least one autistic patient who was a sweet sensuous child but seemed utterly lacking in curiosity—not, I came to think, because it was being defended against, but more because it seems to have hardly been awakened. Or if it had in his early days, it was so disused, it had atrophied. He came in, in a very loving mood one day, and made two toy animals kiss each other most tenderly on the cheeks. But the kissing went on and on and on … and on. I began to think that even Antony and Cleopatra got up and went for a walk, or a cup of coffee occasionally!! Eventually, I began to talk about how I thought the animals might want to climb the hill (of the couch) and see what was over the top. Eventually, he did then move them, slowly and tentatively, up the hill.

I am suggesting that in these situations we are in the realm of deficit in both parts of the inner world, that is, in the self and in the internal objects, and in the relations between self and its objects. Little is expected of either or of the encounter.

It is interesting that Klein herself wrote that "in schizophrenia, in my opinion, the capacity for personification and for transference fails, amongst other reasons, through the defective functioning of the projection mechanism. This interferes with the capacity for establishing or maintaining the relation to reality and the external world" (Klein, 1929, p. 208). This accords closely with the views of Bick, Meltzer, and Tustin on the difficulties of autistic children in using projective identification (Bick, 1968; Tustin, 1981; Meltzer et al., 1975). Klein played actively the part of the naughty boy that her patient could not yet play, and, eventually, he himself was able to take on the role in the play. But what of such patients who can never conceive of defiance or rebellion? Dare we introduce the idea? Is that still psychoanalysis? Where the internal object, and other people, are experienced as dead, and curiosity about them has atrophied, can we introduce aliveness and meaning which is not yet present in the child's inner world, and still be true to our psychoanalytic roots?

There would seem to be certain necessary preconditions for good introjections and internalisations to take place. Analysts are talking about this in terms of technique nowadays—see Joseph, as early as 1975, on the need for containment with patients who are difficult to reach, and Steiner, who stated that containment may need to precede the patient taking responsibility for himself (Steiner, 1993a, 2004). Many of us have found that there is no point telling a desperately fragmented patient that the reason he is so upset today is because of the break he has just had from analysis until he has calmed down enough, first to realise we are back, and then to listen. The calming down is the first problem. Because the need for oxygen takes physiological priority over the need for nourishment, a baby held too close to the breast cannot suck unless and until he can breathe. A baby held too far from the nipple and too precariously in his mother's arms will cling to the nipple with all his might, but may not take in much milk, may not explore the nipple and breast much, and certainly will not enjoy himself. A sure grip not only permits, but may also be a necessary condition for, relaxed pleasurable introjections. Thoughtful introjections depend on secure, even leisurely, background conditions. Wolff has shown that babies first need to be well fed and comfortable in order to be relaxed enough and alert enough to be interested in the world (Wolff, 1965). A distressed baby's curiosity is very different from a satisfied baby's. It is narrower and more limited by its urgency. But here I am adding the point that beyond the sure grip, and the feeling of safety, the object has to be felt to be sufficiently *interesting* in order to attract the baby's attention.

Thus when the baby is not seeking, or has given up seeking, due to dissociation, depression, or autism, a more animated response from us may be required. For Bion's "alpha function" (the function of the mind that makes thoughts thinkable) to operate, the object has to be seen to be worth attending to in the first place. As I have indicated, we often see certain neglected children who are sluggish mentally, suffering from a kind of lifelong, but not a particularly active, depression. They seem to be full of unvalued, not devalued, objects. Here I am thinking more of the consequences of neglect, or in the case of autism, self-neglect, but not trauma, and of depression or despair, rather than terror. I think we see some children where apathy is a result of having never quite felt pulled together.

Conclusion

Klein's great meta-theoretical distinction between the anxieties related to depressive functioning and those of the paranoid-schizoid position involved an incredible breakthrough. Here I am suggesting a further distinction within the paranoid-schizoid position. I am aware that my attempt to group some of these mental states into differing and similar levels of pathology may seem crude. I do think, however, that the idea of a continuum of levels of functioning in ego, self, and the internal objects may provide some degree of structure to our thinking about how best to reach such children. And this is no mere matter of finding the right words. Usually, the feelings in our countertransference have to come first, although, very occasionally, it can be the other way round, as I showed with my pretend greeting to Robbie. The transferential and countertransferential emotional encounters, especially with our more ill patients, are intense and often overpowering. Conversely, and more worryingly, they are sometimes seriously underpowering: nothing seems to matter and our meeting with a particular patient at moments may seem to be bereft of meaning for both parties. These various states of mind and feeling—or lack of it—are taken very seriously by those therapists who work psychoanalytically. Bion taught that if you are bored, study the boredom. Bergstein (2009) also wrote on the relationship of boredom to encapsulated parts of the psyche. Transference and countertransference do not interfere with the work—they are the work's most vital instruments. But although the containment and processing of our countertransference feelings, even without the "right" words, may often be enough to enable the patient to feel understood and to get something from that moment of encounter, this is not always the case. Sometimes the elements in something Bion called "transformation"—the stage beyond containment, where the feeling in the analyst gets returned in a transformed manner to the patient—are more essential than at other times. This is because an emotional experience is transformable in innumerable ways. I have suggested that it may be useful to distinguish the paranoid persecuted states from the more schizoid states, and that with these latter most pathological of cases—states of extreme chronic dissociation, emptiness, or perverse attachments to inhuman, non-human, or sado-masochistic objects—we may need to use the intensity of our feelings, or else our intense alarm about our lack of feeling, in intensified ways.

References

Acquarone, S. (2007). *Signs of Autism in Infants*. London: Karnac.

Alvarez, A. (1992). *Live Company: Psychoanalytic Psychotherapy with Autistic, Borderline, Deprived and Abused children*. London: Routledge.

Alvarez, A. (1995). Motiveless malignity: problems in the psychotherapy of psychopathic patients. *Journal of Child Psychotherapy, 21*: 167–182.

Alvarez, A. (1997). Projective identification as a communication: its grammar in borderline psychotic children. *Psychoanalytic Dialogues, 7*: 753–768.

Alvarez, A. (2010a). Levels of analytic work and levels of pathology: the work of calibration. *International Journal of Psychoanalysis, 91*: 859–878.

Alvarez, A. (2010b). Mourning and melancholia in childhood and adolescence: some reflections on the role of the internal object. In: E. McGinley, & A. Varchevker (Eds.), *Enduring Loss: Mourning, Depression and Narcissism Throughout the Life Cycle*. London: Karnac.

Alvarez, A. (2012a). *The Thinking Heart: Three Levels of Psychotherapy with Disturbed Children*. London: Routledge.

Alvarez, A. (2012b). Under-integrations and integrations at the paranoid-schizoid level. In: *The Thinking Heart: Three Levels of Psychotherapy with Disturbed Children* (pp. 130–143). London: Routledge.

APA. (1994). *Diagnostic and Statistical Manual of Psychiatric Disorders, IV*. Washington, DC: American Psychiatric Association.

Beebe, B., & Lachmann, F. M. (1994). Representation and internalization in infancy: three principles of salience. *Psychoanalytic Psychology, 11*: 127–165.

Bergstein, A. (2009). On boredom: a close encounter with encapsulated parts of the psyche. *International Journal of Psychoanalysis, 90*: 613–631.

Bick, E. (1968). The experience of the skin in early object-relations. In: A. Briggs (Ed.), *Surviving Space: Papers on Infant Observation*. London: Karnac.

Bion, W. R. (1959). Attacks on linking. In: *Second Thoughts: Selected Papers on Psychoanalysis*. London: Heinemann, 1967.

Bion, W. R. (1962). *Learning from Experience*. London: Heinemann.

DeJong, M. (2010). Some reflections on the use of psychiatric diagnosis in the looked after or "in care" population'. *Clinical Child Psychology and Psychiatry*, 15: 589–599.

Fairbairn, W. R. D. (1952). Schizoid factors of the personality. In: *Psychoanalytic Studies of the Personality*. London: Routledge.

Fairbairn, W. R. D. (1954). Observations on the nature of hysterical states. *British Journal of Medical Psychology*, 27: 105–125. Fisher, J. (2011). The emotional experience of K. In: C. Mawson (Ed.), *Bion Today* (pp. 43–63). Hove: Routledge.

Freud, S. (1920). *Beyond the Pleasure Principle. S. E., 18*: 1–64. London: Hogarth.

Gerhardt, S. (2004). *Why Love Matters: How Affection Shapes a Baby's Brain*. New York: Brunner-Routledge.

Green, A. (1995). L'objet et la function objectalisante. In: *Propédeutique* (pp. 229–226). Paris: Editions Champvallon.

Joseph, B. (1975). The patient who is difficult to reach. In: E. B. Spillius, & M. Feldman (Eds.), *Psychic Equilibrium and Psychic Change: Selected Papers of Betty Joseph*. London: Routledge, 1989.

Joseph, N. (1982). Addiction to near death. In: E. B. Spillius, & M. Feldman (Eds.), *Psychic Equilibrium and Psychic Change: Selected Papers of Betty Joseph*. London: Routledge, 1989.

Klein, M. (1929). Personification in the play of children. In: *The Writings of Melanie Klein, Volume I*. London: Hogarth, 1975.

Klein, M. (1935). A contribution to the psychogenesis of manic-depressive states. In: *The Writings of Melanie Klein, Volume III*. London: Hogarth, 1975.

Klein, M. (1937). Love, guilt and reparation. In: *The Writings of Melanie Klein, Volume I*. London: Hogarth, 1975.

Klein, M. (1946). Notes on some schizoid mechanisms. In: *The Writings of Melanie Klein, Vol III*. London: Hogarth, 1975.

Klein, M. (1952). The origins of transference. *International Journal of Psychoanalysis, 33*: 433–438.

Kundera, M. (1982). *The Joke*. Harmondsworth: Penguin.

Likierman, M. (2001). *Melanie Klein: Her Work in Context*. London: Continuum.

Meltzer, D., Bremner, J., Hoxter, S., Weddell, D., & Wittenberg, I. (1975). *Explorations in Autism: A Psycho-analytical Study*. Strathtay: Clunie.

Music, G. (2009). Neglecting neglect: some thoughts on children who have lacked good input, and are "undrawn" and "unenjoyed". *Journal of Child Psychotherapy, 35*: 142–156.

Panksepp, J. (1998). *Affective Neuroscience: The Foundations of Human and Animal Emotions*. Oxford: OUP.

Panksepp, J., & Biven, L. (2012). *The Archaeology of Mind: Neuroevolutionary Origins of Human Emotions*. London: Norton.

Papousek, H., & Papousek, M. (1975). Cognitive aspects of preverbal social interaction between human infants and adults. *Parent Infant Interaction* (CIBA Foundation Symposium No. 33). Amsterdam: Elsevier.

Perry, B. D. (2002). Childhood experience and the expression of genetic potential: what childhood neglect tells us about nature and nurture. *Brain and Mind, 3*: 79–100.

Reid, S. (1999). Autism and trauma: autistic post-traumatic developmental disorder. In: A. Alvarez, & S. Reid (Eds.), *Autism and Personality: Findings form the Tavistock Autism Workshop*. London: Routledge.

Rodriguez, E. (1955). The analysis of a three-year-old mute schizophrenic. In: M. Klein, P. Heimann, & R. E. Money-Kyrle (Eds.), *New Directions in Psycho-analysis: The Significance of Infant Conflict in the Pattern of Adult Behaviour*. London: Tavistock.

Schore, A. (1994). *Affect Regulation and the Origin of the Self: the Neurobiology of Emotional Development*. Hillsdale, NJ: Lawrence Erlbaum.

Segal, H. (1957). Notes on symbol formation. In: *The Work of Hanna Segal*. New York: Aronson, 1981.

Solms, M. (2000). Freudian dream theory today. *The Psychologist, 12*: 618–619.

Steiner, J. (1993a). Problems of psychoanalytic technique: patient-centred and analyst-centred interpretations. In: *Psychic Retreats: Pathological Organisations in Psychotic, Neurotic and Borderline Patients*. London: Routledge.

Steiner, J. (1993b). *Psychic Retreats: Pathological Organisations in Psychotic, Neurotic, and Borderline Patients*. London: Routledge.

Stern, D. N. (2010). *Forms of Vitality*. Oxford: OUP.

Stolorow, R. D., & Lachmann, F. M. (1980). *The Psychoanalysis of Developmental Arrests*. Madison, CT: International Universities Press.

Trevarthen, C. (2001). Intrinsic motives for companionship in understanding: their origin, development, and significance for infant mental health. *Infant Mental Health. Special Issue: Contributions from the Decade of the Brain to Infant Mental Health, 22*: 95–131.

Tustin, F. (1980). Autistic objects. *International Review of Psychoanalysis, 7*: 27–39.

Tustin, F. (1981). *Autistic States in Children*. London: Routledge & Kegan Paul.

Van der Kolk, B. (2009). Proposal to include a developmental trauma disorder diagnosis for children and adolescents in DSM-V. Paper presented at UCLA Trauma Conference, California, July 2009.

Wakschlag, L. S., Tolan, P. H., & Leventhal, B. L. (2010). Research review: "Ain't misbehaving": towards a developmentalized specified nosology for preschool disruptive behaviour. *Journal of Child Psychology and Psychiatry, 51*: 3–22.

Winnicott, D. W. (1945). Primitive emotional development. In: *Collected Papers*. London: Hogarth.

Wolff, P. H. (1965). The development of attention in young infants. In: L. J. Stone, H. T. Smith, & L. B. Murphy (Eds.), *The Competent Infant: Research and Commentary*. London: Tavistock, 1974.

CHAPTER TWENTY-TWO

Balancing on a tightrope of mania: a precarious normality

Judith Jackson

Ⅰn this paper I explore how certain manic defensive organisations can be used to sustain a very fragile sense of self and enable a potentially psychotic eruption to remain in a latent state. I will bring my experience of working analytically with a nine-year-old girl, Victoria, to examine the ways in which she tries to master persecutory anxieties, crippling phobias, and potential fragmentation in order to hold herself together. I hope to show how she tries to convince herself and others that she can function like an ordinary normal child when psychically she is all the time balancing precariously (as my title suggests) on a tightrope of mania. I would also like to highlight some of the technical problems I needed to consider when working with such a patient.

Freud (1917b) stated that mania has as its basis the same contents as melancholia and is, in fact, a way of escaping from that state. Many subsequent writings have stressed the function of omnipotent denial in mania. Klein (1935) suggests that in mania the ego seeks refuge not only from melancholia, which was Freud's understanding, but also in order to escape a paranoid condition that the ego is unable to master. She maintains that mania originates in that very early phase in which the undeveloped ego endeavours to defend itself from the most overpowering and profound anxiety of all, namely, its dread of internalised persecutors and of the id. In other words, in mania the ego attempts to defend itself against the overwhelming anxiety of falling to bits, or, as Hanna Segal (1981) calls it, "atomisation". Henri Rey (1994) states that in manic states or in the manic defence we are no longer concerned with the maternal breast but with the penis,

> which is needed by the subject for the task of reparation: through it he can regain the destroyed object either as a direct substitute by identification or by recreating the contents of the mother, for example, by making her pregnant by filling her empty breasts and so on. The more the

maternal object is destroyed by the subject's attacks, the more must the penis become omnipotent, and the subject by identification, becomes omnipotent also. In this manner, the destroyed state of the object is denied. (1994, p. 18)

Baruch (1997) follows Riviere's (1936) ideas about the use of the manic defence as a highly organised system mobilised against the experience of depressive anxiety and guilt. In his paper he focuses particularly on Abraham's (1919) and Riviere's (1936) description of the nature and form of manic, analytic material, which he calls the "manic narrative", a fake communication, which the patient uses to give an appearance of meaningfulness and truth.

These ideas provided a helpful theoretical landscape, underpinning my attempts to understand the complexity of my child patient's persecutory anxieties and her use of bizarre and manic narratives.

The referral

The existence in Victoria's inner world of the kinds of persecutors outlined by Klein is graphically expressed in my patient's deep anxieties at the point of referral. According to her mother, she was excessively fearful, screaming in terror if left alone, phobic about going to a toilet outside home, believing that snakes, in particular a boa constrictor, would come up out of the toilet. She seemed to be hallucinating, claiming that she actually saw things and that a person would suddenly become a rat or a snake, and this was what alerted her mother to the seriousness of her disturbance. (This suggests that she may have recognised that these were delusions.) Although bright academically and at a competitive girl's school, she had great difficulty in making friends and her mother would constantly be initiating arrangements to make it seem as though Victoria had a successful social life.

History

Victoria is the only child of European professional parents, born one month prematurely when Mother was already forty-five years old. At my preliminary meeting with her parents I learned that Mother had initially had to express milk for her; following this, despite being instructed by her doctor only to breast-feed for the first six months, she had continued to do so until Victoria was almost three years old. Mother told me that she had begun to wean her at the age of one: weaning had been proceeding successfully until Mother was asked to supply milk for a friend's baby. This baby, Mother said, had colic and needed a supplement for a week or so until her friend regained her own milk. Mother reported that Victoria, who had just begun walking, had entered the room while she was expressing milk. As Mother said, "All hell broke loose" and weaning went out of the window.

Having been brought up in an African country Mother justified her avoidance of weaning by claiming that it was, after all, the chosen child-rearing practice in rural villages. She dismissed her own questions about whether Victoria would remember the incident, claiming she was so young. At the same time as she made the decision to continue breast-feeding, she went back to work on a full-time basis, from early in the morning until early evening. It was not clear to what degree Mother continued to breastfeed Victoria because she felt that this concrete bodily link provided the only emotional link between herself and her daughter or because she felt so guilty about having chosen to return to work. However, when Victoria got into a state about going to nursery school at the age of three, Mother gave up work altogether, although continued to employ nannies and childminders.

Father seemed less emotionally intrusive and contradictory although also less thoughtful about his daughter. He believed that Victoria would grow out of her problems and was quite dismissive of his wife's concerns. He described Victoria as a baby who was so enchanting, beaming at everyone, that "when they took her out for a walk people would give them money for her". He found this extraordinary—as did I when I listened to the story.

It was immediately clear to me that there was considerable tension between the parents. Father conveyed his irritation with his wife's fussing over their daughter; in particular, he got quite fed up with his wife spending ages over Victoria's bedtime and was irritated that his daughter kept on waking up at night and going into their bedroom. He felt that Victoria could be quite manipulative and knew how to get her mother worked up. Father was also clearly irritated with his wife's involvement with an esoteric Chinese religion that involved hourly periods of meditation.

Mother described a number of other disturbing situations, such as Victoria's inability to be on her own. She told me that Victoria would start screaming whenever a playmate had to leave for home and would get into a state if her ways of doing things were not strictly adhered to; a puzzle, for instance, had to be completed on the outside before any of the inner pieces could be fitted in. I was also informed that she could not tolerate being interrupted in a sequence of activity and Mother would have to warn her "at least two hours" before she needed to stop. At the same time her parents described her as very intelligent, generous, and loving, painting a picture of an obsessively enthusiastic girl who also had an excellent memory.

During our meeting I found this mother quite controlling and intellectualising, and noticed that she oscillated between on the one hand having very relevant anxiety about her daughter and on the other hand seeming over-involved in a disturbing and inappropriate way. Over time I gained the impression of a mother who had very confused ideas about boundaries, limits, separation, and what was fair to herself and fair to the child. I wondered if she was both desperate to have a child at that stage of her life, and equally desperate to get back to work in order to regain her identity and be free from Victoria. How difficult was it for her to manage the rough and tumble of an ordinary child growing up? I also wondered about Mother's terror of Victoria's rage when she saw her expressing milk for another baby at a point when she herself was being weaned. Mother's quick reversion to breastfeeding Victoria for another two years in response to "all hell breaking loose", as well as the fact that she was feeding someone else's baby (and, in view of her age, was unlikely to have another baby to feed) suggest that Mother may have had her own difficulties with loss, rivalry, and oedipal issues. How did Victoria experience this? Could one suggest that a child's rage that is not contained grows out of all proportion in the child's mind—it becomes the boa constrictor monster coming out of everywhere to terrify and tyrannise. Perhaps, too, it represents her version of a "poo baby"—the baby she had forever eliminated when she possessed Mother's breast once more. And was she also terrified of Father's rage, as monstrous as her own, so that she feared he could turn into a vicious snake or rat, ready to attack or even eliminate her, for occupying so much of Mother's attention? I was also interested in her intrusion into her parents' bedroom at night, even as an older child, with bad dreams and unmanageable terrors. How much was there a hidden rage at her exclusion from the parental relationship, perhaps exacerbated by the fact that she was an only child? I was, at this point, challenged by many questions.

The analysis

Victoria is a very solid, pleasantly plain-faced girl with long sandy-coloured hair which she continually remodels—during, between, and throughout the analytic sessions. Her capacity to be articulate and even entertaining was there from the outset, as was her rapid, manic flood of narratives (Baruch, 1997).

Extracts from first session

> After some initial anxiety, which I addressed, and after spelling out the nature of the setting (inviting her to say whatever was in her mind, including dreams, and indicating that her box was for her use only), Victoria launched into a nonstop narrative of all her fears from when she was very little, many of which I had already heard from her mother, although Victoria brought many more examples. This rapid outpouring took me by surprise. She seemed particularly upset about the cruelty of some friends and the way they humiliated her. She stressed that she couldn't be alone without getting frightened. She hated the dark and needed the light on. While telling me this she looked at my light. This was the first noticeable reaction to the room. I suggested that she was perhaps worried about the light in the room, perhaps too because she came late in the afternoon, at a time when it would start getting darker here. Would my room, I suggested, become a frightening place for her too, and would I, like the cruel friends she had been describing, laugh at her fears? She tried to brush away my words, insisting that it wouldn't really be like that. I continued, however, saying that she was also telling me that there were many things that frightened her and that what was most frightening was when she was in the dark and alone with these fears; when she looked at my light perhaps she was also looking to me to see whether I would understand what all these fears were about; whether I could shed some light on them?
>
> Victoria agreed and added that she would go up to her parents' room at night when she was frightened and that she still did that now sometimes. She was also frightened of rats and all sorts of other creatures in her room. She told me that she once had a dream about a bat flying around in her room and another, which had to do with her hamster escaping: he was in her bedroom, she said, like a rat, and could get out through the various chutes linking parts of the cage together. Another dream was about the hamster in a heap of blood in the cage. Having described this, she told me that her mother had a dream last week about going away for a week; everybody forgot to feed the hamster and it died. She half laughed. I interpreted that although she tried to laugh at that, she seemed very frightened of all sorts of dangerous things happening or coming into her room, but perhaps too, of all sorts of very dangerous things coming out of her mind which she was starting to see. "Yes," she said, continuing about being

afraid of people—her parents, friends—all turning into snakes and coming to get her; she supposed she would then be a snake too, she quickly added. She told me a further dream about horrible monsters—creatures coming out of her uncle's pool, which was dirty and green. Then she said that she didn't get frightened if she had to go down chutes and slides and things like that, or when driving a car very fast in the traffic, but she was more frightened with adults than with children—adults seemed to want to reassure her whereas children also seemed to have the same sorts of fears. She continued to talk rapidly, giving other examples of the things that frightened her and then described an occasion that led her to hide in the headmistress's cupboard room to avoid tidying up—she hated tidying up and her room was always in such a mess—and another time when she had been frightened of a hole in the skirting board.

At this point I noticed her eyes wandering around my room. I commented that she was perhaps suddenly worried about the cupboards in my room and had noticed that one was a bit open—that she didn't know where they led to and what was inside them. She sort of agreed, a bit embarrassed. (Perhaps she might also have been afraid of "tidying up"—tidying up her mind would mean getting to know it more and where things belong, which itself would be quite disturbing). I continued, suggesting that perhaps she was also afraid—was my mind a safe place where she could voice all these fears? She nodded, and told me that once she poked her mother's eye when she was little and her mum had to go to hospital and she was very worried about that—about what she had done to her mum. I suggested that she was afraid not only of dangerous things outside that could get out and threaten her, but also of the things she could do that could be dangerous—dangerous to me too. She agreed, adding that she didn't know if she was real or not—was she a character in somebody else's dream? How did she know she really existed? (This was a very unusual thing for a girl of this age to say, perhaps also revealing a disturbance in her relationship to the other whereby she could not take her own existence for granted. One might wonder whether this originated in her very early experiences of being a premature infant with limited or confusing contact with her mother.)

The session continued in the same vein. Victoria said that she knew she had an imagination and that these things weren't really there but this didn't stop her from feeling very frightened. I suggested that she felt that the most frightening thing was to be left alone with what went on her in her mind.

In this first session I was not only aware of how these fears, dreams, and hallucinatory experiences flooded the session, but was immediately struck by her verbal precocity. As the session continued, however, I also began to sense something strangely paralysing in the atmosphere. Retrospectively I noticed I was saying things that seemed appropriate—she seemed to agree and go along with me—but was she really able to listen? It seemed to be too dangerous to stop and let me in, as though she used her words to create a safe world, and provided she could stay with these words—and cage me in—then, perhaps, I would not be dangerous and change into something terrifying. It was as if she had come for a talking cure and used words quite concretely to evacuate her experience of being overwhelmed and persecuted. In a sense, one might say that she had already started to poke my eye out because I was so flooded by all her talk that I was not really able to register my experience of her in the session and see properly for myself what was happening. Perhaps she was already starting to control and fix me into position.

She did this quite concretely with her eyes as well as her talk. Retrospectively I could see that I might become a dangerous animal, something called "An Analyst" who had to be caged in, and not allowed out into her mind, except where she provided the material for me to whizz up and down on, like her hamster in the cage. But it may also have been that when she said "Yes", she did think the interpretations were right, but she was also finding a way to join up with what I said so that she didn't experience me as a separate person who could have an impact on her, or who could be potentially dangerous. This may be similar to the devices that Maria Rhode (personal communication, 2015) suggests many high-functioning autism spectrum disorder (ASD) children, or some Asperger's children, are very adept at making use of. Children who have had a lot of nasty interventions when little, including being fed through a tube, can also have a similar way of talking.

By the end of that first week, my room did indeed become the frightening place of her inner world and she was screaming that she didn't want to come. It seemed as though talking about her terrors concretised them and stirred up terrible persecutory fears that she had been trying to control with her narratives. Fortunately, her mother believed in the work of the analysis and was firm in bringing her back after the weekend. I am not sure that anything I thought I understood at the time helped. Instead, what seemed important was that we both continued to survive but, perhaps more significantly, her manic strategies began to take wing and as the analysis progressed, all her symptoms and fears apparently "disappeared".

I began to notice that as she spoke to me, she sat with her foot resting on her toy box, and managed to tilt the box, balancing it so that it looked as if it was on the verge of toppling over, though it never did. In a sense this typified her behaviour and chatter; she seemed to keep herself psychically tilted so that she appeared to be an ordinary, friendly latency girl with much to say, bright and funny often, but concealing her bizarre thoughts and feelings. She seemed desperate to prove to both of us that she was never anxious and that her life was full of activities. Weekends in particular had to be filled up in this way, but I came to experience her endless chatter about her day at school, or social arrangements, as all quite hollow and it had very little resonance inside me. I could also begin to notice that it was very often "off-centre". She seemed to put things together in a sort of conglomeration as though it all made sense, but making it very hard to find any meaning.

When she turned to draw, however, something of her bizarre state of mind was more clearly exposed. She would draw monstrous faces, contorted and enmeshed, one face showing many different perspectives, features without heads containing them, clothes without bodies wearing them, eyes on their own anywhere and everywhere. The pages would all run into each other and, unlike most children who would choose a clear space or a new page to draw something different on a different day, she would draw in-between other drawings, confusing the detail, the sequence, the sense of time past and present.

I wondered whether this had to do with a very early lack of containment leading to a feeling that she had no boundaries and no stable physical orientation—she did not know which way was up, as though her sense organs had not been integrated into her body. It also seemed to indicate a lack of corporeal solidity: the clothes without bodies inside and the way she created drawings in a space that was already full suggested that she felt like a ghost but also signalled that Mother was felt to be full of other people or things. (These issues about bodily solidity and embodiment are very characteristic of children on the autistic spectrum, although not exclusively so).

In one session she drew some doves, which were supposed to be flying in either direction, this way or that; then she sketched a face that could be a girl but also a monster, an elegant woman, a witch—apparently very clever—a lesson in reversible perspectives. I gradually learned that it was not helpful to translate such material as though the transference had the same meaning for both of us as it so easily became "stuff" that could fly in any direction. Her communications invariably could not be thought about and processed. I also slowly began to hear her "pseudo latency" chat with a different ear. She seemed to be unconsciously encasing herself in some kind of manic cage of talk that limited the eruptions of these paranoid and fragmented feelings. It became a carapace, very much as Bick (1968) describes. At times her manic activities were focussed on writing witty, but cruel, limericks, usually about friends who had upset her, for example:

> There was a young girl called Corrine
> who smelt like a rotten dustbin
> she looked really foul
> and at night she did growl
> for a loyal and nice friend to suck in.

Through such rhymes, Victoria revealed an awareness of a nasty cruel part of herself, and the potential for reversible perspectives (who was Corrine—her friend, or herself?) was contained in all she did. She created several versions of her own alphabet, a sort of private code, which was very illuminating—and very common to many ordinary nine- or ten-year-olds—and was, again, used to keep her world out. In a similar sort of way she appeared to have an ordinary mode of communication, wearing the clothes of an ordinary, normal child, to cover up her very fragile sense of self. Later on in the analysis, she had a dream that was very telling:

> Mrs Smith, her teacher, gave the class a clean piece of paper on which to do their homework. Her friend Mary Jane (who features constantly as an alter ego) said, "Oh good, I love clean white sheets" and started ticking it. Victoria said, "But how can you tick when you haven't done the sums yet?" Mary Jane then quickly added a few crosses. Victoria was irritated as this didn't make any difference.

This dream beautifully conveys the way she rushed past and foreclosed any experience that she had or might have in a way that left her mind empty and ticked off—or crossed out—so that nothing could be thought about and processed. There seemed to be a similar dynamic in the transference where I would be tempted to tick or cross out something before it was properly understood. But the dream also conveyed that there was the beginning of some introjection of my observing function, an observing self, who could sometimes question this a bit more.

Who and where was I in all of this? Was I like a mother who was totally immersed in all her daughter's narratives and activities, a sort of taxi service, fetching and carrying her from one to another, losing a sense of direction and often without a mind of my own? Was I in projective identification with the emotional functioning of her experience of her mother, who, amongst other things, could not process her daughter's reaction to losing the breast? I noticed how I could slip into switching off. At other times I became aware of feeling quite exhausted listening to her, and having to concentrate intently in order to follow her, otherwise I would lose her in an instant, despite her attempts to entertain or occupy me. Was she, in fact, intending me to be lost and not to find her, using her talk to render me impotent? Or was she projecting such a state of mind (her internal mother?) into me?

Vignette

In one session, after all sorts of endless narratives, I showed her that perhaps she wanted me to get lost, so that I shouldn't really notice what was happening. She looked up and said, "I went with my friend to Hampton Court maze. I was worried that we wouldn't be able to find our way back and it was getting dark. It was a good job though that we could." I interpreted: "You are relieved if I can find you, that I am not lost, even though you want to camouflage and disguise what you feel, creating mazes round me with your many tales, so that I'm to be in the dark and not properly know where you are." Victoria asked to go to the toilet. When she returned she said cheerily something about her mum receiving a notice about a trapeze-artist camp for children where you could swing ropes and jump on trampolines like in a circus. "Really sounds like fun," she added in her inimitable way.

I felt despair that she had already evacuated me as an object who could find her; that I was not simply to be lost, but also impotent, watching a quite brilliant trapeze artist balancing on her tightrope of mania. But she also may have needed to use the toilet to avoid having to notice that what she did impacted on me. Was I then experienced as a defective container from which she needed to swing and bounce away? Was it her persecutory guilt at that moment that needed to be defended against? But equally, am I experienced as a figure, such as the mother in her mind (as well as externally) who encourages her to swing up high, away from her fears and anxieties and camouflage herself as a bright, happy child.

I would now like to describe more fully a session from further on in the analysis that is fairly typical of many in the way she talks, but where I was able to make contact with her and where we could see the temporary collapse of her manic defences.

Session

This was a Monday session in June in the second year of analysis. Victoria came in look-ing thoughtful and at first she didn't say anything. Then she told me about sleeping in the clubhouse in the garden with Sally and her brothers. They had sleeping bags and mattresses and all settled down but the boys were talking all the time and she kept on telling them to keep quiet—she had a headache from it. Then Nanny came and agreed with her that they should settle down. But then she and Sally couldn't sleep so they got up and went out into the garden and saw a "figurehead" through the window—it was her mother. She motioned to her mother that they couldn't sleep—her mother phoned Sally's mother and then they went to Sally's place (in the same block of flats). She then described how Sally had a chair like mine in the room. She went over to my chair and showed me how it was built and how two chairs were joined together to make a bed—Sally slept on top and she slept underneath. She described the bar over her head—how she could hardly move and when she wanted to scratch her back, Sally told her to stop moving so much. Then Sally's duvet fell on top of her because the two chairs moved apart and then she couldn't move and couldn't breathe. In the morning she heard Sally talking—to herself, she thought—but Sally denied this and said, "I'm not—my brother is here." She had also heard her making funny noises in the night. Victoria then described the awful breakfast Sally's mother had prepared of strawberries and bananas, which Sally and her brother didn't want to have. Victoria said how delicious it was and ate it all up.

Without stopping, she went on to describe what happened on Sunday—that Mary Jane was going on a picnic, that she asked Mary Jane or maybe Mary Jane phoned her. At first she wasn't invited along so she then phoned Hilary and arranged to go out with her. And then Mary Jane phoned her back and asked her to go with them: she said that she had already made arrangements and couldn't but she really would have liked to go on the picnic, she acknowledged wistfully. She continued without pausing about how she went with Hilary handing out leaflets to various shops in the village advertising an all-day marathon of music at Hilary's school: she felt rather grown-up to be involved in this activity. Afterwards they went to a hamburger bar and just sat there and eventually a man came and offered them the menu saying they couldn't just sit there without ordering. She didn't order but the others did—she just wanted something to drink.

Occasionally while she was talking she took out her lip balm and smeared her mouth with it. She continued to speak about her time with Hilary, about the various complications of her relationship to Mary Jane and about who was and wasn't a best friend. She was prepared to go on and on—at which point I interrupted her.

I interpreted that she seemed to have had a marathon weekend with all these activities going on non-stop and there seemed to be a marathon in the session today too. "Oh no," she said. "On Saturday I didn't do anything—just stayed at home—maybe I went shopping a bit with my dad—only Saturday night and Sunday." Then she told me more about Sunday's barbeque with Hilary—as from this weekend, she was no longer a vegetarian. Then Hilary went home and she had a bath and did her homework.

(I was aware of already feeling quite flooded, as though I too was instructed to choose something from her menu when I just wanted an ordinary drink of water, so to speak. At the same time I also sensed that she could not cope with her defences being challenged—or, was she perhaps experiencing me as unable to cope with her marathon too? Who was the overwhelmed child and who was the overwhelmed mother? There seemed to be no third position, no father who could intervene effectively. It was difficult to know how to how to make contact in a helpful way. Clearly she could pretend to eat my "delicious" breakfast, while secretly experiencing my analytic food as quite awful.)

I suggested that she was in fact telling me that all this noise and busyness and all this talk was quite disturbing and exhausting—that it was quite a strain—it even gave her a headache and tummy ache. (I realise now that I was instinctively just picking up her affective experience. This was probably more containing for her in all likelihood than trying to make all sorts of links and attribute some symbolic meaning to her material, which would probably have overwhelmed her.)

She denied this and told me it was a lot of fun (rather thin, I thought.) She then took her drawing book, scribbled on one page, and turned it over and told me that she was looking forward to getting a CD player. She proceeded to draw what she later showed me was her CD player with the CD open to reveal the music. She said she was getting speakers. (She seemed to have these already!). Then she briefly showed me that the scribbles had been her attempts to draw the storm as she had been sketching last week, but she couldn't do it properly. She continued without pause … "I hope my mum will remember all the ingredients for cookery tomorrow …"

I indicated that perhaps she was not quite sure if I remembered how stormy she was feeling the previous week about her friends and their treatment of her. I said that I thought she wanted to fill her mind up with another kind of music today so that all those angry and upset feelings were replaced by a marathon of activities where she was included and not left out and not teased so horribly by her friends. I added that I also thought that when she was talking non-stop in the session she was trying to connect me with all of her weekend so that we were joined together like the two chairs—like two speakers—in a non-stop way, as though we had been together all the time, because otherwise she might become quite stormy here too.

She now got on the couch and touched the wall as though marking it, pressing her fingers against it. Then she tied a bow on her waist and untied it, playing with it a few times. She told me she hadn't got a best friend at the moment but Hilary was quite a good friend. She took the lip salve and rubbed it on her lips, smelled it, opened and tightened the lid a few times, playing with it. She tucked it under the fold of the blanket and kept it there tucked up while she flicked her fingers in a jazzy sort of style (like autistic "stimming"?). She was silent during all of this and lying properly on the couch with her feet on the mat. (This seemed like an important shift in the session as I felt she became depressed and more in touch with the emptiness, envy, jealousy, and exclusion. It was very painful to acknowledge not having a best friend. This was quite poignant.)

I spoke in a gentle tone suggesting that she seemed to be listening to some music in her head right now—having her own ongoing, non-stop playing, all conducted by her. Perhaps, I suggested, she didn't want to listen to me talking, especially about the weekend?

Victoria denied this and said she had a habit of flicking her fingers. Then she told me that she had a headache and felt sleepy.

I persisted, however, and suggested that she was trying to flick something away that disturbed her but she couldn't—it didn't work—something was still there in her head.

She then talked about Mary Jane being offered a prize if she won the scholarship—she was singing and whistling a bit in-between her talk. She carried on about the various girls and scholarships and who would get what and who knew how to get the best results—she went on and on about which friend would know and who would win and of course Mary Jane didn't stand a chance. She again took the lip salve, sucked it and used it; she was lying face down on the cushion and then seemed to want to curl up. (I now had a different experience of her, as though she was a much younger child.)

I took up that she seemed to want to comfort herself today with the lip salve, like a baby wanting to find a teat. I said that I thought she wished I would come in like a nanny—a mother—and know that all these voices and activities and competitiveness going round and round in her head didn't let her rest at all; they gave her a headache and exhausted her. I suggested that she wanted to get close to me too, to have me give her some comfort away from all that—which, being on the couch, the cushion, and coming back to me today, seemed to offer her.

"Yes," she said. She then turned the other way, facing the wall, curled up, her hand on a blanket wrapped around the bottle, and went to sleep for the rest of the session. I had to wake her up when we reached the end.

We can see in this session the way the mania affords her no resting place. She created such a restless, endlessly mobile expressway in her talk, that she had no comfortable or comforting object to turn to, no internal object to contain her, process her experiences for her, and be the alpha functioning maternal object (Bion, 1962) that she so needed. She seemed trapped between either "Don't talk/Don't move" or a carapace of mania where no storm could be allowed in or contained or tolerated. The material—the bed of two chairs, locked into one another, so that I found I couldn't move easily in the session—also suggested that she knew somewhere that she had to resort to mechanical connections to get me under her control and to control her own impulses and feelings.

I was also aware of how difficult it was to know what would be valuable to say to her. For quite a while I had several ideas while she was talking but it did not seem useful to say anything. When she described the chair she had to sleep under, which she linked to the chair in my room, was she unconsciously creating an oedipal couple with me in which I would not be able to move? Her manic descriptions of how much she was doing during the weekend was an attempt to join us together so that I was involved in every detail of her weekend. At the same time it was an attempt to deny exclusion and the pain of not being my "best friend". The material also conveys her feeling of emptiness without her analyst and the analytic space, and her unconscious manic strategy of filling that space and joining us together. Her descriptions of how much she was doing during the weekend might also be her attempt to project exclusion and envy, which, at the end of the day, did not really work and created unmanageable strain. We can also see how she desperately had to find a way to roll away or flick away all this strain. In this session we therefore get a picture of how she was desperately trying to appear normal but she grotesquely wasn't. (We can thus see how her manic marathon of social activities and apparently active social life could encourage her parents to believe she was a happy, ordinary child; that, at worst, she was just a funny or odd little girl who talked a lot.)

I struggled to process all of this and eventually did manage to address the strain she was under, her attempts to flick away her chaotic and disturbing feelings, which tormented her and could not be properly processed, as well as the way she sought to flick me away if I tried to show her what she was doing. I think that focussing on the strain enabled her to feel understood. I could then be experienced as a containing figure, linked to a mother who could pick up an agitated baby and convey a feeling of comfort, allowing the baby to be able to settle down and go to sleep. I did not experience the going to sleep as a withdrawal, splitting off in a negative sense, but as a relief that she could find some respite.

It was very evident that the mania was relentless; it went on and on. She once told me about a hopscotch game she had created which she considered quite brilliant: it had so many rules, all contradicting one another, so that if you got to one end, you had to turn around and get to the other end and the game was never-ending—no way could it be resolved. It seemed a fitting analogy: hopping here and there, but going nowhere, is how I experienced her in the sessions. There were moments, however, when I had a sense of her knowing in a profound way that she was not properly connected, not really the same as other girls. Furthermore, there was sometimes a genuine linking up with me when I did seem to be on the ball with her. She would listen intently, swallow, look uncomfortable and often say "Yes" quite directly, or disagree with me equally directly, rather than defensively, and correct me in my use of language if she felt I was not accurately describing something. For instance, when I interpreted her feeling worried about her move to secondary school, which occurred two years into the analysis, she told me she was not exactly worried but was nervous. In a sense she was right; worry would indicate a capacity to think about this; nervousness seemed to suggest a general state of mind that did not exactly have the same capacity for definition. However, I often found it difficult to know whether she was presenting me with an accurate description of her mind or putting me in my place, very much like a patronising parent would a slow-witted child. (I could imagine her father, a high-powered academic, doing this.)

At the end of the second year of analysis, the parents were pushing to end the treatment, just as they had at the end of the first year when all her symptoms disappeared. They were concerned that the analysis would impinge on the demands of secondary school. There was also an attempt to reduce the number of sessions. I was, however, still very concerned about her and remained firm in my conviction that the analysis needed to continue. At about this time she had a peculiar "spell" where she sat and stared into space in the classroom and alarmed her teacher. This was at the time of the scholarship exams, which fortunately worried the parents enough to trust me to continue. They also recognised that the pressure of the exams threatened Victoria and they withdrew her from the round of tests. I was also very worried about how she would negotiate the move to secondary school.

The mania continued in an accelerated form when she started at her new school. She rushed round all the lunchtime clubs, enrolling in each one—drama, chess, maths, and many more. Similarly, she was desperate to make friends and moved in and out of all sorts of casual encounters that never took hold. She tried to convince me it was all great fun. She was however, particularly concerned about her timetable at school, having to move to different classrooms for different subjects, and this coincided with a different timetable in the analysis as I now had to offer her different times. Thus nothing seemed secure and reliable; she had even lost the containment of having a "home" in one room. Mother, too, was in a state about which class group she would belong to, afraid she would be with girls who, in the past, had provoked her quite cruelly. Thus although from time to time there was an idea that Victoria no longer needed analysis, there was also a great resurgence of anxiety with this new move. Such anxieties are part of the ordinary developmental tasks of coping with a new school; but with Victoria, there was always a sense that she did not have the psychical equipment to manage, except by maintaining a whirlwind of activities that appeared normal, that "held" her precariously through this time and enabled her to survive, very like the constellation of "second skin" defences written about by Bick (1968).

Nonetheless, Victoria was able to continue in analysis for three and a half years and when we ended, she was more integrated, more able to process her experience of herself, and her manic defences had lessened considerably.

Discussion

Victoria was a child who came across as not properly connected to reality, in a profound and disturbing way. She seemed to be continually trying to put herself together, but like the description of the two chairs that were supposed to create a proper place to sleep, the result ended up being disturbing and bizarre. She seemed to live in a perpetual state where mad things assailed her.

What was taking place for these internal links to have been dismantled in such a disturbing way? Certainly in her early childhood, her shock and rage when she discovered that her mother was expressing milk for another baby and "all hell broke loose", and the ensuing subsequent development of hallucinatory, terrifying creatures suddenly appearing, as if ready to attack her, suggest some massive projection of fragments of her internal aggression. These may have been directed against a mother (combined figure) who had, until then been totally preoccupied with her. The attacked and disturbed external and overwhelmed internal mother, who submitted to her fury, may have led the way to further persecutory guilt. Victoria's agitated insistence with arranging a frame for her puzzles also points to her experience of not finding an object strong enough to tolerate difficulties, a focussed maternal eye, which cannot be easily poked into (as well as not being dangerously intrusive). But the vignette about getting lost also reveals how she could also perhaps contribute to her propensity to attack the links when she could not face knowing about her painful feelings, fears, and potential awareness of her guilt. Instead, the continuous manic whirlwind of talk, which whizzed her and her objects around, created a false carapace, which, at times, she seemed to idealise. Her "Mary Jane" dream, for instance, also suggested that she somewhere believed that she was so brilliant she would never have to struggle for answers; that she was omniscient and would know everything before she was asked. Similarly, her clever alphabet and biting limericks offered her a sense of superiority, presumably preferable to feeling small, humiliated, and enraged—and often confused. "Omnipotence replaces thinking and omniscience replaces learning from experience in a disastrously confused, undeveloped and fragile ego" (O'Shaughnessy, 1981, p. 149). But the dream also suggested that she wanted some help with this.

There were serious technical difficulties in working with her. Betty Joseph (1985) maintains that

> much of our understanding of the transference comes through our understanding of how our patients act on us to feel things for many varied reasons; how they try to draw us into their defensive systems; how they unconsciously act out with us in the transference, trying to get us to act out with them; how they convey aspects of their inner world built up from infancy ... experiences often beyond the use of words, which we can often only capture through the feelings aroused in us, through our countertransference, used in the broad sense of the word. (p. 157)

In this analysis, I had continually to monitor and process my countertransference and learn how to listen to Victoria in a way that resonated inside me. For much of the time it seemed more crucial to examine the function of my patient's talk than its content. Bion (1962) came to understand that psychotic patients employ a different type of projective identification, which, in addition to being a mechanism of defence, is the very first mode of communication between mother and infant—it is the origin of thinking. He emphasised the crucial significance of a mother's capacity for "reverie", her capacity to contain and transform her infant's experience, so that it can be tolerated and known. If the infant is not too persecuted or too envious, he will introject and identify with a mother who is able to think, and he will introject his own now modified feelings. This process gradually transforms the infant's entire mental situation and underpins a reality ego, which has unconsciously internalised at its core an object with the capacity to think, that is, to know psychic qualities in itself and others. "In such an ego there is a differentiation between conscious and unconscious, and the potential also to differentiate between seeing, imagining, phantasising, dreaming, being awake, being asleep. This is the normal mind, the achievement of which depends on both mother and infant" (O'Shaughnessy, 1981, p. 179).

When Victoria, in the first session, asked, "How do I know I am real?" and described her hallucinatory experiences and terrified feelings, we see a mind that not only does not feel normal, but is also not firmly embedded in reality. Furthermore, the manic defences that dominated her functioning, and the experience of the analysis, revealed, through projective identification into me, an experience of an internal mother without a mind, who ticked or crossed off experiences, without properly processing them and transforming them. As I have suggested, I became aware of how I could use my "analytic understanding" in a similarly manic omnipotent way. It seemed, at such times, that I was in projective identification with her internal overwhelmed, intellectualising, non-understanding mother, invariably talking another language, involved in my "esoteric religion"—psychoanalysis—and out of touch with her communications. Who was who at such times? Was I mirroring her, trying to be balanced and normal too, being everywhere and nowhere? Brenman Pick (1985), in her seminal paper on the countertransference, writes: "The analyst needs to work through the experience of feeling like an overwhelmed mother threatened with disintegration by an interaction with the overwhelmed baby" (1985, p. 46). I believe this was the crucial work of this analysis. The more I could stay with my own unconscious enactments and process them, the more effective I became in addressing her manic defensive organisation, so that she gradually became more able to stay with her psychic pains and her hatred of a reality that was not under her omnipotent control. I learnt that with such a patient it was important to stay with her affective state, rather than to have an expectation that she had an understanding of meaning. I had to bear "being lost" and not knowing where I was without defending against that undesirable and quite threatening state of mind. It was not always clear what she could not bear to let in at any moment. I had to experience being encaged by her talk and manic narratives before I could find ways of freeing my mind and finding a third position (Britton, 1989). In a sense, I had to experience being an infant with a confusing and intrusive object filling me up, as well as feeling like a first-time ill-equipped mother, overwhelmed by all that I had to manage. And often I failed. The analysis brought all of this to the fore in the wake of a torrential tsunami of persecutory anxieties and manic defences that were failing to withstand the onslaught of potential psychotic breakdown. My patient, however, attempted to hold on to her "normality", albeit relentlessly on a tightrope of mania, and was desperate enough to begin to face her own internal nightmares and her struggle with her reality, as well as her attempts to triumph over and to control me. In this way she allowed the carapace to be at least partially dismantled.

References

Abraham, K. (1919). A particular form of neurotic resistance against the psychoanalytic method. In: *Selected papers on Psychoanalysis* (pp. 303–311). London: Hogarth, 1927.

Baruch, G. (1997). The manic defence in analysis: The creation of a false narrative. *International Journal of Psychoanalysis, 78*: 549–559.

Bick, E. (1968). The experience of skin in early object-relations. *International Journal of Psychoanalysis, 49*: 484–486.

Bion, W. R. (1962). A theory of thinking. In: *Second Thoughts*. New York: Jason Aronson, 1967.

Brenman Pick, I. (1985). Working through in the counter-transference. In: E. Bott Spillius (Ed.), *Melanie Klein Today. Vol. 2. Mainly Practice*. London: Routledge, 1988.

Britton, R. (1989). The missing link: parental sexuality in the Oedipus complex. In: J. Steiner (Ed.), *The Oedipus Complex Today*. London: Karnac.

Freud, S. (1917b). Mourning and melancholia. *S. E., 14*: 237–258. London: Hogarth.

Joseph, B. (1985). Transference: the total situation. In: E. Bott Spillius (Ed.), *Melanie Klein Today. Vol. 2. Mainly Practice*. London: Routledge, 1988.

Klein, M. (1935). A contribution to the psychogenesis of manic-depressive states. *International Journal of Psychoanalysis, 16*: 145–174.

O'Shaughnessy, E. (1981). W. R. Bion's theory of thinking and new techniques in child analysis. In: E. Bott Spillius (Ed.), *Melanie Klein Today. Vol.2. Mainly Practice*. London: Routledge, 1988.

Rey, H. (1994). The schizoid mode of being and the time-space continuum (before metaphor). In: J. Magagna (Ed.), *Universals of Psychoanalysis in the Treatment of Psychotic and Borderline states*. London: Free Association.

Riviere, J. (1936). A contribution to the analysis of the negative therapeutic reaction. *International Journal of Psychoanalysis, 17*: 304–320.

Segal, H. (1981). *The Work of Hanna Segal*. New York: Jason Aronson.

CHAPTER TWENTY-THREE

Psychoanalytic work with an adopted child with a history of early abuse and neglect

Margaret Rustin

Introduction

The institutional context for the case I shall discuss in this chapter is an important one and records an important moment in the development of child psychotherapy in the UK. The background in theoretical developments within Kleinian and post-Kleinian thinking is equally important, and I shall first address these two aspects of the framework which together made clinical work of this kind possible.

In the 1960s, individual courageous child psychotherapists began to attempt psychoanalytic work with children with very severely deprived and compromised early life experiences (Boston, 1972). This was a time in which hopefulness about the potential impact of analytic work with severe disturbances in children was at its height in the London psychoanalytic community. There was considerable enthusiasm for child analysis from informed parents and child psychiatric colleagues, a growing demand for training, and a National Health Service network of clinics employing the still tiny number of qualified child psychotherapists to which a wide range of children in difficulties were being referred. The inherited wisdom of the child guidance tradition had been that "milieu" therapy (Dockar-Drysdale, 1990) was needed for children whose start in life had not provided a relationship with a "good enough" object. Psychoanalysis was deemed to require an already established internalised good maternal figure as a starting point.

Bion's elaboration of Klein's account of the early development of mind (Bion, 1962) was immediately seen by child analysts and psychotherapists to offer them something vital. His theory of maternal reverie, that, is the openness of the mother's mind in her care of her baby to receiving awareness of profound infantile anxieties and her capacity to transform these "nameless dreads" into meaningful emotional experience, described how a mind was formed through relationship with a more mature being whose attentive and attuned responsiveness created the building blocks of meaning and thinking. The language of container/contained (Bion, 1970) made sense of the chaotic, unpredictable behaviour of young children whose anxieties had not been contained or given meaning in contexts of disorganised, neglectful, or abusive early parenting. Projective identification, thus reconceptualised as communication, and not only as intrusive and aggressive, opened up a new vista. If the fragmentation and intensity of these children's experiences could be "gathered" (Meltzer, 1967) in a transference relationship it seemed possible that normal forms of development could be set in motion and their pathological defences be replaced by states of mind that would enable them to benefit from relationships, to grow, to feel more bearable emotions, and to learn.

This new psychoanalytic vertex required new techniques—classical interpretation of anxieties and defences was not tolerable or useful to patients whose minds could not yet conceive thoughts. The thinking and "dreaming" in Bion's terms about the earliest infantile fears as described by both Bion (1962) and Bick (1968) had first to be done by the mother or, in the clinical context, by the analyst. This kind of realisation also led, for example, to Steiner's (1993) formulation of "analyst-centred" interpretations as the necessary precursor to interpretations that focus on the mind and experience of the patient.

Prior to many of these theoretical formulations, Bick's invention of infant observation (1964) for child psychotherapists at the start of clinical training had already proved to be immensely important in helping therapists find a way of being with children whose unformed minds were fragmented or liable to melt-down. The discipline of closely observing the emotional interchange of mothers and babies and of not intervening was a good basis for sustaining observation under pressure, and of receiving what a child needed to project without rushing to give it back. The patience and mental space needed to take in and hold on to what was being communicated in often primitive nonverbal ways was a capacity that infant observation nourished and supported (Rustin, 2015). Child psychotherapists were therefore particularly attuned to the theorisation deriving from Bion's insights, eager to link their clinical and observational experience with his conceptualisations.

The Tavistock Clinic in the 1970s played a particular role in this evolution of clinical practice with children. The strong tradition of infant observation (Rustin, 2009), the clinic's commitment to work towards *national* mental health, meaning the population as a whole, not only the privileged minority who might have knowledge of and access to psychoanalysis, and the multi-disciplinary teams available to contribute to the care of patients led to the formation of a workshop studying and consulting to the institutions that were caring for severely deprived children—initially children's homes, and later mainly foster care—and exploring the potential for individual psychotherapy with these troubled children and adolescents (Boston & Szur, 1983). A large number of children were taken on for treatment and their therapy presented in the workshop, and this resulted in a growing conviction in the possibilities for internal change in the children, more understanding of the conditions that were required for this (long-term therapies, ongoing work with carers, close supervision to support therapists, institutional tolerance of much acting-out by the children, community liaison, especially with schools), and more understanding of the tremendous strain often placed on adoptive and foster families who gave these children shelter. There was also a keen appreciation of what a multi-disciplinary clinical research workshop could offer its members. The high levels of anxiety, mental pain, and uncertainty—and, indeed, in twenty-first-century terms, "risk"—that therapy with these children entailed, was contained by the structured process of the group's work. It supported clinicians taking risks in the best sense.

As child psychotherapy has gradually spread across the UK, one trend that stands out is the high level of referral of children in the care system for psychotherapy, and this remains one of the major ways in which public mental health clinics make use of child psychotherapists. Some modest but significant research work on process and outcome with this population has aided the recognition of the relevance of psychotherapy for children who have been neglected or maltreated in their early years (Kennedy & Midgley, 2007).

The case

The case I shall now discuss is probably fairly representative of many children adopted by parents eager to help children who had suffered a catastrophic start in life. Not infrequently, the families found that the children brought serious difficulties with them, which were very disturbing to their parents and others. My patient Tim was a boy aged eight when I began to see him once a week. This followed some months of intensive (three times a week) psychoanalytic psychotherapy with a colleague who unexpectedly became seriously ill. She hoped to return to work with him in due course, but this proved not possible. I therefore continued to see him, and the therapy ended when he was twelve and a half and had made a successful move into secondary school.

This case highlights some important contemporary issues in analytic work with children. The question of frequency is of course a very important one in psychoanalysis generally at this time. Although I only ever saw my patient once a week, I believe we had a psychoanalytic relationship. Despite the high level of acting out in his sessions in the early years, which I shall describe, it was possible to sustain a focus on transference/countertransference dynamics, and the work we did addressed deep levels of internal object relationships.

My patient seemed to lack a sense of belonging to the human family when I first met him. He had been adopted at age five, and the picture of himself as an outsider was painfully enacted in the family context. In his therapy, I felt pushed to extremes of anxiety and doubt about my capacity to hold on.

Tim's history

When Tim came to the S family aged three and three quarters, he joined a family in which there was already one adopted son, Jack, aged seven at that time. The couple very much wished to have a family, and had decided they would adopt when it became clear that Mrs S would be unable to bear a child. In Jack they had already taken on a child with appalling early experiences. When a second boy became available for adoption, they agreed to go ahead, although family circumstances at that particular time were stressful and Mrs S was under a good deal of strain.

Tim's early years had been chaotic and full of tragedy. His birth mother was a prostitute, herself brought up in care as an adolescent. Her first child had been removed and subsequently adopted. Following several terminated pregnancies, she gave birth to Tim. Tim and she lived in at least six different places in his first three months of life. She separated from his father because of serious violence a few months later and the following year she married another man who was in and out of prison. He is said to have disliked Tim, who, however, seems to have had a special place in his mother's troubled heart. Another child was born in the following year, and Tim and his sibling spent numerous periods in local authority care on a voluntary basis. When Tim was two years old, there was a fire in their home and this little brother did not survive. Tim was taken into care and plans made for his future. He is said to have been Mother's favourite. She never gave her consent to his adoption, though she failed to turn up for the final court hearing, and so it went ahead.

When Tim came into care aged two and a quarter, his behaviour in the foster family indicated a history of sexual abuse, which was investigated and broadly substantiated. At this time, he was described as being delayed in development: he had little speech, and could not feed himself. His behaviour was extremely sexualised, and he called everyone Mummy. His mother had weekly access visits. When she failed to turn up, Tim became obviously depressed. After more than a year in foster care and a nursery placement, he had improved greatly and adoption began to be considered for him. However, when Tim went to live with the Ss he became withdrawn; he avoided eye contact and regressed to indiscriminate behaviour.

Referral

When the Ss came to the Tavistock clinic some years later, originally because of their concern about Jack, they gradually began to share their worries about Tim. They described his secretiveness, his lying, his aggression towards other children, his sexualised behaviour, and later also spoke of their (particularly mother's) tremendous difficulty in getting close to him. They described their very first encounter with Tim when he was three and a half: he was roller skating along the pavement of a busy road at high speed, in the opposite direction from his foster home. Now aged seven, Tim would disappear if he hurt himself or felt ill and curl up in his bed silently. Mother felt wounded by this refusal of care, but was able to tell us later on that she felt she had not loved Tim when he first came to the family. In fact she said she had sometimes hated him: she felt so involved with Jack that there was nothing left for Tim. Father, however, felt closer to him. It is important to note here that consistent long-term support was provided for these parents by a very skilled psychiatric social worker throughout the period of their children's treatment.

Following the discovery of sexual play between the boys, Mr and Mrs S wanted therapy to be considered for Tim; Jack had already had one year's treatment. A psychotherapy assessment revealed Tim's extreme anxiety about his capacity and urge to destroy, but also gave a picture of a needy and expressive little boy. Some months later, therapy began on an intensive three times a week basis.

His first therapist had a very difficult two terms of work with him. After a brief seductive interlude, tremendous violence erupted. Tim wreaked havoc in the therapy room and disturbed his therapist deeply by his ruthlessness and inaccessibility. Unfortunately, she then became unexpectedly ill, and this entailed some months' absence from the clinic. What was to be done?

Both Tim and his parents were in a highly upset state about Tim's therapy and its interruption, and it seemed necessary for the clinic to provide some holding for Tim through these months. This is the point at which I became involved. I agreed to see Tim weekly, until his therapy could resume.

Beginning therapy

In his first session with me, his challenging behaviour was immediately evident as he explored the room, attempting to poke holes in the ceiling tiles and to attract his brother's attention during his session, which was taking place at the same time elsewhere in the clinic, by semaphore-like antics at the window. However, he then became fascinated by the project of making a parachute. He used a small plastic bag that had contained some of the toys I provided for him, to which he fixed strands of Sellotape, linked together to represent an open parachute. He showed me that he wanted it to land gently, but anything he used to attach to the parachute turned out to be too heavy and to cause an immediate crash to the ground. He was both persistent and frustrated by the unsuitability of Sellotape for his purpose, and he left still intent on pursuing this idea and with a promise to try with string next week.

In the next couple of weeks he tested out my boundaries in every possible way, and also invented an elaborate game, which, he told me, was so that I would be trapped as a prisoner. The following session was missed due to a heavy snowfall that prevented the family reaching the clinic. When he next came, Tim's response to this began with a renewed interest in the parachute theme, which led me to talk about the shock of the missed session the week before. Perhaps, I suggested, it had felt like crashing to the ground when he realised they would not get here. His activities developed into a desperate effort to take control of the room and of me. This included a sequence in which he used the desk lamp to enact being an optician who then turned out to be a torturer, shining the light into my eyes and staring at me with a fiercely cruel expression. He was enraged when I turned my head away.

Turning his attention elsewhere, he crawled around under the furniture and the room was filled with a faecal smell. Next he tried to make a 999 (emergency) call on the telephone. Any comment from me elicited "Fuck off" or a snarl, with the exception of a brief interlude when he wanted to explain to me where he lived and drew a detailed map of the part of London where his home was. After I had thwarted his attempts to flood the room, he again became friendlier and started to tell me a version of the story of Cyrano de Bergerac in which his interest was focused on Cyrano's difficulty in getting a drink because his long nose always got in the way. I was able to talk to him about the idea that his intrusive nosiness about me and my room might in fact be preventing him getting something good from me.

In these early months of work there were many sessions that brought me to the edge of my capacities as a therapist. Tim threatened my peace of mind with a bewildering variety of weapons and I often felt close to hopelessness about being able to find the part of him that might respond to understanding. I would wake up on Thursday mornings, which was the day of his session, feeling very anxious and physically fearful—would I manage to keep the session within some bearable degree of control? My fears ranged from his dangerous behaviour at the high window, with which he thrilled to torment me, to concern for my room and its contents and for my own physical integrity; not so much direct fear of how he would hurt me, although this did happen, but more subtle assaults, which left me feeling abused and exposed. This was sometimes a physical reality, as when he held on to a handful of my hair as if to pull it out by the roots, but more often it was mental cruelty that left me feeling shattered.

I spent large chunks of sessions feeling that I had nowhere to put myself—Tim would commandeer all the furniture and I would feel lost and homeless in my room. I experienced shame and helplessness, knowing that he would jeer at whatever I said and feeling huge and foolish. He once spoke of me as one of the smelly vagrants on the River Thames embankment, telling me I lived in a cardboard box, and at that moment I certainly felt exposed to the cruelest elements of his personality in an unprotected way.

This experience of shame (Cregeen, 2009) I came to understand better later on in our work, when there was a session in which Tim enacted a sexual scene before me. He climbed on top of the wall cupboard in my room on which he could lie full-length, quite high up. Prior to this he had been scribbling abusive and sexually explicit words on the wall in red pen and he took the pen up with him, taunting me even more pointedly from above my head. As he lay there, I had to stand quite close to make sure he did not tumble down as he writhed around, and in a state of wild excitement he began to enact intercourse in a grossly lewd and noisy fashion, declaiming that I was desperate to touch him because he was so fantastic. The horror and pain evoked in me was difficult to bear. I felt I was being made to feel what the toddler Tim had endured, an excruciating awareness of his mother's life as a prostitute to which he had been exposed, simultaneously excited and humiliated. The mixture of his great love for her, and the ugly violation of her better self and his infantile vulnerability had, I believe, stirred up intense shame and confusion. The impact on his oedipal development of this premature exposure to adult sexual activity, doubtless heightened by the experience of actual sexual abuse, was alive in the room, and it was possible for me to speak to him about this. After describing what he was doing, I said that he wanted me to know about a little Tim who felt terribly upset when he imagined me in this room with a horrible Tavistock Daddy. He wanted to show me that his mind today was full of a sexy show-off Mummy—me, who enjoyed making him feel left out and forcing him to see things he could not bear. Perhaps there was a long-ago Tim who felt tormented by things Mummy did that he could not get out of his mind.

His response was very moving and unexpected. He quietened, asked me to help him climb down, and then fetched a cloth from the sink and washed all the red graffiti from the wall. He did this with extraordinary care and there was a deep silence in the room. It took him quite a long time.

Signs of development

I now want to describe some elements in the therapeutic process that represented the thrust towards his claiming a place in my mind and a sense for my patient that he did belong somewhere (Rustin, 2006), even though this was a fragile conviction always easily disturbed by separations.

I think a degree of safety entered into Tim's relationship with me when it was realised that the original idea of his returning to his first therapist was not practical and that I needed to continue with him on a long-term basis. Tim began to show me occasional searing glimpses of his painful memories. His vulnerability to hurt had always been evident whenever there was any possibility in our all-too-frequent physical struggles that he could be hurt. He behaved as if his skin had no solidity at all, and although at times I wondered if he wanted me to be guilty and anxious about the risk of hurting him, I mainly felt that he believed himself to lack any protective covering. In one session, when there had been a long series of confrontations between us as to the limits of what I would allow, as I held on to him up on the desk that was by the window, panting with the effort involved in preventing him kicking me or wriggling out of the window, I said to him, "Tim, one of my tasks is to take care of your body and of mine, not to let you or myself get hurt if I can prevent it. That is why I am holding you now, because you are not safe near the window when you are upset." The fighting tension went out of his body and he curled up in a heap, crying very softly. After a few minutes he whispered to me "Nobody ever took care of my body." I talked to him about his worries as a little boy that nobody cared for him, his belief that he could only rely on making himself feel big and strong to survive all the frightening things in the world, and his hope that I would understand all of this. I sat close to him, speaking very quietly, and with the conviction that my going on talking to him was very important. He could not see me because he was curled up like a foetus, but I thought the sound of my voice was soothing to him, and that my words also would mean something.

At one point when I had been speaking of his baby experiences, he said very quietly "I don't want to talk about that any more now." On another occasion he had spent the first half of the session fighting me by hurling things from behind a barricade made of all the movable furniture in the room. Then he began to construct a camp inside all this heap of furniture, using the blanket I provided as a roof. Curled up, completely hidden from me inside his safe haven, he communicated by weak cries and moans that he was starving and dreaming of food that was out of reach.

A crucial sequence of sessions took place after one Christmas break. Just before that holiday, he had been telling me with unusual freedom and pleasure about his school play, which was about convicts in nineteenth-century London who were to be transported to Australia. His part was to play one of the convicts, and he described the prison ships and the farewell to friends and family on the last morning, and sang a poignant song about losing his homeland and all that he loved. He had a sweet singing voice and narrated this whole story with great feeling, making me think about the profound links between individuality and mother-infant communication (Malloch & Trevarthen, 2010). When he returned after the holiday, he had two sessions before his brother's therapy sessions resumed, and these visits to the clinic seemed to hold special meaning for him. His mother was bringing *just him*, not Tim merely as an attachment to the older child he believed to be the favourite. He looked around my room after a brief explosive entry and suddenly it seemed he had a brainwave. He began to move all the furniture systematically into different positions, not in a jumble, but in order to create a quite new room. The physical labour involved in this was immense, and as I was concerned about the weight of some items, I offered to help him, which he accepted. We were co-operating like two furniture removers. He decorated the newly positioned desk with a plant and objects from his drawer of toys, which he said were to be ornaments, and created a little corner for himself, almost completely enclosed, where he could draw on the low table, kneeling on the blanket and pillow, while I sat and watched on a chair that he placed for me just by him. I had a conviction that Tim felt at home in a quite new way now that he had devised a way of making the room his own so dramatically. He began each of the following sessions by repeating this sequence.

One week into this sequence of sessions I received a message from Mr S cancelling all the family's sessions because of illness. Seven minutes after the usual start of Tim's session, I received a phone call from reception saying that Tim was in fact waiting for me: clearly there had been a muddle and the message given to me was wrong. I hastily prepared to receive Tim, which took a few minutes, and we therefore began about ten minutes late. Predictably enough, we had a terribly difficult session. He ran ahead and blocked me out of the room, and, in the end, I had to force my way in. There followed a long sequence of provocative and risky behaviours—spitting, hurling items, blood-curdling threats. The one quieter moment involved his playing with a wobbly tooth, eventually pulling it out triumphantly. But Tim then immediately stared in a very anxious way at his tooth, convinced that he had pulled out some flesh with it and would now have what he called a "black hole" in his mouth. In the last few minutes of the session he turned my room into as big a mess as he could, maliciously commenting that it would take me a long time to clear up.

A crucial session

The following week started more calmly, and to my amazement we even entered the consulting room together, the first time this had been achieved in many months.

Straightaway but with a surly expression on his face, he began to move the furniture around. He accepted my help with the desk in quite a friendly way—negotiating which end to move, etc.—while I talked about his wanting to make the room feel his own today. The atmosphere seemed tense and volatile. When he moved towards the chest of drawers, he very violently slammed shut the drawer that contained his toys and materials. Then he bent to scratch at his leg just below the knee, a bit secretively, with his back to me. I wondered aloud if he might have a sore leg but be unsure about showing me. He came closer and told me, "It itches—it's a bite." I said, "When you want to bash and hurt something, the hurt seems to bounce back at you and leave you feeling hurt." Then he fetched the rug and lay down on the sofa, now under the window, and wrapped himself up completely inside it. Just as he had been preparing to do this I suggested pulling the blind down as the room was getting rather hot. I decided to go ahead and do this, though it involved leaning over him to reach the window, which felt uncomfortably close. However, he remained peaceful. He lay still inside the rug briefly, then he seemed to be scratching at something—and I wondered aloud what was feeling wrong. He replied, but I could hardly hear, and then he spoke again. It sounded like "shady and cool". I talked to him about his searching for protection from the sun, which felt too hot today, and then went on to speak about last week when he had also wanted some protection. I talked about his sore mouth last week, thinking of the hurt leg today—and I mentioned the loose tooth. "I got one pound for my tooth," he interrupted in a lively tone. "Did you?" I replied and added: "You were pleased that I remembered about your tooth and feel friendlier when you know I have remembered you. Perhaps needing to wrap yourself up today was linked with feeling hurt?" He emerged, and with great seriousness rolled up the pillow inside the rug, using the whole floor to do this as a neat package, then placed this in his table-corner.

He then looked round the room appraisingly. He fetched some water for the plants from the sink using the watering can. First, the spider plant on top of the tall cupboard—delicately removing a couple of dead leaves. "Where is the bin?" he said and added, "It's not growing; there aren't any little ones yet." Then he moved to the plant on the window sill. "Do you water the plants?" he asked me, in a friendly tone of voice. I spoke of his questions about whether I keep in mind the things that are important to him from week to week and whether I know how to look after growing things and provide what they need. He said seriously that I should take the plants out of the room when other children come in here; a younger child might pull bits off. I spoke about his doubt about allowing his different feelings to be in the room together. The younger wild and angry little Tim who has often wanted to attack me and my plants and my room is feared by the more thoughtful Tim here just now who would like the plants and himself to grow.

Tim again scanned the room with careful attention. He fetched his drawing book and pencil and settled down in a corner to sketch the watering can, which he placed with the utmost care in a position from which he could see it well, as if he were an artist in his studio, setting up a still life. I sat on the couch and after a while spoke of his uncertainty about how close he wanted me to be today. Usually he puts a chair for me just by him, but today his mixed feelings made that seem impossible. I linked this to the upset of last week's delayed start, and his uncertainty about whether I am to be trusted. He looked up as if light were suddenly dawning, and rearranged the room to put my chair in its usual place. Then he said, "You can sit there if you want." I spoke of his not being sure if he dare tell me that this is what he wants when he is not sure if I want to be with him—when I wasn't there at the right time last week, he felt it was evidence that I did not want him. I moved to sit by him and look at his drawing. After a few minutes he realised this altered the light and shade on the paper, and asked me to move again, showing me the light problem that was altering his composition. I moved away to re-create the original situation. He asked if he could show the picture to his father at the end. I said that we would keep that in mind and think about what this meant today. I suggested that he was wanting to find a father part of myself who will see that Tim is learning from me and recognise what he feels is a good and hard-working aspect of himself. As he carried on drawing, I talked about how interested he was in light and shade today, perhaps wondering if his own light and dark feelings towards me might be able to connect up. He responded by looking behind the desk to his right, which is a very dark part of the room, particularly so on this occasion because of the bright sunshine outside. I said he now felt interested in looking into the darker places. He mouthed into the dark space "Hello, hello", and asked if I heard the echo. I spoke of his wish that I listen to a "baby" Tim that wants to explore inside himself and me.

Just as he was preoccupied with this game, he became aware of sirens outside in the road. "What's that?" he asked. I wondered what he imagined. "Murder … there's been an accident, someone's hurt … fire … there's a cat on a roof … someone's threatening to commit suicide." Then he made another reference to a fire, someone being hurt and the ambulance getting there in time, as if recalling something he knew about. This was particularly poignant since I knew that a younger sibling had in fact died in a fire and that this had been the trigger for his being removed from his mother's care. I said Tim was thinking that today the emergency services, which he wants me to have ready for many disasters between us, might be getting there in time with the right intervention, the right ideas. Last week he had felt when I came late that a catastrophe had taken place—he was afraid I was hurt or dead, and afraid that he would be left without help, as he had worried when Mrs P was ill and had to stop her work with him. Today he felt more hopeful that he could get a message to me about his worries about himself and me, that he felt I understood how frightened he was, like a cat stranded on a roof. This made him feel that a rescue might be possible and a disaster not have to happen.

He began to curl up under the little table, making a bigger space by propping the table up on one set of legs. "It's nice under here," he said with satisfaction. I said he felt he had been able to settle down with me today, and that it was like finding a safe home. Then gradually the atmosphere changed—perhaps as he noticed the evidence of some paint marks he had previously made under the table. He began to pull at the desk drawers. I said he was now wanting to poke inside all my space and find out about what did not belong to him. "Where is the phone?" he asked angrily. I said he was full of questions today about me and my room and the other people I was connected with, and was remembering the phone that used to be here. I reminded him that he knew that I had removed it because it had been too upsetting for him and too interfering to our work.

He then asked for his paints and a little water. I remarked on his wanting me to keep firmly in mind how risky things often are here, being mindful of so many struggles over dirty water, which he loved to squirt round the room. Tim said he would be very careful, and asked for just a little water in the pot. He started to paint black under the table, lying on his back and doing it from underneath. I wondered whether he could tell me about what he was doing. "All black," he said, "so no-one else can use it." As he painted I talked about Tim wanting to take over all the space here, to fill my mind up completely with him; I linked this to last week when he had felt cheated, and wanted to cover me with his spit. He had felt this would be like a label, that I was Tim's, to keep anyone else off me, because he felt he made me so disgusting no one else would want me. Perhaps the black paint was also a bit like that. He went on painting very carefully the underneath of the table. I reminded him about his idea that if other children came in here they would want to spoil me and all my things, as he had told me earlier when he said that a little child might pull off the leaves of my plant. The other children he had in mind seemed to be like the attacking, greedy, and possessive parts of himself. I talked about how much he wished to make me into a Mrs Rustin with a label on saying "Keep out" to all the other children. "It's not only the children," he said quietly. I said this was important, he was correcting me, and explaining that he could not bear to think of anyone else being with me, children or grown-ups (and at this moment I thought with pain of his mother's life as a prostitute). "I'm doing well, aren't I?" he said, in a reflective tone. As he painted with notable care he suddenly said, "Has anyone died in the Tavi?" I asked if he could tell me any more about this question. He could only repeat it. I then said I had two ideas I wanted to share with him. Last week he had felt very afraid that I had died, but he had also been afraid that he had died in my mind, and that I had forgotten him or no longer cared about him. For little Tim this felt like my letting him die or even killing him. Now we were near the end of our session today and he was again feeling worried about whether I would be keeping him alive in my mind until next week and whether he would be able to remember me. I suggested that when it was time for our session to end he felt confused about whether I was sending him away because we had done our work for today and he could feel ready to go or whether I was throwing him out in a cruel way, as he had felt last week. We spent the last few minutes clearing up together. Tim was obviously quite anxious about his mother telling him off about the paint water that had got on to his clothes, and he picked up his sketchbook to show his father the drawing he had done in the waiting room. I thought this was to reassure himself, as his drawing would be appreciated.

Discussion

This session seemed to me to herald the possibility that links can be sustained for long enough for some modification in Tim's severely split relationship to his internal mother to take place. The acutely breathless, volatile, and edgy atmosphere of many prior sessions gives way here to some sense of rhythm, to my having enough time to say things and his having time to listen. I knew that something important had happened when we entered the room *together*. The dimension of time (Canham, 1999) was present in his mind—he wondered if I watered the plants in-between times and told me (this is unprecedented) something that links last week and this, in the news about his tooth money, something that links his external world with the therapy world. This contrasted with his usually acutely anxious desire to seal off the mayhem of the consulting room and our time together from the rather charming boy he presents himself as in the waiting room, where he is a great favourite of the receptionists.

Once the space of the week between sessions is present for him, so are the other children who come to see me, and indeed not only children, as he himself remarks. I am perceived not as someone he must master and control because I am an unwilling and untrustworthy slave but as someone who could be asked for something and who will not be offended if the most important thing for him is not always myself—it could be that the drawing, which links him with his daddy, is what provides something solid to hold on to at the point of separation.

The technical question he posed for me rather relentlessly was what I could afford to risk. Black paint all over the floor, and on me, for example. The important point, I think, was that I was not to know and must endure the pain of taking the risk. If I imposed too many limits, I implied no trust at all in his potential for responsible behaviour, but I had to live with this knowledge of his capacity for sadistic delight in cynical trickery, alongside the appreciation of being understood and finding meaning.

Broader reflections

The clinical process with Tim highlights some central Kleinian and post-Kleinian concepts, which have proved particularly relevant to work with abused and deprived children. Klein's (1936) originality in describing the intense neediness of the infant for responsive maternal care was to see that the infant's anxieties arose not only from the fact of initial total dependence but also from the urgent pressure to be relieved of the terror aroused by his own overwhelming impulses. She conceptualised the baby's love and hate as rooted in the life and death instincts with which the infant is confronted from the start of life. The role of the mother can then be understood as not only the provision of physical care for the baby to ensure survival and growth, but also of psychological receptivity to modify his fears of abandonment. Bion's development of a theory of the growth of mind that showed the process of preverbal communication between infant and mother taking place through the mechanism of projective identification, maternal reverie, and understanding, elaborated Klein's description of the object-relatedness of the baby from birth onwards.

Tim's sensitivity to any feelings of loss of safety is more than understandable from the point of view of his early experience. Frequent brief episodes of being cared for by unknown people when his mother could not cope, a preoccupied mother with no stable home and abusive partners, the death of a sibling, permanent loss of mother's care and subsequent loss of a foster-mother when placed for adoption, all added to by the loss of his first therapist, exposed him to a repeated experience of existential threat. The absence of a reliable external parental figure meant that his internal world was peopled by figures he suspected and could not trust. The volatility in his relationship with me was, however, as became clear, due not only to his vulnerability to believing me to be another abandoning maternal figure but also to the unpredictable upsurges of violent mistrust and hatred that threatened him with having nowhere to project his aggression. If I was not there, could he survive? "Has anyone died in the Tavistock?" he asked, and I think at depth this question referred to his anxiety about both his lost internal maternal object and his own endangered healthy self. The frightening black hole of his lost tooth and his marked sense of painful bodily vulnerability both express the visceral quality of a very early fear of loss of life, of absence of protection from deathly anxieties. Bick's description of early infantile states (Bick, 1964, 1968) and Tustin's later work on this theme (Tustin, 1992) have become classics for child psychotherapists in much of their work with severely disturbed children.

The growth of capacities for observation, reflection, and memory is what can modify the profound insecurity of the infant. The child who has had many changes of primary carer early in life has, however, a particular area of loss with respect to memory. The story of his early life is not known to the parents who are bringing him up. In my work with Tim, I thought my giving him evidence of my capacity to recall details from earlier sessions was very important to him. It provided him with an experience of my having a functioning memory that could store what was relevant and draw on it. In later work with him, it was his growing ability to distinguish past, present, and an imagined future, that seemed to usher in his readiness to work towards ending his therapy.

A second critical issue was of course the question of whether things could be put right. What balanced Klein's deep concern with the distinctive forces in mental life was not only her attention to the balance of love and hate in the personality but also her discovery of the impulse to repair. In the early months of work with Tim it was precisely the absence of any sense of concern about the impact of his ruthless behaviour that was most disturbing to me. This echoed what greatly upset his parents, who feared that his habitual lying and complete refusal to acknowledge any fault presaged a psychopathic delinquent future. It was, therefore, of great significance when reparative and creative behaviour emerged (Segal, 1957). His willingness to tackle clearing up the pornographic mess he had made in daubing my wall opened up the possibility of the creative use of art materials to explore internal and external reality.

His artistic expansiveness also represented oedipal development. The dominant configuration at the start was one in which parental intercourse was represented as continuous, violent, ugly, and perverse, something inflicted on the child in order to torment him with feelings of exclusion, powerlessness, and humiliation. At the start in the countertransference, one of my striking experiences was the loneliness I felt, not only the loneliness of the neglected infant that Tim often projected on to me, but also the loneliness of having no adult to turn to in my own mind. No doubt this had something to do with my feeling echoes of his mother's unsupported circumstances in his first two years, but I also saw it as a broken oedipal link in which I as mother could find no father during the sessions. Sometimes I found myself needing to talk to a colleague afterwards to recover a sense of reality and my awareness of potential support. The oedipal triangle was, therefore, marked by its frequent absence (O'Shaughnessy, 1989). When Tim began to draw—and also when he could use paper to write, in the form of messages, thoughts that were too difficult to say out loud—mental space seemed present in a new way. Symbolic expression went hand in hand with new possibilities with respect to the oedipal triangle. Tim and father could have a link of which I was the observer, as described by Britton (1989) and at the same time I could find my mind at work freely, able to be in intercourse with my psychoanalytic intuition and intellectual resources afresh.

Looking back at my title, one could say that what is unavoidable when there is serious early abuse and neglect as well as loss is that the therapist is going to have to survive being badly treated and feeling neglected over a long period. Only if the child can feel that she has really taken in what it means to count for nothing, to face much cruelty, and to believe one is alone in the world is there going to be the possibility of his discovery of a mind that can take the measure of his experience and not throw it back at him. To do this work, the psychoanalytic concepts I have mentioned were a vital resource. Also needed is an institution able to acknowledge the clinical necessities of adequate time for such work, team support, and recognition of an inevitable degree of disruption of the physical environment as well as of the state of mind of the therapist. However, these are the children likely to be a huge cost to themselves, their families, and the wider society in future years if left without therapeutic help. It is a remarkable thing that psychoanalysis has provided us with theories that make it possible to intervene and to make a difference, and it is vital that such work should be protected in the future.

References

Bick, E. (1964). Notes on infant observation in psychoanalytic training. *International Journal of Psychoanalysis, 45*: 558–566.

Bick, E. (1968). The experience of the skin in early object relations. *International Journal of Psychoanalysis, 49*: 484–486

Bion, W. R. (1962). A theory of thinking. *International Journal of Psychoanalysis, 53*: 308–315.

Bion, W. R. (1970). *Attention and Interpretation*. London: Tavistock.

Boston, M. (1972). Psychotherapy with a boy from a children's home. *Journal of Child Psychotherapy, 3*: 53–67.

Boston, M., & Szur, R. (Eds.) (1983). *Psychotherapy with Severely Deprived Children* London: Routledge.

Britton, R. (1989). The missing link: Parental sexuality and the Oedipus complex. In: J. Steiner (Ed.), *The Oedipus Complex Today: Clinical Implications* (pp. 83–101). London: Karnac.

Canham, H. (1999). The development of the concept of time in fostered and adopted children. *Psychoanalytic Inquiry, 19*: 160–171.

Cregeen, S. (2009). Exposed: phallic protections, shame and damaged parental objects. *Journal of Child Psychotherapy, 35*: 32–48.

Dockar-Drysdale, B. (1990). *The Provision of Primary Experience: Winnicottian Work with Children and Adolescents*. London: Free Association.

Kennedy, E., & Midgley, N. (Eds.) (2007). *Process and Outcome Research in Child Adolescent and Infant Psychotherapy: A Thematic Review*. London: NHS London.

Klein, M. (1936). Weaning. In: *The Writings of Melanie Klein, Vol. 1* (pp. 290–305). London: Hogarth, 1975.

Meltzer, D. (1967). *The Psychoanalytic Process*. London: Heinemann.

Malloch, S., & Trevarthen, C. (Eds.) (2010). *Communicative Musicality: Exploring the basis of human companionship*. Oxford: OUP.

O'Shaughnessy, E. (1989). The invisible Oedipus complex. In: J. Steiner (Ed.), *The Oedipus Complex Today*. London: Karnac.

Rustin, M. E. (2006). Where do I belong? Dilemmas for children and adolescents who have been adopted or brought up in long-term foster care. In: J. Kenrick, C. Lindsey, & L. Tollermache (Eds.), *Creating New Families*. London: Karnac.

Rustin, M. E. (2009). Esther Bick's legacy of infant observation at the Tavistock: some reflections 60 years on. *International Journal of Infant Observation, 12*: 29–42.

Rustin, M. E. (2015). Infant observation: A method of psychoanalytic learning and an influence on clinical practice. In: A. Elliott, & J. Prager (Eds.), *The Routledge Handbook of Psychoanalysis in the Social Sciences and Humanities*. London: Routledge.

Segal, H. (1957). Notes on symbol formation. *International Journal of Psychoanalysis, 38*: 391–397.

Steiner, K. (1993). *Psychic Retreats*. London: Routledge.

Tustin, F. (1992). *Autistic States in Children*. London: Routledge.

CHAPTER TWENTY-FOUR

"At times when I see your face thinking, I am thinking as well": a plea for an organising object

Gianna Williams

In this chapter I would like to share my thoughts about some specific aspects of work with patients who have been at the receiving end of projections. I have long been interested in this "second failure of containment" (Williams, 1996, 1997a). I began by defining it as a "reversal of the container-contained relationship", but subsequently realised that the terms "container-contained" should actually be changed. The word "containment" does not apply when a child is projected into, because nothing is being contained. I suggested that, in this case, the terms "container-contained" should be replaced by the terms "receptacle" and "foreign body" (Williams, 1997b).

Patients whose projections are contained internalise, according to Bion (1962), an organising object capable of performing alpha function. Following this line of thought, one can hazard the hypothesis that patients who are projected into also internalise an object but, in their case, a disorganising object performing a disorganising function.

I have suggested that this function could be called omega function to signify that it is the obverse of alpha function. It interferes with thinking clearly and it creates confusion. The perception of internal chaos is disturbing to many patients.

Both in my own clinical experience and in the experience of students and colleagues I have supervised, there is a strong countertransference feeling that some of the patients, in part, were longing for an object that could put some order in place, an order that could counteract the disorganisation.

Initial requests for help in this direction can be communicated in a very concrete form. For instance, Daniel, an eighteen-year-old I will refer to later in this chapter, told me in a session when he was wearing odd socks: "I wish you could come to my house and help me clear up the jumble of clothes on the floor of my bedroom." Clothes coming out of the washing machine

347

apparently formed a "sand hill" out of which Daniel extracted items in a haphazard way, "As I have done in the morning with my socks," he added, looking at his feet.

I felt a strong impulse in the countertransference to actually go to Daniel's house and concretely help him. Reflecting on my strong countertransference feelings, on my strong wish to help Daniel "put some order", I had the measure of the strength of his plea for an organising object.

I would like to emphasise here as I have done elsewhere (Williams, 1997b) that being a "receptacle" of projections is, for a child, a worse predicament than the one described by Bion as the experience of "nameless dread" (Bion, 1962). This is the experience of a child whose projections are not received, but are stripped of meaning and returned as "nameless dread". The child is left with an "internal projective-identification-rejecting object", a "wilfully misunderstanding" object.

When a child's projections are not received and the child is also projected into, a second failure of containment occurs. When we work with such patients we need to know that they will expect and fear to be projected into again in the analytic relationship. Indeed some of them can be very defensive (Williams, 1997a) for a long time and it is not easy to detoxify the transference relationship from the expectation and fear of a projecting object.

I have learned—also by making some mistakes—that it is important to be perceptive about the first glimpse of a plea for an "organising object" and to contain the anxiety evoked by disorganisation in the patient.

In the following selection of clinical examples, I will illustrate the moments when disorganised patients are able to say "Please help me to tidy up", "Please help me to think more clearly". These cases include a retrospectively improved understanding of patients I saw a long time ago. In some of these patients the disorganising function operated both at an emotional and at an intellectual level, while in other cases it operated only in the emotional sphere.

Sarah

Many years ago (Henry [Williams], 1969) I wrote about Sarah, a very disturbed little girl who had been emotionally (not intellectually) disorganised by traumatic circumstances. When she was seven years old, two years after she started treatment, she told me: "My digestive system is not very good; you digest the food for me in your stomach and give me back what goes into my bloodstream." Sarah was a child emotionally disorganised by what I later termed "omega function", but she was longing for an object performing alpha function (Bion, 1962). She was very precise in saying that her digestive system was not very good because she implied that she had an emotional stomach. She was in fact just asking to be helped with emotional digestion. Sarah's intellectual functioning was not impaired—she could think—but she needed help with making emotional sense of her experiences. It is more common for children who are projected into, to be not only emotionally but also cognitively and intellectually disorganised—as in the case of Solange.

Solange

Solange was a black child adopted by French parents who temporarily lived in London. When they returned to their home country Solange's analysis had to be interrupted, but both she and her parents continued therapeutic work in France.

Solange's parents had lived for some years in the African country where they adopted her. Mother had had a number of miscarriages. She was very distressed by her failure to bring a pregnancy to successful conclusion, and both parents were seen individually both in England and in France. Father also needed to be helped with unprocessed mourning as there had been serious trauma in his family.

When Solange was two and a half years old she surprised her mother by asking her, as she was getting her ready for her bath, "Why is it that my skin is black and your skin is white?" Mother was overwhelmed by panic and she answered impulsively: "It is because when you were born we were in Africa and all children that are born in Africa have black skin." Mother could not hold back her tears and asked her husband to continue bathing Solange. By the time Solange had begun analysis at the age of six, the parents had been helped to tell their daughter the truth about her adoption.

When she started treatment, Solange had some intriguing learning difficulties. She could not read a whole word. She could also only write a word if the letters were spelled separately but not if the word was dictated to her as a whole. The disorganisation in the thinking and linking in this case, as well as in the emotional realm, expressed itself in Solange's not being able to hold a word together. This type of learning difficulty was overcome fairly early in my work with Solange. It disappeared in parallel with her growing capacity to allow me to make links and attempt to make sense of her feelings. This included, for instance, her strong, often very angry, reactions to weekend breaks and analytic holidays.

Early on in her analysis, Solange started to draw rudimentary maps to show me the route between where she lived and the place where I saw her. Her parents had given her a globe, which she brought to her sessions. With great precision she would show me where England was and also the country where she was born. When we approached the end of our work together (Solange's father was preparing to be transferred for his work back to France) Solange drew a rudimentary map showing the relationship between France and England, but she put a very small channel between the two countries and a bridge over the channel. She said that there was already a tunnel, but she did not like it because it was under the sea. She knew that they were planning to build a bridge.

Fortunately we had generous notice of her father's work transfer and a long period of analysis to work through Solange's tempestuous feelings about saying goodbye. The phantasy of the bridge over a tiny strip of water was part of her denial of our separation, which was a painful one for me as well. I approached this denial very gently, following Anne Alvarez's suggestion that one could avoid bursting a bubble in a violent way, by saying: "How right it would be for it to be so …" (Alvarez, 1992). So I started by telling Solange that it would really be good, it would be "right", if London and Paris were so close, because we would then be within walking distance and I could walk to Paris to see her four times a week. I obviously implied with the tone of my voice: "Pity this is not the case."

Even though I approached the denial with caution, when Solange came to accept that our work together would come to an end, I was confronted with the anger and the grievances of a lifetime. I became the mother who had abandoned her. I knew that the work of mourning would continue with the new analyst with whom Solange would resume analysis in Paris, but it was important for me to hold in the transference Solange's feelings about the abandoning object, to help her to tolerate the painful link between "where it hurts and why it hurts" (Williams, 1997a).

There was, in the depths, a great longing in Solange to be helped to think clearly about the truth, however painful it was going to be.

This longing to be helped to think was still very much present in Solange's work with the analyst she saw in Paris. This colleague sent me the notes of a touching session when Solange had said to her: "You know … at times when I see your face thinking, I am thinking as well."

The working through of a process of mourning touched on an extremely sensitive area for Solange's parents as well. They both needed to be helped to mourn in order not to project into Solange as Mother had done, when she linked the colour of Solange's skin with the fact that she was born in Africa. This false link could be seen as the quintessence of minus K, in terms of Bion's grid, but it was just an isolated defence against unmetabolised psychic pain in the mother. These parents were not functioning on the negative grid of -L-H-K. They were not "wilfully misunderstanding" parents (Bion, 1962), but needed a great deal of help in dealing with their psychic pain. They needed to be helped in their mourning before they could help Solange face the anger and pain about having been given up for adoption by her natural mother.

Solange was a much-loved child and her case is one of the many examples where I felt that it was the projection of unprocessed psychic pain and trauma in the parents, and not necessarily severe parental mental illness, that disorganised the child. However, there are also cases where the projections from the parents and consequent disorganisation in the child are due to the parents' severe disturbance. This was true of the case of Daniel, the patient I mentioned at the beginning of the paper.

Daniel

Daniel was a severely bulimic and suicidal boy whom I started seeing, in a National Health Service institution, when he was eighteen years old. I saw him initially non-intensively and gradually increased his sessions to four per week.

Daniel told me in his first assessment session that he had been born ten weeks premature. I was to learn later that doctors had told his mother that it was unlikely that he would survive. Mother had become pregnant with a "replacement baby" (Reid, 1992) when Daniel was still in the incubator.

There had been a great deal of domestic violence in Daniel's family. His father was addicted to alcohol and drugs and died from a drug overdose when Daniel was in his teens. Daniel's mother had to be taken many times to hospital, on one occasion with a broken jaw, having been hit by her husband with his fist during a row. The parents separated and mother and children lived for a time in a hostel for survivors of domestic violence. Mother had a number of psychotic breakdowns. On one occasion, she tried to set fire to a sofa and Daniel, aged ten at the time, extinguished the fire with buckets of water before the firemen arrived. On many occasions Daniel and his brothers had to be put in temporary foster care while mother was readmitted to a psychiatric hospital. When I started seeing Daniel, he was still living at home with his brothers and his mother. She was, at the time, capable of holding down a job.

Daniel was diagnosed as being at serious suicidal risk. I saw him in close conjunction with a psychiatrist and, with his help, made arrangements for possible admission to hospital when I took my first holidays. On one occasion, during this analytic break, Daniel came to see the psychiatrist I worked with, but he never needed to be admitted to hospital.

Daniel was sure that he would at some point in his life end up in a psychiatric hospital because his mother had been hospitalised and she kept telling him that he was "just like her". She had been like Daniel, first anorexic and then bulimic. Daniel was convinced that he would just "fall into a groove traced by mother's life". She had actually told him that he would be cleaning toilets at the airport like her when he was forty-five and Daniel was very "porous" (Williams, 1997b) to mother's projections. It is in my work with Daniel that I visualised the parental projections experienced by some patients as being like a wind blowing through metal filings. This is a metaphor inspired by a conversation with Esther Bick (personal communication, 1974) who told me, when supervising my work with a child, that a "parent's attention holds together the parts of a child's personality, like a magnet gathers metal filings". The effect of a disorganising "omega function" can be described with an inversion of Bick's metaphor.

Daniel said that he was full of "nasties" and that he got rid of them when he binged on white bread, which acted like blotting paper. After being sick he felt "clean inside" for a short while, during which he could sit at his desk in front of the window, and look out. At such times he felt he could concentrate and study.

When I started seeing Daniel he was in the first year of his sixth form and he was an A-star student. He had always been academically able. He told me with pride that his teacher had made him stand on a table in primary school and asked him to recite his times tables and spell difficult words. No doubt this was a request, in his transference to me, for mutual idealisation. As in the case of Sarah, it was thought-provoking to be confronted with such a marked division between Daniel's emotional life and his capacity to learn. There was certainly no evidence that Daniel would be cleaning toilets when he was forty-five, but when he felt full of "nasties" his logic failed him.

I have described my work with Daniel in some detail in an earlier publication (Williams, 1997b), in which I focused on his eating disorder. I will not return, in this paper, to that aspect of his treatment, but I will focus on him as an example of a child who had internalised a disorganising object performing a disorganising ("omega") function.

I find that patients who are unable to think clearly because of "the wind scattering the metal filings" in their minds, are more likely to long, at some point in their treatment, for an organising object, a "magnet gathering the metal filings".

The countertransference evoked by patients like Daniel is different from the one evoked by patients who need to protect themselves from psychic pain by using confusion and "attacks on linking" (Bion, 1959) as a defence. A clear-cut separation of these categories is artificial and I wish to avoid such generalisation, as Daniel was not immune to attacks on linking.

I will give an example of such an occurrence: after some months of having overcome his bulimic symptoms, Daniel resumed his bingeing and vomiting during one of my summer breaks. He spoke about it in passing as if I should not notice. I remarked on it and he answered angrily that it was a waste of time talking about his bingeing because I had said so often that this was not *the* problem. This was a striking -K (Bion, 1962), an obvious distortion of my interest in exploring with him the meaning of bingeing, in the context of our relationship.

Indeed a "bingeing" state of mind continued to manifest itself in an area that did not bear a relationship with food. At a time when the actual bulimic symptoms had receded, Daniel's bingeing state of mind manifested itself in voracious reading. On a Thursday Daniel wrote a letter to me that I that would receive on Friday, the day when he had no session:

> I have only seen you today and I am already here writing. I have read almost every minute since our meeting. I have started reading Plato for my essay, then I remembered that I had not finished the Joyce book I was reading. I left Plato and I started reading Joyce. It is now eleven at night. I have read a little bit of Plato, a little bit of Joyce, I have almost finished Wilde's amazing *Portrait of Dorian Gray* but I can't remember very much about it. Then I started reading Plato again, but I can't stay with anything. If I could come to a session tomorrow, you could help me to find some rhyme and reason in what is happening.

Although a bulimic pattern is clearly present in Daniel's binge reading, it is clear that he was not asking me in this letter to perform the function of blotting paper (the white bread that absorbed the nasties). He did not wish me to help him *evade* his experience but to *modify* it (Bion, 1962). He did not wish to evacuate his confusion as he did with his bulimia, but he was asking for me to help him to put some order in his mind, to be helped to think.

The wish to be helped to think more clearly was adumbrated in earlier descriptions of how Daniel felt when he was bingeing. He said he was "running around like a headless chicken". He also spoke of "thoughts racing through his mind at 150 miles per hour". He called them thoughts, but it was clear that they were not thoughts he could think or talk about, but something more akin to flying debris.

It is interesting that in spite of strongly resenting weekends and holiday breaks, even referring to my analytic fifty minutes as Greenwich *mean* time, Daniel spoke in more than one session about having missed a paternal function, a limit setter and a time keeper in his family. He spoke about playing in the courtyard of a council house with other children when he lived in the north of England. On long summer evenings, he was left to play outside to his heart's content. Nobody at home appeared to notice his absence. A child's father called him from his flat and he put out of the window "a great big hand" to tell him to go home. This was a great big hand that said "We are missing you, we notice your absence": a protective paternal hand, very different from the "great big hand" of Daniel's violent father.

The lack of a protective paternal function was present in Daniel's complaint about the handle missing on the door of his bedroom. The door was always ajar and at any moment a "missile" could come through the door. An example of a "missile" was mother barging in and telling him that she would kill herself because she had discovered that he had binged again and he "would never change".

Similar "missiles" came in my direction from Daniel when, just before one of my first holiday breaks, he said: "If I killed myself it would give a kick-start to the family". It certainly gave a kick-start to my Christmas holiday.

The need to project the "fear that the baby may die" (Bion, 1962) is understandable in a boy whose mother had given him up for dead when he was in the incubator. This fear had to be experienced and contained by me in the Christmas break I mentioned above. Daniel said I could not go if I really knew how much he "felt like quitting". My taking a break was the consequence of "malignant misunderstanding" (Britton, 1998). I was to feel all the guilt he had wished his mother to feel for having abandoned him in the incubator.

It turned out to be not so dramatic: Daniel spent his holiday at the house of a friend, Nigel, who had been left with his older brother because "the parents had gone to have a holiday in the sun". So they all spent Christmas day with Nigel's maternal grandparents and Daniel was never sick during that time, but full of commiseration for the friend "abandoned" by the selfish sexual couple. Nigel's parents represented a marked improvement in terms of Daniel's internal landscape from the couple of suicidal mother and drug-addicted father—a couple raising an oedipal grievance, a different type of grievance.

I wish to stress again that patients who have been traumatised, projected into, and disorganised by "frightened or frightening parents" (Main & Solomon, 1986) are far from being immune from attacks on linking. I have given an example of such attacks in Daniel's twisting my interpretation about bulimic symptoms not being the problem we should talk about.

If I try to describe my countertransference in my work with Daniel, I certainly would not say that he was permanently thirsting for clarity, but I felt that the internalisation of chaotic objects seemed to have generated in him a longing, which at times I felt was very palpable, for containment and help in thinking thoughts. He longed for an alpha function that could counteract the presence of a disorganising object and a disorganising function in his internal landscape.

The feelings evoked in the countertransference by patients like Daniel are very different from the feelings evoked by patients who need to attack linking and thinking as their main defence against psychic pain.

I would like to make a brief reference to one such patient, an adolescent I saw non-intensively for six years. I will select material from the time in his treatment when he was firmly devoted to attacks on linking (Bion, 1959) and most reluctant to be helped to think.

Martin

Martin was a patient I began seeing when he was fourteen and had a reading age of six. I have described him as "doubly deprived" (Henry [Williams], 1974; Williams, 1997a) because he suffered serious deprivation in his early life. But he also developed defences that often tied the hands of those who were trying to help him and attacked the mind that was trying to understand him.

For a long time it was very hard to reach him (Joseph, 1975). He was attending his sessions very regularly, but meeting my attempts to make some contact with him with stony silence or brief sentences such as "I have got no time for your rubbish" or "Tough, you have got to suffer ..."

I struggled to understand the countertransference evoked in me by Martin, and eventually, by trial and error, I came to realise that he treated me like an annoying child trying to get the attention of an impervious object. Perhaps that was what I "had to suffer". I had to experience the feelings of a child who is demanding attention and being fobbed off by a parent who is otherwise engaged.

At times, while ignoring the "annoying child" (me), Martin was looking at his nails, or he looked at his reflection in his sunglasses. On one such occasion he combed the fur around the hood of his parka with a comb as if it were beautiful hair. His movements were gentle and feminine, and contrasted sharply with the knuckle rings he was wearing on his right hand. He seemed to be in the skin of, in projective identification with, a vain and hard object (Klein, 1946). There must have been something that touched him as I tried in various ways to suggest what he may wish for me to feel. He said, on one occasion, "If you understand something about me, keep it for yourself, will you?" So perhaps I was understanding something about him!

Only very gradually and always in the here and now of the transference, I attempted to share with him the notion that he was splitting and projecting a part of himself, a needy child, into me while being himself in projective identification with a vain and hard object that he idealised.

Needless to say I did not inflict on him interpretations using psychoanalytic jargon. In one of his usual brief communications Martin told me one day, "You are talking to a brick wall" and I wondered if perhaps he wished me to know how it felt to hit one's head against a brick wall. He responded with a surprisingly long sentence and a complex one for a child who had been assessed as suffering from severe learning difficulties: "There is only one way to find out if you are a brick wall or not. You hit your head against a brick wall. If it hurts, you are not." Martin certainly wished to imply that he was much wiser than me. He knew how to avoid psychic pain. He knew how to avoid being hurt and how to dispose of his psychic pain: you cannot be hurt if you identify with a hard/brick-wall object.

On one occasion he gave me a graphic demonstration of one of his techniques for avoiding psychic pain. He was holding a piece of string in his hands and cut it with a penknife saying "My hurt is not my hurt, I execute it!" This was a very graphic demonstration of how he attacked links.

Martin had developed an amazing skill in breaking links in his mind and between our minds. I needed to protect myself from the risk of links being broken in my mind. Martin's link-breaking defences were directly proportional to his dread of being put in touch with his psychic pain. The following example conveys perhaps the extent of his defences.

Martin was Afro-Caribbean. He had internal doubtful alliances (Rosenfeld, 1971) but he had also an external "friend", a white boy who also had learning difficulties. One day, they both skipped school and Martin should have come to his session at lunchtime. He decided to cancel and entered a phone booth (it was the 1970s) with the intention of calling the clinic. He hit his face with the door of the booth and some blood came out from a small cut on his eyebrow. The friend laughed at him and said: "I did not know black people had red blood like us". Martin punched the friend with his knuckle rings and ran to the clinic where I was waiting for him. He was not very late. It was a rainy day and he arrived with a wet face and some blood showing on his eyebrow. He was full of rage and, after he told me what had happened, I unwisely referred to tears, perhaps tears of rage. Martin caressed his knuckle rings and told me, looking straight into my eyes: "You can get your face wet with blood, with rain, with tears and yours is going to be wet with blood before mine is wet with tears" (Henry [Williams], 1974).

Unlike Daniel, Martin did not wish for me to help him find some "rhyme and reason". He feared that my attempts to find a meaning, to make emotional sense, risked to take him closer to the most dreaded link: the one between where it hurts and why it hurts. In my experience, many learning difficulties originate from the avoidance of that central link and improve—as they did with Martin—when that link can be tolerated. For a long time, he preferred to live in an illiterate world because he could not tolerate being helped to read the meaning of his feelings. He asked me: "Why don't you get rid of that man that runs around your head putting together all the data? Why don't you throw him out of the window and let him have a bit of fresh air?"

Like Sarah, whom I quoted at the beginning of the paper, Martin intuited one of the central metaphors of Bion's theory—in this case about the central role of an attack on the analytic couple in the attack on the analyst's work. As Bion put it:

> … the couple engaged in a creative act are felt to have an enviable emotional experience. He [the patient] being identified with the excluded party has a painful emotional experience […] [his] hatred contributed to the murderous attacks on that which links the pair, on the pair itself and the object generated by the pair. (Bion, 1959)

Conclusion

In this chapter I have attempted to describe the predicament of patients who find it difficult to put order in their mind, at least partly, as a consequence of having internalised a disorganising object. I found that, in some of these patients, there was a wish to be helped to think more clearly. This wish to think clearly emerged early in the analytic relationship and it was important to be receptive to the patient's plea for an organising object.

Unlike Solange, who seemed to experience relief when she told her analyst: "At times when I see your face thinking, I am thinking as well", Martin chose "attacks on linking" as one of his main defences. For a long time this impaired his capacity to learn but provided him with a protection against the psychic pain that he anticipated as intolerable.

Keats's words in "Ode to a nightingale" (Keats, 1970) beautifully describe the dread of thinking in patients like Martin:

> Where but to think is to be full of sorrow
> And leaden-eyed despairs.

References

Alvarez, A. (1992). *Live Company: Psychoanalytic Psychotherapy with Autistic, Borderline, Deprived and Abused Children*. London: Routledge.

Bion, W. R. (1959). Attacks on linking. *International Journal of Psychoanalysis, 40*: 308–315.

Bion, W. R. (1962). *Learning from Experience*. London: Heinemann.

Britton, R. (1998). *Belief and Imagination: Explorations in Psychoanalysis*. London: Routledge.

Henry [Williams], G. (1969). Some aspects of projective mechanisms in the Jungian theory, *Journal of Child Psychotherapy, 2*: 43–56.

Henry [Williams], G. (1974). Doubly deprived. *Journal of Child Psychotherapy, 3*: 15–28.

Joseph, B. (1975). The patient who is difficult to reach. In: P. L. Giovacchini (Ed.), *Tactics and Technique in Psychoanalytic Therapy, Vol. 2: Countertransference*. New York: Jason Aronson.

Keats, J. (1970). Ode to a nightingale. In: M. Allott (Ed.), *The Complete Poems of John Keats*. London: Longman.

Klein, M. (1946). Notes on some schizoid mechanisms. In: *The Writings of Melanie Klein, Vol. 3: Envy and Gratitude and Other Works* (pp. 1–24). London: Hogarth, 1975.

Main, M., & Solomon, J. (1986). Discovery of a new, insecure-disorganised/disoriented attachment pattern. In: M. Yogman, & T. B. Brazelton (Eds.), *Affective Development in Infancy* (pp. 95–124). Norwood, NJ: Ablex Press.

Reid, M. (1992). Joshua—Life after death: The replacement child. *Journal of Child Psychotherapy, 18*: 109–138.

Rosenfeld, H. (1971). A clinical approach to the psychoanalytical theory of the life and death instincts: an investigation into the aggressive aspects of narcissism. *International Journal of Psychoanalysis, 52*: 169–178.

Williams, G. (1996). Capovolgimento del rapport fra contenitore e contenuto. In: C. Candelori (Ed.), *Dolore mentale e conoscenza*. Bologna: Cosmopoli.

Williams, G. (1997a). *Internal Landscapes and Foreign Bodies*. London: Karnac.

Williams, G. (1997b). Reflections on some dynamics of eating disorders: "no entry" defences and foreign bodies. *International Journal of Psychoanalysis, 78*: 927–941.

PART IV

APPLIED CONTRIBUTIONS

A perfect poem of tears: grieving as depicted in Federico García Lorca's *Lament for Ignacio Sánchez Mejías*

Shelley Rockwell

Ignacio Sánchez Mejías, a daring, well-known, and beloved bullfighter, was gored by the bull Grenadino in Manzanares, Spain, a small town south of Madrid, on 11 August 1934. He died of gangrene from this wound thirty-six hours later in a Madrid clinic. Almost exactly two years later the poet Federico García Lorca was executed by the Falange Espanola party (Franco's fascist police), on 18 August 1936 near Granada, Spain, in a spot known as the Fuente Grande.

Lorca was reported to have told a close friend, "Ignacio's death is like mine, the trial run for mine …" and his biographer Ian Gibson wrote "that in death, even as in life, his and Ignacio's destinies were inseparably linked" (1989, p. 391). Damoso Alonso, a poet and friend, wrote: "Lorca's work, in its persistent oneiric imagery, reflects on every page the poet's obsession with death" (p. 202). He was known to have a strange compulsion: "the need to act out his own demise and burial." Salvador Dalí included Lorca in many paintings, and in 1926 he painted him in a recumbent position, a "corpse imitation posture" (pp. 145–146). Lorca was both terrified and enamoured by death, his own in particular. The poem, "Lament for Ignacio Sánchez Mejías" (Lorca, 1955d), represents the culmination of his preoccupation, his creation of an "immense poem of grief", echoing Edmund Wilson's (1941) description of James Joyce's *Finnegan's Wake* as an "immense poem of sleep".

Several months after Mejías' death, near the end of October 1934, Lorca gave a first reading of his poem, 220 lines long in four sections. We can read this poem as a double grieving, one for the past and the loss of Mejías, and at the same time his own felt-future's death. Lorca's lament is a powerful and poignant illustration of a conscious and deliberate case of narcissistic identification.

This has been described by Ignês Sodré as follows:

> Massive projective identification *with the object* (a process first described by Anna Freud (1937) as "identification with the aggressor") implies a phantasy of "becoming" the object—or a particular aspect or version of the object … whereas the object "becomes" the self … (2015, p. 44, original italics)

Freud also described this kind of identification: "[t]he ego wants to incorporate this object into itself, and in accordance with the oral or cannibalistic phase of libidinal development in which it is, it wants to do so by devouring it" (1917e, pp. 249–250).

In this paper I will explore how Lorca incorporated his beloved friend's destiny, his very death. The reader witnesses Lorca's movement from the concrete to a symbolic and more separated form of identification. We do consider massive identification to be pathological, but in this poem I will show how "becoming" Mejías was necessary and adaptive for the poet's process of mourning.

In Hanna Segal's classic and brilliant paper "A psycho-analytical approach to aesthetics" she writes: "The task of the artist lies in the creation of a world of his own" (1952, p. 489). And in describing Marcel Proust's work:

> … to sacrifice himself to the re-creation of the dying and the dead. By virtue of his art he can give his objects an eternal life in his work. And since they represent his internal world too … he himself will no longer be afraid of death. (p. 491)

Further on she writes:

> The artist withdraws into a world of phantasy, but he can communicate his phantasies and share them. In that way he makes reparation, not only to his own internal objects, but to the external world as well. (p. 499)

Segal draws on the work of the German historian and philosopher, Wilhelm Dilthey and his concept of *"nacherleben"*, meaning "after having lived through it". Segal writes that for the reader an "unconscious re-living of the creator's state of mind … is the foundation of all aesthetic pleasure (p. 500).

Turning to the aesthetics: the focus of this paper is the aesthetics of Lorca's poem, the ways in which he creates a "lived in, having lived through it" experience for his reader. Lorca created a work of art that allowed him to "live through" the death that he anticipates is coming very close; in this poem the past, present, and future are integrated into one experience. As Thomas Ogden writes in his discussion of Robert Frost's poem, "Acquainted with the night", "[t]he poem is not a poem about a walk: the poem is a walk" (1999). The reader too suffers grief, has a mourning.

Lorca's "Lament" is an elegy. The elegy has ancient roots (found in Theocritus's 3000 BC "First idyll" (Sacks, 1985, p. 23)) and has two meanings: "to speak well of" and as a "cry of grief". Both are found in Lorca's poem.

Lorca has fashioned his own form of elegy in which the poem is imbued with *"duende"* spirit, described by Lorca as follows: "so in all ages Spain is moved by the duende, for it is a country of ancient music and dance where the duende squeezes the lemons of death …" (1955b, p. 64).

And *"duende"* originates from

> Gypsy siguiriya [which] is the prototype of deep song … it comes from the first sob and the first kiss (p. 10) … [and is a] perfect poem of tears … the melody cries, and so does the poetry. (1955a, p. 17)

And additionally, Edward Hirsch (himself a fine poet and teacher) wrote:

> … the concept of duende … was associated with the spirit of earth, with visible anguish, irrational desire, demonic enthusiasm, and a fascination with death. It is an erotic form of dark inspiration … The incantatory quality of the *repetition gives the rhythmical feeling of death blowing through an endless present*. (2002, pp. 10–12, my italics)

And turning to the psychoanalytics: an essential part of the work of mourning is, as Freud points out in "Mourning and melancholia", the testing of reality. He says that "in mourning time is needed for the command of reality-testing to be carried out in detail, and that when this work has been accomplished the ego will have succeeded in freeing its libido from the lost object" (Freud, 1917e, p. 252).

Lorca's relentless repetition drives his poem, and the mourner, towards integration—the repetition changes in quality as does the splitting and denial that move closer to reality, increasingly allowing the integration of inner and external reality. In addition, the imagery becomes less concrete, more free and symbolic—moving from the physical to the mental and finally to the spiritual. As the narrator's narcissistic relation to his lost object loosens, there is a decreased identification with his object and a softening of the poet's controlled hold on reality. The reader "lives through" the development of grief, in all its vicissitudes, including splitting and denial, idealisation, manic and obsessional features, longing and pining, fury and hatred. Lorca writes a lament that is "anti-melancholic"—the mourner has arduously and painfully let go of his beloved Mejías, thereby internalising him as a gentle presence.

"Cogida and death"

What follows here are the first two of the three stanzas that comprise the first of four sections of the poem.

> At five in the afternoon.
> It was exactly five in the afternoon.
> A boy brought the white sheet
> *at five in the afternoon.*
> A frail of lime ready prepared
> *at five in the afternoon.*

The rest was death, and death alone
at five in the afternoon.

The wind carried away the cottonwool
at five in the afternoon.
And the oxide scattered crystal and nickel
at five in the afternoon.
Now the dove and the leopard wrestle
at five in the afternoon.
And a thigh with a desolate horn
at five in the afternoon.
The bass-string struck up
at five in the afternoon.
Arsenic bells and smoke
at five in the afternoon.
Groups of silence in the corners
at five in the afternoon.
And the bull alone with a high heart!
at five in the afternoon.
When the sweat of snow was coming
at five in the afternoon,
when the bull ring was covered in iodine
at five in the afternoon.
death laid eggs in the wound
at five in the afternoon.
At five in the afternoon.
Exactly at five o'clock in the afternoon.

Mejías' hour of death is the centre around which all facts of reality arrange themselves. The chant "at five in the afternoon", comprising twenty-eighty of the first section's fifty-two lines, continuously alternates with a small, specific, and shatteringly realistic detail of Mejías' goring.

This alternation between the beat of time and the concrete facts of the goring develops a forward-backward rhythm, opening up time and space as does a spade in hard-packed soil, not so much by digging straight down but through a forward-backward pulse, loosening up the soil, making it permeable, allowing the seeping-in of water and air—processing of facts of death, to break up what is frozen, numb—the shock of this death.

Reality enters in the third line in the figure of "A boy [who] brought the white sheet … A frail of lime ready prepared …"—the white sheet announces death, the covering of the bull-fighter with a sheet and the frail (bucket) of lime used to aid the body's decomposition. Cotton wool is used to cover the ears of the horse(s) or the nostrils of the bull; oxide, crystal, and nickel are afloat in the air.

Repetition is defined in the *New Princeton Encyclopedia of Poetry and Poetics* as follows: "When a line, phrase, or even a sound is repeated, the experience of the first occurrence is continuously maintained in the present in each subsequent recurrence" (Preminger & Brogan, 1993, p. 1036).

The poet clings to the hour of death, the chant of time beats on us—and he recreates the ring and the goring, sinking into the sensory detail, coming to know, to feel what happened in the external world from the inside.

Freud described this duality as follows: "... respect for reality gains the day ... [and its] orders ... are carried out bit by bit, at great expense of time and cathectic energy, and in the meantime the existence of the lost object is psychically prolonged" (1917e, pp. 244–245).

Freud described the parallel quality of mourning; the lost object's presence is maintained, alongside the effort to comprehend the reality of death. This parallel quality of mourning is found in the poem's alternation of the details of time and of death.

The emotional climate deepens in the middle of the second stanza, the poet's pounding description moving closer to the bullfight; *now* life and death, soul and body "wrestle", as in leopard with dove, (bull's) horn with (fighter's) thigh. These lines (twelve to fifteen) are in the present tense whereas the first eleven lines are written in the past. The poet has slipped from recounting to immediate experience; the reader may feel the horn in the thigh.

Shifting again to the past tense, the "bass-string struck up" introduces the deep low music of death into the air, the sound of a dirge. Still at a distance, the first reference to an audience appears—"Groups of silence in the corners ... And the bull alone with a high heart!" The spectators are silenced, horrified, and the bull triumphant.

We move yet closer to Mejías' death in the following lines: "When the sweat of snow was coming ... when the bull ring was covered in iodine ..." At the time of great pain or illness our body shivers and sweats in shock, heat and cold coming together; Lorca expresses this beautifully in the "sweat of snow". The use of iodine for such an injury is useless, as "[d]eath laid eggs in the wound". The narrator has grasped reality, shock has lessened: the bull's goring of Mejías' thigh, the eggs that herald the onset of gangrene—life comes from an egg, and now death must be born(e).

The poem continues:

> A coffin on wheels is his bed
> *at five in the afternoon.*
> Bones and flutes resound in his ears
> *at five in the afternoon.*
> Now the bull was bellowing through his forehead
> *at five in the afternoon.*
> The room was iridescent with agony
> *at five in the afternoon.*
> In the distance the gangrene now comes
> *at five in the afternoon.*
> Horn of the lily through green groins
> *at five in the afternoon.*
> The wounds were burning like suns
> *at five in the afternoon,*
> and the crowd was breaking the windows
> *at five in the afternoon.*
> At five in the afternoon.

Ah, that fatal five in the afternoon!
It was five by all the clocks!
It was five in the shade of the afternoon!

"A coffin on wheels is his bed", begins the third and final stanza of the first section—and following the last line of the second stanza, "Exactly at five o'clock in the afternoon." Lorca has included "exactly" and "o'clock" in his refrain, which contributes to its quality of a formal announcement—to himself. The assemblage of fact has convinced the narrator that Mejías has died and in need of his coffin.

Edward Hirsch (2002) refers to the Madrid newspaper's account that Mejías' coffin had left the chapel "at exactly five o'clock". Hirsch continues:

> Lorca seized on this as the inevitable hour of reckoning ... this line "filled my head like the tolling of a bell and I broke into a cold sweat thinking that such an hour was waiting for me, too. Sharp and precise like a knife. The hour was the awful thing." Five in the afternoon is also "the traditional opening hour of the bullfight." (pp. 24–25)

The "coffin on wheels" may refer to the ambulance, which was delayed, that carried Mejías to the Madrid clinic, as the ring's infirmary was considered inadequate. He contracted gangrene, dying a painful and delirious death two days later. It was observed that in his delirium at the end, Mejías shook so violently his bed rolled (Gibson, 1989).

Now the chanting shifts in quality, becoming less incessant, less torturing, not so full of accusation—that is, "How could you let this happen to him, to me?"—instead developing into a soothing incantation. As the narrator is increasingly receptive to the reality of his loss, simultaneously less manic and filled with "pining", (Klein wrote, it is the "longing to regain ... the good object ... including feelings of sorrow and concern" (1940, p. 348)), he falls into the physicality of the dead Mejías; we become entangled with the poet's entanglement with his lost object.

We read, ears are full of the sound of flutes and clatter of bones, Mejías' bones, the rattle of death. "Now the bull was bellowing through his forehead"—taking over Mejías' mind and head. Man and bull are one, and the poet too is consumed with the "bellow", visually the "room was iridescent with agony". Lorca continues, "In the distance the gangrene now comes", bringing the smell of decomposition to the mourner. The final image of this third stanza is tactile, related to the skin, "Horn ... through ... green groins ... wounds were burning like suns ..."

The breaking of windows standing for the boundaries dissolving between the reader and poet, Lorca and Mejías—we see the poet has lost himself in Mejías' dying body, a luminous agony fills the mind, a conglomerate sensory image forms: hearing, seeing, smelling, and feeling on the outside and inside of our bodies, in the very surround of the air. There is a breakdown of the differentiation between subject-object, inside-outside. The identification of mourner with his lost object is close to complete. Having fallen into the dead body, he feels the burn and heat of the "green groins".

Herbert Rosenfeld described this action when he reported his patient's dream:

> He [the patient-dreamer] saw a famous surgeon operating on a patient, who observed with
> great admiration the skill displayed by the surgeon … Suddenly the surgeon lost his balance
> and fell right into the inside of the patient, with whom he got so entangled that he could
> scarcely manage to free himself. He nearly choked, and only by administering an oxygen
> apparatus could he manage to revive himself. (1949, p. 49)

Hence a kind of massive simultaneous projection/introjection has occurred: doctor falls into
the stomach of his patient, the poet into his lost object—oxygen/psychoanalysis can retrieve
the surgeon/analyst; poetry restores the mourner. As listeners we fall into the narrator's falling
into the lost loved object.

From this sensual and primal place Lorca indulges one more time, giving in to the demand
and necessity for calling out the hour, a going back as if to a touchstone.

The poet doubles his repetition; "five" appears five times in this section's final five lines—
and is written with variations. Lorca repeats the refrain in bold print (in contrast to the earlier
italics), he adds exclamation points to the last three lines, and adds the word "fatal"—breaking
the relentless continuity.

The repetition is further broken when "Ah" replaces "At" as the starting word of the phrase:
"Ah, that fatal five in the afternoon!" Poetry and psyche move together—in replacing the hard
stress (accent) of "t" with "h"—that is, the hard beat "at" with the soft stress of "ah", a crucial
change in sound and feeling develops as the "ah" gives a moan, a breakthrough of suffering, as
described by Klein—manic control is loosened, repetition changed, the narrator's yearning and
desire for Mejías more fully felt. It is important to note this is true only in the English translation by Stephen Spender and J. L. Gill (Lorca, 1955d), as the Spanish original does not turn from
"t" to "h"; instead "A" becomes elongated in "Ay", which does give, in its own way, a "cry of
anguish" (Garvey, 2016).

> If … the mourner is able to surrender fully to his feelings, and to cry out his sorrow about the
> actual loss … there is a relaxing of the manic control over [his] internal world … and goodness
> and love [are] increasingly experienced within. (Klein, 1940, p. 359)

The poem's discontinuity continues in the fourth refrain: "It was five by all the clocks!", asserting the deadly hour as a communal event, felt by all; by virtue of owning or reading a clock that
reads "five in the afternoon" one, too, suffers the "fatal" hour. The mourner longs to believe his
loss is universal.

The final development, "It was five in the shade of the afternoon!", occurs in the last two
lines. These are complete sentences, not phrases, more formal and less chant-like, developing a
picture of the mourner in a fuller use of his own mind as he emerges from a massive identification with Mejías.

The poem, at the end of the first section, has turned, the poet communicates a moan of grief;
"all the clocks" brings in the wish for a shared grief; and "shade" recaptures for the mourner

an atmosphere with its lack of light at that fatal hour, the approaching dusk as the darkness of death. The narrator's grief travels into the voice, deep in the chest as a moan, then pushes itself out into the world of "clock-readers" and finally right back in time, to the beginning, that moment of loss and the ensuing darkness there in the bullring.

"The spilled blood"

I will not see it!

    Tell the moon to come
for I do not want to see the blood
of Ignacio in the sand.

I will not see it!

    The moon wide open.
Horse of still clouds,
and the grey bull ring of dreams
with willows in the barreras.

I will not see it!

Let my memory kindle!
Warn the jasmines
of such minute whiteness!

I will not see it!

Lorca continues to rely on repetition; moving from an adhesion to the hour of death and its concrete circumstance to flat-out denial and angry defiance: "I will not see it" in its varied forms, shouted fifteen times—what will not be seen—the blood of Ignacio. The poet's repetition provides a crucial splitting: "I will not see", a particular kind of denial inherently *knowing*, something must be turned away from, blocked from sight. Reality *has* been seen and must be denied. As in the first section, the second contains an alternation between negation and acceptance. And the quality of splitting has changed, moving the poet closer to reality, the distance between the two realities less extreme, the poet simultaneously protests and accepts the bullfighter's loss of his body, blood, and vitality. Klein wrote: "Without partial and temporary denial of psychic reality the ego cannot bear the disaster ..." (Klein, 1940, p. 349).

And Beckett's well-known refrain captures this particular double quality of denial: "I can't go on. I'll go on ..." (1960, p. 176).

The first short three stanzas, bracketed by four lines of "I will not see it", plead for the moon "to come ... wide open". This atmosphere of moonlight, clouds, dreams, and kindled memory, softens the too real "blood / of Ignacio in the sand".

The poem continues:

> The cow of the ancient world
> passed her sad tongue
> over a snout of blood
> spilled on the sand,
> and the bulls of Guisando,
> partly death and partly stone,
> bellowed like two centuries
> sated with treading the earth.
> No.
> I do not want to see it!
> I will not see it!

Alan Josephs, a well-known and respected American scholar of Ernest Hemingway, Spanish culture, and, particularly, the bullfight, followed the Columbian matador, César Rincón, for four seasons through Spain, France, and South America. Joseph's respect for and understanding of the bull and the bullfighter is conveyed below as he helps us grasp Lorca's love for the "cow of the ancient world". There exists a

> fascination, awe … [and] veneration … [in] many Mediterranean and Near Eastern religions of antiquity … [but most importantly] love of the animal, love of its physical beauty, its strength, its character, and above all love of its unmitigated wild bravery. The toro bravo [brave bull] is the descendant of the wild, prehistoric *bos primigenius*, the aurochs of antiquity, precisely the bull that so fascinated the great cave painters of southern France and Spain. (2002, pp. 3–5)

Now the reality of one bullfighter's spilled blood encroaches; the narrator looks at the blood and shouts his refusal to look in the next breath: "No./I do not want to see it!/I will not see it!" But—he has looked, the "sad tongue" has touched him.

The poem goes on:

> Ignacio goes up the tiers
> with all his death on his shoulders.
> He sought for the dawn
> but the dawn was no more.
> He seeks for his confident profile
> and the dream bewilders him.
> He sought for his beautiful body
> and encountered his opened blood.
> I will not see it!
> I do not want to hear it spurt
> each time with less strength:
> that spurt that illuminates

the tiers of seats, and spills
over the corduroy and the leather
of a thirsty multitude.
Who shouts that I should not come near!
Do not ask me to see it!

Until this moment in the poem the bullfighter has gone unnamed; here he gains his name: "Ignacio goes up the tiers" and, in a Christ-like reference, "with all his death on his shoulders". Now no longer only a "thigh" or a "he", he comes into his own as a glorious and individual torero, beloved but separate, not of the same mind and body as the poet. Ignacio seeks for his own aliveness, a "dawn … his confident profile … his beautiful body … and the dream bewilders him … encounter[ing] his opened blood."

After this development, the narrator turns in the next line, "I will not see it"—nevertheless the mourner has again fallen into his lost object: "I do not want to hear it spurt/each time with less strength". The reader also lives through it as it "illuminates/the tiers of seats, and spills/ over …/a thirsty multitude …"—thirsty for death, we imagine.

His eyes did not close
when he saw the horns near,
but the terrible mothers
lifted their heads.
And across the ranches,
an air of secret voices rose,
shouting to celestial bulls,
herdsmen of pale mist.
There was no prince in Seville
who could compare with him,
nor sword like his sword
nor heart so true.
Like a river of lions
was his marvelous strength,
and like a marble torso
his firm drawn moderation.
The air of Andalusian Rome
gilded his head
where his smile was a spikenard
of wit and intelligence.
What a great torero in the ring!
What a good peasant in the sierra!
How gentle with the sheaves!
How hard with the spurs!
How tender with the dew!
How dazzling in the fiesta!

> How tremendous with the final
> *banderillas* of darkness!

Alan Josephs writes regarding the feelings that drive the historical tradition of bullfighting:

> the man is meant to kill the bull … and it is always the matador's task to make the death … as graceful, as inspiring, and as beautiful as possible … His performance is a ritual enactment of the myth of the man-god who kills the bull-god, the hero who through skill and art, conquers the primal force of nature. (p. 10)

Lorca praises Mejías: "His eyes did not close/when he saw the horns near"—even as the fatal goring approaches, the brave bullfighter maintains his "grace" and does not lose sight of the bull, his impending death. And now Mejías, accepting the fate of his "terrible mothers" ("… probably the Fates, Morai or Parcae, whose influence is exerted at birth" (Maurer, 2002, p. 944)) joins the celestial realm of ancient bulls and fighters "of pale mist".

Nowhere in this sixth stanza of the poem's second section does Lorca shout "I will not see it!" He has seen. And the poem in its entirety turns here. The poet recognises Ignacio is lost to him, and in the ninth line—"There was no prince in Seville/who could compare with him"—turns to elegy in a more traditional sense, that is, "to speak well of" (Sacks, 1985, p. 23). As the poet accepts, for the moment, Ignacio's spiritual presence, his absent physical being—he is free to recount the wonders of this once-living man.

Thus elegy becomes eulogy: a prince, his sword, his heart, strength, "his smile was a spikenard [precious ointment]/of wit and intelligence." He is a "great torero … a good peasant …"—gentle contrasts with hard, tender with dazzling, ending: "tremendous with the final/*banderillas* [wooden shafts] of darkness!" This stanza ends with Ignacio's greatness as a bullfighter, his deft beauty, thus giving to him in poetry what he did not obtain in his final fight with the bull.

The final stanza of section two is as follows.

> But now he sleeps without end.
> Now the moss and the grass
> open with sure fingers
> the flower of his skull.
> And now his blood comes out singing;
> singing along marshes and meadows,
> sliding on frozen horns,
> faltering soulless in the mist,
> stumbling over a thousand hoofs
> like a long, dark, sad tongue,
> to form a pool of agony
> close to the starry Guadalquivir.
> Oh, white wall of Spain!
> Oh, black bull of sorrow!

> Oh, hard blood of Ignacio!
> Oh, nightingale of his veins!
> No.
> I will not see it!
> No chalice can contain it,
> no swallows can drink it,
> no frost of light can cool it,
> nor song nor deluge of white lilies,
> no glass can cover it with silver.
> No.
> I will not see it!

The mourner is strengthened through splitting—ferocious denial, rhapsodic idealisation—and is better able to face the earthy reality of death: "But now he sleeps without end. /Now the moss and the grass/open with sure fingers/the flower of his skull." The body's disintegration is anticipated, resulting in stunning poetry: "And now his blood comes out singing ... sliding ... faltering ... stumbling ... like a long, dark, sad tongue,/to form a pool of agony/close to the starry Guadalquivir" (the longest navigable river in Spain, and here as a metaphor for the Milky Way).

The repetition of "now", three times, emphasises the immediacy of a development in the mourner: exactly in this moment he can allow himself to imagine the decomposition of Mejías' body, its very corporeality and vulnerability so close and clear.

The blood moves "along ... on ... in the mist ... over hoofs and horns ... marshes and meadows". Hence one metaphor, the hated denied blood, is transformed into a thing of moving beauty. Segal wrote (quoting Rodin): "We call ugly that which ... suggests illness, suffering, destruction ... But let a great artist get hold of this ugliness; immediately he transfigures it—with a touch of his magic wand he makes it into beauty" (1952, p. 502).

And now the poet halts: a moan ensues, four lines begin with "Oh"; the first three are held tightly with alliteration and assonance: "white wall ... black bull ... hard blood"; this compression opens with a "nightingale", Ignacio's singing blood. Lorca's poetics open space, encouraging integration in the face of stark extremes, black-white, soft-hard.

This integration is followed by a change of heart; the last stanza is comprised of nine lines, each containing a negative, no, nor, not. The poet's outpouring of refusal explains to the reader that Mejías' blood *cannot* be held by chalice or drank by swallow—no frost can cool—no covering over by lilies, song, glass, or silver is possible. The poet cannot bear to continue, to hold in his own mind what cannot be stopped, the flowing blood of his beloved friend including his own foreseeable blood.

"The laid out body"

> Stone is a forehead where dreams grieve
> without curving waters and frozen cypresses.
> Stone is a shoulder on which to bear Time
> with trees formed of tears and ribbons and planets

I have seen grey showers move towards the waves
raising their tender riddled arms,
to avoid being caught by the lying stone
which loosens their limbs without soaking up the blood

For stone gathers seed and clouds,
skeleton larks and wolves of penumbra:
but yields not sounds nor crystals nor fire,
only bull rings and bull rings and more bull rings without walls.

Now, Ignacio the wellborn lies on the stone.
All is finished. What is happening? Contemplate his face:
death has covered him with pale sulphur
and has placed on him the head of a dark minotaur.

All is finished. The rain penetrates his mouth.
The air, as if mad, leaves his sunken chest,
and Love, soaked through with tears of snow,
warms itself on the peak of the herd.

What are they saying? A stenching silence settles down.
We are here with a body laid out which fades away,
with a pure shape which had nightingales
and we see it being filled with depthless holes.

Who creases the shroud? What he says is not true!
Nobody sings here, nobody weeps in the corner,
nobody pricks the spurs, nor terrifies the serpent.
Here I want nothing else but the round eyes
to see this body without a chance of rest.

Here I want to see those men of hard voice.
Those that break horses and dominate rivers;
those men of sonorous skeleton who sing
with a mouth full of sun and flint.

Here I want to see them. Before the stone.
Before this body with broken reins.
I want to know from them the way out
for this captain strapped down by death.

I want them to show me a lament like a river
which will have sweet mists and deep shores,

to take the body of Ignacio where it loses itself
without hearing the double panting of the bulls.

Loses itself in the round bull ring of the moon
which feigns in its youth a sad quiet bull:
loses itself in the night without song of fishes
and in the white thicket of frozen smoke.

I don't want them to cover his face with handkerchiefs
that he may get used to the death he carries.
Go, Ignacio; feel not the hot bellowing.
Sleep, fly, rest: even the sea dies!

Stone winds its way through the first four stanzas, appearing five times: "Stone is a forehead where dreams grieve/... Stone is a shoulder on which to bear Time ..." Stone holds the dreaming mind, providing a comforting shoulder ... and we see both mind and body are held. Lorca mingles the concrete and the symbolic, as the stone also has an important literal significance, as in the slab on which the body lies, and the stone above the grave; similarly to the blood in section two, an interweaving of the concrete and the symbolic.

Now given over to stone, "Ignacio the wellborn lies on the stone. /All is finished." Mejías is free to go the way all bodies will, "rain penetrates his mouth ... air ... leaves his sunken chest,/ and Love, soaked through with tears of snow ..."; the beauty and glory of Ignacio's body, "laid out which fades away ... pure shape which had nightingales ... being filled with depthless holes." Death is endless, boundless: "A stenching silence settles down." We again experience the actual physicality of Mejías' death, its crushing collapse; Lorca imagining his own demise, and the final rotting of the body painfully at hand.

The last stanza, one of the most beautiful in the entire poem, reveals the agonising conflict of mourning: "I don't want them to cover his face with handkerchiefs/that he may get used to the death he carries", followed by, "Go, Ignacio; feel not the hot bellowing. /Sleep, fly rest: even the sea dies!" Side by side lie a demand for illusion—if they don't cover his face he won't be dead—and the necessary acceptance of his loved one's departure: "Sleep, fly rest"—a giving permission, allowing the bullfighter his own proper and real ending, inevitably his own self.

"Absent soul"

The bull does not know you, nor the fig tree,
nor the horses, nor the ants in your own house.
The child and the afternoon do not know you
because you have died for ever.

The back of the stone does not know you,
nor the black satin in which you crumble.
Your silent memory does not know you
because you have died for ever.

The autumn will come with small white snails.
misty grapes and with clustered hills,
but no one will look into your eyes
because you have died for ever.

Because you have died for ever,
like all the dead of the Earth,
like all the dead who are forgotten
in a heap of lifeless dogs.

Nobody knows you. But I sing of you.
For posterity I sing of your profile and grace.
Of the signal maturity of your understanding.
Of your appetite for death and the taste of its mouth.
Of the sadness of your once valiant gaiety.

It will be a long time, if ever, before there is born
an Andalusian so true, so rich in adventure.
I sing of his elegance with words that groan,
and I remember a sad breeze through the olive trees.

The poem's fourth and last section is somber, full of resignation, bitterness, and acceptance. The need for repetition remains; "Because you have died forever" is repeated four times in four stanzas in a section with a total of six stanzas. "Does not know you"—repeated five times and intimated many more—is the absolute definition of death; a fear of death is the fear of no longer being known or remembered, not held in the mind of any living person.

Final acceptance takes this form. Ignacio cannot be known, in the present and forever; will not be known again. Not the bull who killed him, nor any other bull, will ever know him. The list continues: "the fig tree … horses … ants in your own house. / The child and the afternoon … back of the stone … the black satin in which you crumble." But most painful is the realisation that Ignacio will never know himself again: "Your silent memory does not know you …" Mejías' relationship to his own self is lost—others lose him but worse is that he has lost himself, his own life. Animate and inanimate entities will not know Ignacio, and time will pass, "autumn will come" (and go) with no heed of his death. Nothing on this earth stops for death. Despair leads to an eruption of anger and bitterness: "like all the dead of the Earth … who are forgotten/ in a heap of lifeless dogs." Ignacio is not a dead lifeless dog, but the poet expresses his fury at Mejías' death, essentially name-calling—"You cur! How dare you do this to me"—and perhaps Lorca's own wish *is* to forget and turn his back in hatred and contempt. And yet, the poet can recover his love and turn to his poetic task.

The poet sings of his singing, his recognition that poetry and song provide genuine solace, language and thinking are perhaps the only real resolution. The poet and the reader are filled with sad resignation. We note that this is the single stanza holding five lines. This fuller stanza, in length and feeling, marks the final turn of the poem, towards a way of living and being with loss, no longer addressing Mejías, but the world: "I sing of his elegance with words that groan, /and I remember a sad breeze through the olive trees." It is generally assumed that Lorca intended these lines for his own gravestone. And it is known that he and Mejías shared a special love for the olive tree: as a child, Mejías played at being a bull-fighter, the wind in the branches of the olive trees standing for the bull; Lorca took great pleasure roaming through the groves of his family's farm as a child (Gibson, 1989).

Lorca wrote in his own way about mourning when he described "The duende wounds. In the healing of that wound, which never closes, lies the strange, invented qualities of a man's way" (Lorca, 1955b, p. 67). The work of mourning is never completely finished.

Melanie Klein's clinical cases from her 1940 paper "Mourning and its relation to manic-depressive states"

In this paper Mrs Klein described two patients in the throes of mourning: a mother loses her young son, and a son loses his elderly mother. Klein described a normal mourning in the first instance, and, in the second, a more complicated mourning in which manic defences inhibit progress.

Klein's second patient (Mr D) dreams, the night before his mother's death, as follows:

> He saw a bull lying in a farmyard. It was not quite dead, and looked very uncanny and dangerous. He was standing on one side of the bull, his mother on the other. He escaped into a house, feeling that he was leaving his mother behind in danger, and that he should not do so; but he vaguely hoped that she would get away. (p. 364)

In one association the patient recalled a story in which a man was kept lying on the ground as a bull stood over him for hours, threatening to crush him if he moved, a reversal of his dream when he and his mother stood over the bull. Further on he recounted that a friend of his had a bull, which looked ghastly and had damaged some buildings on the family farm. D "urgently advised him to keep the bull under control".

A conversation between death and life is described by David Grossman (2011) in a prose poem written after his son's death:

> —how life and death
> stand face-to-face
> cooing at each other.

And in his essay, "Poem of the bull," Lorca wrote:

> They say that the torero goes to the ring to earn money, prestige, glory, applause ... but this is not true. He goes to the ring to be alone with the bull, an animal he both fears and adores, and *to whom he has much to* say ... Each person in the audience fights the bull along with the torero ... And thus the torero plays the leading role in a collective drama. (Lorca, 1955c, pp. 97–98, my italics)

In another essay, "Play and theory of duende", he wrote:

> The duende is at his most impressive in the bullfight, for he must fight both death, ... and geometry— ... The bull has his orbit, and the bullfighter has his, and between these two orbits is a *point of danger*, the vertex of the terrible play. (1955b, p. 69, my italics)

Mrs Klein's patient, Mr D, and his mother are (in the patient's dream) poised over the bull, at a vertex. Who will remain with the bull and die—and who will escape?

The bull must stand for the terrible allure of his mother as she is dying—"uncanny, dangerous, not quite dead" and in his associations the bull is "ghastly ... out of control and damaging" representing his own drive towards death, to follow his mother.

Thus, there is a moment of decision for Mr D, as his mother will surely die (in fact does the next day), but as with Mrs A, the first patient, who has lost her son, what choice will Mr D make? Mrs A's dream was as follows:

> She was flying with her son, and he disappeared. She felt that this meant his death—that he was drowned. She felt as if she, too, were to be drowned—but then she *made an effort and drew away from the danger*, back to life. (Klein, 1940, p. 358, my italics)

At one crucial moment, at a vertex, both Mr D and Mrs A dis-identify with their object—pulling back from drowning, escaping the bull, they choose to go on living, which has required a letting go of their lost object. This, then, is the individual's conversation, internally, between life and death.

We see, as depicted in the "Lament", that Lorca "decides" to live, to loosen his identification with Mejías, thus his mourning for a beloved friend—and his own future anticipated death—is successful, and he—and we—are left with the lovely sad breeze of poetry through the olive trees, standing for a feeling, a surround of feeling and sound, very quiet, perhaps discernible only to the griever, and in the background of ongoing life—serving as a reminder and a link to the lost object who is repaired and whole—his death painfully and arduously accepted.

Lorca did live, but almost exactly two years later was murdered. An official document was obtained by the *Guardian* in 2015 (Kassam, 2015) containing "the first ever admission by Franco-era officials of their involvement in the death ... of playwright and poet Federico García Lorca ... in 1936."

Ian Gibson (1989, pp. 446–458) speculated that Lorca might have escaped in various ways from his particular hiding spot in Grenada, where it was inevitable he would be picked up and murdered. Lorca was an "enemy" of the fascists on at least three counts: politically he was an active and charismatic communist; as a radical artist, poet, dramatist; and in his personal life, for his sexual orientation. It is worth noting that he was killed the day after his brother-in-law (a young socialist doctor) dared, at this terrible time, to become the town's mayor.

Mejías, too, was unable to avoid the lure of death; he came to the ring again after having retired seven years earlier, and being considered by many to be too old and physically unfit, thus returning in complicated and difficult personal circumstances. After the goring he insisted on the long ride (twelve hours) to the Madrid clinic rather than allow the local infirmary to care for him.

In the end, perhaps for both Lorca and Mejías, to die and be remembered for their daring in the "bullring" was preferable to living unknown; the lure of beautiful death more powerful than the love of ordinary life.

References

Beckett, S. (1960). *The Unnamable*. London: Faber & Faber.

Freud, S. (1917e). Mourning and melancholia. *S. E., 14*: 237–258. London: Hogarth.

Garvey, P. (2016). Personal communication. June, 2016.

Gibson, I. (1989). *Federico García Lorca: A Life*. New York: Pantheon Books.

Grossman, D. (2011). *Falling out of Time*. New York: Vintage.

Hirsch, E. (2002). *The Demon and the Angel: Searching for the Source of Artistic Inspiration*. New York: Harcourt.

Josephs, A. (2002). *Ritual and Sacrifice in the Corrida: The Saga of César Rincón*. Gainesville, FL: University Press of Florida.

Kassam, A. (2015). Federico García Lorca was killed on official orders, say 1960s police files. *The Guardian*, 23 April 2015.

Klein, M. (1940). Mourning and its relation to manic-depressive states. In: *Love, Guilt, and Reparation and Other Works 1921–1945: The Writings of Melanie Klein, Vol. 1.* (pp. 344–369). New York: Simon & Schuster, 1975.

Lorca, F. G. (1955a). Deep song. In: *In Search of Duende* (pp. 1–27). New York: New Directions, 1998.

Lorca, F. G. (1955b). Play and theory of duende. In: *In Search of Duende* (pp. 56–72). New York: New Directions, 1998.

Lorca, F. G. (1955c). Poem of the bull. In: *In Search of Duende* (pp. 95–100). New York: New Directions, 1998.

Lorca, F. G. (1955d). *The Selected Poems of Federico García Lorca* (Trans. J. L. Gill, & S. Spender). New York: New Directions, 2005.

Maurer, C. (2002). *Federico García Lorca: Collected Poems*. New York: Farrar, Straus & Giroux.

Ogden, T. (1999). The music of what happens. *International Journal of Psychoanalysis, 80*: 979–994.

Preminger, A., & Brogan, T. (1993). *New Princeton Encyclopedia of Poetry and Poetics*. Princeton, NJ: Princeton University Press.

Rosenfeld, H. (1949). Remarks on the relation of male homosexuality to paranoia, paranoid anxiety and narcissism. In: *Psychotic States: A Psychoanalytic Approach*. London: Hogarth, 1965.

Sacks, P. (1985). *The English Elegy: Studies in the Genre from Spenser to Yeats*. Baltimore, MD: The Johns Hopkins University Press.

Segal, H. (1952). A psycho-analytical approach to aesthetics. In: R. V. Frankiel (Ed.), *Essential Papers on Object Loss* (pp. 485–507). New York: New York University Press, 1994.

Sodré, I. (2015). Who's who? Notes on pathological identifications. In: *Imaginary Existences: A Psycho-analytic Exploration of Phantasy, Fiction, Dreams, and Daydreams* (pp. 41–55). London: Routledge.

Wilson, E. (1941). *The Wound and the Bow: Seven Studies in Literature*. New York: Farrar, Straus & Giroux, 1978.

CHAPTER TWENTY-SIX

Narcissism and ugliness in *King Lear*

Richard Rusbridger

I would like to discuss the picture that Shakespeare gives us in *King Lear* (1608) of a personality organisation based on splitting and idealisation; how Lear uses fragmentation as an attempted defence against reality; and how shame acts as an obstacle to his recognising how he relates to his objects.

Two papers of Hanna Segal's have been in my mind when I have been thinking about Lear: first, her 1958 paper about the analysis of an old man; and, second, her 1952 paper about aesthetics, which I think helps us in evaluating Lear's state of mind at the end of the play. I have also had in mind her views on narcissism.

In the first paper, about the old man (Segal, 1958—one of the first papers about the analysis of older patients), Segal does not make a connection with Lear, though it seems to me that there are a number of parallels. She describes the eighteen-month analysis of a man who came for analysis at seventy-three following a psychotic breakdown characterised by depression, hypochondria, and paranoid delusions. His relationships in his family of origin were characterised—like Lear's—by marked splitting. He loved his oldest brother but hated the next two; he loved one sister but remembered only rejection from his second sister; he described his mother as cold and rejecting but he idolised his father as well as fearing him. Segal thought that the patient had an unconscious terror of ageing and death. He tried to manage this by denial, splitting, and idealisation. His attitude to his own three children replicated his attitude to his parents and siblings: he idealised his only son, and adored one daughter while complaining constantly about the other. Segal thought that he projected his younger self into his son, loving him as he felt that his own father had loved him; and he thought of himself as having been very youthful until his breakdown. But at the same time he felt persecuted by a much hated son-in-law. Some of the parallels with Lear will be clear.

In the analysis, the patient initially idealised the analyst. However, after the first holiday, this idealisation broke down, as did his idealisation of his son, of whom he had to recognise that he lived a life of his own. He was gradually able to admit his fantasy that only an ideal version of the analyst (an ideal mother or father) could save him from death—a thin defence, as she was simultaneously felt to be able to kill him by withdrawing her protection. He was slowly able to see how his greed and hatred were aroused by the inbuilt deprivations of analysis; and how his projection of his fury into his analyst led to his perception of her, and of what she gave him, as poisonous and persecutory. He and his analyst were able to link some of these feelings with his rage at the age of two at having been weaned. In the course of the analysis his attitude to death altered markedly. He was able to talk freely about his sorrow at the thought of losing something he was now able to enjoy: life. He was much more able to allow his children and grandchildren to have lives of their own, rather than being treated as projections of himself. He lived for a further eleven years after the end of the analysis, continuing to work, part-time, and enjoying life.

The second paper of Segal's I referred to is her 1952 paper on aesthetics, published when she was thirty-four. She describes artists as being especially capable of tolerating deep depression, and more so than ordinary neurotics. She believes that in their work they seek to make reparation through their creativity for damage caused in fantasy and reality. The artist's audience, seeing or hearing his or her work, is drawn, by the sensuous qualities of the work, into identification with the artist. This identification enables the audience vicariously to enter the artist's state of mind, and perhaps thereby to develop their own capacity for similar feelings. Segal suggests that this confrontation with destructiveness, and its containment and partial resolution, are detectable in the work of art by the presence of ugliness, contained by the formal aesthetic structures of the art concerned. The ugliness is a necessary component, expressing and standing for destructiveness; while its partial containment is evinced by the formal structure of the work's form, on numerous levels simultaneously. This emphasis on the necessary presence of ugliness provides a criterion for discriminating between great art, which confronts depression and destructiveness, and sentimental art, which does not; and (in a play) between the depiction of an authentic confrontation of destructiveness and a sentimental evasion of it. I think that this touchstone is particularly helpful in appraising the changes in the depiction of Lear's state of mind in the course of the play.

At the start of the play, Lear brings together his three daughters, promising them each a share in his kingdom, in proportion to the intensity of their declaration of love for him. Two of his daughters, Gonoril (the spelling in the first printed version of the play, the First Quarto of 1608) and Regan, do as he expects, and falsely declare their impossibly ideal love for him:

> Sir I do loue you more than words can weild the matter:
> Dearer than eye-sight, space or libertie, …[1] (1:1:49)

Sight, clear-sightedness in relation to the truth, is one of the key recurrent images in the play: here, Gonoril indicates that her view of love is based on false vision. Lear is pleased and rewards her and Regan. His third daughter, Cordelia, however, refuses to be false:

> Vnhappie that I am, I cannot heaue
> My heart into my mouth: I loue your Maiesty

> According to my bond, nor more nor lesse....
> Why haue my Sisters Husbands, if they say
> They loue you all? (1:1:90)

Her answer is reasonable, but from Lear's point of view is very provocative. Her answer moves beyond the incestuous, oedipal bond to her father implied in Lear's demand. It implies instead the existence of time, development, loss, and death. Lear explodes into uncontrollable rage, insults Cordelia, and banishes her from his court with great cruelty ("we/Haue no such Daughter" (1:1:253)). His language is grandiose and arrogant, and his reference to a goddess of the pagan underworld links him with darkness and evil:

> ... by the sacred radiance of the Sunne,
> The misteries of *Hecatt* and the night ...
> Heere I disclaime all my Paternall care ... (1:1:101)

This pagan allusion contrasts with the King of France's reply, with its biblical resonance:

> Fairest *Cordelia* that art most rich being poore,
> Most choise forsaken, and most loued despisd ... (1:1:240)

The Earl of Kent tries to intervene, telling Lear to "See better", but Lear accuses *him* of arrogance ("straied pride" (1:1:158)) and tells him

> Peace, *Kent*. Come not betweene the Dragon and his wrath. (1:1:113)

Kent is a figure of symbolic goodness in the play, linked by his surname with Dover, home of goodness and emblem of renewal in the play. He can perhaps be seen as one of the early psycho-analysts, following his patient around, loyally trying to get him to understand the implications of his actions, without bossing or bullying.

Lear's test of his daughters is absurd: he is out of touch with reality and is in an omnipotent state of mind. He actually believes that he can command precise quantities of love from people, and has no idea that his daughters have feelings that he cannot control. Their only purpose is to please him better. In his world, nothing is outside his control. The lies of Gonoril and Regan become part of a network of lies that sustain his illusion of omnipotence. His rage is directed at the only intrusion into his mad world—Cordelia's statement. Her words evidently convey ordinary truth, but for Lear they represent a massive threat to his psychic system. If he were to accept what she says, the rest of his beliefs would become untenable.

Lear, like Segal's elderly patient, seems to be reacting to the onset of old age, and the threat of death (Jaques, 1965). Both represent loss of power and potency, as well as separation from his daughters. He has had a lifetime of power and control, but there are some indications in the play that he has always had psychological difficulties (Regan, as well as blaming his age for his behaviour ("vnruly waywardnes, that infirme and cholericke yeares bring with them" (1:1:287)), says "hee hath euer but slenderly knowne himselfe" (1:1:282)).

How can we understand this kind of psychotic rage, which treats the truth as something dangerous that has to be expelled, just as Lear expels Cordelia with great cruelty ("We have no such daughter")? I had a patient who would shout at me to be silent, as he pressed his hands over his ears, rather than listen to what I was saying. The underlying issue is the fundamental one of how a person reacts to frustration: does he react according to the "pleasure principle" (*Lustprinzip*) or the "reality principle" (*Realitätsprinzip*) (Freud, 1911b)? Does he retreat into fantasy, as the narcissist or psychotic does if reality means unbearable anxiety, or keep in contact with reality?

In normal development, being able to move from the paranoid-schizoid position towards the depressive position, to take personal responsibility; to feel guilt for damage one goes on doing, in fantasy and/or reality, to people, and to make amends for such damage; and to acknowledge one's dependency on the goodness of others for one's survival, involves the containing, thinking, function of another person's mind. Problems arise if such a function is not available—which may be because of a physical absence of, say, a mother; or because of a psychological absence, as when a mother is depressed. And it is in the absence of a containing, thinking figure of this kind that a baby may have recourse to the kind of omnipotent narcissistic defences that Lear shows. It is notable that there is no reference at all in the play to Lear's mother and only one to his wife (as a dead adulteress—2:4:292); and that the references that there are to women are either hateful or highly idealised. The image of a woman is divided into an ideal and a denigrated figure: one emerging theme of Lear's movement through the play is his gradual progress to accepting the feminine in him (see Kahn, 1988). At first this is equated with the madness of being taken over and possessed by a mother:

> O how this mother [the then term for hysteria, thought to be caused by a wandering womb]
> swels vp toward my hart!
> *Historica passio* downe thou climbing sorrow;
> Thy element's below. (2:4:224)

Kahn links this with the threat of split-off femininity in him: the return of the repressed. Gonoril also despises "milkie gentlenes" in her husband Albany (1:4:322), much like Lady Macbeth. Gonoril also talks about "cowish terror of his spirit/That dares not vndertake [commitments]" (4:2:11). Kahn says that the use of wet nurses was usual until the age of twelve—eighteen months in the gentry and aristocracy in Shakespeare's time. The play, she points out, is full of images suggestive of oral rage at being deprived of a maternal presence. After the wet nursing the infant was returned to his mother, who may by then have seemed a stranger.

Processes of splitting and evacuation of pain are an essential part of normal development. However, if such profound splitting continues—either because of the degree of the external frustration or because of the innate disposition of the baby, or both—then one is considering abnormal development and serious disturbance. Perhaps part of the baby's fantasy during normal thumb-sucking or other self-holding is that he is able to feed himself, be totally in control of his environment and not need anyone. If this continues beyond early life one thinks of this omnipotence as the core of the sort of narcissistic organisation that we can see in Lear. This kind of pathological personality organisation is set up in order to control and evade massive anxiety and to provide a place of fantasied peace and protection. At the start of the play, Lear needs his family to relate to him in a way that sustains his fantasy of being without need: that he is like a baby in omnipotent control of the breast. As Regan and Gonoril strip him of the external signs that might confirm this fantasy, one can imagine a retreat to an even more omnipotent baby state, for example, with him feeling so identified with the breast that in his mind he *is* the breast. (Freud ((1941f) thought that the earliest relation to an object consisted in *being* it, by total identification, rather than *having* it, which implies that it is separate from the self.) He might then think that he can give up all that he has got—the external breast, his kingdom—and everything will still be fine. This would be like a baby that could not accept the reality of being weaned—in the case of an old man like Lear, or like Segal's patient, the reality of being weaned from life.

Amongst the hallmarks of personality organisations of this kind are omnipotence, splitting and, projection, and a particular way of trying to evacuate unwanted parts of the self into others while acquiring, in fantasy, aspects of their personality—the process that Klein (1946) called projective identification. An example of a narcissistic psychic retreat of this kind that I have come across is a sexualised version that appeared in a patient's dream. He was using sausages to penetrate his every orifice, so that he was quite self-sufficient, and in his fantasy both a man and a woman. He also had a dream of being curled up in a self-fellating ball. In both dreams there was someone who could have seen these things going on, and he was very afraid of this being seen—by the onlooker in the dream, and by me and by himself.

Fantasies of this kind can be very shocking to the person themselves when they become aware of them, as in a dream or passing thought, and can lead to feelings of shame. This connects with a theme of shame in *King Lear*, which I will refer to later.

In writing about narcissism, Segal, like Rosenfeld (1964), emphasised the destructiveness entailed in an individual turning away from dependent and loved relationships to asserting that he is the source of goodness. Her primary view is that this is an outcome of a malignant part of the personality: she writes that "The narcissistic structure originates in the paranoid-schizoid position under the dominance of envy and the defences against envy. It depends on the operation of splitting, denial and projective identification" (Segal, 1983, p. 275).

King Lear offers us an opportunity to see how Lear moves to defend himself further when reality impinges too much; and how he also makes some moves in the direction of dependent relations with others—towards depressive position functioning—and what the consequences of this are. Shakespeare shows this move in Lear as being, in addition, a move towards accepting dependency feelings in himself, which are equated with femininity.

As soon as Lear has given away his property to Regan and Gonoril, they treat him with the same cruel quantification with which he has dealt with the two of them and Cordelia: they halve and then quarter the number of his servants, eventually reducing them to none. This schematic reduction in his power and influence, which accurately reflects his own commercialisation of love, challenges his whole defensive system, and he starts to invoke a more desperate defence: that of fragmenting his whole mind and going mad. The plot concerning Lear and his daughters is paralleled by a subplot about the Duke of Gloucester, another self-deceiving parent with both a good and a bad child, both of whom he similarly misjudges. Gloucester has an agonising journey towards a right vision of his children—symbolised by his blinding, in the way that from Homer and the Bible onwards inner vision has been connected with outward blindness (the insightful but blind Tiresias, in contrast with the seeing but un-insightful Oedipus). Towards the end of the play Gloucester talks of how he could have gone mad, like Lear (though perhaps he does go briefly mad when he asks Edgar to help him to die?). We can understand his view of madness as a process defending against grief and guilt:

> The King is mad, how stiffe [unyielding] is my vild sence,
> That I stand vp and haue ingenious [sensitive] feeling
> Of my huge sorowes, better I were distract [distraught],
> So should my thoughts be fencèd from my griefes,
> And woes by wrong imaginations [false delusions] loose
> The knowledge of themselues. (4:6:271)

As a storm begins, indicating, as so often in Shakespeare, a falling apart of order, internal and external (Gloucester describes how there are "in Cities mutinies, in Countries discords, Pallaces treason, the bond crackt betweene sonne and father" 1:2:120), Lear starts to fragment his mind. A feature of his personality is his great cruelty and envy, especially directed at women and their sexuality. This is perhaps an intrinsic part of personality disorders, which seem in part to have the function of controlling and limiting, while at the same time expressing, sadism. He makes a savagely cruel curse on Gonoril's fertility:

> Into her Wombe conuey stirrility,
> Drie vp in her the Organs of increase ... (1:4:268)

He attacks Regan in a similar vein in Act Two, Scene Four. He cannot accept that he has produced such children, and his loathing of himself is projected into women and sex, to ensure that it is not his fault.

At this time he is still pitying himself for having thankless children. Towards the end of Act One he has a fleeting insight into his own failing: "I did her wrong" (1:5:23)—but then loses it again, as he starts to rave about himself:

> So kind a father! ... Monster Ingratitude! (5:30/36)

And he starts to worry about his own grip on reality:

> O let me not be mad, not mad sweet Heauen:
> Keepe me in temper, I would not be mad. (1:5:41)

Despite this prayer, he would rather break down than experience sorrow, regret, responsibility, which he equates with "weak" femininity. Femininity is denigrated in the play, but is also revealed as representing and enabling a sane relation to reality because it accepts dependency and vulnerability, rather than denying them. *King Lear* is sometimes described as a misogynistic play, but is actually the reverse. The "women's weapons" of which Lear speaks are depicted as manipulative, but also show him as threatened from within by the weapons of his own feelings. He ends with a grandiose flourish of impotent rage:

> O let not womens weapons, water drops,
> Stayne my mans cheekes! ... I will doe such things,
> What they are yet I know not, but they shalbe
> The terrors of the earth, you think Ile weepe,
> No Ile not weepe ...

The stage direction at this point is apt:

> *Storm within.* (2:4:435)

Madness and fragmentation—actualised here in the broken, fragmented syntax, and embodying the ugliness, the un-smoothed-over version of reality, that Segal says is an essential component of great art—are here preferable for Lear to the pain of the depressive position. This perhaps would seem to him to face him with a worse hellish torment, the pain of recognising his own cruelty—and the impossibility of making reparation for it:

> This heart shall breake, in a 100 thousand flaws
> Or ere Ile weepe, O foole, I shall goe mad! (2:3:444)

The swift, short scenes of Act Three show, by the fragmentation of the dramatic structure, the deterioration in Lear's mind, as in Gloucester's. Lear is said to be calling for the destruction of the earth. Now even more desperately omnipotent than he was at the beginning of the play, he would rather destroy the whole world and his whole mind if he can't have things just as he wants them. The connection can be seen with the not uncommon psychotic delusion in schizophrenia of the world ending or being destroyed:

> [He] Bids the wind blow the earth into the sea
> Or swell the curlèd waters boue the maine,
> That things might change or cease ... (3:1:4)

("Maine" here can mean both the sea and the (main)land. Shakespeare uses this poetic compression to convey the confusion of the elements in Lear's mind.) His omnipotence will overcome and destroy nature as well: "Blow, windes, & crack your cheeks" (3:2:1). He talks, with the communicative freedom and condensation of the psychotic, of

> You Sulphrous and Thought-executing fires ...
> and thou all-shaking Thunder, ...
> Smite flat the thicke Rotunditie of the world, [the image suggests a
> pregnant stomach or womb that he is attacking]

> Cracke natures Mold, all Germains [seeds] spill at once
> That makes Ingratefull man (3:2:4)

The fires are both to execute, kill off, any thoughts, but they are also the instant product of his teeming manic rage: his mind is so powerful that he has only to think them and they exist. The masturbatory excitement of his attack on female generativeness is referred to in the spilling of the seeds, the "Germains".

In the middle of his rage, there is a flash of compassion for someone for the first time. Kent has just referred to the "friendship" and "repose" that a hovel they have come across will provide (which here seems to represent a container rather than a retreat). Ambiguously (is he going more mad, or is this part of a redemptive move towards a clearer, more compassionate way of seeing that in the play is linked with movement towards Dover, where Cordelia is based?), Lear says, "My wit begins to turne", and says to the Fool[2]

> Poor fool and knaue, I have one part of my heart
> That sorrowes yet for thee. (3:2:72)

The link between the storm in his mind and that around him on the heath (though the word "heath" is not in fact used in the play) is made explicit:

> this tempestious storme
> Inuades vs to the skin ... This tempest in my mind
> Doth from my sences take all feeling else ... (3:4:6/12)

He again briefly sees the error of his arrogance:

> Poore naked wretches ... I have tane
> Too little care of this, take physicke pompe,
> Expose thy selfe to feele what wretches feele, ...
> And shew the heauens more iust. (3:4:25)

But then he shifts back again, blaming Poor Tom's troubles on Tom's bad daughters (Tom is Gloucester's loyal son Edgar in disguise). Kent tells him, "He hath no daughters sir", but Lear says he must have: unless Kent agrees with him he is a traitor—a traitor to Lear's one-tracked authoritarianism.

John Steiner (1987) has commented that one of the difficulties in emerging from the refuge offered by a narcissistic personality disorder is shame: being seen, both by others and by one-self, to have treated one's objects with such cruelty is felt to be unbearable. People using narcissistic methods of defence and attack will often approach guilt and responsibility, only to turn back into the retreat out of shame. One could say that they use shame, a fear of being seen to have done wrong, as a defence against guilt, a more costly acknowledgement of actually having damaged someone (Conran calls shame "the poison of guilt" (2006, p. 73)). Much analytic work is needed to make a more lasting shift possible. One of the features of the paranoid-schizoid position is a particularly savage and primitive form of superego, and it is the fear of this (as the internal observer, with whom the external observers are equated) being turned on the self that seems to be felt to be unendurable. We can see Lear's cruel superego in his treatment of Regan and Gonoril; and it appears also at the start of the storm scene, where, in giving an example of those whom "the great gods" will expose (a projection of what he feels he deserves), he says:

> Tremble thou wretch that has within thee
> Vndivulgèd crimes, vnwhipt of Iustice … (3:2:51)

He also attacks the "Caytife" (villain) for his incestuous desires. His crushing superego is seen again in his savage attack on the "rascall beadle" of his fantasy (a beadle was a minor law officer of the parish) who is lashing a whore whom he hotly lusts to use, as he says,

> in that kind
> For which thou whipst her. (4:6:155)

This could perhaps be described as insight through projection: we often understand things about ourselves by first seeing them in our friends. Lear accurately diagnoses the beadle's hypocritical denial of his sexualised cruelty, and the beadle's hatred of this in himself, expressed through whipping the woman. In Lear's own disgusted attack on women just before this passage he was doing exactly what he describes the beadle as doing:

> Behold yon simpring Dame …
> The Fitchew [polecat] nor the soyled Horse goes too't
> With a more riotous appetite. (4:6:114)

He goes on to describe the female genitals as "the sulphury pit" of hell—another way, misogyny, in which he separates himself from the horror of submission to dependency on the feminine, the maternal.

We are thus invited to understand that Lear is as sexually excited as he believes the women he is attacking to be—just as he describes the beadle as being—and is as disgusted by this in himself as he is in them, and as punitive towards himself. Lear, perhaps just grasping the extent of his mad cruelty towards women, and specifically Cordelia, is said by Kent to be too ashamed to meet her:

> A soueraigne shame so elbows him, his own unkindnes
> That stript her from his benediction turnd her
> To forraine casualties [the chances of life abroad], … these things
> sting his mind,
> So venomously that burning shame detains him from *Cordelia*. (4:3:42)

The end of the play shows Lear moving towards insight as to reality, and then away from it again. He hints at depressive torment

> I am bound
> Vpon a wheele of fire, that mine owne teares
> Do scald like molten lead ... (4:7:45)

but immediately retreats into self-pity:

> I am mightily abusd ...
> I am a very foolish fond old man
> ... and to deale plainly [which he doesn't quite]
> I feare I am not in my perfect mind ... (4:7:51/58)

He remembers vaguely that he may have injured Cordelia, so she will be justifiably angry with him—but then slides back, via the falsely self-exculpating conjunction "for", into blaming Regan and Gonoril:

> If you haue poyson for mee I will drinke it,
> I know you doe not loue me; for your sisters
> Haue as I doe remember, done me wrong,
> You have some cause, they haue not. (4:7:69)

Cordelia murmurs, collusively (or is it also lovingly, to protect him from further pain?) "No cause, no cause"—but also correctly sees her father's madness: "Still, still, farre wide" (4:7:48).

Lear slips into a sentimental view of his plight in Act Five, abetted by Cordelia. On hearing that he will be sent to prison, he says

> We two alone will sing like birds i'th cage,
> When thou dost aske me blessing, ile kneele downe
> And aske of thee forgiuenes, so weele liue
> And pray, and sing, and tell old tales, and laugh
> At guilded butterflies, and heare poor rogues
> Talk of Court newes ... (5:3:10)

The picture he outlines is sweet, and very easy on himself. Any forgiveness will be neatly bilateral, reciprocal, and symmetrical: Cordelia will primarily want his blessing, as of a religious figure, but he will obligingly ask hers in return. The absence of felt guilt is shown by the verse's blandness in the neat sequence of imagined activities, familiar and stale: "weele liue/And pray, and sing, and tell old tales". The "poor rogues" have replaced the "wretches" of whom he was one earlier, and amongst whom he lived, when he himself was "cut to the brains" and was simply "vnaccommodated man ... such a poore, bare, forked Animall as thou art" (3:4:96, when he was addressing Poor Tom). In his vision, he has in fact become a gilded butterfly in a cage: different in form from the gilded narcissistic king of the start of the play, but not so different in psychic reality. Here we can see the usefulness of Segal's criterion about the necessary presence of ugliness—or is it better expressed as the absence of sentimentality?—in trying to assess whether depressive pain is being faced or evaded. Here ugliness is absent, both in content and in form. Underlying this, though, for the audience, is the sense or horror and almost unbearable pity that Lear can do no other, cannot face his guilt, and has had to become a kind of idiot or simpleton.

We can also see how painful recognising the incompleteness of his journey is: in revising the play for production in 1681, in a version that held the stage for about 160 years, Nahum Tate, later the Poet Laureate, contrived a happy ending. Cordelia falls in love with Edgar, and Lear and Gloucester retire to

> some cool Cell,
> [where they] Will gently pass our short reserves of Time
> In calm Reflections on our Fortunes past". (Tate, 1681, p. 440)

(The tone is very like Lear's in the speech that I have just quoted.) In his introduction, Tate said that if he had not written in a happy ending, "Otherwise I must have incumbred the Stage with dead Bodies, which Conduct makes many Tragedies conclude with unseasonable Jests" (ibid., p. 468). Although Tate says that he thought people would laugh, it seems to have been the unbearableness of the ending that made him tame it. Dr Johnson, one of Shakespeare's early editors, said, "I might relate, that I was many years ago so shocked by Cordelia's death, that I know not whether I ever endured to read again the last scenes of the play till I undertook to revise them as an editor" (Johnson, 1765). The ending of Segal's paper is also striking in its optimistic tone: her patient's brief analysis had, she thought, resolved his difficulties in facing death almost completely, and she describes the patient as having had an ideal death, following a milky drink.

When Cordelia is brought on, hanged, Lear at first sees the reality of the situation clearly:

> Howle, howle, howle, howle … shees gone for euer.
> I know when one is dead, and when one liues,
> Shees dead as earth. (5:3:255)

He is unable to sustain this clarity of sight, and insight, however. As he says, "Mine eyes are not oth best". Calling for a feather with which to test if she is breathing, he says that if she were to live,

> It is a chance which do's redeeme all sorrowes
> That euer I have felt. (5:3:262)

—which of course it could not do: it would be just that—a "chance", not the full reparation and redemption that is beyond his reach. He slips in and out of contact with reality:

> I might have sau'd her; now she's gone for euer. [But then he says:]
> *Cordelia, Cordelia*: stay a little … (5:3:266)

The play ends without sentimentality as to the difficulty—the impossibility—of Lear's emergence from the delusion of his narcissistic retreat. His final words are ambiguous—we don't know if he is asking for his own button to be undone, as he gasps for air as he dies, or if he still believes that Cordelia might possibly be alive:

> And thou no breath at all? Thou'lt come no more,
> Neuer, neuer, neuer, neuer, neuer,
> Pray you vndo this Button. Thanke you, Sir. O, o, o, o. (5:3:303)
> [The later Folio edition adds, after "Sir":]
> Do you see this? Looke on her? Looke her lips,
> Looke there, looke there. [*He dies*].

The play as a whole ends with a speech (given to Albany in the Quarto and to Edgar in the Folio) that seems to offer, in contrast to this pessimistic view of the possibility of Lear's gaining of insight, some idea of the possibility of surviving destructiveness, of a depressive position frame of mind in which there is a capacity for truthfulness and an ability to learn from history:

> The waight of this sad time we must obey,
> Speake what we feele, not what we ought to say ... (5:4:318)

This represents an advance on the premature coda by Albany ("all friends shall tast the wages of their vertue, and al foes the cup of their deseruings" 5:3:273).

In summary, through the extraordinary range and power of Shakespeare's vision and language, we can understand Lear as an elderly man—like Hanna Segal's patient—in the grip of a narcissistic organisation characterised by omnipotence and an entrenched sense of grievance. In response to the certainty of death he uses a method—omnipotence—that all babies use, and all of us continue to use at some time, but which in most people evolves into more mature states of mind. In the face of challenges to his delusional system Lear initially retreats into a fragmented psychotic state. He later makes some progress in acknowledging how destructive his usual pattern of relating is, but is sadly unable to maintain this and returns to a deluded psychic refuge. I have suggested that amongst the reasons for his difficulty in emerging fully from his state of grievance are the feelings of unbearable shame and guilt that he would have to face if he were to do so. Hanna Segal's understanding of the fear of death in the elderly, of narcissism, and of the necessary presence of ugliness in great art enable us to assess the fluctuations in Lear's ability to face the reality of his destructiveness.

Notes

1. The Quarto (1608) and Folio (1622) versions of the play differ considerably. In the main I have followed the Quarto, as recommended by Stanley Wells, the editor of the Oxford Shakespeare edition of the play (Shakespeare, 1608).
2. About the Fool, Conran (2006, p. 76) says, "it seems the King has found a device, to wit the Fool, whereby he may tell himself home-truths which, though coming from within, can be tailored in such a way a not to interfere with the progression of his rage to madness and the avoidance of

grief. In the Fool, according to my reading, Shakespeare anticipates Freud's (1940e) discovery of splitting of the ego." An example of the truths that the Fool tells is his advice against arrogance: "Marke it vncle, haue more then thou shewest, speake lesse then thou knowest" 1:4:130.

References

Conran, M. (2006). Some considerations of shame, guilt, and forgiveness derived principally from *King Lear*. In: I. Wise, & M. Mills (Eds.), *Psychoanalytic Ideas and Shakespeare*. London: Karnac.

Freud, S. (1911b). Formulations on the two principles of mental functioning, *S. E.*, *12*: 213–226. London: Hogarth.

Freud, S. (1941f). Findings, ideas, problems. *S. E.*, *23*: 299. London: Hogarth.

Jaques, E. (1965). Death and the mid-life crisis. *International Journal of Psychoanalysis*, *46*: 502–514.

Johnson, S. (1765). *The Plays of William Shakespeare*. London.

Kahn, C. (1988). The absent mother in *King Lear*. In: M Ferguson, M. Quilligan, & N. Vickers (Eds.), *Rewriting the Renaissance: The Discourses of Sexual Difference in Early Modern Europe* (pp. 33–49). Chicago, IL: University of Chicago Press.

Klein, M. (1946). Notes on some schizoid mechanisms. *International Journal of Psychoanalysis*, *27*: 99–110. (Revised version in M. Klein, P. Heimann, S. Isaacs, & J. Rivière, *Developments in Psycho-Analysis* (pp. 292–320). London: Hogarth, 1952.)

Rosenfeld, H. (1964). On the psychopathology of narcissism: a clinical approach. *International Journal of Psychoanalysis*, *45*: 332–337.

Segal, H. (1952). A psycho-analytical approach to aesthetics. *International Journal of Psychoanalysis*, *33*: 196–207.

Segal, H. (1958). Fear of death: notes on the analysis of an old man. *International Journal of Psychoanalysis*, *39*: 178–181.

Segal, H. (1983). Some clinical implications of Melanie Klein's work: emergence from narcissism. *International Journal of Psychoanalysis*, *64*: 269–276.

Shakespeare, W. (1608). *The History of King Lear* (Ed. S. Wells). Oxford: OUP, 2000.

Steiner, J. (1987). The interplay between pathological organisations and the paranoid-schizoid and depressive positions. *International Journal of Psychoanalysis*, *68*: 69–80.

Tate, N. (1681). *The History of King Lear*. London.

CHAPTER TWENTY-SEVEN

Hedge funds as phantastic objects: a psychoanalytic perspective on financial innovations

Richard Taffler and Arman Eshraghi

"We start with a *blank canvass*. We are trying to *sketch out* a global macro view of the world for the next two years. And we are looking for *wealthy patrons* that want to buy that *piece of art*."

Hugh Hendry, Founder and Chief Investment Officer of the Eclectica Hedge Fund, interviewed in the *Financial Times* (Williams, 2015, italics added)

Overview

Hedge funds are the "darlings" of the investment industry, with currently almost $3 trillion invested in them. These opaque, predominantly unregulated and exclusive investment products, which are only open to wealthy individuals and large investing institutions, possess a mystique and allure that renders them enormously attractive to investors. This is despite their less than stellar performance in recent years. Whereas the large majority of hedge funds are properly constituted and appropriately managed investment vehicles, some are less so, and the important implications of this are expanded upon in the chapter. Specifically in our analysis we draw on psychoanalytic theory, and especially the work of Klein and Bion, to explain the magical appeal of hedge funds to investors, and why they are willing to put so much of their funds and, by extension, their trust into such "exotic" and secretive investment vehicles. In particular, we explain the rapid growth in aggregate hedge fund assets under management until June 2008, followed by their subsequent dramatic collapse, in terms of the conflicting emotions such investments evoke, and, from this, consider the implications of the excitement-generating potential underlying all financial innovations.

Adopting the methodological approach of critical discourse analysis, this chapter explores how hedge funds were represented in the financial press, interviews with hedge fund managers, investor comments, and Congress hearings, before and after the burst of the hedge fund "bubble". In particular, we frame the human need for excitement in this discourse. Our study finds evidence demonstrating how hedge funds can be transformed in the minds of investors into objects of fascination and desire, with their unconscious representation dominating their original investment purpose. Drawing on the insights of the psychoanalytic understanding of unconscious fantasies, needs, and drives as these relate to financial markets, and parallels with dot.com mania, we show how hedge fund investors' search for "phantastic objects" (Tuckett & Taffler, 2008) and the associated excitement of being invested in them can become dominant, resulting in risk being ignored.

We suggest that financial regulators need to recognise explicitly the key role powerful unconscious processes play in all financial activity at both individual and market levels, and the adverse consequences if such understanding is ignored. Public policy implications are that investors need to be protected from the encouragement to act out their unconscious fantasies to their financial detriment via appropriate regulation, and that stricter ethical guidelines for the hedge fund industry may be required. *Caveat emptor* is not an adequate basis on which parts of the financial services sector should be allowed to operate, however "sophisticated" investors might be thought to be. We also argue that the financial and public media need to contain, rather than spread, the excitement associated with innovative financial products, and the individuals behind them. This is one of very few studies concerning investors' emotional attachment to financial innovations, and builds on the emerging field of emotional finance. The conclusions and implications discussed in the chapter go beyond any single financial market or product.

Introduction

Although the first hedge fund was established in 1949 they are a relatively recent but very high profile financial innovation. There is no clear definition of what a hedge fund is. However, broadly speaking, such investment vehicles are loosely regulated and secretive in nature. They are designed for sophisticated and wealthy investors, and aim to earn higher returns while protecting investor capital from downside risk using a wide range of different investment strategies. Importantly, their managers, many of whom become very rich and are celebrated in the financial media, are incentivised by the high fees paid them. Hedge fund assets under management grew at the rate of twenty-five per cent per annum from 1990 to June 2008, peaking at almost $2 trillion, and with the industry then consisting of no fewer than 10,000 hedge funds and funds of hedge funds (funds that invest in hedge funds) (HFR, 2009). In the following six months, however, assets under management collapsed by almost a third following investment losses of around twenty per cent, associated investor withdrawals, and fund closures. Interestingly, despite the hedge fund industry underperforming the S&P 500 by almost ten per cent a year in the five years to the end of 2015 (Preqin, 2016), assets under management had by then increased to over $3 trillion (Preqin, 2016). We will return to this apparent paradox in our discussion section.

This chapter helps to explain the rise and dramatic fall in hedge fund assets under management from 1990 to 2008 by addressing, among other factors, how the unconscious needs and beliefs of market participants may have come to dominate normal investment considerations.

We hypothesise that the fascination with investment vehicles such as hedge funds, and associated unrealistic expectations and wishful thinking, may at least partially be explained in terms of the collective psyche of market participants and their unconscious fantasies (phantasies).

Specifically, we describe how hedge funds came to assume a very different meaning in investor's unconscious reality to their stated aim of providing investment returns less correlated with more traditional asset classes. Based on a psychoanalytic reading of financial markets, we explain how before the hedge fund "bubble" burst, the excitement of investing in what hedge funds represented became divorced from the anxiety associated with the potential consequences of taking on excessive investment risk. Against this backdrop of collective euphoria, all such doubts were dismissed or rationalised away (Tuckett & Taffler, 2008).

However, any such euphoric state is likely to be unsustainable, leading to widespread denial, anger, blame, and panic when reality ultimately intrudes. The emotional trajectory experienced by market participants in this process is a common feature of most asset-pricing bubbles (Kindleberger & Aliber, 2011, pp. 26–33). We argue that the rapid growth and then dramatic collapse of hedge fund assets under management followed a similar trajectory. Hedge funds can be easily represented in the minds of market participants as highly desirable "phantastic objects" due to the financial innovations that many of them claim to represent, the potential opaqueness of their investment strategies, their implicit promise of wealth, their often exclusive nature, and their portrayal in the financial media.

In this chapter we draw parallels between hedge funds as phantastic objects and investors' perceptions of dot.com stocks both during dot.com mania, and after the bubble burst. We suggest many hedge fund investors become emotionally involved with their investments in a similar way, with associated unrealistic expectations and unintended consequences. In particular, we demonstrate the anger and blame felt by investors who had again to relinquish their unconscious desires when ultimately confronted with underlying reality, and to acknowledge that hedge funds are, in principle, just like any other investment vehicle. Finally, we argue that almost any type of investment has the potential to become phantastic in the investor's unconscious. It is therefore important to understand properly the vital role the unconscious plays in investment decision-making, the domain of the emerging field in finance, emotional finance (e.g., Taffler & Tuckett, 2010; Tuckett, 2011; Tuckett and Taffler, 2012). Emotional finance seeks to describe how unconscious processes can drive investment decisions and market behaviour more generally. It studies how the inherently unpredictable nature of financial markets generates powerful feelings of excitement and anxiety leading investors to being caught up emotionally with consequences often not recognised.

We believe that the psychoanalytic understanding of the human mind constitutes a helpful epistemology to explore the issues addressed in this paper. The manner in which hedge funds are perceived by many investors and the media, as demonstrated below, provides implicit evidence that unconscious processes are being acted out in the market for hedge fund investments, with the consequential need for greater regulation to protect investors and stricter ethical codes of behaviour. Whereas most hedge funds seek to act in their clients' best interests, a number, whether consciously or not, may well be exploiting the highly seductive nature of these investment vehicles to investors for their own purposes. It is these cases that are the particular concern of this chapter.

Hedge funds

There is no universally accepted definition of what a hedge fund is. According to a US Securities and Exchange Commission (SEC) definition, "hedge fund" is a "general, non-legal term used to describe private, unregistered investment pools that traditionally have been limited to sophisticated, wealthy investors." The Alternative Investment Management Association stresses their absolute return focus, using a definition based on Ineichen (2003): "A hedge fund constitutes an investment program whereby the managers or partners seek absolute returns by exploiting investment opportunities while protecting principal from potential financial loss."

Essentially, being largely unregulated, hedge funds are able to undertake a wider range of activities than, for example, conventional mutual funds (professionally managed and regulated investment funds that pool money from many investors, and are sold to the general public). They are open to a limited number of typically wealthy individuals and their representatives or investing institutions such as pension funds, endowments, insurance companies, sovereign wealth funds, and banks. Investment processes are determined by each fund's particular strategy and investment approach, which may change from time to time. Their investable universe can, in some cases, be viewed as just that—the universe—ranging from conventional equities and bonds to commodities, currencies, and other financial instruments, etc. They are able to take short positions (i.e., bet against the fall in value of an asset) and use leverage (borrowing) and derivatives (artificially constructed financial instruments deriving their value from the real assets than underpin them) to increase returns at the cost of greater risk, and invest in illiquid (i.e., difficult to sell) assets. They may also tie up their investors' funds for a significant period, imposing restrictions on withdrawals with clear consequences, for example, when investors sought to get their money out in 2008 but could not.

In theory, hedge funds should play an important role in the management of diversified investment portfolios (Stulz, 2007) and improve risk-adjusted portfolio returns. Nevertheless, measuring the performance of hedge funds is difficult. First, hedge funds, being largely unregulated, are not required by law to report their investment returns to any single publicly available database, unlike mutual funds. Although the majority do self-report to one or more of the commercial hedge fund databases available, many do not, making it difficult to measure overall industry performance and managerial skill. Also, because voluntary reporting is often done for marketing purposes, this leads to positive selection bias in commercial database coverage (e.g., Aiken et al., 2013; Jorion & Schwarz, 2014) resulting in a serious overstating of average hedge fund returns (Getmansky et al., 2015). In addition, there is a high attrition rate among hedge funds reporting to commercial databases (Getmansky et al., 2015). It is therefore not possible to measure hedge fund performance accurately, as in the case of mutual funds.

Nonetheless, there is some evidence that a significant percentage of hedge fund managers do have skill. For example, Ibbotson and Chen (2011) find that even after correcting for data biases, returns earned are significantly positive. In addition, a number of authors (e.g., Jagannathan et al., 2010; Jame, 2015; Kosowski et al., 2007) demonstrate top hedge fund performance cannot be explained by luck and can persist; that is, prior returns can help predict future returns.

On the other hand, other authors (e.g., Dichev & Yu, 2011; Gregoriou, 2006; Griffin & Xu, 2009; Malkiel & Saha, 2005) argue hedge fund returns are lower than is commonly supposed.

In particular, Dichev and Yu (2011) show that investors tend to invest in such funds well after their inception, and in widely uneven bursts of capital often chasing past returns. As a result, the *actual* returns they earn are three to seven per cent below conventionally reported ones with real returns close to zero, and much lower than the return on the S&P 500 Index. Also, Chan et al. (2006) demonstrate that a hedge fund manager may be able to report strong and consistent returns over ninety-six months but still be at risk of sudden implosion. Similarly, Stulz (2007) comments that "hedge funds may have strategies that yield payoffs similar to those of a company selling earthquake insurance … [and thus] will have a significant positive alpha [return]—until the quake hits." Indeed, the lack of consistent results across various studies further confirms the difficulties and biases inherent in the measurement and evaluation of hedge fund performance, and the real contribution of hedge fund managers. In addition, most, but not all, empirical studies cover historic periods, not the more recent ones when reported hedge fund returns are very much lower than prior to 2008.

Investors and the allure of hedge funds

In parallel with the remarkable growth in hedge fund assets under management until June 2008, the level of attention paid to hedge funds, both in absolute terms and relative to comparable investment vehicles, rose dramatically. For example, a search in the entire Factiva database of newspaper stories, magazine articles, and the like between 1998 and 2008 for the terms "hedge fund" and "mutual fund" yields an increase of 115 per cent in the frequency of mentions of "hedge fund" compared to only a twenty per cent increase for "mutual fund". Similarly, a simple search in Google Trends shows a forty-six per cent increase in "hedge fund" mentions from 2004 to 2008 in US-based sources, which compares with a twenty-six per cent decline in occurrences of the term "mutual fund" during the same period.

We argue that the rapid increase in the amount invested in hedge fund assets, followed by its sudden collapse in the second half of 2008, may be explained by the unconscious meaning hedge funds have in the minds of investors. To start with, such investment vehicles are conventionally believed to be able to deliver higher returns because of the often complex, sophisticated, and wide range of investment strategies and asset classes available to them. We suggest this implicit promise of wealth can become a key driver of investor fascination with hedge funds whether or not such performance is actually realised. Gregoriou (2006, p. 139) also points out that the lottery-like nature of hedge fund returns and the increased chance of doing very well or very badly, compared, for example, with mutual funds, can further enhance their appeal to investors and lead them to "expect a more thrilling investment ride". In addition, since hedge funds are unconstrained in what they do and able to change their investment strategy freely, investors can easily fantasise, imagining them to be whatever they want them to be.

Another distinctive feature of hedge funds is that a number of prominent funds are run by enormously wealthy managers who are hero-worshipped by the financial media. It is a basic human need to always search for champions that can be cherished and with which to identify. "Star" hedge fund managers, particularly when portrayed in exaggerated and unrealistic ways, can become represented in the minds of market participants as investment gods or gurus, further disconnecting investors from their underlying anxiety about the possibility of loss. That many hedge fund managers are reluctant to disclose their investment rationale for proprietary reasons or to maintain a "mystique" again adds to the attraction of their funds.

Hedge funds' exclusivity also contributes to their magical appeal. Being accredited to invest in a high-profile hedge fund represents membership of an exclusive, elite society of rich and sophisticated individuals. Lowenstein (2000, p. 24) describes the mania associated with Long-Term Capital Management (LTCM) with the observation that "hedge funds became symbols of the richest and the best." (LTCM was a celebrated hedge fund with two Nobel prize winners in economics and the Vice Chairman at the Federal Reserve Bank as principals, as well as employing no fewer than twenty-four PhDs, which collapsed within a month in 1998 and had to be bailed out to avoid bringing down the US financial system.)

> The real appeal of hedge funds, however, was financial snobbery. Investing with one of these titans meant membership in a discreet, truly exclusive private club. Imagine the cachet that came from standing at a reception in Midtown Manhattan in the '90s and listening to other people discuss their mutual funds, dot.com investments, and stock options, and being able to quietly murmur that your money was invested with Soros. (Farrell, 2002)

The role of the investment environment in the transformation of hedge funds to magical and immensely attractive vehicles must also be highlighted. A psychoanalytic reading of dot.com mania demonstrates that investors are always searching for exceptional returns with no downside (Taffler & Tuckett, 2005; Tuckett & Taffler, 2008). Highly leveraged hedge fund structures became attractive in the post-2000 investment environment of low interest rates and abundant capital (Geithner, 2008). Hence, many investors employed splitting, a common mental process whereby they were able to "split off" their knowledge of underlying risk from the excitement of the potential to earn extraordinary returns, thereby avoiding anxieties they would have felt had they brought the two together.

Hedge funds as phantastic objects

The concept of phantasy derives mostly from the writings of Freud (1911b) and Melanie Klein (Spillius, 2001). In his paper "Formulations on the two principles of mental functioning", Freud defines phantasy as a "wish-fulfilling activity that can arise when an instinctual wish is frustrated". Klein, however, regards phantasy as more central and argues that phantasies are not only the constituents of dreams but of all forms of thought and activity.

The term "object" in psychoanalysis refers to the mental image of something or someone in the real world, that is, objective reality. As the object points to the image rather than the actual thing or person, multiple versions of the same object can exist in the minds of different individuals. The phantastic object is thus defined as "a mental representation of something or someone which in an imagined scene fulfils the protagonist's deepest desires to have exactly what she wants exactly when she wants it" (Tuckett & Taffler, 2008). Hence, when discussing phantastic objects, the term "phantasy" suggests the potential of the object for transformation into an exceptionally exciting and desirable mental image. We argue that the thrill, and sometimes euphoria, associated with a successful investment may be explained by the unconscious role the phantastic object plays, be it a winning stock, a top-performing mutual fund, or, as in this paper, a celebrated hedge fund or hedge fund manager.

Freud, in his later thinking, together with Klein, views object relations as central to psychic development. In particular, Klein maintains that object relations arise at the outset, and there is no psychology without object relations (Klein, 1952a). Further, individuals are more susceptible to the phantastic object when a particular sense of reality dominates their thinking. According to Klein (1952b), people make decisions in one of the two basic oscillating states of mind, the depressive (D) state of mind, and the paranoid-schizoid (PS) state of mind. In the D state, we see ourselves and the others more or less as we are, both good and bad. In the PS state of mind, the psychic pain of dealing with undesirable reality is avoided by mentally splitting off the good from the bad. The unconscious search for the phantastic object triumphs over "realistic" judgments when a PS state of mind dominates. In such settings, hedge funds can readily be transformed in the minds of investors into investment vehicles that promise, much like Aladdin's lamp, to fulfil their investors' deepest unconscious desires.

Importantly, once an investor comes to "believe" that a particular hedge fund can earn exceptional returns, he is likely to repress any doubts associated with investing in it. Hence, in the investor's unconscious search for the phantastic object, the hedge fund's stated purpose may well be ignored. When the excitement of investing in the phantastic object takes over, the normal capacity to judge risk breaks down, unless sufficiently large losses literally wake the investor up from his reverie.

Information processing takes on a different purpose when a phantastic object is unconsciously believed to exist. The phantastic object "appears to offer the opportunity to break the rules of usual life and so turn 'normal' reality on its head" (Tuckett & Taffler, 2008), which creates the impression that what was previously considered impossible can, in fact, happen after all. In this respect, there are interesting parallels between hedge funds and internet stocks in the late 1990s. Taffler and Tuckett (2005) describe what happened in the dot.com bubble:

> Conventional firm valuation models based on discountable future cash flows and/or earnings broke down not just in the absence of meaningful historic accounting numbers and realistic forecasts but, crucially, because of the unconscious psychic meanings dot.com stocks possessed as phantastic objects.

Likewise, some hedge funds could have been viewed as latter day dot.com stocks, with their innovative investment strategies, implicit promise of exceptional returns, and media portrayal of their managers changing the rules of business (Taffler & Tuckett, 2005). The anxiety associated with investment risk is thus split off from the excitement, and underlying reality is similarly suspended. In such settings, market participants essentially become a "basic assumption group" that share the same strong belief in the phantastic object. In contrast to the "work group" whose members co-operate in the performance of a task, are clear about their purpose, and act in a rational and constructive manner, individuals in a basic assumption group do not think for themselves (Bion, 1952). Rather, they operate in a particular sense of reality, a PS state of mind, which blocks any attempt to think clearly and independently. Basic assumption group members collectively adopt unconscious defences against anxiety. Their activities, which look chaotic at first, "are given a certain cohesion if it is assumed that they spring from basic assumptions common to all the group" (Bion, 1961, p. 146).

Splitting and projection are evident in basic assumption groups but, according to Bion (1952, 1961), these take the form of one of three "basic assumptions": fight/flight, pairing, and dependence. "All basic assumption groups include the existence of a leader, although in the pairing group … the leader is 'non-existent', i.e., unborn. … [The leader] need not be a person at all but may be identified with an idea or an inanimate object" (1961, p. 155); in our case perhaps the idea of investment outperformance?

In the dependency mode, "one person is always felt to be in a position to supply the needs of the group, and the rest in a position in which their needs are supplied … the basic assumption seems to be that an external object exists whose function is to provide security for the immature organism" (Bion, 1961, p. 74). Clearly, the dependency basic assumption might help explain the interdependence between superstar hedge fund managers and investors relying on them for their own phantasy fulfilment. In such settings, infatuation with the phantastic object accompanies wishful thinking. However, it is important to recognise that any investment in a phantastic object must eventually lead to disappointment. This is both because hedge fund managers are required on one level to live up to their investors' needs to be phantastic objects, and the way they may equally be caught up unconsciously in the same basic assumption group thinking. Hedge fund managers may also be driven to take uncalculated risks due to investors' demands for magic in the form of extraordinary returns. In fact, the real problem may be "not [so much] out-of-control hedge fund managers, but rather overaggressive marketing and over-eager investors" (Cramer, 2006).

Fight/flight refers to the tendency of groups to either attack an object directly or to run away from it in a state of panic. Bion (1952) describes situations of panic that can sweep through crowds, causing people to run away from an unknown, possibly non-existent threat. In this scenario flight offers instant satisfaction of impulses. These types of behaviour are evident in financial markets in the contagious excitement of asset price bubbles where investors simply have to have the phantastic object (Tuckett & Taffler, 2008) and then turn against it in panic when reality intrudes and their idealised phantasy is shown to be just this. In fact, we may view the dramatic collapse in investment in hedge funds in 2008 as directly reflecting how investors turned from fight for possession of the phantastic object to flight, and the attempt to withdraw their funds as quickly as possible.

Pairing is the basic assumption least talked about by Bion but relates primarily to the libidinal, reproductive instincts of groups. In the pairing basic assumption group the feeling of hope is key, based on the collective phantasy of a notional pairing producing a "messiah", although he can never be born. Bion (1961, p. 151) comments: "… the feeling of hope itself … is characteristic of the pairing group and must be taken by itself as evidence the pairing group is in existence, even when other evidence appears to be lacking." The key role collective unconscious wishful thinking or hope of a never to be realised investment jackpot plays in all investment activity is a clear manifestation of pairing basic assumption group behaviour.

The psychoanalytically informed theory of the phantastic object can also explain why, despite the level of competition in the market, hedge fund fees (commonly two per cent of assets and twenty per cent of profits) have remained so high for so long. Once hedge funds become phantastic objects in the minds of investors, they and their managers are consequently deemed infallible, and hence, immensely valuable. Just as one would not wish to be operated on by a heart surgeon who competes on price, so one is not likely to invest with a cut-price hedge fund manager.

When reality finally intrudes, investors feel cheated, and the once dominant feeling of desire for the phantastic object changes to anger and blame. The blame emanating from investors is rarely directed towards themselves. Instead, it is projected outwards at their managers, and more generally at hedge funds as an investment class with all their associated elements of marketing, including the media that helped to spread the investment phantasy. Conversely, hedge fund managers tend to blame overeager investors, regulators, rating agencies, and the financial system as a whole (Sender & Kirchgaessner, 2008). This culture of blame is often intertwined with a hatred of reality, which can destroy the functions of perception such that objective, external reality may not be appropriately acknowledged. When investors in a PS state of mind are eventually let down, this is inevitably associated with the avoidance of feelings of guilt and shame, and the wish to learn from the experience, which would be the appropriate emotional response in a D state of mind.

Hedge funds and their managers in the media: spreading the phantasy

The exciting depiction of hedge funds in the media as money-making machines, and their managers as financial alchemists, can play a key role in their transformation into phantastic objects. Through disseminating cover stories that are "often new, complex, always rather vague and appear clever" (Tuckett, 2009), the media can help eliminate any legitimate doubts that investors might initially have about the phantastic object, and thus further spread the phantasy. Whether this hidden power of media is manipulative has been debated by, for example, Fairclough (2001, pp. 45–46), who cites the professional beliefs and assumptions of media workers as the main factor in "keeping the power of the media discourse hidden from the mass of the population." In the context of hedge funds, however, it is not only the phantasy-provoking nature of the media stories surrounding these investment vehicles, but also their investors' often unconscious search for excitement, and the symbiotic link between these two forces, that contributes to a psychic retreat from underlying reality.

Hedge funds' potential to deliver spectacular performance, as well as the distinctive features of some hedge fund managers, among other factors, contribute to the willingness by the media to cover the individuals running these investment vehicles. Indeed, the media often treat high-performing and exceptionally rich hedge fund managers as celebrities, which, in turn, can attract more investors to hedge funds through unconscious identification and the expectation of earning similar exceptional returns.

Media portrayal of hedge funds in the form of movies (such as *Wall Street* and its 2010 sequel, *Pretty Woman*, *Bonfire of the Vanities*, *The Wolf of Wall Street*, and, most recently, *The Big Short*) and TV broadcasts can further consolidate this phantasy element. Many of these depict very rich and glamorous investment managers who can virtually get anything or anyone they wish for, conveying a sense of their omnipotence to the audience. The depiction of hedge funds and the people associated with them in the press involves similar themes. The media coverage of the Noel sisters, the five daughters of Walter Noel, the founder of Fairfield Greenwich Group—Madoff's largest feeder fund investing $7.6 billion with him, and earning $500 million in the process—provides a good example. With three of their husbands being partners in Fairfield and another running a hedge fund of his own, they were regularly showcased in newspaper and magazine articles with glossy photographs as the *perfect* girls who happen to be "well educated [Harvard, Yale, Brown, Georgetown], well married, and raising a pack of well-behaved, multi-lingual children …" (Stewart, 2002). Needless to say, Fairfield Greenwich went bankrupt when Madoff's fraud (see below) was exposed, losing its investors a large part of their investments.

Despite the secrecy of many hedge funds, there is often little reticence about the wealth of their managers. According to the annual survey by *Alpha* magazine, the world's twenty-five highest-earning hedge fund managers in 2009, after hedge fund returns recovered, earned an average $1,013 million each, up from $464 million apiece in 2008, and $892 million in 2007, for the equivalent but different sets of top twenty-five managers. However, it is not only the exceptional wealth of some hedge fund managers that attracts attention, but also how it is commonly displayed and reported on in the media. For example, Steve Cohen, former owner of the eponymous hedge fund SAC Capital, with personal net worth of $12 billion in 2015 according to *Forbes*, is generally regarded as owning "one of the best privately owned art collections in America". This has over 300 works by Impressionist and contemporary artists including Picasso, Cezanne, Van Gogh, Warhol, and Francis Bacon (Burrough, 2010). He also owns Damien Hirst's celebrated thirteen-foot shark in a tank of formaldehyde with which he is often photographed. (SAC Capital was closed down in 2013 after being fined $1.2 billion to resolve criminal wrong-doing charges and paying $600 million civil penalties for insider trading.)

Ironically, the personal lifestyles of hedge fund managers may often be more carefully scrutinised than their investment strategies. For example, they are often well represented in the wedding announcements of *The New York Times* (Anderson, 2005). The hedge fund industry's unofficial 2006 annual conference, Hedgestock, which took place at a stately home just north of London with the slogan "Peace, love and higher returns", consciously sought to appropriate the trappings of the generation of Woodstock (Timmons, 2006). Similarly, in a 2007 charity fund-raising dinner hosted by Arpad Busson, a high-profile hedge fund manager, Bill Clinton flew in to make a speech, and the celebrity guest list included the likes of popular music icons Madonna and Prince, top fashion designer Valentino, and British actress Elizabeth Hurley (Cadwalladr, 2007):

> Arpad Busson, for example, who manages £5bn through his company EIM, dated Farrah Fawcett [actress] before having two children by Elle Macpherson [model and actress] (they recently parted), while Nat Rothschild, of Atticus Capital, the 46th richest person on this year's *Sunday Times* Rich List, has dated Petrina Khashoggi [model], Ivanka Trump [model] and Natalie Portman [actress], and is good friends with Roman Abramovich [the Russian oligarch and owner of Chelsea Football Club]. According to *Tatler*, Busson is the seventh "most wanted man at a party", while Rothschild is "Britain's most eligible bachelor".

Critical discourse analysis holds on to the underlying assumption that power and language are interlinked (Fairclough & Holes, 1995; Fairclough, 2001). In particular, Fairclough (2001, p. 1) argues that the role of language in producing, maintaining, and changing social relations of power is widely underestimated, hence the importance of analysing discourse in a systematic way. From this vantage point, we suggest that the language used to describe hedge funds and their managers in the media bears witness to their assumed power and mystique. Phrases such as "masters of the new universe", "this generation's robber barons", and "Delphic oracles of finance" are only a few examples of how hedge fund managers used to be portrayed before June 2008 (Anderson & Creswell, 2007; Niederhoffer, 1998). Such exaggerated representations of some hedge fund managers as omnipotent and omniscient beings is typical of the phantastic object, and serves further to dismiss any anxiety related to investing with them. Media portrayal of hedge funds and their managers in this spirit not only adds to the mystique associated with these investment vehicles, but also serves to enhance the hubristic self-perceptions of their high-profile hedge fund managers and, as such, turns them into (human) phantastic objects for their investors. This is consistent with the inherent reflexivity of language, that is, language both mirrors reality and constructs (construes) it in a desired way (Fairclough & Holes, 1995).

For example, James Simons, the president of Renaissance Technologies, and number one in *Alpha's* list of twenty-five highest-earning hedge fund managers in 2008, is described in a *Financial Times* article (White, 2007) as:

> ... the most successful hedge fund manager ever ... [who] does just about everything a little differently ... a prize-winning mathematician and former code-breaking cryptologist ... the king of the quants ... spent $600 million on computers ... [has] an army of PhD's ranging from astrophysics to linguistics.

Another example, an eight-page *Business Week* cover story, describes Philip Falcone, the co-founder of Harbinger Capital Partners who ranked fourth in *Alpha's* list in 2008, as "the Midas of Misery" belonging to a group of vulture investors with "more clout and more imagination ... [who] just might kick-start the economy" (Thornton, 2008). However, following heavy investment losses, by September 2009 Harbinger Capital Partners funds under management were seventy per cent down on their peak of $26 billion a year earlier. Nonetheless, Falcone subsequently invested $2.9 billion of his remaining funds in a speculative satellite communications network that went bankrupt, and in 2013 was banned from the securities industry for five years by the SEC, *inter alia* for market manipulation and misuse of client monies.

A similarly eloquent tone and admiring language is used in *Fortune's* nine-page hagiography of Ken Heebner, a widely-acclaimed hedge fund manager:

> Spend some time with [him] and it becomes clear why. His brain is wired differently. His ideas come faster, his focus is more intense, and his ability to sift through massive quantities of information and zero in on what matters is downright spooky ... Basically, he's the last of the gunslingers—a go-anywhere manager who can be investing in left-for-dead US value stocks one day and red-hot Brazilian growth stocks the next. (Birger, 2008)

Eulogising high-performing hedge fund managers in this way only helps to consolidate the investment phantasy. In the case of Heebner, after producing an unmatched record of outperformance, including a gain of eighty per cent in 2007, his main fund (CGM Focus) fell by over fifty per cent in the second half of 2008, and he had underperformed ninety-five per cent of his peer group in the five years to 2012 (Stein, 2012).

The marketing of hedge funds to potential investors is similarly conducted in a variety of attractive and enticing ways that trigger the (unconscious) need for belonging to an exclusive group. Within this context, it is not surprising that hedge funds can bear singular names such as Dragonback, Eclectica, Richland, Matador, Maverick, Atticus (variously an Ancient Greek philosopher, a Christian martyr, or Atticus Finch, the upstanding and noble hero of *To Kill a Mockingbird* by Harper Lee), Valinor (the Undying Lands in Tolkien's world of fantasy), Kynikos ("dog-like" in Ancient Greek from which the English word "cynic" is derived), Helios (the ancient Greek god of the Sun), Farallon (radioactive islands), Cerberus (three-headed mythological creature), and Appaloosa (a horse breed known for its distinctive physical characteristics) among others.

Hedge funds and the intrusion of reality

The bursting of financial bubbles is not driven by the emergence of new information, rather by the fact that "what people have always known becomes salient in such a way that it can no longer be ignored" (Tuckett, 2009). Once reality intrudes, a strikingly different series of emotions is triggered, which highlights the prototypical emotional reactions to the intrusion of the real world.

With the unfolding of the global financial crisis, and the drying up of liquidity in financial markets in 2008, hedge fund returns collapsed, which, together with investor withdrawals, forced many funds out of business. As hedge fund closures and implosions increased, so did the blame-driven accusations against almost all parties involved, partly fuelled by comments from politicians, regulators, and investment bankers who held hedge funds accountable for the disruptions witnessed in the financial sector. A strong denial of reality, a universal search for scapegoats, and an abundance of anger and blame was a common thread in the range of reactions by investors, hedge fund managers, regulators, and the public.

Denial is an immediate defence mechanism that allows the individual to "avoid awareness of some painful aspect of reality and so diminish anxiety or other unpleasant affects" (Moore & Fine, 1990, p. 50). Such denials of one's involvement with reality are often intertwined with blame and projection, a process whereby "a personally unacceptable impulse or idea is attributed to the external world" (ibid.). When the belief in the existence of the phantastic object is confronted with objective reality, denial can be of the reality itself, or of any personal involvement with it.

An abundance of blaming others, in the absence of any noticeable self-blame, is commonly observed upon the intrusion of reality. For example, in the US Congress hearing on hedge funds, George Soros, ranked fourth in 2008 and second in 2009 in *Alpha's* list of twenty-five highest-earning hedge fund managers, blamed "the financial system itself" for the global financial crisis (Soros, 2008). John Paulson, ranked first in 2007, second in 2008, and fourth in 2009 in the same annual ranking, showed no embarrassment in his testimony by claiming his wealth reflected returns to investors (Paulson, 2008). Likewise, Philip Falcone emphasised he had tried hard to earn his wealth and had not always been fabulously rich:

By 1994, I was so "financially challenged" that the power in my apartment was shut off because I could not afford to pay the electricity bill. That experience, as painful as it was, stayed with me over the years … It is important for the committee and the public to know that not everyone who runs a hedge fund was born on 5th Avenue—that is the beauty of America. (Falcone, 2008).

At the same hearing, James Simons blamed the Securities and Exchange Commission (SEC), the Federal Reserve System (Fed), and credit rating agencies in particular, arguing they did not warn early enough of the dangers ahead:

There is much blame to be shared: the SEC and perhaps the Federal Reserve for taking such a hands-off position … the players all along the chain of creation and distribution of the paper, each of whom should have blown a whistle rather than passing the problem on to the next guy; and finally, and in my opinion the most culpable, the rating agencies, which failed in their duty and allowed sows' ears to be sold as silk purses. (Simons, 2008).

A study of letters to investors written by hedge fund managers to explain their unsatisfactory performance provides further evidence of blame by revealing common patterns. They usually opened with a brief apology, then moved swiftly on to blame other market factors, while working on emotions as well as creating a feeling of human warmth and optimism in the process (Kellaway, 2008). Arguably, the abundance of anger and blame expressed in such letters is consistent with what happens when the phantastic object eventually has to confront reality.

The Madoff fraud: the perfect phantastic object

The $65 billion fraud by Bernie Madoff—who did not actually claim to run a hedge fund, but used feeder funds that were mostly hedge funds or funds of hedge funds—clearly illustrates the seductiveness and power of the phantastic object. First, Madoff successfully exploited investors' unconscious search for the investment phantasy by showcasing the exclusivity of his funds. Investment with Madoff was by invitation only, and considered a great privilege. He would usually emphasise that his funds were closed, which made potential investors even more eager to get in. Investors were "hypnotised by the perceived exclusivity of investing with Madoff and believed that not investing would be foolish" (Arvedlund, 2009, p. 85). Occasionally, Madoff would admit some individuals, claiming "they came from the same world or were related through an uncle of his accountant" (Sender, 2008). One of Madoff's closest investors describes how being initially rejected made investors more willing to part with their money:

In November, I invited a friend and longtime Madoff investor to dinner and literally begged him to get me in. He listened politely, then shook his head slowly. "Forget it", he said. Bernie was closed; Bernie had a multimillion dollar minimum; Bernie didn't need my money. His discouraging response only made me want Bernie all the more. (Seal, 2009).

Second, the language used by Madoff to describe his business and his stated investment strategy (the so-called "split-strike conversion" strategy) further enhanced his image of an omnipotent fund manager. While there was no detailed explanation of what he was doing, Madoff's use of such terminology led to plenty of discussion in internet forums and elsewhere about how it worked and how to replicate it (Caldwell, 2009).

Third, Madoff's apparent extraordinary returns, as well as his reputation in the industry and personal attributes, allowed him to enjoy a perceived edge with both friends and investors. His close friends always had a high opinion of him—one even referring to him as "the most honorable, smart person"—while his investors described him as pleasant and charming (Seal, 2009), and "the benchmark for investors seeking stable returns" (Sender, 2008). His long-time secretary thought there was "a mystique about him—the money, the power, the legend" (Seal & Squillari, 2009). All this, together with Madoff's background and charitable donations, his history of Nasdaq chairmanship, and the SEC's continued approval of his operations, served as cover-ups that led people to trust Madoff as a fund manager. It was not just Madoff who became a phantastic figure, but also the managers of the main feeder funds who invested heavily with him, and who effectively opened the door for more investors to enjoy the privilege of being invested with Madoff.

Fourth, the strength of the Madoff phantasy was such that any attempt to disassociate with it became futile. True Madoff believers increasingly referred to him as "the miracle worker" and wished to see him living happily and well as they felt he deserved it (Seal, 2009). Very little effort was made to question Madoff's investment methods. For example, Madoff's largest investors, such as Fairfield Greenwich, viewed themselves equally as victims in his fraud, despite having apparently failed to notice red flags or reportedly perform required due diligence. However, various studies argue that Madoff investors could easily have discovered the fraudulent nature of the returns series by performing operational due diligence or quantitative analysis (e.g., Bernard and Boyle, 2009; Clauss et al., 2009; Gregoriou & Lhabitant, 2009). The same point is made in the many lawsuits filed by the court-appointed trustee, Irving Picard, charged with recovering money for Madoff's victims *inter alia* against even such large and reputable banking institutions as HSBC and J P Morgan (Masters, 2010; Masters et al., 2011).

The Madoff case illustrates how belief in the phantastic object can lead to such basic assumption group dependency pressure that individuals wishing to warn others against the phantasy are repeatedly ignored, or accused of just not "getting it". Harry Markopolos attempted many times to warn regulators about the Ponzi scheme (earlier investors are paid out with money from later ones) being orchestrated by Madoff, but no one, including the SEC, took appropriate action (Markopolos & Casey, 2010). Likewise, a 2001 article appearing in a hedge fund publication wondered how Madoff's strategy worked by raising some key concerns:

> Skeptics who express a mixture of amazement, fascination and curiosity about the program wonder, first, about the relative complete lack of volatility in the reported monthly returns. But among other things, they also marvel at the seemingly astonishing ability to time the market and move to cash in the underlying securities before market conditions turn negative; and the related ability to buy and sell the underlying stocks without noticeably affecting the market. (Ocrant, 2001).

However, the desirability of investing with Madoff was so strong that any signs of doubt were inevitably repressed. Only when reality intruded on 11 December 2008, did his investors recognise how they had been caught up in phantasy. The unconscious irony of Madoff's favourite sculpture, the four-foot rubber screw behind his desk where he met investors (Seal & Squillari, 2009), can also be noted in this context.

Discussion

On one level, investment is always associated with excitement (Taffler & Tuckett, 2010), and the search for excitement is a universal human activity. In volatile markets, when hedge fund strategies are considered most effective, this excitement is heightened. On this basis, it is not only the intrinsic nature of hedge funds as alternative investment vehicles that explains the apparent investor fascination with them, but also the excitement generated by investing in them. Hedge funds' exclusivity and perceived secrecy, the lottery-like nature of their investment returns, and the often exaggerated media portrayal of their managers and their performance also contribute to such sentiments. Hedge funds as phantastic objects can therefore become a source of emotional attachment for all investors.

Since the end of 2008 the amount invested in hedge funds has almost doubled to over $3 trillion despite the underperformance of the sector compared with the S&P 500 of getting on for ten per cent per annum over the past few years. What is very interesting, also, is how high net worth individuals now account for only a third of hedge fund assets under management compared with two thirds ten years ago, and even then most of their investment is managed professionally on their behalf by "family offices" and private wealth advisors. Institutions such as public and private pension funds, foundations, sovereign wealth funds, asset managers, banks, and insurance companies are now the dominant clients and invest a significant amount of their total assets in this investment class (Preqin, 2016). So, it seems not only wealthy and arguably less financially knowledgeable individual investors, but also prudent and sophisticated institutional investors, may be susceptible to the unconscious lure of the phantastic object and dependency basic assumption group phantasy.

Also, given the lack of regulation, investors need to be able to guard themselves against hedge fund managers being susceptible to acting in their own rather than their clients' interests (Foley, 2015; SEC, 2013). They have the ability and, in principle, the incentive, to overvalue their portfolios, and avoid reporting losses to attract and retain investors (Bollen & Poll, 2009) as well as routinely revising their previous returns history, thereby altering their performance record (Patton et al., 2015). By studying a comprehensive sample of hedge fund due diligence reports Brown et al. (2012), in fact, show how hedge funds frequently misrepresent past legal and regulatory problems. However, the costs of commissioning such reports are prohibitive for smaller investors.

Unlike with carefully regulated mutual funds, where audited information on strategies and performance is readily available, in the case of hedge funds investors are dependent on past performance and associated information self-reported to public databases (Patton et al., 2015), as well as media coverage. This makes responsible reporting even more important and the need to avoid being carried away by the excitement-generating potential of such investment vehicles.

Given the tendency of media coverage to generate investment flows (Ozik & Sadka, 2013), the importance of the financial media following appropriate ethical practices in the reporting of hedge fund activities, and likewise avoiding being caught up in the collective excitement, can also not be emphasised enough.

Had there been stricter regulations and ethical standards in force governing professional conduct in the hedge fund industry, Madoff, for example, could not have so easily orchestrated a fraud of such dramatic proportions. In the post-Madoff era, it is clear that even the most respected firms should not get a pass on the required checks, and investors should not have to tolerate any level of manager obfuscation.

It is, however, important to observe that the transformation of investment vehicles into phantastic objects is not exclusive to hedge funds. Dot.com stocks, house prices, Chinese shares, and the exotic financial instruments purveyed by investment banks designed by their "rocket scientist" PhDs, which were believed to have banished risk forever through magical sleight of hand, and helped stoke the global financial crisis, are other recent examples. In fact, the risks posed by phantastic objects go well beyond financial markets. All technological innovations, whether of a financial nature or not, can become readily phantastic as they run the risk of "temporarily exceeding our ability to use those technologies wisely" (Lo, 2008).

Regulators are human themselves, and thus in theory equally prone to becoming caught up in basic assumption group thinking and a paranoid-schizoid state of mind (as the SEC's inability to detect the Madoff fraud clearly illustrates). They need explicitly to recognise the key role unconscious fantasy plays in all financial activity so they can be more effective in taking appropriate action to prevent investors from being caught up in such a potentially dangerous way with the consequences we see on a regular basis.

Nevertheless, like more traditional mutual funds and other investment vehicles, most hedge funds and funds of hedge funds are properly constituted with appropriate risk controls and exercise proper due diligence. Much of the research evidence suggests that such alternative investment vehicles can potentially play a useful role in diversified investment portfolios. However, excitement, wishful thinking, and idealisation are all part of the potential transformation of hedge funds or any other investment vehicle into phantastic objects. Accompanied by a lack of appropriate oversight by regulators, this inevitably leads investors, however sophisticated, towards splitting off, projecting, and repressing the associated risk and anxiety with undesirable consequences for all parties involved.

References

Aiken, A. L., Clifford, C. P., & Ellis, J. (2013). Out of the dark: Hedge fund reporting biases and commercial databases. *Review of Financial Studies*, 26: 208–243.

Anderson, J. (2005). If I only had a hedge fund. *New York Times*, 27 March.

Anderson, J., & Creswell, J. (2007). Hedge fund managers leading in race for riches. *New York Times*, 23 April.

Arvedlund, E. (2009). *Madoff: The Man Who Stole $65 Billion*. London: Penguin.

Bernard, C., & Boyle, P. (2009). Mr. Madoff's amazing returns: An analysis of the split-strike conversion strategy. *Journal of Derivatives, 17*: 62–76.

Bion, W. R. (1952). Group dynamics: a re-view. *International Journal of Psychoanalysis, 33*: 235–247.

Bion, W. R. (1961). *Experiences in Groups*. New York: Basic.

Birger, J. (2008). America's hottest investor. *Fortune*, 27 May.

Bollen, N. P. B., & Poll, V. K. (2009). Do hedge fund managers misreport returns? Evidence from the pooled distribution. *Journal of Finance, 64*: 2257–2288.

Brown, S. J., Goetzmann, W. N., Liang, B., & Schwartz, C. (2012). Trust and delegation. *Journal of Financial Economics, 103*: 224–234.

Burrough, B. (2010). What's eating Steve Cohen? *Vanity Fair*, 30 June.

Cadwalladr, C. (2007). Close to the hedge. *Observer*, 29 July.

Caldwell, C. (2009). Bernie Madoff's life of make-believe. *Financial Times*, 13 March.

Chan, N., Getmansky, M., Haas, S., & Lo, A. (2006). Systematic risk and hedge funds. In: Carey, M., & Stulz, R. M. (Eds.), *The Risks of Financial Institutions* (pp. 235–330). Chicago, IL: University of Chicago Press.

Clauss, P., Roncalli, T., & Weisang, G. (2009). Risk management lessons from Madoff fraud. In: J. J. Choi, & M. G. Papaioannou (Eds.), *Credit, Currency, or Derivatives: Instruments of Global Financial Stability or Crisis?* (pp. 505–543). Bingley: Emerald.

Cramer, J. J. (2006). After Amaranth. *New York Magazine*, 2 October.

Dichev, I. D., & Yu, G. (2011). Higher risk, lower returns: What hedge fund investors really earn. *Journal of Financial Economics, 100*: 248–263.

Fairclough, N. (2001). *Language and Power*. UK: Pearson Education.

Fairclough, N., & Holes, C. (1995). *Critical Discourse Analysis: The Critical Study of Language*. Harlow, Essex: Longman.

Falcone, P. A. (2008). Statement before the US House Committee on Oversight and Government Reform. 13 November.

Farrell, C. (2002). Before you jump into a hedge fund. *Business Week*, 17 May.

Foley, S. (2015). SEC reveals hedge fund managers' failings. *Financial Times*, 16 October.

Freud, S. (1911b). Formulations on the two principles of mental functioning. *S. E., 12*: 213–226. London: Hogarth.

Geithner, T. F. (2008). Systemic risk and financial markets. Testimony before the House Committee on Financial Services, 24 July.

Getmansky, M., Lee, P. A., & Lo, A. W. (2015). Hedge funds: a dynamic industry in transition. Available at SSRN: http://ssrn.com/abstract=2367007.

Gregoriou, G. (2006). *Funds of Hedge Funds: Performance, Assessment, Diversification, and Statistical Properties*. Oxford: Butterworth-Heinemann.

Gregoriou, G., & Lhabitant, F. (2009). Madoff: A riot of red flags. Available at SSRN: http://ssrn.com/abstract=1335639.

Griffin, J., & Xu, J. (2009). How smart are the smart guys? A unique view from hedge fund stock holdings. *Review of Financial Studies, 22*: 2331–2370.

HFR (Hedge Fund Research) (2009). Year-end 2008 report. Available at www.hedgefundresearch.com.

Ibbotson, R. G., & Chen, P. (2011). The ABCs of hedge funds: Alphas, betas and costs. *Financial Analyst Journal, 67*: 15–25.

Ineichen, A. M. (2003). *Absolute Returns—Risk and Opportunities of Hedge Fund Investing*. New York: John Wiley.

Jagannathan, R., Malakhov, A., & Novikov, D. (2010). Do hot hands exist among hedge fund managers? An empirical evaluation. *Journal of Finance, 65*: 217–255.

Jame, R. (2015). Liquidity provision and the cross-section of hedge fund skill. Available at SSRN: http://ssrn.com/abstract=2284696.

Jorion, P., & Schwarz, C. (2014). The strategic listing decisions of hedge funds. *Journal of Financial and Quantitative Analysis, 49*: 773–796.

Kellaway, L. (2008). Go short on letters to investors. *Financial Times*, 2 November.

Kindleberger, C. P., & Aliber, R. Z. (2011). *Manias, Panics, and Crashes* (6th ed.). New York: Palgrave Macmillan.

Klein, M. (1952a). The origins of transference. *International Journal of Psychoanalysis, 33*: 433–438.

Klein, M. (1952b). Some theoretical conclusions regarding the emotional life of the infant. In: *The Collected Works of Melanie Klein, Vol. III*. London: Hogarth.

Kosowski, R., Naik, N. Y., & Teo, M. (2007). Do hedge funds deliver alpha? A Bayesian and bootstrap analysis. *Journal of Financial Economics, 84*: 229–264.

Lo, A. (2008). Statement before the US House Committee on Oversight and Government Reform. 13 November.

Lowenstein, R. (2000). *When Genius Failed: the Rise and Fall of Long-Term Capital Management*. New York: Random House.

Markopolos, H., & Casey, F. (2010). *No One Would Listen: A True Financial Thriller*. Hoboken, NJ: John Wiley.

Malkiel, B. G., & Saha, A. (2005). Hedge funds: Risk and return. *Financial Analysts Journal, 61*: 80–88.

Masters, B. (2010). HSBC had Madoff warnings in 2001. *Financial Times*, 6 December.

Masters, B., Murphy, M., & Scannell, K. (2011). J P Morgan risk officer warned on Madoff. *Financial Times*, 3 February.

Moore, B. E., & Fine, B. D. (1990). *Psychoanalytic Terms and Concepts*. New York: The American Psychoanalytic Association.

Niederhoffer, V. (1998). *The Education of a Speculator*. New York: John Wiley.

Ocrant, M. (2001). Madoff tops charts: Skeptics ask how. *MAR/Hedge (RIP), 89*: May.

Ozik, G., & Sadka, R. (2013). Media coverage and hedge fund returns. *Financial Analysts Journal, 69*: 963–999.

Patton, A. J., Ramadorai, T., & Streatfield, M. (2015). Change you can believe in? Hedge fund data revisions. *Journal of Finance, 70*: 963–999.

Paulson, J. (2008). Statement before the US House Committee on Oversight and Government Reform. 13 November.

Preqin (2016). Preqin Global Hedge Fund Report. Available at www.preqin.com.

Seal, M. (2009). Madoff's world. *Vanity Fair*, April.

Seal, M., & Squillari, E. (2009). Hello, Madoff! *Vanity Fair*, June.

SEC (2013). Investors Bulletin Hedge Funds. SEC Publ. No. 139 (2/13).

Sender, H. (2008). Members of the "club" who won the allegiance of colleagues. *Financial Times*, 13 December.

Sender, H., & Kirchgaessner, S. (2008). Top hedge fund chiefs blame the system for crisis. *Financial Times*, 14 November.

Simons, J. (2008). Statement before the US House Committee on Oversight and Government Reform. 13 November.

Soros, G. (2008). Statement before the US House Committee on Oversight and Government Reform. 13 November.

Spillius, E., & Bott (2001). Freud and Klein on the concept of phantasy. *International Journal of Psychoanalysis, 82*: 361–373.

Stein, C. (2012). Heebner at bottom for fourth year in five sticks to bet. *Bloomberg.com*, 28 June.

Stewart, K. (2002). Golden in Greenwich. *Vanity Fair*, 31 September.

Stulz, R. (2007). Hedge funds: Past, present, and future. *Journal of Economic Perspectives, 21*: 175–194.

Taffler, R. J., & Tuckett, D. (2005). A psychoanalytic interpretation of dot.com stock valuations. Available at SSRN: http://ssrn.com/abstract=676635.

Taffler, R. J., & Tuckett, D. (2010). Emotional finance: The role of the unconscious in financial decisions. In K. H. Baker, & J. R. Nofsinger (Eds.), *Behavioral Finance* (pp. 95–112). New York: John Wiley.

Thornton, E. (2008). The Midas of misery. *Business Week*, 24 April.

Timmons, H. (2006). "Peace, Love and Hedge Funds", *International Herald Tribune*, 9 June.

Tuckett, D. (2009). Addressing the psychology of financial markets. *Economics: The Open-Access, Open-Assessment E-Journal, 3*: 2009–2040. doi:10.5018/economics-ejournal.ja.2009-40.

Tuckett, D. (2011). *Minding the Markets: An Emotional Finance View of Financial Instability*. Basingstoke: Palgrave Macmillan.

Tuckett, D., & Taffler, R. J. (2008). Phantastic objects and the financial market's sense of reality: A psychoanalytic contribution to the understanding of stock market instability. *International Journal of Psychoanalysis, 89*: 389–412.

Tuckett, D., & Taffler, R. J. (2012). *Fund Management: An Emotional Finance Perspective*. Charlottesville, VA: CFA Institute.

White, B. (2007). The billion dollar boffin. *Financial Times*, 27 April.

Williams, J. (2015). Hugh Hendry stops betting on Armageddon. *Financial Times*, 2 August.

CHAPTER TWENTY-EIGHT

Communicating psychoanalytic ideas about climate change: a case study

Sally Weintrobe

Introduction

This paper is about my work to bring psychoanalytic ideas to bear on the gap between what science tells us about climate change and our willingness to accept the science and act with sufficient urgency to reduce carbon emissions.

Recently I gave a talk on climate change to architects as part of a dialogue with Sue Roaf, Professor of Urban Design at Herriot-Watt University. Her subject was the way most architects are still ignoring climate reality and building high-energy buildings without regard for local ecology. She spoke of the need to move on from unsustainable architecture. Our dialogue opened an international conference organised by Sheffield University on "Architecture and resilience on the human scale" with a session entitled "Bricks and feelings". During the three-day conference I heard presentations from many architects who are now faced with current and future climate devastation, increased flooding and hurricanes, and having to move communities. First, I will reproduce what I said in my talk, then look at psychoanalytic ideas I relied on, and then describe three of the architects' presentations.

The new imagination in a culture of uncare[1]

Introduction

Sue Roaf (2013), in a wonderful phrase, has called for architects to "re-engineer their dreams" to build for a sustainable future. This means nothing less than restructuring the architectural imagination.

The imagination needed for our climate crisis is a caring imagination. My argument is a culture[2] of uncare[3] in the global north[4] actively works to break our felt links[5] with the part that

411

cares. It does this to block change and promote carbon intensive business as usual. I suggest we are all, more or less, influenced by the culture of uncare.

Roaf's phrase, "re-engineering a dream", resonates with a psychoanalytic way of seeing: here, thinking is an inner, psychic, dynamic building project in which we maintain links with care by keeping those we care for nearby us in the internal world of the imagination; close enough to feel touched by them.[6] A main way we break links to care is by spatially rearranging our relationships in the inner world of the mind in order to keep people at a distance.[7] As "distanced others",[8] we do not care as much for them. An internal world[9] with uncare in charge is an internal world in which our relationships have been re-engineered spatially in this kind of way.[10] My argument is that the culture of uncare works to promote this kind of rearranging, which can lead to a distorted inner representation of the external world.

I will look at what sort of caring imagination we need to dream of and to build a sustainable world. I call it the "new imagination". Embracing the new imagination involves repairing broken links with care, and forging new links with care. This can be difficult and painful to do, but can also expand the experience of self and of feeling alive.[11]

A concept I will emphasise is frameworks of care. The capacity to care is not just part of individual character, but depends on these frameworks of care. Architects build them when they build sustainably.

The culture of uncare

A culture of uncare has gained ascendency in the period of globalisation since the mid-1980s. It has, by now, been extensively studied by social and psychosocial scientists, with each scholar naming it in turn the narcissistic, perverse, consumerist, extractive, entitled, arrogant, psychopathic, instrumental, and manically triumphant, culture.[12] All these are aspects of uncare, and together these aspects cohere to form a mindset, which I have called the uncaring mindset. It is organised, narrow minded, short-term minded, avaricious, and it tends to be set and tenacious.

The uncaring mindset is at the heart of the culture of uncare. It is driven by a powerful underlying phantasy,[13] which is that the earth is an idealised indestructible breast/toilet mother, there solely to provide endlessly for us and to absorb all our waste.[14]

The project to globalise the economy was driven by this phantasy. "Grab, grab, grab, now, now, now; undermine as many restraining trade barriers as possible, hide the true costs and let tomorrow go hang" was the order of the day. Laws were framed and trade agreements put in place to facilitate deregulation. Naomi Klein (2014) has described this process in her latest book on climate change, *This Changes Everything*, as has Joel Bakan (2004) in *The Corporation*. Deregulation means people working to undermine frameworks of care that hold excessive greed and exaggerated entitlement in check.

The only possible outcome of globalisation driven by a mindset that sees the earth as a breast/toilet mother was a pileup of social and environmental damage and the biggest problem for drivers of the global economy was how to get people to co-operate with what was an essentially immoral and inherently unsustainable project. Happy carefree consumers were needed to boost profits. The problem for the drivers of globalisation was how to disable the caring part of people.[15] The need was to reverse the human climate so that people would care too little, not too much. To date, trillions of dollars have been spent on undermining care through working to shift peoples' bedrock ego ideals of caring behaviour. Undermining care has been brought about through political framing, mass media, the academe, general culture, and advertising. It has led to a change in the culture of social groups towards greater disregard for science, more materialistic values, and the idea that to feel as free of care as possible is most desirable, rather than being a warning sign that one is living in a gated community, a psychic retreat, within the mind. All this money would not need to have been spent, and would not have been spent, if people were basically uncaring by nature. Instead, people are by nature caring and uncaring.

In my view, the global economy's business plan was to drive uncare and to disable care, specifically in relation to our behaviour as consumers. The need was for people happily to consume more and more products produced in the cheapest possible way to maximise profits. The true cost was climate change[16] and rising social inequality. People's moral qualms, their feelings of responsibility, their anxiety that it would all end very badly, their sense of guilt and their impulse to resist taking part, all stood in the way of the willing co-operation needed.

The new culture that came in had the ideological function of helping people find ways not to care too much about living in a way they knew deep down was morally wrong and unsustainable. The culture's aim was to promote an uncaring mindset. This mindset has trickled down from corporate power, to governments, to social groups, to the individual psyche.

Lawrence Summers' leaked memo

Here is an example of the mindset at a corporate level. In 1991, Lawrence Summers, then President of the World Bank, confided in a leaked confidential memo, "I think the economic logic behind dumping a load of toxic waste in the lowest-wage country is impeccable and we should face up to that. … Just between you and me, shouldn't the World Bank be encouraging more migration of the dirty industries to the Least Developed Countries?"[17] Here is the uncaring mindset writ large: outsource environmental damage to those who are far away and without power. Let them bear the suffering.

When this email was exposed, Summers said he was only joking. Presumably this was because he did not want either the bank or himself, as the bank's leader, to be judged immoral. The problem is that people experience conflict between caring and not caring and feel guilty and ashamed at having their uncare exposed; even if they do not, they know others are likely to judge them. This is the main reason why damaging and inequitable trade treaties are negotiated in secret, away from public scrutiny.

Like others, I was shocked to read of Summers' memo, but I too outsource environmental damage I cause, albeit obviously on a far smaller scale. Here is an example where I saw this clearly.

At the bus stop

I was waiting for the bus, having decided to travel more by public transport to reduce my carbon emissions. It was spitting rain, blowy and cold, and I thought, "I hate waiting for the bus. I wish I'd taken the car". Suddenly, spontaneously, I imagined my grandchildren overhearing my thought. They were now young adults, not the small children they are. In my imagination their world, a future world, was right up close to my world. In my imagination, we were all close enough to hear, see, and touch each other; close enough for me to see the extreme weather they were in and close enough to feel their suffering.

I felt ashamed. Part of my shame was feeling I was so much less of a person than I wished I was, and felt I can be. I felt trivial, fatuous, and grumpy, like a spoiled entitled brat. I had heard myself in a different way and with a different perspective. I think this was because I felt a direct, loving, empathic, link with my grown-up grandchildren. And, because I felt this direct link so keenly, I managed to stay in touch with what I had understood, despite this being painful.

This was that I had, without being consciously aware of it, relocated my own grandchildren to in a faraway place in my imagination, a place I had labelled "the future", and I had done this in order to sever a caring, loving, link with them. I had moved them from being close to being distant so I would not have to feel guilty, ashamed, and anguished about my carbon behaviour. Here I was outsourcing suffering. In my imagination, my grandchildren were now "distanced others", far enough away to be outside the area of my love and concern. I had broken my caring link with their actual future experience so as to assuage my guilt.

I have often thought climate change will affect the lives of my grandchildren. I now realised with real empathy that this was cut off. I had never felt affected like this. Here, I believe I had repaired the loving, caring link between us. I had reversed mental distancing and brought them back close to me where they properly belong. This is the sort mental re-engineering that I think is required.

The mechanism I have described—that of actively breaking loving links to avoid mental pain—is an ordinary human defence mechanism that can usefully protect us from being too emotionally overwhelmed. My point is that the culture of uncare boosts breaking caring links and boosts mental distancing on a daily basis. It does this in many ways and through different branches of the culture. For instance, take our social groups. Mine would be more likely to say, "Don't be so hard on yourself Sally; give yourself a break. Don't be omnipotent. Do you really think that your one tiny action of taking the bus is going to save the world?" They would be less likely to say, "Yes, it's unpleasant waiting for the bus, but stick at it. Perhaps give yourself a break if you are tired or not feeling well. Face how helpless and enraged you can feel that government is not stepping up to tackle climate change.[18] Use these feelings constructively to help you do what you can towards combating climate change." Or, take our newspapers. They mostly airbrush out references to climate change. For example, at his last inauguration as President, Obama spoke about climate change. The main headline across the mass media that day was: Did Beyoncé lip-sync the national anthem?[19] Or, take advertising and general culture. These relentlessly exhort and seduce us to feel entitled to idealised conditions. They encourage the uncaring part of us that I heard in my inner voice at the bus stop.

The aim of this culture is to break links with care and encourage spatial distancing of the victims of our uncare in the internal world of the psyche. The aim is to keep us defended against feeling conflicted and anguished at our collectively damaging way of living.

Disavowal

These distancing strategies are part of disavowal, which is seeing reality but finding ways to remain blind to reality at a feeling level. Disavowal can leave us with highly distorted inner pictures of reality, with people we love far away or in the shadows, with important issues seen as tiny and trivial issues seen as big, with time's steady march arrested to the present tense only, and with the environmental and social violence that we do carefully airbrushed out of the picture. We sanitise our inner landscapes through psychic re-engineering and we do this to protect ourselves from emotional discomfort and pain. The culture, rather than help us face reality, invites us repeatedly to engage in disavowal. In this culture, it is very difficult to resist being drawn in.

Omnipotent thinking

One particularly destructive aspect of disavowal is that it attempts to solve problems omnipotently, that is, through an act of thought, rather than through making genuine repairs. This is magical, "as if",[20] not rational thinking. My mental distancing is an example of "as if" thinking. It was "as if" I could rid myself of guilt and anxiety through an act of thought. I cut my links to care by locating my grandchildren far away, as if this would solve the problem. At one level it does solve the problem, in that it gets rid of consciously experienced guilt. The cost is rationality itself. And, "as if" thinking only leads to problems getting worse, because damaging behaviour is not addressed in reality.

Genuine care involves mourning the phantasy that the earth is an idealised breast/toilet mother, and attempting to address the damage this phantasy has caused. "As if" care is setting ambitious climate targets one knows will not be kept,[21] or apparently minimising the danger, or believing in miracle techno quick fixes, or avoiding hearing any news about the damage, or rubbishing the climate science community, or locating the damage in some future far off place, or preferably doing all these at the same time. All these magical repairs work by cutting felt links with care.

"As if", omnipotent, fake, solutions can be rustled up in an instant. They require no inner psychic work, which is needed to reconnect with care. Connecting and reconnecting with care is the only kind of work that will lead to real repairs being undertaken in the external world. The true aim of omnipotent solutions is to enable business as usual to proceed. Omnipotent thinking is now so widespread in relation to climate change that any troublesome aspect of the problem can apparently be dismissed instantly through an act of thought.

I believe at the bus stop I was in disavowal, operating in "as if" thinking mode. I think its purpose was to avoid shame and guilt while still feeling apparently good and virtuous. In a state of disavowal, I could write about the effect of climate change on my grandchildren without taking greater care to reduce my own emissions and I could push my guilt about this, and push them, to the edges of my mind.

The new imagination

The new imagination is made up of elements that are very old and also very new. It is the caring imagination that we need for now.[22] It is very old, because the ongoing struggle between care and uncare is as old as human kind. Homer described this struggle in *The Iliad*:

> destructiveness, sure-footed and strong, races around the world doing harm, followed haltingly by ... (care), which is lame, wrinkled, has difficulty seeing and goes to great lengths trying to put things right. (Homer, *The Iliad*, 9:11:502ff, in Brearley, 2012, p. 162)

In the new imagination, care no longer appeases uncare. It is no longer led by the nose by uncare like an ineffectual parent clearing up after a self-centered, triumphant, toddler running amok. Care, in the new imagination has come of age. It stands up to uncare. It represents the moment when the human race matures, starts to grow up and face reality.

The new imagination recognises that because of our environmental and carbon crisis, we are a unique generation, tasked with a particularly heavy burden of care about climate change. The last generation did not have the full picture and if we leave taking care to the next generation or even to ourselves tomorrow, it will be too late.[23] The new imagination recognises that we face a full-blown emergency but also knows we can address it, and with existing technology.

One strand of the new imagination is very new historically because only now, with scientific and technological advances and satellite pictures, can we more fully appreciate Earth in her otherness, her majesty, and also as fragile and with limits. We now can see that she comprises complex interconnecting dynamic systems that support life. All this enables us to love her more fully and in a more mature way, and be very concerned when we see her damaged. The new imagination helps us face our true dependency on and indebtedness to the earth. It helps us give up and mourn the narrow-minded phantasy of her as an idealised breast/toilet mother to exploit and think we can control. It opens our eyes to the need to share resources with other humans and other species living now and in the future.

The other strand we need for the new imagination to flourish is a deeper understanding of the mind and of culture. This enables us to take a more sympathetic and a more critical look at ourselves. It helps us to recognise that care is not best understood just at an individual level. Care flourishes when frameworks of care are in place and it withers without these frameworks. I now move to frameworks of care.

Frameworks of care

Awareness of the uncaring side of humanity has led to a recognition of the importance of there being structures in place to contain and limit uncare, hate, and sadism. A framework of care is such a structure. It does two thing: it keeps destructive uncaring social behaviours in check and it actively supports caring social behaviours. Frameworks of care exist at all levels, from laws that prohibit violence and theft, to social groups that disapprove of certain behaviours while also helping people face life's difficulties, to parents who understand how their child feels and also provide discipline where necessary, to the individual inner moral code we have internalised that regulates our behaviour. Frameworks of care help us maintain our living, direct, links with felt care. They also help us mend caring links when these have become severed. They can do this in many ways. We vitally depend on our frameworks of care, and are often not even aware they are in place, only noticing their effects when they start to break down. A civil society depends on them.

When architects build sustainable buildings they build physical structures to keep people safe. With these structures they are also building frameworks of care and this is a profoundly important aspect of their work and the role they play. The frameworks of care they build are vitally necessary for mental health by keeping uncare in check in psychological as well as practical ways. If we live in a low-carbon house, and travel on carbon ultra-light transport, our carbon emissions drop right down. If our buildings are designed to better withstand ravaged elements, we are safer. This enables us to feel that our survival is cared about. An important insight from psychoanalysis is that to be caring we need to feel cared for. This starts in babyhood with parental care.

Architectural frameworks of care can bring us closer to people, nature, and beauty in a way that helps keep our links with care alive. They help us reconnect with being citizens, not just consumers, in the way they arrange social space. All this expands our sense of self, boosts our creativity, and connects us to others in a caring way. It disrupts the self-idealising idea that we are somehow superior to some other people and to other species, and entitled to live cut off from them.

Psychoanalytic ideas

In my talk I draw on a number of psychoanalytic ideas. One is Klein's (1940) representational world, a concept I found vital in talking with architects about the architectural imagination. Klein's representational world is "peopled" with internal objects and part objects, always in dynamic relation to each other. Perhaps her central focus on the driving power of unconscious phantasy, based on these relationships, led her to give such prominence to objects in her depiction of the representational world. In my view, her internal objects seem somehow not to be sufficiently tethered to an internal physical world in the background of things. For Klein, the physical world is first and foremost the mother's body, full of objects, and these objects are taken back inside the self in a to and fro between self and object. But this leaves out the part of the physical world that concerns a person's ecology and the landscape in which she lives.

I believe our theory of the representational world needs to include our representation of the physical world in which our relationships take place, a world that we also relate to. In my work, I have sought to include this background world as part of what we represent through the idea of an internal landscape. Our relationships are mostly internally represented as happening in landscapes. Landscapes figure prominently in our dreams, both natural landscapes (e.g., "I walked along the seashore") and built landscapes (e.g., "I was at the top of a high-rise building looking down at someone far below"). Psychoanalysts, with the exception of Searles (1972), have paid very little attention to landscape and ecology in the representational world. Just as we relate and are attached to objects, we relate and are attached to our landscapes and to the earth that nourishes and sustains us all. I see no reason why landscape should not be included in a fuller account of the representational world; indeed, Klein seems to imply it in referring to an internal *world* of object relationships. The concept of inner landscape was certainly needed when addressing the architectural imagination, which is primarily concerned with the built landscape.

Internal space is another psychoanalytic idea I draw on in my talk, in particular Henri Rey's (1994) discussion of internal space, not as distance or area but in relationship terms as the experience of the space between self and object or objects. Here objects can be experienced as close together or far apart. This idea of Rey's has helped my thinking about the way in which we psychically re-engineer our internal relationships *and* our internal landscapes. Klein's ideas on splitting are important here too. She thought that when we split the object we split the self.

I think we also mentally split apart and fracture our landscapes in split states of mind. Integrating Klein and Rey here, we could say that splitting can involve locating the split-off part in space, for example, defensively projecting a near object to far away. This object might be part of the self, for instance a caring part of the self. For example, I understood one of my patient's dream images—"I was at the top of a high-rise building looking down at someone far below"—to represent her more caring self's capacity to represent an inner situation in which her self had become split into a caring part and a more narcissistic uncaring part that dissociated itself from (looked down on) the caring part by assigning the caring part as distant and far away. The dream image is of split psychic objects located in split psychic landscapes (at the top of the high rise building and on the ground). In a more integrated psychic landscape the self with depressive position capability is more likely to find itself on common ground with others in a shared landscape in the representational world.

In the talk I also make use of Steiner's (1993) idea of the psychic retreat. My argument is that a culture of uncare promotes a *collective* psychic retreat that operates like a defensive pathological organisation. I see disavowal of climate change as primarily stemming from the need of the group to preserve a collective psychic retreat that protects members of the group from having to face conflict, anxiety, and guilt at taking on board that climate change is human caused, which means caused—more or less—by all of us. The self that "lives" in the internal psychic retreat is experienced as split-off from, distanced from, the reality-based self that suffers conflict and that can grieve.

When people say that climate change is a future problem, they may well be operating spitting of this kind. In reality, climate change is a current problem for people in the global south, and climate instability is already impacting on people in the global north. Seeing climate change as a future problem, as I believe I did at the bus stop, involves distancing oneself from the part that cares. In this state of mind, suffering is outsourced to others. The function of the group caught up in a collective psychic retreat is to ensure that conflict and the experience of loss are kept out of conscious awareness.

Bion's (1959) work on forming links and attacks on linking underpins the way in which I talk about internal space in the representational world. The defensive splitting and projection of an object together with a part of the self (Klein always stressed that self was split along with the splitting of the object) and the fracturing of an integrated internal landscape *are* attacks on links, as links rely on "experience-near" relationships with self, with other, and with landscape. With links attacked through psychic re-engineering of mental space, the self can become alienated from experience.

My argument that the culture of uncare boosts self idealisation is informed by psychoanalytic work on idealisation of the self. Abraham (1935) thought identification with an idealised other could be very rapid indeed, based on a primary identification with the idealised parents. This is identification of an omnipotent kind. Here one does not see oneself as having the potential to grow up to become like an idealised parent, but *as* the idealised parent. He thought omnipotent identification could act as restitution of an idealised world at points where idealisation had failed. Self-idealisation is at the heart of destructive narcissism.

Self-idealisation through omnipotent identification with the idealised other is central to the phantasy that the earth is an idealised breast of endless provision. The idealised self drives this phantasy. In the collective psychic retreat, the idealised self becomes the idealised "in-group" that will be spared suffering brought about by climate change. This group does not need to face reality or change. It will be spared because it is special. Others will suffer. This group does not have to mourn the phantasy of endless provision from an idealised breast-earth mother and face the reality that there are limits to what the earth can provide. Self-idealisation is currently show-ing itself as a "Noah's Arc" position. In this way of thinking an in-group will survive climate instability because it is superior and in command of all the resources, while the "outed" group will go under. The Noah's Arc position relies on disavowal.

My fundamental template for a framework of care is Freud's idea of a benevolent civilising superego. Schafer (1960) developed this concept in his paper on the "beloved superego". This superego provides an overarching containing structure, containing with understanding and restraint. In my talk to the architects I do not go into the idea of containment, but it is a key aspect of a framework of care, and my thinking about this has been influenced by Bion's (1962) ideas on container and contained.

Architects' presentations

Architectural frameworks of care and uncare

In listening to many architects' presentations during the conference I saw a caring imagina-tion at work, one that aims to repair frameworks of care and provide containing frameworks for restraining uncare. Most current architecture still sees a building as something to keep nature out and as divorced from its locale and its ecology. My co-presenter Sue Roaf called this "twentieth-century architecture". This kind of building unit tends to be a box that is carbon intensive, often high-rise, and often made of glass. Inside the box, climate is regulated minutely and idealised conditions of comfort are aimed for. The box's most desirable quality is it can be put down anywhere, regardless of its social and material environment and regardless of its impact. Roaf gave as her main example the recent transformation of Dubai from desert to a vast metropolis of shimmering high-rise, high-carbon, glass structures. Anything less appropriate to its environs cannot be imagined.

The architects at this conference discussed the detrimental social and environmental effects of this kind of building. Theirs was a new, different kind of architecture, one that is sustainable and aims to boost people's links with the caring part of their nature. Their kind of architecture represents frameworks of care, both psychological and in the built environment.

Here are three presentations by architects that I think convey this new approach, based on a new architectural imagination.

The Harvard project

Architect Daniel D'Oca from the Harvard School of Design presented the projects of one cohort of his students. Their brief was how to build in order to protect low-lying, low-income, vulner-able communities from increased flooding and sea rise caused by climate change. He reckoned that with sea rise caused by global warming a city such as New York would most likely be protected by having a sea wall built round it. The problem is less wealthy, less protected communities already bearing disproportionate amounts of pollution and extreme weather damage. The students chose New Jersey off Long Island as the site to design for. New Jersey County had agreed to implement the winning design.

This area had suffered badly as a result of Hurricane Sandy, with damage mainly restricted to the low coastal areas. Communities living inland had fared far better. Over 1000 homes were destroyed on the New Jersey coast compared with forty-six inland. The inland area was designated high opportunity (measured by educational opportunities, income, and so on) whereas the coastal area was low opportunity. D'Oca noted that, as so often happens, the poor are hit disproportionately hard.

One plan he described was called "Move on up". This made use of the fact that upland wealthier communities had not realised their legal commitment to build affordable homes. The plan included a provision to move people inland from the coast. One underlying aim was achieving better social integration and aiding the development of a more caring consciousness. This design D'Oca described as a "managed retreat" plan, one that accepted a changed reality, but accepted it not just as a retreat in negative terms but as a new opportunity that could rebuild a caring human spirit.

Another plan was called "Living with the landscape". This involved restoring the coastal landscape in a way that simultaneously made it more resilient to extreme weather and rising sea-level, and a more attractive space to live in, so also promoting psychic resilience. D'Oca said he personally favoured the "Move on up" plan, but New Jersey County accepted the "Living with the landscape" plan. He wondered whether the idea of a managed retreat was too difficult to take on board. In discussion, I linked this with a mindset that preserves a collective psychic retreat that blocks awareness of a changed reality and blocks feelings of mourning.

Creating climate resilient neighbourhoods in Copenhagen and Paris

Here I will contrast two presentations, both concerned with creating climate-resilient neighbourhoods. Climate resilience, for the architects, fundamentally refers to resilience of the human climate.

The first is Saint Kjeld's Kvarter, Copenhagen's first climate-resilient neighbourhood. It combines managing flooding from rain (called cloudbursts) with creating new urban spaces. The spaces are designed to enhance co-operation between people by restoring broken links with care. For example, in Taasinge Square they dug up eighty per cent of the concrete to enable better water drainage, and in the earth liberated by this they built gardens and social spaces. This has had the marvelous effect of raising the spirits of all who live there and who visit. This work was presented by Tina Saaby, Copenhagen's City Architect, who has been described by the Mayor of Copenhagen as like the grain of sand in an oyster: very irritating but seeding pearls.

The second presentation was by Doina Petrescu and colleagues from the R-Urban architectural group's work to create Agrocité in Paris. Agrocité is made up of allotments, a micro-farm whose produce is sold locally, and a school providing professional training in compost-making. There is also a community space and cafe where the food grown on-site is processed and sold at affordable prices. Agrocité was built on disused land that the municipality has recently decided will now be used for a car park. Despite current crowdfunding, petitions, and newspaper coverage, it is likely soon to be covered over with concrete.

While in Copenhagen they are digging up concrete to liberate some life, in Paris they plan to concrete over a sustainable development. This highlights the issue of power and control. So often, carbon intensive business as usual is in charge and these projects flower or wither in the interstices, the vacant lots, dependent on the grace and favour of those currently in power.

I see the underlying issue as how to create conditions in which people can be helped to think with symbols, not concretely, to live in an experience-near way, and to mourn the self-idealising phantasy of superiority and endless entitlement to provision from an idealised breast/toilet. I believe these architects, through the way that they build, and through their awareness of the sorts of frameworks people need to support their capacity to care, have potential to help people reconnect with, and sustain contact with, their capacities to care.

My account of the Paris project may come across as a tale of hopes dashed for a sustainable future. I do not see it that way. At the same time as the model of business as usual is being progressively shown to be malfunctioning, many people, not just architects, are developing and exercising their new imagination, designing, planning, struggling to build a new world in the real world.

These architects have faced conflict, in the self and with the status quo. Rather than proceeding "as if" conflict, pain, and huge effort can be avoided by staying in the retreat of disavowal, they pick up their responsibilities and proceed with a "what if" approach. What if we challenge the existing architectural order? Will we get anywhere? Will it make a difference? Will it show us to have been omnipotent? By challenging the existing order, they put themselves at the sharp end of climate, political, and human reality, which is very different to staying in the retreat.

Here I am using Hanna Segal's discussion of the difference between omnipotent thinking, which proceeds "as if" phantasy is true, and reality-based thinking, which tests phantasy against reality in the real world. My understanding of her point is *all* thinking is based on phantasy, not just wishful thinking. Reality-based thinking tests phantasy in the real world whereas omnipotent thinking proceeds "as if" the phantasy is true and avoids contact with reality.

Listening to the architects brought into focus for me one aspect of the new caring imagination, which is that it needs to be resilient. By resilient I mean being able to operate at the very limits of what humans can stand to bear. There are two main reasons why bearing climate reality is so much harder now than it was. First, the self-idealising phantasy of entitlement to endless provision has by now virtually broken free of restraint, and second, the damage this phantasy has done to frameworks of care and to the environment (both external and internal) has by now been so extensive that we are starting to see the breakdown of systems. The earth system has begun to tip into instability and what Adam Lent (2008) has called "civility" is showing signs of breaking down too. Resilience means being able to keep mounting resistance in a culture of uncare, a culture currently institutionally, defensively, deaf to the caring steps actually needed to face climate change in a genuine way. It means tolerating knowing what the culture of uncare has led to. It means facing that we are in a radical situation, where there is change if we do nothing and change if we do something. It means emerging from the collective psychic retreat in which we still think we can avoid conflict and psychic pain.

I believe that the self-idealising phantasy at the heart of uncare is our modern day manifestation of the death drive. Freud talked about the power of phantasy. He meant unconscious phantasy, and the unconscious self-idealising phantasy has had powerful effects in the external world. It needs bringing to the surface of our cultural awareness.

I believe psychoanalysis has a key part to play in furthering understanding of people's resistance to knowing in a feeling way that climate change is human caused. As psychoanalysts we work with resistance in clinical practice. We understand some of the difficulties involving shame, guilt, embarrassment, and shock entailed in moving out of a psychic retreat, and the temptations to move back into it. John Steiner (2011) has addressed these feelings in *Seeing and Being Seen: Emerging from a Psychic Retreat*. His ideas inform my thinking on how to relate to people about climate change.

Writing from a psychoanalytic perspective about climate change has profoundly changed the way I see a psychoanalytic contribution to social issues in general. I no longer think in terms of applying what can be understood in individual practice to social issues. Rather, it becomes possible to see defences, such as splitting and disavowal, appearing in groups at different levels: within and between social groups and within the individual mind. What one sees is a broadly similar shape appearing at different levels. It would be an error of reductionism to equate all these similar shapes, but I think one can see them all as having what one might call a family resemblance. I remain convinced that individual practice is the testing laboratory where, so far, at least, we have the most rigorous way of interrogating the data we find. We do not have such a rigorous methodology for looking at, for example, disavowal at a governmental level, or the level of the social groups, although extensive work on group processes and institutional defences such as Menzies-Lyth's (1988) has provided a methodology for looking at defences operating at the level of the group. While we need to be cautious about what we claim, this should not stop us from seeing the obvious, which is that we are group animals, and, as Freud (1921c) said, psychoanalysis is the study of groups—we might add, at all levels. I believe we need to do more work on charting similarity in the shape of defences at different levels, certainly not shy away from it.

Notes

1. Keynote opening presentation to "Architecture and resilience on a human scale", international conference held by Sheffield University School of Architecture in 2015. https://www.sheffield.ac.uk/architecture/research/building-resilience/conference

2. Culture includes mass media, government messaging, advertising, cinema, the arts, and our social group culture.

3. I use the term "culture of uncare" rather than "uncaring culture" to emphasise the active way in which this culture seeks to uncouple us from care, that is, to "un-care" us. This culture is not just uncaring in a descriptive sense. It breaks links with care.

4. A culture widely called "American" or "Western" or "of the global north", is increasingly recognised as largely responsible for rising carbon emissions. However, given its rapid spread to all corners of the globe in the period of financial deregulation since the early 1980s, and given recent

shifts in global power relations, it is no longer accurate to talk of a global north/south divide. A huge poster hanging on the wall of the hotel of the Indian government delegation to the 2014 World Economic Forum in Davos highlights this. It said: "India. World's Largest Middle Class Consumer Market by 2030. Join India. Lead the World."

5. Cutting felt links with care was written about by Wilfred Bion in his (1959) paper "Attacks on linking". In Bion's model, links involve directly felt experience of a relationship with the other. The other can include reality. My discussion focuses on the way that severing links with experience leads to dissociation, or more properly, "dis-association" from the part that cares. One might ask if dissociation is present in Ben van Beurden's interview with Alan Rusbridger, then editor of the *Guardian* newspaper. Van Beurden is CEO of Shell. In the interview he acknowledged climate change and the need to reduce emissions, but simultaneously endorsed Shell's expansion of fossil fuel extraction, including tar sands and drilling for oil in the Arctic. He said, "I think about climate change all the time and I think about it not at all" (Rusbridger, 2015).

6. Locating the other far away in the imagination so as not to feel touched by him was described by sociologist Stanley Cohen (2000) as creating the "distant other". I have looked at dehumanising prejudice as one example of distancing the other through spatially rearranging the other as living apart (apart-heid), on the other side of the mental tracks, and through scapegoating and vilification techniques in order to avoid guilt and shame (Weintrobe, 2010a).

7. I have written of how the culture drives us to split our internal world into near and far landscapes, in which we relate to "inferior them" from a separated-off position of "superior us". (Weintrobe, 2012a).

8. There are many examples of creating the distant other to stay in a psychic retreat. For instance, when economist Nicholas Stern (2006) wrote the "Stern review"—which he has now acknowledged did not take the problem of climate change seriously enough—he used an economic model that gave inadequate entitlement to future generations. This is spatial distancing of "those in the future" tucked away and hidden behind the equations. Stern is hardly alone in using the assumptions he did. There is widespread disavowal of genuine consequences for future generations in the models used by economists.

9. Melanie Klein's (1940) concept of the internal world is very useful to understand the way we form an internal representation of the external world, one that can be heavily influenced by phantasy. In Klein's view, relationships feature prominently in the internal world. This is because we are primed to relate and are primarily social as a species. She sees the internal world as literally "peopled" by figures made up of realistic representation and distorting phantasy. My emphasis is on the representation of space internally, often envisioned as inner landscapes.

10. John Steiner (1993) discussed the way that we can form what he called a psychic retreat in the mind. This is an area, often imagined as a sectioned-off place, in which we "arrange" the internal world so as not to be troubled by various sorts of anxiety or feelings of loss. Here, I am suggesting our culture helps foster a collective psychic retreat from anxieties and psychic pain about our damaging environmental and social behaviour.

11. Michael Rustin (2001) has written on structures needed to facilitate care. He says, "In what containing social environments … can human beings tolerate recognition of the truth, and thus of each other's states of mind, desires, needs and sufferings? This is a rather fundamental question

for political and social thought, and is one to which psychoanalysis still has a large contribution to make" (Rustin, 2001, p. 6).

12. Social psychologists have called this mindset "instrumental" (Crompton & Kasser, 2009; Darnton & Kirk, 2011; Kasser, 2002). Sociologists and social commentators have called it "consumerist" (Alexander 2014; Bauman, 2007; Hamilton, 2003; N. Klein, 2000) and "extractive" (N. Klein, 2014). A lawyer has called it pathological and institutionally psychopathic. He distinguishes between a psychopathic corporate culture and individuals who work for it (Bakan, 2004). Psychoanalytic authors have given the mindset various names: "narcissistic" (Lasch, 1991), "narrow-minded" (Brenman, 1985), one of "arrogant greedy entitlement" (Weintrobe, 2010b), "perverse" (Hoggett, 2012; Long, 2008) and involving a sense of "manic triumphalism" (Segal, 2006).

13. Fantasy spelled phantasy indicates the phantasy is, or is mostly, unconscious.

14. See Keene (2012) for discussion of the earth as a breast/toilet mother phantasy.

15. As Freud (1923b) sagely put it, people may not be as moral as they would like to think they are but they are more moral than they realise.

16. Strictly speaking "global warming" refers to the long-term trend of a rising average global temperature and "climate change" refers to the changes in the global climate, which result from the increasing average global temperature. However, the two terms tend nowadays to be used interchangeably. For a discussion see http://www.skepticalscience.com/climate-change-global-warming.htm

17. See Arestis, 1992.

18. See Weintrobe (2012b) for a discussion of how people came to realise after the failed Copenhagen climate summit that governments did not care about them at the level of their survival. It was traumatic to feel this uncared for.

19. See, for example, BBC news 31 Jan 2013. *Beyonce admits to inauguration lip syncing* http://www.bbc.co.uk/news/entertainment-arts-21284398

20. Hanna Segal (1991) has distinguished between "as if" and "what if" thinking. The latter seeks to test a phantasy against reality, by asking what if the phantasy were true. The former ignores reality and proceeds as if the phantasy were true.

21. Argued by Hoggett (2012).

22. Pope Francis' (2015) basic argument in his recent encyclical on climate change is that we need to care.

23. "We are the first generation to feel the impact of climate change and the last generation that can do something about it"(Obama (2014) Remarks by the President at U.N. Climate Change Summit https://obamawhitehouse.archives.gov/the-press-office/2014/09/23/remarks-president-un-climate-change-summit). But Obama does not appear to have embraced the new imagination. At the same time as saying this, he gave Shell Oil the go-ahead to drill for oil in the Arctic. The danger is this is the "as if" disavowing imagination.

References

Abraham, K. (1935). Amenhotep IV (Ikhnaton): A psychoanalytic contribution to the understanding of his personality. *Psychoanalytic Quarterly, 4*: 537–569.

Alexander, J. (2014). https://newcitizenshipproject.wordpress.com/2014/01/22/problem-consumerism-not-consumption/

Arestis, P. (1992). Furore at the World Bank. *New York Times*, 7 February 1992.

Bakan, J. (2004). *The Corporation: The Pathological Pursuit of Profit and Power*. New York: Free Press.

Bauman, Z. (2007). *Consuming Life*. Malden, MA: Polity Press.

Bion, W. R. (1959). Attacks on linking. *International Journal of Psychoanalysis, 40*: 308–315.

Bion, W. R. (1962). *Learning from Experience*. London: Tavistock.

Brearley, M. (2012). Discussion: Unconscious obstacles to caring for the planet: facing up to human nature. In: S. Weintrobe (Ed.), *Engaging with Climate Change: Psychoanalytic and Interdisciplinary Perspectives* (pp. 160–164). London: Routledge.

Brenman, E. (1985). Cruelty and narrowmindedness. *International Journal of Psychoanalysis, 66*: 273–281.

Cohen, S. (2000). *States of Denial: Knowing about Atrocities and Suffering*. London: Polity Press.

Crompton, T., & Kasser, T. (2009). *Meeting Environmental Challenges: The Role of Human Identity*. Godalming, Surrey: WWF-UK.

Darnton, A., & Kirk, M. (2011). Finding frames: New ways to engage the UK public in global poverty. Available at: www.findingframes.org

Freud, S. (1921c). *Group Psychology and the Study of the Ego. S. E., 18*: 67–144. London: Hogarth.

Freud, S. (1923b). *The Ego and the Id. S. E., 19*: 3–68. London: Hogarth.

Hamilton, C. (2003). *Growth Fetish*. London: Pluto Press.

Hamilton, C., & Dennis, R. (2005). *Affluenza: When Too Much Is Never Enough*. Crows Nest, NSW: Allen & Unwin.

Hoggett, P. (2012). Climate change in a perverse culture. In: S. Weintrobe (Ed.), *Engaging with Climate Change: Psychoanalytic and Interdisciplinary Perspectives* (pp. 84–86). London: Routledge.

Kasser, T. (2002). *The High Price of Materialism*. Cambridge, MA: MIT Press.

Keene, J. (2012). Unconscious obstacles to caring for the planet: facing up to human nature. In: S. Weintrobe (Ed.), *Engaging with Climate Change: Psychoanalytic and Interdisciplinary Perspectives* (pp. 144–159). London: Routledge.

Klein, M. (1940). Mourning and its relation to manic-depressive states. *International Journal of Psychoanalysis, 21*: 125–153.

Klein, N. (2000). *No Logo*. New York: Pan.

Klein, N. (2014). *This Changes Everything*. New York: Penguin.

Lasch, C. (1991). *The Culture of Narcissism: American Life in an Age of Diminishing Expectations*. New York: Norton.

Lent, A. (2008). A crisis of civility. *Renewal*, September.

Long, S. (2008). *The Perverse Organization and the Seven Deadly Sins*. London: Karnac.

Menzies-Lyth, I. (1988). *Containing Anxiety in Institutions* (2 volumes). London: Free Association.

Obama, Barak. (2014). Remarks by the President at UN climate change summit. https://obamawhitehouse.archives.gov/the-press-office/2014/09/23/remarks-president-un-climate-change-summit

Pope Francis (2015). Encyclical letter. 24 May. http://w2.vatican.va/content/francesco/en/encyclicals/documents/papa-francesco_20150524_enciclica-laudato-si.html

Roaf, S. (2013). Global green building forum. https://www.youtube.com/watch?v=hE3HcrA-Wa8

Rey, H. (1994). *Universals of Psychoanalysis in the Treatment of Psychotic and Borderline Patients: Factors in Space-time and Language* (Ed. J. Magagna). London: Free Association.

Rusbridger, (2015). The biggest story in the world. *Guardian*, 29 May.

Rustin, M. (2001). *Reason and Unreason*. Middletown, CT: Wesleyan University Press.

Schafer, R. (1960). The loving and beloved superego in Freud's structural theory. *Psychoanalytic Study of the Child, 15*: 163–188.

Searles, H. F. (1972). Unconscious processes in relation to the environmental crisis. *Psychoanalytic Review, 59*: 361–374.

Segal, H. (1991). Imagination, play and art. In: *Dream, Phantasy and Art*. London: Routledge.

Segal, H. (2006). September 11. *Psychoanalytic Psychotherapy, 20*: 115–121.

Steiner, J. (1993). *Psychic Retreats*. London: Routledge.

Steiner, J. (2011). *Seeing and Being Seen: Emerging From A Psychic Retreat*. London: Routledge.

Stern, N. (2006). Stern review on the economics of climate change. HM Treasury. www.National Archives/Gov/UK

Weintrobe, S. (2010a). A dehumanising form of prejudice as part of a narcissistic pathological organisation. In: E. McGinley, & A. Varchevker (Eds.), *Enduring Loss: Mourning, Depression and Narcissism through the Life Cycle*. London: Karnac.

Weintrobe, S. (2010b). On runaway greed and climate change denial: a psychoanalytic perspective. Lionel Monteith Memorial Lecture. *Bulletin Annual of the British Psychoanalytical Society, 1*: 63–75.

Weintrobe, S. (2012a). On the love of nature and on human nature. In: S. Weintrobe (Ed.), *Engaging with Climate Change: Psychoanalytic and Interdisciplinary Perspectives* (pp. 199–213). London: Routledge.

Weintrobe, S. (2012b). The difficult problem of anxiety in thinking about climate change. In: S. Weintrobe (Ed.), *Engaging with Climate Change: Psychoanalytic and Interdisciplinary Perspectives* (pp. 33–47). London: Routledge.

INDEX

Note: italic page numbers refer to figures; numbers preceded by "n" refer to chapter endnotes. Works cited are by Klein, except where otherwise indicated. Melanie Klein is abbreviated to MK in subentries.

Abraham, Karl 119–120, 122, 206, 318, 418; and MK 4, 5, 7, 12, 13, 24, 180
Abram, Jan 45
addiction 217, 220, 220–221, 306
adolescence 64–65, 105–106, 207
adopted children 333–345
aesthetics 360, 370, 377, 378
affective pictograms 127–128
agency *302, 303, 304,* 304–305, 308, 310; and superego 62, 205, 277
aggression 13, 15, 23, 74, 77–79, 106–107, 219; and fire/burning 82–83; and pathological organisations 280, 281, 282, 283, 284
aliveness *see* vitality
alpha elements/function 25, 32, 192, 193, 208, 327; and affective pictograms 127–128; in analytic dyad 133, 134, 135–136, 239, 240, 308; and containment 45, 46, 347; and neglected children 313; and omega function 347, 348, 351
American relational psychoanalysis 75
analyst-centred interpretations 30, 76, 334
analyst–patient relations 10, 19, 25–33, 125–136; and addiction/perversion 217, 218, 220–226; and autistic features *see* "as-if" thinking; and

autistic patients 309–310; bastions in 26, 126, 127; and bi-personal field 26, 243; blockages in 130, 131–135, 157, 188–189; and container/ contained 50–52; and countertransference *see* countertransference; and discipline of memory/ desire/understanding 50, 51–52; and dual identity of analyst *see* irony; and enactments *see* enactments; enclave in 290, 291; envy in 105–108; and generous self 96, 99; and here and now/ history *see* here and now; intersubjectivity in 125, 126, 135–136; intertwining factors in 57, 106, 108, 109–112; jokes in 230–231, 232; and loneliness of analyst 47–48; and mental coherence/incoherence 195–196; and narcissistic self 96–99, 100–101, 156–157; and negative therapeutic reaction 14, 66, 97, 107, 109–110, 111; and object relations 32, 139, 222, 225; and pathological organisations 21–22; and primitive animal self 47; and projective identification 25, 26, 29, 41–42, 43, 47, 63–64, 129, 188–189; and psychic retreat 22; and psychotic patients 129; and self-observation of analyst 130, 131–132; and total situations 33, 126; and transference interpretations 32–33, 86–87; unconscious communication in 135

427